D1487969

Learning Disabilities: Proceedings of The National Conference

Edited by
James F. Kavanagh
Tom J. Truss, Jr.

York Press/Parkton, Maryland

This book was manufactured in the United States of America. Printing and binding by Maple Press, York, Pennsylvania. Cover design by Joseph Dieter, Jr.

Proceedings of the National Conference on Learning Disabilities cosponsored by The Interagency Committee on Learning Disabilities and The Foundation for Children with Learning Disabilities, held January 12–13, 1987 at the National Institutes of Health, Bethesda, Maryland.

Library of Congress Catalog Card Number 88-51466
ISBN 0-912752-19-X
ISBN 0-912752-18-1 (pbk)

Editors' Note

The members of the U.S. Interagency Committee on Learning Disabilities were the National Institute of Child Health and Human Development, National Institute of Neurological and Communicative Disorders and Stroke, National Institute of Allergy and Infectious Diseases, National Eye Institute, National Institute of Environmental Health Sciences, and Division of Research Resources of the National Institutes of Health, the Food and Drug Administration, National Institute of Mental Health, Centers for Disease Control, Environmental Protection Agency, Office of Human Development Services, and Department of Education. The Director of the National Institutes of Health was its chairman, and operational responsibility for the Committee and its activities was assigned to the National Institute of Child Health and Human Development.

FOREWORD

This publication reports the proceedings of the National Conference on Learning Disabilities held in January 1987 on the campus of the National Institutes of Health and sponsored jointly by the U.S. Interagency Committee on Learning Disabilities and the Foundation for Children with Learning Disabilities.

The Interagency Committee was established by the Health Research Extension Act of 1985 (P.L.99-158), enacted by the U.S. Congress on November 20. The Committee was asked to review and assess Federal research priorities, activities, and findings regarding learning disabilities and to report to Congress on a number of issues, including recommendations for future Federal research efforts. A provision of the Act required that the Committee include in its Report a description of findings from research on the cause, diagnosis, treatment, and prevention of learning disabilities. The National Conference on Learning Disabilities was one of several sources of information for the Interagency Committee's Report to Congress, which was transmitted in August 1987. Summaries of the National Conference proceedings were included in that Report.

In developing the Report to Congress, the Committee focused on five topic areas in learning disabilities; these areas formed the five major divisions of the National Conference. For each topic, the Committee commissioned an expert in the field to write a comprehensive review paper that describes recent research in that area as related to the cause, diagnosis, treatment, and prevention of learning disabilities; identifies gaps in knowledge; and makes recommendations for future research. The documents are published here in full, along with commentaries by expert discussants.

These National Conference proceedings are a companion volume to the Interagency Committee's Report to Congress and are the scholarly appendix to it. The proceedings provide extensive up-to-date expert reviews, for the information and guidance of professionals and the general public, of what we know and what we need to know about learning disabilities. The Committee is grateful to the Foundation for Children with Learning Disabilities for its help in support of the National Conference and for providing the funding for publication and distribution of the Conference proceedings.

Duane Alexander, M.D.
Director
National Institute of Child
Health and Human Development

PREFACE

The Foundation for Children with Learning Disabilities (FCLD) was honored to cosponsor the National Conference on Learning Disabilities with the U.S. Interagency Committee on Learning Disabilities. The goal of the FCLD has been public awareness about the frustration and challenge which learning problems bring to children and adults with average and above average intelligence. An extension of the Foundation's public awareness effort during 1987—our 10th Anniversary Year—has been underwriting the proceedings of this important National Conference on Learning Disabilities. To date, the cause and the cure of LD remain unknown. Appropriate support programs in schools, colleges, and vocational institutions, along with informed employers, will make the difference in helping the learning disabled reach their true potential.

As Founder and President of the FCLD and the mother of two LD sons, I was very moved by the opportunity which the Conference provided to bring researchers, parents, and professionals together in dialogue. Strong feelings were shared about both the difficulties and hopes ahead for learning disabled children and adults. The Conference presented the latest findings in education and scientific research, but was followed by discussion related to the everyday struggles of parents and teachers facing the challenge of learning disabilities.

It is my sincere hope that these proceedings of the National Conference on Learning Disabilities will provide the directions for such groups as the Association for Children and Adults with Learning Disabilities (ACLD), the Orton Dyslexia Society, legislators, and grant-makers who shape the future lives of children and adults with learning differences. Special thanks to ACLD's Scientific Studies Committee and others, who stimulated the thinking that led to formation of the Interagency Committee on Learning Disabilities, and, ultimately to this National Conference.

In the name of all parents and professionals who participated in the conference or who read these proceedings, I would like to thank Dr. Duane Alexander, Director, NICHD, and Chairman pro tem of the Interagency Committee on Learning Disabilities, and Dr. James F. Kavanagh, Associate Director, Center for Research for Mothers and Children of the NICHD, and Executive Secretary of the Interagency Committee on Learning Disabilities. Their wisdom guided the planning and execution of a landmark conference which was a formidable undertaking.

This publication is a tribute to over twenty years of effort by families and professionals to understand learning problems and find resources to help learning disabled children succeed in life. The Interagency Committee's report to Congress which preceded this volume is also a new beginning which can bring hope and inspiration to the future. We look forward to the response of Congress to the Report and appreciate the support of the many members of Congress and their staff who share our concern for the learning disabled. Each child is important—each child needs our commitment.

Carrie Rozelle
Founder and President
Foundation for Children
with Learning Disabilities

CONTENTS

Foreword   iv
Preface   vi

PART I: NEUROBIOLOGY OF LEARNING

The Neurobiology of Learning and Memory, Carl W. Cotman
   and Gary F. Lynch   1
Discussion, Albert M. Galaburda   70
Discussion, Richard F. Thompson   73

PART II: SPECIFIC DEVELOPMENTAL DISABILITIES OF READING, WRITING AND MATHEMATICS

Review of Research on Specific Reading, Writing, and
   Mathematics Disorder, Doris J. Johnson   79
Discussion, Margaret Jo Shepherd   164
Discussion, Isabelle Y. Liberman   168
Discussion, Joseph K. Torgesen   174

PART III: DEVELOPMENTAL LANGUAGE DISORDERS

Developmental Language Disorders, Paula Tallal   181
Discussion, Isabelle Rapin   273
Discussion, Katharine G. Butler   281
Discussion, Dorothy M. Aran   285

PART IV: SOCIAL SKILLS DEFICITS

Social Skills and Learning Disabilities: Current Issues and
   Recommendations for Future Research, J. Stephen Hazel
   and Jean Bragg Schumaker   293
Discussion, Tanis Bryan   345
Discussion, Frank M. Gresham   355
Discussion, Hill M. Walker   362

PART V: HYPERACTIVITY/ATTENTION DEFICITS

Attention Deficit Disorder: Current Perspectives,
   Sally E. Shaywitz and Bennett E. Shawitz   369

Discussion, Carol K. Whalen 524
Discussion, Gabrielle Weiss 529
Discussion, James M. Swanson 532

PART VI: SUPPLEMENTARY INFORMATION

Revised Definition of Learning Disabilities 549
Contributors 552
Index 553

PART I: NEUROBIOLOGY OF LEARNING

The Neurobiology of Learning and Memory

Carl W. Cotman

and

Gary S. Lynch

INTRODUCTION

The storage and recall of memories is so constant a part of daily life that it goes largely unnoticed. Yet the ability to encode, catalogue, and recall a vast number of facts and experiences is one of the primary characteristics that defines us as human and distinguishes us as individuals. It is quite appropriate that the biomedical sciences should be concerned with the nature of the machinery in the brain that processes memory and how that machinery becomes disrupted by genetic errors, disease, and pathology.

In this review, we discuss several recent approaches that have led to rapid progress in understanding the "how" and "where" of memory formation, and consider the potential of these advances for treatment of clinical problems. We begin by considering the major questions and goals of the neurobiological analyses of memory. There are really three interlocking areas of concern:

- What is learning, what are the various categories into which it can be subdivided, and are these categories similarly impacted by learning disabilities?
- What answers do we require in a neurological account of learning and memory?

Acknowledgment: The authors are grateful to their colleagues for their contribution and criticisms of the manuscript (M. Baudry, M. Leon, U. Staubli, R. Gibbs, C. Peterson) and to D. Enders and K. Zfaty for editorial and secretarial assistance.

- Why has the analysis of the substrates of memory been so difficult, and are we approaching satisfactory answers?

It is our conclusion that great progress has been made in the past five years in understanding the mechanisms that underlie memory formation. Continued rapid progress can be predicted. In this review, we document the reasons for this new optimism.

WHAT IS LEARNING? BASIC DEFINITION AND SUBTYPES

Learning can be broadly defined as any lasting change in behavior resulting from prior experience. It may seem to be a single phenomenon, but a moment's reflection shows that this is not the case. Consider, for example, the difference between the memory involved in serving a tennis ball and the memory required to answer a question about the capital of the United States. In the first instance, we are not really aware of the specific sequence of muscle movements that produces a successful result, while in the latter, the information is conscious and clearly linked to a series of facts and even experiences. The first type of memory is acquired only after extensive practice. In contrast, a specific fact can be set into memory by a learning episode that lasts only a fraction of a second. Cognitive psychologists have used these and numerous other characteristics to formally dichotomize memory into two broad categories: procedural, skill, or rule memory (typing, bicycle riding, linguistic syntax), and fact or declarative memory (faces, names, semantic aspects of language) (figure 1). While this distinction has evident validity, it gives us only one part of the taxonomy of memory. Tulving (1983), for example, has noted that the fact memory category can be subdivided into two subcategories: simple facts versus "episodes." He argues that the memory for experiences (for instance, dinner last night) is qualitatively distinct in several dimensions from that involved in such simple associations as "Rome:Italy."

These distinctions are important in the present context for two reasons. First, neuropsychological studies over the past ten years have shown that pathology can and often does affect memory in a selective fashion. (Research in this area is described later.) Learning of fact memories appears to involve different, more easily disturbed, brain systems than those subserving procedural memory. Second, neurobiological analyses of learning and memory that intend to explicate these phenomena as found in normal and in brain-injured humans need to take cognizance of the multiple forms and variable sensitives of memory. Themes that frequently appear in this review are the existence of multiple types of learning and memory, the differential effects of injury and disease upon them, and the need for appropriate animal models.

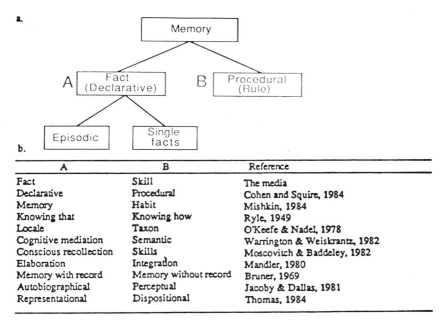

a.

b.

A	B	Reference
Fact	Skill	The media
Declarative	Procedural	Cohen and Squire, 1984
Memory	Habit	Mishkin, 1984
Knowing that	Knowing how	Ryle, 1949
Locale	Taxon	O'Keefe & Nadel, 1978
Cognitive mediation	Semantic	Warrington & Weiskrantz, 1982
Conscious recollection	Skills	Moscovitch & Baddeley, 1982
Elaboration	Integration	Mandler, 1980
Memory with record	Memory without record	Bruner, 1969
Autobiographical	Perceptual	Jacoby & Dallas, 1981
Representational	Dispositional	Thomas, 1984

Figure 1: Memory systems and their taxonomy.
A. General scheme;
B. Alternative nomenclature used for the subtypes in the literature.
(From Squire and Zola-Morgan, 1985)

WHAT DO WE EXPECT OF A NEUROBIOLOGICAL ACCOUNT OF LEARNING AND MEMORY? ASSUMPTIONS AND GOALS

Three levels of neurobiological description are needed for any explanation of learning:

- Synaptic mechanisms: the nature of the stable modifications that actually encode memory, and the types of mechanisms that produce the modifications.
- Brain regions: the location of the regions in the brain associated with the storage, retrieval, and processing of different types of memory.
- Memory "circuits" in brain: the characteristics of the circuitries contained within learning-related brain structures, and how these characteristics are linked to the phenomenologies observed at the other levels of analysis.

In the following discussion, we briefly touch upon the ideas and findings that direct research in each of these three types of analysis. This discussion also serves as an introduction to the more detailed material that follows.

Neuroscientists from the late nineteenth century to the present have assumed that the storage process involves events and alterations occurring in the synaptic contacts between cells. Long-term changes in the functional strength of connections would certainly affect the operation (and hence information processing) of brain networks, and the enormous number of synapses in the human brain provides a reasonable explanation for the astonishing capacity of memory (see below). The search for memory mechanisms in synapses leads naturally to three issues: (1) patterns of physiological activity that trigger the modification process, (2) the chemistries that translate physiological events into stable alterations, and (3) the nature of the long-term changes themselves.

Not all events that trigger responses in the brain are learned. This fact leads to the conclusion that certain distinct patterns of activity are needed to elicit the memory encoding processes. The brain utilizes a host of rhythms in its ongoing activity, and it is tempting to imagine that some subset of these rhythms are learning signals. Recent experiments have provided evidence that this suspicion is correct.

Investigation into the transient chemical events involved in storage constitutes one of the largest and most active areas of research in all of neuroscience. We can assume that the pertinent chemistries are triggered by unusual physiological events, which, once activated, produce very long-lasting changes restricted to specific synapses. The identification of chemical processes that fulfill these requirements is difficult, and the presence of such chemistries is rare. Increasingly, specific hypotheses are being advanced, however, and there is reason to hope that one of them, or a combination of them, will indeed define the "chemistry of memory." The consequences of success in this area would be profound. Beyond its scientific value, the identification of the chemistries that promote memory would open the way for the development of drugs directed to facilitating learning in impaired individuals.

It is also possible to make some reasonable guesses about the nature of the stable changes that are used to encode memory. Synapses, like all components of the neuron, are composed of proteins and lipids that are continuously being broken down and replaced. Since memories can last for years and the chemical constituents of the synapses clearly do not, most theorists assume that the enduring modifications associated with memory involve anatomical changes. It has been known for over a decade that the adult brain can grow new synapses in response to injury, but only recently, physiologically-induced rapidly developing structural modifications have been observed. Whether these effects are indeed the same or similar to those occurring during a learning episode constitutes a pressing issue for research.

Alongside the search for the mechanisms initiating and supporting memory lie the questions of where in the brain learning occurs and of the roles played by different regions in producing it. A point that emerges from the experiments reviewed below is that learning of some type occurs in even very simple nervous systems and that memory storage is found at several levels of the mammalian brain. Yet much evidence leads to a conclusion that in humans the encoding of data and episodes is crucially dependent upon the cortex and the structures lying immediately beneath it in the forebrain. The vast human neocortex (comprising some 80 percent or more of the whole brain) is such an attractive candidate for the repository of memories that most researchers assume that it plays this role. Specific areas of the cortex generate so much of human behavior that it seems almost inevitable that the memories needed for those behaviors are also found in its folds. Moreover, and as noted earlier, the capacity of human memory points to the cortex as the storage site. But subcortical regions are also crucial, at least to the encoding and retrieval aspects of memory, if not to its actual storage. Lesions in the hippocampal region of humans produce a surprisingly selective anterograde amnesia in which patients are unable to store new information, but the patients still retain the greater part of their pre-injury memories. Experiments with primates, and very recently with rats, have also succeeded in identifying a vital function for the hippocampus in the formation of new fact memories. Despite these observations, there is still no satisfactory theory of how the hippocampus and certain other subcortical areas (for example, the amygdala, the midline thalamus) contribute to the encoding of experience, presumably in the neocortex.

Research into memory-related brain structures is closely linked to the search for the causes of learning disabilities and disturbances in memory processing. Indeed, much that we know has emerged from neuropathological work on patients suffering from various types of memory deficits.

MEMORY "CIRCUITS" IN THE BRAIN

Only recently have researchers and theorists begun to tackle the question of what types of networks or circuits are involved in encoding experiences or in complex learned sequences of behavior. Indeed, one might say that work in this area is still in its infancy. We discuss it here because of the great potential it has for connecting the molecular and regional approaches to learning and for providing models against which to test ideas about the causes and possible treatments of disabilities. That is, work over the past five years using computer simulations has shown that networks which incorporate a limited number of neurobiological features exhibit remarkable capacities for processing information. It must be emphasized that these models use rules that are far removed from those employed by brain circuitries. Nonetheless, we can expect to see even more "life-like" networks over the next several years, and with them, new insights into the links between synaptic processes and anatomical organizations in the production of specific aspects of learning and memory. Moreover, progress in network operations already points to certain areas in which neurobiological research is needed for the development of realistic simulations.

WHY IS THE ANALYSIS OF THE NEUROBIOLOGY OF LEARNING SO DIFFICULT? INTERDEPENDENT VARIABLES AND ITS SUBTLE NATURE

Learning and memory have proven to be among the most difficult subjects in the biological sciences. Despite years of intensive research, we still have not agreed upon a single explanation for most of the relevant phenomenology, and only recently have detailed hypotheses about specific aspects of memory begun to appear. Part of the reason for this slow pace is that learning appears to require the coordination of physiopsychological variables that are not themselves part of the encoding and retrieval mechanisms. Indeed, identifying these variables constitutes an important area of research. The area is pregnant with possibilities for clinical application. The dependence of memory functioning on so many general variables, however, makes it difficult to interpret results from the use of pharmacological and pathological approaches employed successfully in the study of nonmemorial behaviors and physiologies. It is often impossible to satisfactorily conclude, for example, if a drug disturbed memory because it interrupted the synaptic chemistries related to storage as opposed to a more nonspecific action on a "background" state needed for these chemistries to operate.

An additional and profound problem, suggested by the seemingly endless capacity of the brain for memory storage, is that the changes required for learning are quite subtle and dispersed. By way of illustration, Standing (1973) presented college students with a series of photographs, each picture being observed for 5 seconds, and then tested the students for recognition the following day. He found that retention could be described as a mathematical function of the number of pictures observed, and the function held from 100 to 10,000 pictures. Feldman (1981) has made an estimate of how much information would have to be encoded in storage to recognize this number of complex pictures: the answer is in the order of 10^{11} "bits." This capacity is barely within the range of the largest computers. Note also that the memory processing of the students did not slow as even more data were added to memory.

These observations lead inevitably to the idea that memory involves changes in a tiny fraction of an extremely large pool of elements.

Such a conclusion makes the task of finding those changes, using current technologies, a formidable one if not impossible. How can one get around this roadblock to the neurobiological investigation of learning? One response that has gained increasing popularity is to study learning or learning-like phenomena in relatively simple "model" systems. The idea is to extract basic principles from these models in which molecular and anatomical details can be studied, and then to use the principles in analyzing learning in the higher regions of the brain.

In the organization of the discussions below, the strategy of proceeding from simple systems to the complexity of the forebrain and cortex is followed. We begin with research on invertebrates, in which simple forms of learning can be directly correlated with changes in identified neurons and synapses. This information is followed by a discussion of studies analyzing conditioning in the far more complicated but still well-defined circuitries found in the brain stem of mammals. This review of learning in the lower brain leads to work on small slices of the hippocampus maintained in vitro and a series of recent and exciting discoveries about the cellular basis of a form of synaptic change that may well be part of mammalian fact memory. After discussing theories about the substrates of memory, we turn to the cerebral cortex and consider recent efforts to develop paradigms for detecting learning-induced changes. Studies in both very young and adult animals are summarized. This material takes us from the question of basic mechanisms to the issue of how different brain regions contribute to different aspects and types of learning. Here we focus on efforts to develop animal models to study the different forms of memory identified in humans and to reproduce specific clinical syndromes. Finally, we briefly mention some recent attempts to place the relationships of brain regions to aspects of learning into the context of the different types of circuits that constitute these regions. In the final sections, we address the issue of the possible neurobiological causes of learning disabilities and the extent to which we can correct or ameliorate them in animal models. We then summarize the field and provide our recommendations for future directions.

DISCOVERING THE BASIC MECHANISMS: FROM SIMPLE TO COMPLEX

INVERTEBRATE MODELS

OVERVIEW

Three models of learning in invertebrates have been studied extensively in the last ten years. They have provided a wealth of information concerning the biochemical and cellular mechanisms involved in the storage of experiences. These are the gill and siphon withdrawal reflex and the tail withdrawal reflex in the sea snail *Aplysia Californica,* classical conditioning in *Hermissenda crassicornis,* and associative conditioning in the mollusc *Limax maximus.*

LEARNING AND MEMORY IN *APLYSIA CALIFORNICA.*

Several defensive reflexes in *Aplysia* exhibit various forms of nonassociative learning (habituation and sensitization), which have both short-term (minutes to hours) and long-term (days to weeks) components. While habituation consists of a decreased behavioral response to a noxious stimulus as a result of repeated experience, sensitization involves a nonspecific enhancement of the response to a test stimulus following a second aversive stimulus applied to another part of the organism (figure 2) (Kandel and Schwartz, 1982).

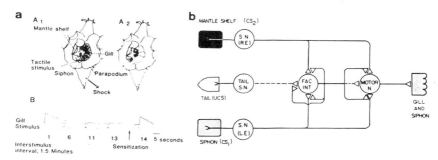

Figure 2: Cellular mechanisms of learning and memory in *Aplysia*
 a: Short-term sensitization of the gill withdrawal reflex
   A1. Experimental arrangement for behavioral studies showing the gill in relaxed position. The reflex is elicited by a water jet to the siphon. The sensitizing stimulus is a noxious stimulus to the tail.
   A2. Gill after withdrawal.
   B. Photocell recordings showing habituation and sensitization of the reflex.
 b: Circuit diagram proposed to underlie the differential conditioning of responses to stimulation of the siphon (CSl) and the mantle shelf (CS2).
(From Kandel and Schwartz, 1982; Hawkins and Kandel, 1984; Byrne, 1985; Goelet et al., 1986)

The connections between sensory neurons and motor neurons controlling these reflexes have been relatively well described anatomically. They exhibit a number of plastic properties including synaptic depression, presynaptic facilitation, and long-term increases in synaptic efficacy. The whole circuitry of these systems can be studied not only in the intact animal but also in isolated preparations. More recently, it was shown that these connections can even be investigated in dissociated cell culture conditions (Belardetti et al., 1986).

The best understood phenomenon in *Aplysia* is sensitization (Kandel and Schwartz, 1982). A sensitizing stimulus in one part of the animal induces the release of a modulating transmitter that produces presynaptic facilitation of many sensory neurons. Presynaptic facilitation increases neurotransmitter release from these sensory neurons when they are subsequently activated, and thus enhances activation of motor neurons and behavioral response. Recently, it has been shown that an elaboration of this mechanism is probably involved in associative learning in *Aplysia*. It is assumed that two sensory pathways make weak subthreshold connections to a common response system and that activity in one sensory pathway (the CS pathway) modifies its response to the facilitatory effect due to the activity in the second pathway (the UCS pathway) if the appropriate temporal association between the two stimuli is present. This hypothesis was tested by using a classical conditioning procedure in which intracellular activation of individual sensory neurons represented the CS and shock to the skin represented the UCS. Paired presentation of the CS and UCS resulted in an enhanced postsynaptic potential to CS presentation (Hawkins et al., 1983).

The molecular and cellular basis for sensitization and for classical conditioning are now known in great detail (at least for the short-term component). Activation of the sensitizing stimulus (or of a sensory pathway) results in the activation of modulatory (facilitatory) interneurons and thus the release of a modulating transmitter (such as serotonin or some neuroactive peptides), which stimulates adenylate cyclase in the cell bodies and terminals of sensory neurons. These events allow the levels of cyclic AMP to increase, which causes the activation of a cyclic AMP-dependent protein kinase and the phosphorylation of some proteins. It has been proposed that one of these proteins is a potassium (K^+) channel or is a protein regulating this ion channel (figure 3). Consequently, there is a decrease in the resting steady-state K^+ current that contributes to the repolarization of the action potential. As a result, the Ca^{++} influx that normally occurs during the action potential is prolonged, which allows greater transmitter release and enhanced activation of the motor neurons responsible for the behavioral response. The short-term sensitization of classical conditioning lasts 15-20 minutes and is due to a prolonged activation of the adenylate cyclase, which provides for the continuous activation of the cAMP-dependent kinase (Kandel and Schwartz, 1982). In associative learning, the activity in the sensory neuron modulates its response to the

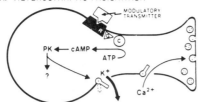
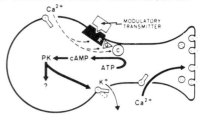

Figure 3:   Model of possible molecular events responsible for heterosynaptic facilitation and activity-dependent neuromodulation.

A.   Heterosynaptic facilitation (responsible for sensitization). In response to the release of a facilitating transmitter (serotonin or peptide), increase in cAMP activates a protein kinase which phosphorylates and closes a K+ channel, allowing a prolonged depolarization of the nerve terminal, an increase influx of calcium, and an increase in transmitter release from the sensory neuron terminals.

B.   Activity.dependent neuromodulation (associative learning). The initial influx of Ca^{2+} due to spike activity modifies the response of the adenylate cyclase complex to a subsequent release of a modulating transmitter.

(From Kandel and Schwartz, 1982; Hawkins and Kandel, 1984; Byrne, 1985; Goelet et al., 1986).

facilitatory transmitter (this mechanism has therefore been termed activity-dependent neuromodulation), and evidence has been presented indicating that this neuromodulation is due to an interaction between Ca^{++} and adenylate cyclase. This would provide an enhanced cyclic AMP synthesis in response to a neuromodulator released by the activation of the UCS pathway in a sensory neuron that has been exposed to the CS and therefore has higher levels of Ca^{2+} due to the influx of Ca^{++} as a result of spike activity.

Little is known concerning the mechanisms responsible for the long-term effects except that structural changes have been shown to take place in the terminals of the sensory neurons (increased number of active zones; Bailey and Chen, 1983). More recently, Kandel and coworkers have shown that protein synthesis is required to establish the long-term modification of synaptic transmission underlying long-term sensitization (Goelet et al., 1986). It has been proposed that signals that initiate short-term memory can initiate, through common intracellular messengers, not only covalent modification of proteins responsible for the short-term effects but also additional steps resulting in the expression of different genes and the formation of lasting traces of experiences.

LEARNING AND MEMORY IN *HERMISSENDA*

For the sea slug *Hermissenda*, light elicits oriented positive movement and foot lengthening, while rotation, a strong aversive stimulus, elicits "clinging" and foot contraction. Paired presentation of light (CS) and rotation of the animal (UCS) produces classical conditioning, with several characteristics similar to that observed in vertebrate systems

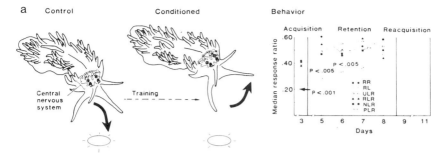

Figure 4: Cellular mechanisms of learning and memory in *Hermissenda*.
      A. Behavior; reduction of phototaxic response as a result of conditioning procedure.
      B. Circuit diagram showing the intrasensory integration from optic stimuli and vestibular information.
(From Alkon, 1984)

(figure 4). In *Hermissenda*, as in *Aplysia*, learning occurs because of the convergence of two sensory pathways on a set of motorneurons responsible for the behavioral response. Analysis of the changes in electrophysiological properties of the sensory neurons responding to light presentation was used to uncover the molecular and cellular mechanisms underlying the learning process (Alkon, 1984).

During acquisition (lasting 1-2 hrs) of the classical conditioning response, there is a prolonged depolarization of the type B photoreceptor. This depolarization is the result of the integrated response of the visual-vestibular network, and accumulates with each paired presentation of the CS and UCS. A marked elevation of intracellular calcium concentration results, which is also accompanied by a reduction of two K^+ currents, respectively termed IA and ICa-K (calcium-dependent K^+ current). During retention (at least 2 days after acquisition), there is no depolarization of the type B photoreceptor and no evidence of an increase in intracellular calcium concentration. However, the reduction in IA and ICa-K amplitude is still present. Furthermore, the rate of K^+ current inactivation is also increased, which suggests that the changes in K^+ currents are due to a modification of the K^+ channels themselves rather than to their density in the soma membrane. The changes in K^+ currents result in an increased sensory cell excitability. It has been demonstrated that these changes are causally related to the learning. The sequence of cellular steps for the production of the long-lasting changes in K^+ currents critically involves membrane depolarization and an increase in intracellular calcium. It does not seem to depend on any particular synaptic transmitter of neurohormones since the same changes can be demonstrated with isolated type B cell somata by repeated injections of a positive current, paired with a light step.

The biochemical mechanisms are not totally elucidated, but there is evidence that the changes are due to the paired activation of a calcium-calmodulin kinase and a calcium-dependent phospholipid-dependent protein kinase (kinase C), and the resulting phosphorylation of specific proteins. It is interesting that similar biophysical and biochemical mechanisms may contribute to neuronal changes observed in rabbit hippocampus following classical conditioning of the nictitating membrane. This classical conditioning has been shown to produce a reduction of postimpulse after hyperpolarization (AHP) measured in pyramidal cells of hippocampal slices (Disterhoft et al., 1986). This AHP reduction, lasting at least 1-2 days and sensitive to activation of protein kinase C, was due, at least in part, to a reduction of ICa-K. Recent experiments seem to indicate that the reduction could be triggered by the expression of new genes in the hippocampus. To our knowledge, this circuitry and the changes in its function have not been simulated with a computer.

LEARNING AND MEMORY IN *LIMAX*

Limax is a terrestrial mollusc. It is a generalist herbivore that employs various mechanisms to optimize its food choices, and in particular to learn to avoid plant odors associated with toxicosis (Gelperin, 1975). The learning procedure by which an attractive plant odor is paired with a bitter taste is identical to typical classical conditioning, with the attractant odor being the CS and the bitter taste the UCS. Following training, the CS is repellent, eliciting an avoidance and rejection response. This classical conditioning paradigm exhibits several of the characteristics of Pavlovian conditioning observed in mammalian systems, such as second-order conditioning and blocking. Although the circuitry responsible for the learning as well as the biochemical and cellular mechanisms underlying the changes in synaptic connectivity are far from being well known, the system has been the subject of a formal computer simulation and is possibly one of the first neural networks to be currently transposed into a silicon chip network (Gelperin et al., 1986).

The advantage of this model is that associative learning can be performed in the intact animal as well as in isolated lip-brain preparations. Alternatively, it is possible to train the intact animal and to assess in vitro the retention of the memory (Gelperin and Culligan, 1984). The circuitry which has been proposed to be responsible for the behavior consists of a set of sensory neurons detecting various characteristics of the odors (or tastes) of plants. The sensory neurons project to a matrix of interneurons (a cataloger). The outputs of the "cataloger" synapse on two control/motor output networks determine the behavioral response of the animal: eat or flee (figure 5).

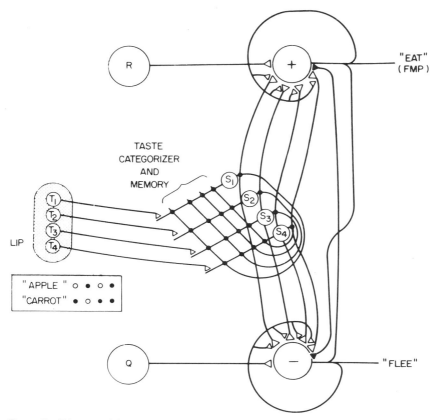

Figure 5: Diagram of the components of the *Limax* stimulation program. (From Gelperin et al., 1986).

The biochemical and physiological properties of the various neurons participating in this circuit are currently being investigated, and there is evidence that traditional transmitters (acetylcholine, dopamine, and serotonin) as well as neuroactive peptides are involved in some aspects of the neuronal control system of feeding. The role of phosphorylation of ion channels in the synaptic changes underlying learning and memory in this system is also currently being investigated. A formal neural model of associative learning has been developed and simulated (LIMAX simulation program), which uses realistic abstractions of real neurons and an algorithm of learning based on Hebbian rules. It is assumed that internal representations of foods are generated and learned by the taste categorizer network and that the associations between the representations and their significance (attractive or repulsive) take place at the level of the control/motor output network. The model accounts for first- and second-order conditioning and makes a certain number of testable predictions.

SUMMARY

The study of learning and memory in invertebrate models has been extremely successful. It has provided a number of fundamental discoveries concerning the biochemical, cellular, and logical mechanisms underlying simple forms of learning:

- A relatively small number of identifiable neurons with known connections is necessary and sufficient to describe the behavioral operation of the system.
- Several well known biochemical/biophysical mechanisms are involved in the regulation of the short-term component of memory. Identification of the mechanisms responsible for the long-term component is actively being pursued. The functioning of some of these systems can be adequately described by a relatively simple theoretical neural network, which allows a dialectic interaction between theory and experimentation.
- Most of the mechanisms thus far identified are present in mammals. This observation raises the possibility that these mechanisms also participate in some of the mammalian learning and memory processes.

SIMPLE SYSTEMS IN VERTEBRATE BRAINS

In study of the vertebrate brain, simple learning paradigms involving brain regions and circuits that can be potentially defined must be used in order to realize an analysis with the precision and definition that has resulted from the research on invertebrates. Great progress toward this goal has been made with the development of several models. The most complete data are on classical conditioning of eye blink response, classical conditioning of forearm position, and the analysis of long-term potentiation in simple in vitro preparations. Long term potentiation (LTP) operates in a two-neuron network. It stores a particular stimulus history, and it appears to play a role in learning in more complex networks.

Other simple systems and approaches have also provided valuable information. Particular areas of note include: plasticity in the vestibulo-ocular reflex (a learning-like behavior resulting from altered visual input; Miles and Lisberger, 1981; Ito, 1984, 1985; Watanabe, 1985), classically conditioned cardiovascular responses (fear learning; Smith et al., 1980; Cohen, 1980, 1982; Kapp et al., 1982; Kesner and Wilbrun, 1974; Gold and Cohen, 1981) and conditioned potentiation of the acoustic startle response (a model of conditioned emotional state). (For a recent review of these other models, see Thompson, 1986).

CLASSICAL CONDITIONING OF EYEBLINK: THE FIRST ILLUSTRATION OF THE ESSENTIAL MEMORY CIRCUIT.

OVERVIEW

Recent evidence suggests that the memory trace for classical conditioning is localized to discrete areas in the brain. The most complete data are from studies of eyelid conditioning (McCormick et al., 1982). Eyelid conditioning exhibits the same basic laws of learning across a wide range of mammalian species, including humans, and is prototypical of classical conditioning of striated muscle responses (Hilgard and Marquis, 1940; Gormezano, 1972; Rescorla and Wagner, 1972; and Prokasy, 1972). This simple form of learning proved valuable for analysis of theoretical issues in learning (Wagner, 1981) and is particularly well suited for neurobiological analysis (Thompson et al., 1976; Disterhoft et al., 1977). This model system of associative learning is the first example where the essential memory trace circuits, and hence the potential locus of the engram, has been identified.

NATURE OF SYSTEM AND PARADIGM

The model uses a simple, well characterized, and robust form of associative learning. Rabbits are trained in a simple Pavlovian task: classical conditioning of the nictitating membrane (NM) and eyelid response. In eyelid conditioning, a brief sound (a tone) is followed by a puff of air to the eye. After a number of pairings of tone and air puff, the eyelid develops a learned closing response to the tone before the puff comes. This is a simple adaptive response that protects the eye. Rabbits and humans learn the eyeblink response equally well.

The paradigm is a standard classical conditioning design: A 350 msec auditory conditioned stimulus (CS) is paired with a 100 msec air puff to the cornea (unconditioned stimulus = UCS), which elicits nictitating membrane (NM) extension and eyelid closure. The UCS is overlapping the last 100 msec of the tone CS. Intertrial intervals are approximately 1 min, and 120 trials per day are usually given. Two types of responses occur during classical conditioning: (1) The unconditioned reflex response (UR) and (2) the classically conditioned eyelid/NM response (CR). Presentation of the UCS (air puff) by itself elicits the unconditioned response or the UR. Pairing a CS (tone) with the UCS (air puff) will ensure that after a few pairings the CS alone comes to elicit a response, called the CR, which is similar if not identical to the response formerly elicited by the UCS. The animal has learned a stimulus-response (CS-UR) relationship. Learning induced by classical conditioning produces the change in behavior that the experimenter records as a CR to the CS.

Aversive learning such as classical conditioning of the NM/eyelid response may occur as two phases, the first involving "conditioned fear" and the second concerned with learned performance of discrete, adaptive motor responses (Prokasy, 1972; Rescorla and Solomon, 1967). A large body of literature implicates opioids in "learned fear," anxiety, and aversive learning (Martinez et al., 1981). Systemic administration of morphine and opiate analogues causes abolition of the CR prior to presentation of the next UCS, but it has no effect on the UR (Mauk et al., 1982). However, if the rabbits are overtrained, morphine has no impact on learning (Mauk et al., 1983). In short, the fear system appears to be essential for the initial learning of the discrete adaptive response. These findings have been suggested to show that the opiate abolition of the learned NM/eyelid response is due to its action on the "conditioned fear" system, which is located in the brain stem and is separate from the memory trace of the discrete adaptive response (Lavond et al., 1984).

KEY BRAIN AREAS IMPLICATED IN THE CHANGES

To understand the physiological substrate of the memory trace, it is important to identify the brain regions that are essential for the acquisition and retention of the conditioned response. Strong evidence from research using lesions, electrophysiological recordings, electrical microstimulation, and microinfusion of drugs supports the view that the memory trace for the eyeblink response is localized rather than widely distributed in the brain.

Where is memory for such a simple learned response stored? Rabbits with the neocortex and hippocampus removed can learn the NM/eyelid response relatively normally (Thompson et al., 1983). The mapping of electrophysiological responses throughout the brain in rabbits has provided important clues. Learning-related increases in unit activity are prominent in certain regions of the cerebellum (both in the cortex and deep nuclei), in certain regions of the pontine nuclei, and in the red nucleus (McCormick and Thompson, 1984). Several regions of the cerebellar cortex and deep nuclei were found where neurons develop patterned changes in firing frequency that precede and predict the occurrence and form of the learned behavioral response (CR) within trials. That is, the pattern of increased neural activity in these areas of the cerebellum formed a "model," in time, of the learned NM/eyeblink response to the tone, but not of the reflex eyeblink to the air puff (figure 6).

Lesions ipsilateral to the trained eye in any of several locations of the cerebellum and related circuits (interpositus nucleus, the middle cerebellar peduncle, the pontine nuclear region, and the dorsal accessory olive) permanently abolish the CR but have no effect on the

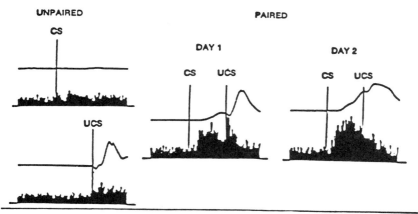

Figure 6: Histograms of unit-recording of the dentate-interpositus nuclei in one animal. The animal was first given random, unpaired presentations of the tone and airpuff and then trained with two days of paired training. Each histogram is an average over the entire day of training indicated. The upper trace represents movement over the NM, with "up" being closure. Each histogram is 9 msec in duration. Note that these neurons develop a model of the CR, but not of the UCR, during learning. (McCormick and Thompson, 1984)

UR (except lesions of the interpositus). None of these lesions prevent learning by the contralateral cerebellum (Lavond et al., 1985; McCormick et al., 1982)

Cerebellar cortical lesions cause only a transient loss of the CR; all lesioned animals eventually relearn (Lavond et al., 1986). It has been suggested that multiple parallel cortical (and interpositus) sites for the memory trace might exist. Collectively, these data suggest that the essential memory trace for this conditioned reflex is localized in the cerebellum. The cerebellum was previously suggested as a possible locus for certain kinds of memory traces having to do with learned movements.

EXACT CIRCUITRIES: THE ESSENTIAL MEMORY TRACE CIRCUIT

The essential memory trace circuit can be defined as the neuronal circuitry from receptors to effectors that is necessary and sufficient for learning and memory in a given training paradigm. As such, its delineation is a major goal of research in this field. Ultimately, these circuits need to be defined for all types of learning.

The pathway that is necessary and sufficient for conveying information about the US to the cerebellar memory trace circuit is composed of climbing fibers from the dorsal accessory olive projecting through the inferior cerebellar peduncle (see figure 7). Electrical microstimulation of the dorsal accessory olive elicits behavioral responses and can be used as an effective US for normal learning of behavioral CR's; the exact behavioral response elicited by stimulation of the dorsal accessory olive is learned as a normal CR to a CS (Mauk and Thompson, 1984).

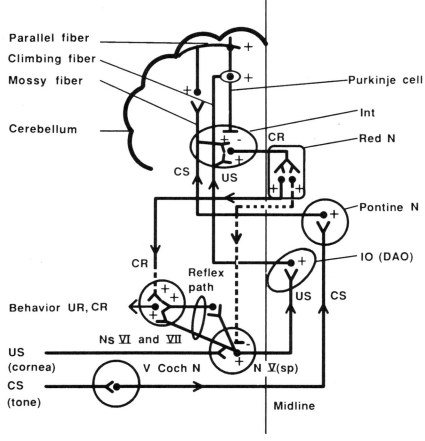

Figure 7: Schematic of hypothetical memory trace circuit for discrete behavioral responses learned as adaptation to aversive events. The US (corneal airpuff) pathway consists of somatosensory projections to the inferior olive (DAO) and its climbing fiber projections to the cerebellum. The tone CS pathway consists of auditory projections to pontine nuclei (Pontine N) and their mossy fiber projections to the cerebellum. The efferent (eyelid closure) CR pathway projects from the interpositus nucleus (Int) of the cerebellum to the red nucleus (Red N) and via descending rubral pathway to act ultimately on motor neurons. The red nucleus may also exert inhibitory control over the transmission of somatic sensory information about the US to the inferior olive (IO), so that when a CR occurs (eyelid closure), the red nucleus dampens US activation of climbing fibers. Evidence to date is most consistent with storage of memory traces in localized regions of cerebellar cortex and possibly interpositus nucleus as well. Pluses indicate excitatory and minuses inhibitory action. (Thompson, 1986).

The essential CS pathway includes mossy fiber projections to the cerebellum via pontine nuclei (lesioning this area abolishes eyelid CR to an acoustic CS; Steinmetz et al., 1986). Electrical microstimulation of the mossy fiber system is an effective CS, producing rapid learning (more rapid than with peripheral CS) when paired with a corneal air puff (Steinmetz et al., 1986). Finally, mossy fiber stimulation as a CS and climbing fiber stimulation as a US yield normal learning of the response elicited by climbing fiber stimulation (Steinmetz et al., 1985). Lesion of the nucleus interpositus, the site where both the CS and the UCS pathways converge, abolishes both the CR and the UR. Thus, in this "reduced" preparation, the essential memory trace is very likely localized to the cerebellum. In the normal animal trained with peripheral stimuli, the possibility of trace formation in brain stem structures has not yet been definitely ruled out.

At present, researchers have only begun to describe the cellular mechanisms involved in this form of learning. High concentrations of gamma-aminobutyric acid (GABA) and GABA receptors have been located in the nucleus interpositus. Microinjections of bicuculline methiodide, a GABA antagonist, selectively and reversibly abolish both the behavioral CR as well as the increment in neuronal firing usually observed in the nucleus interpositus during NM conditioning (Mamounas et al., 1983). This finding suggests that bicuculline produces its selective abolition of the CR through blockage of inhibitory GABAergic synaptic transmission that is in some way essential for generation of the learned response. What kind of other specific chemical processes play a role in classical conditioning of the NM/eyelid response still needs to be elucidated. Little is known about the duration and the neurobiology of the changes underlying the learning of the CR.

SUMMARY

The circuitries responsible for one example of classical conditioning have been clearly identified. In addition, substantial data exist that strongly suggest sites within the circuitry that contain the plasticity necessary for learning. Now that the site(s) have been identified, the cellular and molecular mechanisms await discovery. An important next step is to elucidate the cellular mechanisms involved in this form of learning. It remains to be determined what other training paradigms will share common features with this circuit.

CLASSICAL CONDITIONING OF FOREARM POSITION: SYNAPTIC PLASTICITY AND GROWTH IN LEARNING

OVERVIEW

The neural mechanisms involved in learning of a motor response after repeated trials are of fundamental importance. How is it that conditioned reflexes of arm movement, leg movement, or even body position are learned? These are examples of skill or procedural memory. Unlike simple fact (cognitive) tasks, learning of motor skills, such as riding a bike and balancing, usually requires repeated trials over a considerable period of time. Inherent in such learning is the need to learn a particular body response in reaction to one or more sensory stimuli. The most detailed studies, which have been made in the red nucleus by Tsukahara and co-workers, are concerned with the mechanisms of classical conditioning of limb position. The results of these studies illustrate that new synapse formation appears to occur with conditioning and that the same plastic growth reactions also occur after injury to mediate functional recovery. Thus, the same plasticity mechanisms appear to serve a range of adaptive capacities.

NATURE OF SYSTEM AND PARADIGM

The essential circuitry involved in the control of forearm position is simple and well-defined (figure 8; Tsukahara, 1986). Sensory information from the forearm travels via the spinal cord and the interpositus nucleus to the red nucleus. The red nucleus in turn drives the motor neurons controlling the forearm flexor muscle (biceps branchi). The red nucleus is the key integrative center. In addition to input from the cerebellum, the red nucleus receives input from the cerebral cortex. The red nucleus appears to be essential in avoidance conditioning since rubral lesions abolish conditioned forearm flexion when a tone as a conditioned stimulus (CS) is paired with forearm electric shock as an unconditioned stimulus (US) (Smith, 1970).

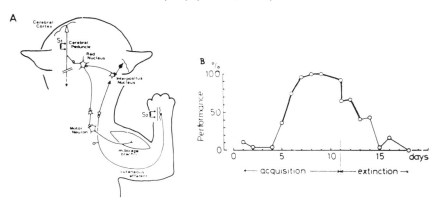

Figure 8: Associative learning mediated by the RN.
   A. Arrangement of experimental setup. CS, conditioned stimulus; US, unconditioned stimulus; CP, cerebral peduncle; IP, nucleus interpositus of the cerebellum; INT, interneuron; Flex, MN, flexor motoneuron.
   B. Change in performance. Abscissa, day after onset of training, CS-US interval of 100 msec. After day 11, the stimulus sequence was reversed to US-CS with an interval of 900 msec.
(Modified from Tsukahara, Oda, and Notsu, 1981)

What is the nature of the synaptic change that occurs upon conditioning? In order to aid in the identification of the primary site of conditioning, outflow from the red nucleus was restricted to the cortical rubral pathway by lesioning other corticofugal (outflow) pathways below the red nucleus (Tsukahara et al., 1981). This experimental procedure eliminated the contribution of the pyramidal tract as well as cortico-ponto-cerebellar and other corticobulbar fibers in reflex. The training procedure involved pairing a subthreshold CS to the cerebral peduncle with an electric shock (US) to the forearm. After pairing the CS-US in close temporal association, an initially ineffective CS elicited flexion of the forelimb. The CS preceded the US by 60-200 msec over about 120 trials per day. At the end of the training session, the flexion responses were tested by changing the CS intensity, and the relationship between the performance score and applied current was determined. Training required several days, consistent with motor learning of skills. Initially, stimulation of the cerebral peduncle elicited no forearm movement. After 7 days of pairing stimulation of the cerebral peduncle with electrical stimulation of the forearm, forearm flexion could be elicited by stimulation of the cerebral peduncle alone. In parallel with the improved performance score, the minimum current to produce 100 percent performance also decreased. The performance was not elicited after a period of several days during which the CS was not paired with the US. Random presentation of US and CS also failed to produce conditioning. These data rule out nonspecific changes in excitability along the conditioned pathway.

KEY BRAIN AREAS AND THE SYNAPTIC MECHANISM OF LEARNING

The site of synaptic change with conditioning could reside in the cortical pathway, in the interpositus pathway, or in subsequent steps that activate the muscle. The probability of firing red nucleus neurons after cortical stimulation increased after conditioning. Such an increase reflected a more effective synaptic input (Oda et al., 1981). Analysis of cortically evoked EPSPs (excitatory postsynaptic potentials) in the red nucleus revealed that a new fast-rising EPSP had emerged that was superimposed onto the normally observed slow-rising EPSP (Tsukahara and Oda, 1981). The primary site of change did not appear to be below the red nucleus or in the interpositus input to the red nucleus. The stimulus intensity required to elicit the performance score after interpositus stimulation did not decline in parallel with that for stimulating the cortical input (Tsukahara et al., 1981). Thus, synaptic transmission through cortico-rubral synapses is associated with conditioning.

The cortico-rubral synapses already present may have increased their strengths, or new synapses may have grown. Studies of partial denervation distal to the red nucleus and on cross union of peripheral nerves suggest the possibility that new synapse formation may have occurred (see Tsukahara, 1986, for a review). As mentioned above, the red nucleus (RN) receives inputs from the ipsilateral cerebral cortex (via the cerebral peduncle) and the contralateral cerebellum (from the nucleus interpositus). Cortical inputs synapse upon the distal dendrites of red nucleus cells, whereas cerebellar inputs synapse upon somatic regions of the cells (Murakami et al., 1982). Correspondingly, electrical stimulation of the cortical inputs produces a characteristic slow-rising dendritic EPSP, whereas stimulation of the cerebellar inputs produces a fast-rising EPSP. These two responses are easily distinguished and predictable on the basis of the location of the afferent terminals relative to the cell body. In the adult, destruction of the cerebellar input causes the cortical input to sprout and form new synapses onto proximal regions of the dendrites. Within ten days after destroying the cerebellar inputs, the rise-time of cortically evoked EPSPs in the red nucleus is significantly reduced. (figure 9). The prediction that cortical fibers had indeed formed new synapses closer to the cell body has since been confirmed by combining lesion studies with electron microscopic examination of cells in the red nucleus (King et al., 1972; Nakamura et al., 1974; Murakami et al., 1982).

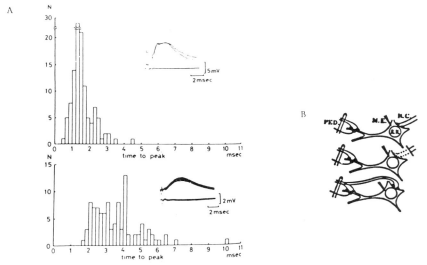

Figure 9: Reactive synaptogenesis in red nucleus. Rise time of corticorubral excitatory postsynaptic potentials induced by stimulating cerebral peduncle after lesion of the nucleus interpositus.
   A. Frequency distribution of time to peak in operated cats (upper histogram) and in normal cats (lower histogram). Specimen records of intracellular and corresponding extracellular records are shown in inset of each histogram.
   B. Diagram of experimental arrangement. R.N., red nucleus neuron: B.C. input from interpeduncular nucleus; PED, input from cerebrum through cerebral peduncle; M.E., microelectrode.
(From Tsukahara, 1986)

Tsukahara and coworkers have also shown that synaptic rear-rangements in the red nucleus can be induced, in the absence of direct lesions, in response to cross-innervation of flexor and extensor nerves of the forelimb (Fuijito et al., 1982; Tsukahara et al., 1982; Tsukahara and Fuijito, 1976). Two to six months after cross-innervation of forelimb nerves, the rise-time of cortically evoked EPSPs in the red nucleus is significantly reduced (Tsukahara et al., 1974, 1975). This effect is restricted almost exclusively to cells innervating the upper regions of the spinal cord where the motor neurons contributing to the affected nerves are located.

Thus, new, fast-rise time EPSPs are seen after lesions, cross- union of peripheral nerves, and conditioning, which suggests a common mechanism. These data also suggest that cortical fibers innervating the distal dendrites of red nucleus cells sprout additional terminals that form synapses along regions of the dendrites more proximal to the cell bodies during the acquisition of the learned response. Indeed, in preliminary experiments Tsukahara and coworkers have reported that, after conditioning, additional cortical synapses have grown onto the cell body of red nucleus neurons. Thus, learning may be mediated by new synaptic growth of a type similar to that seen after partial dener-vation. The mechanisms initiating growth are unknown but may be similar to those involved in reactive synaptogenesis after injury (see Nieto-Sampedro and Cotman, 1985, for discussion).

SUMMARY

Sprouting of cortico-rubral synapses appears to serve as the neurobiological mechanism for learning of a conditioned motor response of limbs. Conditioning occurred over 7 days, when it became maximal. Synaptic growth also mediated functional recovery after cerebellar lesions and after crossing of peripheral nerves. These studies illustrate not only remarkable plasticity of the system but also common use of key, centrally-placed mechanisms for mediating several adaptive responses. An interesting implication of these studies is not only that learning and damage-induced plasticity share a common mechanism but also that the mechanisms in one may predict those in the other.

SYNAPTIC PLASTICITY IN THE HIPPOCAMPUS AS A MODEL OF LEARNING

OVERVIEW

Long-term potentiation (LTP) is an extremely stable form of synaptic facilitation produced in the hippocampus (and elsewhere) by very short periods of high frequency stimulation. LTP exhibits a number of properties expected of a learning mechanism, and it is widely suspected that its substrates are used in behavioral learning. Recent studies have provided a remarkable picture of how LTP is induced, and as a result, describe a specific hypothesis concerning the origins of memory. Pharmacological studies have confirmed that drugs that block a receptor critical for LTP induction also cause a severe anterograde amnesia in rats. This finding constitutes the first (to our knowledge) instance in which neurobiological research pointed to a potent memory-blocking drug.

CHARACTERISTICS OF HIPPOCAMPAL LONG-TERM POTENTIATION

As noted earlier, learning theorists generally assume that the actual encoding process involves particular patterns of activity acting upon a limited number of synapses and resulting in stable, perhaps structural, changes in these synapses. Since any given learning episode affects a small number of widely dispersed contacts, one cannot follow the synaptic events associated with specific memories. However, one could ask the question of whether particular patterns of stimulation do in fact produce the types of effects expected of a learning device. The answer to this is yes.

Brief periods (1/4 to 1 sec) of high frequency stimulation delivered to pathways in the hippocampus cause an increase in synaptic strength that can last for weeks (Bliss and Gardner-Medwin, 1973). Subsequent experiments showed that this long-term potentiation effect has characteristics that are proper for making it an excellent candidate for the process via which memories are formed:

1. Rapid induction;
2. Extreme persistence;
3. Synapse specific: induction of LTP in one group of synapses in a dendritic field does not increase the strength of neighboring contacts (Lynch et al., 1977; Dunwiddie and Lynch, 1978; Andersen et al., 1980) (this feature is assumed by virtually every neurobiological theory of memory);
4. Convergent activity by a group of synapses in the same cell (McNaughton et al., 1978) (many "computational" theories of memory postulate that storage requires convergence);
5. Correspondence of optimal pattern for induction to a naturally occurring brain rhythm ("theta") that appears when an animal is exploring its environment (Larson et al., 1986).

CAUSES AND SUBSTRATES OF LONG-TERM POTENTIATION

Studies from a number of laboratories have provided a satisfactory account of the events that trigger LTP. Considerable progress has also been made in uncovering the modifications that maintain the potentiation. These findings, when considered together, provide a surprisingly detailed picture of how memory might be produced in the mammalian forebrain. Here we list the major events in the LTP sequence.

1. Brief bursts of activity in a collection of input axons with the bursts at 5/second for a second or more (Larson et al., 1986). This pattern corresponds to firing patterns of hippocampal cells under some circumstances.
2. Transient suppression of inhibitory responses with maximum suppression at 200 msec after each burst. This causes successive bursts at 5 sec to elicit longer postsynaptic responses (Larson and Lynch, 1986).
3. Prolonged responses activate a peculiar type of receptor (the N-methyl-D-aspartate [NMDA] receptor) linked to an ion conductance channel that is blocked under normal conditions (Larson and Lynch, 1986). Blockade of these receptors prevents the induction of LTP (figure 10; Collingridge et al., 1983; Harris et al., 1984; Morris et al., 1986).
4. Elevation of internal calcium levels in the region of the synapse in the target cell. Buffering of internal calcium prevents the occurrence of LTP (Lynch et al., 1983).
5. Modification of the numbers of synaptic contacts and possibly alterations in existing contacts (Lee et al., 1980; Chang and Greenough, 1984; Wenzel and Mathies, 1985).

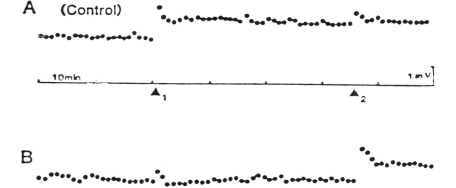

Figure 10:   NMDA receptor antagonist (AP5) blocks long-term potentiation (LTP).
　　　　　A.   LTP in a control preparation. Note the long-lasting increase in response after high frequency stimulation (arrow).
　　　　　B.   LTP does not develop in the presence of DAP5. The trace plots the peak amplitude of the synaptic potential recorded extracellularly.
(Data from Harris et al., 1984)

The structural changes (in step 5) correlate with the magnitude of the LTP effect and appear to be quite stable, and they provide a simple explanation for the extreme persistence of the effect.

The five-step sequence described above does not explain how calcium produces anatomical reorganization. This is a crucial point for any theory of learning. Calcium has been linked to morphological reorganization and alterations in the surface chemistry of simple cells (for example, blood platelets and red blood cells; see Siman, Baudry, and Lynch, 1986), and it is not unreasonable to assume that the processes that it uses in these systems also operate in brain. One candidate mechanism involves a calcium-activated protease (calpain), which degrades cytoskeletal proteins that are integral to the structure of the synapse (see Lynch and Baudry, 1984, for a review). Activation of this enzyme reproduces in synaptic membrane fractions a specific biochemical change (increased uptake and/or binding of glutamic acid) that is found after the induction of LTP (Lynch et al., 1982; Siman et al., 1985). A great advantage of this hypothesis is that calpain's effects (partial breakdown of structural proteins) is irreversible and likely to affect the anatomy of the synaptic region. It seems likely, however, that other calcium-dependent enzymes, such as the protein kinases, are also transiently activated during the induction of LTP and modulate the effects of calpain (see Akers et al., 1986).

LINKS BETWEEN LTP AND LEARNING

The description of how LTP might be elicited in behaving animals is now so detailed that it predicts that certain drugs should influence the learning process. This prediction has been recently confirmed. When infused into the cerebral ventricles, antagonists of the NMDA receptor produce a profound impairment of the ability of the rats to learn spatial locations (Morris et al., 1986). This data memory list is reasonably resistant to a host of other pharmacological treatments. Moreover, this anterograde amnesia is highly selective. Past memories are not disrupted, and the animals are still able to learn simple visual discrimination problems (Morris et al., 1986).

Other studies have shown that inhibitors of the calcium-sensitive protease calpain also disrupt spatial learning as well as the very simple task of learning and remembering that one of two odors leads to a reward. The drugs did not affect avoidance conditioning, in which the rat avoids areas of a cage where mild shocks are administered (Staubli et al., 1984; 1985a).

SUMMARY

Behavioral studies resulting from LTP research have produced new types of amnestic agents, strengthened the idea that the substrates of potentiation are actually used by brain to encode new data, and emphasized again the point that different forms of memory may involve different chemical mechanisms. Recent autoradiographic studies show that NMDA receptors appear to be most concentrated in the hippocampus and widely distributed in different regions of the cerebral cortex (Monaghan and Cotman, 1985). Their distribution may predict the locus of circuits throughout the brain where LTP may occur with learning.

Another type of long-lasting synaptic plasticity (long-term depression) has been described in the cerebellar cortex (Ito et al., 1982; Ito, 1984) but has not been as extensively studied.

CORRELATES OF LEARNING IN CORTICAL CIRCUITRIES

In the preceding discussions, we found that the study of simple systems has yielded a new set of reasonably specific ideas about the way in which learning is etched into neuronal circuitries. We now consider modifications produced in higher brain regions by learning and look for links between these modifications and the mechanisms identified in the research on simple systems. Since one of the themes of this review is learning in humans, we focus attention on forebrain and neocortical structures and consider results of studies of both adult and immature animals.

Any understanding of cognitive dysfunction during development requires knowledge of the mechanisms of early learning that serve the developing organism. Early learning is an important survival mechanism for the young. Learning is used to establish bonds with parents. It adapts the nervous system to particular environments and in general begins to build the encyclopedia of experience for later life. Nervous system circuitry, once set during development, is relatively permanent. Changes that occur in the adult are relatively subtle compared to the impact that disturbances or the environment can have on the developing nervous system. What role does early learning play in establishing nervous system circuitry? What are the critical variables? And what mechanisms predispose the circuitries to particular changes?

Developmental neurobiologists have demonstrated that differential neural activity, including learning, causes the selection of specific neurons and synapses. While early neuronal death in the selection of connections has long been linked to differential neural stimulation, the mechanism by which specific neurons survive has received less attention. It appears that learning may be a selective agent in this process. Information about selection processes may help to provide answers to the question of how normal variation in early experience produces individual differences in the brain and in the expression of behavior.

In the following discussion, two of the more advanced research areas in the field are reviewed, olfactory learning and early visual experience. What is striking about these systems is that the changes produced by learning involve at least some of the same mechanisms, including cellular chemistries, found to be important in the studies of simple systems.

OVERVIEW

Plasticity in the olfactory bulb has proven to be an excellent model of developmental learning. Permanent anatomical, neurophysiological, and behavioral changes occur when normal olfactory stimuli are experienced early in life. Neonatal rats learn to prefer either the odor of their mother or an artificial odor experienced with appropriate tactile stimulation, apparently as a result of a large increase in the size of the glomeruli that are coding for the learned odor. The reorganization of the bulk suppresses the output signal to the piriform cortex. This change indicates the presence of a learned odor. The special neural and behavioral changes associated with early learning can be blocked with an antagonist to the N-methyl-D-aspartate receptor.

NATURE OF THE SYSTEM AND PARADIGM

Norway rat pups learn to approach the odor of their mother (Leon, 1974; Leon and Moltz, 1971; 1972). This preference facilitates mother-young reunions at a time when the young are mobile (Leon, 1983). Pups also learn to prefer and approach nonmaternal odors if they are exposed to them while they receive tactile stimulation of the kind they normally receive from their mother (Leon, 1983; Pedersen et al., 1982). Human neonates acquire an attraction for the odor of their mother within the first weeks of life. They can also acquire a behavioral preference for other odors following early experience (Balogh and Porter, in press; Mac-Farlane, 1975).

The olfactory receptor neurons transduce chemical information into neural signals that are transmitted to second-order neurons within the olfactory bulb. Many olfactory receptor neurons synapse with relatively few mitral, tufted, and periglomerular cells in synaptic structures called glomeruli. The mitral cells project from the bulb to a variety of brain structures, the tufted cells have mostly intra- and interbulbar connections, and the periglomerular cells appear to mediate interglomerular inhibition. Most of the local and centrifugal inhibition is mediated by the inhibitory interneurons, the granule cells (figure 11).

Can experience with a specific odor induce the developing olfactory bulb to a special response to that odor? Pups were exposed to specific odors while receiving tactile stimulation to mimic maternal contact during odor exposure. Peppermint odor was used because rat pups will approach it as if it were a maternal odor (Leon et al., 1977).

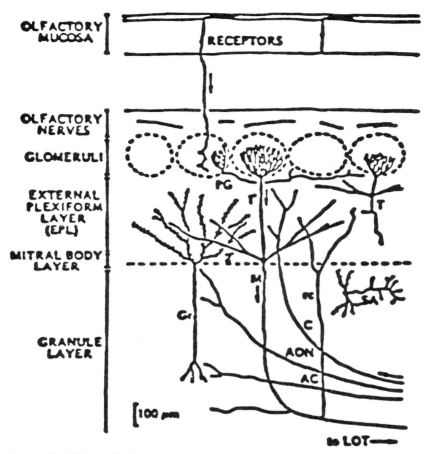

OLFACTORY MUCOSA

RECEPTORS

OLFACTORY NERVES

GLOMERULI

EXTERNAL PLEXIFORM LAYER (EPL)

MITRAL BODY LAYER

GRANULE LAYER

100 µm

to LOT

Figure 11: Olfactory bulb neuroanatomy.

STRUCTURAL CORRELATES OF EARLY LEARNING

The nature of the response to peppermint odor in the olfactory bulbs of 19-day-old odor-learning pups and control pups was examined with the use of 14C 2-deoxyglucose (2-DG) autoradiography. This technique reveals spatially specific activation of the olfactory bulb glomerular layer evoked by different odors (Greer et al., 1981; 1982). The odor-learning pups had 64 percent greater 2-DG uptake in focal areas of the glomerular layer (Coopersmith and Leon, 1984). The levels of uptake in the periventricular core and in other portions of the glomerular layer did not differ between groups. This difference was not attributable to differential respiration of the odor (Coopersmith and Leon, 1984) or to trigeminal system activation (Coopersmith, Henderson, and Leon, 1986). The enhanced 2-DG uptake in the identified glomeruli areas (Coopersmith, Lee, and Leon, 1986) persisted for at least 3 months, the longest period examined.

There was no difference in the number of glomeruli associated with the 2-DG foci; however, the glomeruli of odor-learning pups in these foci were about 20 percent larger than those of controls. Peppermint-learning pups invariably had enlarged glomerular clusters in the area generating the increased 2-DG uptake, while the same area of control pups had no such clusters. These glomerular clusters characteristically protrude from the glomerular layer into the external plexiform layer (EPL). To date, this is the largest localized structural change found in the brain that has been associated with learning.

The enhanced response was clearly associated with learning. Only the pups that were simultaneously stroked and exposed to peppermint had both an increased behavioral preference for the odor and an enhanced neural response for the odor (Sullivan and Leon, 1986). Odor exposure alone or backward pairing of odor and stroking did not induce either an olfactory preference or an enhanced neural response to the odor (Sullivan and Leon, 1986). Indeed, the response appeared specific to this type of learning. Aversive olfactory learning did not evoke an enhanced response to the learned odor (Coopersmith, Lee, and Leon, 1986).

The enhanced response was odor-specific and spatially specific. Peppermint-learning pups showed a significantly higher 2-DG uptake in response to peppermint than that of cyclohexanone-learning pups (Coopersmith, Henderson, and Leon, 1986a). Cyclohexanone-learning pups had an enhanced response to cyclohexanone in another part of the bulb, compared with that of air-exposed control pups (Coopersmith, Henderson, and Leon, 1986a).

It is possible that mitral cell activity is suppressed by early olfactory learning. Single unit activity from mitral cells associated within the identified glomerular areas of odor-learning is suppressed relative to that of control cells (Wilson, Sullivan, and Leon, 1985; Wilson and Leon, 1986). Thus, a learned odor may increase the activity of glomerular layer neurons (periglomerular and/or tufted cells), which may then decrease mitral cell activity. The decrease in mitral cell activity in response to attractive learned odors may produce unique, sharpened signals to the piriform cortex.

Learning caused an enlargement in glomeruli only during the first week of life. Olfactory experience with stroking given to adults did not evoke a special neurobehavioral response. Indeed, the development of the enhanced glomerular response appears to be restricted to olfactory experience given within the first week postpartum (Woo and Leon, 1986). Similar experience, even in the second week of life, was ineffective in evoking the enhanced response.

THE CELLULAR MECHANISM: DECREASED CELL DEATH DURING THE CRITICAL PERIOD

It appears that early olfactory learning saves a greater proportion of the external tufted cells from dying postnatally. The increased number of tufted cells may then contribute both to enlarging the glomeruli and increasing the activation of granule cells in the interior plexiform layer (IPL), thereby inhibiting neighboring mitral cells when a learned odor has activated that glomerular area.

Glutamate receptors of the N-methyl-D-aspartate (NMDA) type have been identified in the neonatal bulb. Blocking them prevents the development of olfactory preference and the enhanced glomerular response in young rats (Lincoln et al., 1986). The specific NMDA antagonist AP5 blocked the enhanced 2-DG uptake in focal areas of the glomerular layer as well as the specific neurobehavioral response to early olfactory learning. Noradrenergic mechanisms may also be involved with early olfactory learning (Sullivan and Leon, 1986).

SUMMARY

Early olfactory experience determines one of the many routes by which the normal olfactory brain will develop. Neonatal rodents, like babies, learn to prefer the odor of their mother when the odor is experienced with appropriate tactile stimulation. The size of select glomeruli increases apparently due to the survival of additional tufted cells, NMDA receptors and therefore neural activity appears to mediate this process. The behavioral, structural, neurochemical, and neurophysiological consequences of early learning have been described for this system.

EARLY VISUAL EXPERIENCE AND TRAINING THE VISUAL SYSTEM

OVERVIEW

A minimum level of normal stimulation is also required for the visual brain to develop along its single normal path. For example, children may permanently lose vision in one eye if vision is temporarily impaired by eye injury early in life, even if the damage to the eye itself heals completely. The nature of the needed visual stimulation has the formal characteristics of a learning situation. It is an activity-dependent process that produces long lasting change in cortical structures. Both pre- and postsynaptic activation are necessary in accordance with the predictions of a Hebbian synapse. NMDA receptor activation and Ca^{2+} ions appear to play a pivotal role.

The organization of the developing visual system depends on neural activity. In the mature visual system, inputs from the two eyes terminate in different laminae of the thalamic relay (lateral geniculate). In turn, the thalamic inputs to the cortex terminate within well-serrated patches or bands in layer IV of the visual cortex (the ocular dominance columns). The segregation of afferents into ocular dominance columns occurs over the course of postnatal development of cats (Shatz, 1983; Shatz and Kirkwood, 1984). While the afferents are initially commingled, the overlapping connections retract and serrate. Suppression of retinal input blocks the segregation. This finding indicates that neural activity is needed for segregation (Archer, Dubin, and Stark, 1982; Mower, Cristen, and Caplan, 1984; Swindale, 1982). Conversely, the segregation of the afferents is facilitated by making the activity patterns from the two eyes dissimilar by alternating occlusion or by causing the eyes to squint (Anderson, Olavarria, and Van Sluyters, 1983; Shantz, Lindstrom, and Wiesel, 1977; Tieman and Tumosa, 1983). Even when the retinal output is suppressed, asynchronous activation of the afferent pathway by electrical stimulation produces the normal segregated pattern; simultaneous activation of the two visual pathways is ineffective (Stryker and Harris, 1986).

Asymmetry in afferent activation from the two eyes also causes an asymmetry in the segregated columns (Blakemore, Gary, Henderson, Swindale, and Vital-Durand, 1980; Hubel, Wiesel and LeVay, 1977). Monocular deprivation causes the size of the patches from the deprived eye to shrink while the size of the patches derived from the other eye expand (LeVay and Stryker, 1979).

The plasticity of this system in response to changes in visual input is restricted to a period early in life (LeVay and Stryker, 1979). In cats, the modifiability of the system in response to differential visual input is correlated with the time during which the patches are segregating (LeVay and Stryker, 1979). In the monkey, segregation is complete at birth, but the plasticity of the system is still present early in life (Blakemore et al., 1980; Swindale, Vital-Durand, and Blakemore, 1981).

MECHANISMS UNDERLYING VISUAL CORTEX ORGANIZATION

The changes in segregation patterns depend on particular patterns of afferent activation. The necessary condition is concurrent activation of both the presynaptic and postsynaptic neurons in the system. This requirement is reminiscent of Hebb's (1949) model for synaptic plasticity during learning. Interestingly, it is also the requirement for long-term potentiation.

If the signals from the two eyes simultaneously converge on their target neuron, their dual connection to the neuron is likely to be stabilized. If, however, the two eyes send information that is out of phase, the two inputs are in competition with each other and one pathway is repressed. Signals from the two eyes must be present within 200-400 msec. Otherwise, the binocular disparity imposes a shift in the segregation of the afferents (Altmann, Luhann, Singer, and Greuel, 1985). When postsynaptic responses are blocked, retinal terminals retract. This observation suggests the need for stabilization of postsynaptic activity in the formation of visual system patterns of organization (Schmidt, 1985; Schmidt and Edwards, 1983).

Both pre- and postsynaptic activity is necessary. Postsynaptic activation alone is insufficient. Postsynaptic activation of target neurons, even with afferent input, is insufficient to induce the normal pattern of visual system organization. Visual information does not influence cortical organization when kittens are paralyzed or anesthetized (Singer, 1979). Similarly, blocking sensory information from the extraocular muscles prevents the expression of ocular dominance despite the fact that the visual information is generating activity in the afferents (Buisseret and Singer, 1983).

Perhaps only the sensory information that is used effectively can influence the development of visual system organization. For example, cats develop a normal organization despite monocular deprivation if the open eye is rotated (Singer, von Grunau, and Rauschecker, 1979). The rotation induces major sensory-motor integration deficits, which induces the animals to use less and less of the unreliable sensory cues. In such animals, the retinal signals are eventually ignored and are ineffective in modifying the cortical organization.

REQUIREMENTS FOR CONCURRENT AROUSING STIMULI

Pairing monocular visual stimulation with electrical stimulation of the reticular formation or the intralaminar nucleus of the thalamus can overcome the inability of anesthetized and paralyzed animals to develop ocular dominance. Conversely, when lesions of the intralaminar nucleus of the thalamus are made, monocular deprivation does not change the cortical neurons from binocular to monocular (Singer, 1982).

These data suggest that the changes in visual input are effective in organizing the system only if attended to or recognized by the brain by means of coincident nonspecific arousal. Thus, only when sensory stimulation is paired with a nonspecific arousing stimulus does cortical plasticity occur. It would be important to determine whether manipulation of the nonspecific arousal system would affect other types of early learning. At present, however, no information is available.

What neural systems may control nonspecific arousal? Cortical neurons continue to respond to binocular visual stimulation after monocular visual restriction if both norepinephrine (NE) and acetylcholine (ACh) are absent (Bear and Singer, 1986). If either NE or ACh is present, cortical afferents segregate properly (Kasamatsu and Pettigrew, 1979; Kasamatsu, Pettigrew, and Ary, 1979; Bear and Daniels,

1983; Daw, Robertson, Rader, Videen, and Cosica, 1984). Thus, both acetylcholine and norepinephrine may mediate the contribution of the nonspecific arousal system in specifying which visual stimulation will affect the organization of the cortical response to subsequent visual stimulation.

Just as with adult learning (Morris et al., 1986), early olfactory learning (Lincoln et al., 1986), and long-term potentiation, NMDA receptor activation also appears to be required for mediating the consequences of early visual experience (Singer, Kleinschmidt, and Bear, 1986).

Is there a final common signal? An influx of extracellular calcium ions into cortical neurons appears to mediate the changes in cortical organization and may be the common signal for mediating plasticity (Singer, 1986). Only when visual stimulation was accompanied by arousing electrical stimulation did the calcium ion pattern suggest such an influx from the extracellular compartment. Visual stimulation alone or arousing stimulation alone neither changed cortical calcium ion levels nor did such experience modify the development of the visual cortex.

SUMMARY

These findings indicate that the normal pattern of visual system development depends on a specific coincidence of visual stimulation and arousing stimulation. An abnormal pattern of visual system organization occurs if either aspect of this early experience is not present. The implication of these findings is that the developing brain circuitry registers environmental signals when the nonspecific arousal system gives significance to an event.

GENERAL COMMENTS ON EARLY LEARNING

The neurobiology of learning during development has not been extensively studied, yet the topic offers great promise for research. Unlike the subtle and often inaccessible changes that appear to occur during adult learning, the changes observed following learning during early life appear quite large and accessible. Indeed, it seems that the developmental processes may amplify small changes that are made early in life and that can be observed by investigators. There is a clear need for more research.

There are indications that some mechanisms are shared by adults and infants following learning. Both glutamate and norepinephrine, for example, have been implicated in the mechanisms underlying both adult and neonatal learning (Morris et al., 1986; Lincoln et al., 1986; Sullivan and Leon, 1986; Gold and Zornetzer, 1984). Similar neural structures involved in adult learning also increase their activity during neonatal learning (Kucharski, Browde, and Hall, 1986).

CORRELATES OF LEARNING IN CORTICAL CIRCUITRIES

ENVIRONMENTAL INFLUENCES ON SYNAPSES

OVERVIEW

The basic structure of the brain is laid down during development and, once formed, is usually thought of as being fixed throughout life. As noted above, however, the number and/or pattern of synapses may serve as a substrate for at least certain forms of learning, and synapses may also change with use. Can environment, the composite influence of learning, experience, and use, produce measurable affects on brain structure? If so, to what degree? It is now clear that the environment and even learning of skills impact on brain structure throughout life, particularly during development.

NEURON STRUCTURE RESPONDS TO THE ENVIRONMENT

Behavioral experience influences the number of dendritic spines and the size of the dendritic tree in the cortex and cerebellum. For example, mice raised for 17 days in an environment where they could exercise and be as active as they liked showed an increase of 23 percent in the number of spines on the dendrites of Purkinje cells beyond that of mice housed in cages with only enough space to allow access to food and water (Pysh and Weiss, 1979). Similar results were obtained in young monkeys. Likewise, rats raised in an "enriched" environment showed an increase in dendritic branching in the occipital cortex (Uylings et al., 1978) as well as an increase in the number of synapses per neuron (Turner and Greenough, 1983) relative to rats raised in an "impoverished" environment. Whether the increase in the number of synapses per neuron is due to additional synapse formation or to the stabilization of existing synapses is not yet clear. Changes in dendritic morphology have also been observed with aging (experience?) in both rodents and humans. Interestingly, dendritic structure often becomes more elaborate with age, perhaps reflecting life-long experience encoded into neuronal structure.

Structural changes are most easily produced in young animals, but similar though less pronounced alterations occur in adults. Recently, for example, Greenough et al. (1985) demonstrated that motor training could directly remodel the apical dendrites of layer V pyramidal cells in the motor cortex of adult rats. Rats have a preferred paw, as humans have a preferred hand. Normally, apical dendritic branching of layer V pyramidal neurons is greater on the side opposite the preferred paw. After 16 days of training to use the nonpreferred paw, branching was greater on the side opposite the preferred paw (figure 12). The experience changed dendritic structure and probably, therefore, synapse patterns. In the experiments of Greenough et al. (1985), the enhanced dendritic branching may have been produced by learning, increased use, or both.

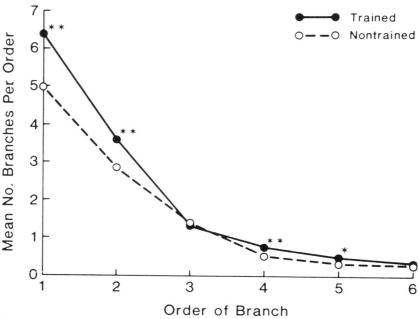

Figure 12: Mean number of branches at each order of bifurcation from the apical dendrite for combined groups. Trained group includes hemisphere opposite trained forelimbs. Nontrained group includes both hemisphere of controls and hemispheres opposite nontrained forelimbs. **p < .001, *p < .001, by analysis of variance.

(From Greenough et al., 1985)

SYNAPSES MAY BE LOST AND REPLACED THROUGHOUT LIFE

Structural changes in the number and pattern of synapses have long been suggested as a plausible mechanism for improved performance with use and for learning and memory. Indeed, recently acquired basic information about synapse turnover adds new strength to this hypothesis. Synapse turnover, defined as the loss and replacement of synapses by nondamaging stimuli, appears to be an ongoing process in at least some areas of the mammalian nervous system. In fact, if learning involves synaptic growth, turnover must occur because we are always learning. Synapse turnover has been well documented in the peripheral nervous system, including the parasympathetic innervation of the ciliary muscle (Townes-Anderson and Raviola, 1978) and the innervation of skeletal muscles by motor neurons (Barker and Ip, 1966), and at sensory nerve endings (Burgess et al., 1974). In the mature central nervous system, perhaps the most remarkable example of stimulus evoked synapse turnover occurs in the hypothalamus and neurohypophysis (see Hatton, 1985). Water deprivation, lactation, or late pregnancy and parturition cause the glial processes and pituicytes to withdraw, which results in (a) the appearance of synaptic contacts between adjacent magnocellular neurons in the supraoptic nucleus, and (b) access of the axon endings to the perivascular space in the neurohypophysis (Hatton, 1985). These events, which are totally reversible, result in increased water retention in the kidneys or a rise in mammary pressure (see Cotman et al., 1981; Cotman and Nieto-Sampedro, 1984).

SUMMARY

Synapse turnover may be the basic mechanism in neuronal remodeling caused by environment. Although relatively little is known about the relationship between synapse turnover and behavior, it seems logical to assume that the ability of the brain to alter its synaptic circuitry in response to stimuli is somehow related to the adaptive abilities of the nervous system. In this sense, synapse turnover is probably involved in improved performance and ongoing learning and memory processes. Learning may accelerate or slow the process and thereby adjust neuronal connectivity. Indeed, as shown by work on the LTP paradigm, changes in synaptic numbers can be rapidly induced in the adult brain.

Can differences in the structure of the mature brain created during development be correlated with learning? Very little data are available for animal models at present if lesion studies and genetic studies are excluded. One pertinent study, however, is that of Lippe et al. (1984). These investigators noted that the rate of two-way avoidance learning in rats and mice is inversely correlated with the size of the intra- and infrapyramidal mossy fiber projection in the hippocampus. In other words, rats that are good learners have a small mossy fiber projection, whereas rats that are poor learners have a larger mossy fiber projection. Furthermore, this relationship is maintained following experimental manipulation of the mossy fiber projection by thyroxin treatment. Thus, rat pups obtained from a line of good learners and injected with thyroxin show an increase in mossy fiber projections and a decrease in their rate of learning as adults. The fact that learning ability is predictable on the basis of mossy fiber anatomy attains special significance in view of age-related increases in mossy fiber terminals in the hippocampus and dentate gyrus of humans (Cassell and Brown, 1984).

Primate Models That Reproduce Specific Clinical Syndromes in Humans

OVERVIEW

Previous discussions in this paper have defined what is meant by "memory," listed and described various types of memories, and discussed how specific animal models have been used to study the mechanisms of memory formation and the relationship between memory and specific structures in the brain. Next, we discuss some of the current thinking regarding the anatomy of memory formation in humans and show how certain animal models have been useful in studying the relationship between limbic lesions and the types of associative memory deficits that have been observed following brain injury in humans.

KEY BRAIN AREAS IN HUMANS IN "MEMORY" CIRCUITS

Amnesia is characterized by an impaired ability to acquire new information and by difficulty remembering at least some information that was acquired prior to the onset of amnesia. Our knowledge of memory formation in humans is based largely on the study of human amnestic syndromes.

At least two areas of the brain appear to be critical to memory formation, the medial temporary lobe region (including the hippocampal formation, amygdala, and temporal stem) and the region surrounding the third ventricle (including the dorsomedial nucleus of the thalamus and mammillary bodies). Medial temporal lobe amnesia is reported to occur following surgical resection of the medial temporal lobes (Scoville and Milner, 1957), following encephalitis (Rose and Symonds, 1960; Drachman and Adams, 1962), following occlusion of the posterior cerebral artery (Benson, Marsden, and Meadows, 1974), and after hypoxic ischemia (Volpe and Hirst, 1983; Squire, 1986). Midbrain diencephalic amnesia is reported to occur in patients with Korsakoff syndrome (Talland, 1965; Victor, Adams, and Collins, 1971; Butters and Cermak, 1980) and as a result of a tumor in the third ventricle (Williams and Pennybacker, 1954). While both syndromes result from damage to limbic structures, the anatomical relatedness of these two types of amnesia is still unclear. Considerable insight has been obtained, however, through the study of a small number of individuals in which severe anterograde amnesia (inability to learn new things) has occurred in the absence of other cognitive deficits. These cases are discussed below.

The first case is that of subject H.M. (Scoville and Milner, 1957; Corkin, 1968). In 1953, H.M. received a bilateral resection of the medial temporal lobes (including the anterior two-thirds of the hippocampal formation, hypocampal gyrus, amygdala, and uncus) in an effort to relieve severe epileptic seizures. Since that time, he has been unable to learn new facts, and he forgets daily events almost as fast as they occur. For example, H.M. is unable to learn a list of words, even after many repetitions, and he is unable to recognize faces he has seen many times over the past years. His memory deficit extends to both verbal and nonverbal material, and it involves information acquired through all sensory modalities.

Despite H.M.'s inability to acquire new information in the form of factual data, his ability to acquire perceptual-motor skills appears to be normal. H.M. successfully learned a mirror tracing task at a rate comparable to controls (Milner, 1968). His speed and accuracy increased in spite of the fact that he had no recollection of having previously performed the task. H.M. also successfully acquired the cognitive skills required for optimal solution to the Tower of Hanoi puzzle (Cohen, 1984). The puzzle consists of three pegs and five blocks of different diameters. The blocks are placed onto the left-most peg in order of decreasing diameter. To solve the puzzle, subjects must move the blocks from the left-most peg to the right-most peg. Only one block can be moved at a time, and a large block can never be placed onto a smaller one. The optimal solution to the puzzle requires 31 moves. H.M. learned the solution at a normal rate across four days of testing and exhibited impressive savings when retested one year later. Again, his acquisition of the cognitive skills required to solve the puzzle occurred despite no recollection of having previously performed the task.

The second case is that of subject N.A. (Teuber, Milner, and Vaughan, 1968; Kaushall, Zetin, and Squire, 1981). In 1960, N.A. received a penetrating brain injury with a miniature fencing foil, producing a lesion in the left dorsomedial thalamic nucleus (Squire and Moore, 1979). Since that time, N.A. has exhibited a severe anterograde amnesia primarily for verbal material, which is consistent with the left-hemisphere localization of his lesion. Nevertheless, he has an intelligence quotient of 124, can make accurate predictions of his own memory abilities, and, like H.M., has no noticeable impairment of higher cognitive functions. Studies have also revealed that, as with H.M., N.A.'s ability to acquire perceptual-motor skill is unimpaired (Cohen and Squire, 1980). A similar finding has recently been reported for patients with Alzheimer's disease (Eslinger and Damasio, 1986). These findings have led to the suggestion that memory for facts (declarative memory) and memory for perceptual-motor skills (procedural memory) are distinct entities, which involve different areas of the brain.

DIFFERENT BRAIN STRUCTURES APPEAR ESSENTIAL FOR FACT VS. RULE MEMORY

The fact that H.M. and N.A. are impaired in their ability to form some memories, but not others, is one piece of evidence supporting the distinction between what are known as fact (declarative) and rule (procedural) memories (see figure 1). Fact memory refers to memories for things which can be stated or "declared," such as word lists, faces, and numbers. Rule memory refers to memories associated with the acquisition of skills or "procedures." Hence, while H.M. and N.A. are impaired in their ability to form declarative memories, their procedural memory abilities are intact. This observation suggests that the processes that underlie declarative and procedural memory formation are functionally and anatomically distinct and that medial temporal lobe and mid-diencephalic structures are involved specifically with declarative memory processes.

MEMORY DEFICITS IN PRIMATES VS. MAN: CLOSE CORRELATIONS

Primate models have been particularly useful for understanding the severe amnestic syndromes observed following medial temporal lobe injury in humans. Normal monkeys were trained to perform a delayed nonmatching to sample (DNMS) task, a task also sensitive to human amnesia (Malamut et al., 1984; Mishkin, 1978; Murray and Mishkin, 1984; Zola-Morgan et al., 1982). The task consists of two trials. On the first trial, the monkey displaces a junk object to obtain a food reward. On the second trial, which can be presented many minutes or even hours later, the monkey is presented the original object together with a novel object, and must displace the novel object to obtain a food reward. Subsequent trials use different pairs of junk objects taken from a large set of several hundred objects. Acquisition of this task requires that the animals be able to distinguish the objects, recall which object was previously presented, and recall the rule that one must displace the novel object to obtain the reward. After being trained to a criterion of 90 correct choices in 100 trials, animals received (1) bilateral ablation of the hippocampal formation, (2) bilateral ablation of the amygdala, (3) ablation of both the hippocampal formation and the amygdala, or (4) no lesion. Although results from different laboratories are somewhat variable, the combined destruction of both the amygdala and hippocampal formation produced a much greater deficit than either hippocampal or amygdala destruction alone (complete destruction of either the hippocampus or the amygdala produced little or no deficit, even when using intertrial intervals lasting several hours). In particular, performance dropped from 90 percent correct responses with delay intervals of a few seconds to near-chance scores after delays of only a minute or two. These results suggest that the deficit is due to the animals' inability to recall which of the two objects had been previously presented.

To further characterize the deficits associated with medial temporal lobe amnesia, monkeys with amygdala and hippocampal lesions were also tested for their ability to perform a delayed matching to sample (DMS) task and an object discrimination task (Malamut et al., 1984). The DMS task is exactly the same as the DNMS task described above except that animals must now learn to choose the more familiar object of a pair to receive a reward. The object discrimination task requires animals to recall which object of a pair of objects had been baited on previous trials and to choose the baited object to get a reward. For example, 20 object pairs are presented in series and one object from each pair is baited. Each day, the same object pairs are presented in the same order, and the same objects are baited. Improved performance requires that animals recall which object in each pair was baited on previous trials. This task is similar to the DMS task in that the associative learning strategy involved (choosing the previously baited object) is the same for each task.

It was predicted that animals which were impaired on the DNMS task would not be able to remember which objects had been previously baited and hence, would perform at chance level on the object discrimination task. Surprisingly, however, animals with combined amygdala/hippocampal lesions were not impaired on this task relative to controls. Animals were significantly impaired on the DMS task (failed to reach criterion within 1,000 trials). However, if the test was run with the baited sample presented twice in rapid succession prior to the test trial, significant improvement was observed. These data suggest that, while a limbic lesion can impair one's ability to form an association between an object and a reward following a single presentation, the ability to form object-reward associations following multiple presentations is unimpaired.

The above findings have been interpreted as providing evidence for two fundamentally different, anatomically distinct, memory systems (figure 13). One system is thought to serve both recognition and association and to utilize a cortico-limbo-diencephalic circuit. This system is used to perform the delayed nonmatching to sample task and is presumed to be impaired in patients with medial temporal lobe amnesia (figure 13a). The other system is thought to involve the acquisition of discrimination habits. This system is thought to mediate the retention of stimulus-response connections, is dependent upon multiple-trial presentation, and is thought to involve a cortico-striatal circuit (see figure 13b). This system is used to perform the object discrimination task and is thought to be preserved in amnestic subjects. Further evidence that performance of the object discrimination task and the DNMS task involve two functionally and anatomically distinct memory systems stems from the fact that infant monkeys (3-4 months old) successfully learned to discriminate long lists of object-pairs about as quickly as adult monkeys, whereas their ability to learn the DNMS task matured much more slowly (Bachevalier and Mishkin, 1984).

The primate models discussed above suggest that severe temporal lobe amnesia will result only following the combined destruction of both the hippocampal formation and amygdala. Destruction of either structure alone produced either a small deficit (hippocampus) or no deficit at all (amygdala). However, a recent case study suggests that selective hippocampal damage alone may produce a severe memory impairment in humans. This case is discussed below.

R.B. was a postal worker who, at the age of 52, suffered a severe ischemic episode (Zola-Morgan et al., 1986). Until his death 5 years later, he exhibited a marked anterograde amnesia on tests of both verbal and nonverbal memory functions. He could not recall a passage of prose

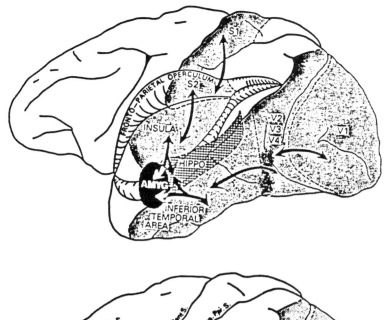

A

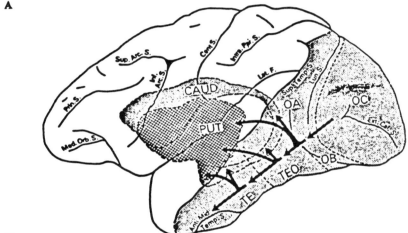

B

Figure 13: Brain structure and circuitries critical for different types of learning in the primate.

    A. Circuitries used for delayed non-match to sample, a task specific for the fact memory system. Circuitries for performing visual or somatosensory-based tasks use many of the same structures, particularly the hippocampus and amygdala.

    B. Circuitries needed for object discrimination tasks when repeated presentation of the object is used for training. Amygdala and/or hippocampus do not produce deficits for these tasks.

(Figures kindly provided in prepublication form by Drs. Mishkin, Murray and Ungerleider)

20 minutes after having heard it or read it, and he could not draw a diagram from memory 20 minutes after having previously drawn it. In addition, he frequently depended on his wife to tell him what had occurred and reported that, if he spoke to his children on the phone,

he did not remember anything about it the following day. This deficit occurred against a background of little, if any, retrograde amnesia, and no sign of other cognitive impairment.

After R.B.'s death, histological analysis revealed a circumscribed, bilateral lesion of hippocampal subfield CA1, extending the full length of the hippocampus. Area CA1 is a region from which major hippocampal efferents emerge, the loss of which effectively isolates a large part of the hippocampal formation. Although minor cell loss was observed in the globus pallidus, the right postcentral gyrus, and the cerebellum, it was concluded that the only damage that could reasonably be associated with the memory deficit was the hippocampal lesion. This finding suggests that selective injury to the hippocampal formation alone can result in severe anterograde amnesia deficits in humans.

SUMMARY

The data from neuropsychopathological studies of human amnestic demonstrate that memory formation processes can be localized to specific structures and circuits in the brain. Animal models have been useful for studying the relationship between specific structures and the formation of specific types of associative memories. Primate models have been particularly useful since the types of memory deficits observed are similar to those seen in humans with medial temporal lobe amnesia. As a result of these studies, a better understanding of the anatomy of memory formation processes in humans is beginning to emerge. Such studies will ultimately lead to a more accurate and precise understanding of the mechanisms by which human associative memories are formed.

RODENT MODELS OF PRIMATE AND HUMAN TEMPORAL LOBE AMNESIAS

OVERVIEW

The discoveries that different neural systems in humans and primates mediate different aspects of memory illustrate the need for rodent behavioral tests that sample simple forms of cognition-linked learning and that respond appropriately to lesions in the hippocampus, amygdala, and dorsomedial nucleus of the thalamus. Most research is conducted with small animals, especially rodents and rabbits. These animals have a sophisticated olfactory system compared to their other sensory systems. Recent data indicate that the learning of olfactory cues in rodents may be a reliable means to probe cognitive-type learning in rodents. In a sense, it makes use of rodent's strengths and man's weaknesses to probe central memory processing systems in both.

The study of human cognitive processes has most often been based on the use of verbal stimuli, not because of an interest in linguistics, but rather because words are excellent stimuli for probing memory processes: they are simple, identifiable, discrete, vast in number, and can be understood equally well by experimenter and subject. Olfactory stimuli are also simple, identifiable, discrete, and numerous, and therefore possess many of the advantages of words. They are, in a sense, a common vocabulary for animals and humans. Olfaction thus provides an opportunity for using laboratory animals to study cognitive processes that are comparable in a very real sense to those experienced by humans.

OLFACTORY CUES DIRECTLY ACCESS MEMORY-RELATED BRAIN STRUCTURES

The olfactory cortex itself is but two neurons removed from the odor receptors in the nasal epithelium (figure 14). The olfactory system thus provides a remarkably direct access to the temporal lobe and midline thalamic regions that are linked by clinical and experimental evidence to memory processing in humans and animals. The olfactory cortex directly innervates the hippocampus, the amygdala, and the dorsomedial nucleus/frontal cortex system. The nature of olfaction and

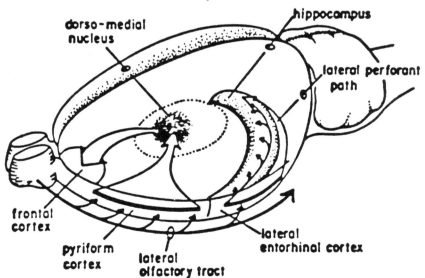

Figure 14: Two olfactory pathways through the telencephalon. The olfactory bulbs (at the front of the brain) generate the massive lateral olfactory tract, which innervates the contiguous pyriform and entorhinal cortices. The first of these projects into the dorsomedial nucleus of the thalamus, a structure that in turn innervates the frontal cortex. The entorhinal cortex produces the perforant pathway, the major afferent of the hippocampal formation.

(From Lynch, 1986)

the evolutionary conservatism of its underlying anatomy allow us to use the same tests in rats and humans. The likelihood that neurobiological discoveries can be transferred to humans is therefore greatly increased.

These anatomical features suggest that olfaction can be used to detect dysfunction in brain systems crucial to memory and cognition. There is experimental evidence for this possibility from patient H.M., who exhibits an anterograde amnesia resulting from damage to the hippocampus and surrounding structures. He is profoundly impaired on even very simple small identification tasks. Severe olfactory deficits have also been reported for amnestic individuals suffering from Korsakoff's syndrome. As discussed below, Lynch, Cotman, and coworkers have found that patients diagnosed as being in the early stages of Alzheimer's disease also have a selective and dramatic impairment in olfactory functioning.

ODOR MEMORIES IN RODENTS APPEAR TO FOLLOW PREDICTIONS OF COGNITIVE LEARNING DEFICITS IN MAN

Fact memories in humans are acquired rapidly and stored in a system of enormous capacity. This observation proved to hold for odor memories in rats as well (Staubli et al., 1986). More important, lesions that separate the olfactory cortex from the hippocampus produced an anterograde amnesia that matched the amnesia seen in humans with hippocampal lesions. Thus the rats appeared to learn new odors when several exposures were closely spaced in time, but they exhibited no memory of this training when tested one hour later (Staubli, Ivy, and Lynch, 1985c). This amnesia does not include memories formed before the lesions (Staubli et al., 1986b), much in the way that patients with temporal lobe/hippocampal dysfunction retain the greater part of their pre-injury memory store. Other experiments have shown that lesions of the dorsomedial nucleus and frontal cortex produce severe impairments in odor learning (Slotnick and Katz, 1974; Eichenbaum et al., 1980), possibly by cutting the links between sensory input and appropriate responses. These studies provide a very simple behavioral test that appears to measure a form of data memory that requires the hippocampus for encoding.

In addition, the circuitries underlying the behavior on these tests are sufficiently defined and simple in design to permit neurobiological experimentation. It has proven possible, for example, to use electrical stimulation of the inputs to the olfactory cortex in the place of odors as sensory cues (Mouly et al., 1985; Staubli et al., 1985) and then follow the physiological events that accompany learning. These latter studies provided evidence that a long-term potentiation occurred as part of the learning process. Thus, there is evidence that much of what has been learned in simple systems is directly applicable to fact learning in the cortex.

The extreme conservatism of the olfactory system raises the possibility that tests that detect damage or circuit dysfunction in rats can also be used in humans. Initial efforts have already yielded some interesting clinical results. The olfactory cortex is now thought to be one of the earliest sites affected by Alzheimer's disease, and tests found to be effective in detecting damage to the cortex in rats did indeed prove to discriminate patients thought to be in the early stages of Alzheimer's from age-matched controls (Kesslak et al., submitted). It would indeed be intriguing to test subjects with learning disabilities on odor learning problems and determine if any observed deficits correspond to impairments found in rats with lesions or subjected to pharmacological manipulations.

SUMMARY

Initial results indicate that many features of olfactory memory in rats match quite well with those used to define what cognitive psychologists refer to as "data" memory. Memory deficits after hippocampal damage in rats resembles the rapid forgetting of new information described for humans with hippocampal and temporal lobe damage. These types of models should prove useful in linking animal studies with studies of humans.

LEARNING IN NEURAL NETWORK SIMULATIONS

In the past five years, there has been a tremendous resurgence of interest in using computers to simulate various aspects of human learning and memory (see McClelland and Rummelhart, 1986, for a series of reviews). An ambition of this effort is to set "computational" constraints that must be met in the operation of brain networks and thereby provide some theoretical basis for the analyses of the networks. The systems modeled thus far incorporate various neurobiological features (for instance, Grossberg and Stone, 1986) but in no case can they be considered as realistic. They usually emphasize mathematical properties derived from physics, such as "simulated annealing" (Hopfield, 1982, 1984; Sejnowski and Rosenberg, 1986; and several others). Some of these models have achieved impressive successes in carrying out human-like learning operations: for example, face recognition (Kohonnen, 1984), feature detection (Feldman, 1981), verbal learning (McClelland and Rummelhart, 1986), and learning to pronounce English (Sejnowski and Rosenberg, 1986). Network models are useful in forming questions about the relationship of the organization and function of anatomical systems to their contributions to learning and memory. For example, the recognition that the comparatively simple olfactory cortex, with its direct connections to hippocampus and other subcortical structures involved in memory, carries out simple forms of data memory operations opens up new possibilities for developing biologically valid network simulations. It is indeed interesting that the internal anatomy of the olfactory cortex and hippocampus does in fact incorporate a number of features that have proven useful in connectionist models (Lynch, 1986). The combination of behavioral data or odor learning in rats and humans with the well defined anatomy and physiology of the olfactory system (Haberly, 1985; for a recent review) would provide powerful limits on the construction and evaluation of a network simulation. If these constraints were to be satisfied, a tool of potentially great utility for exploring ideas about cognitive disabilities would be available.

Although the discussion of "connectionism" and brain circuits takes us from the central theme of this review, it is included to indicate a possible route through which the many aspects of the neurobiology of learning might be synthesized into a coherent theory. If nothing else, the absence of a network theory points to the need for efforts at integration. This need becomes ever more acute as experimental work reveals our understanding of specific aspects of encoding and retrieval.

Computer-based simulations may be useful, and in fact, we predict that they will be a necessary adjunct to studies of learning in higher networks. How does a complex network operate under different conditions? Does a fundamental circuit design serve in several brain areas as a "memory chip," modified and elaborated in special ways for special functions? Currently, models are taking into account the properties of real brain circuitries, exploring their capacities, and predicting their properties. As these models progress, it will be possible, perhaps, to use them to evaluate the consequences of dysfunctions in the optimal types of treatments.

POSSIBLE NEUROBIOLOGICAL CAUSES OF LEARNING DISABILITIES

It is clear from the preceding discussions that the cellular and molecular substrates of learning are accessible to analysis in several vertebrate and invertebrate systems and that excellent progress in understanding them is being made. Clearly, learning depends on the proper operation of defined circuits that transfer information and ultimately store it in a form accessible for retrieval. The substrate often appears to involve molecular changes in existing connections, or as more recent data indicate, actual formation (turnover) of new synapses.

This information, coupled with observations on learning-induced changes in cortical networks and the roles played by subcortical structures in facilitating the encoding process, provides the beginnings of a theory of memory, or at least of its declarative (fact) variation. Advances in neurobiology have also provided us with new insights into possible causes of learning disabilities, and some of them are considered below, along with the relationship between generalized physiological and behavioral "states" and learning. We ask how the concept of "state" can be integrated into a mechanistic, neurobiological account of learning. Our purpose is not to exhaustively explore possible links between neurobiological mechanisms and disabilities but rather to emphasize the steps where learning has "weak links."

GENERAL "STATE" SYSTEMS: POSSIBLE ROLE OF ACETYLCHOLINE, NOREPINEPHRINE, AND SEROTONIN

Neuropsychologists have amply documented the crucial roles played by general body and brain states such as arousal, motivation, and attention. Learning does not occur without a prior focusing of attention and without appropriate motivation. Deficiencies in these states can be expected to have powerful consequences on early learning abilities, and it is likely that disturbances do occur. Perturbations in the machinery that controls arousal, for example, are not uncommon in children, and they present as a hyperkinetic syndrome. Brain states are also known to exert a powerful influence over the body's endocrine system, and hormone levels in turn have been linked to the strengths of the memory trace (see McGaugh, 1983, for a review).

Understanding how brain states variably interact with the learning process, and finding ways of detecting (and correcting) disturbances are areas in which neurobiological research should be encouraged. The discovery that the brain stem contains clusters of neurons that send projections containing catecholamines (dopamine and norepinephrine) and indolamines throughout the brain, including the cortex, has provided part of a description of how the generalized state affects physiological activity in distributed networks. Another major advance has been the appreciation that a group of cholinergic neurons scattered across the basal forebrain is the origin of the major cholinergic projections to cortical and subcortical regions of the forebrain. These cells are responsible for pacing certain cortical (alpha) and hippocampal (theta) rhythms and are almost certainly vital to the learning process. Moreover, recent research has gone far in identifying the target cells, receptors, and ion conductance channels affected by acetylcholine. These findings, coupled with emerging evidence that activation of the cholinergic receptor promotes the turnover of the phospholipids in the neuronal membrane and thereby triggers a series of second "messengers," provide the beginnings of a theory of how a "state" variable acting through the cholinergic system might facilitate the chemistries needed for storage. Certain of these diffusely projecting transmitter systems are known to be disturbed by a specific disease condition and thus become of immediate interest in the search for the etiology of learning disabilities. Cholinergic cells, for example, are at risk in Alzheimer's disease, and the dopamine neurons are damaged by certain diseases (Parkinson's) and pharmaceutical agents.

In reduced model systems, where most of the major progress in the neurobiology of memory is being made, these ancillary states are generally maintained constant and not manipulated, though they are known, in fact, to be potentially important. In the long run, the goal is to translate such psychological constructs into actual neuronal circuitries with a defined transmitter and to pin down the role they may play in altering the primary memory circuits. Thus, for example, the so-called "conditional" transmitters, such as acetylcholine and norepinephrine, are not necessarily in the primary circuit, but they interact with it to facilitate synaptic transmission within the memory processing unit. These and related systems replace the constructs of arousal, motivation, and other states with specific systems.

As more information is collected, it should be possible to define optimal levels of catecholamines, acetylcholines, and other substances for the production of synaptic modification. There data in turn should help in the development of diagnostics and guide the development of appropriate interventions where needed.

ACTIVITY PATTERNS

A logical candidate for the causes of learning disabilities is a perturbation of the machinery that produces specific brain rhythms and patterning of neural activity. We have noted the crucial role played by the cholinergic system in these functions, but more specific processes are also crucial. Inhibitory interneurons are vital to many aspects of network functioning, not the least of which is regulating the rate of cell firing, the intervals between episodes of activity, and brain wave patterns. Research results have demonstrated links between seizures and interneuron operation, and raised the possibility that perturbations in these cells are involved in certain types of epilepsy. Accordingly, we must consider the possibility that milder impairments occur and are part of the etiology of learning disabilities. In any case, the now demonstrated connection between activity patterns and synaptic modification (see above) suggests that analysis of brain waves could be useful in the search for the causes of learning disabilities.

ENCODING MECHANISMS

Perhaps the most obvious candidate for a cause of learning disabilities is in the chemistry that encodes experience into memory. Recent discoveries of receptors that are vital to storage and processing, and formulation of hypotheses involving specific enzymes open the way to exploring the possibility that errors in these mechanisms are responsible for disability.

Interest in this idea is also based on evidence that the same chemistries hypothesized to be linked to synaptic plasticity and learning are at the basis of certain nonmemorial clinical problems. Abnormal activity of the proteolytic enzyme calpain, for example, has been implicated in muscular dystrophy, and has been postulated as responsible for certain neuropathological conditions. As noted, calcium plays a vital role in several models of memory. Disturbances in internal calcium regulatory mechanisms occur as part of several diseases that affect the immature, mature, and aged brain. Perturbations in calcium regulation too mild to produce a disease condition might still be sufficient to impair synaptic plasticity and learning.

INJURY AND INJURY-INDUCED CIRCUITRY REORGANIZATION

Damage to various brain circuitries is another possible cause of malfunctioning. The effect of lesions on the role of specific brain areas in simple learning has been studied extensively. Ultimately, it will be necessary to correlate learning disabilities to injury in specific areas in humans where parallel animal models exist. We are only at a beginning of this search, but some progress is being made. Galaburda and colleagues (1979, 1985) reported that brains of several dyslexic individuals disclosed focal disorganization of the cellular architecture of the language cortex. These abnormalities, found predominantly in left hemisphere persylvian regions, consist of collections of ectopic neurons in layer one and of dysplasia of the underlying cortical layers. These authors reported in addition that the expression of anatomical asymmetry in the language areas of these brains is uniformly anomalous and consistent with the interpretation that they show excessive preservation of undesirable neurons during late corticogenesis (Galaburda et al., 1987). Related research in human and experimental neuropathology (Caviness et al., 1978; Dvorak et al., 1978; McBride and Kemper, 1982) suggests that the cortical alterations described in the dyslexic brains reflect focal injury to the developing brain during late gestation or soon thereafter. Furthermore, many research efforts have addressed the issue of early acquired brain lesions and their effects on the organization of resulting cellular and connectional architectures (see, for instance, Goldman-Rakic and Rakic, 1984). It is possible, therefore, that injurious developmental events lead to the anomalous organization of regional circuitries in portions of the brain involved in language function in developmental dyslexia. Recently, attempts have been made to develop animal models for these types of anomalies (Sherman et al., 1985; Nowakowski, 1986). It is hoped that exact mechanisms involved in injury and reorganization will be found in these efforts.

Concerning another developmental condition, Bauman and Kemper (1985) analyzed the brain of an autistic man at autopsy and found structural abnormalities in the amygdala and hippocampus (key areas in the limbic data memory system) and in the cerebellum (a key area in the procedural memory system). Childhood autism is a developmental disability involving severe social and emotional disturbances including social withdrawal, abnormal interactions with peers, hyperactivity, unusual attachment to objects, and mental retardation. Injury to the hippocampus and amygdala in primates, as noted above, appears to cause selective memory loss but is not observed to create social-emotional disturbances. Recently, however, it appears that the effect of such lesions placed early in development does cause autistic-like behaviors in addition to loss of recognition memory (Bachevalier and Mishkin, 1986; Merjanian et al., 1986). In combination, these findings show that damage to the nervous system can have different impacts, depending on whether it occurs early in life or later as an adult. This type of data further indicates that injury during development and learning has to be studied in its own milieu. It is not possible to extrapolate in all cases from studies involving mature individuals.

It needs to be pointed out that damage to the developing nervous system cannot be considered simply as the removal of specific portions of a circuit. It is now clear that the brain has an inherent capacity to repair itself, particularly for minor injuries. Neurons engage in an active phase of regrowth, which would be predicted to have important consequences on emergent functions. Damage to one or more critical elements during the development of a memory circuit initiates the reorganization of residual circuitry. Undamaged neurons, for example, sprout and replace the connections lost by a process known as axon sprouting or reactive synaptogenesis. When the loss is minor, these responses are probably compensatory and have minor functional impact except to maintain the system. The loss would reduce the redundancy of the system, but the circuits that would form would be expected to be minimally abnormal, much as natural neuronal loss occurs in the course of development. In contrast, major damage to the system, such as the loss of target, can result in entirely bizarre circuitries, even the emergence of new pathways, which could impact on the primary as well as ancillary circuitries. In other words, injury during a critical period early in life causes a cascade of events and the emergence of abnormal circuits. Injuries to the limbic memory system during this phase, for example, might disrupt not only cognitive processing but also the normal development of goals, attitudes, and the emotional coloration of experiences, which are classical limbic system functions. In a way, the injury is interpreted by the brain as an altered signal, which is then encoded into its own repertoire.

CAN LEARNING DISABILITIES BE CORRECTED? PROSPECTS FOR THE FUTURE

Hypotheses about the biological causes of learning disabilities inevitably point to diagnostic techniques and therapeutic measures. One trend in the behavioral neurosciences that should immeasurably facilitate testing of ideas about causes and possible treatments is the emergence of animal behavioral tests that monitor the same types of learning exhibited by humans. The gradual acknowledgement by theorists and experimenters that learning and memory have multiple forms served by different brain systems and possibly different chemistries has brought an appreciation of the urgent need for behavioral measures for use with laboratory animals that can be directly compared with those employed in assessing human capacities.

Another greatly promising development is the identification of learning tests in animal research that can be correlated with identified brain circuits. Modification of these measures for humans could open the way to procedures that might determine whether dysfunction is diffuse or restricted and possibly elucidate something of its nature.

Specific neurotransmitters are being identified that serve to modulate the activity patterns in defined circuitries. In particular, noradrenergic and cholinergic systems appear to have a facilitatory role and can act to enhance synaptic transmission and even long-term potentiation in select brain areas. Previously, in discussing plasticity in the developing visual system, we noted that there is a synergism between cholinergic and noradrenergic systems and that they influence plasticity. Manipulations of both of these systems can facilitate learning and memory in select animal models.

One interesting variant of the conditional transmitter approach to manipulating impairments in learning involves the peripheral hormone system. McGaugh and coworkers have established that levels of peripheral hormones are crucial to the strength of memory and that they act in the amygdala via central norepinephrine cells (McGaugh 1983, 1985; McGaugh and Gold, 1986). This finding raises the possibility of producing selective effects on conditional transmitters by manipulating the endocrine system.

Several manipulations appear to offer promise for improving learning in animal models where there are defined neurological deficits. One powerful intervention has been the use of transplanted neurons. In many instances, this intervention has served to provide an additional source of state-dependent transmitters such as acetylcholine. Thus, for example, select CNS neurons can be replaced by similar types of transplanted cells, with recovery from the specific functional deficits (for reviews, see Cotman, 1985; Cotman and Nieto-Sampedro, 1984; Bjorklund and Stenevi, 1985; Gash et al., 1985). Most appropriately, cognitive deficits caused by cortical or fimbral lesions (Dunnett et al., 1982; Labbe et al., 1983; Kesslak et al., 1986) or associated with old age (Gage et al., 1984) can be restored by transplants of embryonic cells. Particularly effective is the replacement of cholinergic cells. Transplants of dopamine neurons (or even adrenal medullary tissue) are capable of reducing motor deficits caused either by lesions that destroy dopamine cells in the substantia nigra (Perlow et al., 1979; Freed 1983) or by dopamine cell loss with natural aging (Gage et al., 1983). In all these studies, the transplants appear to have acted as an endogenous source of additional transmitter (and perhaps trophic factors) delivered in sufficient quantity onto appropriate receptors (see Cotman and Nieto-Sampedro, 1984). These types of manipulations show that interventions are possible and give valuable information about minimal requirements for improvement in function. They also emphasize the critical role of "state" in brain cognitive function.

Recently, several growth factors, particularly nerve growth factor (NGF), have been identified. NGF can act on CNS neurons to stimulate their survival and growth (see Hefti and Weinger, 1986, for a review). Nerve growth factor was initially thought to work only on peripheral neurons. It has recently been shown that NGF stimulates central cholinergic neurons. Nerve growth factor has also been documented to facilitate behavioral recovery. In fact, a single administration during development causes hyperactivity of the cholinergic system. Thus we are witnessing the beginnings of a new level for possible interventions.

SUMMARY AND CONCLUSION

Over the last five years, results of research on the mechanisms of learning have dramatically expanded the knowledge base. Recent efforts have focused on defining systems for analyzing relatively simple types of learning (sensitization, habituation, and classical conditioning) and for analyzing how physiological activity changes synapses. It is now clear that defined circuits exist for learning, that the site and location of the synaptic change can be localized, and that many specific biochemical mechanisms can be identified.

Invertebrate models are teaching us much about the fundamentals of learning just as the squid axon taught us much about fundamentals of action potentials. Most work on invertebrates involved studies on molluscs as models. The mollusc nervous system is simple and well defined, and its circuits can be outlined. The mollusc *Aplysia Californica* shows a surprising repertoire of behaviors, including long-term sensitization and classical conditioning. Learning appears to take place at a defined set of synapses, where the molecular mechanism has been described to a degree unprecedented for other systems. It involves an increase in cyclic AMP, the phosphorylation of select proteins, and a decrease in the potassium currents. The decreased potassium current increases the duration of the action potential, which causes a larger output of neurotransmitter. In another mollusc, *Hermissenda*, classical conditioning occurs when a light stimulus is paired with a noxious stimulus, such as rotation of the animal. The mechanism appears to involve an inactivation of calcium-dependent potassium currents, which renders the cell more excitable. In the *Limax*, the circuits have been modeled in detail by computer and shown to operate in accordance with the classical rules for conditioning of a mammalian nervous system.

Learning occurs throughout life, from the earliest times after fertilization until the last days of old age. Events learned early in life can dictate later responses. In order to understand learning disabilities, it is essential to define some of the types of learning and plasticity during development. Several exciting advances in model systems have been made for certain types of early learning. Like children, rodent pups learn to recognize key odors early in life, such as those of their mothers. An odor paired with a tactile stimulation during a critical period can alter the behavioral response to that odor. The mechanism appears to involve an increase in the size of the neural network in the olfactory bulb, which processes those odors. NMDA receptors and calcium ions appear to be involved in this early change.

While the primary pathways of the nervous system are laid down at the time of birth, many adjustments and calibrations within these pathways occur in the course of development. The visual system is a premier example where, early in the course of development, the two retinal images from each eye have to be matched, calibrated, and segregated in the proper fashion within the visual cortex. Such changes are clearly activity-dependent, and the proper segregation of the cortical wiring does not occur in the absence of normal neural activity. The development of the system also depends on a nonspecific arousal stimulus. NMDA receptors appear to be involved as in the developing olfactory system.

In rodents, it has been demonstrated that an enriched environment during rearing makes the structure of the visual cortex richer in the arborization of its neurons and in the number of synapses on each cell. Some of these changes are transient, reversing when the environment becomes less complex. Others appear permanent, indicating that the imprint of the environment remains on the cortex and its potential functional properties. Information in the literature suggests that the primate brain can be similarly influenced by experience. It is likely, but not proven, that each sensory system with its associated circuitries can be influenced by early environment and experience. These sensory systems appear to go through critical periods of high plasticity, and once past that period, the system becomes more fixed. It may be that the key areas involved in cognition have a similar critical period for programming various types of learning or learning sets. However, there is no direct evidence at present.

Once the nervous system matures, the basic circuitry is set and serves as a substrate for subsequent operations. Insults early in life can sometimes be compensated for, particularly if they are minor. Such a compensation, however, can often detract from another parallel ability. Learning depends on a combination of different systems, not only for the stimuli that are processed, but also for the type of learning. In a broad sense, the learning of skills or procedures is distinguished from that of certain cognitive tasks, so-called declarative or fact memory. The conditioning of a motor response is an excellent example of skill or procedural learning. A component of a complex motor skill that has been quite well studied is that of learning forearm position. This learning occurs over a time course of a few days and seems to reside within the red nucleus, a key integrative structure where cortical and cerebellar inputs converge. In this nucleus, injury-altered sensory input and conditioning appear to share a common mechanism: the formation of new synapses. These data suggest that the response to injury produced by cell loss shares certain common features and mechanisms with those of adaptive plasticity during learning. More examples are needed. They would enhance this field of study because the information about regenerative plasticity after injury is rapidly increasing.

In the mammalian nervous system, the most elaborate model of basic circuitry and some of the functions of its individual components have been described for a simple type of conditioning called eyelid conditioning, which is a simple form of learning shown equally by humans and animals. A brief tone is paired with a noxious puff of air to the eye. After several pairings, the eyelid closes in response to the tone in order to avoid the noxious air. Learning appears to occur within cerebellar circuitry. Alterations in response pattern appear to involve the hippocampus. Learning of such aversive-conditioned responses involves an initial stage of conditioned fear and a second phase of an adaptive motor response. Opiate-like compounds appear to interfere with the development of the conditioned fear response. The system mediating the conditioned fear response appears to be localized separately from the structures involved in the organization of the discrete motor response. Thus, learning of a simple response, such as eyelid conditioning, has many features and events. These types of multiple events for classical conditioning anticipate the sequence of the events that need to be considered in analyzing learning disabilities.

It is increasingly recognized that cognitive learning (facts, episodes) is the type of learning most relevant to the central needs of humans and their intellectual pursuits. Ironically, this type of learning also appears vulnerable to various neuropathological conditions. Cognitive learning losses in Alzheimer's disease patients, for example, far exceed losses of skill learning.

The development of animal models of such data recognition and processing systems is at an early stage, relative to those for classical conditioning. Tasks like the match-to-sample or nonmatch-to-sample are most commonly employed. Various sensory systems gain access to key components of the data memory system. In rodents, primates, and humans, learning of match-to-sample procedures depends on the function of the amygdala, entorhinal cortex, and hippocampus, which are key components of the limbic memory system. Damage to one or more of these components interferes with the retention of information. A synaptic analog of learning has been identified in these structures and is called long-term potentiation. Stimulation of a pathway at a particular frequency or an association between two pathways causes a long-lasting strengthening of synaptic transmission. At least one form of long-term potentiation appears to involve NMDA receptors. Intracellular calcium activates a sequence of events that alters the morphology of existing synapses and possibly even causes a relocation of some synapses and a growth of others. Cell biological studies have identified an unusual biochemical process that appears capable of producing localized anatomical change in response to elevated calcium levels. Two very recent discoveries strongly support the idea that the substrates for long-term potentiation are used by the brain to encode information: (1) the optimal pattern for eliciting potentiation corresponds to a naturally occurring brain rhythm, and (2) a drug that blocks induction of LTP also causes amnesia. Many important steps have recently been taken in elucidating the molecular mechanisms of long-term potentiation and in defining more than one type of potentiation. Long-term potentiation can probably be modified by steroids; extensive stress, for example, is disruptive of long-term potentiation. The identification of long-term potentiation as a key process in learning and memory has made it possible to use reduced system preparations (for instance, a hippocampal slice) for studies of learning and memory in the mammalian brain and has narrowed the gap between invertebrate and vertebrate models.

Overall, it appears that different types of learning involve different types of record systems and possibly different types, or mixtures of types, of cellular processes. Therefore, our present inability to identify a single mechanism for learning may be due to the absence of a ubiquitous mechanism and to the fact that learning, seen in intact animals, involves a constellation of processes, which, taken together and across brain systems, refine and adjust responses. Thus, when we consider the possible biological origins of learning disabilities, it is vital to identify the type(s) of learning involved.

It is also important to recognize that learning, according to all models so far analyzed, involves sequences of cellular events and that disturbances of any sequence could impair the acquisition and storage of new information. Neurobiological experiments have served to identify events that are at risk. Such events are candidates for the causes of disabilities. Further progress, coupled with information obtained from the study of other instances of brain dysfunction, will lead to new treatment strategies.

RECOMMENDATIONS

Learning and memory is one of the most complex and important tasks that the nervous system executes. People recall what must be hundreds of billions of bits of data and utilize this information in a myriad of ways. The study of learning and memory is in itself subtle and complex. It is truly multidisciplinary research requiring sophisticated behavioral analysis, systems analysis, and expertise in cellular and molecular biology. Inherent in approaches toward a better understanding of the neurobiology of learning disabilities is a need for coordinated investigations involving several levels of analysis. Such efforts need to be fostered in the face of a steady trend toward greater specialization by neuroscientists.

Specific recommendations for research include:

Basic neurobiology: Accelerate research on synaptic plasticity and growth.

- More basic work on synaptic transmission and plasticity within the mammalian central nervous system. Breakthroughs in the understanding of the mechanisms of learning depend on the fundamental information base available. The types of ion channels modified during learning, such as the calcium-dependent potassium channel, were discovered only within the last few years. This basic discovery led immediately major increases in information about the mechanisms of learning.
- Additional projects on the mechanism of synapse formation in the mature brain. There is very little cell biology research on how synaptic contacts are formed, modified, and maintained in the adult brain. These questions are central to any biological theory of learning.
- Definition of the systems that interfere with acquisition and consolidation of information in the various types of learning. In most simple models, factors such as attention and stress, which are components of the normal environment, have been kept constant or minimized. In order to translate animal models to meaningful real-life situations, it is necessary to begin to elucidate interactions between processes.

Neural Behavioral: Identify and develop models of cognitive learning in developing animals.

- Development of accurate animal models for learning disabilities found in humans that can be translated to rodent models. They should be generally accessible to the scientific community and economical to operate. It would be particularly valuable to have such animal models automated and have tasks that access structures amenable to the rigorous analysis needed for molecular studies. It is essential to develop the means to test neurobiological hypotheses where models allow an integrated multilevel analysis.
- Research on learning in animal models during early and later development. At present there is relatively little basic work on learning and memory in animal models that would correspond to ages 5-15 in developing children. This major area is in need of additional research. It is necessary to identify accessible models most suitable to the issues pertinent to childhood learning disabilities.

Animal models and man: Promote integration of animal studies with human conditions.

- Studies that monitor brain function during learning in patients with learning disabilities. What is the relative participation or lack of participation of key structures? New neuroimaging techniques including PET scanning, MRI, and computer averaged EEG are only the beginnings of techniques that may play key roles in elucidating the central structures.
- Detailed anatomical studies of postmortem tissues of the key structures that are believed to be involved in learning disabilities. Sophisticated computer systems exist that allow detailed reconstruction in three dimensions of the various systems. These would not only be valuable for the analysis of the information processing capacity but also for constructing better computer models of relevant brain circuitries, including more information on circuitry in primates and man. Continued work on primates is an essential ingredient for bridging the gap between simple animal models and man.

Computer simulation of networks found in brain: Encourage theoretical work on higher brain function.

- More detailed computer simulations of various cortical-subcortical systems involved in memory. The circuitry and integrative actions of cortical networks are too complex to study without the aid of accurate simulations. They aid in verifying hypotheses from animal studies and also predict new ones to be tested *in vivo*.
- Modeling of expected deficits in circuits to determine functional consequences.

Over the past five years, research in the basic neurobiology of learning and memory has progressed to the point that there is a wealth of new exciting data. The level of interest and activity in the field has reached new heights, and new techniques and concepts are accelerating the acquisition of knowledge. Key components for vigorous programs directed to the understanding of childhood learning disabilities from a basic science viewpoint appear to be largely, if not entirely, in place. Research in learning and memory is inherently multidisciplinary, requiring contributions and coordinated efforts between many individuals and several disciplines. Moreover, it is unlikely that a single solution for learning disabilities will emerge, as it has for various diseases such as polio and infectious diseases.

We recommend that serious consideration be given to establishing research centers especially designed for multidisciplinary studies and amelioration of learning disabilities in children. The centers concept has given new life and direction to the study of Alzheimer's disease as well as to other fields. Centers ideally would infuse major new resources, organize existing ones, and even encourage additional private support. The centers should also provide stability to the area and be the focus of a 5-7 year commitment. We believe that such a major program with appropriate resources would be one major step towards the successful study of a critical national problem.

BIBLIOGRAPHY

Akers, R. F., Lovinger, D. M., Colley, P. A., Linden, D. J., Routtenberg, A. (1986). Translocation of protein kinase C activity may mediate hippocampal long-term potentiation. *Science,* 231:587-589.

Alkon, D. L. (1984). Calcium-mediated reduction of ionic currents: A biophysical memory trace. *Science.* 226:1037-1045.

Altmann, L., Luhmann, H. J., Singer, W., Greuel, J. (1985). Ocular dominance distribution in the striate cortex of kittens raised with rapidly alternating monocular occlusion. *Neuroscience Letters Supplement,* 22:S353.

Anderson, P., Silfvenius H., Sundberg, S. H., Sveen, O. (1980). A comparison of distal and proximal dendritic synapses on CA_1 pyramids in guinea pig hippocampal slices *in vitro* and serotonin release by leupeptin and antipain. *Journal of Physiology,* 307:273-299.

Anderson, P. A., Olavarria, J., Van Sluyters, R. C. (1983). The pattern of ocular dominance columns in areas 17 and 18 of normal and visually deprived cats as revealed in tangential sections of unfolded cortex. *Neuroscience Abstracts,* 9:910.

Archer, S. M., Dubin, M. W., Stark, L. A. (1982). Abnormal development of kitten retinogeniculate connectivity in the absence of action potentials. *Science,* 217:743-745.

Bachevalier, J., Mishkin, M. (1984). An early and late developing system for learning and retention in infant monkeys. *Behavioral Neuroscience,* 5:770-778.

Bachevalier, J., Mishkin, M. (1986). Cortical vs. limbic immaturity: Relationship to infantile global amnesia in monkeys. *Society for Neuroscience Abstracts,* 12:22.

Baddeley, A. (1982). Implications of neuropsychological evidence for theories of normal memory. *Philosophical Transactions of the Royal Society of London Series B,* 298:59-72.

Bailey, C. H., Chen, M. (1983). Morphological basis of long-term habituation and sensitization in Aplysia. *Science,* 220:91-93.

Balogh, R. D., Porter, R. H. Olfactory preferences resulting from mere exposure in human neonates. *Infant behavior and development* (in press).

Barker, D., Ip, M.D. (1966). Sprouting and degeneration of mammalian motor axons in normal and deafferented skeletal muscle. *Proceedings of the Royal Society of London Series B,* 163:538-556.

Bauman, M., Kemper, T. L. (1985). Histoanatomic observations of the brain in early infantile autism. *Neurology,* 35:866-874.

Bear, M. F., Singer, W. (1986). Modification of visual cortical plasticity by acetylcholine and noradrenaline. *Nature,* 320(6058):172-176.

Bear, M. F., Daniels, I. D. (1983). The plastic response to monocular deprivation persists in kitten visual cortex after chronic depletion of norepinephrine. *Journal of Neuroscience,* 3:407-416.

Belardetti, F., Schacher, S., Kandel, E. R., Siegelbaum, S. A. (1986). The growth cones of Aplysia sensory neurons: Modulation by serotonin of action potential duration and single potassium channel currents. *Proceedings of the National Academy of Sciences of the United States of America,* 83:7094-7098.

Benson, D. F., Marsden, C. D., Meadows, J. C. (1974). The amnesic syndrome of posterior cerebral artery occlusion. *Acta Neurologica Scandinavia,* 50:133-145.

Bjorklund, A., Stenevi, U. (Eds.) (1985). *Neural grafting in the mammalian CNS.* Amsterdam: Elsevier.

Blakemore, C., Garey, L. J., Henderson, Z. B., Swindale, N. V., Vital-Durand, F. (1980). Visual experience can promote rapid axonal reinnervation in monkey visual cortex. *Journal of Physiology*, 307:26.

Bliss, T. V. P., Gardner-Medwin, A. T. (1973). Long-lasting potentiation of synaptic transmission in the dentate area of the unanesthetized rabbit following stimulation of the perforant path. *Journal of Physiology (Lond.)*, 232:357-374.

Bruner, J. S. (1969). Modalities of memory. In Talland, G. A. and Waugh, N. C. (Eds.), *The pathology of memory*. New York: Academic Press.

Buisseret, P., Singer, W. (1983). Proprioceptive signals from extraocular muscles gate experience-dependent modifications of receptive fields in the kitten visual cortex. *Experimental Brain Research*, 51:443-450.

Burgess, P. R., English, K. B., Horch, K. W., Stensaas, L. J. (1974). Patterning in the regeneration of type I cutaneous receptors. *Journal of Physiology (Lond.)*, 236:57-87.

Butters, N., Cermak, L. S. (1980). *Alcoholic Korsakoff's syndrome: An information processing approach to amnesia*. New York: Academic Press.

Byrne, J. H. (1985). Neural and molecular mechanisms underlying information storage in Aplysia: Implications for learning and memory. *Trends in Neuroscience*, 8:478-482.

Cassell, M. D., Brown, M. W. (1984). The distribution of Timm's stain in the nonsulphide-perfused human hippocampal formation. *Journal of Comparative Neurology*, 222:461.

Caviness, V. S., Evrard, P., Lyon, G. (1978). Radial neuronal assemblies, ectopia and necrosis of developing cortex: A case analysis. *Acta Neuropathologica*, 41:67-72.

Chang, F. L. F., Greenough, W. T. (1984). Transient and enduring morphological conclats of synaptic activity and efficacy change in the rat hippocampal slice. *Brain Research*, 309:35-46.

Cohen, D. H. (1982). In Woody, C. D. (Ed.). *Conditioning: Representation of involved neural functions*, New York: Plenum.

Cohen, D. H. (1980). In Thompson, R. F., Hicks, L. H., Shvyrok, V. B. (Eds.). *Neural mechanisms of goal-directed behavior and learning*. New York Academic Press, 283.

Cohen, N. J. (1984). Preserved learning capacity in amnesia: Evidence for multiple memory systems. Squire, L. R., Butters, N. (Eds.), *Neuropsychology of memory*. New York: Guildford Press.

Cohen, N. J., Squire, L. R. (1980). Preserved learning and retention of pattern analyzing skill in amnesia: Dissociation of knowing how and knowing that. *Science*, 210: 207-209.

Collingridge, B. L., Kehl, S. J., McLennan, H. (1983). The antagonism of amino-acid-induced excitation of rat hippocampal CA_1 neurones *in vitro*. *Journal of Physiology*, 334:19-31.

Coopersmith, R., Henderson, J, Leon, M. (1986a). Odor specificity of the enhanced neural response following early odor exposure. *Developmental Brain Research*, 27:191-197.

Coopersmith, R., Lee, S., Leon, M. (1986b). Olfactory bulb responses after odor aversion learning by young rats. *Developmental Brain Research*, 24:271-277.

Coopersmith, R., Leon, M. (1984). Enhanced neural response to familiar olfactory cues. *Science*, 225:849-851.

Corkin, S. (1968). Acquisition of motor skill after bilateral medial temporal lobe excision. *Neuropsychologia*, 6:255-265.

Cotman, C. W. (Ed.) (1985). *Synaptic Plasticity*. New York: Guilford Press.

Cotman, C. W., Nieto-Sampedro, M. (1982). Brain function, synapse renewal and plasticity. *Annual Review of Psychology*, 33:371-401.

Cotman, C. W., Nieto-Sampedro, M. (1984). Cell biology of synaptic plasticity. *Science*, 255:1287-1294.

Cotman, C. W., Nieto-Sampedro, M., Harris, E. (1981). Synapse replacement in the nervous system of adult vertebrates. *Physiological Reviews*, 61:684-784.

Daw, N. W., Robertson, T. W., Rader, K. R., Videen, T. O., Cosica, C. J. (1984). Substantial reduction of noradrenaline by lesions of adrenergic pathway does not prevent effects of monocular deprivation. *Journal of Neuroscience*, 4:1354-1360.

Disterhoft, J. F., Coulter, D. A., Alkon, D. L. (1986). Conditioning-specific membrane changes of rabbit hippocampal neurons measured *in vitro*. *Proceedings of the National Academy of Sciences*, 83:2733-2737.

Disterhoft, J. F., Kwan, H. H., Low, W. D. (1977). Nictitating membrane conditioning to tone in the immobilized albino rabbit. *Brain Research*, 137:127-144.

Drachman, D. A., Adams, R. D. (1962). Herpes simplex and acute-inclusion body encephalitis. *Archives of Neurology*, 7:45-63.

Dunnett, S. B., Low, W. C., Iversen, S. D., Stenevi, U., Bjorklund, A. (1982). Septal transplants restore maze learning in rats with fornix-fimbria lesions. *Brain Research*, 251:335-348.

Dunwiddie, T. V., Lynch, G. S. (1978). Long-term potentiation and depression of synaptic responses in the rat hippocampus: Localization and frequency dependency. *Journal of Physiology (Lond.)*, 276:353-367.

Dvorak, K., Feit, J., Jurankova, Z. (1978). Experimentally induced focal micropolygyria and status verrucosus deformans in rats: Pathogenesis and interrelations. *Acta Neuropathologica*, 44:121-129.

Eichenbaum, J., Shedlack, K. J., Eckman, K. W. (1980). Thalamocortical mechanisms in odor-guided behavior. I. Effects of lesions of the medio dorsal thalamic nucleus and frontal cortex on olfactory discrimination in the rat. *Brain, Behavior and Evolution*, 17:255-275.

Eslinger, P. J., Damasio, A. R. (1986). Preserved motor learning in Alzheimer's disease: Implications for anatomy and behavior. *Journal of Neuroscience*, 6:3006-3009.

Feldman, J. A. (1981). A connectionist model of visual memory. In Hinton, R. E., Anderson, J. A. (Eds.), *Parallel Models of Associative Memory*. Hillsdale, N. J.: Lawrence Erlbaum.

Freed, W. J. (1983). Functional brain tissue transplantation: Reversal of lesion-induced rotation by intraventricular substantia nigra and adrenal medulla grafts, with a note on intracranial retinal grafts. *Biological Psychiatry*, 18(11):1205-1267.

Fujito, Y., Tsukahara, N., Oda, Y., Yoshida, M. (1982). Formation of functional synapses in the adult cat red nucleus from the cerebrum following cross-innervation of forelimb flexor and extensor nerves. II. Analysis of newly-appeared synaptic potentials. *Experimental Brain Research*, 45:13-18.

Gage, F. H., Fjorklund, A., Stenevi, U., Dunnett, S. B., Kelley, P. A. T. (1984). Intrahippocampal septal grafts ameliorate learning impairments in aged rats. *Science*, 225:533-535.

Gage, F. H., Dunnett, S. B., Stenevi, U., Bjorklund, A. (1983). Aged rats: Recovery of motor impairments by intrastriatal nigral grafts. *Science*, 221:966-969.

Galaburda, A. M., Kemper, T. L. (1979). Cytoarchitectonic abnormalities in developmental dyslexia: A case study. *Annals of Neurology*, 6:94-100.

Galaburda, A. M., Sherman, G. F., Rosen, G. D., Aboitiz, F., Geschwind, N. (1985). Developmental dyslexia: Four consecutive patients with cortical anomalies. *Annals of Neurology*, 18:222-233.

Galaburda, A. M., Corsiglia, J., Rosen, G. D., Sherman, G. F. (1987). Planum temporale asymmetry: Reappraisal since Geschwind and Levitsky. *Neuropsychologia* (in press).

Gash, D., Collier, T. J., Sladek J. R. (1985). Neural transplantation: A review of recent developments and potential applications to the aged brain. *Neurobiology of Aging*, 6:131-150.

Gelperin, A. (1975). Rapid food-aversion learning by a terrestrial mollusk. *Science*, 189:565-570.

Gelperin, A., Culligan N. (1984). *In vitro* expression of *in vivo* learning by an isolated molluscan CNS. *Brain Research*, 304:207-213.

Gelperin, A., Hopfield, J. J., Tank D. W. (1986). The logic of Limax learning. In Selverston A. I. (Ed.), *Model neural networks and behavior*. New York: Plenum Press.

Goelet, P., Castelucci, V. F., Schacher S., Kandel E. R. (1986). The long- and the short-term memory: A molecular framework. *Nature*, 322:419-422.

Gold, M. R., Cohen, D. H. (1981). A review of electrical stimulation of the brain in context of learning and retention. *Science*, 214:345.

Gold, P. E., Zornetzer, S. F. (1984). The mnemon and its juices: Neuromodulation of memory processes. *Behavioral and Neural Biology*, 38:151-189.

Goldman-Rakic, P. S., Rakic, P. (1984). Experimental modification of gyral patterns. In Geschwind, N., Galaburda, A. M. (Eds.), *Cerebral Dominance: The biological foundation* (pp. 179-192). Cambridge, M. A.: Harvard University Press.

Gormezano, I. (1972). Investigation of defense and reward conditioning in the rabbit. In Black, A., Prokasy, W. (Eds.), *Classical conditioning II: Current research and theory*. New York: Appleton-Century-Crofts.

Greenough, W. T., Larson, J. R., Withers, G. S. (1985). Effects of unilateral and bilateral training in a reaching task on dendritic branching of neurons in the rat motor-sensory forelimb cortex. *Behavioral and Neural Biology*, 44:301-314.

Greer, C. A., Stewart, W. B., Kauer, J. S., Shepherd, G. M. (1981). Topographical and laminar localization of 2-deoxyglucose uptake in rat olfactory bulb induced by electrical stimulation of olfactory nerves. *Brain Research*, 217:279-293.

Greer, D. A., Stewart, W. B., Teicher, M. H., Shepherd, G. M. (1982). Functional development of the olfactory bulb and a unique glomeruli complex in the neonatal rat. *Journal of Neuroscience*, 2:1744-1759.

Grossberg, S., Stone, G. O. (1986). Neural dynamics of word recognition and recall: Attentional priming, learning and resonance. *Psychological Reviews*, 93:46-74.

Haberly, L. B. (1985). Neuronal circuitry in olfactory cortex: Anatomy and functional implications. *Chemical Senses*, 10:219-238.

Harris, E. W., Ganong, A. H., Cotman, C. W. (1984). Long-term potentiation in the hippocampus involves activation of N-methyl-D-aspartate receptors. *Brain Research*, 323:132-137.

Hatton, G. I. (1985). Reversible synapse formation and modulation of cellular relationships in the adult hypothalamus under physiological conditions. In Cotman, C. W. (Ed.), *Synaptic plasticity*. New York: Guilford Press.

Hawkins, R. D., Kandel, E. R. (1984). Steps toward a cell-biological alphabet for elementary forms of learning. In Lynch, G., McGaugh, J., Weinberger, N. (Eds.), *Neurobiology of learning and memory*. New York: Guildford press, 385-404.

Hawkins, R. D., Abrams, T. W., Carew, T. J., Kandel, E. R. (1983). A cellular mechanism of classical conditioning in Aplysia: Activity-dependent amplification of presynaptic facilitation. *Science*, 219:400-405.

Hebb, D. O. (1949). *The organization of behavior*. New York: John Wiley and Sons.

Hefti, F., Weiner, W. J. (1986). Nerve growth factor and Alzheimer's disease. *Annals of Neurology*, 29:275-281.

Hilgard, E. R., Marquis, D. G. (1940). *Conditioning and learning*. New York: Appleton-Century-Crofts.

Hopfield, J. J. (1982). Neural networks and physical systems with emergent collective computational abilities. *Proceedings of the National Academy of Sciences (USA)*, 79:2554-2558.

Hopfield, J. J. (1984). Neurons with graded response have collective computational properties like those of two-state neurons *Proceedings of the National Academy of Sciences (USA)*, 81:3088-3092.

Hubel, D. H., Wiesel, T. N., LeVay, S. (1977). Plasticity of ocular dominance columns in monkey striate cortex. *Philosophical Transactions of the Royal Society of London B*, 278:377-409.

Ito, M. (1985). In Eccles, D. (Ed.), *Recent achievements in restorative neurology I: Upper motor neuron functions and dysfunctions*. Basel: Karger, 222.

Ito, M. (1984). *The cerebellum and neural control*. New York: Raven Press.

Ito, M., Sakurai, M., Tongroach, P. (1982) *Journal of Physiology (London)*, 324:113.

Jaco Jacoby, L. L., Dallas, M. (1981). On the relationship between autobiographical memory and perceptual learning. *Journal of Experimental Psychology: General*, 3:306-340.

Kandel, E. R., Schwartz, J. H. (1982). Molecular biology of learning: Modulation of transmitter release. *Science*, 218: 433-443.

Kapp, B. S., Gallagher, M., Applegate, C. D., Frysinger, R. C. (1982). In Woody, C. D. (Ed.), *Conditioning: Representation of involved neural functions*. New York: Plenum, 581.

Kasamatsu, T., Pettigrew, J. D. (1979). Preservation of binocularity after monocular deprivation in the striate cortex of kittens treated with 6-hydroxydopamine. *Journal of Comparative Neurology*, 185:162-163.

Kasamatsu, T., Pettigrew, J. D., Ary, M. L. (1979). Restoration of visual cortical plasticity by local microperfusion of norepinephrine. *Journal of Comparative Neurology*, 185:163-182.

Kaushall, P. J., Zetin, M., Squire, L. R., (1981). Amnesia: Detailed report of a noted case. *Journal of Nervous and Mental Disease*, 169:383-389.

Kesner, R. P., Wilbrun, M. W. (1974). Modification of the discharge of vagal cardiac neurons during learned heart rate change. *Behavioral Biology*, 10:259.

Kesslak, J. P., Cotman, C. W., Chui, H. C., van den Noort, S., Fang, H., Pfeffer, R., Lynch, G. Novel use of olfaction as a possible probe for diagnosing and monitoring Alzheimer's disease (submitted).

Kesslak, J. P., Nieto-Sampedro, M., Globus, J., Cotman, C. W. (1986) Transplants of purified astrocytes promote behavioral recovery after frontal cortex ablation. *Experimental Neurology*, 92:377-390.

King, J. S., Martin, G. F., Connor, B. (1972). A light and electron microscopic study of corticorubral projections in the opossum, *Didelphis marsupialis virginiana*, *Brain Research*, 38:251-265.

Kohonen, T. (1984). *Self-organization and associative memory.* Berlin: Springer-Verlag.

Kucharski, D., Browde, J. A., Hall, W. G. (1986). Relative regional metabolic changes in the brains of neonatal rats during appetitive olfactory learning. *Society of Neuroscience Abstracts*, 12:751.

Labbe, R., Firl, Jr., A., Mufson, E. J., Stein, D. G. (1983). Fetal brain transplants: Reduction of cognitive deficits in rats with frontal cortex lesions. *Science*, 221:470-472.

Larson, J., Lynch, G. S. (1986). Synaptic potentiation in hippocampus by patterned stimulation involves two events. *Science*, 232:985-988.

Larson, J., Wong, D., Lynch, G. (1986). Patterned stimulation at the theta frequency is optimal for induction of long-term potentiation. *Brain Research*, 368:3,7-35.

Lavond, D. G., Hembree, T. L., Thompson, R. F. (1985). Effect of kainic acid lesions of the cerebellar interpositus nucleus on eyelid conditioning in the rabbit. *Brain Research*, 326:179-182.

Lavond, D. G., Lincoln, J. S., McCormick, D. A., Thompson, R. F. (1984). Effect of lesions of the lateral cerebellar nuclei on conditioning of heart-rate and nictitating membrane/eyelid responses in the rabbit. *Brain Research*, 305:323.

Lavond, D. G., Steinmetz, J. E., Yokaitis, M. H., Thompson, R. F. (1986). Retention of classical conditioning after removal of cerebellar cortex. *Society of Neuroscience Abstracts*, 12:753.

Lee, K., Schottler, F., Oliver, M., Lynch, G. (1980). Brief bursts of high-frequency stimulation produce two types of structural change in rat hippocampus. *Journal of Neurophysiology*, 44:247-258.

Leon, M. (1983). Chemical communication in mother-young interactions. In Vandenbergh, J. (Ed.), *Pheromones and reproduction in mammals* (pp. 39-77). New York: Academic Press.

Leon, M. (1974). Maternal pheromone. *Physiology and Behavior*, 13:441-453.

Leon, M., Moltz, H. (1971). Maternal pheromone: discrimination by preweaning albino rats. *Physiology and Behavior*, 7:265-267.

Leon, M., Moltz, H. (1972). The development of the pheromonal bond in the albino rat. *Physiology and Behavior*, 8:683-686.

Leon, M., Coopersmith, R., Lee, S., Sullivan, R. M., Wilson, D. A., Woo, C. (1986). Neural and behavioral plasticity induced by early olfactory learning. In Krasnegor, N. (Ed.), *Psychobiological aspects of behavioral development*, New York: Academic Press.

Leon, M., Galef, B. G., Behse, J. H. (1977). Establishment of the pheromonal bonds and diet choice by odor pre-exposure. *Physiology and Behavior*, 18:387-391.

LeVay, S., Stryker, M. P. (1979). The development of ocular dominance columns in the cat. *Society of Neuroscience Symposia*, 4:83-98.

Lincoln, J. S., Coopersmith, E. W., Harris, E. W., Monaghan, D. T., Cotman, C. W., Leon, M. (1986). NMDA receptor blockade prevents the neural and behavioral consequences of early olfactory experience. *Society of Neuroscience Abstracts*, 12:124.

Lippe, H. P., Schwegler, H., Driscoll, P. (1984). Postnatal modification of hippocampal circuitry alters avoidance learning in adult rats. *Science*, 225:80-82.

Lynch, G. (1986). *Synapses, circuits and the beginnings of memory.* Cambridge: MIT Press.

Lynch, G., Baudry, M. (1984). The biochemistry of memory: A new and specific hypothesis. *Science*, 224:1057-1063.

Lynch, G., Halpain, S., Baudry, M. (1982). Effects of high-frequency synaptic stimulation on glutamate receptor binding studies with a modified *in vitro* hippocampal slice preparation. *Brain Research*, 244:101-111.

Lynch, G., Laron, J., Kelso, S., Barrionuevo, G., Schottler, F. (1983). Intracellular injections of EGTA block the induction of hippocampal long-term potentiation. *Nature*, 305:719-721.

Lynch, G. S., Dunwiddie, T. V., Gribkoff, V. (1977). Heterosynaptic depression: A postsynaptic correlate of long-term potentiation. *Nature*, 266:737-739.

MacFarlane, A. (1975). Olfaction in the development of social preferences in the human neonate. In *The human neonate in parent-infant interaction* (pp. 103-117). Amsterdam: Ciba Foundation.

Macrides, F., Schoenfeld, T. A., Marchand, J. E., Clancy, A. N. (1985). Evidence for morphologically, neurochemically and functionally heterogenous classes of mitral and tufted cells in the olfactory bulb. *Chemical Senses*, 10:175-202.

Malamut, B. L., Saunders, R. C., Mishkin, M. (1984). Monkeys with combined amygdala-hippocampal lesions succeed in object discrimination learning despite 24-hour inter-trial intervals. *Behavioral Neuroscience*, 5:759-769.

Mamounas, L. A., Madden, J., Barchas, J. D., Thompson, R. F. (1983). Microinfusion of bicuculline into dentate/interpositus region abolishes classical conditioning of the well-trained rabbit eyelid response. *Society of Neuroscience Abstracts*, 9:830.

Mandler, G. (1980). Recognizing: The judgment of previous occurrence. *Psychological Review*, 87:252-271.

Martinez, J. L., Rigter, H., Jensen, R. A., Messing, R. B., Vasquez, B. J., McGaugh, J. (1981). Endorphine and enkephalin effects on avoidance conditioning: The other side of the pituitary-adrenal axis. In Martinez J., Jensen R., Messing, R., Rigter, H., McCaugh, J. (Eds.), *Endogenous peptides and learning and memory processes.* New York: Academic Press.

Mauk, M. D., Thompson, R. F. (1984). Classical conditioning using stimulation of the inferior olive as the unconditioned stimulus. *Society of Neuroscience Abstracts*, 10:122.

Mauk, M. D., Castellano, T. G., Rideout, J. A., Madden, J., Barchas, J. D., Thompson, R. F. (1983). Overtraining reduces abolition of classically conditioned responses. *Physiology of Behavior*, 30:493-495.

Mauk, M. D., Madden, J., Barchas, J. D., Thompson, R. F. (1982). Opiates and classical conditioning: Selective abolition of conditioned responses by activation of opiate receptors within the central nervous system. *Proceedings of the National Academy of Sciences*, 9:7598-7602.

McBride, M. C., Kemper, T. L. (1982). Pathogenesis of four-layered microgyric cortex in man. *Acta Neuropathologica*, 57:93-98.

McClelland, J. L., Rumelhart, D. E. (1986). Parallel distributed processing. Cambridge: MIT Press.

McCormick, D. A., Thompson, R. F. (1984). Responses of the rabbit cerebellum during acquisition and performance of a classically conditioned nictitating membrane eyelid response. *Journal of Neuroscience*, 4:2811.

McCormick, D. A., Clark, G. A., Lavond, D. G., Thompson, R. (1982). Initial localization of the memory trace for a basic form of learning. *Proceedings of the National Academy of Sciences, USA*, 79:2731-2735.

McCormick, D. A., Guyer, P. E., Thompson, R. F. (1982). Superior cerebellar peduncle selectively abolish the ipsilateral classically conditioned nictitating membrane/eyelid response of the rabbit. *Brain Research*, 244:347-350.

McGaugh, J. L. (1983). Hormonal influences on memory. *Annual Review of Psychology*, 34:297-323.

McGaugh, J. L. (1985). Peripheral and central adrenergic influences on brain systems involved in the modulation of memory storage. In Olton, D. S., Gamzu, E., Corkin, S. (Eds.), *Memory dysfunctions: An integration of animal and human research from preclinical and clinical perspectives*. New York: Academy of Sciences, 444:150-161.

McGaugh, J. L., Gold, P. E. (1986). Hormonal modulation of memory. In Brush, R. B. and Levine, S. (Eds.), *Psychoendocrinology*. New York: Academic Press.

McNaughton, B. L., Douglas, R. M., Goddard, G. V. (1978). Synaptic enhancement in fascia dentata: Cooperativity among inactive afferents. *Brain Research*, 157:277-293.

Merjanian, J., Bachevalier, J., Crawford, H., Mishkin, M. (1986). Socio-emotional disturbances in the developing rhesus monkey following neonatal limbic lesions. *Society of Neuroscience Abstracts*. 12:23.

Miles, F. A., Lisberger, S. G. (1981). Plasticity in the vestibulo-ocular reflex: A new hypothesis. *Annual Review of Neuroscience*, 4:273.

Milner, B. (1968). Disorders of memory after brain lesions in man. Preface: Material-specific and generalized memory loss. *Neuropsychologia*. 6:175-179.

Mishkin, M. (1978). Memory in monkeys severely impaired by combined but not separate removal of amygdala and hippocampus. *Nature*. 273:297-298.

Mishkin, M., Malamut, B., Bachevalier, J. (1984). Memories and habits: Two neural systems. In Lynch, G., McGaugh, J. L., Weinberger, N. M. (Eds.), *Neurobiology of learning and memory*. New York: Guilford Press.

Monaghan, D. T., Cotman, C. W. (1985). Distribution of N-methyl-D-aspartate-sensitive L-^{3}H-glutamate binding sites in rat brain. *Journal of Neuroscience*, 5:2909-2919.

Morris, R. G. M., Anderson, E., Lynch, G. S., Baudry, M. (1986). Selective impairment of learning and blockade of long-term potentiation by an N-methyl-D-aspartate receptor antagonist, AP5. *Nature*. 319:774-776.

Moskovitch, M. (1982). Multiple dissociations of function in amnesia. In Cermak, L. (Ed.), *Human memory and amnesia*. Hillsdale, N. J.: Lawrence Erlbaum Assoc., 337-370.

Mouly, A. M., Vigouroux, M., Holley, A. (1985). On the ability of rats to discriminate between microstimulations of the olfactory bulb in different locations. *Behavioral Brain Research*, 17:45-48.

Mower, G. D., Christen, W. G., Caplan, C. J. (1984). Absence of ocular dominance columns in binocularly deprived cats. *Investigative Opthalmology and Visual Science (ARVO abstr.)*, 25 (Suppl.):214.

Murakami, F., Katsumaru, H., Saito, K., Tsukahara, N. (1982). A quantitative study of synaptic reorganization in red nucleus neurons after lesion of the nucleus interpositus of the cat: An electron microscopic study involving intracellular injection of Horseradish Peroxidase. *Brain Research*. 242:41-53.

Murray, E. A., Mishkin, M. (1984). Severe tactual as well as visual memory deficits follow combined removal of the amygdala and hippocampus in monkeys. *Journal of Neuroscience*, 4:2565-2580.

Nakamura, Y., Mizuno, N., Konishi, A., Sato, M. (1974). Synaptic reorganization of the red nucleus after chronic deafferentation from cerebellorubral fibers: An electron microscope study in the cat. *Brain Research*, 82:298-301.

Nowakowski, R. S. (1986). Abnormalities in neuronal migration in the hippocampal formation of the NZB/B1NJ mouse. *Neuroscience Abstracts*, 12:317.

Nieto-Sampedro, M., Cotman, C. W. (1985). Growth factor induction and temporal order in CNS repair. In Cotman, C. W. (Ed.), *Synaptic plasticity*. New York: Guilford Press.

O'Keefe, J., Nadel, L. (1978). *The hippocampus as a cognitive map*. London: Oxford University Press.

Oda, Y., Kuwa, K., Miyasaka, S., Tsukahara, N. (1981). Modification of rubral unit activities during classical conditioning in the cat. *Proceedings of the Japanese Academy, Series B*. 57:402-405.

Pedersen, P. E., Williams, C. L., Blass, E. M. (1982). Activation and odor conditioning of suckling behavior in 3-day-old albino rats. *Experimental Psychology: Animal Behavior Processes*, 8:329-341.

Perlow, M. J., Freed, W. J., Hoffer, B. J., Seiger, A., Olson, L., Wyatt, R. J. (1979). Brain grafts reduce motor abnormalities produced by destruction of the nigrostriatal dopamine system. *Science*, 204:643-647.

Prokasy, W. F. (1972). Developments with the two-phase model applied to human eyelid conditioning. In Black, A., Prokasy, W. (Eds.), *Classical conditioning II: Current research and theory*, New York: Appleton-Century-Crofts.

Pysh, J. J., Weiss, G. M. (1979). Exercise during development induces an increase in Purkinje cell dendritic tree size. *Science*, 206:230-232.

Rescorla, A., Wagner, A. R. (1972). A theory of Pavlovial conditioning: Variations in the effectiveness of reinforcement and non-reinforcement. In Black, A., Prokasy, W. (Eds.), *Classical conditioning II: Current research and theory*, New York: Appleton-Century-Crofts, 64-99.

Rescorla, R. A., Solomon, R. L. (1967). Two-process learning theory: Relationships between Pavlovian conditioning and instrumental learning. *Psychological Review.* 74:151-182.

Rose, F. C., Symonds, C. P. (1960). Persistent memory deficit following encephalitis. *Brain*, 83:195-212.

Ryle, G. (1949). *The concept of mind.* San Francisco: Hutchinson.

Schmidt, J. T. (1985). Formation of retinotopic connections: Selective stabilization by an activity-dependent mechanism. *Cellular and Molecular Neurobiology*, 5:65-84.

Schmidt, J. T., Edwards, D. L. (1983). Activity sharpens the map during the regeneration of the retinotectal projection in goldfish. *Brain Research*, 269:29-39.

Scoville, W. B., Milner, B. (1957). Loss of recent memory after bilateral hippocampa lesions. *Journal of Neurology, Neurosurgery, and Psychiatry*, 20:11-21.

Sejnowski, T. J., Rosenberg, C. R. (1986). *NETtalk: A parallel network that learns to read aloud.* Baltimore: Johns Hopkins University.

Shatz, C. J. (1983). The prenatal development of the cat's retinogeniculate pathway. *Journal of Neuroscience*, 3:482-499.

Shatz, C. J., Kirkwood, P. A. (1984). Prenatal development of functional connections in the cat's retinogeniculate pathway. *Journal of Neuroscience*, 4:1378-1397.

Shatz, C. J., Lindstrom, S., Wiesel, T. N. (1977). The distribution of afferents representing the right and left eyes in the cat's visual cortex. *Brain Research*, 131:103-116.

Sherman, G. F., Galaburda, A. M., Geschwind, N. (1985). Cortical anomalies in brains of New Zealand mice: A neuropathological model of dyslexia? *Proceedings of the National Academy of Sciences (USA)*, 82:8072-8074.

Siman, R., Baudry, M., Lynch, G. (1986). Calcium-activated proteases as possible mediators of synaptic plasticity. In Edelman, G., Cowan, W. M., Gall, W. (Eds.), *Dynamic aspects of neocortical functions.* New York: Wiley.

Siman, R., Baudry, M., Lynch, G. (1985). Glutamate receptor regulation by proteolysis of the cytoskeletal protein fodrin. *Nature*, 315:225-227.

Singer, W. (1979). Central core control of visual cortex functions. In Schmitt, F. O., and Worden, F. G. (Eds.), *The neurosciences fourth study program.* Cambridge: MIT Press.

Singer, W. (1982). Central core control of developmental plasticity in the kitten visual cortex: I. Diencephalic lesions. *Experimental Brain Research*, 47:209-222.

Singer. W. (1986). Activity-dependent self-organization of synaptic connections as a substrate of learning. *The Dahlem Workshop Report: Neural and molecular mechanisms of learning.* Berlin: Springer-Verlag.

Singer, W., von Grunau, M., Rauschecker, J. (1979). Requirements for the disruption of biocularity in the visual cortex of strabismic kittens. *Brain Research*, 171:536-540.

Singer, W., Kleinschmidt, A., Bear, M. F. (1986). Infusion of an NMDA receptor antagonist disrupts ocular dominance plasticity in kitten striate cortex. *Society of Neuroscience Abstracts*, 12:786.

Slotnick, B. M., Katz, H. M. (1974). Olfactory learning-set formation in rats. *Science*, 185:796-798.

Smith, A. M. (1970). The effects of rubral lesions and stimulation on conditioned forelimb flexion responses in the cat. *Physiology and Behavior*, 5:1121-1126.

66

Smith, O. A., Astley, C. A., DeVit, J. L., Stein, J. M., Walsh, K. E. (1980). Functional analysis of hypothalamic control of the cardiovascular responses accompanying emotional behavior. *Federation Proceedings: Federation of American Societies of Experimental Biology,* 39:2487.

Squire, L. R. (1986). Mechanisms of memory. *Science,* 232:1612-1619.

Squire, L. R., Moore, R. Y. (1979). Dorsal thalamic lesion in a noted case of chronic memory dysfunction. *Annals of Neurology,* 6:503-506.

Squire, L. R., Zola-Morgan, S. (1985). The Neuropsychology of Memory: New Links Between Humans and Experimental Animals. *Annals of the New York Academy of Sciences,* 444:137-149.

Standing, L. (1973). Learning 10,000 pictures. *Quarterly Journal of Experimental Psychology,* 25:207-222.

Staubli, U., Baudry, M., Lynch, G. (1984). Leupeptin, a thiol-proteinase inhibitor, causes a selective impairment of spatial maze performance in rats. *Behavioral and Neural Biology,* 40:58-69.

Staubli, U., Baudry, M., Lynch, G. (1985a). Olfactory discrimination learning is blocked by leupeptin, a thiol-proteinase inhibitor. *Brain Research,* 337:333-336.

Staubli, U., Fraser, D., Faraday, R., Lynch, G. (1986a). Olfaction and the "data" memory system in rats. *Behavioral Neuroscience,* in press.

Staubli, U., Fraser, D., Kessler, M., Lynch, G. (1986b). Studies on retrograde and anterograde amnesia of olfactory memory after denervation of the hippocampus by entorhinal cortex lesions. *Behavioral and Neural Biology,* in press.

Staubli, U., Ivy, G., Lynch, G. (1985c). Denervation of hippocampus causes rapid forgetting of olfactory memory in rats. *Proceedings of National Academy of Sciences (USA),* 81:5885-5887.

Staubli, U., Roman, F., Lynch, G. (1985b). Selective changes in synaptic responses elicited in a cortical network by behaviorally relevant electrical stimulation. *Society of Neuroscience Abstracts,* 11:837.

Steinmetz, J. E., Lavond, D. G., Thompson, R. F. (1985). Classical conditioning of skeletal muscle responses with mossy fiber stimulation CS and climbing fiber stimulation US. *Society of Neuroscience Abstracts,* 11:982.

Steinmetz, J. E., Logan, C. G., Rosen, D. J., Lavond, D. G., Thompson, R. F. (1986). Lesions in the pontine nuclear region selectively abolish classically conditioned eyelid responses in rabbits. *Society of Neuroscience Abstracts,* 12:753.

Stryker, M. P., Harris, W. A. (1986). Binocular impulse blockade prevents the formation of ocular dominance columns in cat visual cortex. *Journal of Neuroscience,* 6:2117-2133.

Sullivan, R. M., Leon, M. (1986). Early olfactory learning induces an enhanced olfactory bulb response in young rats. *Developmental Brain Research,* 27:278-282.

Sullivan, R. M., Leon, M. (1986). Implication of norepinephrine in olfactory learning in infant rats. *Society of Neuroscience Abstracts,* 12:124.

Swindale, N. V. (1982). Absence of ocular dominance patches in dark reared cats. *Nature,* 290:332-333.

Swindale, N. V., Vital-Durand, F., Blakemore, C. (1981). Recovery from monocular deprivation in monkey. III. Reversal of anatomical effects in the visual cortex. *Proceedings of the Royal Society of London,* B 213:435-350.

Talland, G. A. (1965). *Deranged memory.* New York: Academic Press.

Teuber, H. L., Milner, B., Vaughan, H. G. (1968). Persistent anterograde amnesia after stab wound of the basal brain. *Neuropsychologia,* 6:267-282.

Thomas, G. J. (1984). Memory: Time Binding in organisms. In Squire, L. R., Butters, N. (Eds.), *Neuropsychology of memory.* New York: Guilford press, 374-384.

Thompson, R. F. (1986). The neurobiology of learning and memory. *Science,* 233:941-952.

Thompson, R. F., Berger, T. W., Cegavske, C. F., Patterson, M. M., Roemer, R. A., Taylor, T. J., Young, R. A. (1976). A search for the engram. *American Psychologist,* 31:209-227.

Thompson, R. F., Berger, T. W., Madden, J. (1983). Cellular processes of learning and memory in the mammalian CNS. *Annual Review of Neuroscience,* 6:447-491.

Tieman, S. B., Tumosa, N. (1983). ^{14}C-2-Deoxyglucose demonstration of the organization of ocular dominance in areas 17 and 18 of the normal cat. *Brain Research,* 267:35-46.

Townes-Anderson, E., Raviola, G. (1978). Degeneration and regeneration of autonomic nerve endings in the anterior part of rhesus monkey ciliary muscle. *Journal of Neurocytology,* 7:583-600.

Tsukahara, N. (1986). Synaptic plasticity in the red nucleus and its possible behavioral correlates. In Cotman, C. W. (Ed.), *Synaptic plasticity.* New York: Guilford Press.

Tsukahara, N., Fujito, Y. (1976). Physiological evidence of formation of new synapses from cerebrum in the red nucleus neurons following cross-union of forelimb nerves. *Brain Research,* 106:184-188.

Tsukahara, N., Oda, Y. (1981). Appearance of new synaptic potentials at cortocorubral synapses after the establishment of classical condition. *Proceedings of the Japanese Academy, Series B.* 57:389-401.

Tsukahara, N., Fujito, Y., Oda, Y., Maeda, J. (1982). Formation of functional synapses in adult cat red nucleus from the cerebrum following cross-innervation of forelimb flexor and extensor nerves. I. Appearance of new synaptic potentials. *Experimental Brain Research,* 45:1-12.

Tsukahara, N., Hultborn, H., Murakami, F. (1974). Sprouting of corticorubral synapses in red nucleus neurons after destruction of the nucleus interpositus of the cerebellum. *Experientia,* 30:57-58.

Tsukahara, N., Hultborn, H., Murakami, F., Fujito, Y. (1975). Electrophysiological study of formation of new synapses and collateral sprouting in red nucleus neurons after partial denervation. *Journal of Neurophysiology,* 38:1359-1372.

Tsukahara, N., Oda, Y., Notsu, T. (1981). Classical conditioning mediated by the red nucleus in the cat. *Journal of Neuroscience,* 1:72-79.

Tulving, E. (1983). *Elements of episodic memory.* Oxford: Clarendon.

Turner, A. M., Greenough, W. T. (1983). Synapses per neuron and synaptic dimensions in occipital cortex of rats reared on complex, social or isolation housing. *Acta Stereologica Supplement,* 2:239-244.

Uylings, H. B. M., Kuypers, K., Diamond, M. C., Eltman, W. A. M. (1978). Effects of differential environment on plasticity of dendrites of cortical pyramidal neurons in adult rats. *Experimental Neurology,* 62:658-677.

Victor, M., Adams, R. D., Collins, G. H. (1971). *The Wernicke-Korsakoff Syndrome.* Philadelphia: F. A. Davis.

Volpe, B. T., Hirst, W. (1983). The characterization of an amnesic syndrome following hypoxic ischemic injury. *Archives of Neurology,* 40:436-440.

Wagner, A. R. (1981). A model of automatic memory processing in animal behavior. In Spear, N., Ritter, R. (Eds.), *Information processing in animals: Memory mechanisms.* Hillsdale, NJ: Erlbaum.

Warrington, E. K., Weiskrantz, L. (1982). Amnesia: A disconnection syndrome. *Neuropsychologia,* 20:233-248.

Watanabe, E. (1985). *Neuroscience Research,* 3:20.

Wenzel, J., Matthies, H. (1985). Morphological changes in the hippocampal formation accompanying memory formation and long-term potentiation. In Weinberger, N., McGaugh, J., Lynch, G. (Eds.), *Memory Systems of the Brain* (pp. 150-170). New York: Guilford Press.

Williams, N., Pennybacker, J. (1954). Memory disturbances in third ventricle tumours. *Journal of Neurology, Neurosurgery, and Psychiatry,* 17:115-123.

Wilson, D. A., Leon, M. (1986). Localized changes in olfactory bulb single unit response to learned attractive odors. *Society of Neuroscience Abstracts,* 12:123.

Wilson, D. A., Sullivan, R. M., Leon, M. (1985). Odor familiarity alters mitral cell response in the olfactory bulb of neonatal rats. *Developmental Brain Research,* 22:314-317.

Woo, C. C., Leon, M. (1986). Temporal characteristics of the enhanced neural response following odor experience in rats. *Society of Neuroscience Abstracts.* 12:123.

Zola-Morgan, S., Squire, L. R., Amaral, D. G. (1986). Human amnesia and the medial temporal region: Enduring memory impairment following a bilateral lesion limited to field CA1 of the hippocampus. *Journal of Neuroscience,* 6:2950-2967.

Zola-Morgan, S., Squire, L. R., Mishkin, M. (1982). The neuroanatomy of amnesia: Amygdala-hippocampus versus temporal stem. *Science,* 218:1337-1339.

DISCUSSION

Albert M. Galaburda

In his introduction to the book *The Mindful Brain* by Mountcastle and Edelman, Professor Frank Schmitt states that "theories based on partial systems are subject to the component-systems dilemma that bedevils all attempts at biological generalization." He goes on to state that "until now no detailed, self-consistent theory has been proposed that specifies and functionally characterizes the operational repertoires at the level of molecules, individual neurons, or groups (circuits) of neurons, and that explicitly defines the postulated information-processing mechanism." The paper by Cotman and Lynch also makes the strong point that the correct approach to the study of the neurobiology of learning and memory, and by corollary extension, of learning and memory disorders, involves the making of no assumptions as to the level of analysis. It is incorrect, therefore, to decide *a priori* that explanations must always be reductionistic in nature or that there is a preferred approach. Rather, as the paper under discussion clearly suggests, the level of analysis must be appropriate to the level of behavior under investigation.

Some of the behaviors that interest students of developmental learning disorders involve complex cognitive processes that are likely to be widely distributed in neural networks. Although these behaviors are ultimately explainable by a composite of individual activities of receptors on genes, cytoplasmic organelles, and cell surfaces, they are likely to involve probabilistic phenomena that can best be described in terms of large-scale neural organization. I have been told, for instance, that the shape of a feather is dictated to a major extent by local molecular epigenetic events. However, the evolution of feathers came about as a result of the interaction between the whole feather (the whole bird, for that matter) with the physical characteristics of the flight environment. It would be difficult, therefore, to comprehend the ultimate shape of the bird's wing and its feather arrangement beginning with the analysis of the molecular events involved in the formation of each subunit barb. In this sense, the investigation of behaviors and their appropriate anatomical substrates at multiple levels is more likely to provide useful answers to the diagnosis and treatment of the various learning disorders.

Physicians are cognizant of the fallacy of making assumptions about level. Thus, for instance, a patient may experience shortness of breath for a variety of reasons: some may be explained by molecular defects, such as is the case in some anomalous hemoglobins, or in the altered acid/base balance of uncontrolled diabetes; others may be explained by straightforward gross anatomical parameters, such as is the case in obstruction of the upper airways by a foreign body such as an aspirated piece of meat. The explanation might implicate the external environment, such as is the case in severe air pollution or extreme altitude.

Analogously, learning disabilities may result from agents acting at one or several levels. In some instances, one may be witnessing the effects of an abnormal social environment—for instance, through substandard education. In the cases where the brain itself is implicated, the abnormalities may best be described at the gross anatomical level such as in holoprocencephaly. Perhaps the anatomical substrate is best described at the level of abnormality in neural circuitries, such as appears to be the case in a group of individuals with developmental dyslexia. Thus, we have described abnormal collections of neurons with disorganized lamination of cortical neurons involving language-relevant areas of the brains of several dyslexic individuals. The anatomical abnormality may, on the other hand, be cellular in nature, a possibility we have suggested to explain the findings in Down syndrome. Explanations at the molecular level, in contrast, may be the only ones suitable for many of the disorders of attention, as may be surmised from the pharmacological literature on this subject. Molecular-level descriptions implicating enzymatic defects explain the changes where the accumulation of sulfatide is seen in the cytoplasm of affected neurons in a condition producing mental retardation and known as metachromatic leukodystrophy.

I find it heartwarming to see represented at a conference on learning disability a paper that discusses the neurobiology of learning from synaptic mechanisms in invertebrates to large-scale networks of neurons in man and nonhuman primates. Although the choice of such a paper addresses the unique importance of neurobiological explanations, it also makes the more general statement that the problem of learning disability must be tackled at multiple levels, from the social, to the psychological, to the neurobiological. Thus far, most approaches have been leveled at social and psychological interactions.

I would like to end with one additional comment. Malfunction of a system such as the brain does not necessarily imply that the brain is at fault; as we have seen, it may reflect the actions of a noxious environment. However, even if the discovery is made that certain types of learning disorders can be explained by the presence in the population of unusual brains, this does not necessarily imply that this oddity is indeed pathological in nature, and may in fact reflect normal variability. Much of the work that has been carried out on learning and memory—and the summary paper under discussion attests to this fact—fails to take account of individual variability. I have been told that even certain aplysias refuse to retract their gills under established experimental paradigms. Thus, even some lowly animals learning with relatively simple nervous systems can demonstrate individuality and a certain probabilistic nature in their behavior. The extremely complex nervous systems and behaviors that we are ultimately interested in, namely those of learning human beings, most likely exhibit the additive uncertainties of their component basic units. Only recently have some neurobiologists and cognitive scientists begun to tackle the problem of diversity and its mechanisms. I believe that those studies, carried out on the shoulders of the information we now have on the neurobiology of learning, will shed much light on the issue of learning differences and disabilities. The paper by Cotman and Lynch represents, therefore, a starting point.

DISCUSSION

Richard F. Thompson

It is a pleasure to be here today to speak to you about this terribly important topic, important to all of us.

First, I would like to compliment Drs. Cotman and Lynch for producing what I think is the very best synthesis and current overview of the neurobiology of learning and memory that I've read. It is an elegant job. Not only do they give a very comprehensive and up-to-date account, but they also manage to convey the enormous excitement that exists in this field today.

Over the past couple of years, I have been chair of a working group for a committee of the National Academy of Sciences. The goal of the committee was to prepare what is called a ten-year report in the behavioral and social sciences, identifying the areas of research that are most exciting and most promising, and are most likely to lead to important breakthroughs in the next ten years. My subcommittee was able to convince the parent committee that the psychology of learning and memory is perhaps the most exciting field in this broad area. So, we agree, Carl.

I think that the general message conveyed by Cotman and Lynch is important and particularly relevant for this conference because they stress the fact that memory is not a unitary "thing" in the brain. There was an old notion that memories are distributed widely and diffusely throughout the brain. This is clearly not the case.

Work in the last ten years has shown that, in fact, there are several different kinds of memory phenomena or processes and several different kinds of memory circuits in the brain, circuits that subserve these different aspects of memory. By the same token, in reading over the papers prepared for this conference, particularly those by Dr. Tallal and Dr. Johnson, it is very clear that there are a number of different kinds or aspects of learning disabilities. I think that as a result of the recent work on the neurobiology and psychobiology of learning and memory, we, for the first time, have a chance of developing a rational neurobiological, theoretical basis for understanding the many different kinds of learning disabilities.

I'd like to pick up on one example that Dr. Cotman mentioned in his talk, the remarkable impairment in the patient H. M. It is remarkable in two ways: what is impaired (declarative memory) and what is not impaired (procedural memory). In mirror reading, you simply hold up an English text to a mirror and read in the mirror. Try it some time; it is very difficult. But with practice, you can learn to read mirror English almost as fast as you read normal English.

H. M. was presented with this task. It takes a number of days to learn. He learned it completely normally. This is not merely a simple motor skill, it is a complex cognitive kind of skill; but he learned it with no difficulty whatever. Consider yourself in this task, having learned mirror reading, and compare yourself with H. M. You would be given a list of words presented in mirror English. You'd read them quite well, and H. M. would be presented with the words and he would read them quite well. Then, afterwards, we would question you and H. M. as to what words you read. You would remember many of the words. H. M. has no memory at all for any words he read.

But the point is that he has learned to mirror read normally. It is my impression, in reading over the other papers prepared for this conference, that many aspects of learning disabilities in children involve this kind of complex skill learning. Carl also alluded in his talk to the work that has been done recently in my laboratory, and he covers it at length in his paper.

Our work is concerned with an elementary kind of skill learning, and without going into any of the details, let me say that our evidence is now quite strong that the memories for this kind of skill learning are stored in a brain structure called the cerebellum. In fact, we think that a great many memories of this type are stored in the cerebellum. Furthermore, nature seems to have designed this system in a very special way. There are only two anatomical inputs to the cerebellum. One is called mossy fibers; the other is called climbing fibers.

It appears that the mossy fibers are the "learning" inputs. They give rise to the synaptic connections that appear to develop modifiability with training. The other input, which is anatomically quite distinct and different, the climbing fiber input, is the "teaching" or reinforcing input, the input that provides the instruction for the learning synapses to learn.

So we have, if you will, a very elegant system that seems to be specifically designed for a certain kind of learning. If so, then the cerebellum may be much involved in human disabilities in skill learning.

Drs. Cotman and Lynch quite properly stressed long-term memory and the nature of long-term memory formation in their major discussions of both declarative, or fact, and procedural, or skill learning. There is one other aspect of learning and memory that I think is worth mentioning, short-term memory. Again, reading over the other papers, it appears that some aspects of learning disabilities in children may relate to short-term memory processes.

There is some very exciting recent work by Patricia Goldman Rakic, Joachum Fuster, and others that appears to identify a particular area of the monkey prefrontal lobe in the sulcus principalis region that has a specific role in short-term memory processing, where the memory of a spatial location must be maintained in the absence of the external object. In other words, when the object isn't there, monkeys and humans can remember that it was there. This kind of memory depends on the tissue of the sulcus principalis and its interconnections with the parietal and temporal association areas.

Finally, an important fact stressed by Dr. Galaburda: The brain is not a set of different circuits doing totally different things. It is a very complex, interacting system, a system made up of many subsystems.

For example, as the frontal lobe evolved, it evolved enormously from monkeys to apes to humans. By the same token the new areas of the cerebellum have evolved in close association with, and are tightly interconnected with, these new association areas of the cerebral cortex.

So, if we make the overly simplified and strong assumption that the cortical systems, the hippocampus and cerebral cortex, are more concerned with declarative or fact memories and that the cerebellar system is more concerned with skill memories, it is very clear that the two systems are tightly interconnected and that they interact and function as one complex system.

However, abnormalities in one or another aspect of these systems could very well produce many of the kinds of learning disabilities we are so anxious to treat.

PART II: SPECIFIC DEVELOPMENTAL DISABILITIES OF READING, WRITING, AND MATHEMATICS

REVIEW OF RESEARCH ON SPECIFIC READING, WRITING, AND MATHEMATICS DISORDERS

Doris J. Johnson

INTRODUCTION AND DEFINITION

Learning disabilities are but one of many developmental disorders that concern families, educators, psychologists, physicians, and others in this country and abroad. As is well known to most people in the field, the term LD was selected to represent a heterogeneous group of children, who, until the 1960's, were given minimal attention in schools (Kirk, 1963). Although these disorders had been noted by doctors, teachers, and others for decades, there were few provisions for special services, with the exception of a few private schools and clinics (Bender, 1956; McGinnis, 1963; Cruickshank et al., 1961; Strauss and Lehtinen, 1947; Frostig, 1968; Orton, 1937; Gillingham and Stillman, 1956; Myklebust, 1954).

Often, because there were no special programs, such children were placed with the deaf, the mentally retarded, or the emotionally disturbed. Others remained in regular classes or dropped out of school. With the combined efforts of professionals and parents, recognition of this population was finally achieved. By the time Public Law 94-142 was passed in 1975, it was apparent that substantial numbers of children needing special education were unlike groups of children with limited sensory acuity, physical capacity, or mental ability.

One of the greatest concerns was for pupils with specific reading disabilities, since advancement in school and in many occupations depends upon the ability to understand and use written language. While problems of mathematics were observed, less emphasis was given to these disorders in remediation and research. Recently, the importance of mathematics literacy has been acknowledged (Glenn, 1978), and more studies have been reported in new journals in mathematics.

As services for the learning disabled were being mandated, there were also concerns for the disadvantaged, the underprivileged, the delinquent, and the illiterate. Therefore, Federal programs such as Head Start and Right to Read were established for children in poverty areas, and efforts were made to foster literacy. Work on reading, writing, and arithmetic was also being conducted and funded through several professional organizations. As funding patterns changed, as new programs were developed, and as national concerns regarding literacy were expressed, the distinctions between learning disabilities and other types of underachievment became more difficult to determine, particularly with the influx of bilingual, bicultural children in public schools. In recent years, more difficult concerns have been raised, such as who should be classified as handicapped, who should be served, and where and how.

As handicapped children were mainstreamed into the regular class, the educational task became even more difficult. The criteria for classifying children as mentally retarded also changed in some states. For example, at one time, in certain locations, children with IQ scores below 79 were placed in rooms for the educable mentally handicapped. Now, with the emphasis on mainstreaming, with the use of generic categories (for instance, "mildly handicapped"), and with concerns regarding the assessment of mental ability, many youngsters with IQ scores between 90 and 70 (and perhaps lower) are in the regular class. Such youngsters are often diagnosed as learning disabled, even though they may not demonstrate a discrepancy between their own ability and achievement. Thus, the incidence of learning disabilities (LD) and mental retardation (MR) has changed in some states. In certain cases, these changes may be positive in that early stimulation might have prevented more serious retardation.

CURRENT ISSUES RELATED TO INCIDENCE AND IDENTIFICATION

School administrators and other professionals within the field of learning disabilities are concerned about the increasing numbers of individuals classified in this group. According to the Sixth Annual Report to Congress on the Implementation of the Education of the Handicapped Act, prepared by the Office of Special Education, U.S. Department of Education (1984), LD is the fastest growing category within special education. In 1982-83, almost 4 percent of school children in the United States were classified as LD. Of those receiving special services, 40 percent of those in special education were in LD programs. Yet, these numbers are not distributed equally geographically. Keogh (1986a) reported that 63 percent of the handicapped children from age 3 to 21 in Rhode Island were considered LD, but only 26 percent were so classified in Alabama. All of these social, cultural, and educational issues, together with developments and concerns in the field of learning disabilities, have prompted local, State, and Federal agencies and many professional groups to carefully reexamine the procedures for identifying children with special needs.

Concerns over increasing incidence, problems in program eligibility criteria, adequacy of test instruments, instructional variables, and service delivery have fostered many discussions, appointments of task forces (Chalfant, 1985), and research symposia to investigate ways of resolving the problems (Vaughn and Bos, 1987). The concerns also have led to the development of new definitions (National Joint Committee on Learning Disabilities [NJCLD], 1981; Hammill et al., 1987) and position papers related to definition (Association for Children and Adults with Learning Disabilities [ACLD], 1985). While these newer definitions and positions are not unanimously accepted, most professionals agree that LD refers to a heterogeneous population. Even within a single area of underachievement such as reading, clinicians, neuropsychologists, and specialists in other areas have identified subtypes.

While several professional organizations have agreed to accept the NJCLD definition, the ACLD has not, in part because of its lack of attention to the nonacademic, nonverbal disorders manifested among LD individuals and also because of the lifelong nature of the condition. In addition, learning disabilities are not simply an academic handicap; nonverbal processing may also be impaired. The ACLD emphasized the selective impairments in LD in contrast to global disorders of the mentally deficient.

Schools typically use the 1975 Federal definition (P.L. 94-142); however, schools are often faced with dilemmas and problems related to funding, personnel, and facilities. Some find that the only placement available for children with reading or writing problems is in the LD program. Therefore, whether the children meet the specific requirements for LD or not, they may be so labeled. In fact, findings from the University of Minnesota Institute have emphasized that it was difficult to differentiate underachievers from students with specific learning disabilities. Ysseldyke et al., (1983) concluded that "the special education decision-making process is one in which a student is referred, often for vague and subjective reasons; automatically tested, often with technically inadequate devices; usually placed by a team meeting; and is the object of decisions made less on data than on subjective teacher or student variables and on inconsistent and indefensible criteria (p. 87)."

In response, McKinney (1983) said that these problems are well documented elsewhere in the literature. Yet he and others disagreed with these conclusions because other learning disability institutes did identify specific deficits in information processing and in adaptive behavior among LD students. According to McKinney, the failure of the Minnesota Institute "to find differences between LD and other underachievers is not surprising, since most psychometric measures that meet acceptable criteria for reliability and validity are correlated with achievement, and both groups have underachievement in common

(p. 137)." McKinney says that further research on specific types of information processing deficits in LD children is needed.

Even though a more replicable body of data needs to be generated, it has been recommended that because of these issues related to program eligibility, school-identified learning disabled students should not be used as research subjects without further assessment (Keogh, 1986b) and without control groups (Torgesen and Wong, 1986; Wong, 1986). At least for the present, research definitions and criteria for program eligibility should be considered separately.

Most definitions and criteria include some mention of an ability-achievement discrepancy. That is, in order to be classified as learning disabled, an individual must manifest a discrepancy between potential and achievement. In order to quantify the degree of underachievement, several formulae have been developed, all with good intentions; but they have been criticized because of mathematical flaws (Shepherd, 1980). While some States adhere to strict quantitative standards, others use tests combined with clinical judgments.

Numerous concerns regarding tests for both mental ability and achievement have been raised. Evaluation of mental ability is of particular concern to those working with the disadvantaged and the bilingual. Tests also can be misused with the handicapped, including the learning disabled. This reviewer feels that one must be cautious in mandating any particular test or combination of tests for learning disabilities. The results might improperly place a subject in the mentally retarded or "slow learning" category (a problem prior to the establishment of LD as a category). One would not, for example, give a verbal IQ test to the deaf or a performance IQ test to the physically handicapped. Similarly, children with language disorders should not be given only verbal IQ measures, nor should those with visual-motor disorders be given only performance tests for mental ability. Given the great heterogeneity of the handicapped population, it is unlikely that specific tests for mental ability and achievement can be mandated for school placement, even though the tests have excellent reliability and validity. Rather, tests chosen should not require skills associated with the primary symptoms. If such tests are used, they should be interpreted with care. Stated differently, if the field accepts heterogeneity of problems, some flexibility in test selection must be considered. Mandated test batteries seem ill advised at this time.

GENERAL ISSUES RELATED TO TESTS

Many tests used to measure learning disabilities have been criticized for their technical inadequacies and lack of proper validity (Ysseldyke, 1983; Ysseldyke et al., 1980, 1982, 1983). Clearly, professionals within the field must be aware of these problems; however, the critics should not discourage researchers from looking for measures to investigate hypotheses about processing or from developing new tests. This reviewer recommends that teams of professionals work together on test construction. These teams should include the best possible people in measurement, assessment, and learning disabilities. Such tests might be developed as part of a contract with one or more Federal agencies.

In the construction or selection of tests, however, it is important to remember that most tests assess multiple functions (Johnson, 1987a), particularly those for higher levels of achievement and cortical function such as reading comprehension, written language, or mathematics. Failures on these measures could be due to disorders of conceptualization, receptive or expressive language, decoding, memory, and other skills.

Most achievement tests are screening measures at best. Thus, even with highly reliable and valid measures for both IQ and achievement, one might not identify specific learning disabilities unless other procedures are used. Many of the authors of articles in *Focus on Learning Problems in Mathematics* emphasize this point. Many reading and spelling tests fail to provide sufficient data regarding rule acquisition, application, or automaticity. Thus, if one suspects on the basis of reading errors that a child's problems are related to phonological sequencing, few tests are available that provide sufficient data across a wide age range to test for this skill. Hence, this reviewer feels that certain experimental procedures (such as linguistic awareness) may need to be converted to standardized tests. The new decoding test is a good example (Richardson, 1985).

MEASUREMENT OF INTELLIGENCE

According to most definitions, individuals with LD are not primarily mentally retarded; no strict criteria, however, are provided in Federal rules and regulations. Individual states and school systems have thus developed guidelines and specified which tests can be used and whether full-scale, verbal, or performance measures should be used. Measurement specialists often argue that only full-scale scores be used, yet, as stated previously, many special educators and parents are concerned that children with specific language disorders or visual-spatial-motor problems may be misclassified if only full-scale IQ scores are used. Specialists in infant assessment also feel that global scores tend to mask patterns of strengths and weaknesses (S. Cohen, 1983).

Several reviews of intellectual levels of learning disabled students have led Stanovich (1986) and others to conclude that the IQ levels of many LD samples are lower than average and fall in the 87 to 93 range (Piotrowski and Siegel, 1986). Stanovich (1986) reported that the mean IQ score of children labeled LD does not approximate 100, but is usually closer to 90. He cites one study in which the mean performance IQ score was 89; another study, a performance IQ of 92; still another, of 91; and a fourth, of 94. A large sample from the Child Service Demonstration Centers in 21 states had a median IQ score of 93. Torgesen and Dice (1980) found the mean IQ score of LD groups was 6 points lower than that of control groups.

This reviewer found many exceptions to these reports, particularly in journals and books on dyslexia. Studies by Haines and Torgesen (1979), Johnson, Blalock, and Nesbitt (1978), Cullen, Boersma, and Chapman (1981), Vogel (1986), and Wong (1980) all reported IQ scores above 100.

In a large study in three school systems, Myklebust et al., (1971) reported a mean verbal IQ score of 102 for the LD group and 104 for the controls. Performance IQ scores for the two groups did not differ; both were above 100. More recently, Blalock (1987) has reported a mean verbal IQ score of 106 and a performance IQ of 103 for a group of 93 learning disabled adults.

Differences in school samples (public or private) and clinic samples also should be noted. The former may include more slow learners because of the selection procedures. In certain school systems, above-average or gifted LD children are occasionally denied services because they are not "severely" underachieving. Yet, they may not be performing at the level of their own ability. Consequently, many families with financial resources seek private services. Thus, the above-average or gifted LD students may not even be included in the school population. Children in private schools for dyslexics frequently have above-average and even superior intellectual ability (Rawson, 1968).

Burns (1984) has discussed several issues regarding the relatively low IQ scores reported in the literature and explained the differences by using the bivariate normal probability distribution. Piotrowski and Siegel (1986) have contended that Burns' explanation is insufficient and that more comprehensive explanations related to referral and placement practices are needed.

Several investigators have analyzed intellectual patterns of LD students to determine whether characteristic profiles would emerge. In a review of 24 studies, Dudley-Marling et al., (1981) concluded that high performance IQ:low verbal IQ was not necessarily characteristic of the group, though some studies found such a pattern. Nor is subtest scatter an indicator of LD, since normals also show discrepancies. While many studies of poor readers have noted low performance on arithmetic, digit span, coding, and information subtests, few LD individuals actually conform to this pattern. Therefore, differential diagnosis should not be made on the basis of pattern analysis of the Wechsler Intelligence Scale for Children (WISC).

In general, most professionals in LD now recommend that school-identified LD populations not be used for research without testing for intelligence and other factors in more depth. This issue is critical not only with regard to the incidence of LD but also for programs of intervention and studies of prognosis. Students with overall low ability probably need assistance with most subjects and usually profit from generalized "good" instruction and study skills. However, these general approaches may not be sufficient for the average or above-average student who has quite specific problems in decoding, written language, or other areas. Comprehensive diagnostic studies also should include a broad base of information, including the family and developmental history, if we are to explain patterns of performance. Several studies reviewed for this report indicate that parental expectations, socioeconomic levels, teacher expectation, and other variables contribute significantly to a child's level of achievement.

COGNITIVE ACHIEVEMENT BATTERIES

In recent years, several new tests have been developed to study various aspects of cognition and achievement. In certain instances, they are used rather than other standardized IQ tests. One used rather widely is the Woodcock-Johnson Psycho-Educational Battery (1977). According to Woodcock (1978), the battery includes several individually administered standardized tests to measure cognitive abilities, scholastic aptitudes, achievement, and interest. The validity of the battery was evaluated with a sample of LD subjects by Ysseldyke, Algozzine, and Shinn (1980), who concluded that the battery has some convergent validity but little discriminant validity relative to various cluster scores or for specific uses. The technical characteristics of the battery appear to be adequate, but the extent to which one can clearly distinguish aptitudes, abilities, or achievement is not resolved.

Smith and Rogers (1978) explored the reliability of standardized assessment instruments used with LD children, and reported high internal consistency reliabilities for the WISC-R[evised], the Metropolitan Achievement Tests, and the Peabody Individual Achievement Tests. They also concluded that the overall psychometric properties of these instruments did not change much when administered to LD children and that the test results were as reliable for LD subjects as for any other group.

ALTERNATIVE APPROACHES TO ASSESSMENT

Future studies of intelligence and intervention may be strengthened by incorporating concepts of clinical or diagnostic teaching or by using dynamic assessment (Brown and Ferrara, 1985; Ferrara, Brown, and Campione,1986; Feurerstein, 1979). Ferrara et al. state that most tests of intelligence measure what a person knows at a given point in time rather than what the person can learn. Stated differently, the instruments test the products of experience rather than the processes used to produce the knowledge base. Therefore, these investigators designed forms of evaluation to augment data from more traditional tests, which they call *dynamic assessment*. It is similar to clinical or diagnostic teaching in that the goal is to study the amount of instruction needed to bring individuals to a specified level of competence. Those who adhere to theories of Vygotsky refer to this as the "proximal zone of development." According to Ferrara et al., (1986), this zone is defined as an inverse function of the number of prompts needed for children to achieve successful independent performance within a problem domain and for them to subsequently maintain and transfer their acquired knowledge to increasingly different types of problems. Children with wide proximal zones are efficient learners in a particular domain and can capitalize on a relatively small amount of assistance. Those with narrower zones require more intervention in order to achieve.

These concepts are relevant for LD, since Ferrara et al. found that average IQ children required more prompts to reach learning criteria than those with higher intelligence. Transfer flexibility was also related to IQ. That is, higher IQ children needed less assistance than average IQ children.

SEVERITY VS. PATTERNS OF PERFORMANCE

In order to reduce the number of children in LD programs, it has been recommended that such children demonstrate a *severe* discrepancy between ability and achievement. Such a plan, however, will not guarantee a "clean" LD population. It would simply screen out a group of severe underachievers and may even prevent some LD students from obtaining services. Even the best IQ and achievement tests will yield a heterogeneous group. Unless the experimenter evaluates many aspects of learning, specific patterns of problems may not be elicited.

Stated differently, *severity* should not be the sole criterion for selecting poor readers or writers if we are to advance the body of knowledge in the field and identify unique problems, subgroups, or patterns. Consideration of an analogy from sensory impairments is useful. A school nurse may detect severe hearing or visual problems, but other tests will be needed to determine the type of disorder and needs. The fields of audiology emerged as psychoacousticians, experimental psychologists, and others defined units of measurement and developed tests to identify types of hearing impairments, which in turn, guide the selection of appropriate hearing aids and intervention procedures, and in some cases, note the site of lesion.

For patterns of performance to emerge, a wide range of tests and background data on many groups of children in various regions of the country are needed. As long as test batteries include only measures of ability and achievement, there may be no differentiation between LD and other poor achievers. Even with control groups and with reliable, valid achievement tests, other data are needed. One would expect adult illiterates, for example, to have difficulty decoding nonsense words. The *overall* psychoeducational pattern of performance of the new immigrant, however, presumably would be different from that of a native speaker who is unschooled or poorly motivated, and different from that of a motivated, poor reader who has had every opportunity for good instruction.

GENERAL DEVELOPMENTS IN RESEARCH

Despite the problems related to definition, program eligibility criteria, and educational management, a considerable body of knowledge has emerged about LD from the use of more rigorous procedures for studying learners in both experimental and naturalistic settings. As is well known, much of the early research in the LD field in the 1930's and 1940's began with descriptions of learner characteristics—that is, with detailed descriptions of behavior and performance in one or more areas of learning. The investigations—then and now—undoubtedly reflect the background of the investigators and the populations they have studied. Early on, the research focused on those handicaps that were most visible, such as perceptual-motor deficits, behavior problems, and severe language and reading disorders. Some, but not all, practitioners emphasized perceptual deficits. Many others focused directly on the language or reading problems of the children. Hence, even though people criticized parts of Orton's theory (1937) because of his focus on perception, it is important to remember that his remedial approach incorporated a very systematic, analytic approach to decoding. He, together with many early theorists and clinicians, emphasized the relationships between one or more parameters of oral language, reading, writing, and mathematics.

While research results have indicated that most poor readers do not have primary perceptual deficits, learning disabilities are not synonymous with reading disabilities; nor are they synonymous with underachievement. Yet, perceptual-motor deficits cannot be overlooked for handwriting and other physical activities. One only has to step inside a classroom for learning disabled children or into a room of adults with learning disabilities to observe that several of them are, indeed, poorly coordinated. They often have difficulty with self-help skills such as tying shoes, folding paper to fit into envelopes, and using various measuring devices. Typically, they also have rather serious problems in handwriting and arithmetic. Thus, while perceptual-motor theories might not explain *reading* disabilities, they cannot be ignored when studying the needs of the total population. Many adults with nonverbal perceptual-motor disabilities have more serious problems in obtaining and maintaining jobs than those with severe reading disorders (Johnson and Blalock, 1987). In general, many early studies provided rather global observations of individuals with relatively severe and obvious disorders. In some respects, this same tendency is evident in countries where work in special education or dyslexia is just beginning (Bogdanowicz, 1985; Marfo et al., 1986).

Other approaches to research have emerged from the fields of adult aphasia, language pathology, and neuropsychology, many of which have provided the hypotheses and symptomatology for investigations of subtypes. They also fostered the development of tests for specific types of disorders, such as word retrieval (German, 1986), spelling (Boder and Jarrico, 1982), and written language (Myklebust, 1965; Hammill and Larsen, 1981).

During the last decade, following the criticism of the literature of earlier periods, more experimental studies were conducted, and new bodies of knowledge have emerged (Ceci, 1986; Doehring et al., 1981; Doris, 1986; Farnham-Diggory, 1986; Fisher and Athey, 1986; Keogh, 1986; Kavale and Forness, 1985; Gray and Kavanagh, 1985; Malatesha and Aaron, 1982; Pavlidis and Fisher, 1986; Perfetti and Hogaboam, 1975; Rumelhart, 1977; Stanovich, 1986; Torgesen and Wong, 1986; Vellutino, 1983). Several new journals, together with results of research from the LD institutes as well as Myklebust's five-volume series, *Progress in Learning Disabilities*, offer new theory and data.

Often, however, studies are conducted in only a single area of underachievement such as reading, spelling, or arithmetic; or, in contrast, researchers investigate the characteristics of LD children in general. Neither approach provides the kind of information needed for an overall understanding of learning disabilities. While rigorous, theoretically based research is necessary to understand learning disorders, more studies are needed to investigate relationships across many areas of learning in several different special populations. Such studies will not be possible unless investigators have the time, funding, and opportunity to measure more areas of learning.

Some indications of relationships between areas of learning come from neuropsychologists and others who explore patterns of performance between reading, spelling, and arithmetic (Rourke, 1978; Rourke and Finlayson, 1978). Many investigators have demonstrated relationships among various aspects of oral language and reading through subtype investigations (Denckla, 1985; Doehring et al., 1981; Lyon and Watson, 1981; Mattis, French, and Rapin, 1975; McKinney, Short, and Feagans, 1985; Mestre and Gerance, 1986; Satz, Morris, and Fletcher, 1985). Most investigators, however, have not looked broadly across all areas of achievement.

In essence, a field reflects the types of questions that investigators raise and the theories that guide their research (Senf, 1986). For example, neuropsychologists who use models from Luria (1966) tend to look for patterns of learning and behavior to explore possible relationships between brain and behavior. Therefore, in the area of reading, they are apt to select tasks that might be related to posterior and anterior functions. Knowing the function of the frontal lobe, they look for possible disorders of planning, organization, and attention. Some look for problems that might be associated with right or left hemisphere functions (for instance, temporal/analytic versus visual-spatial/holistic). While few draw conclusions about site of lesion in developmental learning disabilities, the emerging preliminary data are of interest for studying patterns of problems, particularly when the results are combined with the new technology for studying brain-behavior relationships.

Experimental cognitive psychologists have developed other theoretical models and paradigms for the study of reading (Bauer, 1977, 1979; Bradley and Bryant, 1985; Rumelhart, 1977; Perfetti and Lesgold, 1977; Stanovich, 1983a, 1983b). Their emphases on cognitive capacity, flexibility, and information processing are frequently used to study good and poor readers. Studies of strategy, capacity, and processing have guided theory and intervention (Torgesen, 1977; Shepherd et al., 1982). Studies of metacognition and cognitive behavior modification (Hallahan et al., 1983) as well as of learner activity have also led to new approaches for intervention (Wong, 1980; Ryan, Weed, and Short, 1986; Koorland, 1986).

Developmental psychologists and psycholinguists have advanced the field through their studies of cognitive development, language, early reading and writing, emergent literacy, problem solving, and social development (Bereiter, 1980; Clarke-Steward,1973; deGoes and Martlew, 1983; Ferreiro and Teberosky, 1979; Read, 1983; Snow and Ferguson, 1977; Temple, Nathan, and Burris, 1982; Vygotsky, 1983). While research approaches vary, the newer investigations of children in naturalistic contexts provide an added dimension for studying learning disabled children. Specialists in LD need to understand the types of behaviors that can be expected at various age levels and to recognize the wide range of individual differences in the normal population.

Research using Piagetian theory may highlight problems of the learning disabled in areas not typically assessed on standardized intelligence measures. Class inclusion, classification, conservation, and formal operations tasks often show the thinking and reasoning problems that Strauss and Lehtinen (1947) saw many years ago (Stone, 1987).

Psycholinguists have examined relationships between parents and children, teachers, and peers (Bryan et al., 1983; Scheffel, 1984). Such research requires very different methodology, coding, and units of analysis. With the use of video tapes, remote control microphones, and other technology, experiments can be undertaken outside the laboratory.

Behavioral psychologists, whose methodology focuses on task analysis, reinforcers, time on task, and carefully controlled instruction, are also helpful in explaining possible reasons for underachievement (Berliner, 1980). The methods of ethnographic research used by anthropologists, sociologists, and others are helpful for conducting observations of individuals in groups.

Theories from the field of motivation are being used to explain possible reasons for school failure (Licht, 1983; Adelman and Taylor, 1983). Studies of motivation over time and in various contexts may provide even more information about the relationships between setting and learner (Deci and Chandler, 1986).

Research on the biological foundations of dyslexia and other learning disabilities is increasing steadily. Studies by geneticists, neurophysiologists, biochemists, anatomists, and electroencephalographers are important for a more complete understanding of learning (Silver, 1985; Preston, Guthrie, and Childs, 1974; Denckla, LeMay, and Chapman, 1985; Geschwind, 1985, 1986; Finucci, Guthrie, Childs, Abbey, and Childs, 1976; Matheny and Dolan, 1974; Thatcher and Lester, 1985; Lewis and Fox, 1985; Bakker and Licht, 1986).

More recently, cross-cultural studies have been conducted. Such studies highlight the nature of learning problems in various languages, cultures, and school systems. They have already illustrated certain universal problems (for instance, linguistic awareness: Leong, 1986) in relation to reading. These investigations require that we look closely at the nature of the language as well as the culture (Matajcek and Sturma, 1986; Sturma, 1985). As educators struggle with problems related to illiteracy, school dropouts, and substance abuse as well as the needs of the handicapped, it will be necessary to move outside the laboratory to examine many environmental factors and values within the home, the school, and community (Cornwall, 1985; Drach and Kleber, 1985; Dyssegard, 1985; Haslum et al., 1985; Tarnapol and Tarnapol, 1980; Tyre and Young, 1985; Wiig, Becker-Redding, and Semel, 1985; Stevenson, 1984; Stevenson, Lee, Steigler, and Luker, 1984).

Each of these fields has its own sets of assumptions, questions, values, and views of human behavior (Chall, 1983). Each can provide data to highlight unique problems or needs of exceptional learners. While we will always need studies of specific skills such as memory, reading, or written language, we also need larger data banks on several groups of children to investigate relationships between biological, cognitive, social, and cultural variables. In some respects, researchers of the past decade have provided many analytic approaches to learning problems. The time has come for more synthesis and integration of research and findings.

ETIOLOGY

Despite the growing concern for learning problems in this country, Brackbill, McManus, and Woodward (1985) reported that *Pay INFO Retrospective* (1982) listed "etiology" as a key descriptor term for only 0.03 percent of original research studies in learning disorders. They further noted that etiology was not included in the classification of studies by major content area in a review by Torgesen and Dice (1980). They suggest a reason for this lack of etiologically based research: it is the lengthy period of time between events in prenatal, perinatal, or early postnatal life and the identification of a learning disability. They also observe, along with others, that it is difficult to establish cause-effect relationships through retrospective studies and even more difficult to conduct prospective studies from the prenatal years through school age. Considering the dramatic changes that occur during early childhood, causal factors are not easily identified. Furthermore, the etiologies of specific reading, writing, or mathematics difficulties are probably neither homogeneous nor unique. The same etiology could contribute to any number of developmental disorders. In addition, many early potential aberrations are subtle and difficult to measure (Brackbill et al., 1985).

Some people feel that little can be done about cause; therefore, emphasis should be given to treatment. However, one needs only to look at treatment of such conditions as rubella, phenylketonuria, Rh negative, retrolentalfibroplasia, and other serious problems of the past to emphasize the need for research on etiology. According to Gallagher (1984), even though research on etiology may never lead to specific treatment plans, it may lead to prevention.

BIRTH WEIGHT

Low birth weight, particularly in preterm babies, has been found to be a high risk factor for a variety of developmental disorders. S. Cohen (1983) has emphasized that the resulting problems may include those related to overall intelligence, motor development, and behavioral disorders as well as to specific learning disabilities. According to Cohen, the mean IQ score for low birth weight babies is lower than average. In most studies, however, it is still within the normal range. Cohen argues against overreliance on a single composite score of intelligence to indicate dysfunction. Specific scores rather than global ones are more useful at all ages. Thus, in studies of high-risk children, scales such as the Bayley Scales have been used since they are divided into components such as vocal/social, eye-hand coordination, object relations, imitation, and manipulation to study patterns of behavior.

Data from the National Collaborative Perinatal Project indicate that there were 2,499 children with learning difficulties in a total group of about 30,000. Among the 2,285 with low birth weights, only 251 were identified as learning disabled. Although learning disabilities were more strongly related to socioeconomic and demographic variables than to birth weight variables per se, the risk was higher (1.3 times) for the low birth weight child.

Reading performance of low birth weight children tends to be slightly below average, but the differences are minimal and not found in all studies (Cohen, 1983). Cohen cites Kitchen et al., (1980), who found no differences in reading ability between low birth weight and normal birth weight children. Drillian et al. (1980), also cited in Cohen, reported lower reading scores only for low birth weight babies whose neurological status was abnormal at one year.

Low birth weight babies do, however, score lower on motor development during both infancy and preschool years (Cohen, 1983). Some studies indicate that motor development scores are lower than mental ability scores. According to Cohen, Knoblock maintains that early motor disorders are an indication of central nervous system problems and that such children are at risk for learning or behavioral disabilities.

Several studies indicate that visual-motor integration is a problem for low birth weight babies. Such problems may interfere with the assessment of intelligence and result in possible misclassification if specific domains of behavior are not analyzed carefully. Cohen quotes Taub, Goldstein, and Caputo (1977), who speculate that the deficit in visual-motor integration may be related to subtle brain dysfunction or to a limitation of brain cell growth to which the visual system may be particularly susceptible. Cohen (1983) feels that impairments in the visual area require further study.

Because the range of performance among low birth weight babies is very wide, Cohen recommends more research on sensory processing in infancy. She cites investigators who speculate that the relative immaturity of the visual system at birth makes it vulnerable to problems from exposure to visual stimulation before term (Friedman, Jacobs, and Werthmann). Korner (1981), also cited in Cohen (1983), says that the problems may be due not to insults but to the preterm birth, which may have disrupted or slowed the maturation.

Longitudinal studies of low birth weight infants who have suffered intraventricular hemorrhage are also needed. This reviewer also recommends more careful followup study of people who are known to have had strokes or other illnesses in early childhood. Several such persons came to our adult clinic for assistance in reading comprehension, written language, and higher levels of learning, long after they had been dismissed as "cured" by physicians, speech pathologists, or special educators.

BIRTH COMPLICATIONS, MEDICATION, AND MATERNAL FACTORS

In a review paper on obstetrical trauma, Creevy (1983) summarized several studies, most of which fail to isolate a single event. Rather, multiple factors related to both pregnancy and birth complications may be involved. Studies do not indicate, for example, that learning disabilities are caused by hypoxia and trauma. The ideal study, however, with absolute standardization of all medical records and adequate control of variables, has not been conducted. For now, Creevy recommends that obstetrical interventions be minimized until they have been demonstrated to be beneficial and safe enough for their benefits to outweigh risks. He feels that obstetricians may have an impact on the future incidence of learning disabilities by acting to decrease the incidence of prematurity, to minimize the use of drugs during pregnancy, labor, and delivery, to avoid or treat those conditions that may lead to hypoxia in utero, to avoid traumatic delivery, and to foster positive maternal attitudes toward pregnancy, birth, and the infant.

With regard to prenatal drugs, Gray and Yaffe (1983) reported on epidemiological studies indicating a slight increase in the risk for learning disabilities in children whose mothers took barbiturates. These authors, however, emphasize that the findings do not imply causation, and they are concerned about medication in maternity. They found that hospital mothers (those who chose to deliver in a hospital) did not differ in the number of health-related problems during pregnancy, but they resorted to drugs as the therapy of choice more often than mothers in free standing birth centers or home mothers (those who chose to have deliveries at home). The authors were concerned about the relatively large number of drugs administered during labor or delivery that had not been approved for that purpose by the Food and Drug Administration. Concerning drugs for which there were published reports, they found more than one-half of those consumed or administered contained one or more ingredients that could have an adverse effect on the fetus. They reported that more than two-thirds of nonprescription products used by pregnant mothers carried no labels of warning to pregnant women.

Overall, the Brackbill et al. study (1985) indicated that mothers knew little about the drugs they consumed during pregnancy and less about those administered during childbirth. They found that home mothers were better informed than were hospital mothers, and concluded that there was more "informational gatekeeping" in the latter group. This reviewer feels that these findings may vary somewhat with socioeconomic and educational levels of the mother.

In a review of maternal infections (rubella, cytomegalovirus, herpes simplex, varicella, syphilis, tuberculosis, and toxoplasmosis), Sever (1983) concluded that some infections affect the central nervous system of the fetus and produce brain damage. However, these children are often multiply handicapped. Thus, most studies have not distinguished children with learning disabilities from those with other developmental disorders. More research is needed to investigate specific types of neurological dysfunction that may result from perinatal infections.

Similar conclusions regarding smoking and alcohol consumption were drawn by Streissguth (1983). Chronic alcoholism typically produces fetal alcohol syndrome (and subsequent mental retardation), and moderate alcohol usage may be damaging; however, learning disabilities and alcohol consumption need further systematic study.

Streissguth cited a study by Shaywitz, Cohen, and Shaywitz, who found that of 87 children referred to the Yale Learning Disorders Clinic, 15 were born to mothers who were alcoholic during pregnancy. While intelligence fell in the low average range, all had been referred for school failure and all but one were hyperactive. According to Streissguth, more long-term studies are needed to see if there are different etiologies of learning disabilities, mental retardation, and other conditions.

In Streissguth's review of studies on smoking, at least three investigations show a relationship between cigarette smoking during pregnancy and children's subsequent performance on several cognitive and behavioral measures, including learning difficulties, hyperactivity, neurological soft signs, and hyperkinesis. She says, however, that none of the studies adjusted for alcohol usage and that most did not consider social class, maternal education, birth order, and other factors that could have produced the same outcomes.

ENVIRONMENTAL FACTORS

Many citizens here and abroad are concerned about environmental pollutants and the possible consequences for health, learning, and behavior (Thatcher and Lester, 1985). According to Needleman (1983), many industrial chemicals find their way into the environment, at high doses, and several are neurotoxic. He stresses the need to know which agents can pass through the maternal placenta. The effects of some toxins may express themselves in immediate, dramatic ways, but lesser amounts need to be studied over time. Lead toxicity has been recognized for centuries. In Needleman's studies of 4,000 infants, maternal lead exposure was related to increased risk for minor congenital anomalies. More controlled research is needed to study the impact of other substances on fertility, fetal death, congenital anomalies, intrauterine growth, and central nervous system function. The Scientific Studies Committee of the ACLD has sponsored numerous conferences on this topic at national conventions.

GENETIC FACTORS

From the time that dyslexia and other developmental disorders were first detected, questions regarding genetic factors have been raised (Hinshelwood, 1907; Guttman, 1937; Drew, 1945). DeFries and Decker (1982) quote Thomas, who in 1905 said that congenital word-blindness was often found in families where more than one member were affected. Since then, there have been many reports of familial patterns, including the frequently cited monograph of Hallgren (1950; see also Childs and Finucci, 1983; Decker and DeFries, 1980 and 1981; DeFries, 1985; Owen, Adams, Forrest, Stolz, and Fisher, 1971; Ansara et al., 1981; Decker and Vandenberg, 1985; DeFries and Baker, 1983; Drew, 1945; Finucci and Childs, 1983; Finucci, Guthrie, Childs, Abbey, and Childs, 1976).

Sophisticated genetic models have allowed for more rigorous research. Following a detailed description of genetic models, subject selection, and test performance in their longitudinal study, DeFries and Decker (1982) concluded that there is evidence for a familial factor in reading disability but that the evidence is not yet sufficient for demonstrating a specific genetic influence. There is some positive indication for the polygenic threshold model and for autosomal, recessive inheritance in females. The authors report, however, that no single-gene model was found to account for the transmission of reading disability in all proband families. They feel that the most definitive evidence for major gene influence may come from linkage studies, where associations between a chromosome marker and reading problems are observed over several generations. They quote Smith, who provided tentative evidence for such a relationship between a marker on chromosome 15 and a dominantly inherited form of reading disability.

Perhaps no single-gene model will answer all of the questions because of the heterogeneity of the population. Thus far, DeFries and Decker have found no evidence for profile similarity between probands and parents, but they strongly recommend that other typologies of reading disabilities be put to similar validity tests in the future.

Because reading disability is highly heritable, DeFries and Decker (1982) feel that the establishment of the mode or modes of inheritance has both theoretical and practical significance. The results of their program have already demonstrated the significance of family data for risk analysis, for predicting long-term consequences of reading disability, and for subtype validity. Finucci (1978) also emphasized the importance of studying the genetics of reading disability. This reviewer, however, feels that such studies should not be limited to reading. Disorders of spoken language, writing, and mathematics also should be considered, and family histories of learning problems should be known to educators, psychologists, and others doing research within a school system. In addition, comprehensive studies of children and adults with various types of known genetic disorders may be useful in studying learning problems that co-occur.

CHILDHOOD ILLNESSES

Several important studies of the impact of otitis media have been conducted (Silva et al., 1985; Reichman and Healy, 1983; Silva, Chalmers, and Stewart, 1986). Data suggest that persistent otitis media with effusion is of sufficient significance to warrant continued longitudinal studies. Overall, Silva et al. found that early impairments related to language, intelligence, and reading became less marked with age, but that the trend needed more investigation. The problem also needs to be considered in relation to overall health, socioeconomic status, and family circumstances.

A summary of many studies edited by Kavanagh (1986) indicated that recurrent otitis media with effusion represents a hazard to the development of children. In some instances, fluctuating hearing loss interferes with hearing for many years. Lags in early development also have ramifications for later language development. These delays may subsequently interfere with higher cognitive functions.

Other illnesses of consequence in LD include encephalitis, certain forms of meningitis, Reye's syndrome, and similar conditions. These, together with known accidents and trauma, are sometimes thought not to have long-term consequences for learning if the child is very young. This has not always been the case, at least in our clinic population. Residuals may be manifested in higher level functions, attention, and memory.

Head trauma patients are typically studied by neurologists and neuropsychologists, and such persons may be placed in LD programs. Diagnosticians and teachers should be aware of the attention, memory, and organizational problems of this group. Certain trauma cases provide hypotheses for studying similar co-occurring problems among children with developmental disorders.

INTERACTION OF BIOLOGICAL, SOCIAL, CULTURAL, AND EDUCATIONAL FACTORS

While continued research will be needed on specific facets of etiology, development, and school achievement, many investigators encourage the use of complex interactional models that incorporate both biological and social factors (Sameroff, 1979; Breitmayer and Ramey, 1986). Breitmayer and Ramey cite the work of Zigler and Cascioney, who found that children labeled as "culturally familially retarded" had a number of minor neurological dysfunctions or abnormal medical histories. According to Shonkoff (1982), however, since few children show gross neurological abnormalities and since mild retardation occurs almost exclusively in economically disadvantaged families, the etiology of mild retardation is frequently attributed to environmental influences. Recent studies have attempted to specify the features of disadvantaged environments that may be related to retarded development.

According to Breitmayer and Ramey, relatively low levels of social stimulation and verbally unresponsive maternal behaviors have been implicated. Features of the physical environment are also high-risk factors. These include intense auditory stimulation and lack of orderliness in the home. (This reviewer feels that such factors should be observed in households of middle and upper-middle socioeconomic status families as well as in households of the culturally disadvantaged.)

Breitmayer and Ramey have also found that specific child characteristics may exacerbate the effects of certain environmental factors and may be related to sex differences. For example, according to Bradley and Caldwell (1980) and Wachs (1979) (cited in Breitmayer and Ramey), the cognitive development of male infants is more sensitive than that of females to the detrimental effects of noise, confusion, and disorganization in the home. Inactive, placid infants also show more sensitivity than active infants to environmental deprivation.

Many studies during the 1970's such as those by Birch and Gussow (1970) and Sameroff and Chandler (1975) indicated that perinatal complications of all kinds occurred most frequently among the socioeconomically disadvantaged. Complications related to prematurity and intrauterine growth were associated with intellectual impairment and school problems, particularly if the child was reared in disadvantaged circumstances.

Hanshaw et al. (1976) found that silent cytomegalovirus (CMV) infection often resulted in intellectual impairment in lower-class children but not in middle-class children. However, this reviewer feels that long-term studies of both groups are needed, since deficiencies in some of the processes required for higher level skills (for instance, problem solving and comprehension) may not be observed during early childhood.

Breitmayer and Ramey reviewed several studies of possible significance for LD, including those of Lewis, Bartels, Campbell, and Goldberg (1967), who found that throughout the first year of life, infants with 1-minute Apgar scores of 7, 8, or 9 showed less efficient distribution of attention to visually presented stimuli than infants with scores of 10. Similarly, Caron, Caron, and Glass (1983) found that within a sample of full-term nonsuspect infants, those classified as "optimal" on the basis of perinatal circumstances were superior to those classified as "nonoptimal" in their ability to abstract relational information from visually presented stimuli at 12, 18, and 24 weeks. Given the problems of abstraction noted at later ages in the learning disabled (Friedman, 1984), longitudinal studies of these youngsters are needed. According to Breitmayer and Ramey, these behaviors may adversely affect the child's interaction with the environment, and under certain circumstances, may result in cognitive deficits that could become cumulative over time. In general, Sameroff and Chandler (1975) have suggested that middle-class environments may provide experiences that are sufficiently supportive to overcome the effects of adverse circumstances, including perinatal stress.

While these "transactional" models are more dynamic than others, they are also more difficult to control, since it is assumed that the environment is constantly changing and that the child plays a role in shaping it. Therefore, one needs to study multiple variables, including the child's motivation and response characteristics.

With regard to intervention, studies of high-risk infants indicate that outcomes were better when day care centers incorporated specific compensatory educational experiences in contrast to generalized care (Breitmayer and Ramey, 1986) and when stimulation began as early as 6 weeks to 3 months of age. In general, studies are needed to investigate biological vulnerability (including genetic factors) and subsequent environmental insufficiency as cumulative risk factors.

PREDICTION

Most studies of prediction are conducted with the hope that early identification of a disorder can alleviate serious problems and emotional overlay. Mercer, Algozzine, and Trifiletti (1979) provided an overview of the theoretical models for prediction and discussed the differences between those using single instruments as predictors, multiple-instrument batteries, teacher ratings, and parental involvement. Generally, multiple instruments are more effective.

The analysis of single instrument approaches completed by Mercer et al. (1976) indicated that the Metropolitan Readiness Test was a better predictor than the Lee-Clark Readiness Test or the California Test of Mental Maturity. In their review of prediction using language tests, they found that the type of educational intervention greatly influenced achievement. Thus, the "hit rate" declines when children receive good intervention.

The Bender Gestalt test has often been used to predict reading ability and is included in several followup batteries. According to Keogh and Smith (1970), a good score on this test is typically followed by good achievement, but low scores are not necessarily predictive. Keogh found that tests used for prediction are better when they are closer to the skill being assessed. Thus, knowing letter names would be a better predictor for reading achievement than performance on the Bender Gestalt test.

One of the more comprehensive, multiple-instrument batteries was developed by deHirsch, Jansky, and Langford (1966) and Jansky and deHirsch (1972). They began with 37 variables and found that chronological age at school entrance was a significant predictor of reading achievement in second grade but that predictions for girls were more accurate than those for boys. (The age factor requires further investigation, since other studies found that it did not predict achievement.) While their conclusions are not totally free from criticism, the investigators did show the importance of language, particularly expressive language. This finding is noteworthy, since most school readiness tests are given in groups and require only listening and paper and pencil tasks. The best predictors in the Jansky-deHirsch index included letter naming, picture naming, sentence repetition, word matching, and the Bender Gestalt test. Jansky and deHirsch also looked at instructional variables and reported better achievement among children in classes taught by teachers who were rated "high" by their principals compared with achievement among those in classes whose teachers were rated "average" or lower.

The Jansky-deHirsch battery has been criticized because of the lack of cross validation. That is, results were obtained by applying the index to the group on which it was developed. Feshback, Adelman, and Fuller (1974) used the deHirsch index to predict reading achievement at second grade and reported their overall hit rate was 73 percent, with a relatively high number of false positives. Since other studies reported similar results, Mercer et al. (1979) felt that the indices lacked strong empirical support.

Another major battery was developed by Satz, Friel, and Fletcher as a part of a longitudinal study of 473 boys. According to Mercer et al. (1979), the overall hit rate was adequate, but false negatives tended to be overrepresented (those in need of treatment but not identified). This result may be due to the limited amount of oral language sampling in the Satz battery. False positives were also overrepresented (children identified but not in need of treatment). As with other batteries, the tasks seemed appropriate for identifying low-risk children, but problems arose in the selection of specific children for intervention.

In a study of 1,052 children in a midwestern state, Busch (1980) found that the best predictors included the ability to recognize upper and lower case letters and beginning sounds. The latter item is similar to the research of Bradley and Bryant (1985) on auditory categorization. The second best predictor in the Busch study was measured intelligence, also an important consideration with regard to classification and labeling of LD children. The third factor was the Behavior Rating Scale of Hardin and Busch (a checklist for use by the classroom teacher).

Chronological age is not necessarily a good predictor of reading achievement. Developmental age, as measured by the Gesell School Readiness Screening Test, however, has been found to predict, in kindergarten children, success and failure in school and in later years. While fine distinctions cannot be made with the Gesell test, developmentally immature children often have difficulties. Therefore, good developmental prekindergarten programs to enhance readiness are recommended.

Although most studies show the importance of language and linguistic awareness in contrast to visual processing as a predictor of reading ability (Liberman et al., 1985; Shankweiler and Liberman, 1972), a study of printing errors in kindergarten has predicted academic performance (Simner, 1982). Children were asked to print letters and numbers from memory (after immediate presentation). Results showed that form errors (an overall change in the actual shape of the letter) correlated reliably with academic performance at the end of kindergarten and first grade. While there are limitations in this study, such findings should not be ignored, particularly with regard to visual access, memory, and early writing skills. In addition, Simner indicated that attention problems may have contributed to poor performance.

Badian (1982) used the Wechsler Preschool and Primary Scale of Intelligence (WPPSI) to identify young children at risk for reading disability. While scatter on this test has not been particularly predictive, she hypothesized that certain cluster factors related to conceptual, spatial, and sequential processes might be significant. She began with a group of 72 children who appeared to be at risk for LD at age 5, and at followup 3 years later, she found 32 poor and 40 good readers. Both groups had average intelligence at age 5 and had received similar help. The poor readers were superior in WPPSI conceptual- and acquired-knowledge factors and verbal IQ. Their general patterns were conceptual spatial sequential. The pattern for good readers was spatial sequential conceptual. These findings are of interest, since many poor readers have short-term sequential memory problems (Torgesen and Goldman, 1977).

Mercer et al. (1979) cited several studies in which teachers themselves were better able than the Metropolitan Readiness Test to predict reading problems. Some, but not all, investigators suggested that years of experience in teaching improves accuracy of prediction. Ratings by teachers are most effective for identifying children in need—or not in need—of special programming. Keogh and Smith (1970) found that only false positive mistakes were made. Thus, some children might be placed in special programs unnecessarily. Given these findings, Mercer et al. feel that teacher perceptions, together with good checklists, offer more advantages than either single or multiple tests. Parental involvement also can add to the prediction. Colligan (1981) found that parental descriptions of a child's general development as well as the children's knowledge of letters and numbers were particularly helpful. The children's knowledge could be related to parental expectancies.

Since young children have had limited schooling and test-taking experience, Mercer et al. suggest that December might be the best time to administer a prediction battery. This timing also allows for intervention during the remainder of the year.

In general, multiple test batteries together with teacher and parent ratings seem the most beneficial. Teacher perceptions play a major role because teachers know the content and forms of instruction used in the school.

In planning research on prediction, one cannot ignore the overall curriculum and expectancies within a school. For this reason, each community or school should develop its own plan. Such plans should include more than reading readiness if predictions about overall school performance are to be made.

There is now a significant body of research to suggest that new and different measures need to be added to the typical school readiness tasks including linguistic awareness, segmenting, and rhyming. Traditional readiness tests usually have subtests of vocabulary, listening comprehension, visual discrimination, auditory discrimination, copying, and in certain instances, mathematics. None, however, because they are given in groups, adequately assesses numerous auditory and expressive language processes. Hence, one of my recommendations is to work closely with professionals from the fields of test construction, psycholinguistics, experimental psychology, audiology, and others in order to develop more highly refined procedures to identify possible processing deficits.

In addition, it is important to realize that the rudimentary instruction for reading, writing, and mathematics begins long before children enter school. In fact, it begins with the first picture book, with the naming of letters on toy blocks, with counting fingers and toes, or with seriating pots and pans. A host of cognitive and oral language skills forms the basis for later reading, writing, and arithmetic. Children develop rudimentary story grammar from listening to stories; they learn to differentiate pictures from print and letters from numerals, and they learn that in English we read from left to right and from top to bottom. All of these factors highlight the importance of early detection and early intervention (Kirk, 1986; Lerner et al., 1987).

RESEARCH ON READING DISABILITIES AND DYSLEXIA

BACKGROUND

The number of research studies and books on reading disabilities/dyslexia has increased dramatically during the last decade. Many new volumes have provided multidisciplinary perspectives on this complex problem (Ceci, 1986; Gibson and Levin, 1975; Gray and Kavanagh, 1985; Malatesha and Aaron, 1982; Pavlidis and Fisher, 1986; Pearson, 1984; Pirozzolo, 1979; Duane and Leong, 1985; Stanovich, 1986; Torgesen and Wong, 1986; Vellutino, 1983). These perspectives highlight the importance of incorporating theories, models, and research paradigms from various fields in the study of readers and reading performance.

As one might expect with such a complex process as reading, investigators tend to focus on one or more components such as word recognition, vocabulary, decoding with and without context, text comprehension, and/or specific subskills. Others focus on the type, quality, and organization of the text, motivation, interests of the reader, class size, age at school entrance, and methods of instruction. For an overview of significant research, the *Handbook of Reading Research* (Pearson, 1984 edition) is recommended. This volume provides various perspectives and excellent research summaries from the field of reading. There is no entry in the index, however, either for dyslexia or for learning disabilities, though there are many studies comparing good and poor readers. An excellent chapter on individual differences by Spiro and Myers (1984) gives a fine, historical overview of research, going back to the turn of the century, when investigators attempted to assess mental abilities, interests, and attitudes. With the advent of more complex theoretical models, powerful statistical procedures, and computers, more investigations using correlational patterns were conducted.

Several researchers, using factor analytic techniques, looked for correlates of overall reading skill. Others compared good readers and poor readers on a single hypothesized component, such as syntactic competence or the use of context to facilitate word recognition. Still others based their work on an examination of patterns of reading errors or miscues (Goodman and Goodman, 1977). According to Spiro and Myers, current approaches, which incorporate elements of previous research, have the advantage of more finely specified and experimentally validated cognitive, information-processing models. The entire January 1987 issue of the *Journal of Learning Disabilities* was devoted to research on information processing.

Spiro and Myers remind us that studies of individual differences can be mere artifacts of subject classification procedures and statistical regression to the mean. This factor is particularly relevant for research if school-identified LD subjects are used without controlling for intelligence. Concerns about causal inferences, reliability, generalizability, and ecological validity have also been expressed. With regard to the latter, Spiro and Myers note that experimental tasks are frequently stripped down and isolated for scientific study. They feel that "all the precisely controlled studies of memory for nonsense syllables that can be imagined will not lead people to process more natural verbal materials in a like fashion" (p. 475). They say that the goal of precision with cognitive correlates must not be achieved at the expense of "rendering the results of that research inapplicable to real, naturally occurring reading situations in which the conceptually separable aspects of cognitive processing must function together as part of an integrated system" (p. 476).

This reviewer wishes to underscore these points, and would add another factor regarding "stripped down" experimental tasks. We know, from long experience in the field, that many LD children respond to structure and reduction of task demands and therefore may perform better on highly structured experimental tasks. While such tasks yield valuable information about performance in a particular context, they may not provide the data necessary for a comprehensive view of reading. Shankweiler and Liberman (1972), Vellutino (1977), and others, for example, found that poor readers have few problems with reversals and sequencing. Our own work with adult poor readers produced similar results (Johnson, 1986). When given highly structured lists to read, the adults had very few reversals. However, when the task demands increased and more difficult texts to read or longer lists to decode were given, more transpositions and reversals were evident. This does not mean that direct work on visual processing is necessary, but it does say something about the range of tasks that need to be included in an evaluation.

Analogous problems are evident in oral language disorders. It is not uncommon to find different articulation errors on tests of single words, sentence repetition, and conversation. The latter, like reading tasks, requires the integration of multiple features and attention to several rules. Therefore, in order to more specifically define an individual's reading performance, it is helpful to use an assessment battery that includes both oral and silent reading of words, sentences, and context with varying degrees of difficulty and familiarity. In the future, more studies should be designed with larger numbers of experimental tasks to investigate error patterns.

RECENT APPROACHES AND THEORIES

As the field of reading developed, several theoretical models emerged, some of which have been classified as predominantly "bottom-up" or "outside-in." Proponents of these models emphasize that readers go through a series of processing stages from small units of the text to larger ones. Thus, features of letters are detected, and strings of letters are identified as words. In turn, these are incorporated into sentences and text meanings (Gough, 1972). The opposing, or "top-down," model emphasizes the importance of background knowledge and activity of the reader while working with text. That is, meaning is actively constructed; it is not in the text.

More recently, there has been an emphasis on reading as an interactive process. According to Spiro and Myers (1984), a key feature of the interactive models is that all of the interacting processes share a total system of limited capacity. Thus, bottom-up and top-down processes not only influence and facilitate each other; they may also interfere with each others. For example, if too many resources are used by bottom-up processes, the ability to execute top-down processes may be reduced. Such problems could occur either because of decoding problems or because of the child's misconception of the reading process. The latter can be observed among readers who focus so heavily on phonics that they try to "sound out" sight words such as *the, does*, and *said*.

Spiro and Myers (1984) feel that the dominant view of reading today is an interactive one (Stanovich, 1980; Rumelhart, 1977). That is, "processing goes on from bottom-up and from top-down, either simultaneously or alternatingly" (p. 483). They say that these two kinds of processes operate under a limitation; the processes require cognitive effort such as memory span or directed consciousness and must operate within a system that as a whole may be limited in the amount of cognitive effort that can be supported at any one time. That is, both bottom-up and top-down processes must share a limited processing capacity.

This issue needs to be considered in future studies of dyslexics of different mental and verbal ability. Those with superior mental ability and memory often have a remarkable capacity to hold information from the preceding text or portion of a sentence while decoding an unfamiliar word. Other readers, however, had such short-term memory spans that they could not remember more than two or three words from the preceding text.

There is now substantial evidence to suggest that whenever a component process requires much effort or is not automatic (LaBerge and Samuels, 1974), less capacity remains for other processes. This concept led to the "bottleneck" hypothesis of Perfetti and Lesgold (1978), who found that, in general, poor readers failed to comprehend and process text because of an inability to decode; that is, the decoding created a bottleneck that interfered with text comprehension (Perfetti and Hogaboam, 1975). More recently, Perfetti has developed a verbal efficiency theory.

In special education, the idea of automaticity is not new. Many years ago, Berko (1966) said "brain damaged" children failed to "automatize" behavior as readily as normals. Therefore, they had to propositionalize ("think about") various activities in order to perform. For example, during the writing process, if children have to consciously think about how to form a letter, revisualize it, retrieve words, and organize words into a sentence, there is little cognitive space for ideation. In addition, processes that are normally adequate may deteriorate (Johnson and Mykelbust, 1967).

According to Spiro and Myers (1984), things are rarely as simple as they seem on the surface. For example, processes can be mutually facilitative. Hence, one needs to know more about complementary facilitations, unidirectional bottlenecks, and other processing interdependences.

Theories regarding cognitive capacity, processing capacity, and utilization of compensatory strategies are crucial as one considers the intellectual, linguistic, and achievement levels of learning disabled children. In the future, it may be beneficial to carefully examine children in the low average, average, and high average mental ability range with and without oral language disorders to explore their spontaneous selection of strategies and compensatory techniques in reading. Larger groups of children should be studied longitudinally to examine their use of "top-down," "bottom-up," and interactive processing. Single studies are comparable to "snap shots" when we need multiple episodes of reading over time in various contexts.

RESEARCH RELATED TO DECODING AND WORD RECOGNITION

Many studies of poor readers indicate that their primary problems are related to faulty decoding, phonological/linguistic awareness, short-term auditory memory, and/or lexical access (Catts, 1986; Das, Bisanz, and Mancini, 1984; Downing, 1979; Johnson and Hook, 1978; Leong, 1986; Mann, 1986; Torgesen and Goldman, 1977; Mann and Liberman, 1984). Whether investigators have been in the field of psychology, reading, or neuropsychology, they have concluded that more problems are related to verbal or linguistic deficits than to visual processing disorders. Explanations, however, vary somewhat with the theories and background of the investigators. Shankweiler and Liberman (1972) developed an excellent line of research on reading, devised tasks to assess linguistic awareness, and now have a large body of evidence indicating that poor readers are less able than good readers to use phonologic strategies. Liberman et al. (1985) said that this linguistic deficiency is related to lexical access and representation in short-term memory. She emphasized that reading problems result not from auditory or visual processes but from linguistic deficits. Further evidence for this hypothesis comes from many international studies quoted by Liberman et al. (1985).

For the last decade, Vellutino (1977) has provided evidence to show that specific reading disabilities are not caused by disorders of visual perception, cross-modal transfer, or visual verbal deficits, but are due to linguistic coding. His conclusions were based on a series of studies showing that poor readers did not differ from normals on various nonverbal tasks, such as pattern matching. He theorized that facility in storing and retrieving words for reading requires an awareness of multiple attributes, including semantic, phonological, syntactic, graphic, and orthographic features. Following a series of tasks requiring memory, learning of words and pseudo-words, and segmentation, Vellutino found that poor readers were significantly impaired in phoneme analysis and that they performed significantly below the level of normal readers on free recall and picture-syllable tests. He concluded that they were generally less proficient in phonological coding.

More recently, Vellutino et al. (1985) explored reasons for reversals and found that errors accrue because of a lack of analytic attitude in word identification, not because of a deficiency in perception. According to Vellutino, it is conceivable that some poor readers have specific deficits that impair either whole word identification or phonetic decoding, and he hypothesized a relationship between phonological processing and code retrieval as well as lack of experience that leads to deficient lexical and semantic development. He added (and this reviewer agrees on the basis of experience with language impaired children and adults) that severely impaired readers may be impaired in all language domains. Several writers in the *Orton Society Bulletin* during the 1950's and 1960's made similar statements. So also did people who began by studying children with oral language disorders. For this and other reasons, more comprehensive test batteries with numerous oral language, linguistic awareness, and reading, writing, and mathematics tasks need to be developed with large numbers of both normal and LD children at various age, IQ, and grade levels. Only then will it be possible to investigate the interaction of multiple systems, forms of instruction, and instructional methods.

In an excellent summary on individual differences in reading, Stanovich (1986) reported that word decoding ability accounts for a large proportion of the variance in reading skills at all levels. The variance is primarily the result of differences in phonological abilities rather than visual processes. He (1980) hypothesized that poor readers try to compensate for their problems with word recognition by overrelying on top-down processes. Samuels (1987) found that poor readers often use the letter as the unit of recognition. This strategy places heavy demands on short-term memory. Consequently, comprehension is a slow and labored process. Samuels concluded that the size of the processing unit should be increased with practice. Practice influences automaticity, which in turn, increases the size of the visual unit.

Other studies indicate that learning disabled poor readers tend to look at the first letter of words and guess from context. When their miscues are analyzed, poor readers often substitute words that are graphically similar to the target word. As a result, both meaning and syntax may be disrupted.

A number of investigators have reported specific deficits in short-term memory among poor readers (Bauer, 1977, 1979; Tarver et al. 1976; Torgesen and Goldman, 1977). Others have focused more on the role of semantic memory (Swanson, 1986). While preliminary findings are promising, the interaction between short-term, long-term, semantic, and episodic memory requires further investigation with various types of reading tasks, such as mono- versus multisyllabic words, words of various semantic classes, sentences with varying syntactic complexity, familiar and unfamiliar texts, and oral and silent reading. The use of spontaneous and directed strategy also should be continued.

While there is a growing body of evidence about the nature of word recognition problems, more comprehensive batteries are needed on the same groups of subjects since the reader's use of context is linked to type of content, word frequency, and level of difficulty (Pearson, 1984).

Several studies indicate that disabled readers have difficulty learning to apply contextual aids in identifying unknown words. While some poor readers *may* not take advantage of the cues, other poor readers, perhaps because of underlying oral language or auditory memory problems, *can* not take advantage of the cues. In order to explain these differences, more pretest or posttest evaluations of language skills should be included in future research. Such evaluation is important, not only for reading but also for written language since poor readers often omit word endings and relational words. These omissions appear later in their writing and may interfere with precise meanings in the text (Johnson and Blalock, 1987).

RESEARCH ON READING COMPREHENSION

Studies of word recognition need to be supplemented with more studies of comprehension, since many poor readers have problems understanding spoken vocabulary, sentences, and discourse (Carlisle, 1983; Pflaum, Pascarella, Auer, Augustyn, and Bostwick, 1982). Evidence comes from both clinical investigations and research on subtypes of reading disorders (Lyon and Watson, 1981; Levi et al., 1984; Lyon, 1983; Mattis, French, and Rapin, 1975). To investigate the interactions between decoding and comprehension, one might have groups of (1) poor decoders with receptive and/or expressive language disorders, (2) poor decoders without oral language problems, and (3) mixed groups. A fourth group might include those who have good listening and decoding skills, yet cannot infer word meanings from context. John Carroll (1977) argued for the development of a "WOC" scale from which one might determine whether reading comprehension problems are related to written language, oral language, or conceptualization. Similarly, Johnson and Myklebust (1967) said it was necessary to investigate "inner language" disorders (that is, disorders of meaning) as well as many parameters of oral language in evaluating poor readers. Recently, Friedman (1984) found that a group of language impaired children performed below the levels of both deaf and normal children on a nonverbal classification task. Thus, it appears that some children, very early, fail to abstract criterion attributes.

Generally, studies of comprehension are more difficult to conduct than word recognition because experimental variables are less easily controlled. Consequently, Frank Smith (1979) says that there are more studies of "bottom-up" processes and lower level skills. Recently, however, several new approaches to the study of comprehension have been developed. Rather than using traditional reading tests, investigators have attempted to determine more about the subjects' understanding by asking them to talk about their comprehension of the text while reading. Others analyze oral reading miscues, retelling of stories, and recall of main ideas and supporting details (Golinkoff,

1975-76; Stein and Glenn, 1979; Williams and Taylor, 1982). Analyses of questions asked by both the teacher and learner are made in order to explain possible reasons for comprehension difficulties.

Many of these studies indicate that poor readers have problems in comprehension that cannot be totally explained by decoding difficulties. (Guthrie, 1973; Weaver and Dickinson, 1979; White, Pascarella, and Pflaum, 1981).

Excellent reviews of research and instruction on comprehension are included in the *Handbook of Reading Research*. In many studies, however, the subjects had limited pretesting for conceptual development and receptive and expressive language. In order to examine individual needs and possible subtypes of problems, more investigations of prerequisite skills are needed (Calfee, 1982), including studies of the interaction between decoding, oral language, and reading comprehension (Bryan et al., 1983; Pflaum, 1980; Pflaum and Bryan, 1980; Pflaum and Pascarella, 1980). In addition, it is essential to evaluate the readers' domain and specific knowledge, particularly in areas such as science and social studies. Some poor readers have acquired extensive information from observation and listening, which they use when responding to questions.

At the present time, there are no standardized tests to compare oral language and reading (that is, the same vocabulary, syntax, and content). In addition, there are few good receptive language tests, particularly at the upper grade levels, to determine whether a student might have problems listening to lectures in class. Tasks such as the Peabody Picture Vocabulary Test (Dunn and Dunn, 1981) are useful, but they do not assess multiple word meanings, subtleties of vocabulary, figurative language, and many aspects of morphology, all of which may be deficient among the learning disabled (Groshong, 1987).

Evidence for listening comprehension problems among poor readers comes from Fleisher et al. (1978, cited in Spiro and Myers, 1984) and others. Nahmias (1981) found that when poor readers were given texts they could decode, they still had difficulty comprehending the passages. Their listening skills were also below those of the control group. Thus, one cannot assume that problems are unique to reading. For this reason, we are cautious in recommending tape recorded text books or giving oral examinations to poor readers unless listening comprehension has been carefully evaluated. Certain LD adults whom we have tested could not comprehend material that was read to them. One 24-year-old who had been advised to take examinations for the "print handicapped" could decode every word on the form but did not even understand the meaning of "print handicapped." Similar problems have been noted in unique populations such as the "hyperlexics," who can decode but not comprehend (Huttenlocher and Huttenlocher, 1972; Healy and Aram, 1986).

This is not to say that listening and reading comprehension tasks are identical. Maria and McGinitie (1982) and Spiro and Myers (1984) emphasize that reading comprehension involves the acquisition of a set of new processing skills (beyond those needed for simple decoding), including the use of structural features within the text, new vocabulary, and representational features such as parenthesis. More procedures are needed to determine how well students learn *from* reading. Poor readers often have difficulty inferring word meaning from text.

Several studies cited by Stahl and Fairbanks (1986) indicate that poor readers need and profit from direct vocabulary instruction. Whether their vocabulary deficiencies result from oral language deficits or from lack of experience in reading needs further investigation. According to Stahl, poor readers made the greatest progress when new words were defined in combination with examples of word usage. When only a definition or an example was given, neither was sufficient.

Pany, Jenkins, and Schreck (1982) explored the use of three methods of vocabulary instruction and found that both good readers and poor readers learned and remembered new words when a practice method of instruction was employed. They learned fewer word meanings when teachers gave them synonyms, and the least when new words were presented in context. Wong, in Vaughn and Bos (1987), discussed the need for more carefully controlled intervention whereby the same words are taught using different procedures.

For several years, Blank (1985) has emphasized the need for more work at the sentence level. In fact, she states that the basic unit of meaning is the sentence, not the word; sentences depend upon the presence of "noncontent" words. Noncontent words appear less frequently than content words and are less accessible. In her experiments with good readers and poor readers, she found that the performance of the better students was less affected by frequency and class of word than was the performance of the less skilled (but normal) readers. Of equal interest were Blank's results in spelling. Among third graders, she found that 67 percent of the single-syllable words they misspelled were noncontent words, whereas only 33 percent were content words. A similar pattern was observed among fifth graders. Given these findings, together with research on decoding, she designed a program to teach content words with an emphasis on phonics, but other analytic procedures were used for noncontent nonphonetic words ("are," "whose," "could"). Children must realize the role that noncontent words play in structuring language into meaningful units. For automaticity, Blank says that one must go beyond word-by-word procedures. Words must be chunked into larger units by meshing content and noncontent words (for instance, "to the house"). These recommendations should be considered when basal readers are selected for poor readers since phonologically controlled reading texts contain rather unnatural sentences ("Dan can fan"; "can Dan fan?"). Sentences of this type interfere with the child's ability to predict words in context and to understand relational words in the text.

STRATEGY STUDIES IN READING AND READING COMPREHENSION

According to Schumaker et al. (1982), learning strategies are the techniques, principles, or rules needed to facilitate the acquisition, manipulation, integration, storage, and retrieval of information in various situations and settings. Emphasis is on teaching students how *to learn* rather than on specific content. Self-questioning techniques help students learn to make quick surveys, scan for questions, and rehearse. The Kansas Institute staff (Schumaker et al., 1982) developed "Multipass," which involves use of strategies, modeling, rehearsal and practice, testing, and feedback. Results led to the conclusion that LD adolescents could be taught a complex strategy and that they enjoyed it. Students in this Kansas study were reading at or above the fourth grade level, however, and the investigators did not know whether Multipass would be effective with those reading at a lower level. This reviewer also noted that the mean IQ score was 91, with some as low as 80, so generalized strategy training was probably needed. With an increase in text difficulty, students may need more specific work in decoding or in vocabulary.

In a study using questioning strategies, Wong (1979) found that questions increased the main ideas among the LD group but had little effect on the normals. She felt that the normals were already spontaneously asking questions and that the LD students were perhaps less active learners. Wong did not present IQ data for her group, but she said that the members of it had adequate intelligence on the WISC. Some of the variance within and between the groups could be attributed to differences in intelligence or decoding levels. One of the Columbia Institute studies showed that poor readers have difficulty not with main ideas but with linguistic cue words.

In another study of reading comprehension and memory, Wong (1980) found that a simple "questions/prompts" procedure facilitated processing of implied information in LD second and sixth graders. She concluded that their initial performance reflected a "production deficiency" and that they were inactive learners who did not assume responsibility for their own learning. Poor performance could also be related to the phenomenon of learned helplessness or to lack of motivation following years of failure and loss of initiative. Therefore, students rely increasingly on the teacher to generate strategies for them.

This reviewer also hypothesizes that many problems begin with language disorders in early childhood, which in turn, alter the parent-child interaction and the adult guidance offered. In a puzzle board problem-solving task with young normal children and LD children, Sammarco (1984) found that the mothers of normal children provided many prompts and cues to assist their children's performance. In contrast, perhaps because the language impaired children lacked the vocabulary and/or perceptual-motor development to perform the task, their mothers tended to place the puzzle pieces in the board for them. Thus, it is recommended that early intervention with both parents and teachers be provided to help them select the prompts or cues that foster more independent cognitive control.

Research on reading intervention indicates that students can and should be taught flexible strategies. In a study of LD students and normal students at three grade levels, Dowdy, Crump, and Welch (1982) found that proficient readers paid attention to the information most relevant to their purpose but that poor readers were less flexible and more bound to the print. The authors emphasized that LD students should be encouraged and taught to read for a variety of purposes. Ultimately, students should learn how to set their own purpose for reading and to ask relevant questions of the instructors. Gibson and Levin (1975) found that good readers adjust their reading styles with the purpose (that is, scanning, focusing). Apparently, some poor readers do not vary their approaches. In addition, current research indicates that there is a need to teach readers to ask their own questions.

SUBTYPES OF READING DISORDERS

In a new volume on *Biobehavioral Measures of Dyslexia*, Satz, Morris, and Fletcher (1985) provide an excellent overview of both theoretical and methodological issues related to the study of dyslexia. One of the major issues is the unitary deficit hypothesis versus the multivariate and/or multidisciplinary approach. Among the unitary approaches, the authors cited Hagen's strategy/deficiency hypothesis of short-term memory, Satz and Van Nostrand's maturational lag hypothesis, Cruickshank's perceptual-deficit hypothesis, Vellutino's verbal mediation hypothesis, and others.

Many clinicians and investigators have attempted to identify subgroups of poor readers. Satz et al., (1985) review the methodological problems and contend that further work on typology is needed. Initially, subgroups were defined on the basis of clinical evidence (Johnson and Myklebust, 1967; Boder, 1971; Mattis, French, and Rapin, 1975). Later studies using Q-factor techniques (Doehring, 1984; Doehring et al., 1981; Rourke, 1978) and cluster analyses (Lyon, 1983; Satz et al., 1985) were completed. Other procedures discussed by Maletesha and Aaron (1982), Kinsbourne (1982, 1986), Dykman, Ackerman, and Holcomb (1985), Petrauskas and Rourke (1979), Lovett (1984), and Doehring (1984) provide a good overview of needs and problems in identifying subgroups.

While controversies over the existence of certain subtypes continue, most investigators have found that the majority of dyslexics have some identifiable type of verbal deficit. The types of problems manifested, however, depend upon the number and kinds of measures used.

Some investigators, but not all, have found a visual subtype. Perhaps the questions should not be whether there is a pure visual subtype, but rather whether any poor readers have visual processing problems, and if so, of what type. Vellutino found no evidence for visual processing deficits, and Liberman (1983) found no evidence for visual memory disorders since poor readers could remember Chinese characters as well as good readers. Others, however, have identified reversals and visual accessing problems. Often these are manifested in writing, spelling, and in arithmetic.

Benton (1985) feels that the question of visual processing is not closed. While reading clearly requires the abstraction of feature and rules from oral language, it also requires abstraction of orthographic features. This necessitates visual processing.

With the development of new theoretical models, it will be helpful to explore the pros and cons of each for purposes of studying exceptional populations. Theories and data from normal development are essential, but they may not be specific enough to detect and highlight the unique patterns of deficits among people with learning disabilities. More studies comparing the symptoms and error patterns of acquired and developmental dyslexia may be helpful (Baddeley, Ellis, Niles, and Lewis, 1982; Coltheart, Masterson, Byng, Prior, and Riddock, 1983; Coltheart, Patterson, and Marshall, 1980). Theoretical constructs from neuropsychology and brain function will probably be useful in guiding future investigations, but they will need firm grounding in normal development. In particular, emphasis should be given to levels of linguistic rule acquisition and application. Kinsbourne (1982) says that the task of developing appropriate measures is forbidding unless one is informed by an understanding of mental development. He feels it is important to incorporate developmental principles along with those from neuropsychology.

NEUROPHYSIOLOGICAL CORRELATES OF READING

EYE MOVEMENT RESEARCH

During the 1950's, several studies explored the role of eye movements in poor readers, most of which indicated that faulty eye movements were not the cause of reading disorders but a reflection of other problems. Now that more sophisticated procedures have been developed, new studies using eye movement data as dependent variables have been completed. According to Rayner (1986), the amount of time a reader looks at parts of a text is important in specifying underlying cognitive processes associated with reading (Rayner, 1978; Just and Carpenter, 1980).

Rayner has emphasized the distinction between developmental dyslexia as opposed to acquired reading disorders. In cases of acquired dyslexia, the brain damage that results in language or reading disorders may also result in abnormalities of the oculomotor system. While the focus of this review is on developmental disorders, it is important to emphasize the need for obtaining histories when studying school-identified learning disabilities. In our clinical samples, parents have reported histories of infant strokes and childhood illnesses such as encephalitis or meningitis, which may result in ocular disorders. If researchers select poor readers without obtaining a history, these problems may be overlooked.

According to Rayner (1978; 1986), normal children show clear developmental trends. Fixation duration decreases, saccade length increases, and the frequency of regressions decrease with age and with proficiency in reading. Lefton et al., (1979) found that poor readers showed less of a developmental trend, and according to Rayner (1986), several researchers found that eye movements of dyslexics were different from those of normal readers. Explanations of cause, however, differ.

Pirozzolo (1979) precategorized dyslexics into those with language deficits and those with visual-spatial disorders, and he used a battery to study visual half-field and saccadic latencies. While subjects read tests above or below their reading levels, their eye movements were recorded. On the basis of differences in saccadic latency, he found that normals and language-deficit dyslexics moved their eyes faster to the right than to the left, whereas the visual-spatial dyslexics moved their eyes faster to the left than to the right. Therefore, he concluded that for visual-spatial dyslexics, processing in the right hemisphere was more efficient than in the left hemisphere. He felt that the language-deficient group had some type of left hemisphere disorder.

Other researchers have found that the eye movement patterns of language-deficit dyslexics were normal in nonreading tasks (Stanley, Smith, and Howell, 1983; Brown et al.,1983; Adler-Grindberg and Stark, 1978; Olson et al., 1983) but abnormal in reading tasks. Rayner (1986) and others feel that these patterns reflect the difficulty readers have when processing language. Some investigators have found that dyslexics tend to move their eyes to the left in both reading and nonreading tasks. Pirozzolo (1979) said that they have a higher frequency of return sweep inaccuracies.

Pavlidis (1981), has reported greater differences among all dyslexics on both nonreading and reading tasks. By using a lights test in which subjects fixate on a target that moves from left to right or right to left across a screen, he found that when the target moved from left to right, the dyslexics had significantly more right-to-left saccades than the normal readers. In contrast, he found that "backward readers" (those whose IQ levels or whose sociological or educational factors were the cause of underachievement) did not differ from the controls. Critics of his approach, who attempted to replicate his findings, did not obtain the same results. Brown et al., (1983), Olson et al., (1983), and Stanley et al., (1983) found that dyslexics did not differ from controls in the frequency of regressions on the lights test. Pavlidis (1986), however, continues to report significant differences. The equipment, tasks, units of measurement, and types of analyses could account for the differences and the contradictory results in studies of saccadic latency among dyslexics.

Visual half-field studies are also somewhat inconclusive. McKeever and VanDeventer (1975) and Yeni-Komshian, Isenberg, and Goldberg (1975) found a right visual field superiority for word recognition among dyslexics, but Olson (1973) found a reduced right field superiority in poor readers. According to Rayner (1986), there are probably several reasons for the differences in these results. First, he and others (Pirozzolo, Rayner, and Hynd 1983) feel that subject selection is a major factor. Rayner argues for careful preselection of dyslexics who have linguistic or visual-spatial deficits. This reviewer would also argue for less preselection and a more comprehensive test battery of large groups of dyslexics who could be studied longitudinally. Since there is still disagreement within the field as to whether there are subgroups, it would be helpful if several researchers could agree upon a similar comprehensive test battery, including full-scale verbal and nonverbal intelligence tests, several language tests, and visual-spatial measures. The type of reading test used for subject selection may also influence the subject pool. Investigators who choose poor readers on the basis of silent reading tasks may find different correlations from those who use oral reading tasks.

Studies of perceptual span have also been inconclusive. Rayner, however, concludes from results of a study by Underwood and Zola (1986) that reduced perceptual span is probably not a major factor in dyslexics.

It is possible that reading styles and eye movement are related. In a study of this subject, Olson et al., (1984) called one group of disabled readers "plodders." They displayed few regressions between words and rarely skipped words on forward movements. A second group, called "explorers," showed more regressions and word-skipping movements. Olson and his colleagues found no differences among subjects with either low performance or low verbal IQ scores, and that "plodders" and "explorers" were equally distributed among their samples. Thus, they concluded that there was no evidence of distinct subgroups.

Pirozzolo and Hansch (1982) stated that a considerable amount of knowledge about reading disorders has accumulated during the past decade but that our understanding of the causes is still relatively primitive. They emphasize the complexity of the reading process as well as the numerous mechanisms that govern such functions as visual perception, memory, and language.

McConkie and Zola's (1985) review shows that various techniques involved in the monitoring of eye movements can play an important role in understanding ongoing reading processes. They feel that research techniques involving the monitoring of eye movements provide powerful ways of studying the processing that takes place during reading. Ultimately, such techniques may play an essential role in the diagnosis of reading disorders.

NEURODIAGNOSTIC STUDIES

Duane (1986), Obrzut and Hynd (1983), and others have recently provided a critique of several neurodiagnostic procedures used in the study of dyslexia. Duane feels that procedures for studying brain-behavior relationships may provide diagnostic information, but more studies are needed for validation. He reminds us that the primary diagnostic tools for dyslexia include measurements of reading and intellectual function. Given the fact that most acquired dyslexia is related to a disturbance in the left hemisphere (Geschwind, 1985, 1986), many neuropsychologists, physicians, and others have speculated about disturbances in developmental dyslexia.

ANATOMY OF DEVELOPMENTAL DYSLEXIA

Autopsies of normal brains have indicated differences in the width and surface area between the right and left hemispheres, particularly in the superior temporal region. As one might expect with developmental disorders, there are few autopsies of individuals with specific learning disabilities or dyslexia. Nevertheless, those that have been performed increase the evidence for biological foundations of these disorders. Duane cites several researchers who found in autopsied dyslexics a wider left temporal plane in 65 percent of the cases studied, a wider right temporal plane in 11 percent, and equality in 24 percent. Other studies of brains of developmental dyslexics (Galaburda and Kemper, 1979) indicate that, while the left hemisphere was wider than the right, the temporal planes were of equal size. Disordered cortical cellular arrangement was observed in the left hemisphere, particularly in language areas of the brain. Witelson (1983) studied the brain of a 62-year-old dyslexic and found bilateral temporal cortical cellular anomalies.

In 1968, Drake studied a 12-year-old boy who died from a cerebellar hemorrhage. Prior to death, he had a history of enuresis, asthma, hyperactivity, dizzy spells and "blackouts," reading, writing, and calculation problems, and recurrent left frontal headaches (quoted in Pirrozolo and Hansch, 1982). On the basis of the autopsy, Drake argued that the headaches were related to the vascular malformation and that the condition might have been a minor seizure disorders. There was some indication of an atypical gyral pattern in both parietal lobes, but Drake was reluctant to draw conclusions about the reading problems.

More recently, with the support of the Orton Dyslexia Society, Galaburda (1986) and his colleagues have been studying brains of dyslexics. Galaburda says that the biological substrate(s) of dyslexics has yet to be specified, but a few clues are emerging. Although the types of neuroanatomical alterations observed are not unique to developmental disorders, what is special is the frequency and particularly the distribution of the alterations. All of the brains studied thus far had developmental anomalies in the cerebral cortex and some had alterations in subcortical structures. In four cases, there was symmetry of the hemispheres rather than asymmetry. The alterations consisted of disordered cellular architecture as well as the presence of neural elements in areas from which they were normally absent. Generally, the lesions showed a predilection for the site of the anterior speech zones in the inferior frontal gyrus and in the posterior tempero-parietal region (the posterior language zone).

Of some significance, Galaburda feels that these anomalies originate in fetal life and cannot result from damage at birth or from postnatal processes. The disorder probably occurred during the period when young neurons were migrating to their positions in the cortex—probably between the 16th and 24th week of gestation. According to him, the effects are more severe during the latter period (between week 20 and week 24).

BIOCHEMICAL FACTORS

Wender, cited in Pirozzolo and Hansch (1985), feels that learning disabilities may be caused by biochemical imbalances in the brain. Evidence seems to point to a monoaminergic deficiency, since some youngsters with attention deficits respond to substances such as methylphenidate, dextroamphetamine, and caffeine, which are presumed to act upon the bioamines: dopamine, serotonin, and norepinephrine (p. 220). More recent studies, however, indicate that the drug effect may not be as specific as it was once thought to be.

COMPUTERIZED TOMOGRAPHY

Computerized tomography (CT) scans permit the visualization of the brain without significant radiation hazards. Studies by LeMay (1976) and Galaburda indicate that cerebral hemispheric asymmetries are observable within the general population and that, generally, the left hemisphere is somewhat larger. There may be a relationship between extent of cerebral asymmetry shown by CT scan and hand preference. Right-handers had a longer left hemisphere posteriorly, a wider left hemisphere posteriorly, and a wider right hemisphere anteriorly. Left-handers, in contrast, demonstrated either a reversed asymmetry or no asymmetry. Duane, however, cites some technical difficulties with these studies, including sample size of the population and differences in measurement. However, evidence for asymmetries have also been reported by Weinberger et al., (1982) and by Chi et al., (1977). Emerging data seem to suggest that hemispheric asymmetry may be established as early as the end of the second trimester of gestation.

Reversed asymmetry in dyslexia has been noted by Hier et al. (1978). Since the results of CT scan revealed wider right than left posterior hemispheres, they hypothesized that these findings were related to lower verbal IQ than performance IQ and to history of language delays. Duane (1986) noted, however, that there was considerable variation in IQ scores. In addition, there was no control population.

A second investigation, conducted by Rosenberger and Hier (1980), included a more heterogeneous LD population. Of 53 subjects, 22 were found to have reversed asymmetry, with the right parietal area wider than the left. Rosenberger and Hier concluded that reversed asymmetry constituted a risk factor for language and academic problems. Duane (1986), however, noted again that more data related to educational experience and other variables should have been included, such as age range, type of educational experiences, and handedness.

More recently, Haslam et al. (1981) studied 26 right-handed males, age 9 to 13, who had full-scale IQ scores above 80 and were underachieving in reading by 2 years. "Soft neurological signs" were found in 50 percent of the group, and 6 had a history of early language problems. The control group was younger, in order to control for reading performance. Haslam et al. found no correlation between dyslexia and reversed asymmetry, and they hypothesized that reading disabilities and hemispheric symmetry or asymmetry might be genetically determined. Further investigations of dyslexic families could provide additional insights into these theories.

Duane (1986) has concluded that CT scans are probably not routinely warranted for diagnosis, but he feels that they should not be ignored in future research. In addition, Denkla et al., (1985) reported few CT scan abnormalities among neurologically impaired children. As with all investigations, however, careful selection of subjects with maximum family, personal, and psychoeducational data will offer more insights into the nature of brain-behavior relationships.

ELECTROENCEPHALOGRAM

Various forms of the electroencephalogram (EEG) have been used in studies of dyslexia and learning disabilities. Drake (1968) and others have summarized certain limitations. Despite years of EEG research, Hughes (1982) has said that further study is required to determine whether specific EEG patterns relate to specific reading disorders. When sex, age, and handedness have been controlled, reading disabled subjects have generally showed an EEG pattern different from that of normals, but more multidisciplinary approaches are needed to verify these observations (Hughes, 1985).

The EEG is useful in the diagnosis of reading epilepsy (Forster, 1975). In this condition, seizures may occur while the subject is reading quietly or aloud. Seizures consist of a jaw jerk, vocalization if the patient is reading aloud, and usually a transient disturbance in consciousness. The latter may lead to loss of place in reading and is often noted simply as a disorder of attention. Of importance is the fact that repeated evocation of minor seizures may lead to a major motor seizure. According to Forster, the EEG pattern frequently shows a spike followed by a slow wave. He says that the pattern is not generalized, but usually occurs over the anterior portion of the head and predominantly over the left hemisphere.

BRAIN ELECTRICAL ACTIVITY MAPPING

One of the more recent, promising research tools for studying dyslexia and related disorders is the technique called brain electrical activity mapping (BEAM) (Duffy et al., 1980). The procedures allow for more analyses of EEG recording under various activities as well as averaged evoked responses. Data are presented on a visual screen. Results of the procedures have been able to differentiate dyslexics from nondyslexics, particularly in the left posterior hemisphere and in the paramedian frontal region. While these results are impressive, further evidence is needed with larger samples before this tool can be considered for diagnostic use (Duane, 1986). The procedure would also be useful in the study of nondyslexic learning disabled subjects—for example, those with mathematics or nonverbal disorders.

MAGNETIC RESONANCE IMAGING

Magnetic resonance imaging (MRI) procedures have been used to investigate various human conditions, since there are no known hazards (Duane, 1986). MRI permits the investigator to study sections of the brain sagittally as well as lower regions of the brain not observable with CT scan. Duane says that MRI is more sensitive to alterations in white matter content in the brain. While no aberrations in white matter have thus far been identified in dyslexics postmortem, future studies may be warranted.

CROSS-CULTURAL STUDIES OF DEVELOPMENTAL DYSLEXIA

In an attempt to understand the basic nature of dyslexia and to investigate questions of incidence, several researchers have looked to the nature of the orthography as a partial explanation. As early as 1906, Claiborne suggested that reading disabilities were less frequent among Spanish children. Stevenson (1984) said that there are differences in the characteristics of reading disabilities in English, Japanese, and

Chinese groups but no differences in either prevalence or severity among the groups.

Lindgren, Renzi, and Richman (1985) recently designed a study to examine whether the phonetic regularity of a language can significantly influence the prevalence and pattern of developmental dyslexia. Demographically matched samples of fifth grade children in Italy (N=448) and in the United States (N=1,278) were evaluated on a number of neuropsychological tests. Findings indicated that dyslexia is more prevalent in the United States but that the problems in both countries are strongly associated with disorders of verbal processing. U.S. dyslexics tended to have more visual-motor deficits. Lindgren et al. also found a greater dissociation between reading comprehension and decoding in the Italian children than in the U.S. children.

The investigators explained their findings by describing English as having a "deep" orthography. (A deep orthography is efficient and relatively predictable for the skilled reader.) This finding is in keeping with the generalizations put forth by Liberman and the Haskins group. Italian and other languages have a "shallow" orthography, which encourages reliance on surface phonology. (It seems that some poor readers treat the English language as if it *were* shallow, particularly in spelling). Lindgren et al., like Luria, feel that there are interactions between neurocognitive deficits and the characteristics of the language being read.

Findings from the analyses indicated that U.S. and Italian dyslexics were poorer than control children at decoding nonsense words but that decoding was a greater problem for the U.S. children. While some of these differences could be related to amount and quality of instruction, a number of authors agree that we must make reading-speech connections more explicit in early reading instruction to prevent failure.

SEX DIFFERENCES IN DYSLEXIA

Many studies have indicated that the incidence of reading disabilities is higher among males than among females (Ackerman, Dykman, and Oglesby, 1983). Yet some investigators have revealed no specific cognitive differences or patterns of problems between the groups (Johnson and Blalock, 1987).

A major review of studies of sex differences in dyslexia edited by Ansara et al., (1981) has been published by the Orton Dyslexia Society. In chapter 1, Finucci says that more boys than girls are poor readers but that the extent of the discrepancy varies with the definition and selection of subjects. She feels that females tolerate deficits in reading and spelling more than males. (Researchers in the area of mathematics have drawn similar conclusions.) In addition, the mechanisms through which the effects of genes or experiences produce differences are as yet unknown.

Anne Peterson reviewed the literature (Ansara et al., 1981) on spatial tasks and says that males are frequently found to be better than females. She says, however, that many females excel at spatial tasks and many males are poor spatial visualizers. Peterson says that the variability among females and among males is usually larger than variability between groups.

According to McGuinness in a review of language and auditory processing tasks (Ansara et al., 1981), the strongest predictor of reading ability is phonological encoding and a general "language facility," and females are more adept in both. According to Weber, the rate of maturation may be more pertinent than sex itself. Some differences, according to Widen, also may be related to the use of different approaches to tasks. McKeever says that the bulk of the evidence is against simple (that is, direct) sex effects on the hemispheric lateralization of verbal processes.

RESEARCH IN WRITTEN LANGUAGE

Research in the area of writing has increased dramatically during the last decade. Theoretical models from psycholinguistics, developmental and cognitive psychology, and education have generated new perspectives and research (Bereiter, 1980; Gregg and Steinberg, 1980; Britton et al., 1975; Frederiksen and Dominic, 1981; Halliday and Hassan, 1976; Litowitz, 1981; Nystrand, 1982; Phelps-Gunn and Phelps-Terasaki, 1982; Scardamalia and Bereiter, 1983).

A review of studies of literacy from the late 1800's and early 1900's reveals that the predominant focus was on form and, to a certain extent, moral content. In one turn-of-the-century text, students were taught appropriate posture, techniques for quill sharpening, use of a pen, and subskills leading to perfect penmanship. Spelling and grammar drills were used together with practice-copying of sentences, many of which contained a moral principle. Emphasis in schools was on form, memorization, and drills.

Up until the 1940's, schools generally had separate classes for penmanship, orthography, grammar, and composition, and students were evaluated on their spelling, grammar, and punctuation. Changes in the curriculum resulted in broader subject matters, such as language arts and social studies. Some educators advocated an even broader approach, where the emphasis was on communication, life skills, and self-preservation. These changes, together with notions about communication, pragmatics, and language usage stimulated more research on the functions of reading and writing than on form. Periodically, however, educators worry about whether we are teaching the "basics" because of the poor writing observed among students.

Part of this problem may be related to the amount of time devoted to writing instruction in schools. A survey from two major Eastern cities reported in *Phi Delta Kappan* (1979) found that the weekly amounts varied considerably from teacher to teacher and that systems of evaluation varied as well. While most teachers felt writing was important for self-expression, they tended to grade a student's work on the basis of spelling, grammar, and form rather than creativity or quality of ideas. Because of curricular differences, research on writing must be considered in relation to values, expectancies, and kind of instruction.

Two standardized tests for written language have been used frequently in learning disabilities. They are the Picture Story Language Test (PSLT) (Myklebust, 1965) and the Test of Written Language (TOWL) (Hammill and Larsen, 1981). The PSLT measures productivity, sentence length, syntax, and abstractness/concreteness. The TOWL measures thematic maturity, language usage, spelling, and handwriting. While both tests have been criticized for the types of stimuli used (pictures) and for other technical factors, there are few other measures of spontaneous writing that yield age or grade level scores. Both tests provide perspectives on what can be expected across age levels. In addition, the PSLT has been used with large numbers of exceptional children including the deaf, mentally retarded, behaviorally disturbed, and learning disabled (Myklebust, 1973). Often, standardized measures need to be supplemented with criterion reference measures to define more specific problems and to plan instruction (Weiner, 1980).

Writing, like reading, has been studied by professionals from many disciplines. Often, those with a neuropsychological perspective focus on specific modality processing deficits (Boder and Jarrico, 1982; Boder, 1971) or on relationships between reading and writing, such as acquired dyslexia without agraphia. In contrast, those with a developmental perspective tend to look at the types of discourse, syntax, or spelling patterns used by children at various age levels. In the opinion of this reviewer, both perspectives may be needed in order to identify unique problems among the learning disabled. In some instances, we found that the neuropsychological perspective needed to be supplemented with more data pertaining to rule application (Trout, 1973). That is, it was insufficient to investigate modality-specific problems without incorporating rule generalization. It is essential to understand the types of errors made by young children. In contrast, broad developmental norms may be insufficient to identify specific types of errors. The type of task may also influence the findings. If, for example, one studies spelling by using only words based on frequency of occurrence, one might not be able to identify problems related to rule acquisition, application, automaticity, or monitoring. Furthermore, there are no tests of spelling that investigate performance across spontaneous, dictated, and recognition tasks. The forms of input and modes of response are particularly important when studying problems of the learning disabled (Johnson and Blalock, 1987). Individuals with revisualization or retrieval problems, for example, may perform much better on recognition than on recall spelling tests. Similarly, handwriting, syntax, and other aspects of writing may deteriorate during complex written language tasks.

HANDWRITING

While letter formation may be less important than ideation and actual written language, it is obvious that severe visual-motor deficits can interfere with the ability to convey ideas to others. Poor handwriting may result from disorders of visual-spatial processing, revisualization, visual-motor integration, motor planning, and other factors. Neuropsychologists often do comprehensive analyses of visual, tactual, and proprioceptive functions to examine the source of the problems (Kinsbourne, 1986; Rourke and Finlayson, 1978).

In recent years, more research on the development of handwriting has provided additional data regarding performance at various age levels. These are helpful in determining whether a child should receive special services (Thomassen and Teulings, 1983).

Without help, many people with learning disabilities may have significant problems vocationally and socially. In a few instances, we observed adults whose handwriting was so unstable that they were unable to cash their own traveler's cheques. With the advent of computers, word processors, and other technology, people with these disorders may be able to create legible copy (McDermott and Watkins, 1983). However, it is important to realize that at least some of the same visual-motor skills needed for handwriting are also needed for typing.

SPELLING

Studies of spelling during the early childhood years have been greatly enhanced through the work of Read (1983), Temple, Nathan, and Burris (1982), and others, who analyzed the spontaneous writing of youngsters who had not been formally taught to spell. They found that beginners do not spell words perfectly but reflect what they have abstracted from the printed word. Their spelling patterns reveal what they have abstracted from both oral language and the orthography. Usually, children begin using global strategies or first letters, and progress to using letter names (if they have been taught) and syllabic units. Later, they acquire orthographic principles (Frith, 1980).

A significant volume on spelling edited by Frith (1980) emphasized that spelling should be considered a linguistic process, not simply a skill requiring memory. In order to spell, one must abstract features and principles of the orthography for generalization to occur. If rule application is expected, more than memory is needed.

Both reading and spelling require the ability to analyze language into its component parts, an ability called "linguistic awareness" by Mattingly, Liberman, and others. According to Shankweiler and Liberman (1972), effective use of an alphabetic code requires active awareness of the phonological structure of the language. They also stress the importance of morphological knowledge.

Smith, in Frith (1980), argues against views of reading and spelling that conceptualize graphemic, phonemic, and semantic representations as simple single-level structures. Syntactic information and phonemic and graphemic structures of the entire word are also used in spelling. In addition, etymological factors, such as information about the language in which a word originated, influence pronunciation and spelling.

In English, regularities in spelling are not related directly to the surface phonology, but rather to an underlying form closely related to meaning (Venezky, 1970). In words such as "sane" and "sanity," critical parts of each word may be spelled alike, have similar meanings, and be pronounced differently. Therefore, one cannot use reading or spelling programs that focus only on phonemic decoding strategies.

Bryant and Bradley (1980) and Smith claim that reading and spelling require different components of linguistic ability. Whereas reading can be done with visual clustering strategies, spelling requires a phonological component that is absent from reading. In general, the reader-speller is a multilevel information processor who uses numerous levels, including graphemic, phonetic, low-level phonemic, high-level phonemic, morphemic, lexical, syntactic, semantic, and etymological knowledge. Tasks such as reading aloud or silently, proofreading, and spelling require selection of different levels. While some people make more errors on dictated tests, Johnson and Blalock (1987) reported that LD adults made more morphosyntactic, segmenting, and morphographemic errors during spontaneous writing than on dictated spelling tasks.

Several investigators have found differences in "linguistic sensitivity" among educated adults. Poor spellers at the college level were less successful than good spellers in abstracting regularities at the surface phonetic level and in using morphophonemic representation. More recently, Liberman et al. (1985) and Vogel (1986) have found that poor readers had more difficulty than normals with the acquisition and usage of morphological rules for spelling. Poor readers and writers also have problems applying rules in novel situations (Berry, 1961; Johnson and Hook, 1978).

Several studies indicate that a phonological strategy is particularly difficult for individuals who cannot segment or manipulate sounds in words (Bradley and Bryant, 1979; Frith, 1980). There is some indication, however, that such individuals acquire the rules in the same way but at a slower rate (Gerber, 1984). Nelson, in Frith (1980), studied spelling errors of dyslexics (mean age, 11 years) and normal children (mean age, 7 years) and found that the former made no more phonetically inaccurate or orthographically illegal errors than the normals. She concluded that they were delayed in acquiring spelling knowledge rather than in applying it. Nelson hypothesized that spelling can take place via two routes, a phonemic-graphic route and a direct semantic-graphemic route. Other studies also indicate that dyslexics made no more letter order errors or phonetically inaccurate spellings than the normal subjects. Perhaps, however, some individual subjects do make idiosyncratic mistakes.

Gerber (1984) viewed spelling as a type of problem-solving activity, and he found that learning disabled children were less flexible in their use of spelling strategies than normals. Therefore, he suggested a problem-solving approach to instruction. More recently, Gerber and Hall (1987) provided an excellent review of information-processing approaches to spelling.

Several studies have been undertaken to identify poor spellers, using the Boder classification scheme (1975; Boder and Jarrico, 1982). This test differentiates poor spellers into dysphonetic, dyseidetic, and mixed types. While this measure is useful for some purposes, it is generally insufficient for identifying subjects with morphological problems.

According to Barron, in Frith (1980), children might not benefit from reading and spelling programs that place too much emphasis either on phonics or on "look-say" methods. He says that exclusive emphasis on one strategy over another might encourage children to "overspecialize" in one type of strategy and deter them from acquiring others. Harris, Gray, and other reading specialists emphasized the need for multiple strategies many years ago.

Several studies have found that poor spellers with severe memory deficits performed significantly more poorly on tasks requiring short- and long-term recall of words. They hypothesized that poor spellers may require alternate means of studying words and more trials to achieve.

Studies from the Columbia Research Institute have documented the importance of directed study. Instructional emphasis was given to reduced unit size, distribution practice, and training for transfer. Investigators concluded that instruction should incorporate classic principles of learning and remedial teaching (Bryant, Fayne, and Gettinger, 1980). This reviewer would agree as long as the training emphasizes linguistic awareness, the nature of the alphabetic code, rules, and principles (Bailet, 1985; Beers and Henderson, 1980; Hanna and Hanna, 1971).

While rules may be useful, Sloboda, in Frith (1980), discussed several reasons why rules are not sufficient for perfect spelling, one of which is related to individual differences in the use of visual imagery. These differences allow visualizers to outperform nonvisualizers in certain instances. While he acknowledged the role of phonological, morphological, and morphographemic rule systems, he saw imagery as something that operates on the "end product" of a spelling process. Average spellers spell by rule, but good spellers spell some words by rote and they have additional strategies available that they can evoke when rules do not suffice.

Tenny, in Frith (1980), examined visual processes in spelling and found that imaging what two alternative spellings look like was less helpful than actually seeing them. In addition, she found that seeing words in an unfamiliar form was less helpful than seeing them in a familiar form. Research on the ability to generate various spelling alternatives may provide more insights into spellers' knowledge of orthography as well as imagery. Hoff (1985) found LD sixth graders were able to generate fewer options than normals reading at similar grade levels.

Wing and Baddelly (1980) and Hotopf, in Frith (1980), using information processing theories, hypothesized that spelling errors are slips of the pen as opposed to errors of convention, which arise in a temporary storage buffer. Thus, delays in retrieval might be imposed by the mechanical constraints in writing (a major factor for some LD subjects). While Wing and Baddelly say that they barely "scratched the surface" with their distributional analysis, further investigations with good spellers and poor spellers may be promising.

Barron, in Frith (1980), has suggested that lexical access problems may play a role in spelling. This reviewer agrees, and has observed many students who have both word retrieval problems and revisualization difficulties that interfere with rapid spelling. Some students report that they cannot visualize letters, particularly capital cursive forms (Trout, 1973).

Black children are often overrepresented in special education, and spelling by groups of black children and others who use nonstandard English deserves special study. During the 1960's, several studies highlighted teachers' awareness to rules used by speakers of "black" English. While there are probably many reasons for the findings, Farnham-Diggory (1978) found that black children prefer a visually based strategy in spelling, whereas white children of the same age prefer a phonemically based strategy (quoted in Frith, 1980). Such a finding may be open to many interpretations (including delay in linguistic awareness), and the topic warrants further investigation.

Desberg et al., in Frith (1980), studied the relationship among reading, spelling, and mathematics achievement scores and dialect in a group of black elementary school children and found that those who had better standard English were better readers and spellers than children who did not. In contrast, achievement in mathematics was not related to dialect. According to Venberg, we may need to find a better way to make rules more explicit both for dialect speakers and for LD children, particularly since many of the latter enter school with speech and language defects. All of these findings, together with findings by neuropsychologists, provide the basis for further study. Questions regarding patterns of delay and difference are still of interest.

WRITTEN SYNTAX

Years ago, Myklebust (1965, 1973) completed several studies of written language development and found that LD children generally wrote significantly fewer words, fewer sentences, and fewer words per sentence at nearly all age levels than did normals. Syntax was particularly deficient. Errors included word omissions, additions, and substitutions as well as faulty punctuation. Using the same test, Poteet (1980) found that LD children did not differ on the overall syntax scale but that they made more punctuation errors. Research with the Test of Written Language (Hammill and Larsen, 1978) resulted in similar findings. Poplin et al. (1980) found that LD children were lower than normals on the subtests for capitalization and punctuation. Differences across studies may be related to severity of the language disorder.

Many investigators applied Hunt's T-unit analysis to the study of written language (1965, 1970). Hunt defines the "T" unit as one main clause and any subordinate clause or nonclausal structure that is attached to or embedded in it. In general, T-unit length increases with the age of the writer and, therefore, can be considered a reflection of syntactic maturity but not of syntactic complexity. Most studies found no differences in number of T-units used by LD and normal subjects.

Vogel and Moran (1982), using a "deep" structure procedure, found LD college students differed from a comparison group in their use of compound, complex, and compound-complex sentences. Vogel (1985), however, reported that when capitalization and punctuation were ignored and types of T-units were analyzed, there were no significant differences. More recently, Vogel (1986) found that LD college writers differed on variables related to subordination and embeddedness. Using a sentence-combining task, Gregg (1982) found that LD college subjects made more syntactic errors that distorted meaning than either normal college freshmen or basic writers in the same school.

Morris and Crump (1982) examined various properties of text and found no significant difference in T-units, but they detected group differences in vocabulary development. This finding warrants further investigation to determine whether the problems were related to disorders of language comprehension, word retrieval, or linguistic flexibility.

WRITTEN DISCOURSE

Several theorists emphasize writing as an *activity* and the *process* of writing as well as the *product.* Hence, researchers observe writers during the writing process, the composing process, prewriting and rewriting activities, and monitoring. Protocol analyses are also used to describe what writers think about when writing (Fredericksen and Dominic, 1981; Flowers and Hayes, 1980; Gregg and Steinberg, 1980). Fredericksen and Dominic examined four factors: (1) cognitive (capacities of the writer); (2) linguistic (dealing with forms and uses of writing), (3) communicative (the audience and author's voice), and (4) contextual (the situation, purpose, and function of writing).

Litowitz (1981) says that writers must be able to control lexical access, spelling, handwriting, grammar, organization, audience, and structure of the text. Given the limitations of information processing discussed earlier, it is clear why writing is such a problem for most LD students. Bereiter (1980) and other theorists in Greg and Steinberg (1981) liken the writing process to that of a juggler managing multiple constraints. At times, a writer must "throw away" a constraint while concentrating on a specific objective.

Several studies of the process of composition indicate that poor writers engage in less prewriting and revising activities than good writers, perhaps because LD writers' faulty handwriting and spelling make it nearly impossible for them to reread their work. Some decode so slowly that they tire while rereading; others have not been taught how to proof, revise, and edit. The consequences of these deficits are evident in the adult examples discussed by Shaughnessy (1977) and others.

According to Flowers and Hayes (1977), poor writers tend to produce content based more upon the writer's own discovery of his or her subject matter than upon a clear, understandable presentation of material to readers. They, like younger writers, have more difficulty in taking the perspective of the reader (Litowitz, 1981). The writer must be aware of what the audience needs to know and at the same time cope with the physical distance between himself and the audience. Thus, considerable metacognitive and metalinguistic awareness is needed for writing. According to Shaughnessy (1977), the orientation of poor college writers assumes that readers understand what is going on in the writer's mind and therefore need no introduction or explanation.

While few studies have examined perspective-taking of LD writers, C. Cohen (1983) found that normal children displayed significantly greater awareness than their LD peers who were reading at comparable levels. She found, whether the writer and reader shared the same information or whether the writer possessed more knowledge than the reader, that normal writers appeared to be more skilled than LD subjects in accommodating readers. While writing places exceptional demands on an individual, diagnosticians should note whether such problems are unique to writing or whether they are related to all forms of communication.

Bereiter (1980) taught children how to ask questions of themselves while writing (that is, carry on an internal dialogue) in order to think about what the reader needs to know. A reason why writing is so difficult is that the writer must communicate with an imagined audience. Britton et al. (1975) said that writing practice should include writing for self, for familiar audiences, and for unfamiliar people. Phelps-Gunn and Phelps-Teraski (1982) also discuss the need for helping LD students write various forms of discourse since each form demands different cognitive skills. Instruction should be provided in writing narration, description, exposition, and argument.

Research using computers and word processors is promising but is not conclusive (Torgesen, 1986). While some studies indicate that performance improves (Greenfield, 1984), others report no change. More information about each individual, the curriculum, and program are needed to interpret the data.

RESEARCH IN MATHEMATICS

According to Bell, quoted by Moses (1984), mathematics has been called the "queen and servant of the sciences" since its generality and freedom from specific content is an accomplishment of abstraction and logic. Bell says that analysis of problems with symbolic arithmetic operations and numbers takes us beyond elementary arithmetic as taught in schools into more basic realms of auditory and visual information processing, perception, and symbolic interpretation of numbers and symbols. A highly complex set of neuropsychological processes underlies even the simplest arithmetic operations. Thus mathematics, like reading, language, or writing, requires the integration of component skills that must be mastered and automatized for problem solving.

Several investigators in adult aphasia, developmental psychology, neuropsychology, mathematics education, and special education have attempted to delineate factors related to mathematics performance. Kosc (1974, 1981) and Cohn (1971), for example, identified four cognitive factors: language, memory, logical reasoning, and visual-spatial abilities. In addition, Kosc (1974) found relationships between general mental ability and mathematics, and Badian (1983) identified a specific numerical ability. Chalfant and Scheffelin (1969) reported that general intelligence, verbal ability, spatial ability, reasoning, and approach to problem-solving all played a role in mathematics. More recently, strategy use has been studied by Conner (1983) and Fleishner and Garnett (1979).

In addition to cognitive factors, Gerstmann (1940) identified a syndrome that included disturbances in calculation, agraphia, right-left disorientation, and finger agnosia. Others have found that these problems do not necessarily co-occur (Benton, 1961; Spellacy and Peter, 1978).

Unfortunately, mathematics has not received as much attention as reading and writing in learning disabilities. Yet, its importance cannot be denied. Johnson and Blalock (1987) found that many adults in their clinical sample (N=93) had difficulty with one or more aspects of mathematics and arithmetic. While most understood the basic operations, their overall independence and social maturity was limited by their difficulties with computation and mathematical reasoning. In a survey of 112 adolescents, Johnson, Blalock, and Nesbitt (1978) found that 63 were underachieving in mathematics or arithmetic.

Deer (1985) quotes McLeod and Crump (1978), who said that only 10 percent of LD students have severe deficits in mathematics but that over one-half required at least supplemental instruction, especially at the intermediate and secondary levels (McLeod and Armstrong, 1982). Deficiencies commonly cited include problems related to regrouping in addition, subtraction and multiplication, long division, place value, basic operations, and measurement (Cawley, Fitzmaurice, Shaw, Kahn, and Bates, 1979).

LOGICAL REASONING

Logico-mathematical abilities, according to Piaget, are basic to learning mathematics. The concepts of greatest importance include number, classification, and conservation or invariance (Copeland, 1984).

Anderson, Richards, and Hallahan (1980) found that learning disabled boys, ages 8-12, showed a cognitive delay in hierarchical classification (class inclusion). Their ability was similar to that of children several years younger. Stone (1987) found that some learning disabled adults with average Wechsler Adult Intelligence Scale (WAIS) scores displayed difficulty on higher level Piagetian tasks (formal operations) and mathematics.

In a study of conservation and mathematics achievement, Derr (1985) reported that many 9- to 12-year-old children with severe mathematics disabilities had not developed the concept of conservation, even though they had average mental ability (IQ score of approximately 90). She concluded that this lag may restrict their ability to understand mathematics instruction but that further analyses are needed to determine whether the problems are conceptual or linguistic, since many Piagetian tasks require verbal explanations. Fincham (1979) found no difference in conservation ability between LD and normal children, but he did not study those with specific mathematics problems.

LANGUAGE AND MATHEMATICS

The role of language in the acquisition of mathematics has been studied by several investigators. Earp and Tanner (1980) report that a student's success in mathematics is inextricably interwoven with the student's level of language sophistication. Aiken (1972) says that the first hurdle a student faces in learning mathematics is to understand the language, including its vocabulary, syntax, semantics, and function. Sharma (1981) feels that mathematics is a bona fide "second language" and that many children fail because they have not acquired it. Beilin (1975) has outlined the properties of mathematics that make it a language, such as its representational function and communicative function, including such natural properties as the lexicon, syntax, and grammar.

Thus, it seems reasonable to assume that children who have problems with oral language may have difficulty with one or more aspects of mathematics. In a followup study, Hall and Tomblin (1978) found that language impaired children scored significantly lower than articulation impaired children on tests of mathematics in grades 3 through 6. The authors hypothesized that the language of instruction may have accounted for some of the problems but that general problems of symbolic representation, including nonlinguistic symbols, should be considered. This hypothesis is in keeping with the observations of Inhelder (1976), who reported that dysphasic children may have underlying problems in symbolic representation that go beyond language.

In a review of 112 learning disabled children, Johnson and Blalock (1987) found that 75 had oral language and/or auditory processing disorders and that 45 of the 75 were underachieving in mathematics. Problems with multiple word meanings, complex syntax, and understanding of comparative terms were observed.

Reduced auditory memory span is common among both mathematics disabled children and poor readers. Many studies of poor readers reveal low scores on both the digit span and the arithmetic subtests of the WISC (Wechsler, 1974a, 1974b).

In a study of measurement, James (1975) found that LD children did not differ from the normals in overall understanding of the concept; however, the control group gave more ambiguous explanations than their normal peers. He concluded that the verbal report of the controls did not reliably reflect the nature of their conceptual structure.

Several studies reported by Aiken (1971, 1972) and by Wiig and Semel (1976) indicate a relationship between syntactic complexity and the ability to solve verbal mathematics problems. Aiken found that training in both vocabulary and syntax aided problem solving. Larsen, Trenholme, and Parker (1978) found that the syntactic complexity of mathematical problems influenced eighth-grade subjects' problem-solving ability, and felt that the language in mathematics textbooks should be analyzed.

VISUAL-SPATIAL FACTORS

Fleischner and Frank (1979) found that several components of mathematical achievement are related to visual-perceptual ability, including the ability to store visual arrays of objects, to code them with regard to their membership in a numerical category, and to manipulate stored images to accomplish operations. Their research further indicated that visual perception emerged as a probable good predictor of mathematics achievement since, in several cases, visual-perceptual measures accounted for more of the variance in arithmetic achievement than did IQ. If these findings are replicated, it seems plausible to suggest the use of concrete material when introducing mathematical concepts. Not all mathematics problems, however, are related to disturbances in visual perception.

Ceci and Peters (1980) found that their group of dyscalculics did not differ on most visual measures used. However, their subjects were less well defined and their test battery was not as comprehensive as that of Fleischner and Frank. Ceci and Peters did find that the dyscalculics performed below the normals on a task of visual closure. These studies, however, have questionable comparability because the terms "perception" and "perceptual deficit" are used loosely in the literature for a wide range of skills, without a delineation of the cognitive requirements of each task.

Often, the problems are more evident on tasks requiring visualization and memory. Battista (1980) reported that spatial visualization (a task requiring more mental manipulation) correlated with problem-solving ability. Male college students scored higher on spatial ability measures than did females.

Several years ago, Johnson and Myklebust (1967) noted that students with mathematics problems were often deficient in social perception as well as in visual-spatial-motor coordination and handwriting. Rourke (1978) reported similar findings. More recently, Badian (1983), using the Myklebust Pupil Rating Scale, investigated the personal-social characteristics of mathematics underachievers and found that children with a disability in mathematical computation may be at risk for impulsive and possibly antisocial behavior. Immaturity and lack of responsibility were also noted. Therefore, she has recommended more investigations of children with good reading and poor mathematics ability.

ARITHMETIC STRATEGIES

Columbia University Institute findings have supported the hypothesis that LD students have a general delay or disability in the development and use of age-appropriate cognitive strategies. Fleischner, Garnett, and Shephard (1980) found that LD students attempted significantly fewer problems than normals on timed tests of basic arithmetic facts. An analysis of protocols led them to believe that LD students relied on overt counting procedures, which, in turn, led to studies of strategy use. Using Groen and Parkman's classification scheme, the Columbia group defined a *reproductive* strategy as one that reflects an automatized, habituated response with short latencies and no signs of counting. (The assumption is that children often know the answer from memory.) In contrast, *reconstructive* strategies involve more overt manifestations of counting, such as the use of fingers and manipulatives. The Columbia group found that LD students used more reconstructive strategies than normal subjects, and said that the LD students were slower than their peers to develop and apply strategies for encoding and retrieving information.

Results of intervention studies showed that LD students learn arithmetic facts when they are provided with systematic direct instruction that includes cumulative and distributed practice through attractive games and activities. Learning to mastery enhances retention of facts.

The Columbia group also developed problem-solving programs that emphasized (1) procedural knowledge (helping the student understand that a problem exists and that skills to develop, execute, and monitor a cognitive plan for responding to it are needed; (2) information derived from the problem, such as what is given and what is asked; and (3) task-specific knowledge, such as knowing when a two-step procedure must be employed and which computational operation is needed. In general, they found that LD students lacked the ability to devise and implement cognitive plans for executing complex tasks. A recent summary of their investigations was reported by Garnett and Fleischner (1987).

Another successful study using cognitive strategy training was conducted by Montague and Bos (1986). The procedures enabled students to read, understand, carry out, and check verbal mathematic problems encountered in the general mathematics curriculum at the secondary level.

In the future, it would be beneficial to investigate, in more depth, the characteristics of subjects in relation to their performance. Until researchers know more than subjects' overall IQ and achievement levels, it may be difficult to determine whether there are subtypes of mathematics disorders.

NEUROPSYCHOLOGICAL PERSPECTIVES

Rourke (1978), using a neuropsychological perspective, analyzed the reading, spelling, and arithmetic performance of a group of LD children and found three subgroups. The first was uniformly deficient in all three areas. Another was better in arithmetic than in either reading or spelling, but was still performing below expectancy. The third had normal reading and spelling performance with impaired performance in arithmetic. Cawley et al. (1979) found subgroups at three different ages and a set of discriminators.

More recently, Badian (1983) identified five groups: (1) difficulty in reading and writing mathematical symbols; (2) spatial difficulties; (3) difficulty in understanding operations; (4) attentional-sequential problems (difficulty with facts, multiplication tables, and inconsistent usage); and (5) a mixed type.

Using models from Luria and from Lewis, Golden, and Moses, Moses (1984) suggests four different types of problems associated with lesions in various areas of the brain. While one cannot expect such clear-cut problems with developmental cases, the types do provide a basis for studying problems that co-occur. For example, patients with dysfunctions of the frontal lobe often lack an understanding of what is required for task solution. Hence, they try to solve the problem on the basis of fragmentary impressions. In addition, they cannot inhibit impulsive guesses that are based on incomplete information. Thus, if a guess is disconfirmed, the attention and focus of the patients change from one stimulus cue to another. Moses says that these patients have difficulty with perceptual analysis (taking fragmentary cues out of context) and try to generalize to the situation. Response disinhibition is seen regardless of the sensory input. The patients make errors whether the problem is presented visually or aurally. They tend to remember fragmented details without an identified goal or strategy. They have no plan and, consequently, fail to appreciate the significance of their errors and fail to learn from them. Often they appear careless and unconcerned about their performance. While neurologically based disinhibition can be mistaken for poor motivation, Moses says that these patients lack the basis for independent, goal-directed, motivated problem-solving. He also says that they may have problems in shifting cognitive sets (such as with addition and/or subtraction).

Moses says that a second type of mathematics disorder results from temporal lobe dysfunction. In these cases, the people comprehend number structure and can formulate a general plan or solution, but they have difficulty with oral presentations or recall of intermediate steps.

A third type results from left parietal-occipital dysfunction. These patients show confusion of arithmetic symbols, reversals, and disintegration of number structure. At times, extra placeholders may be inserted or needed ones omitted.

Moses says that in right hemisphere dysfunction, the visual-spatial element, not the symbolic content, is disturbed. Subjects may misalign numbers and show other evidence of visual-spatial disorganization. Moses finds that these people are task-oriented, and can repeat directions and execute plans.

Despite the evidence of mathematics problems in known cases of brain damage, Cawley and Richstone (1984) say that it is not known whether individuals referred to as learning disabled have neurological impairments, nor is it known that all who manifest mathematics problems are learning disabled or neurologically impaired. These authors, like many neuropsychologists, found that some LD individuals have greater deficits in mathematics than in reading, others have greater problems in reading than in mathematics, and still others have nearly equivalent disorders in both (or all) areas of learning.

According to Cawley and Richstone, language seems to mediate complicated tasks in mathematics, but there is little evidence regarding the relative contributions of verbal labeling and spatial perception in simple tasks, such as counting or one-step addition problems. They feel that in most individuals, the left hemisphere is dominant for language as well as certain kinds of logic. While the right hemisphere has a logic (or intuition), it is based more on simultaneous processing. And they say that mathematics consists of both logic and intuition.

Cawley and Richstone have found that more work on brain and learning has been done in language and reading than in mathematics. This reviewer agrees and hopes that Galaburda will be able to secure brains of people with serious nonverbal and/or mathematical problems as well as those with dyslexia. Cawley and Richstone say that the corpus callosum may play an even greater role in mathematics than in reading.

A review of several studies of mathematics and EEG led Cawley and Richstone to conclude that hemispheric specialization, when described globally as either right or left, might be too limiting a construct. Subject-matter content as well as cerebral or cognitive styles may need to be considered. Presumably, several areas of the brain are accessed during even simple arithmetic operations.

PREDICTION

Several factors other than learner characteristics may predict mathematics achievement. Guerrieri (1979) found that the amount of formal education of parents was the best predictor. About 40 percent of the variance in the mean mathematics scores of eighth graders was accounted for by this variable. While less significant, the students' perception of parental expectations, the students' own expectations, and parental interests in school were also related. Neither sex nor race was a good predictor.

The role of instruction is probably greater in mathematics than in either reading or writing. Cawley and Richstone (1984) cite an earlier study of Cawley, Kahn, and Tedesco in which they found (after looking at 1,300 LD profiles) that they could identify a child's school and the person who tested the child by examining the test battery and results.

In an examination of arithmetic achievement, it is helpful to examine the data from studies by Tarnopol and Tarnopol (1979). Grade-level scores on the Wide Range Achievement Test (WRAT) for students in a state university graduate school of education in California ranged from 3.9 to 18.9. The Tarponols found no differences between males and females. In contrast, Australian graduate education students were more homogeneous. Their scores ranged from 6.9 to 15.9, with a median grade-level of 12.8. The education-mathematics majors scored from 9.0 to 19.5, with a median score of 14.7.

These findings amplify the need for maintaining high standards for both regular and special education teachers. Problems in mathematics achievement may be directly related to faulty instruction. The Tarnopols wondered how graduate students in education could pass courses in tests and measurements with such low computation ability. They recommended the screening of teachers for arithmetic disabilities, enrollment in rigorous and individualized remedial mathematics courses, and upgrading arithmetic courses for in-service.

INTERVENTION STUDIES

Many textbooks in the field of learning disabilities provide summaries and comparisons of various approaches (Adelman and Taylor, 1983; Myers and Hammill, 1982; Lerner, 1985). The ways in which one characterizes a philosophy or program depends on the degree to which the methods have been described, the perceptions of the writer, and a host of other factors. Myers and Hammill (1982) differentiate broad-based systems for teaching the learning disabled from those designed more specifically for particular areas such as reading and mathematics. Such a distinction is important since there are no methods for learning disabilities per se. Rather, there are general approaches or philosophies or methods for teaching reading, decoding, spelling, handwriting, etc. As one might expect, research on intervention tends to focus on specific disabilities so variables can be controlled. The problem is that these small studies are often decontextualized and are not always described in relation to the total educational program or curriculum. For example, even with highly structured programs such as Gillingham and Stillman (1956), one can assess the effectiveness of the decoding and spelling methods, but procedures for comprehension would need further elaboration.

Investigators should be aware that all educational programs, for both normal and atypical learners, are based on the value systems of the culture, the community, and the school. In some systems, these values are made explicit whereas in others they are only implied. Some special educators, for example, emphasize remediation for longer periods of time in hope that the students will learn to read, write, or calculate and eventually minimize the discrepancy between potential and achievement. Others feel it is better to use compensatory strategies, such as tape recorders for the nonreader, to insure maximum knowledge and, perhaps, better motivation. Some educators use external reward systems whereas others work toward intrinsic motivation (Adelman and Taylor, 1983). Whatever the orientation, however, most educators assume that the individual is capable of learning and change. Yet the goals, expectancies, and direction for change will vary.

Recently Kirk, in Vaughn and Bos (1987), said that intervention procedures can be classified into two broad types: (1) the ecologic or organizational, which deals with the environment or delivery systems in which the child is remediated, and (2) the specific strategies of instruction, which are designed for the child's inherent difficulties. The methods for research, according to Kirk, include quantitative research, single-subject, ethnographic approaches, and case studies. He says that research on intervention is more complex than experimental research on a single variable in human learning. In addition, he feels that studies are needed to investigate rate of learning in various service delivery systems. This reviewer agrees but feels that data on motivation and long-term attitude toward learning, adjustment, and independence will also be needed to examine the overall impact of special education.

Wong, in Vaughn and Bos (1987), says that intervention research in LD is needed and will likely increase with the development of more empirical data on thinking skills and cognitive strategies. Among relevant issues raised by Wong are the role of affective variables, individual versus small group instruction, general and domain-specific strategies, ecological validity, maintenance, and transfer.

Given the complexity of these issues and the heterogeneity of the population, it is difficult to identify comprehensive intervention studies. Nevertheless, there are some findings that provide the bases for future hypotheses and research. First, several studies cited earlier in this paper highlight the effectiveness of early intervention. Hence, it is important to continue practices of early identification and instruction.

Findings from studies of early literacy and reading problems in the early grades highlight the importance of early training in rhyming, linguistic awareness, and auditory categorization (Bradley and Bryant, 1985). Many of the current reading readiness programs need to be supplemented with training in these areas. School readiness assessment programs need more tasks to assess oral expressive language and linguistic awareness.

Many studies reported by Chall (1983) have indicated the need for a code emphasis during the early stages of reading. And given the body of research on decoding difficulties, we need continued studies of the best approaches to teaching the code. Efforts should be made to explore the rate of rule acquisition, application, and automaticity. Studies of automaticity combined with more research on "time on task" could be combined.

Several studies from the Columbia University Institute emphasize the need for training flexible strategies. Poor readers who depend solely upon either top-down or bottom-up processing will be less effective than those who incorporate both. In the Columbia studies of reading comprehension, the LD subjects frequently failed to make use of linguistic cue words. This suggests that work on the code should be combined with any aspect of vocabulary, syntax, or semantics that is deficient. Approaches that foster a more analytic, reflective style, with emphasis on active questioning on the part of the reader, also hold promise.

Research on all aspects of written language should continue. Now that there are more developmental theories and data to guide future investigations, broad-based studies that include careful assessment of cognition, oral language, reading, and writing are recommended. Data from recent research on spelling (Frith, 1980) should be incorporated in new spelling programs for young children. Emphasis should be given to heightening their awareness of the alphabetic code. Studies from England and elsewhere also indicate a need for helping students write for different audiences in various content areas.

Mathematics, an often overlooked (or undertaught) area, should not be ignored in future programs for the learning disabled. New research in *Focus on Learning Problems in Mathematics* provides the basis for direct instruction in vocabulary, in the language of mathematics, and in procedures. While drill and practice for automaticity are needed, several investigators have emphasized that meaning must precede drills. Others have reported the need for careful selection of media, including manipulatives, finger mathematics, and visual presentations for students who cannot remember or image figures and relationships. Plans and strategies for various operations also are needed (Fleischner, 1985; Piper and Deshler, 1985; Levy and Schenck, 1981; Wood and Dunlap 1982; Sundberg, 1982). While direct instruction is beneficial, these findings should not be taken to mean that every student needs or profits from the same presentation. Hence, one cannot ignore the attributes of the learner and patterns of error.

Over the years, other "remedies" have been proposed. In a symposium on learning disabilities, Millichap (1977), a neurologist with training in biochemistry, summarized a list of treatments that are still unproven. These included patterning exercises, visual training, vestibular stimulation, biofeedback alpha-wave conditioning, hypoallergenic diets, hypoglycemic diets, and orthomolecular and megavitamin therapy. More recently, Levinson (1981) has recommended the use of antimotion medication for treatment of dyslexia. Dr. Richard Masland has critiqued this work in a 1986 issue of *Orton Society Perspectives* and concluded that no controlled studies have been done to prove that the treatment is effective.

In a survey of research on psychotropic drugs in the treatment of reading disorders, Aman (1982) said that there were no findings to suggest the use of anxiolytic drugs in specific reading disorders. Short-term studies of stimulants with hyperactive children indicated some beneficial effects on learning-related skill (for instance, attention), but long-term followup studies were unable to document lasting drug-related gains in academic achievement. A recent investigation by Chase, Schmitt, Russell, and Tallal (1984) did suggest that Piracetam may be beneficial for some individuals with reading disorders but that further long-term studies are needed.

The Role of Media in Learning

Several important investigations have explored the effect of various media on learning and behavior (National Intitute of Mental Health, 1982; Pearl et al., 1982; Rice, Huston, and Wright, 1982). Greenfield (1984) provides an excellent summary of studies that are relevant for special educators. She describes, for example, the differences in language heard on radio and language heard on television. The former is more like written language since the announcer must provide the context, specific vocabulary, and complete sentences whereas language on TV is more fragmented. Greenfield says, however, that television has unique codes for certain time and space concepts that may be difficult for young children and people from other cultures to understand, such as panning and zooming of the camera.

Greenfield (1984) discusses the merits of using word processors and computers and feels that they provide excellent means for editing and interchange, particularly when children work in small groups. Torgesen and Wolf (1986) and Trifiletti et al. (1984) summarize the pros and cons of using microcomputers.

PROGNOSIS AND OUTCOME

Most longitudinal studies, followup investigations, and case reports indicate that learning disabilities are rarely "cured." The problems persist well into adulthood (Miles, 1986; Kline, 1982; Zigmond and Thornton, 1985; Baker, Decker, and DeFries, 1984; Finucci, Gottfredson, and Childs, 1986; Forell and Hood, 1986; Horn, O'Donnell, and Vitulano, 1983; Hoffman et al., 1987). Spreen (1982), in an excellent overview of studies, found that people who were initially thought to have only reading disabilities tended to have problems in most school subjects and in many areas in life. Their disorders interfered with occupations, socialization, and personal affairs. Outcomes are negatively influenced by the presence of even minimal neurological impairments (soft signs). While concerns about delinquency have been expressed, Spreen said that the relationship between such problems and LD have probably been overstated.

Reading disabled people find that their careers are limited and that they may need to enter low-status, low-paying jobs, even though they have excellent mental ability and motivation. Most, however, find employment and can live independently. There are, of course, those whose problems are so severe that they need special living arrangements and considerable supervision at work. Johnson and Blalock (1987) found that adults with low performance and mathematics disorders were often most lacking in vocational opportunities and skills.

According to Spreen (1982), discrepancies in outcomes are probably due, in part, to differences in mental ability. Studies of subjects with low IQ scores (80 and below) tend to yield less optimistic outcomes than those with average or above mental ability (Rawson, 1968). Spreen says, however, that there is no clear relationship between adult reading achievement and intelligence. The fact that there are so many new programs for LD college students attests to the fact that LD students are often motivated to achieve, yet lack the skills for independence in higher education (Cordoni, 1982).

SUMMARY AND RECOMMENDATIONS

On the basis of this review, it is evident there are many needs in the field, none of which are easily solved in a country with a diverse population, where each school system develops its own curriculum. We cherish the freedom to design individual programs of instruction and research, and to generate alternative approaches for education. As a nation, we are, in general, concerned about individuals who, for one reason or another, are unable to profit from the experiences provided in our schools. Hence, we have laws, rules, regulations, and services for those with special needs.

Because of the current concerns in general education as well as in learning disabilities, it is suggested that a National Advisory Council for Research in Learning Disabilities be established. The purpose of such a council would be to integrate findings from the most rigorous research in various disciplines and to offer guidance for future investigations. The purpose would *not* be to promote any particular theory, but to diminish the gaps between research, assessment, and education. These are age-old issues, but given the concerns expressed by parents, educators, and administrators, several approaches and questions might be addressed. If such a council is appointed, it should, like the Research Council on Mathematics include both researchers and practitioners. Depending upon the issues, parents and administrators might also be included.

A major concern is the differentiation of the learning disabled from other underachievers. Plans should be developed for a series of longitudinal studies with comprehensive test batteries. As stated earlier, level of severity should not be the sole criterion for determination of services. Mild, moderate, and severe conditions are observed with all handicaps. Test batteries that include only measures of intelligence and reading or mathematics achievement provide data about only one facet of learning and do not provide sufficient data to examine patterns of errors across many areas of achievement. While research will always be needed in specific areas such as decoding or spelling, poor performance in any one of these is insufficient for identifying subgroups of learning disabilities. Subtypes of reading disabilities are not synonymous with subtypes of learning disabilities (McKinney, 1986; McKinney, Short, and Feagans, 1985).

A comprehensive assessment should include, at a minimum, an evaluation of all areas of potential underachievement specified in the definition. This includes assessment of listening (that is, auditory receptive language); oral expressive language, including word retrieval, syntax, articulation, and language usage; many components of reading, including single words and context, decoding, and comprehension; several facets of writing, including handwriting, spelling, syntax, and discourse; mathematical reasoning and computation; and various aspects of nonverbal behavior related to social perception, such as nonverbal communication and orientation. Without such comprehensive studies, the relationships between one or more areas of achievement may go unrecognized and untreated in special education. Problems in reading, written language, and mathematics, for example, may be related to the same underlying language comprehension disorders. Similarly, visual-spatial disorders that interfere with handwriting may also interfere with mathematics, self-help skills, and many occupations. Yet, unfortunately, each subject matter is often studied separately.

Therefore, it is recommended that other approaches to classification be considered (Keogh, 1986b). Several clinicians, neuropsychologists, and researchers have already begun to identify certain problems that co-occur. It may be beneficial for a research advisory council to select a comprehensive test battery that several people would agree upon, which could be administered to several groups of children in various geographical regions of the country. It is hypothesized that certain patterns of learning and performance would occur irrespective of socioeconomic levels (though other factors may influence the severity). As an analogy, one finds similar linguistic characteristics with Broca's and Wernicke's aphasia whether the adult is in a nursing home or in a private rehabilitation center, or in a rural area or urban area of the United States. While level of severity and type of care might differ, the symptomatology is similar. I would like to suggest that we try to define "prototypical" or "exemplar" cases that have common profiles or patterns of deficits. Most clinicians are aware of at least some types and might collaborate on definition and topology. These, in turn, could be validated more empirically.

Other recommendations include the following:

- A common nomenclature for research and practice should be established. Many studies are difficult to compare because of the varied terminology used across disciplines. Terms such as "perception," "word identification," "phonological coding," and "linguistic awareness" do not always represent the same phenomenon or skill. Therefore, at least for purpose of clarity, investigators should, at the very least, define terms and indicate how a particular skill was measured.

- To close the research, diagnosis, and remediation gap, it may be helpful to have groups of investigators work closely with experts in measurement and test construction to develop more reliable and valid tests. Since many experimental tasks are highly predictive of reading achievement, they should be used more systematically, together with other readiness tests.

- All experimenters should be encouraged to define the attributes of their subjects more specifically. To simply specify intellectual and achievement levels is insufficient, given the other biological, social, and cultural variables that play a role in learning. In many respects, our task as investigators, diagnosticians, and administrators resembles a giant class inclusion exercise in which we are required to identify sets and subsets of learners. Studies should include as much detail as possible about the attributes of both the experimental and the control groups, particularly if generic labels such as "good" and "poor" readers are used. Criteria for both inclusion and exclusion of all subjects should be specified. Control groups drawn from regular classrooms often contain children with a wide range of mental ability and achievement. Therefore, both upper and lower levels of ability and performance should be noted. Data regarding the number of subjects who failed to meet the criteria for an experiment also provide the reader with additional perspectives about the population, tests, and experimental measures used.

- Special emphasis should be given to studies of LD children with different mental age levels. As indicated earlier, gifted children may be eliminated from services if they are not underachieving in relation to grade placement. Investigations of strategy selection and usage would be particularly interesting to explore with children of low average, average, and above average mental ability. Researchers in mathematics have found that gifted students with learning problems make types of errors that are different from the types made by those with less ability. The former abstract principles easily but make computation errors because of carelessness or failure to monitor. It is hypothesized that similar patterns of performance would be noted in written language as well.

- Special emphasis should be given to long-range planning for gifted LD students in order to help them actualize their potential. For example, the School of the Art Institute of Chicago recently employed an LD teacher to help talented students with theory and history courses.

- Future research will be strengthened if investigators provide descriptions of settings from which groups are drawn. Factors such as class size, curriculum, overall makeup of the group, expectancies, type of school and home environment, socioeconomic levels, sex and race, and parents' education and occupation all add to our understanding of learning and learning disabilities.

- To achieve a more replicable body of literature, studies should provide a description of experimental tasks including content, formats, directions, materials, reinforcement, and other pertinent details.

- Attributes of intervention methods also should be specified. There is a tendency for use of overly general terms such as "whole word," "phonics," or "multisensory" to describe certain approaches. Unless one has taught exceptional children, investigators may not realize the problems associated with the word "method." In reading, for example, one needs to define the type of orthography, class of word, type of sentence structure, whether the method is analytic or synthetic, type of content, familiarity of content, type of rule learning (implicit or explicit), mode of input, and forms of response. Terms such as "direct teaching" also tend to be somewhat ambiguous. Information regarding the theoretical rationale, objectives, content, scope, and sequence is needed.

- Long-term, prospective studies of intervention need to be conducted to explore the interaction of biological, social, cultural, and educational variables. Descriptions of service delivery models including parental programs of intervention, preschool programs, special schools, self-contained categorical vs. noncategorical placements, resource rooms, and itinerant programs should be provided. Detailed analyses of multiple variables within the learner and the environment should be made of children who make the most and least progress. Efforts should be made to characterize the type of setting, environment, and stimulation in which learners thrive best.

- The mental health of children, their families, and teachers also require study. Knowing the physical and emotional strains associated with stress, we should try to examine the pressures, placements, and procedures that interfere with the well-being of all concerned. While one cannot avoid certain types and levels of stress, I am concerned about the long-term consequences of multicategorical rooms after interviewing over 200 LD adults. Many found that the rooms with behaviorally disordered and mentally retarded children created environments that were not the best for learning and added to their loss of self-esteem. I also am concerned about stress on teachers in such rooms. The attrition rate of teachers in special education is increasing, not because the teachers are necessarily dissatisfied with their profession but because they are "worn out" from dealing with behavior problems. Some have elected to take lower paying teaching jobs in private centers in order to be able to work with more homogeneous groups of children.

- Studies of types of mental health services for the LD population, particularly at the upper levels, should also be investigated. Informal discussions with adults have revealed that many prefer and have profited from short-term problem-solving approaches in contrast to more dynamic therapy in which they were required to review early childhood memories.

- While I was asked to review reading, written language, and mathematics problems, I would also like to emphasize the need for studying both nonverbal disabilities and generalized conceptual (meaning) disorders. Both types of problems may result in relatively serious social and vocational limitations. Often these individuals have the ability to decode, spell, and compute, but they fail to comprehend the significance of words and symbols. Some, but not all, have very high verbal and low performance IQs. These people are often of great concern to their families because of their inability to take care of their daily needs and to obtain work.

- Now that several good programs of intervention have been developed, there should be videotape libraries for teachers and parents to use. Programs such as those developed by Bradley and Bryant (1985) for linguistic awareness have been well researched. Educators often need to see demonstrations of the procedures in order to fully understand how to use them. Tapes for higher level decoding and reading comprehension approaches also would be beneficial.

- Research on career awareness and vocational rehabilitation should be combined with efforts in business and industry. Our experience with LD adults indicates that the typical paper and pencil aptitude tests provide limited data about problems and modifications that may be needed on the job.

- Every effort should be made to integrate theory and practice. In a new volume on learning disabilities (Vaughn and Bos, 1987), several leaders in the field (including Keogh, McKinney, Torgesen, Kavale, and Lyon) emphasized the importance of theory-based research. Many of the authors in the volume provided excellent recommendations for future research in the field. Theory has also been emphasized by theorists in the fields of reading, written language, and mathematics (Gibson, 1975; Martlew, 1983; Kintsch, 1977; Kintsch and van Dijk, 1978; Resnick and Ford, 1981).

- In order to strengthen both research and practice, Martin (1987) highlights the need for studying policy-related issues. He says that the legislation in P.L.94-142 reflects the most humane and progressive instincts in our society. According to Martin, the law was passed by Congress not because of special interests but because of a genuine need articulated jointly by parents and professionals.

- Finally, all studies related to etiology should be continued. While we will probably always need special education programs, it is far better to direct at least some of the energy toward prevention. Collaborate studies with neurologists, biologists, geneticists, physicians, educators, and others will hopefully add to our understanding of both normal and atypical learning.

BIBLIOGRAPHY

Ackerman, P., Dykman, R., Oglesby, D. (1983). Sex and group differences in reading and attention disordered children with and without hyperkinesis. *Journal of Learning Disabilities*, 16:407-415.

ACLD definition of the condition: Specific learning disabilities (1985). *ACLD Newsbriefs*, No. 158, 1-3.

Adelman, H., Taylor, L. (1983). *Learning disabilities in perspective*. Glenview, IL: Scott, Foresman.

Adler-Grinberg, D., Stark, L. (1978). Eye movements, scanpaths and dyslexia. *American Journal of Optometry and Physiological Optics*, 55:557-570.

Aiken, L. Jr. (1972). Language factors in learning mathematics. *Review of Educational Research*, 42:359-385.

Aiken, L. (1971). Verbal factors in mathematics learning: A review of research. *Journal of Research in Mathematics Education*, 2:304-313.

Aman, M. (1982). Psychotropic drugs in the treatment of reading disorders. In Malatesha, R., Aaron, P. (Eds.), *Reading disorders: Varieties and treatments* (pp. 453-471). New York: Academic Press.

Andersson, K., Richards, H., Hallahan, D. (1980). Piagetian task performance of learning disabled children. *Journal of Learning Disabilities*, 13:501-505.

Ansara, A., Geschwind, N., Galaburda, A., Albert, M., Gartrell, N. (Eds.) (1981). *Sex differences in dyslexia*. Towson, MD: The Orton Dyslexia Society.

Baddeley, A., Ellis, N., Niles, T., Lewis, V. (1982). Developmental and acquired dyslexia: A comparison. *Cognition*, 11:185-199.

Badian, N. (1986). Nonverbal disorders of learning: The reverse of dyslexia? *Annals of Dyslexia*, 36:253-269.

Badian, N. (1984). Can the WPPSI be of aid in identifying young children at risk for reading disability? *Journal of Learning Disabilities*, 17:8-11.

Badian, N. (1983). Dyscalculia and nonverbal disorders of learning. In Myklebust, H. R. (Ed.), *Progress in learning disabilities*: Vol. 5 (pp. 235-264). New York: Grune & Stratton.

Badian, N. (1982). The prediction of good and poor reading before kindergarten entry: A four-year follow-up. *Journal of Special Education*, 16:309-318.

Bailet, L. (1985). *Spelling rule application skills among learning disabled and normal spellers*. Doctoral dissertation, Northwestern University.

Baker, L., Decker, S., DeFries, J. (1984). Cognitive abilities in reading-disabled children: A longitudinal study. *The Journal of Child Psychology and Psychiatry and Allied Disciplines*, 25:111-117.

Bakker, D., Licht, R. (1986). Learning to read: Changing horses in mid-stream. In Pavlidis, G. T., Fisher, D. F. (Eds.), *Dyslexia: Its neuropsychology and treatment* (pp. 87-96). New York: Wiley.

Barakat, M. (1951). A factorial study of mathematical ability. *The British Journal of Psychology* (Statistical Section), 4:137-156.

Battistia, M. (1980). Interrelationships between problem solving ability, right hemisphere processing facility and mathematics learning. *Focus on Learning Problems in Mathematics*, 2:53-60.

Bauer, R. (1977). Short-term memory in learning disabled and nondisabled children. *Bulletin of the Psychonomic Society*, 10:128-130.

Bauer, R. (1979). Memory acquisition and category clustering in learning-disabled children. *Journal of Experimental Child Psychology*, 27:365-382.

Beatty, L., Madden, R., Gardner, E., Karlsen, B. (1976). *The Stanford Diagnostic Mathematics Test*. New York: Harcourt, Brace, Jovanovich.

Beers, J., Henderson, E. (1980). *Developmental and cognitive aspects of learning to spell*. Newark, DE: International Reading Association.

Beilin, H. (1975). Development of the number lexicon and number agreement. In *Studies in the cognitive basis of language development*. New York: Academic Press.

Bender, L. (1956). Research studies from Bellevue Hospital on specific reading disabilities. *Bulletin of the Orton Society*, 7:1-3.

Benton, A. (1961). The fiction of the Gerstmann syndrome. *Journal of Neurology, Neurosurgery, and Psychiatry*, 24:176-181.

Benton, A. (1985). Visual factors in dyslexia: An unresolved issue. In Duane, D. D., Leong, C. K. (Eds.), *Understanding learning disabilities: International and multidisciplinary views* (pp. 87-96). New York: Plenum.

Benton, A., Hutcheon, J., Seymour, E. (1951). Arithmetic ability, finger-localization capacity and right-left discrimination in normal and defective children. *American Journal of Orthopsychiatry*, 21:756-766.

Bereiter, C. (1980). Toward a developmental theory of writing. In Gregg, L., Steinberg, R. (Eds.), *Cognitive processes in writing*. Hillsdale, NJ: Erlbaum.

Berko, M. (1966). Psychological and linguistic implications of brain damage in children. In Mecham, M., Berko, M., Berko, F., Palers, M. (Eds.), *Communication training in childhood brain damage*. Springfield, IL: Charles C. Thomas.

Berliner, D. (1980). Allocated time, engaged time, and academic learning time in elementary school mathematics instruction. *Focus on Learning Problems in Mathematics*, 2:27-40.

Berry, M. (1961). *Berry-Tablott language test: Comprehension of grammar*. Rockford, IL.

Birch, H., Gussow, J. (1970). *Disadvantaged children: Health nutrition and school failure*. New York: Harcourt Brace.

Blalock, J. (1987). Intellectual levels and patterns. In Johnson, D., Blalock, J. (Eds.), *Adults with learning disabilities: Clinical studies* (pp. 47-66). Orlando: Grune & Stratton.

Blank, M. (1985). A word is a word—or is it? In Gray, D. B., Kavanagh, J. F. (Eds.), *Biobehavioral measures of dyslexia* (pp. 261-277). Parkton, MD: York Press.

Boder, E. (1971). Developmental dyslexia: Prevailing diagnostic concepts and a new diagnostic approach. In Myklebust, H. R. (Ed.), *Progress in learning disabilities*: Vol.2 (pp. 293-321). New York: Grune & Stratton.

Boder, E., Jarrico, S. (1982). *The Boder test of reading-spelling patterns*. New York: Grune & Stratton.

Bogdanowicz, M. (1985). Therapeutic care of children with reading and writing difficulties in Poland. In Duane, D. D., Leong, C. K. (Eds.) *Understanding learning disabilities: International and multidisciplinary views* (pp. 263-267). New York: Plenum

Brackbill, Y., McManus, K., Wooward, L. (1985). *Medication in maternity: Infant exposure and maternal information* (Monograph Series No. 2). Ann Arbor: University of Michigan International Academy for Research in Learning Disabilities.

Bradley, L., Bryant, P. (1979). The independence of reading and spelling in backward and normal readers. *Developmental Medicine and Child Neurology*, 21:504-514.

Bradley, L., Bryant, P. (1985). *Rhyme and reason in reading and spelling* (Monograph Series No. 1). Ann Arbor: The University of Michigan International Academy for Research in Learning Disabilities.

Bradley, R., Caldwell, B. (1980). The relation of home environment cognitive competence and IQ among males and females. *Child Development*, 51:1140-1148.

Breitmayer, B., Ramey, C. (1986). Biological nonoptimality and quality of postnatal environment as codeterminants of intellectual development. *Child Development*, 57:1151-1165.

Britton, J., Burgess, T., Martin, N., McLeod, A., Rosen, H. (1975). *The development of writing skills* (pp. 11-18). London: MacMillan Education.

Brown, A., Ferrara, R. (1985). Diagnosing zones of proximal development. In Wertsch, J. W. (Ed.), *Culture, communication, and cognition: Vygotskian perspectives* (pp. 273-305).

Brown, B., Haegerstrom-Portnoy, G., Adams, A., Yingling, D., Galin, D., Herron, J., Marcus, M. (1983). Predictive eye movements do not discriminate between dyslexic and control children. *Neuropsychologia*, 21:121-128.

Brown, C. (1983). *Childhood learning disabilities and prenatal risk: An interdisciplinary data review for health care professionals and parents.* Skillman, NJ: Johnson & Johnson.

Bryan, T., Pearl, R., Donahue, M., Bryan, J., Pflaum, S. (Spring 1983). The Chicago Institute for the study of learning disabilities. *Exceptional Education Quarterly: Research in Learning Disabilities: Summaries of the Institutes,* 4(1):1-22.

Bryant, N., Fayne, H., Gettinger, M. (1980). *"LD efficient" instruction in phonics: Applying sound learning principles to remedial teaching* (Tech. Rep. No. 1). New York: Teachers College Columbia University Research Institute for the Study of Learning Disabilities.

Bryant, P., Bradley, L. (1980). Why children sometimes write words which they do not read. In Frith, U. (Ed.), *Cognitive processes in spelling* (pp. 355-370). New York: Academic Press.

Bryant, P., Bradley, L. (1983). Psychological strategies and the development of reading and writing. In M. Martlew (Ed.), *The psychology of written language* (pp. 163-178). Chichester, England: Wiley.

Bryant, P., Bradley, L. (1980). Why children sometimes write words which they do not read. In Frith, U. (Ed.), *Cognitive processes in spelling.* New York: Academic Press.

Burns, B. (1972). *The effect of self-directed verbal commands on arithmetic performance and activity level of urban hyperactive children.* Unpublished manuscript, Boston College.

Burns, E. (1984). The bivariate normal distribution and the IQ of learning disability samples. *Journal of Learning Disabilities,* 17(5):294-295.

Busch, R. (1980). Predicting first-grade reading achievement. *Learning Disability Quarterly,* 3:38-48.

Buswell, T., John, L. (1926). *Diagnostic studies in arithmetic* (Supplemental Educational Monograph No. 30). Chicago: University of Chicago Press.

Calfee, R. (1982). Cognitive models of reading: Implications for assessment and treatment of reading disability. In Malatesha, R., Aaron, P. (Eds.), *Reading disorders: Varieties and treatments* (pp. 151-176). New York: Academic Press.

Carlisle, J. (1983). Components of training in reading comprehension for middle school students. *Annals of Dyslexia,* 33:187-202.

Caron, A., Caron, R., Glass, P. (1983). Responsiveness to relational information as a measure of cognitive functioning in nonsuspect infants. In Field, T., Sostek, A. (Eds.), *Infants born at risk: Perceptual and physiological processes* (pp. 181-209). New York: Grune & Stratton.

Carroll, J. (1977). Developmental parameters of reading comprehension. In Guthrie, J. (Ed.), *Cognition curriculum and comprehension.* Newark, DE: International Reading Association.

Carroll, J., Chall, J. (Eds.) (1975). *Toward a literate society.* New York: McGraw-Hill.

Catts, H. (1986). Speech production/phonological deficits in reading-disordered children. *Journal of Learning Disabilities,* 19(8):504-508.

Cawley, J. (Ed.) (1985). *Cognitive strategies and mathematics for the learning disabled.* Rockville, MD: Aspen.

Cawley, J., Miller, J. (1986). Selected views on metacognition, arithmetic problem solving, and learning disabilities. *Learning Disabilities Focus,* 2(1):36-48.

Cawley, J., Richstone, E. (1984). Brain, mathematics and learning disability. *Focus on Learning Problems in Mathematics,* 6:13-40.

Cawley, J., Fitzmaurice, A., Shaw, R., Kahn, H., Bates, H. (1979). Word problems: Suggestions and ideas for learning disabled children. *Learning Disability Quarterly,* 2:25-41.

Cawley, J., Miller, J., School, B. (1987). A brief inquiry of arithmetic word-problem-solving among learning disabled secondary students. *Learning Disabilities Focus*, 2(2): 87-93.

Ceci, S. (Ed.) (1986). *Handbook of cognitive social and neuropsychological aspects of learning disabilities.* Hillsdale, NJ: Erlbaum.

Ceci, S., Peters, D. (1980). Dyscalculia and the perceptual deficit hypothesis: A correlational study. *Focus on Learning Problems in Mathematics*, 2:11-14.

Chalfant, J. (1985). Identifying learning disabled students: A summary of the National Task Force Report. *Learning Disabilities Focus*, 1(1):9-21.

Chalfant, J., Scheffelin, M. (1969). *Central processing dysfunctions in children: A review of research.* Bethesda, MD: U.S. Department of Health, Education, and Welfare.

Chall, J. (1983a). *Learning to read: The great debate* (2nd ed.). New York: McGraw Hill.

Chall, J. (1983b). Literacy: Trends and explanations. *Educational Researcher*, 12(9):3-8.

Chase, C., Schmitt, L., Russell, G., Tallal, P., (1984). A new chemotherapeutic investigation: Piracetam effects on dyslexia. *Annals of Dyslexia*, 34:29-48.

Chi, J., Dooling, E., Gilles, F. (1977). Left right asymmetries of the temporal speech areas of the human fetus. *Archives of Neurology*, 34:346-348.

Childs, B., Finucci, J., (1983). Genetics, epidemiology, and specific reading disability. In Rutter, M. (Ed.), *Developmental neuropsychiatry*. New York: Guilford Press.

Clarke-Steward, K. (1973). Interactions between mothers and their young children: Characteristics and consequences. *Monographs of the Society for Research in Child Development*, 38 (6-7, Serial No. 153).

Cohen, C. (1983). *Writers' sense of audience: Certain aspects of writing by sixth grade normal and learning disabled children.* Unpublished doctoral dissertation, Northwestern University.

Cohen, R. (1983). Reading disabled children are aware of their cognitive deficits. *Journal of Learning Disabilities*, 16:286-289.

Cohen, R. (1971). Arithmetic and learning disabilities. In Myklebust, H. R. (Ed.), *Progress in learning disabilities*: Vol. 2. New York: Grune & Stratton.

Cohen, S. (1983). Low birthweight. In Brown, C. C. (Ed.), *Childhood learning disabilities and prenatal risk: An interdisciplinary data review for health care professionals and parents* (pp. 70-78). Skillman, NJ: Johnson & Johnson.

Colligan, R. (1981). Prediction of reading difficulty from parental preschool report: A three-year follow-up. *Learning Disability Quarterly*, 4:31-37.

Coltheart, M., Masterson, J., Byng, S., Prior, M., Riddoch, J. (1983). Surface dyslexia. *Quarterly Journal of Experimental Psychology*, 35A:469-495.

Coltheart, M., Patterson, K., Marshall, J. (Eds.) (1980). *Reading disabilities: The interaction of reading, language, and neuropsychological deficits.* New York: Academic Press.

Condus, M., Marshall, K., Miller, S. (1986). Effects of the keyword mnemonic strategy on vocabulary acquisition and maintenance by learning disabled children. *Journal of Learning Disabilities*, 19(10):609-613.

Connolly, A., Wachtman, W., Pritchett, E. (1971). *Key math diagnostic arithmetic test.* Circle Pines, MN: American Guidance Service.

Connor, F. (1983). Improving school instruction for learning disabled children: The Teachers' College Institute. *Exceptional Education Quarterly: Research in Learning Disabilities: Summaries of the Institutes*, 4(1):23-44.

Cooper, C., Odell, L. (1978). *Research on composing: Points of departure.* Urbana, IL: National Council of Teachers of English.

Copeland, R. (1984). *How children learn mathematics* (4th ed.). New York: Macmillan.

Coppola, R. (1985). Recent developments in neuro-imaging techniques. In Gray, D. B., Kavanagh, J. F. (Eds.), *Biobehavioral measures of dyslexia* (pp. 63-69). Parkton, MD: York Press.

Cordoni, B. (1982). Services for college dyslexics. Malatesha, R., Aaron P. (Eds.), *Reading disorders: Varieties and treatments* (pp. 435-448). New York: Academic Press.

Cornwall, K. (1985). The specific reading difficulty versus dyslexia debate in the United Kingdom. In Duane, D. D., Leong, C. K. (Eds.), *Understanding learning disabilities: International and multidisciplinary views* (pp. 237-244). New York: Plenum.

Creevy, D. (1983). Obstetrical trauma. In Brown, C. C. (Ed.), *Childhood learning disabilities and prenatal risk: An interdisciplinary data review for health care professionals and parents* (pp. 66-70). Skillman, NJ: Johnson & Johnson.

Cromer, F. (1974). Structural models for predicting the difficulty of multiplication problems. *Journal for Research in Mathematics Education,* 5:155-166.

Cromer, R. (1980). Spontaneous spelling by language disordered children. In Frith, U. (Ed.), *Cognitive processes in spelling.* London: Academic Press.

Cruickshank, W. (1985). Learning disabilities: A series of challenges. *Learning Disabilities Focus,* 1(1):5-8.

Cruickshank, W. et al. (1961). *A teaching method for brain-injured and hyperactive children.* Syracuse: Syracuse University Press.

Cullen, J., Boersma, F., Chapman, J. (1981). Characteristics of third-grade learning disabled children. *Learning Disability Quarterly,* 4:224-230.

Dangel, H., Bunch, A., Coopman, M. (1987). Attrition among teachers of learning disabled students. *Learning Disabilities Focus,* 2(2):80-86.

Das, J., Bisanz, G., Mancini, G. (1984). Performance of good and poor readers on cognitive tasks: Changes with development and reading competence. *Journal of Learning Disabilities,* 17:549-554.

Deci, E., Chandler, C. (1986). The importance of motivation for the future of the LD field. *Journal of Learning Disabilities,* 19(10):587-594.

Decker, S., DeFries, J. (1981). Cognitive ability profiles in families with reading disabled children. *Developmental Medicine and Child Neurology,* 23:217-227.

Decker, S., DeFries, J. (1980). Cognitive abilities in families with reading disabled children. *Journal of Learning Disabilities,* 13:517-522.

Decker, S., Vandenberg, S. (1985). Colorado twin study of reading disability. In Gray, D. B., Kavanagh, J. F. (Eds.), *Biobehavioral measures of dyslexia* (pp. 123-135). Parkton, MD: York Press.

DeFries, J. (1985). Colorado reading project. In Gray, D. B., Kavanagh, J. F. (Eds.), *Biobehavioral measures of dyslexia* (pp. 107-122). Parkton, MD: York Press.

DeFries, J., Baker, L. (1983). Colorado Family Reading Study: Longitudinal analyses. *Annals of Dyslexia,* 33:153-162.

DeFries, J., Decker, S. (1982). Genetic aspects of reading disability: A family study. In Malatesha, R., Aaron, P. (Eds.), *Reading disorders: Varieties and treatments* (pp. 255-279). New York: Academic Press.

deGoes, C., Martlew, M. (1983). Young children's approach to literacy. In Martlew, M. (Ed.), *The psychology of written language* (pp. 217-236). Chichester, England: Wiley.

deHirsch, K., Jansky, J., Langford, W. (1966). *Predicting reading failure.* New York: Harper & Row.

Denckla, M. (1985). Issues of overlap and heterogeneity in dyslexia. In Gray, D. B., Kavanagh, J. F. (Eds.), *Biobehavioral measures of dyslexia* (pp. 41-46). Parkton, MD: York Press.

Denckla, M., LeMay, M., Chapman, C. (1985). Few CT scan abnormalities found even in neurologically impaired learning disabled children. *Journal of Learning Disabilities,* 18(3):132-135.

Derr, A. (1985). Conservation and mathematics achievement in the learning disabled child. *Journal of Learning Disabilities,* 18:333-336.

Doehring, D. (1984). Subtyping of reading disorders: Implications for remediation. *Annals of Dyslexia,* 34:205-216.

Doehring, D., Trites, R., Patel, P., Fiedorowicz, C. (1981). *Reading disabilities: The interaction of reading, language, and neuropsychological deficits.* New York: Academic Press.

Doris, J. (1986). Learning disabilities. In Ceci, S. (Ed.), *Handbook of cognitive social and neuropsychological aspects of learning disabilities:* Vol. 1 (pp. 3-54). Hillsdale, NJ: Erlbaum.

Dowdy, C., Crump, D., Welch, M. (1982). Reading flexibility of learning disabled and normal students at three grade levels. *Learning Disability Quarterly* 5:253-263.

Downing, J. (1979). *Reading and reasoning.* New York: Springer-Verlag.

Drach, W., Kleber, E. (1985). Legasthenia in German speaking countries: Concept and research in reading-writing difficulties. In Duane, D. D., Leong, C. K. (Eds.), *Understanding learning disabilities: International and multidisciplinary views* (pp. 245-256). New York: Plenum.

Drake, W. E., Jr. (1968). Clinical and pathological findings in a child with a developmental learning disability. *Journal of Learning Disabilities,* 1:486-502.

Drew, A. (1945). A neurological appraisal of familial congenital word-blindness. *Brain,* 79:440-460.

Duane, D. D. (1986). Neurodiagnostic tools in dyslexic syndromes in children: Pitfalls and proposed comparative study of computed tomography, nuclear magnetic resonance, and brain electrical activity mapping. In Pavlidis, G., Fisher, D. F. (Eds.), *Dyslexia: Its neuropsychology and treatment* (pp. 65-86). New York: Wiley.

Duane, D., Leong, C. (1985). *Understanding learning disabilities: International and multidisciplinary views.* New York: Plenum.

Dudley-Marling, C., Kaufman, N., Tarver, S. (1981). WISC and WISC-R profiles of learning disabled children: A review. *Learning Disability Quarterly* 4:307-319.

Duffy, F., Denckla, M., Bartels, P., Sardini, G., Kiessling, L. (1980). Dyslexia: Automated diagnosis by computerized classification of brain electrical activity. *Annals of Neurology,* 7:421-428.

Dunn, L. (1981). *Peabody picture vocabulary test (Revised).* Circle Pines, MN: American Guidance Service.

Dykman, R., Ackerman, P., Holcomb, P. (1985). Reading disabled and ADD children: Similarities and differences. In Gray, D. B., Kavanagh, J. F. (Eds.), *Biobehavioral measures of dyslexia* (pp. 47-62). Parkton, MD: York Press.

Dyssegaard, B. (1985). The Danish approach to special education. In Duane, D. D., Leong, C. K. (Eds.), *Understanding learning disabilities: International and multidisciplinary views* (pp. 221-228). New York: Plenum.

Earp, N., Tanner, F. (1980). Mathematics and language. *Arithmetic Teacher,* 28:32-34.

Farnham-Diggory, S. (1986). Time, now, for a little serious complexity. In Ceci, S. (Ed.), *Handbook of cognitive social and neuropsychological aspects of learning disabilities:* Vol. 1 (pp. 123-158). Hillsdale, NJ: Erlbaum.

Fennema, E. (1974). Mathematics learning and the sexes: A review. *Journal for Research in Mathematics Education,* 5:126-139.

Ferrara, R., Brown, A., Campione, J. (1986). Children's learning and transfer of inductive reasoning rules: Studies of proximal development. *Child Development,* 57:1087-1099.

Ferreiro, E., Teberosky, A. (1979). *Literacy before schooling.* Portsmouth, NH: Heinemann.

Feshback, S., Adelman, H., Fuller, W. (1975). Early identification of children with high risk of reading failure. *Journal of Learning Disabilities,* 10:639-644.

Feurestein, R. (1979). *The dynamic assessment of retarded performers. The learning potential assessment device, theory, instruments, and techniques.* Baltimore: University Park Press.

Finchman, F. (1979). Conservation and cognitive role-taking ability in learning disabled boys. *Journal of Learning Disabilities* 2:29-44.

Finucci, J. (1985). Approaches to subtype validation using family data. In Gray, D., Kavanagh, J. F. (Eds.), *Biobehavioral measures of dyslexia* (pp. 137-154). Parkton, MD: York Press.

Finucci, J. (1978). Genetic considerations in dyslexia. In Myklebust, H. R. (Ed.), *Progress in learning disabilities:* Vol. 4 (pp. 41-63). New York: Grune & Stratton.

Finucci, J., Gottfredson, L., Childs, B. (1986). A follow-up study of dyslexic boys. *Annals of Dyslexia,* 35:117-136.

Finucci, J., Guthrie, J., Childs, A., Abbey, H., Childs, B. (1976). The genetics of specific reading disability. *Annals of Human Genetics,* 40:1-23.

Fisher, D., Athey, I. (1986). Methodological issues in research with the learning disabled: Establishing true control. In Pavlidis, G., Fisher, D. F. (Eds.), *Dyslexia: Its neuropsychology and treatment* (pp. 23-36). New York: Wiley.

Fisk, J., Rourke, B. (1983). Neuropsychological subtyping of learning-disabled children: History, methods, implications. *Journal of Learning Disabilities,* 16(9):529-531.

Fleischner, J. (1985). Arithmetic instruction for handicapped students in the elementary grades. *Focus on Learning Problems in Mathematics, 7*:26-37.

Fleischner, J., Frank, B. (1979). Visual-spatial ability and mathematics achievement in learning disabled and normal body. *Focus on Learning Problems in Mathematics, 1*:7-22.

Fleischner, J., Garnett, K. (1979). *Arithmetic learning disabilities: A literature review* (Research Review Series 1979-1980, Vol. 4). New York: Columbia University Teachers College Research Institute for the Study of Learning Disabilities.

Fleischner, J., Garnett, K., Shepherd, M. (1980). Proficiency in arithmetic basic fact computation of learning disabled and nondisabled children. *Focus on Learning Problems in Mathematics, 2*(4):47-56.

Fleischner, J., Nuzum, M., Marzola, E. (1987). Devising an instructional program to teach arithmetic problem-solving skills to students with learning disabilities. *Journal of Learning Disabilities, 20*(4):214-217.

Fleischner, J., O'Loughlin, M. (1985). Solving story problems: Implications of research for teaching the learning disabled. In J. Cawley (Ed.), *Cognitive strategies and mathematics for the learning disabled.* Rockville, MD: Aspen.

Flowers, L., Hayes, J. (1980). The dynamics of composing: Making plans and juggling constraints. In Gregg, L., Steinberg, E. (Eds.), *Cognitive processes in writing.* Hillsdale, NJ: Erlbaum.

Forell, E., Hood, J. (1986). A longitudinal study of two groups of children with early reading problems. *Annals of Dyslexia, 35*:97-116.

Forster, F. (1975). Reading epilepsy, musicogenic epilepsy, and related disorders. In Myklebust, H. R. (Ed.), *Progress in learning disabilities:* Vol. 3 (pp. 161-178). New York: Grune & Stratton.

Frederiksen, C., Dominic, J. (Eds.) (1981). *Writing: The nature, development, and teaching of written communication:* Vol. 2. Hillsdale, NJ: Erlbaum.

Friedman, J. (1984). *Classification skills in normally hearing/achieving, oral deaf, and language impaired preschoolers. A study in language and conceptual thought.* Unpublished doctoral dissertation, Northwestern University.

Frith, U. (Ed.) (1980). *Cognitive processes in spelling.* New York: Academic Press.

Frostig, M. (1968). Education for children with learning disabilities. In Myklebust, H. (Ed.), *Progress in learning disabilities:* Vol. 1 (pp. 234-266). New York: Grune & Stratton.

Galaburda, A., Kemper, T. (1979). Cytoarchitectonic abnormalities in developmental dyslexia: A case study. *Annals of Neurology, 6*:94-100.

Galaburda, A. (1986). Animal studies and the neurology of developmental dyslexia. In Pavlidis, G. T., Fisher, D. F. (Eds.), *Dyslexia: Its neuropsychology and treatment* (pp. 39-50). New York: Wiley.

Gallagher, J. (1984). Learning disabilities and the near future. *Journal of Learning Disabilities, 9*:571-572.

Garnett, K., Fleischner, J. (1983). Automatization and basic fact performance of normal and learning disabled children. *Learning Disability Quarterly, 6*(2):223-230.

Garnett, K., Fleischner, J. (1987). Mathematical disabilities. *Pediatric Annals, 16*(2):159-176.

Gerber, M. (1984). Orthographic problem-solving ability of learning disabled and normally-achieving students. *Learning Disability Quarterly, 7*:157-164.

Gerber, M., Hall, R. (1987). Information processing approaches to studying spelling deficiences. *Journal of Learning Disabilities, 20*(1):23-33.

German, D. (1986). *Test of word finding.* Allen, Texas: DLM Teaching Resources.

Gerstmann, J. (1940). Syndrome of finger agnosia, disorientation for right and left, agraphia and acalculia. *Archives of Neurology and Psychiatry, 4*:389.

Geschwind, N. (1985). The biology of dyslexia: The after-dinner speech. In Gray, D. B., Kavanagh, J. F. (Eds.), *Biobehavioral measures of dyslexia* (pp. 1-19). Parkton, MD: York Press.

Geschwind, N. (1985). The biology of dyslexia: The unfinished manuscript. In Gray, D. B., Kavanagh, J. F. (Eds.), *Biobehavioral measures of dyslexia* (pp. 1-19). Parkton, MD: York Press.

Geschwind, N. (1986). Dyslexia, cerebral dominance, autoimmunity, and sex hormones. In Pavlidis, G. T., Fisher, D. F. (Eds.), *Dyslexia: Its neuropsychology and treatment* (pp. 51-64). New York: Wiley.

Gibson, E. (1975). Theory-based research on reading and its implications for instruction. In Carroll, J., Chall, J. (Eds.), *Toward a literate society* (pp. 288-320). New York: McGraw-Hill.

Gibson, E., Levin, H. (1975). *The psychology of reading.* Cambridge, MA: MIT Press.

Gillingham, A., Stillman, G. (1956). *Remedial training for children with specific disability in reading, spelling, and penmanship.* Cambridge, MA: Educators Publishing Service.

Ginsburg, H., Barody, A., Russell, R. (1982). Children's estimation ability in addition and subtraction. *Focus on Learning Problems in Mathematics,* 4:31-46.

Gittleman-Klein, R., Klein, D. (1976). Methylphenidate effects in learning disabilities: Psychometric changes. *Archives of General Psychiatry,* 33:655-669.

Glenn, J. (Ed.) (1978). *The third R: Towards a numerate society.* New York: Harper & Row.

Golinkoff, R. (1975-76). Comprehension in good and poor readers. *Reading Research Quarterly* 4:623-659.

Goodman, K., Goodman, Y. (1977). Reading: A search for miscues. *Harvard Educational Review,* 47(3):317-333.

Goodstein, H. (1981). Error analysis in verbal problem solving. *Topics in Learning and Learning Disabilities,* 1:31-45.

Gough, P. (1972). One second of reading. In Kavanagh, J. F., Mattingly, I. (Eds.), *Language by ear and by eye.* Cambridge, MA: MIT Press.

Gray, D. B., Kavanagh, J. F. (Eds.) (1985). *Biobehavioral measures of dyslexia.* Parkton, MD: York Press.

Gray, D. B., Yaffe, S. (1983). Prenatal drugs. In Brown, C. C. (Ed.), *Childhood learning disabilities and prenatal risk: An interdisciplinary data review for health care professionals and parents* (pp. 45-49). Skillman, NJ: Johnson & Johnson.

Greenfield, P. (1984). *Mind and media.* Cambridge, MA: Harvard University Press.

Gregg, K. (1982). *An investigation of the breakdown in certain aspects of the writing process with college age learning disabled normal and basic writers.* Unpublished doctoral dissertation, Northwestern University.

Gregg, L., Steinberg, R. (Eds.) (1980). *Cognitive processes in writing.* Hillsdale, NJ: Erlbaum.

Greenfield, P. (1984). *Mind and media: The effects of television, video games, and computers.* Cambridge, MA: Harvard University Press.

Groshong, C. (1987). Assessing oral language comprehension: Are picture-vocabulary tests enough? *Learning Disabilities Focus,* 2(2):108-115.

Guerrieri, C. (1979). Predictors of eighth grade mathematics achievement. *Focus on Learning Problems in Mathematics,* 1:69-73.

Guthrie, J. (1973). Reading comprehension and syntactic responses in good and poor readers. *Journal of Educational Psychology,* 65:294-299.

Guttman, E. (1937). Congenital arithmetic disability and acalculia (Henschen). *British Journal of Medical Psychology,* 16:16-35.

Guyer, B., Friedman, M. (1975). Hemispheric processing and cognitive styles in learning-disabled and normal children. *Child Development,* 46:658-668.

Haines, D., Torgesen, J. (1979). The effects of incentives on rehearsal and short-term memory in children with reading problems. *Learning Disability Quarterly,* 2:48-55.

Hall, P., Tomblin, J. (1978). A follow-up study of children with articulation and language disorders. *Journal of Speech and Hearing Disorders,* 43:227-241.

Hallahan, D., Hall, R., Ianna, S., Kneedler, R., Floyd, J., Loper, A., Reeve, R. (1983). Summary of research findings at the University of Virginia Learning Disabilities Research Institute. *Exceptional Education Quarterly: Research in Learning Disabilities: Summaries of the Institutes,* 4(1):95-114.

Hallgren, B. (1950). Specific dyslexia: A clinical and genetic study. *Acta Psychiatrica et Neurologica* (Suppl. 65).

Halliday, M., Hassan, R. (1976). *Cohesion in English.* London, England: Longman.

Hammill, D., Larsen, D. (1981). *Test of written language.* Austin, TX: Pro-Ed.

Hammill, D., Leigh, J., McNutt, G., Larsen, S. (1987). A new definition of learning disabilities. *Journal of Learning Disabilities,* 21(2):109-113.

Hanna, R., Hodges, R., Hanna, J. (1971). *Spelling: Structure and strategies.* Boston: Houghton Mifflin.

Hanshaw, J., Scheiner, A., Moxley, A., Gaev, L., Abel, V., Scheiner, B. (1976). School failure and deafness after "silent" congenital cytomegalovirus infection. *New England Journal of Medicine*, 295:468-470.

Haslam, R., Dalby, J., Johns, R., Rademaker, A. (1981). Cerebral asymmetry in developmental dyslexia. *Archives of Neurology*, 38:679-682.

Haslum, M., Morris, A., Butler, N. (1985). A cohort study of special educational needs in ten-year-olds in the United Kingdom. In Duane, D. D., Leong, C. K. (Eds.), *Understanding learning disabilities: International and multidisciplinary views* (pp. 13-26). New York: Plenum.

Healy, J., Aram, D. (1986). Hyperlexia and dyslexia: A family study. *Annals of Dyslexia*, 36:237-252.

Hedley, C., Baratta, A. (Eds.) (1985). *Contexts of reading*. Norwood, NJ: Ablex.

Hier, D., LeMay, M., Rosenberg, P., Perlo, V. (1978). Developmental dyslexia: Evidence for a subgroup with a reversal of cerebral asymmetry. *Archives of Neurology*, 35:90-92.

Hoff, L. (1985). *An investigation of knowledge of graphemic options for spelling in normal and learning disabled children*. Unpublished dissertation, Northwestern University.

Hoffman, F., Shelson, K., Minskoff, E., Sautter, S., Steidle, E., Baker, D., Bailey, M., Echols, L. (1987). Needs of learning disabled adults. *Journal of Learning Disabilities*, 20(1), 43-52.

Hollander, H. (1986). Learning disability among seriously delinquent youths: A perspective. In Pavlidis, G. T., Fisher, D. F. (Eds.), *Dyslexia: Its neuropsychology and treatment* (pp. 231-245). New York: Wiley.

Horn, W., O'Donnell, J., Vitulano, L. (1983). Long-term follow-up studies of learning-disabled persons. *Journal of Learning Disabilities*, 16(9):542-555.

Hoy, C. (1982). *An investigation of certain components of division with learning disabled and normal sixth-grade boys*. Unpublished doctoral dissertation, Northwestern University.

Hughes, J. (1985). Evaluation of electrophysiological studies on dyslexia. In Gray, D. B., Kavanagh, J. F. (Eds.), *Biobehavioral measures of dyslexia* (pp. 71-86). Parkton, MD: York Press.

Hughes, J. (1982). The electroencephalogram and reading disorders. In Malatesha. R., Aaron. P. (Eds.), *Reading disorders: Varieties and treatments* (pp. 234-253). New York: Academic Press.

Hunt, G. (1985). Math anxiety—where do we go from here? *Focus on Learning Problems in Mathematics*, 7:29-40.

Hunt, K. (1965). *Grammatical structures written at three grade levels*. Urbana, IL: National Council for Teachers of English, Report No. 3.

Hunt, K. (1983). Sentence combining and the teaching of writing. In Martlew, M. (Ed.), *The psychology of written language* (pp. 99-125). Chichester, England: Wiley.

Hunt, K. (1975). Recent measures in syntactic development. In Larson, R. (Ed.), *Children and writing in the elementary school* (pp. 55-69). New York: Oxford.

Hunt, K. (1970). Syntactic maturity in school children and adults. *Monographs of the Society for Research in Child Development*, 35:1-44.

Huttenlocher, R., Huttenlocker, J. (1973). A study of children with hyperlexia. *Neurology*, 23:1107-1116.

Inhelder, B. (1976). Observations on the operational and figurative aspects of thought in dysphasic children. In Morehead, D., Morehead, A. (Eds.), *Normal and deficient child language*. Baltimore: University Park Press.

James, K. (1975). *A study of the conceptual structure of measurement of length in normal and learning disabled children*. Unpublished doctoral dissertation, Northwestern University.

Jansky, J., deHirsch, L. (1972). *Preventing reading failure*. New York: Harper & Row.

Johnson, D. (1987a). Assessment issues in learning disabilities research. In Vaughn, S., Bos, C. (Eds.), *Research in learning disabilities: Issues and future directions*, (pp. 141-149). Boston: College-Hill Press.

Johnson, D. (1987b). Nonverbal learning disabilities. *Pediatric Annals*, 16(2):133-144.

Johnson, D. J. (1986). Remediation for dyslexic adults. In Pavlidis, G. T., Fisher, D. F. (Eds.), *Dyslexia: Its neuropsychology and treatment* (pp. 249-262). New York: Wiley.

Johnson, D., Blalock, J. (Eds.). (1987). *Adults with learning disabilities: Clinical studies.* Orlando: Grune & Stratton.

Johnson, D. J., Blalock, J. (1982). Problems of mathematics in children with language disorders. In Lass, N., McReynolds, L., Northern, J., Yoder, D. (Eds.), *Speech, language, and hearing:* Vol. 2. Philadelphia: Saunders.

Johnson, D. J., Blalock, J., Nesbitt, J. (1978). Adolescents with learning disabilities: Perspectives from an educational clinic. *Learning Disability Quarterly,* 1:24-36.

Johnson, D. J., Hook, P. (1978). Reading disabilities: Problems of rule acquisition and linguistic awareness. In Myklebust, H. R. (Ed.), *Progress in learning disabilities:* Vol. 4 (pp. 205-222). New York: Grune & Stratton.

Johnson, D. J., Myklebust, H. (1967). *Learning disabilities: Educational principles and practices.* New York: Grune & Stratton.

Just, M., Carpenter, P. (1980). A theory of reading: From eye fixations to comprehension. *Psychological Review,* 87:329-354.

Katz, A. (1980). Cognitive arithmetic: Evidence for right hemisphere mediation in an elementary component stage. *Quarterly Journal of Experimental Psychology* 32:69-84.

Kavale, K. (1987). Theoretical quandaries in learning disabilities. In Vaughn, S., Bos, C. (Eds.), *Research in learning disabilities: Issues and future directions* (pp. 19-29). Boston: College-Hill.

Kavale, K., Forness, S. (1985). *The science of learning disabilities.* San Diego: College Hill Press.

Kavanagh, J. F. (Ed.) (1986). *Otitis media and child development.* Parkton, MD: York Press.

Keogh, B. (1986a). Future of the LD field: Research and practice. *Journal of Learning Disabilities,* 19(8):455-460.

Keogh, B. (1986b). A marker system for describing learning-disability samples. In S. Ceci (Ed.), *Handbook of cognitive, social, and neuro-psychological aspects of learning disabilities:* Vol. 1 (pp. 81-94). Hillsdale, NJ: Erlbaum.

Keogh, B., Babbitt, B. (1986). Sampling issues in learning disabilities research: Markers for the study of problems in mathematics. In Pavlidis, G., Fisher, D. (Eds.), *Dyslexia: Its neuropsychology and treatment* (pp. 9-22). New York: Wiley.

Keogh, B., Smith, C. (1970). Early identification of educationally high potential and high risk children. *Journal of School Psychology,* 8:285-290.

Kinsbourne, M. (1986). Models of dyslexia and its subtypes. In Pavlidis, G. T., Fisher, D. F. (Eds.), *Dyslexia: Its neuropsychology and treatment* (pp. 165-180). New York: Wiley.

Kinsbourne, M. (1982). The role of selective attention in reading disability. In Malatesha, R., Aaron, P. (Eds.), *Reading disorders: Varieties and treatments* (pp. 199-214). New York: Academic Press.

Kintsch, W. (1977). On modeling comprehension. *Educational Psychologist,* 14:3-14.

Kintsch, W., van Dijk, T. (1978). Toward a model of text comprehension and production. *Psychological Review,* 85:363-394.

Kirk, S. (1963). Behavioral diagnosis and remediation of learning disabilities. Proceedings, Conference on exploration into the problems of the perceptually handicapped child (First Annual Meeting), 1-7.

Kirk, S. (1987). Intervention research in learning disabilities. In Vaugh, S., Bos, C. (Eds.), *Research in learning disabilities: Issues and future directions* (pp. 173-180). Boston: College-Hill.

Kirk, S. (1986). Redesigning delivery systems for learning disabled students. *Learning Disabilities Focus,* 2(1):4-6.

Kline, C. (1982). Dyslexia in adolescents. In Malatesha, R., Aaron, P. (Eds.), *Reading disorders: Varieties and treatments* (pp. 389-408). New York: Academic Press.

Koorland, M. (1986). Applied behavior analysis and the correction of learning disabilities. In Torgesen, J. K., Wong, B. Y. L. (Eds.), *Psychological and educational perspectives on learning disabilities* (pp. 297-328). Orlando, FL: Academic Press.

Kosc, L. (1974). Developmental dyscalculia. *Journal of Learning Disabilities,* 7:164-177.

Kosc, L. (1981). Neuropsychological implications of diagnosis and treatment of mathematical learning disabilities. *Topics in Learning and Learning Disabilities,* 1:19-30.

LaBerge, D., Samuels, S. (1974). Toward a theory of automatic information processing, *Cognitive Psychology*, 6:293-323.

Larsen, S., Hammill, D. (1976). *Test of written spelling.* Austin, TX: Pro-Ed.

Larsen, S., Trenholme, B., Parker, R. (1978). The effects of syntactic complexity upon arithmetic performance. *Learning Disability Quarterly*, 1:80-85.

Lefton, L., Nagle, R., Johnson, G., Fisher, D. (1979). Eye movement dynamics of good and poor readers: Then and now. *Journal of Reading Behavior*, 11:319-328.

LeMay, M. (1976). Morphological cerebral asymmetries of modern man, fossil man, and nonhuman primate. *Annals of the New York Academy of Sciences*, 280:349-366.

Leong, C. (1986). The role of language awareness in reading proficiency. In Pavlidis, G. T., Fisher, D. F. (Eds.), *Dyslexia: Its neuropsychology and treatment* (pp. 131-148). New York: Wiley.

Lepore, A. (1979). A comparison of computational errors between educable mentally handicapped and learning disability children. *Focus on Learning Problems in Mathematics*, 1:12-33.

Lerner, J. (1985). Learning disabilities: Theories, desists and teaching strategies. Boston: Houghton Mifflin Co.

Lerner, J., Mardell-Czudnowski, C., Goldenberg, D. (1987). *Special education for the early childhood years.* Englewood Cliffs, NJ: Prentice-Hall.

Lesgold, A. (1983). A rationale for computer-based reading instruction. In Wilkenson, A. C. (Ed.), *Classroom Computers and Cognitive Science* (pp. 85-105). New York: Academic Press.

Levi, G., Piredda, M. (1986). Semantic and phonological strategies for anagram construction in dyslexic children. *Journal of Learning Disabilities*, 19:17-22.

Levi, G., Musatti, L., Piredda, M., Sechi, E. (1984). Cognitive and linguistic strategies in children with reading disabilities in an oral storytelling test. *Journal of Learning Disabilities*, 17:406-410.

Levin, J. (1981). Estimation techniques for arithmetic: Everyday math and mathematics instruction. *Educational Studies in Mathematics*, 12:421-434.

Levinson, H. (1981). *A solution to the riddle dyslexia.* New York: Springer-Verlag.

Levy, W. (1979). Dyscalculia: Critical analysis and future directions. *Focus on Learning Problems in Mathematics*, 1:41-52.

Levy, W., Schenck, S. (1981). The interactive effect of arithmetic and various reading formats upon the verbal problem solving performance of learning disabled children. *Focus on Learning Problems in Mathematics*, 3:5-12.

Lewis, M., Bartels. B., Campbell, H., Goldberg, S. (1967). Individual differences in attention: The relation between infants' condition at birth and attention distribution within the first year. *American Journal of Diseases of Children*, 113: 461-465.

Lewis, M., Fox, N. (1985). Issues in infant assessment. In Brown, C. C. (Ed.), *Childhood learning disabilities and prenatal risk: An interdisciplinary data review for health care professionals and parents* (pp. 78-84). Skillman, NJ: Johnson & Johnson.

Liberman, I. (1983). A language-oriented view of reading and its disabilities. In Myklebust, H. R. (Ed.), *Progress in learning disabilities:* Vol. 5 (pp. 81-102). New York: Grune & Stratton.

Liberman, I., Rubin, H., Duques, S., Carlistle, J. (1985). Linguistic abilities and spelling proficiency in kindergarteners and adult poor spellers. In Gray, D. C., Kavanagh, J. F. (Eds.), *Biobehavioral measures of dyslexia* (pp. 163-176). Parkton, MD: York Press.

Licht, B. (1983). Cognitive-motivational factors that contribute to the achievement of learning disabled children. *Journal of Learning Disabilities*, 16(8):483-490.

Lindgren, S., Renzi, E., Richman, L. (1985). Cross-national comparisons of developmental dyslexia in Italy and the United States. *Child Development*, 56:1404-1417.

Litowitz, B. (1981). Developmental issues in written language. *Topics in Language Disorders*, 1:73-89.

Lovett, M. (1984). The search for subtypes of specific reading disability: Reflections from a cognitive perspective. *Annals of Dyslexia*, 34:155-178.

Luria, A. (1966). *Higher cortical functions in man.* New York: Basic Books.

Lyon, G. (1983). Learning-disabled readers: Identification of subgroups. In Myklebust, H. R. (Ed.), *Progress in learning disabilities:* Vol. 5 (pp. 103-134). New York: Grune & Stratton.

Lyon, G., Watson, B. (1981). Empirically derived subgroups of learning disabled readers: Diagnostic characteristics. *Journal of Learning Disabilities,* 14:256-261.

Malatesha, R., Aaron, P. (1982). *Reading disorders: Varieties and treatments.* New York: Academic Press.

Mann, V. (1986). Why some children encounter reading problems: The contribution of difficulties with language processing and phonological sophistication to early reading disability. In Torgesen, J. K., Wong, B. Y. L. (Eds.), *Psychological and educational perspectives on learning disabilities* (pp. 133-159). Orlando, FL: Academic Press.

Mann, V., Liberman, I. (1984). Phonological awareness and verbal short-term memory. *Journal of Learning Disabilities,* 17:592-599.

Mardell, C. (1972). *The prediction of mathematical achievement from measures of cognitive processes.* Unpublished doctoral dissertation, Northwestern University.

Marfo, K., Walker, S., Charles, B. (Eds.) (1986). *Childhood disability in developing countries: Issues in habilitation and special education.* New York: Praeger.

Maria, K., MacGinitie, W. (1982). Reading comprehension disabilities: Knowledge structures and non-accommodating text processing strategies. *Annals of Dyslexia,* 32:33-59.

Marshall, N., Glock, M. (1978-79). Comprehension of connected discourse: A study into the relationships between the structure of text and information recalled. *Reading Research Quarterly,* 14:10-56.

Martin, E. (1987). Learning disabilities and public policy: A role for research workers. In Vaugh, S., Bos, C. (Eds.), *Research in learning disabilities: Issues and future directions* (pp. 203-210). Boston: College-Hill.

Martin, L. (1986). Assessing current theories of cerebral organization. In Ceci, S. (Ed.), *Handbook of cognitive, social, and neuropsychological aspects of learning disabilities:* Vol. 1 (pp. 425-440). Hillsdale, NJ: Erlbaum.

Martlew, M. (Ed.) (1983). *The psychology of written language.* Chichester, England: Wiley.

Matejcek, Z., Sturma, J. (1986). Language structure, dyslexia, and remediation: The Czech perspective. In Pavlidis, G. T., Fisher, D. F. (Eds.), *Dyslexia: Its neuropsychology and treatment* (pp. 203-214). New York: Wiley.

Methany, A., Dolan, A. (1974). A twin study of genetic influence in reading achievement. *Journal of Learning Disabilities,* 7:99-102.

Mattis, S., French, J., Rapin, I. (1975). Dyslexia in children and young adults: Three independent neuropsychological syndromes. *Developmental Medicine and Child Neurology,* 17:150-163.

McConkie, G., Zola, D. (1985). Eye movement techniques in studying differences among developing readers. In Gray, D. B., Kavanagh, J. F. (Eds.), *Biobehavioral measures of dyslexia* (pp. 245-260). Parkton, MD: York Press.

McDermott, P., Watkins, M. (1983). Computerized versus conventional remedial instruction for learning-disabled pupils. *Journal of Special Education,* 17:81-88.

McGinnis, M. (1963). *Aphasic children.* Washington, DC: Alexander Graham Bell Association for the Deaf.

McKeever, W., VanDeventer, A. (1975). Dyslexic adolescents: Evidence of impaired visual and auditory language processing associated with normal lateralization and visual responsibility. *Cortex,* 11:361-378.

McKinney, J. (1984). The search for subtypes of specific learning disability. *Journal of Learning Disabilities,* 17:43-40.

McKinney, J., Short, E., Feagans, L. (1985). Academic consequences of perceptual-linguistic subtypes of learning disabled children. *Learning Disabilities Research,* 1(1):6-17.

McKinney, M. D. (1983). Contributions of the institutes for research on learning disabilities. *Exceptional Education Quarterly,* 4(1):129-144.

McLeod, T., Armstrong, S. (1982). Learning disabilities in mathematics-skill deficits and remedial approaches at the intermediate and secondary level. *Learning Disability Quarterly,* 5(3):305-311.

McLeod, T., Crump, W. (1978). The relationship of visuo-spatial skills and verbal ability to learning disabilities in mathematics. *Journal of Learning Disabilities*, 11:237-241.

Mercer, C., Algozzine, B., Trifiletti, J. (1979). Early identification: An analysis of the research. *Learning Disability Quarterly*, 2:12-24.

Mestre, J., Gerace, W. (1986). The interplay of linguistic factors in mathematical translation tasks. *Focus on Learning Problems in Mathematics*, 8:59-72.

Miles, T. (1983). *Dyslexia: The pattern of difficulties*. Springfield, IL: Charles C. Thomas.

Miles, T. (1986). On the persistence of dyslexic difficulties into adulthood. In Pavlidis, G. T., Fisher, D. F. (Eds.), *Dyslexia: Its neuropsychology and treatment* (pp. 149-164). New York: Wiley.

Millichap, G. (Ed.) (1977). *Learning disabilities and related disorders*. Chicago: Yearbook Medical Publishers, Inc.

Montague, M., Bos, C. (1986). The effect of cognitive strategy training on verbal math problem solving performance of learning disabled adolescents. *Journal of Learning Disabilities*, 19:26-33.

Morris, N., Crump, W. (1982). Syntactic and vocabulary development in the written language of learning disabled and non-learning disabled students at four age levels. *Learning Disability Quarterly*, 5:163-172.

Moses, J. (1984). Neurological analysis of calculation deficits. *Focus on Learning Problems in Mathematics*, 6:1-12.

Myers, P., Hammill, D. (1982). *Learning disabilities: Basic concepts, assessment practices, and instructional strategies*. Austin, TX: Pro-Ed.

Myklebust, H. (1954). *Auditory disorders in children*. New York: Grune & Stratton.

Myklebust, H. (1965). *Development and disorders of written language:* Vol. 1. New York: Grune & Stratton.

Myklebust, H. (1973). *Development and disorders of written language:* Vol. 2. New York: Grune & Stratton.

Myklebust, H., Bannochie, M., Killen, J. (1971). Learning disabilities and cognitive processes. In Myklebust, H. (Ed.), *Progress in learning disabilities:* Vol. 2 (pp. 213-251). New York: Grune & Stratton.

Nahmias, M. (1981). *Inferential listening and reading comprehension of discourse in normal and reading disabled children*. Unpublished doctoral dissertation, Northwestern University.

National Institute of Mental Health (1982). *Television and behavior: Ten years of scientific progress and implications for the eighties* (Vol. 1: Summary Report). Rockville, MD.

National Joint Committee for Learning Disabilities. *Learning disabilities: Issues on definition*. Unpublished manuscript, 1981. (Available from Drake Duane. NJCLD Chairperson, c/o The Orton Dyslexia Society, 8415 Bellona Lane, Towson, MD 21204).

Needleman, H. (1983). Environmental pollutants. In Brown, C. C. (Ed.), *Childhood learning disabilities and prenatal risk: An interdisciplinary data review for health care professionals and parents* (pp. 38-45). Skillman, NJ: Johnson & Johnson.

Nystrand, M. (Ed.) (1982). *What writers know: Language process and structure of written discourse*. New York: Academic Press.

Obrzut, J., Hynd, G. (1983). The neurobiological and neuropsychological foundations of learning disabilities. *Journal of Learning Disabilities*, 16(9):515-520.

O'Loughlin, M., Fleischner, J. (1980). *Story problem solving: Implications of research for teaching children with learning disabilities* (Tech. Rep. No. 12). New York: Columbia University Teachers College, Research Institute for the Study of Learning Disabilities.

Olson, M. (1979). Instructional strategy for the severely gifted. *Focus on Learning Problems in Mathematics*, 1:87-110.

Olson, M. (1973). Laterality differences in tachistoscopic word recognition in normal and delayed readers in elementary school. *Neuropsychologia*, 11:343-350.

Olson, R., Kliegel, R., Davidson, B. (1983). Dyslexic and normal readers' eye movements. *Journal of Experimental Psychology: Human Perception and Performance*, 9:816-825.

Olson, R., Kliegel, R., Davidson, B, Foltz, G. (1984). Individual and developmental differences in reading. In Waller, T. G. (Ed.), *Reading research: Advances in theory and practice*. New York: Academic Press.

Orton, S. (1937). *Reading, writing, and speech problems in children.* New York: Norton.

Owen, F., Adams, P., Forrest, T., Stolz, L., Fisher, S. (1971). Learning disorders in children: Sibling studies. *Monographs of the Society for Research in Child Development, 36:* No. 4.

Pany, D., Jenkins, J., Schreck, J. (1982). Vocabulary instruction: Effects on word knowledge and reading comprehension. *Learning Disability Quarterly,* 5:202-215.

Pavlidis, G. (1981). Sequencing eye movements and the early objective diagnosis of dyslexia. In Pavlidis, G., Miles, T. (Eds.), *Dyslexia research and its applications to education.* Chichester: J. Wiley.

Pavlidis, G. (1986). The role of eye movements in the diagnosis of dyslexia. In Pavlidis, G., Fisher, D. (Eds.), *Dyslexia: Its neuropsychology and treatment* (pp. 97-110). New York: Wiley.

Pavlidis, G., Fisher, D. (Eds.) (1986). *Dyslexia: Its neuropsychology and treatment.* New York: Wiley.

Pearl, D., Bouthilet, L., Lazar, J. (Eds.) (1982). *Television and behavior: Ten years of scientific progress and implications for the eighties* (Vol. 2: Technical Reviews). Rockville, MD: National Institute of Mental Health.

Pearson, P. D. (Ed.) (1984). *Handbook of reading research.* New York: Longman.

Pelham, W. Jr. (1986). The effects of psychostimulant drugs on learning and academic achievement in children with attention-deficit disorders and learning disabilities. In Torgesen, J. K., Wong, B. Y. L. (Eds.), *Psychological and educational perspectives on learning disabilities* (pp. 259-295). Orlando, FL: Academic Press.

Perfetti, C., Goldman, S. (1976). Discourse memory and reading comprehension skill. *Journal of Verbal Learning and Verbal Behavior,* 15:33-42.

Perfetti, C., Hogaboam, T. (1975). The relationship between single word decoding and reading comprehension skill. *Journal of Educational Psychology,* 67:461-469.

Perfetti, C., Lesgold, A. (1977). Discourse comprehension and sources of individual differences. In Just, M., Carpenter, P. (Eds.), *Cognitive processes in comprehension* (pp. 215-237). Hillsdale, NJ: Erlbaum.

Petrauskas, R., Rourke, B. (1979). Identification of subtypes of retarded readers: A neuropsychological multivariate approach. *Journal of Clinical Neuropsychology,* 1:17-37.

Pflaum, S. (1980). The predictability of oral reading behaviors on the comprehension of learning disabled and normal readers. *Journal of Reading Behavior,* 12:231-236.

Pflaum, S., Bryan, T. (1980). Oral reading behaviors in the learning disabled. *Journal of Educational Research,* 73:252-258.

Pflaum, S., Pascarella, E. (1980). Interactive effects of prior reading achievement and training in context on the reading of learning disabled children. *Reading Research Quarterly,* 16:138-158.

Pflaum, S., Pascarella, E., Auer, C., Augustyn, L., Boswick, M. (1982). Differential effects of four comprehension facilitating conditions in LD and normal elementary school readers. *Learning Disability Quarterly,* 5:106-116.

Phelps-Gunn, T., Phelps-Terasaki, D. (1982). *Written language instruction: Theory and instruction.* Rockville, MD: Aspen.

Piotrowski, R., Siegel, D. (1986). The IQ of learning disability samples: A reexamination. *Journal of Learning Disabilities,* 19(8):492-493.

Piper, E., Deshler, D. (1985). Intervention considerations in mathematics for the LD adolescent. *Focus on Learning Problems in Mathematics,* 7:38-51.

Pirozzolo, F. (1979). *The neuropsychology of developmental reading disorders.* New York: Praeger.

Pirozzolo, F., Hansch, E. (1982). The neurobiology of developmental reading disorders. In Malatesha, R., Aaron, P. (Eds.), *Reading disorders: Varieties and treatments* (pp. 215-232). New York: Academic Press.

Pirozzolo, F., Rayner, K., Hynd, G. (1983). The measurement of hemispheric asymmetries in children with developmental reading disabilities. In Hellige, J. B. (Ed.), *Cerebral hemispheric asymmetry: Method, theory, and application.* New York: Praeger.

Polatajko, H. (1985). A critical look at vestibular dysfunction in learning disabled children. *Developmental Medicine and Child Neurology,* 27:283-292.

Poole, M. (1983). Socioeconomic status and written language. In Martlew, M. (Ed.), *The psychology of written language* (pp. 335-375). Chichester, England: Wiley.

Poplin, M., Gray, R., Larsen, S., Banikowski, A., Mehringt, T. (1980). A comparison of components of written-expression abilities in learning disabled and non-learning disabled students at three grade levels. *Learning Disability Quarterly*, 3:46-53.

Poteet, J. (1980). Informal assessment of written expression. *Learning Disability Quarterly*, 3:88-98.

Preston, M., Guthrie, J., Childs, B. (1974). Visual evoked responses (VERs) in normal and disabled readers. *Psychophysiology*, 11:452-457.

Rashotte, C., Torgesen, J. (1985). Repeated reading and reading fluency in learning-disabled children. *Reading Research Quarterly*, 20:180-188.

Rathmell, E. (1978). Using thinking strategies to learn the basic facts. In Suydam, M. (Ed.), *1978 Yearbook of the National Council of Teachers of Mathematics*. Reston, VA: National Council of Teachers of Mathematics.

Rawson, M. (1968). *Developmental language disability: Adult accomplishments of dyslexic boys.* Baltimore: Johns Hopkins Press.

Rawson, M. (1986). Developmental stages and patterns of growth of dyslexic persons. In Pavlidis, G. T., Fisher, D. F. (Eds.), *Dyslexia: Its neuropsychology and treatment* (pp. 3-8). New York: Wiley.

Rayner, K. (1978). Eye movements in reading and information processing. *Psychological Bulletin*, 85:618-660.

Rayner, K. (1983). Eye movements, perceptual span, and reading disability. *Annals of Dyslexia*, 33:163-173. New York: Academic Press.

Rayner, K. (1986). Eye movments and the perceptual span: Evidence for dyslexic typology. In Pavlidis, G. T., Fisher, D. F. (Eds.), *Dyslexia: Its neuropsychology and treatment* (pp. 111-130). New York: Wiley.

Read, C. (1983). Orthography. In Martlew, M. (Ed.), *The psychology of written language* (pp. 143-162). Chichester, England: Wiley.

Reeve, R., Hall, R., Zakreski, R. (1979). The Woodcock-Johnson Tests of Cognitive Ability: Concurrent validity with the WISC-R. *Learning Disability Quarterly*, 2:63-69.

Reichman, J., Healey, W. (1983). Learning disabilities and conductive hearing loss involving otitis media. *Annual Review of Learning Disabilities*, 1:39-45.

Reisman, F., Riley, J. (1979). Teaching mathematics to LD adolescents. *Focus on Learning Problems in Mathematics*, 1:67-73.

Resnick, L., Ford, W. (1981) *The psychology of mathematics for instruction.* Hillsdale, NJ: Erlbaum.

Rice, M., Huston, A., Wright, J. (1982). The forms of television: Effects on children's attention, comprehension, and social behavior. In Pearl, D., Bouthilet, L., Lazar, J. (Eds.), *Television and behavior: Ten years of scientific progress and implications for the eighties*: Vol. 2 (Technical Reviews). Rockville, MD: National Institute of Mental Health.

Richardson, E. (1985). The reliability, validity, and flexibility of the decoding skills test. In Gray, D. B., Kavanagh, J. F. (Eds.), *Biobehavioral measures of dyslexia* (pp. 279-296). Parkton, MD: York Press.

Riedsel, C. (1984). The mathematics learning problems of the gifted and/or talented in mathematics. *Focus on Learning Problems in Mathematics*, 6:81-86.

Rosenberger, P., Hier, D. (1980). Cerebral asymmetry and verbal intellectual deficits. *Annals of Neurology*, 8:300-304.

Rourke, B. (1978). Reading, spelling, arithmetic disabilities: A neuropsychologic perspective. In Myklebust, H. (Ed.), *Progress in learning disabilities*: Vol. 4 (pp. 97-120). New York: Grune & Stratton.

Rourke, B., Finlayson, M. (1978). Neuropsychological significance of variations in patterns of academic performance: Verbal and visual-spatial abilities. *Journal of Abnormal Child Psychology*, 6:121-133.

Rumelhart, D. (1977). Toward an interactive model of reading. In Dornic, S. (Ed.), *Attention and performance*: Vol. 6. Hillsdale, NJ: Erlbaum.

Ryan, E., Weed, K., Short, E. (1986). Cognitive behavior modification: Promoting active self-regulatory learning styles. In Torgesen, J. K., Wong, B. Y. L. (Eds.), *Psychological and educational perspectives on learning disabilities* (pp. 367-397). Orlando, FL: Academic Press.

Salomon, G. (1979). *Interaction of media cognition and learning.* San Francisco: Jossey-Bass.

Sameroff, A. (1979). The etiology of cognitive competence: A systems perspective. In Kersley, R., Sigel, I. E. (Eds.), *Infants at risk: Assessment of cognitive functioning* (pp. 115-151). Hillsdale, NJ: Erlbaum.

Sameroff, A., Chandler, M. (1975). Reproductive risk and the continuum of caretaking casualty. In Horowitz, F. D. (Ed.), *Review of child development research*: Vol. 4 (pp. 187-244). Chicago: University of Chicago Press.

Samuels, S. J. (1987). Information processing abilities and reading. *Journal of Learning Disabilities*, 20(1):18-22.

Sammarco, J. (1984). *Joint problem solving activity in adult-child dyads: A comparative study of language disorders.* Unpublished doctoral dissertation, Northwestern University.

Satz, P., Morris, R., Fletcher, J. (1985). Hypotheses, subtypes, and individual differences in dyslexia: Some reflections. In Gray, D. B., Kavanagh, J. F. (Eds.), *Biobehavioral measures of dyslexia* (pp. 25-40). Parkton, MD: York Press.

Scardamalia, M., Bereiter, C. (1983). The development of evaluative, diagnostic, and remedial capabilities in children's composing. In Martlew, M. (Ed.), *The psychology of written language* (pp. 67-95). Chichester, England: Wiley.

Scheffel, D. (1984). *An investigation of discourse features of mother-child verbal interaction with normal and language impaired children.* Unpublished doctoral dissertation, Northwestern University.

Schumaker, J., Deshler, D., Ellis, E. (1986). Intervention issues related to the education of LD adolescents. In Torgesen, J. K., Wong, B. Y. L. (Eds.), *Psychological and educational perspectives on learning disabilities* (pp. 329-365). Orlando FL: Academic Press.

Schumaker, J., Deshler, D., Alley, G., Warner, M., Denton, P. (1982). Multipass: A learning strategy for improving reading comprehension. *Learning Disability Quarterly*, 5:295-304.

Senf, G. (1986). LD research in sociological and scientific perspective. In Torgesen, J. K., Wong, B. Y. L. (Eds.), *Psychological and educational perspectives on learning disabilities* (pp. 27-53). Orlando, FL: Academic Press.

Sever, J. (1985). Maternal infections. In Brown, C. C. (Ed.), *Childhood learning disabilities and prenatal risk: An interdisciplinary data review for health care professionals and parents* (pp. 31-38). Skillman, NJ: Johnson & Johnson.

Shankweiler, D., Liberman, I. Y. (1972). Misreading: A search for causes. In Kavanagh, J., Mattingly, I. (Eds.), *Language by ear and by eye.* Cambridge, MA: MIT Press.

Sharma, M. (1979). Children at risk for disabilities in mathematics. *Focus on Learning Problems in Mathematics*, 1:63-94.

Sharma, M. (1981). Using word problems to aid language and reading comprehension. *Topics in Learning and Learning Disabilities*, 1:61-71.

Shaughnessy, M. (1977). *Errors and expectations: A guide for the teacher of basic writing.* New York: Oxford University Press.

Shepard, L. (1980). An evaluation of the regression discrepancy method for identifying children with learning disabilities. *Journal of Special Education*, 14:79-80.

Shepherd, M., Frank, T., Solar, R., Gelzheiser, L. (1982 May). *Progress Report.* New York: Columbia University Teachers College Research Institute for the Study of Learning Disabilities.

Shonkoff, J. (1982). Biological and social factors contributing to mild mental retardation. In Heller, K. A., Hohzman, W. H., Messick, S. (Eds.), *Placing children in special education: A strategy for equity* (pp. 133-181). Washington, DC: National Academy Press.

Siegel, L., Heaven, R. (1986). Categorization of learning disabilities. In Ceci, S. (Ed.), *Handbook of cognitive social and neuropsychological aspects of learning disabilities*: Vol. 1 (pp. 95-122). Hillsdale, NJ: Erlbaum.

Silva, P., Chalmers, D., Stewart, I. (1986). Some audiological, psychological, educational and behavioral characteristics of children with bilateral otitis media with effusion: A longitudinal study. *Journal of Learning Disabilities, 19*(3):165-169.

Silva, P., Stewart, I., Kirland, C., Simpson, A. (1985). How impaired are children who experience persistent bilateral otitis media with effusion? In Duane, D. D., Leong, C. K. (Eds.), *Understanding learning disabilities: International and multidisciplinary views* (pp. 27-38). New York: Plenum.

Silver, L. (1985). A review of current and future directions in biomedical research in learning disabilities. In Duane, D. D., Leong, C. K. (Eds.), *Understanding learning disabilities: International and multidisciplinary views* (pp. 39-46). New York: Plenum.

Simner, M. (1982). Printing errors in kindergarten and the prediction of academic performance. *Journal of Learning Disabilities, 15*:155-159.

Smith, C. (1986). The future of the LD field: Intervention approaches. *Journal of Learning Disabilities, 19*(8):461-472.

Smith, F. (1979). Conflicting approaches to reading research and instruction. In Resnick, L., Weaver, P. (Eds.), *Theory and practice of early reading*: Vol. 2. Hillsdale, NJ: Earlbaum.

Smith, M., Rogers, C. (1978). Reliability of standardized assessment instruments when used with learning disabled children. *Learning Disability Quarterly, 1*:23-31.

Smith, S., Goldgar, D., Pennington, B., Kimberling, J., Lubs, H. (1986). Analysis of subtypes of specific reading disability: Genetic and cluster analytic approaches. In Pavlidis, G., Fisher, D. F. (Eds.), *Dyslexia: Its neuropsychology and treatment* (pp. 181-202). New York: Wiley.

Snow, C., Ferguson, C. (Eds.) (1977). *Talking to children: Language input and acquisition.* Cambridge, England: Cambridge University Press.

Spellacy, F., Peter, B. (1978). Dyscalculia and elements of the developmental Gerstmann syndrome in school children. *Cortex, 14*:197-206.

Spiro, R., Myers, A. (1984). Individual differences and underlying cognitive processes. In Pearson, P. D. (Ed.), *Handbook of reading research* (pp. 471-504). New York: Longman.

Spreen, O. (1982). Adult outcome of reading disorders. In Malatesha, R., Aaron, P. (Eds.), *Reading disorders: Varieties and treatments* (pp. 473-498). New York: Academic Press.

Spreen, O., Haff, R. (1986). Empirically derived learning disability subtypes: A replication attempt and longitudinal patterns over 15 years. *Journal of Learning Disabilities, 19*:170-180.

Stahl, S., Fairbanks, M. (1986). Effects of vocabulary instruction. *Review of Educational Research, 56*(1):72-110.

Stanley, G., Smith, G., Howell, E. (1983). Eye-movements and sequential tracking in dyslexic and control children. *British Journal of Psychology, 74*:181-187.

Stanovich, K. (1986). Explaining the variance in reading ability in terms of psychological processes: What have we learned? *Annals of Dyslexia, 35*:67-96.

Stanovich, K. (1980). Toward an interactive-compensatory model of individual differences in the development of reading fluency. *Reading Research Quarterly, 16*:32-71.

Stanovich, K. (1983a). Individual differences in the cognitive processes of reading: I. Word decoding. *Annual Review of Learning Disabilities, 1*:57-65.

Stanovich, K. (1983b). Individual differences in the cognitive processes of reading: I. Text-level processes. *Annual Review of Learning Disabilities, 1*:66-71.

Stein, N., Glenn, C. (1979). An analysis of story comprehension in elementary school children. In Freedle, R. (Ed.), *New directions in discourse processing.* Norwood, NJ: Ablex.

Stevenson, H. (1984). Orthography and reading disabilities. *Journal of Learning Disabilities, 18*(3):132-135.

Stevenson, H., Lee, S., Steigler, J., Lucker, W. (1984). Family variables and reading: A study of mothers of poor and average readers in Japan, Taiwan, and the United States. *Journal of Learning Disabilities, 17*:150-156.

Stone, C. A. (1987). Abstract reasoning and problem solving. In Johnson, D., Blalock, J. (Eds.), *Adults with learning disabilities: Clinical studies* (pp. 67-80). Orlando: Grune & Stratton.

Strauss, A., Lehtinen, L. (1947). *Psychopathology of the brain-injured child.* New York: Grune & Stratton.

Streissguth, A. (1983). Smoking and drinking. In Brown, C. C. (Ed.), *Childhood learning disabilities and prenatal risk: An interdisciplinary data review for health care professionals and parents* (pp. 49-56). Skillman, NJ: Johnson & Johnson.

Sturma, J. (1985). The study of dyslexia in Czechoslovakia. In Duane, D. D., Leong, C. K. (Eds.), *Understanding learning disabilities: International and multidisciplinary views* (pp. 257-262). New York: Plenum.

Sundberg, T. (1982). Fingermath and the learning disabled child. *Focus on Learning Problems in Mathematics,* 4:35-40.

Svien, K., Sherlock, D. (1979). Dyscalculia and dyslexia. *Bulletin of the Orton Society,* 23:269-276.

Swanson, H. (1986). Multiple coding processes in learning-disabled and skilled readers. In Ceci, S. (Ed.), *Handbook of cognitive social and neuropsychological aspects of learning disabilities:* Vol. 1 (pp. 203-228). Hillsdale, NJ: Erlbaum.

Swanson, H. L., Rhine, B. (1985). Strategy transformations in learning disabled children's math performance: Clues to the development of expertise. *Journal of Learning Disabilities,* 18(10):596-603.

Tarnopol, L., Tarnopol, M. (1980). Arithmetic ability in Chinese and Japanese children. *Focus on Learning Problems in Mathematics,* 2:29-48.

Tarnopol, L., Tarnopol, M., Yamaguchi, K. (1984). Arithmetic achievement in three Japanese schools: Lower, middle, and upper socioeconomic. *Focus on Learning Problems in Mathematics,* 6:13-40.

Tarnopol, M., Tarnopol, L. (1979). Brain function and arithmetic disability. *Focus on Learning Problems in Mathematics,* 1:23-40.

Tarver, S., Hallahan, D., Kauffman, J., Ball, D. (1976). Verbal rehearsal and selective attention in children with learning disabilities: A developmental lag. *Journal of Experimental Child Psychology,* 22:375-385.

Taylor, H., Fletcher, J., Satz, P. (1982). Component processes in reading disabilities: Neuropsychological investigation of distinct reading subskill deficits. In Malatesha, R., Aaron, P. (Eds.), *Reading disorders: Varieties and treatments* (pp. 121-147). New York: Academic Press.

Temple, C., Nathan, R., Burris, N. (1982). *The beginnings of writing.* Boston: Allyn & Bacon.

Thatcher, R., Lester, M. (1985). Nutrition, environmental toxins and computerized EEG: A mini-max approach to learning disabilities. *Journal of Learning Disabilities,* 18(2):287-297.

Thomassen, A., Teulings, H.-L. H. (1983). The development of handwriting. In Martlew, M. (Ed.), *The psychology of written language* (pp. 179-213). Chichester, England: Wiley.

Thornton, C. A. (1978). Emphasizing thinking strategies in basic fact instruction. *Journal for Research in Mathematics Education,* 9(3):214-227.

Torgesen, J. (1986). Computer assisted instruction with learning disabled children. In Torgesen, J., Wong, B. Y. L. (Eds.), *Psychological and educational perspectives on learning disabilities* (pp. 417-435). Orlando, FL: Academic Press.

Torgesen, J. (1977). Memorization processes in reading-disabled children. *Journal of Educational Psychology,* 69:571-578.

Torgesen, J. (1986). Using computers to help learning disabled children practice reading: A research-based perspective. *Learning Disabilities Focus,* 1(2):72-81.

Torgesen, J., Dice, C. (1980). Characteristics of research on learning disabilities. *Journal of Learning Disabilities,* 13:531-535.

Torgesen, J., Goldman, T. (1977). Verbal rehearsal and short-term memory in reading disabled children. *Child Development,* 48:56-60.

Torgesen, J., Wolf, N. (1986). Computers and reading instruction: Lessons from the past promise for the future. In Pavlidis, G., Fisher, D. (Eds.), *Dyslexia: Its neuropsychology and treatment* (pp. 279-296). New York: Wiley.

Torgesen, J., Wong, B. Y. L. (Eds.) (1986). *Psychological and educational perspectives on learning disabilities.* Orlando, FL: Academic.

Trifiletti, J., Frith, G., Armstrong, S. (1984). Microcomputers versus resource rooms for LD students: A preliminary investigation of the effects of math skills. *Learning Disability Quarterly*, 7:69-76.

Trout, S. (1973). *A neurological approach to the analysis of written spelling disorders.* Unpublished doctoral dissertation, Northwestern University.

Tyre, C., Young, P. (1985). Action research for dyslexic pupils: Parents as full partners. In Duane, D. D., Leong, C. K. (Eds.), *Understanding learning disabilities: International and multidisciplinary views* (pp. 151-158). New York: Plenum.

Underhill, R. (1986). An introduction to the Research Council. *Focus on Learning Problems in Mathematics*, 8:5-18.

Vaughn, S., Bos, C. (Eds.) (1987). *Research in learning disabilities: Issues and future directions.* Boston: College-Hill Press.

Vellutino, F. (1983). Childhood dyslexia: A language disorder. In Myklebust, H. R. (Ed.), *Progress in learning disbilities*: Vol. 5 (pp. 135-173). New York: Grune & Stratton.

Vellutino, F. (1977). Alternative conceptualizations of dyslexia: Evidence in support of a verbal-deficit hypothesis. *Harvard Educational Review*, 47(3):334-354.

Vellutino, F., Scanlon, D. (1985). Verbal memory in poor and normal readers: Developmental differences in the use of linguistic codes. In Gray, D. B., Kavanagh, J. F. (Eds.), *Biobehavioral measures of dyslexia* (pp. 177-214). Parkton, MD: York.

Venezky, R. (1970). *The structure of English orthography.* The Hague: Monton.

Vogel, S. (1985). Learning disabled college students: Identification, assessment, and outcomes. In Duane, D. D., Leong, C. K. (Eds.), *Understanding learning disabilities: International and multidisciplinary views* (pp. 179-204). New York: Plenum.

Vogel, S. (1986). Syntactic complexity in written expression of college writers. *Annals of Dyslexia*, 35:137-157.

Vogel, S., Moran, M. (1982). Written language disorders in learning disabled college students: A preliminary report. In Cruickshank, W., Lerner, J. (Eds.), *Coming of age*: Vol 3 (The best of ACLD 1982). Syracuse: Syracuse University Press.

Vygotsky, L. (1983). The prehistory of written langue. In Martlew, M. (Ed.), *The psychology of written language* (pp. 279-292). Chichester, England: Wiley.

Wachs, T. (1979). Proximal experience and early cognitive-intellectual development: The physical environment. *Merrill-Palmer Quarterly*, 25:3-41.

Wade, J., Kass, C. (1986). Component deficit and academic remediation of learning disabilities. *Journal of Learning Disabilities*, 19:23-25.

Wagner, R. (1986). Phonological processing abilities and reading implications for disabled readers. *Journal of Learning Disabilities*, 19(10):623-629.

Weaver, P., Dickinson, D. (1979). Story comprehension and recall in dyslexic students. *Bulletin of the Orton Society*, 29:157-171.

Wechlser, D. (1974a). *Manual for the Wechsler Intelligence Scale for Children—Revised.* New York: Psychological Corporation.

Wechsler, D. (1974b). *Wechsler Preschool and Primary Scale of Intelligence—Revised.* New York: Psychological Corporation.

Weinberger, D., Luchins, D., Morihisa, J., Wyatt, R. (1982). Asymmetrical volumes of the right and left frontal and occipital regions of the human brain. *Annals of Neurology*, 11:97-100.

Weiner, E. (1980). The diagnostic evaluation of writing skills (DEWS): Application of DEWS criteria to writing samples. *Learning Disability Quarterly*, 3:54-59.

White, C., Pascarella, E., Pflaum, S. (1981). The effects of sentence construction on the comprehension of learning disabled children. *Journal of Educational Psychology*, 73:697-704.

Wiig, E., Becker-Redding, U., Semel, E. (1983). A cross-cultural, cross-linguistic comparison of language abilities of 7- to 8- and 12- to 13-year-old children with learning disabilities. *Journal of Learning Disabilities*, 16(10):576-585.

Wiig, E., Semel, E. (1976). *Language disabilities in children and adolescents.* Columbus, OH: Charles E. Merrill.

Williams, J. (1986). The role of phonemic analysis in reading. In Torgesen, J., Wong, B. Y. L. (Eds.), *Psychological and educational perspectives on learning disabilities* (pp. 399-416). Orlando, FL: Academic Press.

Williams, J., Taylor, M. (1982). *Factors in the comprehension of expository text in normally achieving and learning-disabled children* (Tech. Rep. No. 18). New York: Research Institute for the Study of Learning Disabilities.

Wilsher, C., Atkins, G., Manfield, P. (1985). Effect of Piracetam on dyslexic's reading ability. *Journal of Learning Disabilities*, 18:19-25.

Wilson, B., Baddeley, A. (1986). Single case methodology and the remediation of dyslexia. In Pavlidis, G., Fisher, D. F. (Eds.), *Dyslexia: Its neuropsychology and treatment* (pp. 263-278). New York: Wiley.

Wing, S., Baddelly, A. (1980). Memory and spelling. In Frith, U. (Ed.), *Cognitive processes in spelling*. New York: Academic Press.

Witelson, S. (1983). Neuroanatomical asymmetry in the human temporal lobes and related psychological characteristics: Final Report. US NINCDS contract number N01-NS-6-2344.

Wong, B. (1980). Activating the inactive learner: Use of questions/prompts to enhance comprehension and retention of implied information in learning disabled children. *Learning Disability Quarterly*, 3:29-37.

Wong, B. (1979). Increasing retention of main ideas through questioning strategies. *Learning Disability Quarterly*, 2:42-47.

Wong, B. (1986). Problems and issues in the definition of learning disabilities. In Torgesen, J. K., Wong, B. (Eds.), *Psychological and educational perspectives on learning disabilities* (pp. 3-26). Orlando, FL: Academic Press.

Wong, B. (1987). Conceptual and methodological issues in interventions with learning disabled children and adolescents. In Vaughn, S., Bos, C. (Eds.), *Research in learning disabilities: Issues and future directions* (pp. 185-196). Boston: College-Hill.

Wong, B., Wilson, M. (1984). Investigating awareness of teaching passage organization in learning disabled children. *Journal of Learning Disabilities*, 17:477-482.

Wood, M., Dunlap, W. (1982). Applications of drill and practice. *Focus on Learning Problems in Mathematics*, 4:15-22.

Woodcock, R. (1978). *Development and standardization of the Woodcock-Johnson Psycho-Educational Battery*. Higham, MA: Teaching Resources Corporation.

Woodcock, R., Johnson, M. (1977). *Psycho-Educational Battery*. New York: Teaching Resources.

Woodcock, R., Johnson, M. (1977). *Woodcock-Johnson Psycho-Educational Battery*. Boston: Teaching Resources Corporation.

Wormach, L. (1980). Sex differences in factorial dimension of verbal logical mathematical and visuospatial ability. *Perceptual and Motor Skills*, 50:445-446.

Yeni-Komshian, G., Isenberg, D., Goldberg, H. (1975). Cerebral dominance and reading disability: Left visual field deficit in poor readers. *Neuropsychologia*, 13:83-94.

Ysseldyke, J. (1983). Current practices in making psychoeducational decisions about learning disabled students. *Annual Review of Learning Disabilities*, 1:31-38.

Ysseldyke, J., Algozzine, B., Regan, R., Potter, M. (1980). Technical adequacy of tests used by professionals in simulated decision making. *Psychology in the Schools*, 17:202-209.

Ysseldyke, J., Algozzine, B., Shinn, M., McGue, M. (1982). Similarities and differences between low achievers and students classified learning disabled. *Journal of Special Education*, 16:73-85.

Ysseldyke, J., Thurlow, M., Graden, J., Wesson, C., Algozzine, B., Deno, S. (1983). Generalizations from five years of research on assessment and decision making: The University of Minnesota Institute. *Exceptional Education Quarterly: Research in Learning Disabilities: Summaries of the Institutes*, 4(1):75-93.

Zigmond, N., Thornton, H. (1985). Follow-up of postsecondary age learning disabled graduates and drop-outs. *Learning Disabilities Research*, 1(1):50-55.

DISCUSSION

Margaret Jo Shepherd

My task is to react to Dr. Johnson's research review within ten minutes. Although the time is short, I have chosen to speak, first, about the purpose of this meeting. As I understand the purpose, we are here to consider the status of scientific knowledge about a group of developmental disorders of childhood.

The title of our program refers to these disorders as "learning disabilities," but the research reviews which we will hear summarized today and tomorrow have different titles. Dr. Johnson's review, for example, is entitled, "Review of Research on Specific Reading, Writing, and Mathematics Disorders."

We have also come together to discuss ways to increase knowledge about these developmental disorders, believing that the more we know, the more likely it will be that we can help. Among us are members of a Government committee, the Interagency Committee on Learning Disabilities. Their task is to prepare a report to Congress which may guide the way public monies for research on these disorders are allocated and spent in the future.

The questions before us today and tomorrow, then, are: What do we know about these developmental disorders? What do we need to learn? How should we go from what we know to what we need to learn? Behind these questions are the lives and futures of many people.

My reactions to Dr. Johnson's review are set in the context of these questions and my understanding of the purpose of the meeting. My reactions take the form of two recommendations. Each is a general, rather than specific, response to Dr. Johnson's review.

First, I believe that the time has come to assign the term "learning disabilities" to historical accounts of research on these developmental disorders. The time has come to recognize that the term "learning disabilities" is, as the textbooks say, a general term which subsumes several more specific concepts about developmental disorders of childhood. I believe that the time has come to reconsider the origin and meaning of the term and to replace it with a taxonomy of those disorders which it subsumes.

Developmental disorders that present during the years when children are in school might be described as "developmental written language disorders" and "developmental arithmetic disorders," or these same disorders might be described as "developmental reading disorder," "developmental writing disorder," and "developmental arithmetic disorder." A taxonomy which lists each academic disorder separately would be consistent with the title of Dr. Johnson's review.

Without endorsing a psychiatric diagnosis of these disorders, I suggest that the taxonomy of specific developmental disorders in *The Revised Third Edition of the Diagnostic and Statistical Manual of Mental Disorders (DSM-III-R)* published by the American Psychiatric Association is a better heuristic for research than the term "learning disabilities." In fact, the format for this meeting is a better heuristic for research than the title of the program for this meeting.

"Learning disabilities" is a seductive term. It implies a diagnosis. The term was, in fact, suggested for the purpose of obtaining needed special education services in the public schools. A term that serves to rally support for special education is not necessarily a diagnosis. Special educators serving emotionally disturbed (should we call them "behaviorally disordered"?) students know this only too well.

When a child is described as "learning disabled," we typically think that we know a lot about that child. When we stop to think about it, though, we are not exactly sure of what we do know. Does "auditory processing deficit" really tell us something? The term "learning disabilities" and other terms associated with it seduce us into thinking that we have knowledge, but that knowledge is often an illusion.

Because it is a term with broad implications, "learning disabilities" also encourages us to look for the cognitive deficit which is at the heart of the learning disability. The upshot of that search over the past twenty years is a plethora of cognitive deficits that are all attributed to children and adolescents described as "learning disabled." Special education and psychology texts lead us to believe that learning disabilities are associated with multiple cognitive deficits. It is surprising, given the cognitive deficits attributed to these children, that we can distinguish them from children who are mentally retarded.

Throughout her review and in her summary, Dr. Johnson urges us to find an integrated perspective on learning disabilities. She urges us to draw generalizations from the research which has been done with children and adolescents described as "learning disabled."

The problem with the research conducted over the past twenty years, however, is that we cannot summarize findings across studies. We cannot summarize, or generalize, from these studies for two reasons. First, we know very little about the characteristics of the subjects who participate in most of the studies. Second, given what we do know about the way children are classified as "learning disabled," we have good reason to believe that the characteristics of the subjects vary from study to study. So, there is a logical argument against drawing general conclusions from research that has been conducted with subjects described as "learning disabled."

The main concern that I have with the term "learning disabilities" is that I believe that it diverts us from conducting the studies which might provide us with answers to some very important questions. There is so much that we need to know, for example, about developmental reading disorder. We need to know whether reading disorder occurs in one form or in many forms. We need to know whether children with a reading disorder always have a spelling and writing disorder also or if these disorders can be disassociated. We need to know much more about the relationship between reading disorder and speaking and listening disorders. We need to know whether reading disorder always co-occurs with some form of oral/aural language disorder or whether there are, in fact, some intelligent children who have difficulty learning to read but otherwise have intact language skills.

The list of "don't know's" could go on and on. The members of the Subcommittee on Specific Developmental Disorders for DSM-IIIR were faced with the sobering task of *creating* information about these disorders. Their creations may or may not be accurate. What, for example, is the age of onset for developmental reading disorder? What is the course for developmental arithmetic disorder?

From what I have heard thus far this morning, my second recommendation may emerge as the major theme of this Conference. The disorders subsumed under the term "learning disabilities" are *developmental* disorders. They emerge over time and affect skills and knowledge which normally developing children acquire over time. Further, the nature of the skill changes over time. A 6-year-old first learning to read does not read as he will 6 months later. Not surprisingly, therefore, the symptoms of these disorders change over time.

To understand these developmental disorders, we will have to watch acquisition and we will have to map change. Watching one child or one group of children grow from 5-years-old to 12-years-old will cause us to think differently about these disorders than we do as a consequence of sampling behavior, at one point in time, from a group of 5-year-olds and a group of 12-year-olds. Until we do careful, longitudinal studies, we will not be able to locate the primary problems and separate them from the problems that are the resultants of primary problems.

At present, in the absence of data from longitudinal studies, we are terribly confused about cause and consequence with these youngsters. We know, for example, that oral vocabulary increases as a result of experience with reading, but we are quite willing to say that a 12-year-old who cannot read also has a vocabulary "deficit" and imply that the deficit is in some way implicated as a cause of the reading disorder.

The experience of reading may have a significant effect on other aspects of language as well. If this is so, language "deficits" identified among 12-year-olds who cannot read may be a consequence rather than a cause of the reading disorder.

These comments about the term "learning disabilities" have been made with reference to research, because that is the agenda for this Conference. There are important issues with regard to services to children, also, but those are very sensitive and complicated issues. Nobody wants to take services away from children who need them.

Those of us who are special educators associate the term "learning disabilities" with Samuel Kirk. Dr. Kirk was my teacher. From him I learned, among many things, that special education can be intelligent as well as caring. I have been troubled by the confusion surrounding the term "learning disabilities" for some time.

When Dr. Kirk came to Teachers College in the spring of 1986, I took the opportunity to talk with him about the term and the confusion surrounding it. In our conversation, he said many things which he has said in public on several occasions over the past twenty years. He talked about his determination to get special education for children who needed but were not receiving it. He talked about his dismay over finding children in classes for the mentally retarded who did not belong there. He recalled listening to a psychologist struggle to explain "dyslexia" to a 12-year-old.

Dr. Kirk spoke, with great feeling, about the need to separate these disorders from implications of brain damage. He talked about children and their families and he talked about hope. And then he said about the term learning disabilities, "I never thought it had the properties of a diagnosis."

DISCUSSION

Isabelle Y. Liberman

We should be grateful to Dr. Doris Johnson for her thoughtful review of the major issues relating to definition, identification, and remediation of learning disabilities and for a remarkably comprehensive summary of what has been learned from research. I am delighted to have the chance to lend my support to many of the recommendations she proposes and to add one or two of my own, particularly in regard to that large and important group of the learning disabled whose special problem is reading.

I have chosen to touch upon two points: the importance of theory-driven research and the need for improvements in the training of teachers in reading instruction.

I would agree with Dr. Johnson that a balanced, broad-spectrum behavioral test battery is a critical ingredient for research in reading disabilities. In practice, however, such test batteries have not been very successful. As Doehring et al. (1981) have suggested, the results of most large-scale studies are ambiguous. In their view, and I would agree, this is because the test batteries used are typically not based on any coherent theory about what functions might or might not be involved in the reading process. The global measures of language, memory, and intelligence that constitute the typical comprehensive battery, even when psychometrically rigorous, have failed because they do not measure the right functions, or else measure them in such a way that the result is possibly influenced by other quite irrelevant factors (Calfee, 1977).

Let us consider some functions that one might want to test in a search for the root causes of reading disability. A little reflection and a modicum of common sense would suggest that problems in reading might have something to do with language since it is a language that is being read. So language would surely be a prime candidate for consideration. But concern with language at the level of the usual clinical divisions of auditory receptive language and oral expressive language is not enough. I would instead consider the problems raised by the orthography, that is, by the particular way in which our alphabetic writing system conveys the language that is being read.

We know that in an alphabetic writing system, the orthography taps into the language at the phonological level—that is, it represents the basic building blocks of language, the consonants and vowels. We also know from research (Liberman, Cooper, Shankweiler, and Studdert-Kennedy, 1967) that in spoken language, consonants are not separate sounds but are combined into consonant-vowel syllables. We might suppose therefore that it might not be immediately apparent to the learner that words have an internal structure of separable units that can be represented by the letter units of the orthography. Tests of this hypothesis have been carried out many times in many different languages in many different countries, and in all the results I know about, the hypothesis has been confirmed. It is indeed difficult for young children (Blachman, 1983; Fox and Routh, 1980; Goldstein, 1976; Helfgott, 1976; Liberman, Shankweiler, Fischer and Carter, 1974; Zifcak, 1981) and, in fact, for illiterate adults (Byrne and Ledez, 1983; Liberman, Rubin, Duques, and Carlisle, 1985; Marcel, 1980; Morais, Cary, Alegria, and Bertelson, 1979) to understand that a word like "bag," which in speech seems to be a single, indivisible monosyllable, has an internal structure of three separate segments that can be represented in print by three different letters. We are not surprised, therefore, to find in study after study around the globe that reading success is strongly associated with the degree to which the child or adult has acquired this understanding of the internal linguistic structure of words, or phonological awareness, as it has been called. To cite only a few studies, there is the work in Belgium by Alegria, Pignot, and Morais (1982); in England by Bradley and Bryant (1983); in Australia by Bryne and Ledez (1983); in the States by Read and Luyter (1985) and Treiman and Baron (1981) as well as by my colleagues and me, Liberman (1973) and Mann and Liberman (1984); in Sweden by Lundberg, Olofsson, and Wall (1980); in Argentina by de Manrique and Gramigna (1984); and in Italy by Cossu, Shankweiler, Liberman, Tola, and Katz (in press).

If this understanding of phonological structure is difficult for the beginner to attain but is nonetheless so critical for reading success, it should not only be assessed but should also be trained where deficient (Liberman and Shankweiler, 1979). The next obvious question to ask is whether it can be trained. Recent research tells us that the analysis of words into their constituent elements can be taught successfully even to very young children (Content, Morais, Alegria, and Bertelson, 1982; Olofsson and Lundberg, 1983), and furthermore that teaching children how to carry out this analysis can markedly improve the reading proficiency of many (Bradley and Bryant, 1983; Vellutino, 1985).

With all this as background, we can now raise a further question: whether the poor reader's inability to analyze words into their constituent elements reflects a general cognitive deficiency in analytic ability, or is, alternatively, specifically linguistic in nature. Procedures for instruction and remediation could, of course, be drastically affected by the answer to that question. The research to date suggests that it may be specifically linguistic. Thus, a recent study (Morais, Cluytens, and Alegria, 1984) has shown that disabled readers aged 6 to 9 were poorer than normal readers in segmenting words into their constituent parts, but performed as well as normal readers in a task that required them to deal in a similarly analytic way not with words but with musical tone sequences. In another study (Pratt, 1985), poor readers in the third grade and in adult education classes both had greater difficulties than normals with three different measures of phonological analysis but not with a nonlanguage analytic task identical in format to one of the two linguistic tasks. Thus it would appear that the deficiency was not due to some general analytic disability, but was specifically language-related.

A comprehensive test battery would need to take into account this question of specificity not only with regard to analytic ability but also with regard to other abilities that have been found to correlate with reading deficiency. For example, many studies agree that short-term memory is deficient in children with reading problems (Shankweiler, Liberman, Mark, Fowler, and Fischer, 1979). We have considered that an efficient memory buffer is required to hold words while the reader (or listener) is making sense of the larger units—phrases and sentences—that the words form. But there again, we can ask whether the underlying difficulty is specifically linguistic or more general. Research to date suggests that the memory problems of poor readers are material-specific—that is, they occur with linguistic tasks but not when the materials to be remembered are outside the linguistic realm—for example, faces, nonsense designs, and spatial arrays (Katz, Shankweiler, and Liberman, 1981; Liberman, Mann, Shankweiler, and Werfelman, 1982). Here again, the designers of a test battery would need to keep this distinction in mind.

In fact, the designers of a test battery would do well to consider not only how language abilities may be related to other cognitive abilities but also how the subsystems of language—the phonological, syntactic, and semantic subsystems—are interrelated. For example, it is known that disabled readers are poor in naming objects and have trouble comprehending complex sentences. Surprisingly, recent results (Katz, in press; Crain and Shankweiler, in press) suggest that their difficulty may be phonological in nature, and not semantic or syntactic, as one might initially have expected. In these cases, difficulties in the phonological component gave rise to problems in other linguistic domains.

Of course, no one would suggest that deficiencies in these rather specific domains of language could possibly be the sole cause of all reading disabilities. But if not all reading disabilities are linguistically based, we must ask: What characterizes those that have other sources? Can their performance be distinguished from that of children whose disability appears to be related to language? Here, comparisons among children with specific reading retardation, attention deficits, hearing loss, arithmetic disabilities, and both high and low IQ will be critical.

I would suggest that we already have sufficient knowledge to guide the development of a test battery that would be useful in these endeavors. Moreover, to effect change, we need not wait for all the answers to come in. As I have intimated earlier, there is a wealth of information from laboratories around the globe that could be put to use in preventing reading disabilities in many children and in remediating the problems of others. Here, we encounter a major roadblock in the form of the inadequate training of teachers. Much of the criticism being leveled at teachers is, in my opinion, unfair. It is unfair because the problem is not with the teachers but with how they are being taught in the schools of education. In the first place, even for the teacher who is being trained to teach in the elementary grades, reading instruction is often squeezed into a one-semester so-called methods course along with mathematics, science, social studies, health education, and I expect lately, morals and sex education. Even when more time is allowed, what we have come to call the ordinary methods of instruction in reading may leave much to be desired.

Teachers of beginning reading, for example, are being trained to teach reading in an alphabetic orthography without ever being taught how an alphabetic orthography represents the language or indeed why it is important for beginning readers to explicitly understand the internal structure of words that the orthography represents. The prospective teachers are not being taught the critical role that this kind of phonological awareness can play in the child's mastery of the alphabetic principle even though its relevance has been confirmed over and over again, as we have seen. In fact, they are all too often provided with an instructional procedure that directs them specifically not to trouble the child with details of how the orthography works. Luckily, many children will pick up the alphabetic principle on their own—that is, they simply begin to discover for themselves the commonalities between similarly spoken and written words. These children turn out to be the ones with strength in phonological awareness.

Unfortunately, the many children with weakness in phonological awareness may never discover on their own how the alphabet works and will simply join the ranks of the millions of functional illiterates with their little stores of memorized words and no strategies for deciphering a new word. (An example would be the man in an adult education class who could recognize the word *photograph* but had no idea of how to decipher the word *peg*.) Some of these children with deficient phonological awareness may eventually be led to discover what they need to know by individualized instruction with a special education teacher. But meanwhile they will have lost precious time for the practice that is essential in the mastery of any skill. I would ask why we should require children to fail before we teach them what they need to know. Why not introduce them to the alphabetic principle at the start of instruction in reading? Indeed, why not introduce teachers to what they need to know to prevent failure?

REFERENCES

Alegria, J., Pignot, E., Morais, J. (1982). Phonetic analysis of speech and memory codes in beginning readers. *Memory & Cognition,* 10:451-456.

Blachman, B. (1983). Are assessing the linguistic factors critical in early reading? *Annals of Dyslexia,* 33:91-109.

Bradley, L., Bryant, P. E. (1983). Categorizing sounds and learning to read—a causal connection. *Nature,* 301:419-421.

Byrne, B., Ledez, J. (1983). Phonological awareness in reading disabled adults. *Australian Journal of Psychology,* 35:185-197.

Calfee, R. C. (1977). Assessment of independent reading skills: Basic research and practical applications. In Reber, A. S., Scarborough, D. L. (Eds.), *Toward a psychology of reading.* Hillsdale, NJ: Erlbaum.

Content, A., Morais, J., Alegria, J., Bertelson, P. (1982). Accelerating the development of phonetic segmentation skills in kindergarteners. *Cahiers de Psychologie Cognitive,* 2:259-269.

Cossu, G., Shankweiler, D., Liberman, I. Y., Tola, G., Katz, L. (in press). Awareness of phonological segments and reading ability in Italian children. *Applied Psycholinguistics.*

Crain, S., Shankweiler, D. (in press). Syntactic complexity and reading acquisition. In Davison, A., Green, G., Herman, G. (Eds.), *Speech in the laboratory, school, and clinic* (pp. 331-375). Cambridge, MA: MIT Press.

Doehring, D., Trites, R., Patel, P. (1981). *Reading disabilities: The interaction of reading, language, and neuropsychological deficits.* New York: Academic Press.

Fox, B., Routh, D. K. (1980). Phonetic analysis and severe reading disability in children. *Journal of Psycholinguistic Research,* 9:115-119.

Goldstein, D. M. (1976). Cognitive-linguistic functioning and learning to read in preschoolers. *Journal of Educational Psychology,* 68:680-688.

Helfgott, J. (1976). Phoneme segmentation and blending skills of kindergarten children: Implications for beginning reading acquisition. *Contemporary Educational Psychology,* 1:157-169.

Katz, R. B. (in press). Phonological deficiencies in children with reading disability: Evidence from an object-naming task. *Cognition.*

Katz, R. B., Shankweiler, D., Liberman, I. Y. (1981). Memory for item order and phonetic recoding in the beginning reader. *Journal of Experimental Child Psychology,* 32:474-484.

Liberman, A. M., Cooper, F. S., Shankweiler, D. P., Studdert-Kennedy, M. (1967). Perception of the speech code. *Psychological Review,* 74:431- 461.

Liberman, I. Y. (1973). Segmentation of the spoken word and reading acquisition. *Bulletin of the Orton Society,* 23:65-77.

Liberman, I. Y., Mann, V., Shankweiler, D., Werfelman, M. (1982). Children's memory: Recurring linguistic and non-linguistic material in relation to reading ability. *Cortex,* 18:367-376.

Liberman, I. Y., Rubin, H., Duques, S. L., Carlisle, J. (1985). Linguistic skills and spelling proficiency in kindergarteners and adult poor spellers. In Gray, D. B., Kavanagh, J. F. (Eds.), *Biobehavioral measures of dyslexia.* Parkton, MD: York Press.

Liberman, I. Y., Shankweiler, D. (1979). Speech, the alphabet, and teaching to read. In Resnick, L. B., Weaver, P. A. (Eds.), *Theory and practice of early reading:* Vol. 2 (pp. 109-134). Hillsdale, NJ: Erlbaum.

Liberman, I. Y., Shankweiler, D., Fischer, F. W., Carter, B. (1974). Explicit syllable and phoneme segmentation in the young child. *Journal of Experimental Child Psychology,* 18:201-212.

Lundberg, I., Olofsson, O., Wall, S. (1980). Reading and spelling skills in the first school years, predicted from phonemic awareness skills in kindergarten. *Scandinavian Journal of Psychology,* 21:159-173.

Mann, V., Liberman, I. Y. (1984). Phonological awareness and verbal short-term memory: Can they presage early reading problems? *Journal of Learning Disabilities,* 17:592-599.

deManrique, A. M. B., Gramigna, S. (1984). La segmentacion fonologica y silabica en ninos de preescolar y primer grado (Phonologic and syllabic segmentation in preschool and first grade children). *Lectura y Vida*, 5:4-13.

Marcal, A. (1980). Phonological awareness and phonological representation: Investigation of a specific spelling problem. In Frith, V. (Ed.), *Cognitive process in spelling* (pp. 373-403). London: Academic Press.

Morais, J., Cary, L., Alegria, J., Bertelson, P. (1979). Does awareness of speech as a sequence of phonemes arise spontaneously? *Cognition*, 7:323-331.

Morais, J., Cluytens, M., Alegria, J. (1984). Segmentation abilities of dyslexics and normal readers. *Perceptual and Motor Skills*, 58:221-22.

Olofsson, O., Lundberg, I. (1983). Can phenomeic awareness be trained in kindergarten? *Scandinavian Journal of Psychology*, 24:35-44.

Pratt, A. (1985). The relationship of linguistic awareness of reading skill in children and adults. Unpublished doctoral dissertation, University of Rhode Island.

Read, C., Luyter, L. (1985). Reading and spelling skills in adults of low literacy. *Remedial and Special Education*, 6(6):43-52.

Shankweiler, D., Liberman, I. Y., Mark, L. S., Fowler, C. A., Fischer, F. W. (1979). The speech code and learning to read. *Journal of Experimental Psychology: Human Learning and Memory*, 5:531-545.

Treiman, R., Baron, J. (1981). Segmental analysis ability: Development and its relation to reading ability. In MacKinnon, G. E., Waller, T. G. (Eds.), *Reading research: Advances in theory and practice: Vol. 3*. New York: Academic Press.

Vellutino, F. (1985). Phonological coding: Phoneme segmentation and code acquisition in poor and normal readers. In Gray, D. B., Kavanagh, J. F. (Eds.), *Biobehavioral measures of dyslexia*. Parkton, MD: York Press.

Zifcak, M. (1981). Phonological awareness and reading acquisition. *Contemporary Educational Psychology*, 6:117-126.

DISCUSSION

Joseph K. Torgesen

Although the basic tone of Dr. Johnson's paper is positive, it contains many reminders that our field is currently in a state of some disarray, in both its scientific and its applied aspects. Her recommendations focus clearly on several things that can be done immediately to improve knowledge and practice in this area. For example, I support strongly her recommendations that call for increased attention to the technical aspects of research and the way it is reported.

I recently wrote a paper with the lengthy title of "Thinking about the future of research in learning disabilities by distinguishing between issues that have answers and those that do not" (Torgesen, in press). Many problems in present research and practice are solvable from present knowledge, but there are others whose solutions are not immediately apparent. We must clearly explicate and work on the first type of problem, and must continue to search for workable solutions to the second. In my view, much of the research on reading, writing, spelling, and mathematics disorders at present is plagued by three areas of ambiguity.

First, we often do not know whether the disabilities we are describing are a cause of academic difficulty or whether they are its result. Recent work from developmental psychology (Siegler, 1983) has documented the pervasive impact that domain-specific content knowledge has on children's ability to perform many kinds of intellectual tasks. Children with poor reading skills obviously do not have the same kind of access to knowledge as children who acquire good reading skills in the early elementary grades. There is good evidence, for example, that lack of reading skills affects the acquisition of vocabulary knowledge (Anderson, Hiebert, Scott, and Wilkenson, 1985), and it almost certainly also affects the development of other language skills and types of general knowledge.

In addition to content knowledge, early reading failure can also affect the acquisition of procedural knowledge required by most complex tasks. For example, poor readers are exposed to an instructional environment different from that of good readers, almost from the beginning of elementary school. Children who easily master the decoding aspects of reading are given much more instruction and practice focused on comprehension of written material than are poor readers (Brown, Palinscar, and Purcell, 1986). As a result of this extra practice and instruction, they become more able to engage in the complex strategies required to comprehend text than do children who have difficulty mastering word reading skills. Thus, it is possible that many of the reading and language comprehension difficulties identified in older poor readers result from lack of instruction and practice in comprehension that is given in school only *after* more basic reading skills are mastered.

Dr. Johnson pointed out the need for more longitudinal research, and I strongly support this recommendation as one important way of dealing with the problems of causal inference in our work.

Another thing that we often do not know in our research is to whom it generalizes. Reviews of research in our field often end up comparing apples to oranges because research samples are selected by so many different criteria. One important problem in this area involves control of general ability level. A key concept in differentiating children with specific learning disabilities from other poor learners is that specific-learning disabled children are supposed to have a specific, isolated intellectual disability in the presence of at least average general learning aptitude. Because the technical methods for controlling general aptitude in past research have been so poor (Crowder, 1984), it is possible that many of the intellectual difficulties thought to be characteristic of children with specific learning disabilities are actually associated with mild but pervasive intellectual deficits in the samples being studied.

Apart from the problem of better IQ controls, which is a problem we clearly know how to do better on, is the issue of which aspects of general ability to control. There are no easily defensible conventions about which aspects of "intelligence" to control when selecting samples of LD children. Do we, for example, equate our samples with normal learners on general measures of both verbal and nonverbal aptitude, or do we require that they show normal intellectual ability in only one of these areas? Of course, whatever decision we make will have a direct impact on what we find in our research. If we control only for nonverbal intelligence, we are very likely to find that our learning disabled sample will show a broad variety of verbal deficits.

One solution to this problem would require that we stop using the unqualified term "learning disabilities" in the title of our research reports. Our subject selection procedures should be openly guided by our particular assumptions about the nature of the abilities we are studying. Thus, we might have some studies of "language-impaired learning disabled children," others of "learning disabled children with average full-scale IQs," or perhaps others of "learning disabled children with above average verbal intelligence." Further, as I suggest in more detail later, we should also refer to our subjects in terms of the major academic task or tasks that they are deficient in rather than as generally learning disabled. In any event, the titles of our research papers and proposals should reflect more clearly that generalization is limited to groups selected by similar criteria.

A final set of things we are often confused about is how to apply our findings toward helping learning disabled children perform better in school. The problem of assessing disabilities in a way that will have useful instructional implications has been with us from the beginnings of our field. However, the recent development of new paradigms in cognitive psychology holds promise for strong advances in this area in the near future.

A brief look at the history of our field provides convincing evidence that much of our difficulty in developing a useful understanding of learning disabilities is due to the fact that we were influenced by psychological theory that was inadequate to understanding performance on complex, real-life tasks such as reading and mathematics. This theory focused on the discovery of mechanisms of learning that were supposed to be independent of context and age. These "general principles" of learning were studied in laboratory tasks that were far removed from the types of tasks required in everyday learning. As a consequence of being influenced by this kind of psychological theory, students of learning disabilities sought to identify general learning abilities, such as auditory or visual processing skill, that could be identified, discussed, and treated independently of reading and mathematics learning contexts (Torgesen, 1986).

However, as Anne Brown and Joseph Campione (1986) have documented in a recent article in the *American Psychologist,* a dramatic alteration in the type of learning theory favored by cognitive psychologists has occurred over the last ten years. Rather than specifying general learning principles that apply across task domains, newer learning theories now attempt to explain the acquisition of knowledge and procedures required on complex, everyday learning tasks. These learning theories are closely tied to a *specific task context,* and they attempt to describe all the procedures and knowledge required to accomplish a given task at different levels of expertise. Brown and Campione suggest that this type of research is paving the way for a breakthrough in the treatment of learning disabilities because "now it is feasible to focus diagnosis on the extent to which a child can operate efficiently with the knowledge required to perform a specific academic task" (p. 1062).

In my judgment, there are two striking examples of effective use of such task-specific learning theories and assessment in recent work on learning disabilities. The first is the work on efficient phonological processing as a precursor to the attainment of effective decoding skills in reading. The identification of phonological processing problems in reading disabled children grew out of a well developed theory of the role of this type of linguistic skill in acquiring beginning reading skills (Liberman, Liberman, Mattingly, and Shankweiler, 1980). It is now apparent that training procedures focusing on such skills can have an important impact on how well children respond to early reading instruction (Wagner and Torgesen, 1987).

The other example of benefits deriving from recent research on reading involves training comprehension skills in poor readers. A series of recent published reports, particularly exemplified in the work of Brown and Palinscar (1987), have shown dramatic improvements in the ability of poor readers to comprehend text after they receive training and practice in the use of more sophisticated comprehension strategies. These instructional procedures were directly derived from research and theory that indicate an important role for consciously directed strategies in comprehending text.

In conclusion, I am optimistic about the future of research and practice in our field, primarily because we are now supported by learning theories that promise to help us bring research and practice together in ways that have not occurred before. Although we are plagued by a number of complex issues affecting the delivery of services to LD children, it is my hope that better, more useful knowledge about learning problems will help us to solve many of them.

REFERENCES

Anderson, R. C., Hiebert, E. H., Scott, J. A., Wilkenson, I. A. G. (1985). *Becoming a nation of readers.* Washington, DC: National Institute of Education.

Brown, A. L., Campione, J. C. (1986). Psychological theory and the study of learning disabilities. *American Psychologist, 14:*1059-1068.

Brown, A. L., Palinscar, A. S. (1987). Reciprocal teaching of comprehension strategies: A natural history of one program for enhancing learning. In Borkowski, J., Day, J. D. (Eds.), *Intelligence and cognition in special children: Comparative studies of giftedness, mental retardation, and learning disabilities.* New York: Ablex.

Brown, A. L., Palinscar, A. S., Purcell, L. (1986). Poor readers: Teach, don't label. In Neisser, U. (Ed.), *The school achievement of minority children: New perspectives.* NJ: Lawrence Erlbaum Assoc.

Crowder, R. G. (1984). Is it just reading? *Developmental Review, 4:*48-61.

Liberman, I. Y., Liberman, A., Mattingly, I. G., Shankweiler, D. (1980). Orthography and the beginning reader. In Kavanagh, J., Venezky, R. (Eds.), *Orthography, reading and dyslexia.* Baltimore, MD: University Press.

Siegler, R. S. (1983). Information processing approaches to development. In Mussen, H. (Ed.), *Charmichael's Manual of child psychology.* New York: John Wiley & Sons, Inc.

Torgesen, J. K. (1986). Learning disabilities theory: Its current state and future prospects. *Journal of Learning Disabilities, 19:*399-407.

Torgesen, J. K. (in press). Thinking about the future by distinguishing between issues that have answers and those that do not. In Vaughn, S., Bos, A. C. (Eds.), *Issues and future directions for research in learning disabilities.* San Diego: College-Hill Press.

Wagner, R. K., Torgesen, J. K. (1987). The nature of phonological processing and its causal role in the acquisition of reading skills. *Psychological Bulletin, 101:*192-212.

PART III: DEVELOPMENTAL LANGUAGE DISORDERS

DEVELOPMENTAL LANGUAGE DISORDERS

Paula Tallal

[AUTHOR'S NOTE: This paper comprises a description of the current research findings on the definition, associated characteristics, diagnosis, prognosis, prevalence, causes, and treatment of developmental language disorders. Each section reviews the current literature and also focuses on future research needs as well as clinical needs as they ultimately relate to issues of prevention. The section on linguistic characteristics and subtypes of language impaired children (deviance or delay), language testing, and cognitive development was contributed by Dr. Susan Curtiss, a developmental psycholinguist at the University of California, Los Angeles. The section reviewing language intervention research was coauthored by three speech research pathologists: Dr. Lesley Olswang and Dr. Catherine Mateer at the University of Washington and Dr. Barbara Bain at the University of Montana. Another speech pathologist, Dr. Christine Sloan, from Halifax, contributed the section on interventions for auditory perceptual and phonological disorders. Several of my students from the neuroscience, psychology, and linguistics programs at the University of California, San Diego, reviewed relevant portions of the literature incorporated in this paper. These include: Sharon Hendricks, Dianne Dukette, Randy Ross, and Tony Mauro. The work of my own laboratory reviewed in this report has been funded by the National Institute of Neurological and Communicative Disorders and Stroke, the National Institute of Mental Health, and the MacArthur Foundation.]

DEFINITION

Language is one of the most complex of all human functions. Normal language development requires the integration of sensory, attentional, perceptual, cognitive, motor, and linguistic functions. When one or more of these functions fails to develop normally, language development may be delayed or disordered. Consequently, global mental retardation, hearing impairment, autism, paralysis, malformation of the vocal apparatus (as in cleft palate), emotional disturbance, and frank neurological dysfunction (such as seizure disorder or brain lesions) are conditions that commonly predispose a child to fail to develop normal language at or near the expected age. Language disorders that arise in the presence of one or more of these predisposing peripheral or central impairments are considered to be resulting symptoms of the more pervasive disorder rather than the primary disorder itself. Children with significant hearing loss, for example, often have resulting language deficiencies; however, such children are not considered to be primarily language impaired. Similarly, language dysfunction can also result from acquired postnatal brain injuries to the areas of the brain that subserve language in the adult. Such language dysfunction is referred to as *acquired aphasia.* Although children with language disorders that are secondary to other primary disorders may share many characteristics associated with children who have primary or specific developmental language disorders, language disorders that are considered secondary are not the focus of this paper.

There are children with seriously compromised language development that cannot be attributed to any of the above-mentioned common causes. These children appear to be developing normally in all areas except language. Early observational descriptions of children with such specific language impairment (LI) focused on their similarity to adult aphasics. The disorders were defined in terms of presumed underlying brain dysfunction or etiology as opposed to linguistic dysfunction (Myklebust, 1954; McGinnis, 1963; de Ajuriaguerra et al., 1976).

Benton (1964) was the first to suggest that there is a distinct clinical syndrome, which he termed developmental aphasia.[1] It is characterized by a child who shows a relatively specific failure of normal language functions in the absence of the factors that often provide the general setting in which failure of language is usually observed: deafness, mental deficiency, motor disability, or severe personality disorder. The failure can manifest itself either as a disability in expressive language only, with near normal receptive language, or as a disability in both

---

[1]The terms developmental aphasia or dysphasia and specific developmental language delay, deficit, disorder, or impairment are used interchangeably in this paper.

receptive and expressive language. Benton further noted that the interrelationship between language disability and articulation disorder is inconsistent. That is, some developmentally aphasic children also demonstrate impaired development of speech articulation whereas others do not.

Though developed almost two decades later, nomenclature of the American Psychiatric Association (DSM-III, 1981) unfortunately adds very little information to the definition of developmental language disorders originally proposed by Benton (1964). Like Benton, the DSM-III divides developmental language disorders into two basic types: the expressive type, which is characterized by a failure to develop vocal expression of language despite relatively intact comprehension of language; and the receptive type, which is characterized by a failure to develop both comprehension and vocal expression of language. Developmental articulation disorder is listed as a separate diagnostic category, distinct from developmental language disorders. An articulation disorder is characterized by a failure to develop consistent articulations of the sounds of speech. Although these are distinct diagnostic categories in the DSM-III, research has demonstrated a complex interrelationship between phonological development (the development of the perception and production of speech sounds) and language development. It is now widely accepted that there are many LI children who have concomitant speech articulation disorders and that there are also LI children who exhibit normal articulation. Conversely, there are children with disordered articulation in the absence of developmental language delay (Aram and Kamhi, 1982; Wolfus et al., 1980).

Even a cursory look at these definitions of specific developmental language disorders clearly demonstrates that they are definitions by exclusion. That is, children are defined as developmentally language impaired on the basis of clinical tests that demonstrate aspects of their development that are not responsible for their language problems. The definition, by default, implies that the disorder is specific to language, and is developmental or congenital rather than acquired.

ASSOCIATED CHARACTERISTICS (INCLUSIONARY CRITERIA)

Although clinical definitions have tended to focus on exclusionary criteria, primarily for the purpose of differential diagnosis, research has focused on developing inclusionary criteria based on investigations demonstrating profiles that are characteristic or associated with developmental language delay. Research in the field has focused on two main approaches: (1) investigating in more detail the receptive and expressive linguistic development of language impaired children (the psycholinguistic approach); and (2) investigating in such children the perceptual, motor, and cognitive mechanisms that are presumed to be prerequisites for normal language development (the neuropsychological approach).

Determining the patterns of language acquisition in LI children has been a major focus of research. The central questions to be answered are: (1) What is the nature of language acquisition in the LI child? (2) Is language acquisition in the LI child merely delayed, or is it deviant as well as delayed? To answer these questions, the grammars of LI children must be characterized with respect to the linguistic representations and grammatical principles embodied in each linguistic component (phonology, morphology, syntax, and semantics), including different levels of grammar (that is, D-structure, S-structure, logical form, phonetic form). In addition, to determine patterns of the acquisition of grammar in the LI child, analyses of the internal changes in their grammar at consecutive stages must be made. Only through such analyses can the nature of language acquisition be ascertained. Such analyses, however, require knowledge of linguistic theory; and for the most part, linguistic theory has not informed the description of language disorders in children. Rather, what has been documented are largely many linguistic phenomena associated with the language development of LI children. Descriptions converge to build a picture where certain phenomena are characteristically associated with language learning in the LI child. These are detailed below.

PHONOLOGY

In phonology, two main questions are addressed: (1) whether LI children are using normal phonological principles in their acquisition; and (2) whether LI children are acquiring the language-particular facts of the target language (in this case, English). Most phonological studies of LI children have been concerned with the second question, and most of them deal with English-specific rules of allophony, phonemic distinctions, and syllable structure.

Numerous studies have examined the phonetic realization of segments and syllables in the speech of LI children (Compton, 1970; Ingram, 1976; Oller, 1973; Campbell and Shriberg, 1982; Shriberg et al., 1986). The consistent conclusion was that LI children demonstrate, on the whole, phonological processes that are nearly identical to those found in the grammars of younger, normal children (syllable and segment simplification and assimilation as reflected by cluster reduction, final consonant deletion, substitution of one stop for another or of stops for spirants). In general, however, these studies are actually concerned with the phonetic specification of segments or segment combinations, and as a result, they indicate that the phonetic processes extant in the speech of LI children are normal. Unfortunately, the studies say little about their phonology—that is, for example, whether LI children are acquiring and making use of the actual phonological rules of adult English. Nonetheless, the studies suggest (albeit indirectly) that in many instances, underlying phonological representations of individual lexical items are normal.

A few studies stand out as exceptions; they address the first question raised above (Camarata and Gandour, 1984; Leonard, 1985; and to a lesser extent, Leonard and Leonard, 1985). Camarata and Gandour are able to show, by utilizing a rather straightforward phonological analysis (in this case, that of examining the distributional facts for the occurrence of certain phonetic segments), that what looks like an aberrant and unprincipled system on the surface reveals an output of a normal phonological rule, one that just does not happen to hold for English. In this case, the important distinction is made between the acquisition of language-particular facts versus what is a possible phonological rule. In the Leonard and Leonard study, the importance is demonstrated of looking at even word-level phonetic context in capturing the rules a child may be using. Although the authors do not appear to appreciate the larger theoretical context into which their findings could be placed (as evidence in support of the theory of consonant-vowel [CV] or skeletal phonology, and as evidence to indicate that LI children, like normal children, appear to know and make use of phonological tiers in their language acquisition), once again they are able to make generalizations about data that, without consideration of contextual phonetic information, could not have been observed. In addition, as with the Camarata and Gandour study, Leonard and Leonard are able to suggest a rule in the child's system that can be motivated phonetically (as is the case with almost all known phonological rules). This suggests that normal underlying phonological principles are at play, even when the language-particular facts have not been mastered. Leonard (1985) proposes a specific mechanism to account for how both LI and young, normal children arrive at distorted productions of target words. Although he does not offer an explanation for phonological disorders themselves, he argues convincingly for strong similarities between LI and much younger normal children in both their surface and underlying lexical phonologies.

While the above data suggest a delay in the phonological acquisition of LI children, an additional and important finding emerging from studies of their phonological development is that early acquired forms persist, or coexist in free variation with later acquired forms, over protracted periods of time (Lorentz, 1972; Edwards and Bernhardt, 1973; Salus and Salus, 1973; and to a lesser extent, Ingram, 1976). As the acquisition of new phonological forms presumably reflects changes in the grammar that should rule out old forms, the coexistence of distinct and competing phonological representations is a phenomenon that potentially marks the phonological development of LI children as deviant. It suggests that LI children may be constructing grammars that tolerate a variance in representations that would be disallowed in the normal course of acquisition. Such grammars might then be the result of abnormal acquisition processes. Free variation of competing forms might, however, reflect specific production difficulties rather than differences in grammar per se, and only an analysis of a variety of phonological phenomena over successive stages in phonological development can help to decide between these possibilities. The situation remains an unexplored and potentially critical area for further investigating the issue of delay versus deviance.

MORPHOLOGY

There are perhaps three primary questions to be addressed in the area of morphology: (1) Do LI children know the principles underlying word formation and acquire normal word-formation rules? (2) Do LI children acquire the word-formation rules of English normally? (3) Does inflectional and other nonlexical morphology bear the same relationship to syntax and phonology in the grammars of LI children as it does in the grammars of normally developing children?

There are few, if any, studies that address the first two questions directly. Most studies in this area have examined the acquisition of specific morphemes and not knowledge of word formation per se. It is striking, however, that no study reports the creation of impossible (in the sense of not allowed by human grammars) word forms by LI children. Moreover, no study reports the use of noun morphology with verbs or vice versa. While English is a less than ideal target language in this regard, given its paucity of bound morphology and the phonetic isomorphism of many of the relevant forms that exist, the data on acquisition of nonlexical morphology in LI children suggest that their grammars embody both normal general principles and correct language-particular rules for word formation. Their use of inflectional morphology also shows consistent and accurate syntactic classification of both roots and inflectional morphemes.

Some work has been done examining the interaction of morphology with phonology in LI children (Smit and Bernthal, 1983; and Camarata and Gandour, 1985). Predictably, there is a clear interplay between the phonetic abilities of LI children and the realization of many morphological inflections. However, there are no data to suggest that morphology and phonology interact in an abnormal way in this population.

Most studies pertaining to acquisition of morphology in LI children have concentrated on the acquisition of specific morphemes, the order in which they are acquired, and the relationship between occurrence of particular morphemes in the speech of LI children and "grammatical stage" as defined by measures of mean length of utterance (MLU). Ingram (1972), Kessler (1975), Johnston and Schery (1976), and Steckol (1976), for example, studied the acquisition of a predefined set of inflectional and free-standing grammatical morphemes about which there are considerable data on normal acquisition. They examined the order in which these morphemes were acquired and the stage (determined by MLU—that is, the mean number of words per sentence) at which they appeared. In each of these studies, LI children appeared to acquire the morphemes in approximately the same order as normal children, but neither their earliest occurrence nor the point of mastery occurred at the same developmental stage as that of normal children. Typically, LI children produced specific morphemes at earlier stages than normal children, but did not control them until later stages. A somewhat more enlightened study (Johnston and Kamhi, 1984) reveals that LI children differ from normals in that the LI children tend to produce constructions requiring the use of more grammatical morphology, but then omit more of these forms in obligatory environments.

These studies, then, suggest that with respect to order of acquisition of nonlexical forms, LI children evidence normal acquisition patterns, but that with respect to the relationship between morphological acquisition and syntactic "stage," LI children may exhibit deviance. Here, as before, informed linguistic analyses are called for. Length of an utterance tells us little about its internal syntactic structure. Although MLU has been widely used as an index of grammatical development, studies of acquisition of languages with considerably richer morphological systems than English demonstrate the inadequacy of such measures rather clearly (e.g., Hyams, 1983; Berman, 1981). Children learning a language with an elaborate morphology such as Hebrew, German, or Italian, for example, use inflectional morphemes even in single-word utterances—that is, utterances with the simplest syntactic structures possible. Johnston and Kamhi also point out the inadequacy of MLU as a measure even when considering only rather superficial syntactic factors. What is needed, then, are studies of the relationship between the acquisition of actual syntactic structures and acquisition of morphology, on the order of studies of normal acquisition (for example, Hyams, 1983, 1986; Klein, 1985). Such analyses will determine whether particular changes in the syntax are systematically linked to concomitant acquisition in morphology (e.g., acquisition of the "finite/infinite" clause distinction linked to acquisition of tense morphology). Only then will we have direct evidence as to whether the acquisition of morphology in LI children is normal or not.

SYNTAX

The central questions about syntax are: (1) Do LI children appear to construct grammars embodying universal syntactic principles? (2) Do LI children show normal acquisition patterns in the instantiation of these principles for English? (3) Do LI children show normal patterns for acquiring English-specific syntactic phenomena?

Studies of syntax rarely address these questions. For the most part, they consist of taxonomic-type investigations of the syntactic forms used by LI children. Menyuk (1964) and Leonard (1972) found that LI children used "normal" noun phrase, auxiliary, and verb phrase (NP, AUX, and

VP) structures as well as structures involving embedded clauses (complements and relatives). Morehead and Ingram (1973) found that LI children on the whole used particular syntactic categories and structures less frequently than normal age-matched peers, but with the same frequency as normals matched for MLU. Johnston and Kamhi (1984) found that LI children typically have difficulties with acquisition of grammatical markers in general.

Very few studies in this area have been guided by syntactic theory. Early exceptions, which undertook to perform early-version transformational grammar analyses on the speech of LI children, found on the whole that LI children produced sentences that involved fewer distinct phrase structure and transformational rules than did normal peers (Morehead and Ingram, 1973; Menyuk, 1964; Lee, 1966). Researchers in this area have failed to utilize more current syntactic theory, however, and syntax perhaps more than any other component of the grammar has been underinvestigated.

Nonetheless, two findings that have emerged are worth noting. Both of them are reported in Lee (1966). She considers, among other things, the fact that LI children frequently produce ungrammatical utterances. First, Lee observes that in many cases, LI children produce ill-formed sentences that result from using semantically appropriate lexical items whose syntactic requirements lie outside their syntactic competence. For example, children may use verbs like "guess" or "think," which require a sentential complement (in most cases) before their grammars can generate sentential complements. This may be a phenomenon that occurs in normal acquisition as well, but the extent to which such potentially problematic asynchronies exist in the grammars of LI children may be abnormal and may provide an important clue regarding the character of grammar building in this population. Lee's second noteworthy observation is that LI children produce ungrammatical utterances consisting of word strings that appear to lack any internal syntactic structure. This raises the disturbing possibility that in at least some instances, long past the earliest stages of "beginning to talk," LI children may be constructing utterances outside the framework of a grammar. Since the examples Lee presents do not appear to be social formulas or other typically automatic or "extragrammatical" utterances, this phenomenon could be a marker of clearly deviant language development.

Since the distinction between children with preschool language impairments and those evidencing school-age developmental dyslexia may be at least partially artificial, one study of adult developmental dyslexics deserves mention here. Kean (1984) conducted a linguistic investigation into the syntactic abilities (judgment, interpretation, and processing) of adults who were dyslexic as children. She found that the adult dyslexics failed to make correct grammaticality judgments for sentences involving construal of pronouns and anaphors, and in addition, incorrectly interpreted sentences involving certain kinds of referential dependencies. In both cases, the sentences causing problems for the dyslexics involved the Binding principles—that is, syntactic constraints governing the interpretation and dependency relations of different classes of noun phrases, such as R-expressions (regular nouns), pronouns, and anaphors (reflexives and reciprocals). What Kean found, therefore, was an anomaly or deficit in a specific aspect of syntactic knowledge. Although only a pilot study, her findings raise very specific questions concerning the syntactic abilities of this and other disordered populations. What is especially important about this work with dyslexic adults is that the generalizations concerning their performance could be made only through Binding Theory, part of current syntactic theory. Other generalizations concerning patterns in the performance of LI children will also be observable and characterizable only through a theory about the knowledge base in question.

Clearly, much more research on the syntax of LI children is called for. The essential questions in this area remain completely unanswered. For the most part, syntax in LI children has been taxonomized, not characterized. This is an unfortunate state of affairs, as an examination of the syntax of LI children may shed the clearest light on whether or not they have specifically linguistic deficits. There is no question, however, that productive research in this area—work that can lead to important generalizations about the syntax of this population— will have to be informed and guided by linguistic theory. Only then can basic questions concerning the LI child's acquisition of even the most fundamental properties of human syntax be addressed.

Some of these questions are currently being studied as part of the San Diego Longitudinal Evaluation of Outcomes of Preschool Impairments in Language, a study funded by the National Institute of Neurological and Communicative Disorders and Stroke (Tallal and Curtiss, 1980-1988). In this study, 100 children with specific developmental language impairments and 60 age- and IQ-matched controls were carefully selected at age 4, based on quantitative inclusionary and exclusionary criteria. These children have been extensively studied longitudinally for 5 years to assess their neuropsychological (sensory, perceptual, motor, cognitive) development as well as their receptive and expressive language (phonological, morphological, semantic, syntactic, and pragmatic) development. The study also includes an additional group of 30 children matched to the "language-age" of the language impaired children at their entry into the study at age 4 years.

Some of the questions being addressed include:

(1) Are LI children deviant or delayed in their language development?

(2) What is the role of nonlinguistic sensory, perceptual, motor, or cognitive deficits in language impairments?

(3) Do preschool impairments in language development predict subsequent intellectual development, academic achievement, and/or social and emotional development?

(4) Are there different profiles or subgroups of language impairment, and if so, do they predict different developmental outcomes?

Preliminary results from this study (hereafter referred to as the San Diego longitudinal study) are reported in appropriate sections of this review.

SEMANTICS

The major questions to be addressed in the area of semantics are: (1) Do LI children acquire a normal lexicon, wherein words are learned, represented, and used in a normal manner; and (2) Do LI children learn to map propositional meanings onto linguistic structures in a normal fashion?

Work on semantics suffers in general from the absence of a coherent theory of semantics or semantics acquisition. Therefore, the work on semantics in children with language disorders has proceeded in much the same fashion as equivalent work on normal language acquisition. Both of the above questions have been addressed, with a concentration on the acquisition of meaning relations between words and, more recently, acquisition of individual lexical items themselves.

Research into the acquisition of meaning relations in LI children has found that such children express the same range of thematic roles as do normal children. Freedman and Carpenter (1976), for example, found no differences between normal and LI children in the semantic roles they encoded in their utterances at the earliest stages of speech. Leonard et al. (1976, 1978) also found no differences in the range of semantic roles expressed between LI children and age-matched normal peers, but did find differences in the frequencies with which specific roles were expressed when age-matched peers were used, with LI children tending to use earliest acquired semantic relations more frequently. These differences disappeared when language-matched peers were used for comparison.

It is difficult to know what to make of these findings. These studies examined only a relatively small set of possible semantic categories, which may have left areas of difference unexplored. Moreover, the set considered may represent semantic primitives or primes—an unlearned, basic set of meaning relations. Evidence from Brown (1973), Bowerman (1973), Greenfield and Smith (1976), and many others studying the earliest stages of language production suggest that this may be the case, since even the youngest and least linguistically developed children in these studies express all of the semantic roles used in the above-mentioned studies of LI children. However, using a more extended set of semantic categories, including those of irrealis, intentionality, causative, obligation, and temporality, Curtiss and Tallal (1985) in the San Diego longitudinal study again found no differences between LI and language-matched normals on the range of categories expressed.

Differences between groups also failed to show up when considering degree of unsemantic or semantically ill-formed propositions.

The expression of multipropositionality has, however, been shown to differentiate between at least some LI and controls matched for language age. Johnston and Kamhi (1984) found that LI children expressed fewer logical propositions per utterance, even while producing utterances that were comparable in length to those of MLU-matched normals. This resulted from the increased use by LI children of simple progressive aspect and greater use of motion verbs whose obligatory arguments can be expressed within a single proposition. In the Curtiss and Tallal study, in contrast, there was a significant difference only between a particular subgroup of LI children and both the other LI children and the age-matched normals, on the extent to which they could express multipropositionality.

Recent studies have also examined the nature of lexical acquisition (Leonard et al., 1982; Chapman et al., 1983; Schwartz and Leonard, 1985; Camarata and Schwartz, 1985). To date, these studies are consistent in their findings. LI children appear to acquire lexical items in a normal manner. What is especially intriguing is the possibility raised by the findings of Leonard et al. (1982) and Chapman et al. (1983) that LI children may also acquire vocabulary at the same rate as normal children. A mismatch between a normal rate of acquisition on the one hand and areas of lexical impairment on the other may give rise to some of the production abnormalities noted in the lexical acquisition patterns of LI children (for example, the concomitant use of early, semantically overextended words alongside semantically more restricted synonyms). This kind of lexical variation, where more advanced or fully specified lexical entries coexist and are used alongside less fully specified entries to express the same meaning, whether or not they arise as a result of a normal rate of lexical acquisition combined with more delayed lexical development in other areas, once again raises the possibility of deviance in the grammar. This, as well as all other areas of semantic representation and use, clearly needs further investigation.

PRAGMATICS

Although not technically part of the grammatical system, a major rule system interfacing with grammatical knowledge is the pragmatic system, the rules governing the use of language in context. In examining the nature of pragmatic function in LI children, the question of whether these children are more globally communicatively impaired can be addressed. In addition, in language development and in mature language use, form and function interact in important ways. It is of specific interest, therefore, to determine if children impaired in the acquisition of linguistic form are also impaired in the social and communicative functions of language.

Questions to be asked in this area include: (1) Do LI children exhibit normal patterns of communication? (2) Are LI children able to use their linguistic knowledge in the service of communication in a normal fashion—that is, do they adequately and appropriately map their linguistic knowledge onto the rules of social discourse?

This area of investigation has grown considerably. Prior to the last decade, the pragmatic abilities of LI children had yet to be explored. In the last decade, however, a multitude of studies have been conducted, but results to date are somewhat inconsistent.

One area that has been examined is conversational participation—that is, the ability to appreciate the reciprocal nature of conversation and to adequately and appropriately play both speaker-initiator and listener-respondent. Bartak et al. (1975) found that, unlike autistic children, LI children were quite skilled in their conversational participation, both as initiators and as respondents. In contrast, Stein (1976), Watson (1977), and Sheppard (1980) found that LI children show somewhat restricted conversational participation, relying more heavily than other children on back channel (e.g., nonverbal) devices. These findings indicate a lower degree of responsiveness and assertiveness in conversational interactions. Fey et al. (1981), Jacobs (1981), Prelock et al. (1981), Van Kleeck and Frankel (1981), Fey (1981), and Fey and Leonard (1984), supporting the early study by Bartak et al., found that LI children do not exhibit deficits in conversational participation, especially when compared with children who are somewhat comparable linguistically. These latter studies reveal the importance of not confounding linguistic-pragmatic factors with factors such as age, cognitive maturity, and personality. They also point to the importance of separating the ability to perform certain pragmatic acts from the linguistic means with which those acts are performed. A more restricted range of linguistic devices for performing conversational acts may be expected in children who have linguistic deficits. They do not, in themselves, however, indicate pragmatic deficits. Curtiss and Tallal's (1985) findings from the San Diego longitudinal study support this contention. They found that the range of pragmatic acts children display in a conversational dyad can be extensive and comparable across LI and language-matched normals. They also found that the degree of conversational initiative that LI children display may depend on their particular performance strengths and weaknesses. This finding somewhat complicates matters. Different expressive-receptive performance profiles were associated with different degrees of conversational initiative, which, it appears, may be more related to linguistic facility in handling particular situational contexts or tasks than to linguistic maturity per se. Moreover, this study suggests that pragmatic performance may change quite dramatically over time.

A second area of pragmatic function that has been investigated is the ability to regulate discourse—that is, the ability to provide feedback regarding a partner's communicative effectiveness. Watson (1977) found that LI children request clarification less often than normal children. In contrast, Fey (1981) and Griffin (1979) report that LI children request clarification as often as normals and use the same types of devices to do so. Most studies in this area (see Stein, 1976; Hoar, 1977; Gale et al., 1981), however, report that LI children are less versatile in the means by which they request clarification, consistently relying on the already given structure of the interlocuter's utterance to do so. These latter findings again point out the difference between linguistic limitations and pragmatic ones.

A third area of pragmatics has been speech act range—that is, the set of functions that utterances are intended to serve. In general, findings in this area mirror those found in other pragmatic areas studied. When linguistic abilities are not considered (Geller and Wollner, 1976), LI children may appear to be deficient compared to normal children. However, when linguistic and other potentially confounding factors are noted, no such deficits are found (Fey et al., 1978; Ball and Cross, 1981; Snyder, 1978; Curtiss and Tallal, 1985), although a more restricted set of linguistic means to express intention or function is again often noted.

Another pragmatic ability which, when investigated, has led to inconsistent results, is the ability to "code switch"—that is, the ability to produce stylistic variations to suit the social situation. Fey and Leonard (1984) report that LI children failed to simplify their speech when talking to younger children. Shatz and Gelman (1973) and Sachs and Davin (1976), however, found that many young normal children also fail to make stylistic adjustments when talking to adults or babies. In contrast, Fey (1981), Fey et al. (1981), and Messick and Newhoff (1979) found that LI children appropriately modify their speech to the age and status of their conversational partners.

The bulk of the evidence on pragmatic function seems to indicate that LI children are not globally, communicatively impaired. Specific task factors may give rise to the appearance of pragmatic deficits, but no pragmatic dysfunctions have consistently been demonstrated. As knowledge of pragmatic ability in the normal population increases, however, new areas to investigate are revealed. It may yet be the case that LI children will be shown to have pragmatic deficits in addition to deficits in other areas already known to exist.

The studies of LI children detailed above reveal the important distinction between the mastery of rules of grammar on the one hand and the use or performance of this knowledge on the other. LI children differ from normal children and from each other in their ability to map their linguistic knowledge onto pragmatic acts. This distinction between linguistic knowledge and use is one that may be of major importance in characterizing the impairments that LI children display, as is made clear in considering the issue of linguistic subgroups.

One finding that consistently arises in studies of LI children is that not all LI children perform similarly. Three subgroups are widely recognized, including: some LI children who comprehend significantly more than they produce (expressively impaired); some who speak remarkably well, given how poorly they perform on tests of comprehension (receptively impaired); and some who seem significantly impaired across the board, regardless of task or performance domain.

Although the three performance profiles referred to above define hallmark characteristics of LI children, key questions regarding the subgrouping of this population remain unanswered. For example, do LI children also fall into subgroups based upon nonlinguistic performance factors? (See Wilson, 1986, for a review of this area.) Are the classical subgroupings of LI children meaningful linguistically—that is, are the performance characteristics peculiar to each of these subgroups generalizable along grammatical lines? Are performance strengths and weaknesses, which define subgroup membership, consistent over time—that is, are such subgroupings meaningful clinically? (See Rapin and Allen, 1983, for a review of this area.)

Attempts to define subgroups along linguistic dimensions have recently been made (Aram and Nation, 1975; Wolfus et al., 1980). Such studies report a number of distinct patterns of linguistic abilities that distinguish among LI children and consequently suggest ways to define subgroups based on more detailed characteristics of performance. Results of some of these studies, however, are in conflict with each other. In the Wolfus study, for example, semantic performance did not correlate significantly with phonological ability, whereas the two areas did correlate significantly in the Aram and Nation study. Other results, though not conflicting, are difficult to interpret. In both studies, for example, syntactic production did not correlate significantly with semantic ability, but semantic and syntactic ability did correlate when receptive syntax was the relevant measure. Furthermore, both studies defined subgroups by performance mode deficits, yet the specific constellation of linguistic abilities correlating with these subgroups differed substantially in the two studies.

As part of the San Diego longitudinal study, these questions pertaining to subgroupings are being investigated. Data from its first two years yield some surprising answers (Curtiss and Tallal, 1985). In this study, LI children were classified into four subgroups based on their standardized test performance at the time they were selected into the study: (1) *receptively impaired:* those whose expressive language age exceeded their receptive language age by a minimum of 4 months; (2) *expressively impaired:* those whose receptive language age exceeded their expressive language age by at least 6 months but was within 1 year of their chronological age; (3) *severely impaired:* those whose expressive and receptive language ages were both more than 1 year below their chronological age; and (4) *mildly impaired:* those whose expressive and receptive language ages only when averaged together placed the child more than 1 year below the child's chronological age. All of the groups were compared each year longitudinally on their ability to comprehend and produce several different clusters of linguistic structures, each of which shared a particular linguistic structure or principle. There were two noteworthy results. First, the pattern of performance across clusters was the same for all of the subgroups. Even more interesting, however, subgroup 2 (the expressively impaired group) outperformed subgroup 1 on every cluster, regardless of the structural linguistic parameters involved. The quantitatively, but not qualitatively, different result obtained suggests that the impairment (or set of impairments) of both groups may be somewhat task-dependent and may lie principally in an area other than linguistic knowledge per se, since the linguistic signal has the same properties regardless of which performance channels it must pass through. A major difference between these two groups, then, may be that subgroup 2's performance is enhanced or at least unimpeded by certain parameters of structured tasks, whereas subgroup 1's performance is compromised in the same circumstances. Second analyses point to the same conclusion.

In a second set of analyses, Tallal and Curtiss performed detailed linguistic and conversational analyses of free speech data from 30 of the LI children and 30 language-matched normals. The 30 LI children represented 10 children from each of the first three subgroups. First, detailed pragmatic analysis was performed. The only significant difference found between subgroups was that in year 1 of the study, subgroup 1 (receptively impaired) showed significantly more conversational initiative than the other subgroups and the normal children. Aside from this difference, however, the three subgroups in the first two years of the study did not differ significantly from each other, either in pattern or in level of communicative performance, across the numerous parameters evaluated. Second, in evaluating semantic performance, the use and appropriateness of 24 separate semantic roles or structures and semantic ability were examined. Despite the numerous opportunities for differences to be noted, only one significant difference between groups emerged. Subgroup 1 produced significantly more multipropositional utterances than subgroup 2. This was true in the first-year (4-year-old) and second-year (5-year-old) children in the study. Regarding syntactic performance, once again a rich variety of parameters was examined. At year 1 of the study, significant differences between subgroups were noted. Subgroup 2 used a significantly smaller range of syntactic structures than the other three groups, and subgroups 2 and 3 demonstrated significantly poorer control of syntactically complex structures and produced a significantly higher percentage of ungrammatical morphological and syntactic structures. By year 2 of the study, however, there were no longer significant differences between subgroups. Importantly, these results demonstrate that test performances that showed large expressive language differences between the different subgroups of 4-year-old LI children did not translate into significant differences in syntactic, semantic, or communicative performance in spontaneous speech by age 5. Moreover, even during the first year of the study, few differences between subgroups emerged, except in the area of syntax. These results again suggest that something other than knowledge of the linguistic system per se may be what is differentiating LI children so consistently into subgroups on the basis of standardized test performance. In support of this interpretation is the fact that production of specific linguistic structures was successful (well-formed) on one production task (sentence completion, for example) but unsuccessful (ill-formed or omitted) on another (spontaneous speech). Such differences appear to be related directly to the capacity to handle task-specific features—that is, to couple linguistic knowledge with particular nonlinguistic requirements. Furthermore, although some children succeeded more often with sentence completion than on spontaneous speech, while others performed in the opposite pattern, children within the same subgroup generally appeared to perform similarly. These results are consistent with the hypothesis that the classical subgroupings of LI children relate to psycholinguistic and neuropsychological impairments in this population rather than to factors pertaining to their acquisition of linguistic knowledge. These unexpected data, implicating neuropsychological rather than linguistic deficits as the potential basis of these classically recognized subgroups of LI children, make it imperative that we take even more seriously hypotheses that characterize LI children as having neuropsychological rather than primary linguistic deficits.

NEUROPSYCHOLOGICAL (PERCEPTUAL/MOTOR) CHARACTERISTICS

There is no doubt that LI children have difficulty with various aspects of linguistic processing and/or production. Deviation in the development of linguistic performance may be attributable, for example, to difficulty acquiring higher order semantic or syntactic rules. It is also possible, however, that linguistic deficits could result from more primary perceptual and/or motor problems, such as difficulty in detecting signal change, in discriminating temporal or spectral features, or in integrating, storing in memory, or producing different aspects of complex signals over time. Such processes may be a necessary prerequisite to normal language function. Until we can effectively rule out malfunctions in these more primary perceptual, memory, and motor mechanisms, it will be extremely difficult to differentiate between disorders that may arise at different stages of language processing and production.

Clinical descriptions of LI children have consistently reported perceptual motor and memory deficits. These clinical impressions have been supported by numerous research studies (see Tallal, 1981, for review). The studies of Tallal and colleagues over the past 15 years have demonstrated highly significant and consistent nonverbal temporal, perceptual, motor, and memory deficits in LI children (Tallal and Piercy, 1973a, 1973b, 1974; Johnston et al., 1981; Tallal et al., 1981; Stark et al., 1983; Tallal et al., 1985). These studies demonstrate that LI children are specifically impaired in their ability to discriminate as well as sequence rapidly presented nonverbal stimuli, and hence, remember them. For example, whereas normal children required only 8 msec between two 75 msec tones to respond correctly to their temporal order, LI children required, on average, 300 msec to even discriminate between the tones. This result, replicated in numerous studies using nonverbal auditory, visual, tactile, and cross-modal stimuli, demonstrates that LI children are specifically impaired in their ability to respond correctly to nonverbal sensory information that enters the nervous system quickly in time (simultaneously or in rapid succession) and that the amount of time required by LI children for sensory information processing is orders of magnitude greater than that demonstrated by normal children. Similar temporal deficits in nonverbal temporal motor planning have also been observed in LI children (Johnson et al., 1981; Tallal et al., 1985a, 1985b; Bishop and Edmundson, in press). It is important to emphasize that these highly consistent and significant deficits characteristic of LI children are demonstrated both for processing and for producing nonverbal temporal patterns. There are no significant differences between LI and normally developing children on other tasks of information processing and production not requiring rapid temporal integration, or even on the same tasks of temporal integration when stimuli are presented more slowly. Thus, this nonverbal temporal deficit is: (1) large in magnitude, (2) specific, and (3) highly replicable across populations of specifically LI children. Importantly, children with articulation disorders (without language disorder) and children with reading disorders (without oral language disorders) have been shown to perform normally on temporal tasks (Stark and Tallal, 1980; Tallal and Stark, 1982). However, reading impaired children with concomitant oral language deficits (and phonological decoding difficulties) did show this pattern of temporal perceptual impairment (Tallal, 1980a,b).

The relationship between these nonverbal processing deficits and the verbal disorder of LI children was investigated by Tallal and Piercy (1974, 1975), who published data that provided, for the first time, a direct link between basic nonverbal processing deficits and basic speech perception deficits in LI children. Using computer synthesized speech, which allows for precise control of the acoustic spectra of individual speech sounds, Tallal and Piercy demonstrated that LI children were specifically impaired in their ability to discriminate and sequence precisely those speech sounds that incorporated rapidly changing acoustic spectra (stop consonant-vowel syllables). Importantly, these same children were unimpaired in their ability to respond correctly to speech sounds that were either steady state in nature (isolated vowels) or had been synthesized in such a way as to slow down the rate of acoustic change (stop consonant-vowel syllables with extended format transitions). Thus, these studies demonstrated that LI children are not equally impaired in processing all speech sounds. Rather, they have specific difficulty processing only those speech sounds that are characterized by rapidly changing acoustic spectra that are critical for their discrimination (Tallal and Stark, 1981). Further study demonstrated that these children's errors in speech production were similar to their errors in speech perception. That is, those speech sounds that rely on brief temporal cues for their discrimination were not only most often misperceived by these children but also were most frequently misproduced or omitted in their speech output (Stark and Tallal, 1979; Tallal et al., 1980a, 1980b). On the basis of these results linking a specific nonverbal temporal processing deficit directly to the pattern of speech perception and speech production deficits in LI children, Tallal hypothesized that basic neural deficits in temporal analysis and production may preclude or delay the development of normal speech perception and production and thus may impinge on normal language development.

Tallal and colleagues (Stark, Mellits, Kallman) have investigated this hypothesis by assessing the degree of receptive language impairment in a large group of LI children. They hypothesized that if the specific temporal perception deficits of LI children were directly related to their receptive language impairment, the degree of their perceptual impairment should predict the degree of their receptive language impairment. The results of multivariate analyses demonstrated a highly significant relationship ($r = .85$, $p < .001$) between the degree of nonverbal temporal perceptual impairments and receptive language impairments in LI children (Tallal et al., 1985a). This study demonstrated quantitatively that temporal perceptual abilities alone could account for over 72 percent of the variance associated with the receptive language deficits of LI children (Tallal et al., 1985a).

Although specific developmental language impairment has clinically been defined primarily by exclusion, research has now provided reliable evidence of specific temporal perceptual/motor profiles that appear to be positively associated with LI children. The extent to which these specific temporal variables alone could correctly classify (diagnose) children as language impaired or normal has also been addressed by Tallal and colleagues (Tallal et al., 1985b). The results of discriminate function analyses indicated that a combination of six perceptual and motor variables, when taken in combination, could classify correctly 98 percent of the subjects studied as either normally developing or language impaired. These six variables included: (1) rate of multisyllabic word production; (2) discrimination between speech syllables, incorporating brief format transitions; (3) discrimination of simultaneous touches to the fingers; (4) cross-modal (auditory-visual) integration rate; (5) visual integration rate; and (6) double simultaneous tactile stimulation to the hands and/or cheek. These variables had in common the need to perceive or produce basic sensory information quickly in time. Using these six variables alone, Tallal and colleagues were able to correctly classify 31 of the 32 LI children participating in the study as language impaired and all 36 of the control subjects as normal. Importantly, none of these variables assessed what are commonly considered higher level linguistic functions or used standardized language assessment procedures employed clinically to assess language impairments.

The results of this now large series of studies demonstrate that a specific temporal perceptual/motor mechanism is grossly impaired in LI children. The degree of temporal perceptual/motor impairment: (1) is highly predictive of the degree of receptive language impairment in these children; (2) appears to co-occur in the vast majority of children with specific developmental language disorders; and (3) may well be a "marker variable" for language impairment.

READING PROFILES

Importantly, reading impaired children with concomitant oral language disorders as well as specific decoding (phonics) deficits have also been shown to manifest a pattern of neuropsychological deficits similar to those described for LI children (Tallal, 1980a, 1980b). However, reading impaired children who do not have concomitant oral language deficits or difficulty learning phonics rules do not show these specific temporal perceptual/motor deficits (Tallal and Stark, 1982). Thus, Tallal has suggested a developmental hypothesis which postulates that a specific neurological temporal mechanism may disrupt phoneme perception and production, resulting first in delayed language acquisition in young children and subsequently in delayed reading acquisition in older children. This hypothesis suggests that certain developmental language disorders and developmental reading disorders may result from the *same underlying neurological deficit* and may differ only in the *age* of the child and in the learning skills being acquired at different ages.

Recent results from the San Diego longitudinal study support this hypothesis. These results demonstrate the remarkable predictive outcome of early language impairment (developmental dysphasia) to subsequent reading impairment (developmental dyslexia). Preliminary results of this longitudinal study demonstrate, on discriminant function analysis, that by age 6 years, 78 percent of the LI subjects (selected at age 4) can be correctly classified on the basis of their spelling scores, 86 percent on their reading vocabulary scores, and 87 percent on their reading comprehension scores alone. By age 7 years, 75 percent of the LI subjects are correctly classified on the basis of spelling scores alone, 81 percent on reading vocabulary, and 80 percent on reading comprehension. Similar results have been found in all previous longitudinal studies reporting a high incidence of dyslexia in children with early language impairments (Strominger and Bashir, 1977; Hall and Tomlin, 1978; Aram and Nation, 1975; Silva, 1980, 1983; Stark et al., 1984).

Longitudinal studies directly demonstrate the co-occurrence of developmental language disorders and developmental reading disorders in the same children at different ages. Nonetheless, these disorders continue to be defined, diagnosed, conceptualized, and treated as distinct clinical and research entities. This distinction is evidenced by the separation between professionals serving language impaired children and reading impaired children, in both their clinical and their theoretical training. Whereas speech pathologists and audiologists serve language impaired children, special educators and reading specialists serve reading impaired children. Conferences on developmental dysphasia (developmental language disorders) rarely include papers on developmental dyslexia (reading impairment) and vice versa. Significantly, even the National Institutes of Health has two separate institutes for overseeing research on these disorders. Whereas language impairments (aphasia) fall under the auspices and responsibilities of the National Institute of Neurological and Communicative Disorders and Stroke, research on reading impairments (dyslexia) falls within the domain of the National Institute of Child Health and Human Development. Similarly, the DSM-III classifies developmental language and reading disorders separately. The results of longitudinal research studies, however, clearly demonstrate that it may be the *age* of the child rather than the *neurological basis* that differs between developmental language and developmental reading disorders. Continuing to separate these developmental communication disorders ultimately fails the many children who "progress" from language impaired to reading impaired. Although not all reading impaired children have concomitant oral language deficits (Tallal and Stark, 1982), these research findings suggest that a very high percentage of LI children have some degree of delayed reading acquisition, in most instances profound. Continued separation of these disorders may potentially impede progress toward the eventual treatment and prevention of these communication learning disorders.

COGNITIVE CHARACTERISTICS

For more than 20 years, LI children have been operationally defined as having normal nonverbal intelligence and normal cognitive capacity. The conclusion that LI children had normal nonlinguistic cognition was drawn probably because, in order to make differential diagnoses of specific language impairment, as opposed to mental retardation, children had to perform within normal limits on nonverbal portions of standardized intelligence tests. Research on this point, however, remains controversial. Some studies suggest that LI children may exhibit deficits or delays in nonlinguistic areas of cognition, and other studies refute this interpretation.

LI children have demonstrated difficulties with many different nonverbal aspects of cognition: means/ends knowledge (what children do to obtain objects or to cause actions) (Snyder, 1978); interpreting and drawing inferences from visually depicted events (Mackworth et al., 1973; Otto et al., 1973); classification (Johnston and Ramstad, 1978); figurative thought (thought involving visual mental representations), including haptic problem-solving, seriation, and mental rotations (Kamhi, 1981; de Ajuriaguerra, 1976); rule and hypothesis formulation (Kamhi et al., 1984); and short-term memory processes, especially with respect to parameters relating to memory capacity (Kircher and Klatzky, 1985).

On the basis of this and other research, some researchers have hypothesized that LI children do not have a selective language deficit but have a more general representational deficit that underlies both their linguistic and nonlinguistic difficulties (Morehead, 1972; Morehead and Ingram, 1973; Inhelder, 1966, 1976; de Ajuriaguerra, 1976). The finding that LI children exhibit deficits in representational abilities across a range of tasks and at different points in development is consistent with this view. Such deficits could explain some of the specific impairments noted in the language development of this population. For example, the delay in speech onset, the protracted rate of lexical acquisition, the impoverished range of semantic functions and relations expressed, and the limited propositional complexity of speech could all be the linguistic reflections of representational and conceptual impairments. Moreover, deficits in rule formulation and in hypothesis testing could have equally significant negative consequences for language acquisition.

Such conclusions, however, are premature. First, many investigations of nonlinguistic cognition in LI children have failed to find any such deficits in this population. (See Stark et al., 1983, for review.) Studies of the symbolic play of LI children have produced equivocal results (Lovell et al., 1968; Terrell et al., 1984), as have investigations of operative thought (Inhelder, 1966; Johnston and Ramstad, 1978). In addition, several of the studies cited above, which purported to find evidence of nonlinguistic cognitive deficits of LI children, presented data from which alternative conclusions could easily be drawn. Johnston and Weismer (1983), for example, concluded that LI children possess an impairment of visual imagery, even though these children did not differ significantly from control children either in the accuracy of their judgments or in the number of training trials needed to reach criterion on a mental rotation task. The LI children did respond significantly more slowly on the task. This observation may simply imply that such children were motorically slow. In another study, Kamhi et al. (1984) concluded that LI children evidence deficits in hypothesis testing ability and in nonlinguistic symbolic abilities. The data do not support these conclusions. LI children performed normally on a concept acquisition task and on a discrimination learning task (in terms of number of trials needed to reach criterion). Significantly more LI children than controls, however, were unable to verbalize the correct solution to this latter task. This is hardly a surprising result, given that these are, by definition, language impaired children. The LI children also performed significantly worse on a haptic recognition test, from which the authors concluded that such children possess a general problem with symbolic representation. Clearly, a more parsimonious explanation for these data would be that the LI children have a problem with cross-modal sensory integration (in this case, tactile sensation-visual recognition), as reported by Tallal et al. (1981).

Second, theory in both linguistics and psycholinguistics supports the contention that linguistic and nonlinguistic rules and representations may differ considerably (Chomsky, 1980; Curtiss, 1982, in press; Demopoulos and Marras, 1986). Therefore, there is no a priori reason to assume that a child with linguistic representational difficulty would necessarily also have nonlinguistic representational difficulty. However, this remains an interesting theoretical question.

Third, not all LI children evidence nonlinguistic deficits; in almost every study cited, at least some of the LI children performed normally on nonlinguistic, cognitive measures. This finding indicates that LI children do not comprise a single, homogeneous population. Therefore, the fact that many LI children manifest a range of developmental dysfunctions that could impair their language acquisition does not preclude the possibility that a subgroup of these children have a truly selective linguistic deficit.

There is currently no conclusive evidence as to whether the various cognitive deficits that LI children demonstrate stem from a single underlying impairment or whether they are causally related. However, an investigation into possible relationships between the linguistic and nonlinguistic cognitive deficits in these children would be germane to at least two important issues in the cognitive sciences: (1) Are language, mental imagery, and other symbolic abilities separate faculties of mind, embodying distinct cognitive principles, or are they different manifestations of a single set of cognitive principles? (2) Which perceptual and/or cognitive abilities are prerequisites for language acquisition? Because the LI child commonly shows perceptual as well as cognitive deficits, a rigorous examination of linguistic, cognitive, and perceptual function, in the same impaired population, could provide crucial evidence about the fundamental relationships between language development and aspects of cognition and perception that are not strictly linguistic. The first such study, wedding linguistic, cognitive, and neuropsychological investigations of the same population, is currently underway as part of the San Diego longitudinal study.

SOCIAL-EMOTIONAL CHARACTERISTICS

Investigating the role that language may play as a mediator in emerging social and emotional development in children has occupied a central position in the field of developmental social cognition. It has been suggested that a child gains with the development of language a new and powerful means of classifying logical connections and developing reasoning skills that enable the child to differentiate emotional and conceptual domains and gain mastery within them (Hassibi and Breuer, 1980).

Thus, it might be expected that serious developmental language impairment could have a profound impact on social and emotional development. Indeed, LI children offer a unique opportunity for evaluating the potential relationship between emerging language (or lack thereof) and social and emotional development. Despite the potential for studying this important developmental issue, few empirical studies of the social and emotional status of LI children have been reported until recently. This is obviously a fruitful area for continued research.

The studies by Cantwell et al. (1980) and Baker et al. (1980) provided perhaps the first comprehensive review and new information on the relationship between speech and language disorders and psychiatric disorders in children. These authors report the results of a comprehensive psychiatric evaluation of 100 consecutive cases of children seen in a community speech and hearing clinic. Psychiatric diagnosis of this cohort revealed the presence of a diagnosable psychiatric disorder, according to DSM-III criteria, in approximately 50 percent of the group studied. It is important to note, however, that included as "diagnosable psychiatric disorder" were diagnoses of developmental disorders such as reading and mathematics deficits and attention deficit disorder. Baker et al. (1980) reported a differential degree of these disturbances in children with various linguistic profiles. Children with speech articulation problems, without concomitant language disorders, were found to show the least prevalence for these DSM-III diagnoses. Children with speech and language disorders or language disorders alone were most at risk for these DSM-III diagnoses.

Approaching the association between emotional and speech disorders in children from another direction, Chess and Rosenberg (1974) evaluated the incidence of speech disorders among children referred for psychiatric treatment. They found that over a 3-year period, 24 percent of all children referred for psychiatric therapy had some type of language disorder. Psychiatric diagnoses for these children included cerebral dysfunction, developmental lag, thought disorder, and neurotic behavior disorder. However, these authors suggest that without longitudinal studies assessing the relationship between language and social-emotional development in children, it would be difficult to determine whether emotional disorders are primary or whether the resultant stresses of language delay themselves create a high probability of secondary compensatory behaviors, such as withdrawal or other kinds of intrusive actions. The authors suggest that these protective and defensive maneuvers may be more easily noted and referred for treatment than the speech or language problem, and, in fact, that speech or language problems may often be wrongly understood as derivative and secondary to an underlying neurotic mechanism rather than vice versa.

Issues pertaining to direction of causality might be addressed in a longitudinal study by looking specifically at very young children. Stephenson and Richman (1978) report the only study that has focused exclusively on the preschool age child. These authors conducted a comprehensive epidemiological study of 3-year-olds living in a London suburb. They found that, of the random sample of 700 children studied, 14 percent displayed behavioral problems. However, 59 percent of the children with language delay displayed behavioral problems. Unfortunately, it is not clear from this study that only children with specific developmental language delay were included in the LI group or whether age was a relevant factor. Children with language delay secondary to other developmental disabilities, such as general mental retardation, social deprivation, hearing loss, or infantile autism, were also represented in the population. Thus, the extent to which behavioral problems are associated with other developmental disabilities cannot be parceled out from those associated specifically with language disabilities. This methodological criticism, unfortunately, must be applied to all of the studies previously reported and reviewed here. Similarly, even the most recently published study on the topic (Beitchman et al., 1986) fails to distinguish specific developmental language impairment from language delay secondary to mental retardation, infantile autism, hearing loss, paralysis or malformation of the oral musculature, or frank neurological insult or acquired aphasia. Thus, a clear association between developmental language disorder and emotional disorders has been reported, but to date it is not clear to what extent the relationship is specific to language per se or to other primary disabilities that include delayed language as outcomes.

As part of the San Diego longitudinal study, Tallal et al. (1987) have reported the prevalence of social and emotional disturbance in 4-year old LI children. This study differs methodologically in three important ways from previously reported studies pertaining to social and emotional sequelae of developmental language disorders: (1) only 4-year-old children who had only recently been diagnosed as specifically language impaired were included; (2) subjects were rigorously tested to quantitatively establish that they were both significantly language impaired and that the impairment was specific to expressive and/or receptive language (children with speech problems only or with other neurological, mental, or physical problems were excluded); and (3) a well-matched control group was included. The results of this study also differ from those reported previously. With the use of Achenbach's standardized child behavior checklist (1979, 1980, 1982), it was found that for total scores representing social and emotional attributes, the mean and standard deviations were significantly different between the normal group and the LI group, with the LI group receiving higher scores, which suggested a greater degree of emotional disturbance. However, further analysis demonstrated that only one of the eight individual behavior scales, developed by Achenbach from this checklist to pinpoint specific areas of psychiatric disturbance, contributed to this significant difference. Similarly, with use of a cutoff of a T-score of 70 or higher to represent clinically abnormal behavior, none of the 49 normal subjects and only 5 of the 81 LI subjects participating in the study demonstrated abnormality at this level. This difference is not significant. The one scale that did significantly differentiate the LI from the normal children (immaturity for the boys and social withdrawal for the girls) on further inspection revealed a high number of neurological as opposed to purely emotional items. These included items such as: speech problems, confused, clumsy, can't concentrate, won't talk, twitches, and accident-prone. Discriminate function analysis demonstrated that these neurological items from the Achenbach Child Behavior Checklist accounted for the significant majority of variance found between groups for the total behavior scores. On the basis of these neurological items alone from the Achenbach scale, 92 percent of the boys and 90 percent of the girls could correctly be classified as LI as opposed to normal, without resorting to the inclusion of the more specifically social or emotional items from the scale.

The results of this recent study demonstrate that 4-year-old LI children are not significantly different from age-match controls in social and emotional development in areas other than those of purported neurological integrity. However, when items assessing aspects of neuropsychological functioning are included in standard child behavior checklists, the overall results demonstrate significant differences between total behavior scores obtained between groups. Without more detailed analysis, the differences may be misinterpreted as social and emotional disturbance. It is important that interpretations pertaining to social and emotional disorders in LI children, based on parent, teacher, or clinical observation, not be confounded with aspects of behavior that may be associated with the originally diagnosed neurological disorder, such as "won't talk" or "speech problems." It will be important to replicate these findings with the use of other techniques, including clinical observation and other standardized methods. It will also be of particular interest to reassess these same children at the end of the longitudinal study (at age 8) to determine whether or not changes have occurred in the social and emotional profiles of LI children assessed in the preschool and subsequently the mid-elementary school years. Although these results suggest that specific developmental language delay is initially neurological rather than emotional in origin, it is possible that these children develop emotional disturbances with increasing age, perhaps as a result of attempting to cope with the stresses produced by their language and learning disabilities, or perhaps as a subsequent manifestation of the neurological processing disorders that characterize these children.

Summary and Limitations: Considerations for Future Research

Three major points arise from this discussion of the definition and associated characteristics of specific developmental language disorders:

- Although important similarities may exist between children with specific developmental language disorders and those with language disorders secondary to other developmental disabilities (such as mental retardation, hearing loss, autism, cerebral palsy, cleft palate, acquired aphasia, or articulation disorders), research has been highly confounded by a lack of careful attention to separation between these different disabilities. Until consistent, standardized inclusionary and exclusionary criteria for selecting subjects for studies of specific developmental language impairment are both established and uniformly applied, it will continue to be virtually impossible to generalize research results from one study to the next and to make progress in our understanding of specific developmental language delay. It is suggested that the number one priority for research be the development of standardized inclusionary and exclusionary criteria and the encouragement of their uniform usage for subsequent Federally or privately funded research in this area. This is not to suggest that priority be placed on research on one population versus another, but rather that more standardized criteria for subject selection be adopted for studying various subgroups of children with various developmental disabilities so that each can be more clearly defined, and studies can be replicated more easily.
- Somewhat paradoxically, there seems to be a higher tendency to merge children with language disabilities that appear to arise from very different etiologies (mental retardation, hearing loss, autism) into a single category for study and treatment than children with primary communication-learning disabilities (specific developmental language disorder and specific developmental reading disorder). Nonetheless, research now strongly documents that for many of these children, their language and reading difficulties may result from similar neurological etiology, manifesting itself differently at different stages of development. It is suggested that future research focused on investigating similarities and differences between children with a variety of developmental disabilities be concentrated more directly on etiology and mechanism rather than surface symptomatology. Continued classification based primarily on symptomatology rather than etiology and mechanism may directly impede progress in research and treatment of learning impaired children.

- The continued adherence to definition by exclusion, in light of the plethora of new information emerging from research pertaining to inclusionary characteristics and varying profiles associated with LI children, impedes progress. It is distressing that the DSM-III (1980) adopted a definition of specific developmental language disorders virtually identical to that published by Benton over two decades ago, suggesting incorrectly that no progress has been made in the ensuing two decades. However, research activity has produced considerable advancements in our knowledge of the definition and associated inclusionary characteristics of children with specific developmental language impairment, particularly pertaining to neurological, neuropsychological (especially temporal perception and production), linguistic, cognitive, and social and emotional profiles. Many of these profiles have been shown to be highly reliable and replicable across many laboratories and groups of subjects. For example, although many different subgroups or profiles of children with language disorders have been identified, temporal/perceptual motor deficits have been shown to both accurately predict level of receptive language impairment and correctly distinguish 98 percent of LI children from normal children, regardless of their subtype. It is therefore unacceptable to continue to diagnose solely on the basis of what is not known about LI children in deference to including in the definition of the disorder what is currently known to characterize these children.

DIAGNOSIS

The issue of diagnosis is closely related to the issue of definition and associated characteristics. For appropriate diagnosis to be made, the inclusionary and exclusionary criteria based on the definition of the disorder need to be operationalized and standardized so that consistency in making differential diagnoses across laboratories and clinics can be established. Once inclusionary and exclusionary criteria have been established, standardized, and uniformly adopted, it must be determined which testing procedures are most appropriate for validly and reliably assessing each aspect of the child's behavior needed to determine these criteria. It is suggested that this discussion of diagnosis be read in conjunction with the previous discussion of the definition and associated characteristics.

The differential diagnosis of specific developmental language delay can be conceptualized as a three-tiered process: (1) establishing that the child is demonstrating significant delay in developing language at or near the expected age; (2) determining whether the language delay is the primary disorder or is secondary to other developmental disabilities such as hearing loss, mental retardation, or autism; and (3) determining the nature of the language disorder and its associated characteristics or subtype, such as receptive and/or expressive language disorder with or without concomitant articulation disorder, perceptual/motor impairments, memory disorder, emotional disturbance, or academic achievement problems.

Determining that language development is significantly delayed in a child depends directly on our understanding of the stages and time course of normal language acquisition. This obvious requirement is, nonetheless, often overlooked in the training of professionals to whom the diagnosis of language impairments in children often falls. Specifically, neurologists, psychiatrists, pediatricians, and even teachers have little or no direct training in normal developmental psycholinguistics and neuropsychology or in speech pathology. Having little or no training in normal language development, it is not surprising that these professionals consistently misinform parents about the seriousness of their concerns for their child's language development and the need for referral to a speech pathologist, audiologist, or neuropsychologist for appropriate assessment and diagnosis. In addition, even the enlightened physician or teacher who does recognize a potential language impairment and refers to an appropriate professional for assessment and diagnosis can be easily frustrated or misled by the results of standardized speech and language assessment. Berk (1984) points out that standardized measures of language are among the worst psychometric tests with respect to reliability and validity.

LANGUAGE TESTING

When children are brought to a clinic because of a suspected language-learning problem, the first order of priority for the clinician is to determine whether or not a speech or language problem exists and to characterize the problem if one does exist. To accomplish this task, systematic methods for assessing, or in some way "measuring," speech and language are required. For many years, language sampling procedures were relied upon, but in the last 25 years an abundance of formal language assessment instruments have been developed and have become available for this purpose. Some of these tests focus on the assessment of abilities hypothesized to underlie or be requisite to language acquisition (for example: auditory perception and memory, representational gestures) rather than on speech or language itself. Some tests focus on particular speech or language abilities and modalities of performance (such as articulation, receptive vocabulary, comprehension of syntax, and expressive morphology). Still others have a more comprehensive focus, testing different components of linguistic knowledge across performance modalities (such as production and comprehension of vocabulary, morphology, or syntax). Some of the more well-known and widely used tests include the Illinois Test of Psycho-linguistic Abilities (ITPA) (Kirk et al., 1968), the Peabody Picture Vocabulary Test (PPVT) (Dunn, 1959), the Berry-Talbott Exploratory Test of Grammar (Berry, 1966), the Assessment of Children's Language Comprehension (ACLA) (Foster et al., 1969), the Northwestern Syntax Screening Test (NSST) (Lee, 1974), the Test of Linguistic Development (TOLD) (Newcomer and Hammill, 1977), the Test for Auditory Comprehension of Language (TACL) (Carrow, 1973), the Carrow Elicited Language Inventory (CELI) (Carrow, 1974), the Token Test (DeRenzi and Vignolo, 1962), and the Clinical Evaluation of Language Functions (CELF) (Semel and Wiig, 1980).

There is seemingly no lack of tests for the clinician to use. Indeed, such tests continue to proliferate. The use of them is routine and assumed essential for the identification and diagnosis of language disorders. Careful examination of the tests currently available, however, reveals serious shortcomings from both a psychometric and a theoretical linguistic perspective. McCauley and Swisher (1984), Spekman and Roth (1984), and Lieberman and Michael (1986), for example, point out numerous flaws across a wide range of speech and language tests, flaws which hold equally true for tests not examined by these authors. Serious psychometric flaws include, for example, inadequate normative samples and test reliability, and failure to achieve test validity in most if not all respects. Most serious among inadequacies are a failure to demonstrate construct validity (the degree to which a test measures the theoretical construct it is intended to measure), content validity (the extent to which, when judged by an expert, the test provides relevant information about the behavior being tested), criterion-related validity (the degree to which performance on the test in question is related to some other measure of the behavior being assessed), and reliability (the consistency with which a test measures a given behavior or ability).

Inadequacies in content and construct validity translate, in linguistic terms, into the absence of a theoretically grounded approach for analysis of linguistic abilities. The consequence of using an assessment instrument whose design is not informed by any theory of language is that it is difficult if not impossible to know what the information gathered from such an assessment means. Unless the practitioner using the test has the necessary expertise to construct the larger picture, as it were, from a child's test scores, even details or profiles of test performance may leave most questions concerning the child's disorder unanswered. This shortcoming on the part of most available language tests is reflective of a problem for the field in general, which, in large part, has proceeded uninformed by linguistic or neuropsychological theory. In spite of the large number of language assessment tests currently on the market, there is still a need for new, carefully designed, theoretically grounded language tests that can differentiate a child with a language disorder from a linguistically normal child by virtue of either a significant developmental delay in linguistic growth or an abnormal pattern of linguistic growth. Such tests will need to be comprehensive in scope, testing each component of linguistic knowledge (semantics, morphology, syntax, phonology) across linguistic activities and performance modalities, in ways that are appropriate and relevant for all the years of language acquisition. They will also need to reveal not only level of performance but detailed patterns of performance, so that the acquisition of specific linguistic rules and general principles of grammar are both revealed. There is also a need for tests to assess the ability of the child to make use of linguistic knowledge in the service of communication.

Finally, the importance of valid, reliable standardization of language tests across large populations of children cannot be overemphasized. Because both the pattern and time course of language have been shown to differ dramatically in normally developing children (see Stark et al., 1982, for review), it is essential that appropriate norms be established if reliable diagnosis of language impairment in children is to be made. Based on such norms, critical decisions pertaining to school placement and treatment would be made that will potentially affect the child's ultimate development. It is a disgrace that these essential decisions are currently being made on the basis of tests that lack validity and reliability and are poorly normed. Only with psychometrically valid tests that are both broad and in-depth in their investigation of communicative and linguistic function and are based on well-established normative data can a language disorder be adequately identified or characterized.

The validity and reliability of different test procedures (imitation, sentence-completion, object manipulation, picture-pointing) for revealing a child's linguistic or communicative competence is also a much discussed and important topic. The issue involves whether or not a particular task may consistently incorrectly estimate a child's linguistic abilities, perhaps because of memory or other processing factors involved in the task or because of the nonlinguistic cognitive load it imposes. We do not enlarge upon these questions here, but for some interesting and informative discussions of the topic, see, for example, Slobin and Welsh (1973); Prutting et al. (1975); Daily and Boxx (1979); Connell and Myles-Zitzer (1982); Lust et al. (in press); and Hamburger and Crain (1982, 1984).

Despite the numerous problems with testing and with available tests, the clinician must nonetheless make an evaluation of a child's language. The importance of including a language sample as part of the assessment procedure is now widely recognized; and in the hands of a skilled practitioner, the sample can be used to great benefit in evaluating, at a minimum, the expressive language and communicative performance patterns of a child. The sample must be used in conjunction with a well-designed formal language test. A promising, soon-to-be-published candidate test, which has been used very successfully in the San Diego longitudinal study and which is currently being normed with LI children and normal children from the ages of 2 to 9 years, is the CYCLE (Curtiss and Yamada, to appear). Articulation tests and other carefully designed and relevant nonlanguage perceptual, motor, memory, and cognitive tests must also be included in the diagnosis of language disorders. Test development and standardization based on the principles discussed here are also critically important for assessing associated characteristics of LI children in a reliable manner.

DIFFERENTIAL DIAGNOSIS

Once it has been established that a child is delayed in language development, it is important to determine whether the language delay is the primary disability or the symptom of a more primary developmental disability such as hearing loss, mental retardation, deformity or paralysis of the oral musculature, or autism. Assessments by an audiologist, child psychologist, speech pathologist, pediatric neurologist, and psychiatrist are in order to rule out these other disabilities as the primary cause of the language disorder. Again, standardized, valid, and reliable procedures are needed for assessment of hearing, oral-motor integrity, and psychiatric disturbance in young children. These areas are not discussed in detail in this paper. However, due to their importance to the appropriate differential diagnosis of developmental language disorder, particularly as the disorder is differentiated from mental retardation, issues pertaining to intelligence testing of potentially LI children are discussed.

Specific developmental language delay is, by definition, a disorder that is specific to language development and thus must be differentiated from more general mental retardation. Therefore, it is essential that in addition to demonstrating that language abilities of a child are significantly below what would be expected based on the child's chronological age, it is important to establish that they are also significantly discrepant from what would be predicted based on the child's mental abilities. Thus, a child who demonstrates language and general cognitive abilities that are both significantly, but equally, behind the child's chronological age would not fit the diagnosis of specific developmental language impairment, since language in such cases cannot be demonstrated to be discrepant from other mental capacities. It is, therefore, critical that the assessment of intelligence and language not be confounded. That is, for children suspected of language disorders, intelligence tests that have been developed to assess intelligence without the need for understanding complex verbal instructions or for giving verbal responses must be utilized. For a child with specific developmental language delay who is given an auditory verbal, language-loaded intelligence test such as the Stanford Binet (Terman and Merrill, 1973), the McCarthy Scales of Children's Ability (McCarthy, 1970), or the Peabody Picture Vocabulary Test (Dunn, 1959), the resultant IQ score will reflect the child's language disorder, not necessarily the child's cognitive abilities. According to Wilson (1986), the LI child may do very well with visually mediated cognitive and visual-constructional tasks, but a measure such as the Stanford Binet IQ score, which is heavily verbally loaded, does not appropriately reflect that child's cognitive or conceptual abilities, since the scores are masked by the linguistic demands required by such tests to demonstrate cognitive and conceptual abilities. Wilson and Wilson (1977) compared IQ scores obtained from preschool LI children based on the Stanford Binet, the McCarthy Scales of Children's Abilities, the Hiskey-Nebraska Test of Learning Aptitude (Hiskey, 1966), and the Pictorial Test of Intelligence (French, 1964). The mean IQ scores increased significantly and systematically across the four tests, as language loading on the tests decreased. The mean IQ score of the LI group ranged from 62 on the Stanford Binet to 92 on the Pictorial Test of Intelligence. Thus, on the basis of the intelligence tests selected to assess cognitive ability, the same child could be diagnosed as mentally retarded or as specifically language impaired, depending on the extent of verbal loading incorporated in the test. Thus, it is inappropriate to use language-based tests such as the Stanford Binet, the verbal or full-scale IQ score of the Weschler Intelligence Scales for Children (Weschler, 1963), or the Peabody Picture Vocabulary Test to determine intelligence or mental age of a child demonstrating delayed language development. Tests not requiring comprehension of complex verbal instructions or verbal responses, such as the Leiter International Performance Scale (Leiter, 1969), the Ravens Colored Progressive Matrices for Children (Raven, 1956), the Hiskey-Nebraska Test of Learning Aptitude, or the performance scales of the Weschler Intelligence Scales for Children, must be used for assessing intelligence in a child suspected to have a language disorder. In using such nonverbal tests of intelligence, it is necessary to demonstrate a discrepancy between developmental language age and both chronological age and mental age for a diagnosis of specific developmental language disorder. Similarly, significant discrepancies between intelligence scales, with performance (nonverbal) IQ outstripping verbal IQ, are indicative of specific developmental language delay.

Just how discrepant must a child's language development be from chronological and mental age to consider the discrepancy diagnostic of a specific language disorder? Concomitantly, is degree of discrepancy at one age or developmental stage equally significant to that at another age? Is a discrepancy of 1 year between mental age and language age in a 4-year-old, for example, synonymous with a 1-year discrepancy in an 8-year-old? Is it more appropriate to use: (1) a cutoff score (for example, two standard deviations from a given mean score); (2) degree of deficit (for example, language age more than one year below chronological or mental age), or (3) language quotient (for example, language age less than 75 percent of chronological age)? These issues have not been investigated, and there is no established, uniform procedure either for clinical practice or for research. Again, this lack of uniformity pertaining to such a basic diagnostic issue impedes progress in both research and treatment for LI children.

PATTERNS OF LANGUAGE DISORDER

Once it has been established that a child is significantly delayed in language acquisition, and a differential diagnosis has established that the impairment is specific to language, the pattern of language disorder and accompanying characteristics can be assessed. Standardized clinical tests can assess receptive (comprehension) aspects of language separately from expressive (production) aspects. Articulation impairment can also be assessed separately from receptive and expressive language disorder. Although there are many tests that claim to assess auditory discrimination, auditory perception, and auditory memory functions in children, these tests uniformly suffer because they confound verbal and nonverbal auditory abilities. As each of these tests utilizes words as stimulus material, it is not possible, with these procedures, to distinguish verbal from nonverbal discrimination, and perceptual and memory deficits. Nonverbal perceptual, memory, and motor testing procedures, such as those developed by Tallal (1980c) for use in research with LI children, need to be developed and standardized for clinical diagnostic use if these important neuropsychological components (prerequisites) of language impairments are to be assessed separately from language skills per se. Similarly, methods for assessing social and emotional disturbance in children that do not confound language, learning, and other neuropsychological symptomatology with psychiatric disorder must be developed and standardized for clinical and research use with LI children.

PREVALENCE

In a recent review of prevalence of speech and language disorders in children, Beitchman et al. (1986) state that "despite speech and language disorders being increasingly recognized as a major health problem among young children, known to antedate serious psychosocial problems and academic failure, there are still no reliable data on the prevalence of speech and language disorders among school-age children." As Beitchman further points out, this obvious dearth of information about prevalence is the direct result of the lack of a comprehensive, uniformly applied classification system for speech and language disorders. The literature is very confusing in this area, since speech, language, hearing, and mental retardation are often lumped together in developing estimates of prevalence. Tuomi and Ivanoff (1977) assessed the prevalence of speech disorders as well as language and hearing disorders in kindergarten and first grade children. They found the prevalence of articulation problems to be 25 percent in kindergarten children and 17 percent in first grade children. Fundudis et al. (1979) conducted a study of speech-delayed and deaf children in England. Assessing only for severe forms of delay, these authors report a 4 percent prevalence. Stevenson and Richman (1976) found in a London population of 3-year-olds the prevalence of expressive language delay to be 3 percent and severe expressive language delay to be 2 percent. Between 40 and 50 percent of the same children, however, were mentally retarded. Combining speech and language delay together, Williams et al. (1980) found that 14 percent of males and 8 percent of females had speech and/or language difficulties and that 9 percent had mild impairment and 2 percent were severely impaired. Silva (1980) reported that 3 percent of his sample of 3-year-old children in Dunedin, New Zealand, were delayed in verbal comprehension, 2.5 percent were delayed in verbal expression only, and 3 percent were delayed in both. Beitchman concludes his review as follows:

> It should be clear from the studies of the prevalence of speech defects and language delays-disorders reviewed that serious methodological problems render the validity of the existing data questionable. Non-representative samples, lack of clearly defined criteria for the definition of cases, absence of trained staff and standardized methods, with no evidence of reliability between raters are examples of the problems that have bedeviled existing studies (p. 100).

Beitchman attempted to address these methodological problems in a major prevalence study in Ottawa-Carleton, Canada. In a one-in-three stratified random sample procedure of all 5-year-old English-speaking kindergartners from the Ottawa-Carleton region, children were screened in a three-stage procedure by professional staff. Stage 1 was a speech and language screening. All children scoring below the stage 1 cutoff as well as those in a small random sample scoring above the cutoff were asked to participate in more extensive testing in stage 2. Only those children scoring below the stage 2 cutoff points were identified as speech or language impaired. These children as well as the control sample participated in stage 3 testing. Using standardized receptive and expressive speech and language tests as well as a checklist for voice disorders, stuttering, and dysarthria, the following results were obtained: Of the 1,655 children sampled, 315 failed stage 1. All but 14 (184 boys and 117 girls) agreed to participate in stage 2 testing. Of these, 175 (58 percent) failed at least one of the tests in stage 2 and went on to stage 3.

Significantly, the highest percentage of failure at stage 3 testing separating LI from normal children occurred on the Goldman-Fristoe-Woodcock (1976) test for memory for auditory sequence (44 percent failed). Surprisingly, only 18 percent failed the memory for verbal content portion of the same test. Failure for memory for auditory sequence was consistently higher than that for any other subcomponent of language assessed. Language measures ranged from a low of 0.3 percent failing the grammatical completion portion of the Test of Language Development (Newcomber and Hammill, 1977) to a high of 32 percent failing the spoken language portion of the same test. Thus, the single most powerful indicator of speech and language disorders in this prevalence study was found to be failure on a test of memory for auditory sequence. These results are consistent with those reported by Tallal et al. (1985a,b) and Bishop and Edmundson (in press), which demonstrated that temporal, perceptual/motor deficits are highly predictive of level of receptive language impairment.

The overall prevalence of speech and language disorders reported by Beitchman et al. (1986) was found to be 19 percent, plus or minus 3 percent (at the 95 percent confidence interval). Isolated speech impairments were found in 6.6 percent of boys, while 3.3 percent had speech and language impairment and 8.2 percent had language impairment only. (Total percent of boys affected was 18.) For the girls, 6.7 percent showed speech problems only, 7.1 percent had speech and language problems, and 8.4 percent had language problems only (total: 22 percent). These numbers demonstrate that 20 percent of all 5-year-old children evidenced some form of speech and/or language impairment. It must be kept in mind, however, that all speech and language impairments (including voice disorders and stuttering) were included in this prevalence estimate. Furthermore, estimates of specific developmental language disorder not attributable to other concomitant developmental disabilities, such as hearing loss, mental retardation, neurological impairments, dysarthria, and autism, cannot be derived, since these other developmental disabilities were unfortunately not differentiated or excluded in this study in determining prevalence of language disorder.

In conclusion, to date there are no studies employing appropriate methodology that address the issue of prevalence of specific developmental language disorders. This is an important area for study, but again, progress will depend on the development of standardized, reliable inclusionary and exclusionary criteria for definition and diagnosis of specific developmental language delay and on the development of valid and reliable test instruments.

CAUSES (ETIOLOGY)

In reviewing causes of specific developmental language disorders, the two principal groups of factors that are addressed fall under the broad headings of organic and psychogenic. These are variably referred to under other dichotomies, such as "nature" versus "nurture," or heredity versus environment.

Etiologies can be divided according to intrinsic factors, including such causes as sex-linked chromosomal aberrations, inborn errors of metabolism, the normal influence of gonadal hormones on prenatal brain development, possible effects of excesses or deficiencies of such hormones during critical periods of development, and various neuroanatomical abnormalities that were genetically determined either directly or indirectly by biochemical abnormalities. Such factors could either be transmitted to a child through the genetic material of his parents (often as a homozygous allele) or would reflect a mutation sometime during embryogenesis.

The second class, the extrinsic factors, includes all possible insults to the developing brain during prenatal, perinatal, or postnatal periods. Such insults may result from trauma, seizure, dietary deficiencies (maternal or infant), infections, or exposure of the developing fetus to various teratogens such as heavy metals, drugs (including alcohol), and other environmental pollutants.

Finally, psychosocial factors such as the language-learning environment in which the child is reared, mother-child interaction, and socioeconomic status may have an effect on language development. Factors from each of these classes will be examined and reviewed in order to delineate the possible role each might play, in isolation or combination, in the etiology of developmental language disorders.

GENETIC FACTORS

Beginning in 1926 (McReady) and continuing to the present time (Borges-Osorio and Salzano, 1985; Samples and Lane, 1985), only a few case reports of families with several members having language disorders can be found in the literature. Despite the dearth of case reports of families, it is commonly believed that there may be a genetic basis for specific developmental language deficits (see Ludlow and Cooper, 1983, for review).

In one of the largest group studies to date, Ingram (1959) obtained family histories on 75 probans. Eighteen probans had at least one parent with a history of speech or language difficulty (including delayed speech development, a history of stuttering, and "lisping"). Of the 131 siblings of probans, 30 (23 percent) carried a diagnosis of severe language impairment, this being confirmed by direct observation in 23. In the only other group study found in the literature, which directly evaluated the potential genetic basis for specific developmental language disorders, Hier and Rosenberger (1980) found that 19 of 30 dysphasic children studied had a positive family history of developmental language disorder.

Unfortunately, these studies suffer from serious methodological problems, which include: a lack of objective diagnosis of specific developmental language disorders and also exclusion of hearing impairment, autism, and mental retardation in the probans; parent and sibling diagnosis made by interview rather than by direct observation or testing; and no control group.

Many of these issues are being addressed in the San Diego longitudinal study. As part of this study, issues pertaining to incidence of family history as they relate to a possible genetic basis for specific developmental language disorders are being addressed in 100 LI children with specific developmental language delay, and in age-, IQ-, and socioeconomic status-matched controls. Based again on parent interview rather than direct observation or testing, the following preliminary family history data have been obtained from this population. Families of LI children report an average of 35 ($\pm$ 3) percent of first degree relatives having a history of language and/or learning impairment, as compared to 20 ($\pm$ 3) percent for controls (t = 2.91; p .005). Next, probans were placed into one of three groups: (1) at least one parent impaired; (2) reported history of affected siblings or secondary relatives, but without positive parental history; and (3) no reported primary or secondary relatives with positive histories for language, reading, or writing impairments. When segregated in this fashion, results demonstrated that for the controls, 38 percent fell into group 1, 26 percent into group 2, and 36 percent into group 3. For the LI children, 62 percent were in group 1, 20 percent in group 2, and only 18 percent in group 3 (chi-square = 7.81 [p .02]).

Obviously, the most convincing evidence for genetic influence in language disabilities would be the discovery of a chromosomal abnormality responsible for the defect. Because of the 2 or 3:1 male-female ratio, many investigators have concentrated on the sex chromosomes to address this possibility. Both of the two classical approaches in genetic research have been used in this attempt. In the first, several authors have reported an increased frequency, as compared to the normal population, of sex chromosome abnormalities in children with delayed language acquisition (Garvey and Mutton, 1973; Mutton and Lea, 1980; Friedrich et al., 1982). Unfortunately, the results of these studies also suffer from lack of consistent definition and assessment of LI children and from failure to rule out other diagnoses not specific to the language impairment.

The other approach is to prospectively follow children with sex chromosome abnormalities and watch for development of language difficulties. Although these studies also are replete with methodological problems (specifically: lack of operational definition of language disorders and subject selection criteria), some evidence in support of a hereditary component to specific developmental language disorders may be gleaned from these descriptive case studies. It appears that many children with sex chromosome anomalies have communication impairments, including low verbal IQ relative to performance IQ, and expressive language deficits that persist into adulthood (see Ludlow and Cooper, 1983, for review). Eleven children with abnormal sex chromosomes were compared to ten normal control children in a cyto-genetic study reported by Leonard et al. (1974). Blind evaluations at 1 and 2.5 years of age revealed no clinical abnormalities and no mental retardation among any of the children studied. However, language was considerably delayed by the age of 2.5 years in the children with abnormal sex chromosomes. Other studies evaluating language development in children with abnormal sex chromosomes can be summarized as follows:

- 47 XYY boys. Radcliff (1982) reported that verbal comprehension is not affected.
- 47 XXY boys. Puck et al. (1975) reported that three of four males showed a lag in speech development; Neilsen et al. (1981) reported an increase in frequency of speech difficulties. However, neither of these reports defined these speech and language difficulties or reported any objective measures supporting their conclusions. Graham et al. (1982) reported the only well-controlled, detailed study of language, reading, and spelling abilities of XXY boys. This study compares a group of 14 unselected XXY boys ascertained during a neonatal screening survey with a matched group of 15 normal control boys. Studies demonstrated significant reductions in verbal IQ, expressive language functions, and reading and spelling abilities for the XXY group. The authors suggested that left-hemisphere-based difficulty in auditory processing may underlie some of these deficits. Further study demonstrated significant deficits in both nonverbal and verbal auditory processing abilities for the XXY group. On nonverbal tasks, the XXY group had more difficulty discriminating and sequencing at rapid rates of presentation. Of 11 XXY boys with difficulty sequencing nonverbal tones at rapid rates of presentation, 2 had a primary auditory rate discrimination problem, while the remaining boys, in the absence of auditory rate discrimination problems, appeared to have auditory memory problems or difficulty sequencing at rapid rates of presentation. The XXY group also had difficulty remembering and preserving the serial order of both speech and nonspeech auditorily presented materials. These difficulties were significantly correlated with problems in oral language production and in reading and spelling proficiency. These findings help to clarify previous misconceptions concerning the cognitive abilities of XXY boys and assist in clarifying the bases of the learning disabilities demonstrated by these children during their school years.
- 47 XXX females. These XXX females were reported to have receptive language problems (Pennington et al., 1980) as well as lower verbal IQ (Neilsen et al., 1981). These authors, however, emphasize that the language problems are difficult to evaluate because of general cognitive deficiencies that co-occur in these subjects.

- 45 XO females. These females do not exhibit delays in early speech milestones in the only study reported (Robinson et al., 1979).

Occasionally, autosomal abnormalities have been associated with abnormalities in language development on a case report basis. Examples include partial trisomy 15 (Moedjono et al., 1983) and 18p (Thompson et al., 1986). The infrequencies of these reports indicate that, at best, gross chromosomal abnormalities represent only a small fraction of the language disabled population. However, the occurrence of even these sporadic cases indicates that, with the increasing ability of cytogenetic techniques to find even smaller chromosomal abnormalities, further research may elucidate regions of the genome associated with language disabilities.

Netley (1983), in his review of the subject, concluded that until such time as studies more clearly define, describe, and select for specific language disorders, no firm conclusions can be made pertaining to the genetic basis of specific developmental language disorders. It is clear from review of this scant literature that language impairments per se have rarely been the focus of genetic research. Much more data need to be generated before an informed conclusion pertaining to a genetic basis of language disorders can be drawn.

INBORN ERRORS OF METABOLISM

Recognizable and unique behavioral phenotypes have been described for many genetically determined diseases, and it has been reported that inborn errors of metabolism may impair development and behavior in specific ways (Simopoulos, 1983). These inherited disorders tend to show a wide range of clinical severity, which may be a function of the degree of enzyme deficiency that exists in individual families. Although the incidence of metabolic disorders in the general population is considered to be very low (Nyhan, 1974), it may, in fact, be much higher within a population of children with more subtle cognitive deficits, such as language disorders. This hypothesis is presently being investigated as part of the San Diego Center for Neurodevelopmental Studies.

In many cases, dietary manipulations after birth can overcome or bypass even severe enzymatic defects to the extent that no gross physical, cognitive, or behavioral disturbances appear to develop (Simopoulos, 1983). Unfortunately, such treatment may not entirely preclude the development of residual deficits, such as a language or learning disorder, since secondary biochemical and histological changes are well established in utero for some inherited metabolic diseases.

There is considerable evidence that disorders of language development occur in children treated for various inborn errors of metabolism. Melnick et al. (1981) investigated the linguistic development of 12 children from English-speaking, middle-income families who were treated early in infancy for phenylketonuria (PKU). The researchers measured both receptive and expressive language, short-term auditory memory, hearing, oral-motor function, and articulation. Children were assessed longitudinally for approximately 18 months, beginning at 26 months. Results showed that they had normal IQ, normal development, normal hearing, and no oral musculature deviations. However, 6 of the 12 children (4 males, 2 females) had retarded expressive language development, and 4 of these 6 had receptive language impairment as well. In addition, all of these LI children were significantly below average on tests of short-term auditory memory.

Similarly, Waisbren et al. (1983) found that 7 out of 8 children with galactosemia treated early had substantial speech and language deficits. These children had normal growth, physical development, and mean full-scale IQ, although their mean verbal IQ score was significantly lower than their mean performance IQ score. This pattern is commonly found among LI children. History of language delay was also reported for each child. Like the PKU children described earlier, these galactosemic children had particular problems with expressive language, and were found to score well below average on auditory short-term memory tests.

Speech defects and mental retardation are the most prominent clinical features of histidinemia, an inborn error of amino acid metabolism in which large amounts of histidine accumulate in body fluids because it is not properly metabolized to urocanic acid (Nyhan, 1972). The nature of the speech defect has not been documented; hearing is not impaired in histidinemic patients, and general mental retardation is present only in some. Again, similar to both PKU and galactosemic children, auditory short-term memory deficits have also been reported in these children (Nyhan, 1974). Treatment of established patients with low histidine diet has not proven effective in improving their intellectual deficits, although it may help to normalize their growth if the treatment is started in infancy (Nyhan, 1974). In one family case report (Ghadimi et al., 1961), a 3-year-old girl who had been diagnosed as having PKU was found to have extremely elevated histidine levels in both urine and plasma. Her emotional, social, motor, physical, and intellectual development appeared normal, but she spoke only single words. Other family members were subsequently tested, and it was found that several also had elevated histidine levels. Witkop and Henry (1963) reported that of 10 known cases of histidemia, 9 showed defective speech. These researchers reported that although articulation was often impaired, the deficit appeared to be primarily one of language. Unfortunately, however, no tests were reported that directly differentiated verbal IQ from performance IQ, or receptive language skills from expressive ones. However, not all researchers agree that histidinemia is a primary cause of language disorders in children. Lott et al. (1970) report that of 4 children with histidinemia, only 1 had an abnormal auditory memory span, and none had abnormal speech; 2 of the children had developed normal language, and the other 2 were retarded. They found no evidence that language was impaired any more than other cognitive functions in the 2 retarded children, and concluded that the language deficits reported elsewhere in the literature were not caused directly by the metabolic disorder interfering with brain structures subserving language function but rather may have resulted from hearing loss or general retardation.

There is some evidence that specific developmental language disabilities may also be behavioral sequelae of other genetically transmitted disorders such as Laurence-Moon-Biedl syndrome and deLange syndrome. Despite the fact that these syndromes are characterized by such diverse impairments as retardation and hearing loss, some researchers insist that these other deficits are not commensurate with the profound language disabilities that these patients experience (Garstecki et al., 1972; Moore, 1970). Garstecki et al. (1972) reported that children with the Laurence-Moon-Biedl syndrome, who had normal hearing, were below the 8th percentile for receptive vocabulary and had particular difficulty discriminating speech sounds. Nyhan and his colleagues have studied the behavior of several children with other inborn errors of metabolism: A patient with oculocutaneous tyrosinemia had normal intelligence with a specific learning disability (Ney et al., 1983); two patients with 3-methylglutaconic aciduria and three with ethylmalonic aciduria had isolated disorders of speech development but no other clinical manifestations; and one patient with 4-hydroxybutyric aciduria currently being studied has essentially no development of language (Nyhan, personal communication). Clearly, additional research is needed in this area to resolve discrepancies and to better assess neuropsychological and linguistic development in children with specific inborn errors of metabolism.

HORMONES

Especially before birth, when brain cells are developing rapidly, abnormal hormonal secretions can have permanent effects on brain structure and function and thus on behavior. Genetic defects can cause such abnormalities, but so can events that are environmental from the viewpoint of the fetus. Such events might include drugs taken by the mother during pregnancy (for instance, phenobarbital [Gray and Yaffe, 1983]) or a change in maternal hormone levels in response to severe stress (McEwen, 1983).

McEwen (1983) cautions that the effects of abnormal endocrine signals on prenatal brain development should not be underestimated. Timing is of the essence in the development of brain cells. If neurons are subjected to abnormal influences from hormonal agents secreted at the wrong time or in the wrong amounts, intricate neural circuitry may be disrupted. The effects of hormones on the immature, developing brain are generally greater and longer lasting than their effects on the mature brain. Many of the long-lasting influences of hormones are deduced from experiments in which fetal or newborn rodents are subjected to excesses or deficiencies of key hormones during different periods—for example, thyroid and adrenocortical hormones. Imbalances cause serious, long-lasting, and fairly obvious effects on adult brain function.

Gonadal hormone influences are more subtle, and potentially could influence language development, particularly in boys, in at least three ways. First, prenatal androgens cause the right and left cerebral hemispheres to develop differently, so that the left hemisphere is late to mature (Chi et al., 1977). In fact, the size of the temporal plane of the left cerebral hemisphere does not catch up to that of the right until approximately 31 weeks of gestation (McEwen, 1983). Such delayed growth in the left hemisphere as a result of testosterone may account for the greater frequency of left handedness in males; it also makes the male left hemisphere susceptible to insult for a protracted period of time. Since the left temporal lobe is considered crucial to normal human language development, and since this region in males is far more vulnerable to a wide variety of late prenatal, perinatal, or early postnatal insults than is either the male right hemisphere or the entire female cortex, we are provided with a potential hypothesis of why so many more boys than girls suffer from developmental language disorders.

A second way in which gonadal hormones might influence language development is that there is a differential effect of androgen on the hemispheres, which also may cause the lateralization of brain structure and function to be more pronounced in human males than in human females (McEwen, 1983). Brain-injured females, for example, do not show such marked laterality on verbal or spatial tests as do brain-injured males; androgen-deficient males do less well than normal males on spatial tasks; and androgen-insensitive males do better on verbal than on nonverbal tests, unlike the normal male. This increased lateralization of function in males may increase the chances that congenital defects or brain damage will cause language deficits in boys, since the right hemisphere may be more highly specialized for extra-linguistic functions, such as spatial skills in boys, and thus less able to take over language functions.

Finally, neurons that occupy Wernicke's area in the left temporal lobe are formed before 20 weeks of gestation and migrate to that ultimate location. Since 12 to 20 weeks of gestation is the period of maximum testosterone elevation in developing male fetuses, the hormone may affect some of these developing brain cells. It could influence their division or survival, migration, or the formation of stable connections with other neurons (McEwen, 1983). It is not known how a bloodborne substance that reaches both sides of the brain could have selective effects on one side. McEwen postulates that hormone-receptive cells may not be laid down in equal numbers on both sides of the developing brain, giving rise to an asymmetrical target for hormone action. It is equally plausible, however, that the effects are actually widespread but simply appear to be selective because language, or some underlying perceptual prerequisite to language, is very fine-tuned and thus is more likely to be disrupted by hormonally induced alterations in cerebral development than are other behaviors or cognitive processes.

TERATOGENS

It is well known that numerous environmental contaminants can affect a developing fetus—for example, heavy metals, dioxin derivatives, polychlorinated diphenyl compounds, pesticides, tobacco smoke, alcohol, and others. A broad spectrum of sequelae has been associated with exposure to these various toxins, from abnormalities in the female or male germ cells, on up through development (Longo, 1980). Unfortunately, behavioral teratogenicity in humans is an elusive and poorly defined concept. To date, much of the research on toxins known to damage the central nervous system (CNS) (from both physiological and anatomical evidence) and result in behavioral disorganization in animals has not been extrapolated to humans. Even if it had been, it would be difficult to explain human clinical findings on the basis of existing animal experimental models, since there are major differences between humans and other mammals in their embryological development, biochemistry, and structure and function of various brain regions. This caveat would, of course, apply especially to animal modeling of uniquely human cognitive abilities such as language. However, it is possible that higher mammals could be used in future research to model cognitive or perceptual prerequisites of language that are consistently disordered in language impaired children, such as nonverbal temporal perception or memory.

Neonatal deficits associated with intrauterine exposure to small doses of potential teratogenic agents vary considerably across individuals. For example, of 242 newborns exposed prenatally to polychlorinated biphenyls, some were born small and/or early; some had one or more of labile states, motoric immaturity, increased startle response, and hypoactive reflex; and some had no detectable impairment (Jacobson et al., 1984). These sorts of differences between and within species make it difficult to pinpoint exactly which deficits are consistent sequelae of a particular teratogenic insult.

Some of the best research on the consequences of prenatal toxic insult has been in the area of lead poisoning (Needleman et al., 1979; Bellinger et al., 1986a,b). One detailed investigation of the possible effects of lead on cognitive development, which included extensive language and auditory processing and memory assessment, was conducted by Needleman et al. (1979). Baby teeth were collected from the children, and the dentine was analyzed for lead content. Children whose lead content was above the 90th percentile for the group were classified as "high," and those below the 10th percentile were classified as "low." The "high" children were found to have significantly lower scores than the "low" children on the verbal IQ, but not the performance IQ subscale of the Wechsler Intelligence Scale for Children. "High" children were also significantly impaired on sentence repetition on the Seashore test of auditory perception, on the Token test, on reaction time performance, and on most items of the teachers' behavioral checklist (although not on hyperactivity items). The researchers concluded that children with high lead levels were generally impaired with regard to verbal performance, auditory processing, and sustained attention.

It is clear that much more research is needed in this area. With the exception of the study by Needleman et al. (1979), there appear to be no investigations of the effects of heavy metals on child development that focus on, or even address, language development specifically.

The placenta does not protect the developing embryo and fetus from heavy metal toxins. In addition, most common drugs, including both alcohol and nicotine, cross the placenta readily, and circulation levels in fetal blood are often similar to those in maternal blood. Like heavy metal interactions, drug interactions may be important; it is not known whether the latter are additive or synergistic (Streissguth, 1986). In assessing possible relationships between intrauterine drug exposure and subsequent behavioral and developmental variables, it is also important to control for the many factors impinging on children post-natally, such as family characteristics, diet, schooling, and socio-economic status, which are potentially confounding or at least interactive variables.

One toxic substance that has been shown to affect fetal development at very low levels is alcohol. Dose-response curves are generally steep for developmental toxins but the curve for alcohol exposure is nearly flat—demonstrating adverse fetal effects following only one to two ounces per day during pregnancy (Ob-Gyn News, July 1985). Streissguth (1986) reports that children of light drinkers (less than one drink per day on average) show attentional problems. Children of alcoholic mothers incur many disabilities, including retardation and impairments of learning, speech, attention, and fine and gross motor performance. Unfortunately, there have been no studies that have systematically looked at patterns of language per se in normal IQ children exposed prenatally to alcohol, nor have any studies indicated whether significant differences exist between performance and verbal IQ measures in these children.

As part of the San Diego longitudinal study, thorough medical questionnaires were completed by the biological parents of each subject. Prenatal, perinatal, and postnatal history as well as demographic data were collected. Of the numerous medical history and demographic variables assessed, only questions pertaining to prenatal exposure to teratogens (nicotine, alcohol, drugs) significantly differentiated the LI from the control group (Tallal et al., in preparation).

The effects of prenatal alcohol exposure, in either the first or third trimester of pregnancy, on subsequent neuropsychological and linguistic development is currently being studied by the San Diego Center for Neurodevelopmental Studies. Neurological, neuropsychological, and linguistic development is being assessed in fine-grained detail in children whose mothers either "binge drank" in their first trimester of pregnancy (before they realized they were pregnant) or were given large quantities of alcohol intravenously in their third trimester as a medical treatment for premature labor. The results of these new studies should help clarify the potential role of alcohol in developmental language and learning disorders.

It is known that both prenatal and postnatal administration of phenobarbital (PB) can have a detrimental effect on the biochemistry of the brain. It can also affect hormone levels and, consequently, sexual differentiation. Male rats exposed to PB during gestation showed a marked decrease in testicular synthesis of testosterone on the day of birth, and the level of testosterone remained low throughout adult life (Gray and Yaffe, 1983). When PB is given in high enough doses, male brain development may be irreversibly altered (Clemens et al., 1979). Unfortunately, behavioral sequelae have not been well delineated for these animals. Nothing is known about the effects of prenatal exposure to PB on the acquisition of complex behavior such as language (Gray and Yaffe, 1983).

Other postnatally induced biochemical abnormalities may have specific effects on language development. Early reports of dietary chloride deficiency in infants documented biochemical abnormalities accompanied by delayed growth and developmental milestones. (See Kaleita et al., 1987, for review.) Kaleita et al. (1987) report followup studies of children with a history of ingesting chloride-deficient baby formula (neo-mull-soy/cho-free). Of 10 consecutive cases studied, 6 children showed a consistent profile including language disability, motor incoordination, normal intelligence, and behavioral disturbance. Physical examination was normal.

INFECTIONS

PRENATAL INFECTIONS

Many infections are known to be capable of causing brain damage prenatally, including the cytomegaloviruses, rubella, herpes simplex, varicella, syphilis, tuberculosis, and toxoplasmosis (Sever, 1986). The brain damage may be seen in many forms, including mental retardation, seizures, cerebral palsy, hearing loss, and learning disabilities. Usually, affected children are multiply handicapped; however, most studies have not been reported in sufficient detail (Sever, 1986).

The most promising research in this field to date has concentrated on evaluating outcomes of prenatal exposure to rubella virus. As early as 1970, Weinberger et al. reported that rubella embryopathy may not be clinically evident at birth because of covert symptoms, such as a delay in the expression of certain functions such as language. In addition, mothers may have no history of illness, even though they were exposed. Children with various disabilities such as speech, hearing, or visual disorders of any etiology were tested for the presence of the rubella antibody; the test was positive for 5 of 41 children born in 1964 (the year of the last rubella epidemic). These researchers concluded that although delayed speech was evident in the seropositive children, it was possibly secondary to general psychomotor retardation and/or deafness. The children tended to be small in early infancy and suffered from failure to thrive generally. In 1973, however, Feldman et al. reported that language delay is sometimes the only sequela of prenatal exposure to rubella virus. These researchers tested for the presence of rubella antibody in serum of 12 autistic children, 21 LI children, 25 psychiatric controls (nonlanguage impaired), and 26 normal controls. Three of the autistic children and eight of the LI children tested positive, as did the mothers of these children, as compared with 5 of the 51 other (nonlanguage impaired) children. Thus, there was a significantly higher incidence of seropositivity for rubella virus among LI children than there was among either of the control groups or among the general population. There was no historical evidence of maternal rubella in any of the children, and pure tone audiometry was normal for all.

POSTNATAL INFECTIONS

Otitis media (OM) literally means "inflammation of the middle ear." In this normally air-filled cavity, tiny ossicles transmit the vibrations of the eardrum (which forms the boundary of outer and middle ear) to the cochlea in the inner ear, which converts them into the nerve impulses that the brain perceives as sound. The middle ear is normally open to the atmosphere via the eustachian tube, which allows constant ventilation and maintenance of proper pressure. During the acute stage of inflammation, the middle ear may fill partially with fluid (effusion), usually because a blocked eustachian tube does not allow drainage and ventilation. The result is termed "serous or secretory otitis media." If bacteria infect the effusion, the disease becomes "suppurative." The acute phase lasts about three weeks, and resolution normally can take up to three months (the subacute stage). Effusion lasting longer than three months, or fluctuating improvement, is called chronic (Bluestone, 1983).

The first report examining the effect of middle ear disease (otitis media) on children's language development appeared less than 20 years ago (Holm and Kunze, 1969). While a link was found between a history of the disease and impaired linguistic performance, Holm and Kunze emphasized that this was only a preliminary study. Numerous researchers in the following years also found a correlation between OM and impaired language in various populations, leading some to claim a causal connection. Such reports sparked controversy, however, as none of the studies was able to completely eliminate the possible influence of other environmental factors. Recent reviews have criticized previous work for imprecise methodology and hence faulty conclusions. (See Kavanagh, 1986, for a complete review of this subject.)

In his examination of the controversy, Leviton (1980) attempted to simplify the problem by proposing three direct hypotheses for investigation: first, that children with otitis media are at increased risk for hearing impairment; second, that hearing impairment increases the risk of language and learning disorders; and as a logical conclusion, that children with OM are at increased risk of language disorders.

The first hypothesis Leviton considers is that children with OM are at increased risk for hearing impairment. It is, of course, the dampening presence of fluid in the ear that is usually responsible for hearing loss, although other complications may also cause loss. Because of chronic effusion, the eardrum often perforates, which can cause up to a 30 dB conductive hearing loss. Alternatively, the mucous membrane in the cavity may become thick and fibrous, immobilizing the ossicles (Bluestone, 1983). An early study of OM followed 80 children for 6 months after treatment for the acute phase of an episode of OM, giving each subject 5 audiometric examinations during that time. One-third had no hearing loss after the episode, 55 percent had loss that cleared within the observation period, and 12 percent had loss lasting the entire 6 months and beyond. Loss was defined as a requirement of 15 dB intensity for reception of a pure tone. (Normal subjects require an average of 0 dB [Olmstead et al., 1964]). Kaplan et al. (1973) tested 489 Alaskan Eskimos and found that 19 percent of those with a history of OM had hearing loss of 26 dB or more, compared with 9 percent of those without a history of the disease. Among those with OM, the number of episodes correlated strongly with loss (7 episodes, compared to 3.4 episodes for those who heard normally.) Unfortunately, it is unspecified whether children currently suffering an OM episode were included in the hearing testing. These results are significant, since they bear on the second hypothesis that hearing impairment can lead to language and learning problems.

Audiologists label as "mild" the average 25 dB loss accompanying OM, but investigators have found that the threshold for auditory handicap is age-dependent (Kirkwood and Kirkwood, 1983). It has been suggested that while adults can "fill in" lost input using their well-established grammar and knowledge of how the world operates, children are continuing to form and internalize linguistic rules on the basis of their auditory experience. Therefore, mild hearing loss will be comparatively more damaging to them. As Mustain (1979) points out, the normal ear requires 40 dB intensity to discriminate 90 percent of a group of monosyllabic words. A child with 25 dB loss would then require 65 dB to achieve the same level of discrimination, and normal speech rarely exceeds 50 dB. Menyuk insightfully notes that the fluctuating nature of the loss caused by OM may make it even more damaging. The child receives inconsistent stimuli as hearing improves and deteriorates with the episodes of the disease, and so may find it even more difficult to develop effective listening strategies than a child with consistent mild loss (Menyuk, 1980). It follows logically that if OM causes hearing loss and hearing loss leads to learning or language disability, then OM increases the risk of language disorders. Evidence for the first two hypotheses is not especially controversial, yet studies that set out to consider specifically the third hypothesis have not convincingly proven a causal relationship. The relationship between otitis media, auditory processing, speech processing, and language disorders was the focus of a recent conference sponsored by the National Institute of Child Health and Human Development. A complete, updated review of this topic has been recently published as the proceedings of this conference (Kavanagh, 1986).

Holm and Kunze (1969) administered a battery of speech and language tests to children with a history of OM and to controls. The OM group performed significantly worse on all tests that required the receiving or processing of auditory stimulation or the production of a verbal response. Responses on purely visual or motor tasks or on tasks that allowed yes/no answers did not differ significantly. In addition, the difference in parent rating of abilities reached the .01 level of confidence, in the expected direction. The authors stress that socioeconomic matching was the only control for important factors such as intelligence, motivation, and language stimulation in the home. They suggest that it may well be that a parent who disregards the child's OM until it becomes chronic also provides less language stimulation. Holm and Kunze's results have been replicated in several studies, which have attempted to better control for potentially confounding environmental and demographic variables (Kaplan et al., 1973; Lewis, 1976; Brandes and Ehinger, 1981; Zinkus et al., 1978). Gottlieb et al. (1979) approached the issue from the opposite angle by comparing learning disabled children with significant central auditory processing deficits (group A) with learning disabled children with no evidence of auditory perceptual disturbances (group B). Groups were further divided according to history of OM. Of group A, 46 percent had a history of the disease, a significantly higher prevalence than was found in group B (22 percent). Similarly, 41 percent of group A were delayed in language development compared to 18 percent of group B. The authors concluded that the higher rate of OM in group A indicated that middle ear disease in early life may be an important factor in the development of auditory processing deficits, which, in turn, may compromise development of language and other cognitive functions. A similar theory has been investigated by Eimas and Clarkson (1986).

More recently, prospective studies of infants have helped provide knowledge about hearing impairment and language development during the earliest episodes of OM. Such work will help answer the frequent criticism that retrospective studies cannot provide a causal link since they lack information on early hearing levels. Thelin et al. (1979) administered a behavioral hearing threshold test for speech and a receptive-expressive emergent language scale to 143 infants at 1 year of age. The language quotient correlated significantly (p   .01) with the speech detection threshold, so that poorer hearing led to poorer language skills. Significant articulation and expressive language delays in 47 children between 2 and 5 with confirmed history of at least three OM episodes have also been reported (Lehmann et al, 1979).

Friel-Patti et al. (1982) used auditory brain stem response technology as an objective electrophysiological measure of hearing in 35 infants. Two other independent measures confirmed any hearing impairment or middle ear pathology at 6, 12, and 18 months. A standardized parent interview and observation of the child determined the infants' typical language performance at 12, 18, and 24 months. At study's end, three groups were formed on the basis of number of OM episodes: group 1 had one or none; group 2 had three or more episodes and one-half had ventilation tubes by 18 months; and group 3 had two episodes. Of group 1, 78 percent showed no language delay, and of group 3, 85 percent showed no language delay. In contrast, 71.5 percent of group 2 (the otitis group) showed some delay, with 43 percent demonstrating more than 6 months' delay. Of these patients, 9 had bilateral hearing loss of 25 dB or more, and 4 had abnormal brain stem readings. These results are a clear indication that repeated episodes of OM can lead to language delay, either because of hearing loss, or because the feeling of ill health reduces the infant's attentiveness to stimuli. These results have also been replicated in numerous studies using different methodologies and designs (Silva et al., 1982; Schlieper et al., 1985; Eimas and Clarkson, 1986; Feagans, 1986).

In a large longitudinal study reported by Menyuk (1980), 250 children were followed from birth to age 7 years. Assessment at 7 years indicated continued impact of OM on speech and language development, specifically on expressive language. Four or more episodes appeared to be the critical number affecting long-term impact.

In a review of the types of language, memory, and perceptual difficulties frequently seen in children with OM, Zinkus (1986) points out that many children with OM develop completely normally. Thus, OM does not directly predict developmental language deficits. He concludes that some children may already be at risk for developmental language disorders, and the presence of OM interacts with other causes to lead to their expression. Bishop and Edmundson (1986) found a positive association between parental report of recurrent middle ear disease and perinatal hazards within a language disordered population, but no association within a control group, lending tentative support to this view.

Bishop and Edmundson (1986) also noted that although an increased risk of middle ear disease has been reported in children with specific language delay, this may have resulted because OM is especially likely to be detected and treated aggressively when occurring in association with language impairment, rather than indicating a genuine increase in the incidence of OM in LI children. Two recent studies that screened whole populations for ear disease, and so would not be affected by such a bias, failed to find an association between OM and language disorder (Allen and Robinson, 1984; Fischler et al., 1985).

As part of the San Diego longitudinal study, the question of the relationship between OM and pattern and severity of language disorder is being investigated from a different vantage point. The question raised in this study is not whether OM causes language disorder, but rather whether the pattern or course of language disorder is significantly different in developmentally language impaired children with or without a history of chronic OM. Within the well-defined, selected population of 100 LI and 60 normal children participating in this longitudinal study, 15 LI and 9 normal children had a history of five or more treated cases of OM. Perhaps surprisingly, results of extensive fine-grained analysis have revealed no significant differences in the degree or pattern of neurological, neuropsychological, intellectual, speech, language, or social/emotional development as a factor of OM within either the LI or the normal group. Thus, although previous research has indicated a relationship between OM and LI, the results of this study clearly demonstrate that if OM causes language disorders, the resultant pattern of those disorders is indistinguishable from those caused by other factors (genetic, neurological, teratogenic, etc.). Although there were numerous significant differences found between the LI and the normal children participating in this longitudinal study, these differences cannot be attributed directly to history of OM, since no within-group differences emerged for either normal or LI children as a function of OM. (Tallal et al., in preparation).

BRAIN DAMAGE

Evidence appears to be mixed on whether early brain damage selectively causes language disorders (Hier and Rosenberger, 1980; see Bishop, 1987, for review). On the one hand, Garoutte (1967) argued that prenatal cerebral injuries, severe enough to produce a delay in language acquisition, are generally accompanied by significant mental retardation or other neurological impairments as well. On the other hand, Benton (1964) reported that there is considerable evidence implicating early CNS damage as a causative factor in dysphasia, including: (1) medical histories of cerebral complications such as anoxia, head injury, meningitis, encephalitis, and maternal rubella; (2) increased incidence of neurological "soft signs" such as clumsiness; and (3) higher than normal number of EEG abnormalities.

Eisenson (1969) found that 36 of 73 dysphasic children had positive EEG findings; 22 of these had localized abnormalities, of which 19 were in the left hemisphere. Furthermore, 46 out of 87 LI children were found by Dalby (1977a,b) to have abnormal dilation of the temporal horns (especially the left side) demonstrated by pneumoencephalography. Dalby also found a high rate of cerebellum and brain stem lesions in these children. Among l6 children with a delay in language acquisition, computerized brain tomography (CT) revealed focal abnormality in 6 cases (Caparulo et al., 1981). However, in a subsequent study, Harcherik et al. (1985) used blind assessment of CT scans and more quantitative procedures to compare several groups of children with neurodevelopmental disorders (including 9 cases of developmental language disorder). Results demonstrated no group differences on measures of asymmetry, brain density, or ventricular size. They concluded that language disorder is seldom associated with CT scan abnormality unless accompanied by additional neurological problems.

In a recent study of auditory processing disorders in children with language/learning disabilities, Musiek et al. (1982) reported that 2 to 3 percent of children referred for central auditory disorders were found to have active neurological problems. These included finding (1) a large subarachnoid cyst with no midlatency evoked potential response in one child (although brain stem response was normal); and (2) previously undetected disorders, including severe left ear deficits on dichotic listening tasks, and bilateral deficits on other central auditory processing tests that were strikingly similar to profiles reported for patients who have undergone surgical commissurotomy (split brain).

What type of damage would have to be sustained developmentally in order to produce a selective language disorder, uncontaminated by other cognitive disabilities? The animal literature reveals that large, prenatally induced lesions resulting in substantial cortical loss and displacement did not affect the development of learning behaviors, although much smaller lesions in the same regions in adult animals have had significant effects (Goldman, 1979). Anatomical studies performed after puberty on prenatally lesioned animals indicated that organizational differences in cortical development had taken place, although learning was not impaired and no behavioral deficits were found. Goldman concluded that pre- or postnatal lesions are probably not responsible for marked and long-standing impairments in language development. However, she believes that there may be a lack of, or disordered development of, particular language-related brain regions in dysphasic children. She looks to intrinsic rather than extrinsic factors to explain the phenomenon.

Galaburda and Kemper (1979) agreed with this suggestion that intrinsic focal disorders of cortical development may underlie some cases of specific language and reading disorders. At autopsy, the brain of an adult with a lifelong history of language and reading disorders showed signs of neuroanatomical abnormalities, all confined to the left hemisphere. There was no evidence of neuron loss or gliosis. However, there was a striking area of polymicrogyria, with adjacent molecular layers of the abnormal gyri fused; no normal cortical lamination; and no cell-free layer. These abnormalities were confined to the posterior parts of Heschl's gyrus and to the left planum temporale, an area corresponding roughly to the auditory association region known as Wernicke's area. The remaining auditory fields were relatively unaffected. The cause of this type of malformation is unknown, but in 6 of the 16 autopsy cases of language/learning disorders that have been reported, family history has suggested a genetic component. In 7 of these 16 cases, the polymicrogyria anomaly was restricted to a small, focal area. Galaburda and Kemper (1979) speculated that a familial form of localized polymicrogyria may be responsible for the language impairments of these patients.

Only one child with a specific developmental language disorder has ever come to autopsy (Goldstein et al., 1958). This child had normal hearing, a performance IQ of 97, and a verbal IQ of 76. By 9 years of age, he had acquired some expressive language, but still had considerable difficulty processing speech when it was spoken at a normal rate. His comprehension was reported to be improved when he was spoken to slowly. At autopsy, old, bilateral infarctions of the Sylvian regions and severe retrograde degeneration of both medial geniculate nuclei were found.

Geschwind (1979) has noted that even if there is a lack of visible anatomical change or identifiable biochemical lesion, there may still be a neurological basis for developmental dysphasia. He suggested that since there is a considerable anatomical variation in the normal population, certain brain regions will be developed to a lesser or a greater degree than others in a given individual, and hence, people will vary in the degree to which they will be able to acquire certain skills.

He cites as evidence for this hypothesis that the planum temporale, a brain region which corresponds roughly both to Brodmann's area 22 and to Wernicke's area, is asymmetrical in the "average" human, tending to be approximately one-third larger on the left side than on the right (Geschwind and Levitsky, 1968). This pattern of asymmetry has also been seen in human fetuses and neonates (Geschwind, 1979). However, there is a great deal of variation in this ratio among the human population; one man with a high verbal IQ was found to have a planum temporale that was seven times as large on the left side as on the right, while dyslexics at autopsy have been found to have nearly symmetrical patterns (Geschwind, 1979; Galaburda and Kemper, 1979).

Geschwind (1979) reported that of 24 patients with a history of developmental dyslexia, 10 had a reversal of the normal asymmetry pattern, in that the right parieto-occipital region was wider than the left. These "reversed" dyslexics were significantly more likely to have had delayed onset of language as young children than were the other dyslexics not showing this reversal, and they also had a lower verbal

IQ but not a lower performance IQ than did the other dyslexics. Since this pattern of reversal occurs in 10 to 12 percent of the population, whereas dyslexia occurs in only 1 to 3 percent of the population, Geschwind speculates that this pattern may predispose a child to develop dysphasia and dyslexia if other predisposing factors are also present, such as intrauterine insult. On the basis of these findings, Geschwind postulates that if a child is endowed with a left planum temporale that is unusually small (a reversal of the normal asymmetrical anatomical pattern), problems in acquiring language might result, either because language will be lateralized to a hemisphere less suited to support language function (the right hemisphere) or because the left hemisphere cannot subordinate the right as it normally would, and abnormal interhemispheric interaction is set up. In support of this hypothesis are Eisenson's (1966) findings that LI children developed manual laterality (handedness) very late compared to normal children and that there is a higher than normal incidence of left handedness among these children. Similarly, Arnold and Schwartz (1983) found that of 8 LI children, 6 were right lateralized on a dichotic listening task for language material, compared to only 1 of 8 autistic children. None of the 8 normal children tested showed right lateralization.

While the data supporting Geschwind's hypothesis are striking, they are equally capable of supporting other theories, such as the possibility that genetic anomalies (or even the presence of extrinsic, traumatic factors) rather than normal genetic variation underlie the development of a left temporal lobe that is inappropriately sized or inappropriately lateralized to support normal language function.

It would appear that the left hemisphere, for whatever reason, is the hemisphere most suited to subserve language function. Anatomical evidence suggests that the two hemispheres do not have equal potential early in development. Witelson and Pallie (1973) observed that the left hemisphere is greater in size than the right in neonate humans, while Chi et al. (1977) found that in fetuses the left auditory association cortex is larger than the right by the third trimester. Right/left asymmetry in EEG responses to speech stimuli have been found in infants as young as 6 months (Gardiner and Walter, 1977). Thus, normal language lateralization appears to be not so much a struggle for dominance between the two hemispheres as an outcome of very early development of structures or mechanisms that will mediate language in the left hemisphere.

By adulthood, 95 percent of people are left hemisphere dominant for language (Geschwind, 1979). The right hemisphere is generally severely limited in language use; studies using split brain patients indicate that it can recognize and understand a large lexicon, mostly of concrete words such as nouns and verbs. However, if such patients are forced to rely on right hemisphere function, they cannot learn meaningless nonsense words, their short-term memory is severely restricted, and speech production is virtually impossible (Zaidel, 1979).

Interestingly, the pattern of language as well as auditory perceptual performance of split brain patients using the right hemisphere is strikingly similar to that of children with acquired aphasia (Zaidel, 1979), children treated early for galactosemia (Waisbren et al., 1983), and children with developmental language/learning disabilities with concomitant central auditory processing disorders (Musiek et al., 1982). Similarly, Zaidel (1979) reported that the disconnected right hemisphere, but not the disconnected left hemisphere, is significantly impaired in responding to rapidly presented acoustic information. These deficits are comparable to those reported by Tallal and colleagues for language impaired patients (Tallal and Piercy, 1973, 1974; Tallal et al., 1985; Tallal and Newcombe, 1978).

Consistent with these data, Tallal and Newcombe (1978) showed that adults with focal lesions of the left hemisphere (aphasia) but not the right hemisphere are also impaired in discriminating rapidly presented nonverbal acoustic stimuli, as well as speech contrasts characterized by rapidly changing acoustic spectra. Furthermore, the degree of impairment shown in adult aphasics with left hemisphere lesions on rapid auditory processing tasks correlated highly with the degree of their receptive language impairments ($r = .83$). This is precisely the same pattern of deficits reported for children with developmental language impairment (Tallal et al., 1985). These data demonstrate the superiority of the left hemisphere in processing both rapidly changing acoustic spectra and speech sounds incorporating rapidly changing format transitions. The breakdown of this function, as the result of left hemisphere disruption, appears to be concomitant with speech and language disorders.

Despite the considerable behavioral evidence that demonstrates that LI children have language as well as nonverbal processing disorders consistent with left hemisphere damage, there is still controversy about whether or not such disorders stem from focal brain damage, and if so, about the nature of the damage. It may be that different subtypes of language impairments result from different causal factors. Thus, discrepancies reported in the literature from CT, blood flow, and electroencephalography studies might be resolved by paying more careful attention to behavioral characteristics associated with different types of language disorders and the specificity of these disorders to language.

One final note on this topic is important. Language development of children with early focal brain lesions and even hemispherectomy has been investigated in some detail (Dennis and Whitake, 1977; Woods and Carey, 1979; Woods, 1980; Bishop, 1981, 1983; Vargha-Khadem, O'Gorman, and Watters, 1985). These studies suggest that language impairment resulting from early left hemisphere lesions or left hemispherectomy is different both qualitatively and quantitatively from developmental language disorders. Thus, these studies do not support the hypothesis that specific developmental language disorders result from early localized brain damage.

PSYCHOGENIC EFFECTS

Language is a highly social activity, and language development normally proceeds within the context of a child's social environment. Caregiver-infant interactions determine which language the child will learn, may determine which lexical items the child will first utilize, and may affect linguistic growth more globally. Children raised in extremely impoverished environments may, in certain circumstances, fail to develop language at all (Curtiss, 1977, 1981). However, hearing children of deaf parents, like other children who experience grossly inadequate parental spoken language, have been shown to develop appropriate language skills once exposed to language outside the home (Schiff, 1979; Skuse, 1984). Nonetheless, developmental psychologists have hypothesized that language impairment may be related to, or may be caused by, an impoverished social environment, which is often assumed to be synonymous with low socioeconomic status.

Two separate issues must be addressed. First, is there evidence to support a contention that the type or complexity of language developed by normally developing children is in any way related to the social environment? Second, does the socioeconomic environment of dysphasic children (children who are not simply at the lower end of the language continuum but who represent a population with disordered development) differ significantly from that of nondysphasic children?

With regard to the first issue, Tizard (1983) studied various usages of language (for instance: to categorize, abstract, infer logical relationships, request or give information) and found significant social class differences in the frequency of usage but not in the type of usage. Another study (Fein, 1981) yielded very similar results from an investigation of the sociodramatic play of 45 middle- and lower-class children. This study found that although middle-class subjects verbalized more frequently, the quality of the language used by the two groups did not differ.

A 10-year longitudinal study investigating the linguistic development of 128 British children (Wells, 1983) found that a significant relationship was observed between achievement and socioeconomic status (SES) only after the subjects entered school. This finding implied that lower SES children do not adapt as well or gain as much from the school experience as do children from higher SES environments. In addition, it is now well known that lower SES children suffer from lack of exposure to the standardized procedures used in measuring IQ and various components thereof, including language development (Sandeep, 1981). Either withdrawal from an alien social situation or poor scores on standardized language measures could easily be misinterpreted by the school as evidence of verbal deficits. This misinterpretation may have yielded artifactual data pertaining to SES and language development.

To conclude, current evidence strongly favors the view that the home environments in low SES families provide adequate verbal stimulation for normally developing children. In addition, children of such families display normal verbal cognitive skills that are not significantly different from those of children from higher SES families (Tizard, 1983). It has also been suggested that the quality of language directed at LI children by their parents is deficient. However, studies comparing the language used by parents of LI and control children have failed to find significant differences. (See Conti-Ramsden, 1985, for review.)

With regard to the second issue, it is unfortunate that very few studies of dysphasic children have attempted to control for factors such as SES. Matching LI and control children on the basis not only of "child" variables such as age, IQ, sex, handedness, and so on, but also on the basis of "parent" variables such as parents' educational attainment and family SES would appear to be the simplest way of ensuring that social factors cannot confound results. However, the issue of whether LI children as a group represent a lower than average socioeconomic status is difficult to assess directly due to the fact that parental education level is an important component of determining family SES. Genetic studies have suggested family aggregation of learning disabilities. (See Genetic Factors, previously discussed.) Thus, educational level attained by parents of language-impaired children would be expected to be lower than average, which confounds the issue of SES in these families.

CONCLUSIONS AND FUTURE RESEARCH CONSIDERATIONS

Developmental language impairment, with concomitant temporal auditory processing, motor, and memory deficits, appears to be consistent with a pattern of innate or progressive dysfunction of the left temporal association cortex, which may be due to the presence of a functional deficit within the left hemisphere, to an abnormal state of cerebral asymmetry, or to disordered interhemispheric integration. The mechanism(s) by which this neurological dysfunction occurs is still unresolved. It is likely that an interaction among factors may be responsible (Ludlow and Cooper, 1983). For example, LI children may be predisposed to their condition by having inherited a left temporal lobe that is on the lower end of the continuum of normalcy, as Geschwind (1979) suggests. Conversely, a variety of intrinsic or extrinsic factors may be responsible for an initial induction of a neurological abnormality by causing abnormal cell migration in the brain, by interfering with neurogenesis in regions of the brain where neurons continue to proliferate after birth, by interfering with the normal subtractive neural processes of neuronal death and axon retraction, or by otherwise disturbing the normal development of mylination (Musiek et al., 1982) or of the systems and structures subserving language (Ludlow and

Cooper, 1983; Broman, 1983; Janowsky and Finlay, 1986). It is possible, however, that not all children will be similarly impacted by such disturbances. Certain children may be subject to other intrinsic or extrinsic factors (for example, otitis media), which may interact with the original factors to exacerbate (or perhaps even to compensate for) the original neurological abnormality.

It is also important to remember not only that anatomical asymmetries do occur in the two hemispheres but also that brain development itself is asymmetric. Homologous cortical regions do not develop simultaneously on the two sides. Therefore, factors which affect the brain at a specific point in fetal life may selectively impair the development of specific cortical regions on one side while leaving the other intact (Geschwind, 1979). Thus, the timing of neural insult may be crucial in determining which structures are most affected and, as a result, whether language development, as opposed to other types of development, will be affected.

There is a tremendous need for anatomical studies of the normally developing brain at different stages of development, especially with regard to cytoarchitectonic studies of the organization and timing of development of each area. The study of the brains of dysphasic children who meet with accidental death would also be immensely important.

With regard to the effects of prenatal exposure to teratogens on the developing brain, new procedures need to be developed to (1) determine how to monitor the presence and distribution of metagenic and teratogenic agents; (2) determine what the important threshold levels are; and (3) determine their effects on fetal and infant brain development (Longo, 1980). There is a pressing need for cross-drug comparisons, cross-species comparisons, and improved behavioral and cognitive testing (Gray and Yaffe, 1983). Major limitations of such studies so far include inadequate control of other confounding variables (besides the presence of the teratogen in the prenatal environment), uncertain accuracy of maternal drug histories, and outcome criteria that provide insufficient delineation of subtle developmental delays (Gal and Sharpless, 1984).

There is also a growing need for more longitudinal studies of normal and abnormal development. It is very difficult to answer the most pressing questions about developmental disorders on the basis of studies that cannot assess development over time. In addition, it is increasingly important for future research to gather multidimensional, multidisciplinary data from the same child—behavioral, neurophysiological, anatomical, and biochemical, as well as complete medical, social, and genetic family histories.

TREATMENT

Before embarking on a discussion of the types of interventions that have been developed specifically for language disorders, it is helpful to point out that what constitutes intervention for specific disorders varies widely within the profession of speech-language pathology. This variation is responsible for controversies that exist over what is or what should be treatment for the characteristics associated with specific language impairment, such as auditory processing and memory disorders. Differences in opinion exist regarding the goals of intervention, the form it should take, its content, and the methods to use for evaluating its effectiveness. Some of these differences derive from divergent theoretical positions, such as those regarding the relationship between auditory processing disorders and language disorders. Johnston (1983) points out that, in any survey of language intervention programs, diversity is to be expected because intervention is an extension of a particular theoretical perspective. Johnston challenges professionals engaged in developing intervention programs to take theory based on recent research results seriously and to examine and evaluate the assumptions implicit in intervention practices with reference to that theory.

Controversies in intervention may arise from differences in how speech-language pathologists define their role and responsibility in relation to the management of auditory processing, speech, language, and learning disorders. The role reflects a professional's educational background and experience in clinical training as well as personal bias. Professional associations also contribute to decisions about intervention by defining and restricting areas of responsibility and professional roles. It may be difficult for such roles to keep pace with research advances, and, as such, they may impede therapeutic advances. Similarly, narrow professional boundaries may fail to recognize the multifaceted nature of complex developmental functions such as language. Unfortunately, the child who becomes fractionated for the purpose of treatment among professionals sticking adamantly to their prescribed roles is potentially the big loser.

LANGUAGE INTERVENTION RESEARCH

Leonard (1981) reviewed the literature on training studies that attempted to facilitate LI children's production of language. He examined the studies providing evidence that the reported language gains were attributable to training and not to other factors. Leonard utilized an "outcome" orientation to organize his review. In evaluating intervention research, he examined whether a particular procedure was effective in teaching a new behavior and the extent to which the procedure had generalizable effects. Studies of effectiveness examine the amount and degree a language behavior changes as a result of a treatment procedure. In contrast, studies of treatment effects examine the products of the intervention: that is, what related language behaviors change, and under what conditions. Leonard reported that numerous procedures were successful in teaching linguistic behavior to impaired children. He concluded that, in general, language intervention appeared effective in increasing impaired children's rate of language acquisition. However, variability existed in the amount of success children exhibited. Specifically, children varied in the rate and the ease with which they proceeded through the treatments and in their ability to generalize learning to other settings, people, and behaviors. This variability has been assumed to be related to the specific linguistic behaviors that were taught, the duration of the training, the characteristics of the children being taught, and the measurements utilized.

Leonard's (1981) excellent work has provided a foundation for the current review and an opportunity to follow the direction of language intervention research for more than a decade. The discussion that follows focuses primarily on research studies published since 1981. The dearth of studies reflects the paucity of research on intervention. This is a surprising and disconcerting finding, especially in light of the amount of time clinicians spend in providing intervention.

Intervention research seemed to address one of three broad categories of inquiry: effectiveness of procedures, effects of procedures, and the language acquisition process as applied to LI children. Effectiveness studies included a variety of issues.

EFFECTIVENESS OF PROCEDURES

During the 1970's, the most commonly employed intervention procedures were based on operant conditioning principles. The clinician tightly controlled the antecedent and subsequent events in the treatment paradigm and provided mass trial training. Often the remedial context was a therapy room with minimal materials and equipment. A major thrust in the last five years has been to reduce the amount of structure in treatment and to utilize more naturalistic contexts. Several studies explored the effectiveness of procedures utilizing naturally occurring interactions between children and adults. One such treatment, "incidental teaching," demonstrated effectiveness in increasing preschool children's amount of verbalization and overall language complexity (Warren et al., 1984). The effectiveness of incidental teaching in facilitating language development has been well documented. (See Warren and Kaiser, 1986, for a review of this procedure.) Schwartz et al. (1985) demonstrated the effectiveness of adult-child discourse as a technique for teaching successive single word and multi-word combinations. Discourse offers a natural interaction between speakers, but allows the opportunity for the adult to model linguistic forms and to guide the child's responses. Olswang et al. (1982) also demonstrated the importance of utilizing naturally occurring interactions between adults and children to create a teaching paradigm. In this study, a LI child's functional requesting of objects and actions increased following treatment implemented by the speech-language pathologist and the classroom teacher. The teacher was taught to recognize "request" opportunities and to naturally elicit responses from the child, which, in turn, resulted in increased spontaneous requesting throughout the day and across classroom activities. Treatment using conversational interactions versus the traditional, structured, mass trial training approach shows a change in the focus of intervention. These findings reflect the success of two philosophically different approaches in increasing children's linguistic, communicative performance.

Three studies have compared the relative effectiveness of the naturalistic, interactive treatment procedures to structured approaches. Cole and Dale (1986) and Friedman and Friedman (1980) utilized group designs and found no difference in the linguistic performance between two groups of children receiving the two different treatments. However, Friedman and Friedman (1980) observed a treatment by aptitude interaction; children with lower IQ scores performed better in the structured condition, and children with higher IQ scores performed better in the interactive condition. This finding was not replicated by Cole and Dale (1986). The conflicting results regarding aptitude by intervention interaction may have been due to different subject characteristics, with cognitive abilities being lower in the Cole and Dale study, and to different criteria for defining subjects as being LI. Olswang and Coggins (1984) compared three different interactive teaching procedures, each differing in the amount of structure imposed upon the context and the child. No differences were found between the techniques in teaching children multi-word combinations.

One reason relatively few differences may have emerged regarding the relationship between child characteristics and the effectiveness of different treatment procedures may be the use of group research designs, where individual variation in performance is collapsed into group data. Group designs have contributed important information to the literature regarding overall treatment effectiveness, but the value of such studies lies in their ability to address the broad question of which treatments work, not which treatment works best with which children in teaching different linguistic structures. Time series, or single subject, research designs may allow for the investigation of the learning process, to determine what techniques are most effective with which children. Olswang et al. (1983), for example, examined the lexical learning of four preschool LI children using different stimulus materials. Each child was taught lexical items through picture identification and object manipulation. The authors hypothesized superior learning in the object manipulation condition because all children were in Piaget's sensorimotor stage V or VI of cognitive development. However, results showed that two of the children learned more words more rapidly in the object manipulation condition; one child learned more words in the picture condition; the fourth child showed no preference. The authors interpreted the variation in performance as a reflection of differences between children in language learning processes and "readiness" for learning.

One general criticism of treatment effectiveness research has been a failure to control for maturation. Documenting treatment effectiveness with LI children must demonstrate convincingly that treatment is more effective than maturation alone in changing behavior. Further research is needed to explore the relationship between the success of different treatments and child characteristics, such as IQ, language level, language profile, learning style, and the specific linguistic structures being learned. Looking for a "single, best procedure" for treating all LI children is probably naive and is not supported by intervention research to date. Similarly, placebo-controlled research is also a must if true effect of specific therapies is to be differentiated from effect of individual attention and general stimulation.

TREATMENT EFFECTS

Research investigating treatment effects has focused on what behaviors change and on the conditions under which they change. Treatments are designed primarily to increase the occurrence of a particular target behavior. Learning is judged by the products of the treatment—that is, by the generalized results of the training effort. The ultimate goal of treatment is more effective communicative competence (Rice, 1986). How much training is needed to accomplish this goal has been a research focus for at least the last decade. Numerous studies have addressed this issue by examining response generalization and stimulus generalization. (While these terms have some degree of overlap, they can be viewed separately.) Response generalization refers to changes in behavior that are similar to, but not the same as, target behaviors. Response generalization can be conceptualized as finding that the conditioning of one response has influenced the occurrence of a different although related response (Hughes, 1985). Stimulus generalization refers to the use of the target behavior in different contexts or under stimulus conditions different from those in which it was taught, such as different persons, settings, and time. Researching treatment effects has involved studies in which narrowly defined target behaviors have been treated while the occurrence of related behaviors (response generalization) and the target behaviors in other contexts (stimulus generalization) have been monitored.

Two main issues concerning response generalization are (1) what constitutes a response class and (2) the number of exemplars needed to trigger generalization. Hegde (1980), Hegde and Gierut (1979), and Hegde et al. (1979) have examined response classes by systematically exploring generalization of syntactic structures. Hegde et al. (1979) found that in treating the auxiliary verb ("She's running"), generalization occurred to the copula form ("She's a doctor") but not to the uncontracted auxiliary ("He is swimming"). Hegde's works have identified a response class of "is" verbs, although the parameters of the class remain unclear.

Other studies have illustrated that at least with some LI children, only a few exemplars of the target behavior needed to be directly taught prior to the occurrence of response generalization. In a language comprehension study, Bunce et al. (1985) trained two LI preschoolers in a limited number of preposition + objective exemplars. Generalization to both comprehension and production of untrained words was observed. Connell (1986) also observed response generalization occurring after a limited number of items illustrating that the entity + action semantic relation had been taught. These studies suggest that linguistic "rule learning" can be taught and that teaching can often be efficiently accomplished by exposing LI children to a limited number of training items.

Studying stimulus generalization, Warren and Kaiser (1986) trained preschool LI children to produce a variety of linguistic structures. Monitoring of the children's language in a free play situation revealed that 74 percent of the structures generalized to the nontraining setting, which indicates the success of treatment. A study by Culatta and Horn (1982) systematically examined the generalization process by monitoring LI children's spontaneous production of target syntactic structures in a parallel play situation with the clinician. They reported stimulus generalization occurring early in the treatment. They accounted for this success by the nature of the training procedures, which appeared to naturally evoke the production of the target behavior. Culatta and Horn (1982) and Connell (1982) suggested that rule learning (that is: naturally occurring generalization) can be fostered if treatment programs not only emphasize the components of linguistic rules but also teach children how to use these rules.

Research concerning stimulus generalization again raises the issue of treatment efficiency. Some studies have documented the occurrence of spontaneous generalization of newly learned behaviors to other settings and to other people without direct treatment generalization training (Warren and Kaiser, 1986; Olswang et al., 1986). Other studies such as Culatta and Horn (1982) have suggested that the treatment conditions were directly related to the successful generalization of the learned behaviors. In all of these studies, the entire treatment package resulted in generalization. These treatments, though different, were successful in teaching LI children a generative behavior. No research to date has isolated the components of treatment packages that contribute to, or are responsible for, generalized learning. Such information will contribute to our knowledge concerning the generalization process and to the design of the most effective, efficient training programs.

Measuring stimulus generalization is one way of assessing whether learning is occurring. If a child can use a structure only in the teaching paradigm, one might ask if the child has indeed learned the structure. In a study by Donahue (1984), learning disabled children participated in a program designed to increase their requests for clarification of ambiguous messages and thus to increase their conversational competence. While the children improved in their production of verbal queries in a structured, 20-question task, they did not perform as competently in a referential communication task. Donahue raised the point that the tasks were not similar enough for transfer of skills to occur. Dollaghan and Kaston (1986) taught school-aged children to identify inadequate messages and how to use verbal queries to react to such situations. Skills were taught through a combination of direct instruction, modeling, role playing, and guided discussions. The data showed clear gains in the appropriate use of verbal queries. The conflicting results obtained in the study by Donahue (1984) and in the study of Dollaghan and Kaston (1986) raise several questions: Does lack of stimulus generalization reflect a flaw in treatment in the teaching of rule learning? What is the influence of context on performance? If a client can only produce a behavior in a limited context, what does that result mean? What behaviors should we measure to assess generative language behavior?

Research investigating response generalization needs to be continued to explore the parameters of response classes. Research needs to define the extent to which syntactic, semantic, and pragmatic behaviors are co-related, and thus will co-vary in treatment, and which behaviors will not. Further, research needs to explore the number of training exemplars necessary to achieve a generative, productive response from an impaired child and which types of exemplars better facilitate learning—that is, prototypic or moderately discrepant exemplars. To monitor learning, both response generalization and stimulus generalization need to be addressed. The clinician is faced with the task of determining whether a child has learned a generative, productive behavior. Measuring a variety of behaviors in a variety of settings is essential, but such measuring should not be overly complex. Further research is needed to determine the influence of different tasks on measuring performance and learning. Finally, additional data are needed to define the components of treatment that best facilitate generalization.

LANGUAGE ACQUISITION PROCESS

The third area that intervention research has addressed is the acquisition process. A number of studies have investigated which aspects of the normal language acquisition process apply to impaired children in their learning of language during treatment. Recent research with normally developing children has documented that the acquisition of lexical items proceeds relatively predictably. These children seem to acquire object words more readily than action words and words beginning with sounds in their phonological repertoire versus those not in their repertoire (Leonard et al., 1981; Schwartz and Leonard, 1982). Research examining the lexical acquisition of specific LI children found the same trend (Camarata and Schwartz, 1985; Leonard et al., 1982;

Schwartz and Leonard, 1985). Knowledge of the normal course of lexical acquisition provides clinicians with guidelines for training lexical development in LI children.

Language learning strategies have been another focus of research concerning the language acquisition process. Imitation and comprehension are two strategies documented in the literature on normal learning as being important for language production. Spontaneous, unsolicited imitations seem to herald the onset of spontaneous productions of lexical items and early grammatical structures for many normally developing children (Bloom et al., 1974; Folger and Chapman, 1978; Leonard et al., 1979; Scherer and Olswang, 1984). Intervention studies with LI children have been inconsistent in supporting this finding (Schwartz and Leonard, 1985; Olswang and Coggins, 1984). In general, spontaneous imitations appeared to facilitate lexical acquisition, although differences were noted (Schwartz and Leonard, 1985). Olswang and Coggins (1984) found less of a direct relationship between the emergence of spontaneous imitations and spontaneous productions of multi-word combinations. Comprehension abilities have also appeared to precede production of new forms in normally developing children (Benedict, 1979; Gleitman and Wanner, 1982; Whitehurst, 1982). An implication of this finding has been to train comprehension skills in an attempt to facilitate production. Schwartz and Leonard (1985) and Leonard et al. (1982) found LI children learned lexical items without production practice. This finding supported the observations on normal acquisition that comprehension often precedes production. However, in a training study, Connell (1986) found comprehension training was not sufficient to teach six LI subjects to produce semantic relations meaningfully in their spontaneous language. Thus, the extent to which comprehension precedes production in LI children or the extent to which the pattern of comprehension and production deficits of specific children influence their responsiveness to specific modes of training has not been determined.

A common theme across the intervention studies has been variation in profile of deficit—and hence performance—of clients receiving treatment. Some techniques appear to work particularly well with some children and not with others, and some children seem to use a particular language learning strategy and others do not. Learning a new language ability can be viewed on a continuum from emergence of that particular ability to mastery of the ability. Emergence to mastery of a new behavior proceeds at an uneven rate, often referred to as "growth spurts," and characteristically is accompanied by increased imitations, overextensions, and self-corrections in normally developing children. Evidence supporting the nonlinearity of language learning, as defined by readiness and growth spurts, has continued to accumulate in the literature examining LI children (Gibson and Ingram, 1983; Olswang and Coggins, 1984; Olswang et al., 1983, 1986). Such data suggest that there may be optimum times for direct treatment and also times when benefits from treatment may be negligible. This curve may vary, depending on the profile of language disorder and the age and stage of the child's language development.

Research investigating the acquisition process has contributed important information during the last five years. The data have further supported the use of the normal developmental model for providing clinicians with guidelines for selecting treatment objectives and some teaching strategies. While this model has a very clear role in planning intervention for impaired children, it needs to be evaluated with other models to determine the degree of its effectiveness. Models focusing on functional communication or compensatory strategies may be more appropriate with some children and should be evaluated accordingly.

Language intervention research has paid little attention to determining what is being taught during the treatment process. The answer is unknown as to whether clinicians are capable of teaching compensatory learning strategies (as tools for improving attending and discriminating), underlying concepts (such as spatial concepts underlying the use of prepositions), and/or linguistic rules (for instance, which lexical verbs take objects). Further, how treatment interfaces with the maturation process is unclear. Little evidence is available for suggesting whether treatment induces the emergence of a new structure or only accelerates its mastery.

The role treatment plays in altering the acquisition process of LI children must be defined. Research needs to investigate the learning process to determine whether, in the teaching of different learning strategies, concepts, and/or structures, success is being achieved with children exhibiting different types of deficits. Further, research is needed to explore the timing of treatment to determine if there are optimum times for providing direct stimulation in relationship to such maturational phenomena as readiness and growth spurts. The implication is that treatment will be more beneficial at particular times, and indeed, that treatment is unwarranted at other times.

PROCESSING INTERVENTIONS

Research emphasis is shifting toward improving the understanding of the processing aspects of language acquisition. New technologies available for analyzing and generating well-controlled acoustic stimuli may be one of the most significant forces behind this shift. The use of this technology has enabled researchers to identify the specific acoustic features of speech that contribute to perception (Kuhl, 1982). Auditory neurophysiologists (Kiang, 1980; Delgutte, 1980) are attempting to discover how the auditory nervous system processes these acoustic events and, ultimately, what processes are involved in the perception of speech and hence language. The current theories of speech perception include auditory as well as phonetic levels of processing. These interact with each other as well as with motor functions and levels of linguistic functions. Some of the more recent attempts to formulate intervention programs for LI children, specifically those with comprehension deficits, reflect these current theories (DuBard, 1983; Lasky, 1983; Lasky and Cox, 1983; Butler, 1981, 1984; Sloan, 1980, 1986).

General intervention approaches are represented in the work of Butler (1981, 1984) and Lasky and Cox (1983). These approaches have been developed primarily for school-age children who exhibit language and learning disabilities that reflect basic processing disorders. In these approaches, auditory processing difficulties are seen as a component of the language and learning problems. The general goal of these approaches is to develop methods to use with these children that will facilitate learning in the classroom. Since classroom content is most often presented through oral and written language, these approaches focus on both auditory and linguistic components of processing.

Butler (1981, 1984) uses an information processing model to direct both assessment and intervention of language processing. She suggests that clinicians analyze remediation tasks in terms of stimulus characteristics, processing characteristics, and information load (Butler, 1981). Such aspects as attention, perceptual processing, memory, rehearsal strategies, search procedures, retrieval, processing load, temporal aspects of processing, facilitation of responses, and metalinguistic and metacognitive factors are considered (Butler, 1984). Butler advocates controlling these variables in assessment procedures to determine a child's ability to process verbal information, and then manipulating these same variables in intervention to facilitate the child's information processing strategies.

Although Butler takes a general language processing approach, many of the intervention practices she recommends relate directly to the difficulties that children with auditory processing disorder (ADP) exhibit. She states, for example, that the rate of presentation of stimuli and changes in rate are as important as the semantic content (Butler, 1981). Butler (1984) offers several suggestions for training what might be called "compensatory strategies" so that a child can learn to overcome short-term memory and language processing deficits. These include (1) rehearsal training or deliberate memorizing of critical information, (2) conscious auditory monitoring or vigilance activities for specific lengths of time, (3) permitting the child to control the response rate to speeded tasks, (4) teaching the child self-testing and self-monitoring procedures, (5) teaching subskills or components of tasks before requiring performance of a larger task, (6) teaching mnemonic devices such as chunking, clustering, rhyming, and categorizing, and (7) providing instruction in recall strategies such as active rehearsal or reauditorization.

Lasky and Cox (1983) also take a broad approach to language processing disorders. Their approach considers aspects of the signal and its presentation, the environment, the response required from the child, and the strategies the child uses as factors that affect auditory processing. Intervention practices are recommended that manipulate these factors so as to facilitate listening and learning. Lasky and Cox suggest including in intervention approaches signal manipulations (such as increasing intensity), linguistic strategies (such as using contextual cues), and strategic modifications (repetitions, rehearsing, and preteaching). Manipulations of the presentation rate include the rate of speaking and the rate at which new information is presented. Intervention must find a level at which the child can listen and learn well, then gradually increase the complexity of the signal and rate of presentation. The environment is enhanced by improving the signal-to-noise ratio in the beginning, then gradually introducing competing signals in the environment.

In summary, these general approaches focus primarily on how a child with language processing disorders can be managed in a learning environment. The emphasis is on facilitating comprehension and appropriate responding. These approaches can be viewed as ways to help the child compensate for the difficulties in auditory processing. Unfortunately, empirical support for the effectiveness of the approaches is not provided.

There are few specific and systematic intervention programs for children with processing disorders. Those that are available can be viewed as approaches directed specifically toward improving auditory processing and speech and language perception. They are based on models of speech perception which hold that if one's auditory processing mechanism cannot extract the necessary information from the acoustic signal, inaccurate perception of speech occurs. What is misperceived is likely to be misunderstood. Therefore, accurate and efficient auditory processing and the resultant accurate perception of speech is prerequisite to language learning. While these approaches acknowledge that higher levels of language interact with and influence auditory processing, they suggest in LD children that these higher levels, especially the phonological processes, are likely to be impaired as well because of insufficient or inaccurate input to them in the developing child.

One such specific approach is reported by DuBard (1983) and is a continuation of what is called the Association Method developed by McGinnis (1963). This method is highly structured and systematically organized so that instruction consists of teaching incremental units of language and speech, beginning with phonemes and then gradually including larger and more complex units of communication. The method has been criticized as being contrary to normal language learning. DuBard (1983) points out, however, that the normal child has countless experiences with smaller units of language in the early prelinguistic stage of development—uttering them, storing them, retrieving them, and making proper associations. The LI child, in contrast, does not have such experiences, does not develop these processes to the same extent, and exhibits multiple uncertainties about the units of language and speech. The Association Method is designed to give the LI child these kinds of experiences.

Although McGinnis developed the Association Method for school-age children, emphasizing both oral and written language, DuBard (1983) stresses the auditory training aspect of the method for younger children who are not capable of the necessary articulation or copying skills required in the association technique. She hypothesizes that the auditory processing problem, which includes the processes of identifying, discriminating, and using auditory stimuli, is the major difficulty in LI children. This hypothesis is supported by considerable research with LI children (Tallal et al., 1985, 1987).

A more recently developed program of intervention for APD has been published by Sloan (1985). This program is specifically designed to improve auditory processing so that accurate perception of speech can occur. It focuses on training children to discriminate the distinctive features of speech sounds that are at the basis of the phonologic system. Modifications of the signal and its presentation (auditory cues) are used by the clinician in the beginning to enable the child to distinguish between a minimally distinct pair of speech sounds embedded in a consonant-vowel (CV) unit. As the child progresses in the program, these modifications are faded until accurate identification of each sound in the pair is achieved. Subsequently, the contrast sound pairs are presented in systematically more varied and complex phonetic contexts until accurate identification is achieved in multisyllabic words. Sloan's approach involves intensive auditory training but, at the same time, provides accurate and repetitive input to the phonologic system. Sloan (1980) reported the effectiveness of this method in training a 5-year-old LI child. The child initially required many trials and treatment sessions to be able to distinguish minimal phonetic pairs, such as [t] from [d]. However, once distinctions were acquired, the child was able to generalize training to distinguish features in other consonant contrasts almost immediately.

Other specific treatment approaches that have been published include those of Katz (1983), Katz and Harmon (1981), Tomatis (1978), Musiek (1986), and Lindamood and Lindamood (1975). Musiek (1986) reports some clinical observations that improvements in auditory processing are achieved when children wear personal FM units in the classroom. These are limited output units of the Walkman type, which are comfortable to wear, reasonably priced, and have a 30 to 40 dB gain. They are used primarily to improve the signal-to-noise ratio in the classroom setting, but could be used as high fidelity training systems to amplify specified acoustic features of the speech signal. Shapiro and Mistal (1985) reported on four children with reading, spelling, and auditory processing problems who benefited from high-frequency-enhanced, in-the-ear hearing aids. Musiek reports that while the use of low gain amplification systems looks promising, no empirical data are yet available on their use for APD.

The Auditory Discrimination in Depth (ADD) program developed by the Lindamoods (1975) is an oral-motor approach to beginning reading instruction. This program was developed to train kindergarten and first-grade children in segmentation and blending skills associating awareness of oral-proprioceptive qualities of phoneme production to auditory and visual properties of speech. In a recently completed unpublished doctoral dissertation, Howard (1986) reports the results of controlled research extending over 11 years examining ADD program effects on first-grade entry and exit reading scores as measured by the Woodcock Reading Mastery Tests and the reading subtest from the Iowa Tests of Basic Skills. Analyses of covariance with the pretest as the covariate indicated that first-grade students trained in the ADD techniques made greater gains in word attack and reading achievement in first grade and had higher reading scores in subsequent grades (second through eighth) than students not receiving such training. Kindergarten children trained in ADD techniques entered first grade with higher word attack skills than students not receiving such training. On the basis of these impressive research results, Lindamood has concluded that training specific auditory and visual properties of speech perception and production in young children has a significant effect on their subsequent reading and spelling abilities throughout the elementary school years.

The outlook for intervention for auditory processing disorders is quite promising in light of the renewed research interest in this specific aspect of language disorders. To continue to make advances, however, further research is needed on: (1) the development of auditory processing, psychoacoustic abilities, and speech perception in normal children, (2) the development of auditory and language functions in LI children, (3) the effectiveness of auditory- versus nonauditory-based intervention programs, (4) the development of solid diagnostic methods within the disciplines of audiology and speech-language pathology for the identification of APD, particularly at a young age, and (5) long-term followup of LI children for the purpose of investigating whether deficits in auditory processing persist or are resolved through maturation and/or treatment, and how these deficits relate to reading, writing, and other learning disabilities.

ASSUMPTIONS PERTAINING TO TREATMENT

Documented principles of intervention need to be available for speech-language pathologists to be able to make informed decisions regarding the management of LI children—particularly: who should receive intervention, what behaviors should be treated, how intervention should be conducted, when treatment should be implemented, and for how long. Being accountable in service delivery requires that speech-language pathologists make such decisions confidently and validly. Unfortunately, intervention research has provided speech-language pathologists with only a limited number of principles on which to rely in making these critical decisions about management. Rather than base their decisions on empirically determined principles of intervention, clinicians are forced to decide on whom and what to treat, how to treat, when, and for how long, on the basis of their assumptions about language acquisition and the role of intervention.

In a review of intervention research and clinical decision making, the following list of assumptions appears to guide speech-language pathologists in their work:

- Direct treatment is required for "any child abnormally slow in one or more aspects of language development or [who] has certain biological or behavioral characteristics that place him/her at risk for such a delay in development." (Fey, 1986)
- The earlier treatment can be provided, the better the outcome (Marge, 1972; Menyuk, 1975), and the more people involved in intervention, the better (McCormick and Goldman, 1984).
- "Language intervention . . . can facilitate the child's growth of linguistic abilities and may even help him/her catch up to peers." (Fey, 1986)
- Language intervention will facilitate an impaired child's ultimate linguistic achievement, and without such intervention, the child's potential may not be realized (Leonard, 1983; Fey, 1986).
- Language intervention stimulates overall language development. When this occurs, an individual may be said to have learned a strategy or means of acquiring language, and is able to acquire new forms and functions without receiving systematic instruction on them (Guess et al., 1978; Warren and Kaiser, 1986).

Unfortunately, such assumptions are based on intuition rather than empirical data, as intervention research, thus far, has focused on other issues (treatment effectiveness, effects, and the acquisition process). In fact, these assumptions have not been subjected to research. While most research has not been designed to directly address whom and what to treat, how to treat, when to treat, and for how long, the outcome data do tangentially speak to these questions and suggest some underlying principles for making clinical decisions.

Research results have contributed to the knowledge base that guides two important language intervention decisions: what behaviors to teach, and how to teach them. However, research support for principles addressing whom to treat, when to treat, and how long to treat is quite limited. Clinicians tend to rely on their assumptions and intuition when it comes to making these decisions. "Whom to treat" refers to service delivery decisions and, more often than we wish to acknowledge, to public resources available to fund treatment. A decision of whether a child will benefit most from no treatment at all or from direct treatment planned by a speech-language pathologist and implemented by a parent or classroom teacher should be based on empirical data. Speech-language pathologists have few guidelines regarding which children can benefit from treatment, and if the children are in treatment, which service delivery option would be best. The normal developmental model has been used almost exclusively for determining which children should be enrolled for treatment (Fey, 1986). While this approach has been useful, the assumptions on which such decisions have been based have not been documented. The identification of a language delay using a normal, developmental model speaks only to the extent of a child's handicapping condition; it does not address potential for change under different types of service delivery options. Research identifying principles to guide the decision of "whom to treat" is clearly needed. Uniformity across districts and States, to ensure equity in services based on need (rather than resources), is a critically pressing issue in need of review.

A related question, "when to treat," suggests that there may be an optimum time for direct treatment. Data have indicated that the timing of direct treatment may account for maximum effectiveness and efficiency of behavior change. The lack of robust results in group designs that have compared treatment may reflect the timing variable. Direct treatment in general or even specific procedures may be the most effective in changing behavior at different times during the language acquisition process, from emergence to mastery of new behavior. If such is the case, research must continue to examine the learning process and determine when children are most likely to benefit from intervention.

Theoretical evidence supporting this line of research comes from the works of Vygotsky (1978) and Gottlieb (1976) suggesting that rate of learning may vary, depending upon where a child is in the learning process and upon the influence of "experience" on learning at different points in time. Vygotsky's "zone of proximal development" defines the distance between a child's actual level of functioning and the child's potential level of performance. The "zone" defines a child's potential for immediate change when contextual support is manipulated to enhance performance, which, in turn, reveals a child's ability to learn. Children whose performance can be enhanced by the manipulation of contextual cues are the ones who may benefit most from direct clinical intervention.

Gottlieb (1976) has suggested that rate of change is indicative of how "experience"— in this case, treatment—serves to "regulate maturation, hasten development, and improve performance." Experience can change behavior in different ways, depending upon what the behavior is and where the person is in the learning process. The theory behind the works of Vygotsky and Gottlieb argues for critical learning periods— that is, optimal learning times when change in an organizational process is easily altered, modified, or produced. Indeed, research has supported the concept of readiness and critical learning periods with respect to intervention (Olswang et al., 1983, 1986; Olswang and Coggins, 1984). These studies have provided preliminary evidence that children will perform differently in treatment, depending upon where they are in the learning process. Some behaviors require intensive direct treatment to stimulate change, whereas others require little or no direct treatment. Clinicians need to be responsible and accountable in providing only necessary treatment, in a time frame that is most advantageous to the client. Research is needed to identify critical learning periods for linguistic behaviors and to determine children's behaviors indicating learning readiness. Further studies must explore changing behavior (progress) under different service delivery options (no treatment, direct treatment, and indirect treatment).

Once a child has been enrolled in treatment, the speech-language pathologist must determine how long to provide services. This decision encompasses two aspects of the learning process: (1) how much direct treatment is necessary before automatic transfer of learning occurs; and (2) what the ultimate outcome of intervention is for a particular child and behavior.

The first issue addresses the concept of "instrumental outcomes"—that is, those outcomes that "lead necessarily to other outcomes without further intervention" (Rosen and Proctor, 1981). An ultimate outcome of intervention is communicative competence, but whether direct treatment is needed continuously until that competence is achieved is unknown. Treatment may need to be provided only until an instrumental outcome is achieved; that is, an earlier emerging behavior or performance may herald the mastery of the ultimate desired behavior change. Research findings suggesting that under particular circumstances generalization of new behaviors may not need to be taught to LI children support this notion. Assuming that children need to be treated until "mastery" is achieved appears to be erroneous, and the assumption is costly. Research is therefore needed to define instrumental outcomes, which may vary across children. Furthermore, there is a need to define the methodology for identifying these outcomes in individual children. The latter may be the more feasible undertaking.

Finally, further research is needed to investigate ultimate outcomes. These are performance outcomes indicating that treatment has been a success and that intervention can be completely terminated (Rosen and Proctor, 1981). Deciding how long to keep a child on the therapeutic caseload is difficult, for it forces a clinician to decide if services can be of any further value to an impaired child or family. The main issue is what to define as the ultimate goal of treatment; behaviorally, what is expected from the client? Should "normal" performance be the ultimate achievement? What defines normalcy? Does the definition vary across children? And, finally, how does one measure the ultimate outcome? Expectations regarding language competence must be defined and weighed against different child characteristics. The ultimate goal of intervention must be a socially valid outcome, and yet what this means in terms of the LI child is not known. Longitudinal research is needed to determine which LI children will eventually perform like their normally developing peers and which will not. Both the short- and long-term effectiveness of intervention needs to be evaluated.

The state of the art of language intervention reflects a great need for research to develop principles on which speech-language pathologists can make better clinical decisions. While we know language behaviors can be successfully altered, much remains unknown about the intervention process. The role of the interventionist can be defined only when theoretical issues regarding the nature of language, language disorders, and language change are better understood. This determination will require research investigating the assumptions under which clinicians currently operate. While the practicing clinician can continue to document the efficacy of treatment procedures, systematic, programmatic research is needed to address the major intervention assumptions and to generate principles for making informed clinical decisions regarding whom and what to treat, how best to treat, when, and for how long.

PROGNOSIS

Issues of prognosis of language impairment are important to every other aspect of this review. Indeed, until we know what the long-term effects or outcomes of a disorder are, it is impossible to determine the extent of the problem, and hence, the need for research and treatment. It is important to know, particularly with language disorders, if children are merely delayed in the onset of function or if they will demonstrate long-term deficits as a result of early disability. Given the importance of issues pertaining to prognosis, it is amazing how little empirical information there is on this subject. The few published longitudinal studies evaluating outcomes (prognosis) of language disorders (Strominger and Bashir, 1977; Hall and Tomlin, 1978; Aram and Nation, 1975, 1982; Griffiths, 1969; Silva et al., 1983; King et al., 1982) suffer from two serious methodological flaws: (1) they primarily have been retrospective studies, and (2) they have included children who are highly variable in terms of their age and their physical and intellectual status, and hence, who are not specifically language impaired. Thus, the outcomes reported are difficult to interpret.

The San Diego longitudinal study has been designed specifically to address critical issues pertaining to patterns, profiles, and subtypes of specific early language disorders and the extent to which these subtypes maintain themselves throughout development and are meaningful predictors of subsequent outcomes (prognosis). Many issues critical for both theoretical and clinical understanding of the outcomes of specific developmental language disorders are being addressed. Until these outcomes are understood, appropriate services cannot be provided.

One important question pertaining to outcomes of specifically language disordered children is the degree to which members of subgroups of LI children maintain their subgroup membership over time and whether group membership is related to prognosis. In their longitudinal study, Tallal and Curtiss are administering a set of standardized language measures to each child at the end of each year. They can thereby assess whether each child falls at each year of the study into the same subgroup as at intake. Preliminary analyses have already yielded unexpected and important findings. Children who show primarily expressive language deficits at age 4 appear to show the most rapid and significant progress from that point on. By the second year of the study, more children in this subgroup than in any other subgroup studied tested in the normal range on standardized tests. This tendency for children with primarily expressive deficits to improve dramatically on their test performance after the first year of the study is proving consistent in the later years of the study as well. Although the results of detailed linguistic analyses of the same children suggest that the classical subgroupings may not be relevant regarding what a child may know or have difficulty with linguistically and therefore may not be relevant with respect to language intervention, the results may be exceptionally important prognostically, with children demonstrating receptive language deficits being considerably more at risk for long-term disorders than those with primarily expressive deficits. Similarly, results from this study demonstrate that, unfortunately, the prognosis for a majority of LI children must include subsequent academic failure, especially in areas such as reading and spelling that rely on the same auditory perceptual and phonological building blocks as oral language.

Distressingly, the long-term prognosis for children with early language disorders has yet to be adequately evaluated. Longitudinal studies following LI children throughout the school years and potentially into adulthood must be undertaken to determine the true magnitude of this complex cognitive developmental disorder. Such studies must be multidisciplinary in nature, evaluating etiological, neuropsychological, linguistic, academic, social, and emotional factors in the same child over time. Multisite studies would also be an innovative approach to allow for larger samples of well-selected cohorts to be uniformly studied and for results to be cross-validated.

FUTURE RESEARCH GOALS

Until recently, priority has been given to funding small, isolated, single-variable studies. Few of these studies have pursued a consistent, theoretically driven model or line of research. Not surprisingly, results have been fragmented and have led to disappointingly little integration across studies and, hence, to little advancement of our knowledge of specific developmental language disorders. The National Institute of Neurological and Communicative Disorders and Stroke, the National Institute of Child Health and Human Development, and the National Institute of Mental Health must be commended for recognizing that the pressing clinical and theoretical issues pertaining to complex developmental cognitive disorders must ultimately be addressed by funding complex (multidisciplinary), developmental (longitudinal) studies. Future studies would benefit most from being both practically and theoretically driven. If specific developmental language disorders are ever to be prevented, we must begin first by understanding their etiology (causes) and prevalence in the population, and then develop appropriate treatments. This can never be accomplished if uniformly applied inclusionary and exclusionary criteria for diagnosis are not established and their use encouraged. This goal will rely ultimately on the development and uniform use of well-standardized, reliable, and valid testing procedures.

Future theoretical and technological advances will create increasing demands for more sophisticated, multivariate research designs, data-based management systems, and innovative statistical analysis procedures. The complexity of language development as it relates to all other aspects of child development, by its very nature, must lead to more reliance on increasingly complex, multivariate research designs. In order for the number of variables to be appropriately assessed by such multidisciplinary, multivariate designs, it may be increasingly necessary to move to a more collaborative (less competitive) research arena in the future, where researchers are encouraged to work together across disciplines and sites to develop the large subject populations needed for such research to be successful. The National Institute of Child of Health and Human Development, the National Institute of Neurological and Communicative Disorders and Stroke, the National Institutes of Mental Health, and the MacArthur Foundation are to be highly commended for their leadership into the future, which is demonstrated by the recent advances they have made in breaking down competition and sponsoring (through significant research funding) several large-scale collaborative, multidisciplinary, multisite programs in the area of child development. These first few attempts at cooperation between and across disciplines and geographical locations are already demonstrating exciting and promising breakthroughs.

Developmental language disorders are, fortunately, not life-threatening. However, they may well be life-destroying in many cases. For all our goals for these children ultimately to be reached, we must do everything we can to break down artificial professional and scientific boundaries and to promote collaboration and cooperation.

BIBLIOGRAPHY

Achenbach, T. M. (1979). The child behavior profile: An empirically based system for assessing children's behavioral profiles and competencies. *International Journal of Mental Health*, 7(3-4):24-42.

Achenbach, T. M. (1980). DSM-III in light of empirical research on the classification of child psychopathology. *Journal of the American Academy of Child Psychiatry*, 19:395-412.

Achenbach, T. M. (1982). *Developmental Psychopathology*. New York: John Wiley and Sons.

Adler, S. (1976). The influence of genetic syndromes upon oral communication skills. *Journal of Speech and Hearing Disorders*, 41(1):136-138.

Ajuriaguerra, J. de, Jaeggi, A., Guignard, F., Kocher, F., Maquard, M., Roth, S., Schmid, E. (1976). The development and prognosis of dysphasia in children. In Morehead, E. M., Morehead, A. (Eds.), *Normal and deficient child language*. Baltimore: University Park Press.

Alexander, D. W., Frost, B. P. (1982). Decelerated synthesized speech as a means of shaping speed of auditory processing of children with delayed language. *Perceptual and Motor Skills*, 55:783-792.

Allen, D. V., Robinson, D. O. (1984). Middle ear status and language development in preschool children. *ASHA*, 26:33-37.

Allen, J. T., Gillett, M., Holton, J. B., King, G. S., Pettit, B. R. (1980). Evidence of galactosemia in utero. *Lancet*, 1:603.

Aram, D. M., Kamhi, A. G. (1982). Perspectives on the relationship between phonological and language disorders. In *Seminars of speech and hearing research* (pp. 101-114). New York: Thieme-Stratton.

Aram, D. M., Nation, J. E. (1975). Patterns of language behavior in children. *Journal of Speech and Hearing Research*, 18:229-241.

Aram, D. M., Nation, J. E. (1982). *Child Language Disorders*. St. Louis: C. V. Mosby.

Aram, D. M., Rose, D. F., Rekate, H. L., Whitaker, H. A. (1983). Acquired capsular/striatal aphasia in childhood. *Archives of Neurology*, 40(10):614-617.

Arnold, G., Schwartz, S. (1983). Hemispheric lateralization of language in autistic and aphasic children. *Journal of Autism and Developmental Disorders*, 13(2):129-139.

Baker, L., Cantwell, D. P., Mattison, R. E. (1980). Behavior problems in children with pure speech disorders and in children with combined speech and language disorder. *Journal of Abnormal Child Psychology*, 8:245-256.

Ball, J., Cross, F. (1981). Formal and pragmatic factors in childhood autism and aphasia. Paper presented at the Symposium on Research in Child Language Disorders, Madison, WI.

Bartak, L., Rutter, M., Cox, A. (1975). A comparative study of infantile autism and specific developmental language disorder: I. The children. *British Journal of Psychiatry*, 126:127-145.

Bax, M., Hart, J. (1976). Health needs of preschool children. *Archives of Disease in Childhood*, 51:848-852.

Beitchman, J. H., Nair, R., Clegg, M., Ferguson, B., Patel, P. G. (1986). Prevalence of psychiatric disorders in children with speech and language disorders. *Journal of the American Academy of Child Psychiatry*, 25(4):528-535.

Beitchman, J. H., Nair, R., Clegg, M., Patel, P. G. (1986). Prevalence of speech and language disorders in 5-year-old kindergarten children in the Ottowa-Carleton region. *Journal of Speech and Hearing Disorders*, 51:98-110.

Bellinger, D., Leviton, A., Needleman, H. L., Waternaux, C., Rabinowitz, M. (1986a). Low-level lead exposure and infant development in the first year. *Neurobehavioral Toxicology and Teratology*, 8:151-161.

Bellinger, D., Leviton, A., Rabinowitz, M., Needleman, H., Waternaux, C. (1986b). Correlates of low-level lead exposure in urban children at 2 years of age. *Pediatrics*, 77(6):826-833.

Benedict, H. (1979). Early lexical development: Comprehension and production. *Journal of Child Language*, 6:183-200.

Benton, A. L. (1964). Developmental aphasia and brain damage. *Cortex*, 1:40-52.

Berk, R. A. (1984). *Screening and diagnosis of children with learning disabilities.* Springfield, IL: Charles C. Thomas.

Berman, R. (1981). Regularity vs. anomoly: the acquisition of Hebrew inflectional phonology. *Journal of Child Language*, 8:265-282.

Bernstein, S. P., Musiek, F. E. (1984). Implications of temporal processing for children with learning and language problems. In Beasley, D. S. (Ed.), *Audition in childhood: methods of study* (pp. 25-54). San Diego: College-Hill Press.

Berry, M. (1986). *Berry-Talbott Exploratory Test of Grammar.* Rockford, IL.

Bishop, D. V. M. (1981). Plasticity and specificity of language localization in the developing brain. *Developmental Medicine and Child Neurology*, 23:251-255.

Bishop, D. V. M. (1983). Linguistic impairment after left hemidecortication for infantile hemiplegia? A reappraisal. *Quarterly Journal of Experimental Psychology*, 35:199-207.

Bishop, D. V. M. (1987). The causes of specific developmental language disorder ("developmental dysphasia"). *Journal of Child Psychology and Psychiatry*, 28(1):1-8.

Bishop, D. V. M., Edmundson, A. (1986). Is otitis media a major cause of specific developmental language disorders?" *British Journal of Disorders of Communication*, 21:321-338.

Bishop, D. V. M., Edmundson, A. Specific language impairment as a maturational lag: Evidence from longitudinal data on language and motor development. *Developmental Medicine and Child Neurology*, in press.

Bloom, L,, Hood, L., Lightbown, P. (1974). Imitation in language development: If, when and why. *Cognitive Psychology*, 6:380-420.

Bluestone, C. D., Klein, J. O., Paradise, J. L., Eichenwald, H., Bess, F. H., Downs, M. P., Green, M., Berko-Gleason, J., Ventry, I. M., Gray, S., McWilliams, B. J., Gates, G. (1983). Workshop on effects of otitis media on the child. *Pediatrics*, 71(4):639-651.

Borges-Osario, M. R., Salzano, F. M. (1985). Language disabilities in three twin pairs and their relatives. *Acta Geneticae Medicae et Gemellologica (Roma)*, 34(1-2):95-100.

Bowerman, M. (1973). *Early syntactic development: A cross-linguistic study with special reference to Finnish.* London: Cambridge University Press.

Brandes, P., Ehinger, D. (1981). The effects of early middle ear pathology on auditory perception and academic achievement. *Journal of Speech and Hearing Disorders*, 46:301-307.

Broman, S. H. (1983). Obstetric medications. In Brown, C. C. (Ed.), *Childhood learning disabilities and prenatal risk* (pp. 56-64). Johnson & Johnson Baby Products Company Pediatric Round Table Series.

Brown, R. (1973). *A first language.* Cambridge, MA: Harvard University Press.

Buckholtz, N. S., Panem, S. (1986). Regulation and evolving science: Neurobehavioral toxicology. *Neurobehavioral Toxicology and Teratology*, 8(1):89-96.

Bunce, B., Ruder, B., Ruder, C. (1985). Using the miniature linguistic system in teaching syntax: Two case studies. *Journal of Speech and Hearing Disorders*, 50:247-253.

Butler, K. G. (1981). Language processing disorders: Factors in diagnosis and remediation. In Keith, R. W. (Ed.), *Central auditory and language disorders in children.* San Diego: College-Hill Press.

Butler, K. G. (1984). Language processing: Halfway up the down staircase. In Wallach, G. P., Butler, K. G. (Eds.), *Language learning disabilities in school-age children* (pp. 60-81). Baltimore: Williams and Wilkins.

Calnan, M., Richardson, K. (1976). Speech problems in a national survey: Assessment and prevalences. *Child Care, Health and Development*, 2:181-202.

Calnan, M., Richardson, K. (1977). Speech problems among children in a national survey. Associations with reading, general ability, mathematics and syntactic maturity. *Educational Studies*, 3:55-66.

Camarata, S., Gandour, J. (1984). On describing idiosyncratic phonologic systems. *Journal of Speech and Hearing Disorders*, 49:262-266.

Camarata, S., Gandour, J. (1985). Rule invention in the acquisition of morphology by a language-impaired child. *Journal of Speech and Hearing Disorders*, 50:40-45.

Camarata, S., Schwartz, R. (1985). Production of object words and action words: Evidence for a relationship between phonology and semantics. *Journal of Speech and Hearing Research*, 28:323-330.

Campbell, P., Shriberg, L. (1982). Associations among pragmatic functions, linguistic stress, and natural phonological processes in speech delayed children. *Journal of Speech and Hearing Disorders*, 25:547-553.

Cantwell, D. P., Baker, L., Mattison, R. E. (1980). Factors associated with the development of psychiatric disorder in children with speech and language retardation. *Archives of General Psychiatry*, 37:423-426.

Caparulo, B. K., Cohen, D. J., Rothmann, S. L., Young, J. G., Katz, J. D., Shaywitz, S. E., Shaywitz, B. A. (1981). Computed tomographic brain scanning in children with developmental neuropsychiatric disorders. *Journal of American Academy of Child Psychiatry*, 20:338-357.

Carrow, E. (1973). *Test for auditory comprehension of language*. Austin, TX: Teaching Resources Corporation.

Carrow, E. (1974). *Carrow Elicited Language Inventory*. Boston: Teaching Resources.

Chapman, K., Leonard, L., Rowan, L., Weiss, A. (1983). Inappropriate word extensions in the speech of young language-disordered children. *Journal of Speech and Hearing Disorders*, 48:55-62.

Chase, R. A. (1972). Neurological aspects of language disorders in children. In Irwin, J. V., Marge, E. M. (Eds.), *Principles of language disabilities* (pp. 99-135). New York: Appleton-Century-Crofts.

Chess, S., Rosenberg, M. (1974). Clinical differentiation among children with initial language complaints. *Journal of Autism and Childhood Schizophrenia*, 4:99-109.

Chi, J. G., Dooling, E. G., Gilles, F. H. (1977). Gyral development of the human brain. *Annals of Neurology*, 1:86-93.

Chomsky, N. (1980). *Rules and representations*. New York: Columbia University Press.

Clemens, L. G., Popham, T. V., Ruppert, P. H. (1979). Neonatal treatment of hamsters with barbiturate alters adult sexual behavior. *Developmental Psychobiology*, 12:49-59.

Cole, K., Dale, P. (1986). Direct language instruction and interactive language instruction with language delayed preschool children: A comparison study. *Journal of Speech and Hearing Research*, 29:206-217.

Compton, A. (1970), Generative studies of children's phonological disorders. *Journal of Speech and Hearing Disorders*, 35:315-339.

Connell, P. (1982). On training language rules. *Language, Speech and Hearing Services in Schools*, 13:231-240.

Connell, P., Myles-Zitzer, C. (1982). An analysis of elicited imitation as a language evaluation procedure. *Journal of Speech and Hearing Disorders*, 47:390-396.

Connell, P. (1986). Acquisition of semantic role by language disordered children: Differences between production and comprehension. *Journal of Speech and Hearing Research*, 29:366-374.

Conti-Ramsden, G. (1985). Mothers in dialogue with language-impaired children. *Topics in Language Disorders*, 5:58-68.

Culatta, B., Horn, D. (1982). A program for achieving generalization of grammatical rules to spontaneous discourse. *Journal of Speech and Hearing Disorders*, 47:174-180.

Curtiss, S. (1977). *GENIE: A psycholinguistic study of a modern-day "Wild Child."* New York: Academic Press.

Curtiss, S. (1981). Feral children. *Journal of Mental Retardation and Developmental Disabilities*, 12:129-161.

Curtiss, S. (1982). Developmental dissociations of language and cognition. In Obler, L., Menn, L. (Eds.), *Exceptional language and linguistic theory*. New York: Academic Press.

Curtiss, S., Tallal, P. (1985). On the question of subgroups in language impaired children: A first report. Paper presented at the Tenth Annual Boston University Conference of Language Development.

Curtiss, S. (in press). The special talent of grammar acquistion. In Obler, L., Fein, D. (Eds.), *The neuropsychology of talent and special abilities*. New York: Guilford Press.

Dailey, K., Boxx, J. (1979). A comparison of three imitative tests of expressive language and a spontaneous language sample. *Language, Speech, and Hearing Services in Schools*, 10:6-13.

Dalby, M. A. (1977a). Aetiological studies in language retarded children. *Neuropaediatrie*, 8(suppl.):499-500.

Dalby, M. A. (1977b). Diagnose und aetiologie der dysphasia. In Elstner, W., Karlstad, H. (Eds.), *Dysphasia im kindesalter*. Oslo: Universitetsforlatet.

Delgutte, B. (1980). Representation of speech-like sounds in the discharge patterns of auditory-nerve fibers. *Journal of the Acoustical Society of America*, 63:843-857.

Demopoulos, W., Marras, A. (Eds.) (1986). *Language learning and concept acquisition*, Norwood, NJ: Ablex.

Dennis, M., Whitaker, H. A. (1977). Hemispheric equipotentiality and language acquisition. In Segalowitz, S. J., Gruber, F. A. (Eds.), *Language development and neurological theory*. New York: Academic Press.

DeRinzi, E., Vignolo, L. A. (1962). The token test: A sensitive test to detect receptive disturbances in aphasia. *Brain*, 85:665-678.

Dollaghan, C., Kaston, N. (1986). A comprehensive monitoring program for language impaired children. *Journal of Speech and Hearing Disorders*, 51:264-271.

Donahue, M. (1984). Learning disabled children's conversational competence: An attempt to activate the inactive listener. *Applied Psycholinguistics*, 5:21-35.

DuBard, N. E. (1983). *Teaching aphasics and other language deficient children* (3rd Edition). Jackson: University Press of Mississippi.

Duffy, R., Ulrich, S. (1976). A comparison of impairments in verbal comprehension, speech, reading, and writing in adult aphasics. *Journal of Speech and Hearing Disorders*, 41(1):110-119.

Dunn, L. (1959). In *Peabody picture vocabulary test*. Circle Pines, MN: American Guidance Service.

Dunn, L. M., Dunn, L. M. (1981). *Peabody picture vocabulary test - Revised: Manual*. Nashville, Tennessee: American Guidance Service.

Edwards, M., Bernhardt, B. (1973). Phonological analysis of the speech of four children with language disorders. Unpublished manuscript.

Eimas, P. D., Clarkson, R. L. (1986). Speech perception in children: Are there effects of otitis media? In Kavanagh, J. F. (Ed.), *Otitis media and child development* (pp. 139-159). Parkton, MD: York Press.

Eisenson, J. (1966). Perceptual disturbances in children with central nervous system dysfunction and implications for language development. *British Journal of Disorders of Communication*, 1:21-32.

Eisenson, J. (1968). Developmental aphasia (dyslogia). *Cortex*, 4:184-200.

Eisenson, J. (1969). Developmental aphasia. *Journal of the South African Logopedic Society*, 16(1):15-25.

Elliott, L. L. (1978). Epidemiology of hearing impairment and other communicative disorders. *Advances in Neurology*, 19:399-420.

Evans, C. S. (1973). *A study of selected aural-oral skills of children with various chromosomal abnormalities*. Unpublished master's thesis, University of Tennessee, Knoxville.

Feagans, L. (1986). Otitis media: A model for long-term effects with implications for intervention. In Kavanagh, J. F. (Ed.), *Otitis media and child development* (pp. 192-208). Parkton, MD: York Press.

Fein, G. G. (1981). Sociodramatic play: Social class effects in integrated preschool classrooms. *Journal of Applied Developmental Psychology*, 2(3):267-279.

Feldman, R. B., Pinsky, L., Mendelson, J., Lajoie, R. (1973). Can language disorder not due to peripheral deafness be an isolated expression of prenatal rubella? *Pediatrics*, 52(2):296-299.

Fey, M., Leonard, L., Fey, S., O'Connor, K. (1978). The intent to communicate in language-impaired children. Paper presented at the Third Annual Boston University Conference on Language Development.

Fey, M. (1981). *Stylistic speech adjustments of language-impaired and normal language children.* Unpublished doctoral dissertation, Purdue University.

Fey, M., Leonard, L., Wilcox, K. (1981). Speech style modifications of language-impaired children. *Journal of Speech and Hearing Disorders,* 46:91-97.

Fey, M., Leonard, L. (1984). Partner age as a variable in the conversational performance of specifically language-impaired and normal language children. *Journal of Speech and Hearing Research,* 27:413-423.

Fey, M. (1986). *Language intervention with young children.* San Diego: College-Hill Press.

Fischler, R. S., Todd, N. W., Feldman, C. M. (1985). Otitis media and language performance in a cohort of Apache Indian children. *American Journal of Diseases of Children,* 139:355-360.

Flower, R. (1970). Follow-up studies of "normal" children with delayed speech and language development. *Current Problems in Pediatrics,* 1:1-45. Cited by H. P. Gofman.

Folger, J., Chapman, R. (1978). A pragmatic analysis of spontaneous imitations. *Journal of Child Language,* 5:25-38.

Foster, R., Giddan, J., Stark, J. (1969). *Assessment of children's language comprehension.* Palo Alto: Consulting Psychologists Press.

Freedman, P., Carpenter, R. (1976). Semantic relations used by normal and language impaired children at Stage I. *Journal of Speech and Hearing Research,* 19:784-795.

French, J. L. (1964). *The pictorial test of intelligence.* New York: Houghton Mifflin.

Friedman, P., Friedman, K. (1980). Accounting for individual differences when comparing the effectiveness of remedial language teaching methods. *Applied Psycholinguistics,* 1:151-170.

Friedrich, U., Dalby, M., Staehelin-Jensen, T., Bruun-Petersen, G. (1982). Chromosomal studies of children with developmental language retardation. *Developmental Medicine and Child Neurology,* 24:645-652.

Friel-Patti, S., Finitzo-Hieber, T., Conti, G., Brown, K. C. (1982). Language delay in infants associated with middle ear disease and mild, fluctuating hearing impairment. *Pediatric Infectious Disease,* 1(2):104-109.

Fundudis, T., Kolvin, L., Garside, R. F. (1979). *Speech retarded and deaf children: The psychological development.* London: Academic Press.

Gal, P., Sharpless, M. K. (1984). Fetal drug exposure—behavioral teratogenesis. *Drug Intelligence and Clinical Pharmacy,* 18:186-201.

Galaburda, A. M., Kemper, T. L. (1979). Cytoarchitectonic abnormalities in developmental dyslexia: A case study. *Annals of Neurology,* 6:94.

Gale, D., Liebergott, J., Griffin, S. (1981). Getting it: Children's requests for clarification. Paper presented to the American Speech-Language-Hearing Association, Los Angeles.

Gardiner, M. F., Walter, D. O. (1977). Evidence of hemispheric specialization from infant EEG. In Harnad, S. et al. (Eds.), *Lateralization in the nervous system.* New York: Academic Press.

Garoutte, B. (1967). Cerebral developmental anomalies and disturbances of language. *Journal of Neurological Sciences,* 4:339.

Garstecki, D. C., Borton, T. E., Stark, E. W, Kennedy, B. T (1972). Speech, language, and hearing problems in the Laurence-Moon-Biedl syndrome. *Journal of Speech and Hearing Disorders,* 37:407-413.

Garvey, M., Mutton, D. E. (1973). Sex chromosome aberrations and speech development. *Archives of Disease in Childhood,* 48:937-41.

Geller, E., Wollner, S. (1976). A preliminary investigation of the communicative competence of three linguistically impaired children. Paper given at the New York State Speech and Hearing Association, Grossingers.

Geschwind, N., Levitsky, W. (1968). Human Brain: Left-right asymmetries in temporal speech region. *Science,* 161:186-187.

Geschwind, N. (1968). Neurological foundations of language. In Myklebust, H. R. (Ed.), *Progress in Learning Disabilities:* Vol. 1. New York: Grune and Stratton.

260

Geschwind, N. (1979). Anatomical foundations of language and dominance. In Ludlow, C. L., Doran-Quine, M. E. (Eds.), *The neurological bases of language disorders in children: Methods and directions for research* (pp. 145-153). NINCSD Monograph Series. Bethesda, Maryland: National Institutes of Health.

Ghadimi, H., Partington M.W., Hunter A. (1961). A familial disturbance of histidine metabolism. *New England Journal of Medicine,* 265:221.

Gibson, D., Ingram, D. (1983). The onset of comprehension and production in a language delayed child. *Applied Psycholinguistics,* 4:359-376.

Gibson, E. J. (1969). *Principles of perceptual learning and development.* New York: Appleton-Century-Crofts.

Gibson, K. M., Sweetman, L., Nyhan, W. L., Jakobs, C., Rating, D., Siemes, H., Hanefeld, F. (1983). Succinic semialdehyde dehydro-genase deficiency: An inborn error of gamma-aminobutyric acid metabolism. *Clinica Chimica Acta,* 133:33-42.

Gleitman, L., Wanner, E. (1982). Language acquisition: The state of the art. In Wanner, E., Gleitman, L. (Eds.), *Language acquisition: The state of the art* (pp. 3-48). Cambridge, England: Cambridge University Press.

Gofman, H. P. (1970). Learning and language disorders in children. *Current Problems in Pediatrics,* 1:1-45.

Goldman, P., Alexander, G. E. (1977). Maturation of prefrontal cortex in the monkey revealed by local reversible cryogenic depression. *Nature,* 267:613-615.

Goldman, P. (1979). Development and plasticity of frontal association cortex in the infrahuman primate. In Ludlow, C. L., Doran-Quine, M. E. (Eds.), *The neurological bases of language disorders in children: Methods and directions for research* (pp. 1-16). NINCSD Monograph Series, National Institutes of Health (NIH), Bethesda, Maryland, August.

Goldman, R., Fristoe, M., Woodcock, R. W. (1976). *G-F-W auditory memory tests.* Circle Pines, MN: American Guidance Services, Inc.

Gottlieb, G. (1976). The roles of experience in the development of behavior and the nervous system. In Gottlieb, G. (Eds), *Studies in the development of behavior and the nervous system: Neural and behavioral specificity* (pp. 25-54). New York: Academic Press.

Gottlieb, M., Zinkus, P., Thompson, A. (1979). Chronic middle ear disease and auditory perceptual deficits: Is there a link? *Clinical Pediatrics,* 18(12):725-732.

Graham, J. M. Jr.,, Bashir, A. S., Stark, R. E., Tallal, P. (1982). Auditory processing abilities in unselected XXY boys. *Clinical Research,* 30:118A.

Gray, D. B., Yaffe, S. J. (1983). Prenatal drugs. In Brown, C. C. (Ed.), *Childhood learning disabilities and prenatal risk* (pp. 44-49). Johnson & Johnson Baby Products Company Pediatric Round Table Series.

Greenfield, P., Smith, J. (1976). In *Communication and the beginnings of language: The development of semantic structures in one word speech and beyond.* New York: Academic Press, New York.

Griffin, S. (1979). *Requests for clarification made by normal and language impaired children.* Unpublished master's thesis, Emerson College.

Griffiths, C. P. (1969). A follow-up study of children with disorders of speech. *British Journal of Disorders of Communication,* 4:46-56.

Guess, D., Sailor, W., Baer, D. (1978). Children with limited language. In Schiefelbusch, R. (Ed.), *Language Intervention Strategies* (pp. 101-143), Baltimore: University Park Press.

Hall, P. K., Tomblin, J. B. (1978). A follow-up study of children with articulation and language disorders. *Journal of Speech and Hearing Disorders,* 43:227-241.

Hamburger, H., Crain, S. (1982). Relative acquisition. In Kuczaj, S. (Ed.), *Language Development:* Vol. 2. Hillsdale, NJ: Lawrence Earlbaum.

Hamburger, H., Crain, S. (1984). Acquisition of cognitive compiling. *Cognition,* 17:85-136.

Harcherik, D. F., Cohen, D. J., Ort, S., Paul, R., Shaywitz, B. A., Volkmar, F. R., Rothman, S. L. G., Leckman, J. F. (1985). Computer tomographic brain scanning in four neuro-psychiatric disorders of childhood. *American Journal of Psychiatry,* 142:731-745.

Hassibi, M., Brewer, J. Jr. (1980). *Disordered thinking and communication in children.* New York: Plenum Press.

Hegde, M., Gierut, J. (1979). The operant training and generalization of pronouns and a verb form in a language delayed child. *Journal of Communication Disorders,* 12:23-34.

Hegde, M., Noll, M., Pecora, R. (1979). A study of some factors affecting generalization of language training. *Journal of Speech and Hearing Disorders,* 3:301-320.

Hegde, M. (1980). An experimental-clinical analysis of grammatical and behavioral distinctions between verbal auxiliary and copula. *Journal of Speech and Hearing Research,* 23:864-877.

Hier, D. B., Rosenberger, P. B. (1980). Focal left temporal lobe lesions and delayed speech acquisition. *Developmental and Behavioral Pediatrics,* 1(2):54-57.

Hiskey, M. S. (1966). *The Hiskey-Nebraska test of learning aptitude.* Lincoln, Nebraska: Union College Press.

Hoar, N. (1977). Paraphrase capabilities of language impaired children. Paper presented at the Second Annual Boston University Conference on Language Development.

Holm, V., Kunze, L. (1969). Effect of chronic otitis media on language and speech development. *Pediatrics,* 43(5):833-839.

Howard, M. P. (1986). *The effects of pre-reading training in auditory conceptualization on subsequent reading achievement.* Unpublished dissertation, Brigham Young University.

Hughes, D. (1985). *Language treatment and generalization,* San Diego: College-Hill Press.

Hull, F. M., Mielke, P. W. Jr., Timmons, R. J., Welleford, J. A. (1971). The national speech and hearing survey: Preliminary results. *ASHA,* 13:501-509.

Hyams, N. (1983). *The acquisition of parametrized grammars.* Unpublished PhD dissertation, City University of New York.

Hyams, N. (1986). Core and peripheral grammar and the acquisition of inflection. Paper given at the Eleventh Annual Boston University Conference on Language Development.

Ingram, D. (1972). The acquisition of the English verbal auxiliary in normal and linguistically deviant children. *Papers and Reports in Child Language Development,* 4.

Ingram, D. (1976). *Phonological disability in children.* London: Edward Arnold.

Ingram, T., Mason, A., Blackburn, I. (1970). A retrospective study of 82 children with reading disability. *Developmental Medical Child Neurology,* 12:271-281.

Ingram, T. S. (1969). Developmental disorders of speech. In Vinken, P. J., Bruyan, G. (Eds.)., *Handbook of clinical neurology:* Vol 4 (pp. 407- 442). Amsterdam: North-Holland.

Ingram, T. T. S. (1959). Specific developmental disorders of speech in childhood. *Brain,* 82:450-467.

Inhelder, B. (1966). Cognitive development and diagnosis of mental deficiency. *Merrill-Palmer Quarterly,* 12:299-319.

Inhelder, B. (1976). Observations on the operational and figurative aspects of thought in dysphasic children. In Morehead, D., Morehead, A. (Eds.), *Normal and deficient child language.* Baltimore, MD: University Park Press.

Irwin, R. (1948). Ohio looks ahead in speech and hearing therapy. *Journal of Speech and Hearing Disorders,* 13:55-60.

Jacobs, T. (1981). *Verbal dominance, complexity and quantity of speech on pairs of language-disabled and normal children.* Unpublished doctoral dissertation, University of Southern California.

Jacobson, J. L., Jacobson, S. W., Fein, G., Schwartz, P. M., Dowler, J. K. (1984). Prenatal exposure to an environmental toxin: a test of the multiple effects model. *Developmental Psychology,* 20(4):523-532.

Janowsky, J. S., Finlay, B. L. (1986). The outcome of perinatal brain damage: The role of normal neuron loss and axon retraction. *Developmental Medicine and Child Neurology,* 28:375-389.

Johnston, J., Kamhi, A. (1984). The same can be less: Syntactic and semantic aspects of the utterances of language impaired children. *Merrill-Palmer Quarterly,* 30:65-85.

Johnston, J., Ramstad, V. (1978). Cognitive development in preadolescent language impaired children. In Burns, M., Andrews, E. J. (Eds.), *Selected Papers in Language and Phonology,* Evanston, IL: Institute for Continuing Professional Education.

Johnston, J. , Schery, T. (1976). The use of grammatical morphemes by children with communication disorders. In Morehead, D., Morehead, A. (Eds.), *Normal and Deficient Child Language*, Baltimore, MD: University Park Press.

Johnston, J., Weismer, S. (1983). Mental rotation abilities in language disordered children. *Journal of Speech and Hearing Research*, 26:397-403.

Johnston, J. R. (1983). Discussion: Part I: What is language intervention? The role of theory. In Miller, J., Yoder, D. E., Schiefelbusch, R. (Eds.), *Contemporary issues in language intervention* (pp. 52-57). The American Speech-Language-Hearing Association, Rockville, MD. ASHA Reports No. 12.

Johnston, R. B., Stark, R. E., Mellits, E. D., Tallal, P. (1981). Neurological status of language-impaired and normal children. *Annals of Neurology*, 10:159-163.

Josub, S., Fuchs, M., Bingol, N., Gromisch, D. (1981). Fetal alcohol syndrome revisited. *Pediatrics*, 68:475-479.

Kaleita, T. A., Menkes, J. H., Kingbourne, M. (1987). Neurologic behavioral syndrome associated with infantile dietary chloride deficiency. *Clinical Research*, 35:226a.

Kamhi, A. (1981). Nonlinguistic symbolic and conceptual abilities of language-impaired and normally developing children. *Journal of Speech and Hearing Research*, 24:446-453.

Kamhi, A., Catts, H., Koenig, L., Lewis, B. (1984). Hypothesis testing and nonlinguistic symbolic activities in language impaired children. *Journal of Speech and Hearing Disorders*, 49:169-176.

Kaplan, G., Fleshman, J. K., Bender, T., Baum, C., Clark, P. (1973). Long-term effects of otitis media: A ten-year cohort study of Alaskan Eskimo children. *Pediatrics*, 52(4):577-584.

Katz, J., Harmon, C. H. (1981). Phonemic synthesis: Testing and training. In Keith, R. W. (Ed.), *Central auditory and language disorders in children*, San Diego: College-Hill Press,

Katz, J. (1983). Phonemic synthesis. In Lasky, E. Z., Katz, J. (Eds.), *Central Auditory Processing Disorders: Problems of Speech, Language, and Learning* (pp. 269-295). Baltimore: University Park Press.

Kavanagh, J. F. (1986). *Otitis media and child development*. Parkton, MD: York Press.

Kean, M. L. (1984). The question of linguistic anomaly in developmental dyslexia. *Annals of Dyslexia*, 34:137-154.

Kessler, C. (1975). Post-semantic processes in delayed child language related to first and second language learning. In Dato, D. (Eds.), *Georgetown University Roundtable on Language and Linguistics* (pp. 159-178). Washington, DC: Georgetown University Press.

Kiang, N. Y. S. (1980). Processing speech by the auditory nervous system. *Journal of the Acoustical Society of America*, 63:830-835.

King, R. R., Jones, C., Lasky, E. (1982). In retrospect: A fifteen year follow-up report of speech-language disordered children. *Language, Speech and Hearing Services in Schools*, 13:24-32.

Kirchner, D., Klatzky, R. (1985). Verbal rehearsal and memory in language-disordered children. *Journal of Speech and Hearing Research*, 28:556-565.

Kirk, S., McCarthy, J., Kirk, W. (1968). *Illinois test of psycholinguistic abilities*. Los Angeles: Western Psychological Services.

Kirkwood, C. R., Kirkwood, M. (1983). Otitis media and learning disabilities: The case for a causal relationship. *Journal of Family Practice*, 17(2):219-227.

Kleeck, A. Van, Frankel, D. (1981). Discourse devices used by language disordered children: a preliminary investigation. *Journal of Hearing and Speech Disorders*, 46:250-257.

Klein, S. (1985). A note on UN-verbs. In Goldberg, J., Mackage, S., Twescoat, M. (Eds.), *Proceedings of the West Coast Conference on Formal Linguistics:* Vol. 4. Stanford, CA: Stanford Linguistics Association.

Kuhl, P. K. (1982). Speech perception: An overview of current issues. In Lass, N., McReynolds, L. V., Northern, L., Yoder, D. E. (Eds.), *Speech, Language, and Hearing. Normal Processes:* Vol. 1 (pp. 286-322). Philadelphia: W. B. Saunders.

Landau, W. M., Goldstein, Kleffer, F. R. (1960). Congenital aphasia: A clinicopathologic study. *Neurology*, 10:915.

Lasky, E. Z. (1983). Parameters affecting auditory processing. In Lasky, E. Z., Katz, J. (Eds.), *Central auditory processing disorders: Problems of speech, language and learning* (pp. 11-29). Baltimore: University Park Press.

Lasky, E. Z., Cox, L. C. (1983). Auditory processing and language interaction: Evaluation and intervention strategies. In Lasky, E. Z., Katz, J. (Eds.), *Central auditory processing disorders: Problems of speech, language, and learning* (pp. 243-268). Baltimore: University Park Press.

Lee, L. (1984). *Developmental sentence analysis.* Evanston, IL: Northwestern University Press.

Lee, L. (1966). Developmental sentence types: A method for comparing normal and deviant syntactic development. *Journal of Speech and Hearing Disorders,* 31:311-330.

Lee, L. (1971). *Northwest Syntax Screening Test (NSST),* Evanston, IL: Northwestern University Press.

Lehmann, M. D., Charron, K., Kummer, A., Keith, R. (1979). The effects of chronic middle ear effusion on speech and language development - A descriptive study. *International Journal of Pediatric Otorhinolaryngology,* 1:137-144.

Leiter, R. C. (1969). *Leiter International Performance Scale,* Chicago: Stoelting Co.

Leonard, L. (1972). What is deviant language? *Journal of Speech Hearing Disorders,* 37:427-446.

Leonard, L. (1981). Facilitating linguistic skills in children with specific language impairments. *Applied Psycholinguistics,* 2:89-118.

Leonard, L. B. (1983). Discussion: Part II: Defining the boundaries of language disorders in children. In Miller, J., Yoder, D.E., Schiefelbusch, R. (Eds.), *Contemporary Issues in Language Intervention,* (pp. 107-112). The American Speech-Language-Hearing Association, Rockville, MD. ASHA Reports No. 12.

Leonard, L. (1983). Defining the boundaries of language disorders in children. In Miller, J., Yoder, D., Schiefelbusch, R. (Eds.), *Contemporary issues in language intervention* (pp. 107-112). Rockville, MD: The American Speech-Language-Hearing Association.

Leonard, L. (1985). Unusual and subtle behavior in the speech of phonologically disordered children. *Journal of Speech and Hearing Disorders,* 50:4-13.

Leonard, L., Bolders, J., Miller, J. (1976). An examination of the semantic relations reflected in the language usage of normal and language disordered children. *Journal of Speech and Hearing Research,* 19:371-392.

Leonard, L., Leonard, J. (1985). The contribution of phonetic context to an unusual phonological pattern: A case study. *Language, Speech, and Hearing Services in School,* 16:110-118.

Leonard, L., Schwartz, R., Chapman, K., Morris, B. (1981). Factors influencing early lexical acquisition: Lexical orientation and phonological composition. *Child Development,* 52:882-887.

Leonard, L., Schwartz, R., Chapman, K., Rowan, L., Prelock, P., Terrell, B., Weiss, A., Merrick, C. (1982). Early lexical acquisition in children with specific language impairment. *Journal of Speech and Hearing Research,* 25:554-564.

Leonard, L., Schwartz, R., Folger, K., Newhoff, M., Wilcox, J. (1979). Children's imitations of lexical items. *Child Development,* 50:19-27.

Leonard, L., Steckol, K., Schwartz, R. (1978). Semantic relations and utterance length in child language. In Peng, F., von Raffler-Engel (Eds.), *Language acquisition and developmental kinesics.* Tokyo: University of Tokyo Press.

Leonard, M. F., Landy, G., Ruddle, F. H., Lubs, H. A. (1974). Early development of children with abnormalities of the sex chromosomes: A prospective study. *Pediatrics,* 54(2):208-212.

Levinton, A. (1980). Otitis media and learning disorders. *Journal of Behavioral Pediatrics,* 1(2):58-63.

Lewis, N. (1976). Otitis media and linguistic incompetence. *Archives of Otolaryngology,* 102:387-390.

Liberman, I. Y., Shankweiler, D., Camp, L., Blachman, B., Werlman, M. (1980). Steps toward literacy: A linguistic approach. In Levinson, P. J., Sloan, C. (Ed.), *Auditory Processing and Language: Clinical and Research Perspectives* (pp. 189-215). Grune and Stratton, New York.

Lieberman, R., Michael, A. (1986). Content relevance and content coverage in tests of grammatical ability. *Journal of Speech and Hearing and Disorders*, 51:71-81.

Lindamood, C. H., Lindamood, P. C. (1975). *The A.D.D. program: Auditory discrimination in depth*. Allen, Texas: DLM Teaching Resources.

Longo, L. D. (1980). Environmental pollution and pregnancy: Risks and uncertainties for the fetus and infant. *American Journal of Obstetrics and Gynocology*, 137(2):162-173.

Lorentz, J. (1972). An analysis of some deviant phonological rules of English. Unpublished manuscript.

Lott, I. T., Wheelden, J. A., Levy, H. L. (1970). Speech and histidinemia: Methodology and evaluation of four cases. *Developmental Medicine and Child Neurology*, 12:596-603.

Lovell, K., Hoyle, H., Sidall, M. (1968). A study of the play and language of young children with delayed speech. *Journal of Child Psychology, Psychiatry, and Allied Disciplines*, 9:41-50.

Lubert, N. (1981). Auditory perceptual impairments in children with specific language disorders: a review of the literature. *Journal of Speech and Hearing Disorders*, 46(1):3-9.

Ludlow, C. L. (1979). Research directions and needs concerning the neurological bases of language disorders in children. In Ludlow, C. L., Doran-Quine, M. E. (Eds.), *The Neurological Bases of Language Disorders in Children: Methods and Directions for Research* (pp. 183-192). NINCDS Monograph Series, Bethesda, Maryland: National Institutes of Health.

Ludlow, C. L. (1980). Children's language disorders: Recent research advances. *Annals of Neurology*, 7(6):497-507.

Ludlow, C. L., Cooper, J. A. (1983). Genetic aspects of speech and language disorders: current status and future directions. In Ludlow, C. L., Cooper, J. A. (Eds.), *Genetic aspects of speech and language disorders* (pp. 1-18). New York: Academic Press.

Lust, B., Chien, Y. C., Flynn, S. (in press). What children know about what they say: A study of experimental methods. In Lust, B. (Ed.), *Studies in the acquisition of anaphora: Defining the constraints*.

Mackworth, N., Gradstaff, N., Pribram, K. (1973). Orientation to pictorial novelty by speech disordered children. *Neuropsychologia*, 11:443-450.

Marge, M. (1972). The problem of management and corrective education. In *Principles of childhood language disabilities* (pp. 297-313). New York: Appleton Century-Crofts.

McCarthy, D. (1970). *McCarthy Scales of Children's Abilities (Manual)*. New York: Psychological Corporation.

McCauley, R., Swisher, L. (1984). Psychometric review of language and articulation tests for preschool children. *Journal of Speech and Hearing Disorders*, 49:34-42.

McCormick, L., Goldman, R. (1984). Designing an optimal learning program. In McCormick, L., Schiefelbusch, R. (Eds.), *Early language intervention* (pp. 202-241). Columbus: Charles E. Merrill Publishing Co.

McEwen, B. (1983). Hormones and the brain. In Brown, C. C. (Ed.), *Childhood learning disabilities and prenatal risk* (pp. 11-17). Johnson & Johnson Baby Products Company Pediatric Round Table Series.

McGinnis, M. A. (1963). *Aphasic children: Identification and education by the association method*. Washington, DC: Alexander Graham Bell Association for the Deaf.

McMahon, A. R. (1986). ACLD-Scientific Studies Committee report.

McReady, E. B. (1926). Defects in the zone of language (word-deafness and word-blindness) and their influence in education and behavior. *American Journal of Psychiatry*, 6:267.

Melnick, C. R., Michals, K. K., Matalon, R. (1981). Linguistic development of children with phenylketonuria and normal intelligence. *Journal of Pediatrics*, 98:269-272.

Menyuk, P. (1964). Comparison of grammar of children with functionally deviant and normal speech. *Journal of Speech and Hearing Research*, 7:109-121.

Menyuk, P. (1975). Children with language problems: What's the problem? In *Developmental psycholinguistics: theory and applications* (pp. 129-144). Washington: Georgetown University Press.

Menyuk, P. L. (1980). Effect of persistent otitis media on language development. *Annals of Otology, Rhinology and Laryngology*, 68(Supp.):257-268.

Messick, C., Newhof, M. (1979). Request form: Does the language-impaired child consider the listener? Paper presented to the American Speech and Hearing Association, Atlanta.

Milisen, R. The incidence of speech disorders. In Travis, L. E. (Ed.), *Handbook of speech patholology and audiology* (pp. 619-633). New York: Appleton-Century-Crofts.

Mills, A., Streit, H. (1942). Report of a speech survey, Holyoke, MA. *Journal of Speech Disorders,* 7:161-167.

Moedjono, S. J., Needleman, R., Funderburk, S. J. (1983). Language abnormalities and minimal physical abnormalities in a boy with partial trisomy of chromosome 15. *American Journal of Mental Deficiencies,* 87:659-653.

Molfese, D. L. (1977). Infant cerebral asymmetry. In Segalowitz, S. J., Gruber, F. A. (Eds.), *Language development and neurological theory.* New York: Academic Press.

Moon, C., Marlowe, M., Stellern, J., Errera, J. (1985). Main and interaction effects of metallic pollutants on cognitive functioning. *Journal of Learning Disabilities,* 18(4):217-221.

Moore, M. V. (1970). Speech, hearing and language in deLange syndrome. *Journal of Speech and Hearing Disorders,* 35:66-69.

Morehead, D. (1972). Early grammatical and semantic relations: Some implications for a general representational deficit in linguistically deviant children. Papers and Reports in Child Language Development (no. 4), Committee on Linguistics, Stanford University, Stanford, CA.

Morehead, D., Ingram, D. (1973). The development of base syntax in normal and linguistically deviant children. *Journal of Hearing and Speech and Research,* 16:330-352.

Musiek, F. E., Geurkink, N. A., Kietel, S. A. (1982). Test battery assessment of auditory perceptual dysfunction in children. *Laryngoscope,* 92:251-257.

Mustain, W. (1979). Linguistic and educational implications of recurrent otitis media. *Ear, Nose, and Throat Journal,* 58:62-67.

Mutton, D. E., Lea, J. (1980). Chromosome studies of children with specific speech and language delay. *Developmental Medicine and Child Neurology,* 22:588-594.

National Center for Health Statistics. *Prevalence of selected impairments: United States, 1977.* U.S. Department of Health and Human Services, Hyattsville, MD, 1977 (DHHS Publication No. PHS 81-1562).

Myklebust, H. R. (1954). *Auditory disorders in children: A manual for differential diagnosis.* New York: Grune & Stratton.

Needleman, H. L., Gunnoe, C., Leviton, A., Reed, R., Peresie, H., Maher, C., Barrett, P. (1979). Deficits in psychologic and classroom performance of children with elevated dentine lead levels. *New England Journal of Medicine,* 300(13):689-695.

Netley, C. (1983). Sex chromosome abnormalities and the development of verbal and nonverbal abilities. In Ludlow, C. L., Cooper, J. A. (Eds.), *Genetic Aspects of Speech and Language Disorders* (pp. 179-196). New York: Academic Press.

Newcomer, P. L., Hammill, D. D. (1977). *The Test of Language Development (TOLD),* Austin, TX: Empiric Press.

Ney, D., Bay, C., Schneider, J. A., Kelts, D., Nyhan, W. L. (1983). Dietary management of oculocutaneous tyrosinemia in an 11-year-old child. *American Journal of Disabled Children,* 137:995-1000.

Neilsen, J., Sorensen, A. M., Sorensen, K. (1981). Mental development of unselected children with sex chromosome abnormalities. *Human Genetics,* 59:324-332.

Nyhan, W. L. (1972). Behavioral phenotypes in organic genetic disease. *Pediatric Research,* 6:1-9.

Nyhan, W. L. (1974). Histidinemia. In *Abnormalities in amino acid metabolism in clinical medicine* (pp. 197-205). East Norwalk, Connecticut: Appleton-Century-Crofts.

Oller, D. (1973). Regularities in abnormal child phonology. *Journal of Speech and Hearing Disorders,* 38:36-47.

Olmstead, R., Alvarez, M., Moroney, J., Eversden, M. (1964). The pattern of hearing following acute otitis media. *Journal of Pediatrics,* 65(2):252-255.

Olswang, L., Kriegsmann, E., Mastergeorge, A. (1982). Facilitating functional requesting in pragmatically impaired children. *Language, Speech and Hearing Services in Schools,* 13:202-222.

Olswang, L., Bain, B., Dunn, C., Cooper, J. (1983). The effects of stimulus variation on lexical learning. *Journal of Speech and Hearing Disorders,* 48:192-201.

Olswang, L., Coggins, T. (1984). The effects of adult behaviors on increasing language delayed children's production of early relationship meanings. *British Journal of Disorders of Communication,* 19:15-34.

Olswang, L., Bain, B., Rosendahl, P., Oblak, S., Smith, A. (1986). Language learning: Moving performance from a context-dependent to -independent state. *Child Language Teaching and Therapy,* 2:180-210.

Otto, D., Honck, K. Finger, H. Hart, S. (1973). Event related slow potentials in aphasic, dyslexic, and normal children during pictorial and letter matching. *Proceedings of the Third International Congress of Event Related Potentials of the Brain.* Bristol, England.

Pennington, B., Puck, M., Robinson, A. (1980). Language and cognitive development on 47, XXX females followed since birth. *Behavior Genetics,* 10:31-41.

Petersen, G. A., Sherrod, K. B. (1982). Relationship of maternal language to language development and language delay of children. *American Journal of Mental Deficiency,* 86(4):391-398.

Pinheiro, M. L. (1977). Tests of central auditory function in children with learning disabilities. In Keith, R. W. (Ed.), *Central auditory dysfunction* (pp. 223-256). New York: Grune and Stratton.

Prelock, P., Messick, C., Schwartz, R., Terrell, B. (1981). Mother-child discourse during the one-word stage. Paper presented at the University of Wisconsin Symposium on Child Language Disorders, Madison, WI.

Pronovost, W. (1951). A survey of services for the speech and hearing handicapped in New England. *Journal of Speech and Hearing Disorders,* 16:148-156.

Prutting, C., Gallagher, T., Mulac, A. (1975). The expressive portion of the NSST compared to a spontaneous language sample. *Journal of Speech and Hearing Disorders,* 40:40-48.

Puck, M., Tennes, K., Frankenburg, W., Bryant, K., Robinson, A. (1975). Early childhood development of four boys with 47, XXX karyotype. *Clinical Genetics,* 7:8-20.

Rapin, I., Allen, D. (1983). Developmental language disorders: Nosologic considerations. In Kirk, U. (Ed.), *Neuropsychology of language, reading, and spelling.* New York: Academic Press.

Rapin, I., Wilson, B. C. (1978). *Children with developmental language disability: Neurological aspects and assessment* (pp. 14-42). New York: Academic Press.

Ratcliffe, S. G. (1982). Speech and learning disorders in children with sex chromosome abnormalities. *Developmental Medicine and Child Neurology,* 24:80-84.

Ravin, J. C. (1956). *Coloured progressive matrices.* London: H. K. Lewis Co.

Rees, N. S. (1973). Auditory processing factors in language disorders: The view from Procrustes' bed. *Journal of Speech and Hearing Disorders,* 38(3):304-315.

Rees, N. S. (1981). Saying more than we know: Is auditory processing disorder a meaningful concept? In Keith, R. W. (Ed.), *Central Auditory and Language Disorders in Children.* San Diego: College-Hill Press.

Rees, N. S. (1983). Language intervention with children. In Miller, J., Yoder, D. E., Schiefelbusch, R. (Eds.) *Contemporary issues in language intervention* (pp. 309-316). The American Speech-Language-Hearing Association, Rockville, MD. ASHA Report No. 12.

Rice, M. (1986). Mismatched premises of the communicative competence model and language intervention. In Schiefelbusch, R. (Ed.), *Language competence: Assessment and intervention* (pp. 261-280). San Diego: College-Hill Press.

Rimland, B., Larson, G. E. (1983). Hair mineral analysis and behavior: An analysis of 51 studies. *Journal of Learning Disabilities,* 16:279-285.

Robinson, A., Lubs, H., Nielsen, J., Sorenson, K. (1979). Summary of clinical findings: Profiles of children with 47, XXY, 47, XXX, and 47, XYY karyotypes. *Birth Defects: Original Article Series,* 15:261-266.

Rohr, A., Burr, D. (1978). Etiological differences in patterns of psycholinguistic development of children of IQ 30-60. *American Journal of Mental Deficiency,* 82(6):549-553.

Rosen, A. Proctor, E. (1981). Distinctions between treatment outcomes and their implications for treatment evaluation. *Journal of Consulting and Clinical Psychology*, 49:418-425.

Sachs, J., Devin, J. (1976). Young children's use of age-appropriate speech styles in social interaction and role-playing. *Journal of Child Language*, 3:81-98.

Salus, P., Salus, M. (1973). Language delay and minimal brain dysfunction. Paper presented at the winter meeting of the Linguistic Society of America.

Samples, J. M., Lane, V. W. (1985). Genetic possibilities in six siblings with specific language learning disorders. *American Speech Language and Hearing Association*, 27(12):27-32.

Sandeep, P. (1981). Deprivation and cognitive development in children. *Child Psychiatry Quarterly*, 14(2):47-54.

Scherer, N., Olswang, L. (1984). Role of mother's expansions in stimulating children's language production. *Journal of Speech and Hearing Research*, 27:387-396.

Schiff, N. B. (1979). The influence of deviant maternal input on the development of language during the preschool years. *Journal of Speech and Hearing Research*, 22:581-603.

Schlieper, A., Kisilevsky, M. O. A., et al. (1985). Mild conductive hearing loss and language development: One year follow-up study. *Developmental and Behavioral Pediatrics*, 6(2):65-68.

Schwartz, R., Leonard, L. (1982). Do children pick and choose? Phonological selection and avoidance in early lexical acquisition. *Journal of Child Language*, 9:319-336.

Schwartz, R., Chapman, K., Terrell, B., Prelock, P., Rowan, L. (1985). Facilitating word combination in language-impaired children through discourse structure. *Journal of Speech and Hearing Disorders*, 50:31-39.

Schwartz, R., Leonard, L. (1985). Lexical imitation and acquisition in language-impaired children. *Journal of Speech and Hearing Disorders*, 50:141-149.

Semel, E., Wiig, E. (1980), *Clinical evaluations of language functions*, Columbus, OH: Charles E. Merrill.

Sever, J. L. (1986). Perinatal infections and damage to the central nervous system. In Lewis, M. (Ed.), *Learning Disabilities and Prenatal Risk* (pp. 194-209). University of Illinois Press, Urbana at Chicago.

Shapiro, A. H., Mistal, G. (1985). ITE-aid auditory training for reading- and spelling-disabled children: Clinical case studies. *Hearing Aid Journal*, 26-31.

Shatz, M., Gelman, R. (1973). The development of communication skills: Modification in the speech of young children to indirect directiveness in varying contexts. *Applied Psycholinguistics*, 1:295-306.

Shaywitz, S. E., Cohen, D. J., Shaywitz, B. A. (1980). Behavior and learning difficulties in children of normal intelligence born to alcoholic mothers. *Journal of Pediatrics*, 96:978-982.

Shaywitz, S. E., Caparulo, B. K., Hodgson, E. S. (1981). Development language disability as a consequence of prenatal exposure to ethanol. *Pediatrics*, 68(6):850-855.

Sheppard, A. (1980). *Monologue and dialogue speech of language-impaired children in clinic and home settings: Semantic, conversational and syntactic characteristics.* Unpublished master's thesis, University of Western Ontario.

Sheridan, M. (1973). Children of seven years with marked speech defects. *British Journal of Disorders of Communication*, 8:9-15.

Shriberg, L., Kwiatkowski, J., Best, S., Hengst, J., Terselic-Weber, B. (1986). Characteristics of children with phonologic disorders of unknown origin. *Journal of Speech and Hearing Disorders*, 51:140-161.

Silva, P. A. (1980). The prevalence, stability and significance of developmental language delay in preschool children. *Developmental Medicine and Child Neurology*, 22:768-777.

Silva, P. A., Kirkland, C., Simpson, A. (1982). Some developmental and behavioral problems associated with bilateral otitis media with effusion. *Journal of Learning Disabilities*, 15(7):417-421.

Silva, P. A., McGee, R., Williams, S. (1983). Developmental language delay from three to seven years and its significance for low intelligence and reading difficulties at age seven. *Developmental Medicine and Child Neurology*, 25:783-793.

Silva, P. A., Chalmers, D., Stewart, I. (1986). Some audiological, psychological, educational and behavioral characteristics of children with bilateral otitis media with effusion: A longitudinal study. *Journal of Learning Disabilities*, 19(3):165-169.

Simopoulos, A. P. (1983). Nutrition. In C. C. Brown (Ed.), *Childhood learning disabilities and prenatal risk* (pp. 26-31). Johnson & Johnson Baby Products Company Pediatric Round Table Series.

Skuse, D. (1984). Extreme deprivation in early childhood—II. Theoretical issues and a comparative review. *Journal of Child Psychology and Psychiatry*, 25:543-572.

Sloan, C. (1980). *Auditory processing disorders in children: Diagnosis and treatment* (pp. 117-133). New York: Grune and Stratton.

Sloan, C. (1986). *Treating auditory processing difficulties in children*, San Diego: College-Hill Press.

Slobin, D., Welsh, C. (1973). Elicited imitation as a research tool in developmental psycholinguistics. In Ferguson, C., Slobin, D. (Eds.), *Studies of Child Language Development*. New York: Holt, Rinehart, and Winston.

Smit, A., Bernthal, J. (1983). Voicing contrasts and their phonological implications in the speech of articulation-disordered children. *Journal of Speech and Hearing Research*, 26:486-500.

Snyder, L. (1976). The early presuppositions and performatives of normal and language disabled children. *Papers and Reports on Child Language Development*, 12:221-229.

Snyder, L. (1978). Communicative and cognitive abilities and disabilities in the sensorimotor period. *Merrill-Palmer Quarterly*, 24:161-180.

Spekman, N., Roth, F. (1984). Clinical Evaluation of language functions (CELF) diagnostic battery: An analysis and critique. *Journal of Speech and Hearing Disorders*, 49:94-111.

Sperber, D. (1975). *Rethinking/Symbolism*. Cambridge: Cambridge University Press.

Sperber, D. (1980). Cognition and semiotic function. In Piatelli-Palmarini, M. (Ed.), *Language and learning: The debate between Jean Piaget and Noam Chomsky*. Cambridge, MA: Harvard University Press,

Stark, R., Tallal, P. (1979). Analysis of stop consonant production errors in developmentally dysphasic children. *Journal of the Acoustical Society of America*, 66:1703-1712.

Stark, R., Tallal, P. (1980). Perceptual and motor deficits in language impaired children. In Keith, R. W. (Ed.), *Central auditory and language disorders* (pp. 121-144). Texas: College-Hill Press.

Stark, R., Tallal, P., Kallman, C., Mellits, E. D. (1983). Cognitive abilities of language delayed children. *Journal of Psychology*, 114:9-19.

Stark, R. E., Mellits, E. D., Tallal, P. (1983). Definition of the phenotype: Behavioral attributes of speech and language disorders. In Ludlow, C., Cooper, J. A. (Eds.), *Genetic aspects of speech and language disorders* (pp. 12-15). New York: Academic Press,

Stark, R. E., Bernstein, L. E., Condino, R., Bender, M., Tallal, P., Catts, H. (1984). Four-year follow-up study of language impaired children. *Annals of Dyslexia*, 34:49-68.

Steckol, K. (1976). The use of grammatical morphemes by normal and language impaired children. Paper presented at the American Speech and Hearing Association Convention.

Stein, A. (1976). *A comparison of mothers' and fathers' language to normal and language deficient children*. Unpublished doctoral dissertation, Boston University.

Stevenson, J., Richman, N. (1976). The prevalence of language delay in a population of three-year-old children and its association with general retardation. *Developmental Medicine and Child Neurology*, 18:431-444.

Stevenson, J., Richman, N. (1978). Behavior, language and development in three-year-old children. Journal of Autism and Childhood Schizophrenia, 8(3):299-313.

Streissguth, A. P. (1986). Smoking and drinking during pregnancy and offspring learning disabilities: a review of the literature and development of a research strategy. In Lewis, M. (Ed.), *Learning disabilities and prenatal risk* (pp. 28-67). Urbana-Champaign, IL: University of Illinois Press.

Streissguth, A. P., Clarren, S. K., Jones, K. L. (1985). Natural history of the fetal alcohol syndrome: A 10-year follow-up of eleven patients. *Lancet*, 2:5-91.

269

Strominger, A. Z., Bashir, A. S. (1977). A nine-year follow-up of 50 language delayed children, Chicago. Paper presented at the Annual Meeting of the American Speech Association.

Tallal, P. (1975). Perceptual and linguistic factor in the language impairment of development dysphasics: An experimental investigation with the token test. *Cortex*, 11:196-205.

Tallal, P. (1976). Rapid auditory processing in normal and disordered development. *Journal of Speech and Hearing Research*, 19:561-571.

Tallal, P. (1980a). Auditory temporal perception, phonics and reading disabilities in children. *Brain and Language*, 9:182-198.

Tallal, P. (1980b). Language and reading: Some perceptual prerequisites. *Bulletin of the Orton Society*, 30:170-178.

Tallal, P. (1980c). Perceptual requisites for language. In Schiefelbusch, R. (Ed.), *Non-Speech language and communication* (pp. 449-467). Baltimore: University Park Press.

Tallal, P. (1980d). Auditory processing disorders in children. In Levinson, P. J., Sloan, C. (Eds.), *Auditory processing and language: Clinical and research perspectives* (pp. 81-100). New York: Grune & Stratton.

Tallal, P. (1981). Language disabilities in children: Perceptual correlates. *International Journal of Pediatric Otorhinolaryngology*, 3:1-13.

Tallal, P. (1985). Neuropsychological foundations of specific developmental disorders (language, reading, articulation). In *Psychiatry*: Vol. 3, Chap. 67, (pp. 1-15). Philadelphia: Lippincott Co.

Tallal, P., Dukette, D., Curtiss, S. (1987). Emotional profiles of language-impaired children. *Journal of Clinical and Experimental Neuropsychology*. Submitted for publication.

Tallal, P., Newcombe, F. (1978). Impairment of auditory perception and language comprehension in dysphasia. *Brain and Language*, 5:13-24.

Tallal, P., Piercy, M. (1973a). Defects of non-verbal auditory perception in children with developmental aphasia. *Nature*, 241:468-469.

Tallal, P., Piercy, M. (1973b). Developmental aphasia: Impaired rate of non-verbal processing as a function of sensory modality. *Neuropsychologia*, 11:389-398.

Tallal, P., Piercy, M. (1974). Developmental aphasia: Rate of auditory processing and selective impairment of consonant perception. *Neuropsychologia*, 12:83-93.

Tallal, P., Piercy, M. (1975). Developmental aphasia: The perception of brief vowels and extended stop consonants. *Neuropsychologia*, 13:69-74.

Tallal, P., Stark, R. (1981). Speech acoustic-cue discrimination abilities of normally developing and language-impaired children. *Journal of the Acoustical Society of America*, 69:568-574.

Tallal, P., Stark, R. E. (1982). Perceptual/motor profiles of reading impaired children with or without concomitant oral language deficits. *Annals of Dyslexia*, 32:163-176.

Tallal, P., Stark, R., Kallman, C., Mellits, D. (1980a). Developmental dysphasia: The relation between acoustic processing deficits and verbal processing. *Neuropsychologia*, 18:273-284.

Tallal, P., Stark, R., Kallman, C., Mellits, C. (1980b). Perceptual constancy for phonemic categories: A developmental study with normal and language impaired children. *Applied Psycholinguistics*, 1:49-64.

Tallal, P., Stark, R., Kallman, C., Mellits, D. (1981). A reexamination of some non-verbal perceptual abilities of language-impaired and normal children as a function of age and sensory modality. *Journal of Speech and Hearing Research*, 24:351-357.

Tallal, P., Stark, R., Mellits, F. (1985a). The relationship between auditory temporal analysis and receptive language development: Evidence from studies of developmental language disorder. *Neuropsychologia*, 23:314-322.

Tallal, P., Stark, R., Mellits, D. (1985b). Identification of language- impaired children on the basis of rapid perception and production skills. *Brain and Language*, 25:314-322.

Terman, L. M., Merrill, M. A. (1973). *Stanford-Binet intelligence scale* (3rd ed.). Boston: Houghton Mifflin.

Terrell, B., Schwartz, R., Prelock, P., Messick, C. (1984). Symbolic play in normal and language impaired children. *Journal of Speech and Hearing Research*, 27:424-429.

Thelin, J., Thelin, S., Keith, R., Kazmaier, K., Keenan, S. (1979). Effect of middle-ear dysfunction and disease on hearing and language in high-risk infants. *International Journal of Pediatric Otorhinolaryngology,* 1:125-136.

Thompson, R. W., Peters, J. E., Smith, S. D. (1986). Intellectual, behavioral, and linguistic characteristics of three children with 18p- syndrome. *Journal of Developmental and Behavioral Pediatrics,* 7(1):1-7.

Tizard, B., Hughes, M., Carmichael, H., Pinkerton, G. (1983). Language and social class: Is verbal deprivation a myth? *Journal of Child Psychology and Psychiatry,* 24(4):533-542.

Tomatis, A. A. (1978). *Education and dyslexia.* Fribourg, Switzerland: A.I.A.P.P.

Tuomi, S., Ivanoff, P. (1977). Incidence of speech and hearing disorders among kindergarten and grade one children. *Special Education in Canada,* 51:5-8.

VanDongen, H. R., Loonen, C. B., VanDongen, K. J. (1985). Anatomical basis for acquired fluent aphasia in children. *Annals of Neurology,* 17(3):306-309.

Vargha-Khadem, F., O'Gorman, A. M., Watters, G. V. (1985). Aphasia and handedness in relationship to hemispheric side, age at injury, and severity of cerebral lesion during childhood. *Brain,* 108:677-696.

Vygotsky, L. (1978). *Mind in society: The development of higher psychological processes.* Cambridge: Harvard University Press.

Waisbren, S. E., Norman, T. R., Schnell, R. R., Levy, H. L. (1983). Speech and language deficits in early-treated children with galactosemia. *Journal of Pediatrics,* 102(1):75-77.

Warren, S., McQuarter, R., Rogers-Warren, A. (1984). The effects of mands and models on the speech of nonresponsive language-delayed preschool children. *Journal of Speech and Hearing Disorders,* 49:43-52.

Warren, S., Kaiser, A. (1986a). Generalization of treatment effects by young language-delayed children: A longitudinal analysis. *Journal of Speech and Hearing Disorders,* 51:239-251.

Warren, S., Kaiser, A. (1986b). Incidental language teaching: A critical review. *Journal of Speech and Hearing Disorders,* 51:291-298.

Watson, L. (1977). Conversational participation by language deficient and normal children. In Andrews, J., Burns, M. (Eds.), *Selected papers in language and phonology: Vol. 2.* Evanston, IL: Institute for Continuing Education.

Wechsler, D. (1963). *Wechsler preschool and primary scale of intelligence.* New York: Psychological Corporation.

Weinberger, M. M., Masland, M. W., Asbed, R. A., Sever, J. L, (1970). Congenital rubella presenting as retarded language development. *American Journal of Diseases of Children,* 120(2):125-128.

Wells, G. (1983). Language and learning in the early years. *Early Child Development and Care,* 11(1):69-77.

Whitehurst, G. (1982). Language development. In Wolman, B. (Ed.), *Handbook of developmental psychology* (pp. 367-386). Englewood Cliffs, New Jersey: Prentice-Hall.

Williams, D. M., Darbyshire, J. D., Vaghy, D. A. (1980). An epidemiological study of speech and hearing disorders. *The Journal of Otolaryngology (Supplement),* 7:5-24.

Wilson, B. C., Wilson, J. J. (1977). Early identification, assessment and implications for intervention, Oct. Paper presented at the American Academy for Cerebral Palsy and Developmental Medicine, Atlanta.

Wilson, B. C. (1986). An approach to the neurological assessment of the preschool child with developmental deficits. In Filskov, S. B., Boll, T. J. (Eds.), *Handbook of Clinical Neuropsychology* (pp. 121-171). New York: John Wiley & Sons.

Witelson, S. F., Pallie, W. (1973). Left hemisphere specialization for language in the newborn. *Brain,* 96:641-646.

Witkop, C. J., Henry, F. V. (1963). Sjogren-Larssen syndrome and histidinemia- hereditary biochemical disease with defects of speech and oral functions. *Journal of Speech and Hearing Disorders,* 29:109.

Wolfus, B., Moscovitch, M., Kinsbourne, M. (1980). Subgroups of developmental language impairment. *Brain and Language,* 10:152-171.

Woods, B. T. (1980). The restricted effects of right-hemisphere lesions after age one: Wechsler test data. *Neuropsychologia* 18:65-70.

Woods, B. T., Carey, S. (1978). Language deficits after apparent clinical recovery from childhood aphasia. *Annals of Neurology,* 6:405-409.

Worster-Drought, C., Allen, I. (1929). Congenital auditory imperception (congenital word-deafness): With report of a case. *Journal of Neurology and Psychopathology,* 9:193.

Zaidel, E. (1976). Language, dichotic listening and the disconnected hemispheres. In Walter, D. O., Rogers, L., Fizi-Fried, J. M. (Eds.), *Conference on Human Brain Function.* Los Angeles: Brain Information Service/BRI Publications Office, UCLA.

Zaidel, E. (1979). The split and half brains as models of congenital language disability. In Ludlow, C. L., Doran-Quine, M. E. (Eds.), *The neurological bases of language disorders in children: Methods and directions for research* (pp. 55-86). NINDS Monograph Series, National Institutes of Health (NIH), Bethesda, Maryland, August.

Zinkus, P., Gottlieb, G., Schapiro, M. L. (1978). Developmental and psychoeducational sequelae of chronic otitis media. *American Journal of Disorders of Children,* 132:1100-1104.

Zinkus, P. W. (1979). Perceptual and academic deficits related to early chronic otitis media. In Wolf, D., Gardner, H. (Eds.), *Early symbolization* (pp. 107-116), San Francisco: Jossey-Bass.

DISCUSSION

Isabelle Rapin

Dr. Paula Tallal has prepared a thorough and scholarly review of research concerned with children who do not acquire language as well and as soon as expected. As one would anticipate, she has drawn extensively from the many studies of dysphasic children that she has carried out with a variety of colleagues. I would like to highlight and amplify some of the points in her report that seem particularly important to me and take issue with some others in the light of my clinical experience as child neurologist and of research carried out with my colleagues, Drs. D. A. Allen, B. C. Wilson, D. M. Aram, R. Morris, and others.

I agree with Dr. Tallal that there is a strong need to develop positive criteria for diagnosing dysphasia rather than to rely on negative ones such as lack of hearing loss, mental deficiency, structural or neuromuscular abnormalities of the vocal tract, etc. These positive criteria will need to be validated; they must be efficient and yield clear-cut results. I agree entirely that we do not have well validated standardized measures for differentiating dysphasic children from normally developing ones, or for making a differential diagnosis between dysphasia, mental deficiency, and autism, the other two conditions of preschool children most likely to be associated with deficient language acquisition. (The most important condition of all to consider is hearing loss; there are now reliable neurophysiologic methods for assessing hearing definitively, even in the youngest and most handicapped child. The diagnosis of dysphasia in a child with inadequate development of language requires unequivocal evidence of normal hearing sensitivity.)

We also lack well validated standardized instruments for evaluating children's ability to understand, formulate, and express language, and to use language for meaningful communication and thought. This second set of instruments is required if one's goal is to subtype dysphasic children into homogeneous groups so as to provide these groups with an educational intervention that specifically addresses a child's particular deficits. Subtyping is also required for research into brain-language relationships and for the many other investigations that will be required to gain a deeper understanding of dysphasia.

The point Dr. Tallal makes about the difficulty of measuring cognitive competence fairly in young children with impaired verbal skills needs to be stressed, because even today I see dysphasic children who were mistakenly labeled mentally deficient. Certainly and crucially, nonverbal tests must be used to rule out across-the-board mental deficiency; from a practical standpoint, this may be all that is needed at the time of diagnosis. Dr. Tallal does not discuss in detail whether measures of nonverbal skills, which are "fair" for language impaired and socially deprived children, provide a truly adequate assessment of children's cognitive competence. Nonverbal tests alone cannot be considered valid predictors of later cognitive competence; dysphasic children with less severe language deficits who become competent users of language have a much more favorable overall long-term prognosis than more severely impaired children with equal performance IQs who do not.

Dr. Tallal makes the important point that deficient language acquisition can have multiple causes; that is, genetic factors may play a role in some dysphasic children, while acquired encephalopathic, sociocultural, or all three types of factors are elicited in the histories of others. The history elicits no risk factors in many children. The impression one gets clinically is that either there is no explanation for the child's problem or there are too many possible ones. The fact that there are some four dysphasic (and dyslexic) boys for every girl points to the importance of constitutional factors, presumably genetic ones, in the etiology of dysphasia. It is likely that there are some specific genetic variants of dysphasia that are associated with stereotypical symptoms since at least one well-defined genetic dyslexia has been identified (Smith et al., 1983). Most dyslexics do not suffer from this particular variant, which provides further evidence for etiologic heterogeneity among the dyslexias and, presumably, among the dysphasias.

Although Dr. Tallal does not give an opinion regarding the basic cause (etiology) of dysphasia, as opposed to her theory regarding its pathophysiology (a deficit in the perception of rapidly presented stimuli), she alludes to studies that find strong similarities between dysphasic children and younger normal children; by implication, these studies appear to support the hypothesis of delay in brain maturation rather than deviance in brain function and, possibly, structure. The fact, which Dr. Tallal emphasizes, that dysphasic children are likely to be dyslexic as they grow up underlines the chronicity of their problem and does not support the hypothesis of a simple lag in brain maturation.

The etiology of dysphasia is rarely known and, as stated by Dr. Tallal, it may be multifactorial in at least some children. This etiologic complexity is evident in our multidisciplinary multi-institutional study of preschool dysphasic, autistic, and mentally deficient children, funded by the National Institute of Neurological and Communicative Disorders and Stroke, one of the types of studies Dr. Tallal recommends be carried out. We have found, in the first 86 children examined, that boys outnumber girls by 4 to 1, as expected. In the group, 41 percent of the children are exclusively right-handed, 6 percent exclusively left-handed, and the rest do not have fully established handedness. This high prevalence of non-right-handedness may reflect the young age of the sample; it may also reflect both genetic and acquired factors relevant to the dysphasia. One-third of the children have a family member with a history of dysphasia or learning disability, and 18 percent with a history of an attention disorder. In the group of the dysphasic children, 9 percent were premature, 5 percent being born at 32 weeks or earlier. While three-quarters of the sample had a history suggesting one or more abnormalities in the perinatal period, only some 5 percent of these were considered serious, 10 percent sustained potentially significant postnatal difficulties, 37 percent of the children have a history of 6 or more episodes of middle ear disease, and slightly more than one-half were treated with ventilating tubes. Of the group of dysphasic children, 11 percent have a discernible motor deficit (all of them relatively minor since children with major motor deficits were excluded from the study) and 18 percent have oromotor deficits. (A motor deficit indicates that the child's brain dysfunction is not limited to language.)

There is a paradox inherent in one of the exclusionary criteria used in most studies of dysphasic children; it has to do with "brain damage." "Brain damage" is typically defined by the presence of a clearcut sensorimotor deficit, a history of seizures, or a known structural deficit in the brain. (From a practical standpoint, it makes sense not to include in studies dysphasic children with cerebral palsy who have severe oromotor deficits since it is difficult and frustrating to assess the linguistic skills of a child one can barely understand because of dysarthria—a motor, not language, deficit. It also makes sense to exclude children with uncontrolled seizures or those on toxic doses of anticonvulsants. Whether one should exclude children with occasional seizures or a history of seizures is debatable.) The paradox is that children who do not have a sensorimotor deficit or seizures, yet who are strongly suspected of having sustained a brain insult by virtue of having been a small premature, having had a difficult delivery with perinatal anoxia, or having suffered some other potentially encephalopathic incident, are regularly included in studies of dysphasia. Dr. Tallal also mentions as relevant to the etiology of dysphasia lead poisoning, chromosomal anomalies, and some genetic metabolic brain diseases, conditions known to affect the developing brain.

Excluding children with "brain damage" and including those with suspected brain insults is paramount to saying that structural brain abnormalities do not count so long as they have not declared themselves either by dint of having produced sensorimotor deficits and seizures or by the fortuitous availability of a neuroimaging study that shows an abnormality. It also implies that disorders of higher mental function, including dysphasia, are, of themselves, inadequate evidence for a structural brain dysfunction ("brain damage").

This logically flawed criterion for "brain damage" implies that dysphasia does not have an anatomical substrate. One suspects that this view reflects the prejudice of investigators who believe that dysphasia results from a lag in brain development or that dysphasia is a specific entity with a single etiology and pathophysiology ("neuropsychologic" deficit), rather than results from a variety of subtle or not so subtle structural brain deficits with multiple etiologies affecting one or more of the many systems required for language.

The major issue on which I take exception with Dr. Tallal concerns the nature of dysphasia. She champions the view that the cause of dysphasia is a deficit in processing of rapidly presented sensory information. In other words, dysphasia is not primarily a linguistic disorder; it is secondary to a prelinguistic perceptual deficit. She suggests that the types of language deficits regularly exhibited by dysphasic children are irrelevant surface symptomatology and that progress in research and treatment is impeded by attention to such "psycholinguistic" phenomena.

Language is a multilevel system that requires extraordinarily complex sequential and parallel operations engaging widely distributed brain systems. It seems highly improbable that language would be susceptible to dysfunction at only one operational step. We know from adults with acquired lesions that damage to different language areas of the brain produces different types of aphasia; in fact, one can make at least a rough inference concerning the location of an aphasic patient's pathology based on the observable characteristics of his language. Surely, information about localization of brain lesions in the acquired aphasias of adults is relevant when one is attempting to make inferences concerning the location of brain dysfunction in children with linguistically distinct dysphasic syndromes (Rapin and Allen, 1986).

It is not clear to me how Dr. Tallal proposes to explain by her unitary perceptual theory of dysphasia such language deficits as word-retrieval difficulties, hyperverbal output with poor comprehension, or lack of such "speech-act" pragmatics as question asking and answering in children who can label, comment, and comprehend assertions and commands. Likewise, the ability to understand and ask yes/no questions can exist in children who are unable to ask or answer complex "Wh-" question forms. Are these "psycholinguistic" or "neuropsychologic" deficits?

I have no doubt that there are dysphasic children who have the deficits described by Dr. Tallal (Frumkin and Rapin, 1980). It could even be that children who have these deficits constitute a majority of the dysphasics. This is an empirical question. My colleagues Drs. Allen, Aram, Wilson, and I have attempted to replicate Dr. Tallal's findings in 61 of the preschool dysphasic children in our study, but have found her tests too complicated for children below the age of 4 and extremely difficult to use below the age of 5. We plan to use Dr. Tallal's tasks in older children in future studies to see whether her findings are ubiquitous, as she implies they are, or whether they occur among some but not others of the dysphasic subtypes we have identified.

The next point where my views differ from Dr. Tallal's concerns subtypes among dysphasic children. She divided four-year-old dysphasic children into four groups on the basis of their test performance on standardized instruments: (1) children who were more impaired receptively than expressively, (2) children who were more impaired expressively than receptively, (3) children who were severely impaired for both reception and expression, and (4) children who were less severely impaired for both reception and expression (this latter distinction being one of severity rather than kind). She found that even at age 4, there were relatively few differences among her groups on a variety of language measures, and that by age 5 virtually all differences had disappeared. She interpreted these results as indicating that the children belonged to a single population and as confirming her hypothesis that "the" cause of dysphasia is a deficit in discrimination, sequencing, and remembering nonverbal (and verbal) stimuli presented rapidly and in producing rapid motor acts, including words. It seems improbable that the many possible etiologies of dysphasia mentioned by Dr. Tallal should all produce this one "perceptual-motor" deficit in brain function.

Dr. Tallal did not find that her four groupings provided information regarding patterns of language deficit among the children in her studies. This may have more to do with the tests she used to classify the children than with the children themselves. It is also possible that her tests selected for a particular type of dysphasic child. Dr. Tallal typically provides group results in her studies, although she indicates that there are circumstances where single case studies can yield valuable data. One of the problems with group studies is that they can obscure data from outlier individuals who may be members of subtypes with a low base rate. Subtypes with few members must not be ignored if one wants to obtain a comprehensive neurobehavioral view of dysphasia and if these outlier children require specialized interventions. (This is notably the case of children with the most severe receptive deficit, verbal auditory agnosia, who understand very little or nothing of what they hear, yet are able to acquire language provided it is presented to the visual channel by using signs or the written word.)

Dr. Tallal dismisses two studies (Aram and Nation, 1975, Wolfus et al., 1980) that attempted to subtype dysphasic children on the basis of multivariate analyses of scores on standardized tests of different aspects of language, on the grounds that these studies came up with different subtypes having different deficit correlates. These differing results are not surprising considering that both studies were carried out on relatively small samples of dysphasic children and that they used different instruments and different methods of analysis. Dr. Tallal also does not quote the subtyping study of Wilson and Risucci (1986) based on profiles generated from scores on a neuropsychologic battery or the clinically based subtypes proposed by Rapin and Allen (1983, Resnick et al., 1984, Rapin and Allen, 1986). One suspects that Dr. Tallal believes that standardized instruments are superior to clinical approaches, even though clinical approaches can yield valid and reproducible results, and also even though standardized tests measure a very limited aspect of the children's language competence and most have poor psychometric properties (McCauley and Swisher, 1984). Drs. Aram, Allen, Wilson, and I are currently testing the internal validity of the subtypes we have proposed in the past and possible correspondences among them. We hope to have the opportunity of determining their stability or lack thereof as the children mature. The only way to determine whether behaviorally defined dysphasia subtypes have any biologic reality will be to attempt to correlate them with such independent external validating measures as neuroimaging or mapping of electrophysiologic activity.

There are no formal data as yet to determine whether linguistically defined subtypes among dysphasic children differ in terms of their long-term sequelae. One can anticipate that dysphasic subtypes will blur or seem to disappear, at least to superficial examination, by the time dysphasic children learn to speak more adequately. Yet the children are not "cured" since the majority remain learning impaired and many spell and even read incompetently as adults. They can easily be shown to have persistent language deficits when tested with appropriate instruments.

Dr. Tallal concedes that subtyping may be important prognostically since she found that the probability of a later learning disability is higher in receptively than expressively impaired children. She does not feel that subtyping is relevant as far as intervention is concerned and states that the most efficacious approach is to address the children's auditory processing deficit. Our experience is that, when subtyping is based on an analysis of the children's language disabilities, educationally relevant groupings do emerge (Allen, Mendelson, and Rapin, 1986).

I could not more agree with Dr. Tallal on how inconsistent it is to label the same children dysphasic in the preschool years and dyslexic or learning disabled when they have reached school age. Mattis and colleagues (1975) and members of the Orton Society are among those who have pointed out that the majority of reading impaired children and young adults are language impaired, not visually-perceptually impaired. Most of the learning impaired are dysphasics grown up who present with new symptoms of their deficit. Since most dysphasic children do not "recover," even though most of them eventually learn to speak quite effectively, labeling them language delayed rather than language impaired seems illogical.

Another point of Dr. Tallal's report I should like to discuss concerns the question of whether the emotional and behavior problems of some dysphasic children are primary or secondary to their difficulty communicating. Dr. Tallal states that her sample of 4-year-old dysphasic children did not differ from her matched controls, except for behaviors that may be "associated with the originally diagnosed neurological disorder" (she does not specify what this disorder might be); at least some of the behaviors she mentions ("won't talk," confused, lack of concentration, social withdrawal, and immaturity) could derive from psychosocial as well as neurologic causes. Of course, clumsiness, accident-proneness, and twitches may indeed be signs of a mild motor deficit and of an attention deficit disorder with hyperkinesis that are but other signs of a child's underlying brain dysfunction and not a consequence of his or her language disorder.

There is no doubt that there are dysphasic (as well as hard of hearing and deaf) children who have no behavior or emotional problems. It is my experience, however, that children who have serious comprehension problems, as well as those whose expression is so limited as to prevent them from saying what they have in mind or to render much of what they say incomprehensible even to family members, may become frustrated, negativistic, angry, or withdrawn. Some of these behaviors respond dramatically to interventions to improve the children's communicative ability, which suggests that the behaviors may indeed be secondary to the dysphasia.

I agree completely with Dr. Tallal that markedly aberrant behaviors such as autism and severe hyperkinesis have a neurologic basis and should not be considered social consequences of deficient communication. I should like to make a correction to what Dr. Tallal states: autism does not *cause* the language disorder that is invariably present in autistic children; they are autistic *and* communication impaired and, in many cases, mentally retarded and/or hyperkinetic as well, depending on the extent and location of their brain dysfunction. While I do not have proof for this assertion, there is much clinical evidence to support this view.

With regard to intervention, Dr. Tallal rightly emphasizes that there is a dearth of adequate studies on the efficacy of intervention, whom to treat, how long to treat, and whether some treatments work better than others. I would like to echo her plea for intervention studies that address children's particular deficits specifically (Allen et al., 1986). Intervention and outcome studies are not popular and require just as rigorous a design as experimental studies. It is difficult to get them funded because they take a long time and are thus very expensive. Yet, considering the many millions of public and private monies spent on educational and professional interventions— many of which are probably ineffective—the need for carefully designed studies is obvious.

With few exceptions, intervention studies to date have been small in scale and have not been applied to rigorously defined subtypes of dysphasic children. Dr. Tallal and her associates report that intervention directed at mitigating deficiency in processing of rapid sensory stimuli is efficacious both for dysphasic and learning disabled youngsters. Certainly, presenting language more slowly provides these children with more processing time for all linguistic operations. Helping dysphasic and dyslexic children with phonologic discrimination deficiencies improve their skills is bound to be helpful to them. Whether such a treatment is sufficient or appropriate for all dysphasic children remains to be determined.

REFERENCES

Allen, D. A., Mendelson, L., Rapin, I. (1986). Syndrome-specific remediation in preschool developmental dysphasia. (Presented at the Congress of the International Child Neurology Association, Jerusalem). In French, J. H. et al. (Ed.), Philadelphia, PA, Paul H. Brooks (in press).

Aram, D. M., Nation, J. E. (1975). Patterns of language behavior in children with developmental language disorders. *Journal of Speech and Hearing Research*, 18:229-241.

Frumkin, B., Rapin, I. (1980). Perception of vowels and consonant-vowels of varying duration in language impaired children. *Neuropsychologia*, 18:443-454.

Mattis, S., French, J. H., Rapin, I. (1975). Dyslexia in children and young adults: Three independent neuropsychological syndromes. *Developmental Medicine and Child Neurology*, 17:150-163.

McCauley, R., Swisher, L. (1984). Psychometric review of language and articulation tests of preschool children. *Journal of Speech and Hearing Disorders*, 49:34-42.

Rapin, I., Allen, D. A. (1983). Developmental language disorders: Nosological considerations. In Kirk, U. (Ed.), *Neuropsychology of language, reading, and spelling* (pp. 155-184). New York, NY: Academic Press.

Rapin, I., Allen, D. A. (1986). Syndromes in developmental dysphasia and adult aphasia. (Presented to the Association for Research in Nervous and Mental Diseases, New York, December). In Plum, F. (Ed.), *Language communication and the brain*, New York, NY: Raven Press. (In press).

Resnick, T. J., Allen, D. A., Rapin, I. (1984). Disorders of language development: Diagnosis and intervention. *Pediatrics in Review*, 6:85-92.

Smith, S. D., Kimberling, W. J., Pennington, B. J., Lubs, H. A. (1983). Specific reading disability: Identification of an inherited form through linkage analysis. *Science*, 219:1345-1347.

Wilson, B. C., Risucci, D. A. (1986). A model for clinical-quantitative classification. Generation I: Application to language-disordered preschool children. *Brain and Language*, 27:281-309.

Wolfus, B., Moscovitch, M., Kinsbourne, M. (1980). Subgroups of developmental language impairment. *Brain and Language*, 10:152-171.

DISCUSSION

Katharine G. Butler

I want to express my appreciation to the National Institute of Child Health and Human Development and to the Foundation for Children With Learning Disabilities for permitting me the opportunity to participate in this Conference and to comment upon the work of Dr. Tallal. My comments are divided into three parts: (1) the realities, (2) suggestions for additional areas to be included in the review of research, and (3) recommendations.

THE REALITIES

I would like to congratulate Dr. Tallal and her colleagues on an excellent paper. They have explicated well their findings thus far in the longitudinal research being conducted at San Diego, particularly in the areas of linguistic and auditory processing. Within the constraints of the commissioned papers, it was undoubtedly necessary to limit the scope of the reported work. Thus, it is of interest to language specialists to note that the focus is upon the more severe forms of language impairment. (In fact, Tallal notes that the terms aphasia/dysphasia/specific developmental language delay, deficit, disorders, or impairment are used interchangeably).

In translating the data reported regarding the delivery of services to these children, it may be well to keep in mind that terms such as childhood aphasia or dysphasia are currently in decline with clinical and educational personnel, having given way to such terms as language impairment or learning disabilities. In addition, the DSM-III or DSM-III-R definitions of language disorders (receptive, expressive, and so forth) or academic disabilities (reading, writing) paints with perhaps too broad a brush the entities that are encompassed within the parameters of the term "language impairment." Current nomenclature adopted by speech-language pathologists and others in viewing the "language system" uses a series of subsystems: phonology, morphology, syntax, semantics, and pragmatics. Subspecialization in one or more of these five subsystems serves as a microcosm for the best and worst in the outcomes of a "narrow but deep" research agenda, where, in general, the child phonologist speaks not to a semanticist, and someone interested in grammar may not communicate with those who study pragmatics and so forth. If we have difficulty—and we do—becoming involved with other subdisciplines, the task is much more difficult across disciplines. The synergistic effects of interdisciplinary efforts are sorely needed.

SUGGESTED ADDITIONAL AREAS TO BE INCLUDED IN THE REVIEW OF RESEARCH

Tallal divides current research into studies reflecting the psycholinguistic approach and the neuropsychological approach. It might also be helpful to consider briefly the relatively new and fascinating work in communicative competence, in speech act theory, in the application of information-processing models from cognitive psychology, and in the anthropological and cross-cultural studies of language acquisition and disorders in first and second language learning.

As one reviews the statistics on the changing linguistic, cultural, age, and social-economic-status demographics in the United States, and the projections for the changes anticipated over the next 20 years, it is imperative to bear in mind the influx of limited English-proficient and non-English-speaking children into the nation's day care and school settings. It should lead us to review with care the brain-behavior research in second language learning and to translate the work of applied linguists with adults from across the world to adults and children in the United States who are seen as being at risk for language or learning disabilities. As we said, the demographic shift is to speakers of other languages and limited- English-proficiency individuals. Clinical services for individuals who do not easily attain oral and written proficiency in English will become an important concern. With the increasing Hispanic and Asian rim populations, diagnosis and intervention with language 2 learners who demonstrate developmental or acquired language impairments is an even more complex task than providing such assistance to monolingual (language 1) learners.

The review of the literature might also be expanded to highlight, albeit briefly, the merging literature from ethnographic, anthropological, and child language research that deals with the interactionist viewpoint between caretakers and young children. In addition, the literature on communicative competence among the language impaired is given short shrift, as is the expanding knowledge base in "the language of the schools"—that is, decontextualized language.

If language impairment is implicated in learning disabilities and dyslexia as well as in academic failure, *if* verbal skills are essential to lifelong success and personal contentment, then the literature that addresses the intersection of the learning *of* language *for* learning might well be addressed.

RECOMMENDATIONS

It is critical that children with language and learning disabilities be provided with appropriate services, utilizing not only the basic biological, neuropsychological, and neurological findings but also the new findings in child language, psycholinguistics, communication sciences and disorders, and in special education, learning disabilities, and dyslexia. As we have heard today, nerve growth factors, drug stimulants, and environmental modifications will impact on learning. In addition, work in the developmental aspects of memory processing, in higher-order cognitive processing, in more general learning theory, and in the educational implementation of intervention strategies will provide the bases for modification of intervention procedures. Even more importantly, the potential for prevention of learning disabilities may then become a reality.

As Dr. Cotman has suggested, the synergism between levels of research among a number of disciplines (and based in an interdisciplinary center for learning disabilities) holds great potential.

In accord with Tallal and several of the other authors, I concur in the recommendation that longitudinal studies of major proportions, involving a significant array of interdisciplinary personnel, should be established. Obviously, agreed-upon protocols and collaborative assessment procedures and instruments are essential if we hope to move forward at the intersection of language and learning disorders. Among the team members should be speech-language pathologists and audiologists (preferably conversant with the developmental perspective and the psycholinguistic perspective) who are familiar with the broad array of literature in human communication sciences and disorders. Certainly, particular attention to diagnostic categories and assessment instrumentations would be essential.

In addition to the significant contributions made by these papers, it may be helpful to go beyond the traditional review procedures and/or meta-analytic reviews to a "best-evidence synthesis" approach, procedures that would be intermittently updated. As we are all aware, traditional reviews may suffer from poorly specified criteria for including studies (possibly because the studies themselves have failed to specify selection criteria) and from using statistical significance as the sole criterion for treatment effects. Slavin's 1986 best-evidence approach reflects not only upon statistical analysis but upon the concerns raised by meta-analysis as data are collapsed and manipulated. As health-related findings (as reported in many of these papers) are translated into educational intervention and potential prevention delivery systems, meta-analyses or comprehensive and continuous collection continue to be of importance. In this instance, the interdisciplinary efforts cited above would establish and apply consistent, well-justified, and clearly stated priority *inclusion* criteria for including specific studies, including relevance, methodological adequacy, the minimization of bias, external as well as internal validity, and so forth.

I would make a plea for Federal and private support to assist in the transition from basic to applied research and practice. Breakthroughs at one level, in the last analysis, must be translated to the real world of parents, families, clinics, and educational settings in relation to the needs of the learning disabled, the dyslexic, and the language impaired individual.

Dr. Shepard has advocated assigning learning disabilities as a label to history. I would concur, but only because its original meaning has been lost in the maze of State and local rules and regulations. However, the same may be true of the term "language impairment." Both LD and LI now represent heterogeneous groups whose performance variability on multiple tasks is extraordinary—in fact, so extraordinary that there may be excessive over- or underidentification and labeling of children. One need only view the data collected by the U.S. Department of Education over the years to recognize that the categories of "mental retardation" and "speech impaired" have shrunk dramatically while the "learning disabilities" category has risen equally dramatically. *Who* belongs *where* and *why* are the questions that may be impossible to solve at the practitioner level. Brown and Campione's work (cited by Dr. Torgesen earlier), which reflects a dynamic assessment procedure(s) based upon current learning theory, holds out real hope for improved services, however.

While we await the formation of the highly-recommended multidisciplinary centers for research and the development of further theoretical constructs, Congress should be aware that many children with mild to moderate learning and language impairments are being denied services based upon the fiscal difficulties encountered by State and local education agencies and various constraints borne of funding criteria.

Perhaps there are two important conclusions one can draw from the reports presented here thus far: children in school do not appear in "pure forms" as do children in carefully controlled research samples, and in contrast, practitioners deal with not the "plain vanilla" child but with children who constitute a variety of exotic flavors. Such children are an admixture of difficulties and disorders; it is they that we see most frequently. This fact alone specifies interdisciplinary efforts. Secondly, language is the core of learning. A viable concept whose time has come is that the preschool child learns to use language and the school-age child uses language to learn. Today, we have been engaged in exercising our language skills. Let us now provide children with special needs those same skills.

DISCUSSION

Dorothy M. Aram

Dr. Tallal is to be commended for her admirable summary of a voluminous and fragmented area of study. The following comments serve to underscore several points and in some instances to present an alternative point of view. My comments focus on four major points: (1) definitional issues—that is, the criteria for identifying children with developmental language disorders (DLD); (2) subtypes or differences among children with DLD; (3) the need for research oriented toward the biological and causal basis of DLD; and (4) the importance of achieving a longitudinal perspective of DLD in order to sufficiently address many of the issues central to the study of child language disorders and ultimately to appreciate the impact of DLD upon society.

The area of definitional criteria for DLD is the one in which I have the most basic disagreement with Dr. Tallal's perspective. Dr. Tallal suggests that "the number one priority for research would be the development of these standardized inclusionary and exclusionary criteria and the requirement of their uniform usage for subsequent Federally or privately funded research in this area." Aside from the serious questions of inappropriate control on scientific thought that such a Federally mandated requirement would impose on investigators in this field and the question of what individuals or group of individuals possess this omnipotent knowledge, I object to such a practice for the following reasons.

First, we have not yet identified a sufficient knowledge base to adequately separate DLD from related disorders. For example, while one can state that children with cerebral palsy should be excluded from DLD studies, the actual demarcation between acceptable and unacceptable motor performance among DLD children is far from clear, since many DLD children presumably have a neurological basis for their disorders and present subtle motor abnormalities. Considerable research must first address motor behavior among DLD children before criteria can be anything but arbitrary. A related reason for viewing mandated criteria for defining DLD as premature is that we currently have little to no information about the natural history or long-term developmental course of the associated aspects of behavior that are to serve as criteria. Do we assume that cognitive, motor, emotional, and other statuses do not change over time? At what age can these parameters be reliably predicted? While Dr. Tallal's longitudinal study is beginning to address some of these issues, her study has employed a highly restrictive set of criteria and therefore excluded children whose early deficiency status may have normalized during development. To this point, in a 10-year followup study of preschool children with DLD, we demonstrated that of the 7 children whose IQs tested below 85 during the preschool years, only 3 tests were accurate predictions of IQs obtained during adolescence (Aram, Ekelman, and Nation, 1984). The essential point is that we do not have enough information about the developmental course of these parameters among DLD children to allow us to predict who will and who will not cross diagnostic boundaries over time. Further studies are needed to address these behaviors in more broadly defined DLD groups and to detail the participants' development before we can make informed decisions about appropriate inclusionary and exclusionary criteria.

Finally, as Dr. Rapin has pointed out and as most investigators and clinicians are well aware, even if we did have the knowledge to make these distinctions, we do not yet have available objective, reliable tools to assess these parameters. For example, I know of no psychometrically acceptable measure that can clearly make distinctions between adequate and inadequate oral motor performance in the preschool years. I maintain that to date, decisions regarding emotional, motor, and even cognitive ability are based on more or less informed clinical judgments, with very little use of objective, repeatable measures of these dimensions of behavior. What this all boils down to is that the knowledge and instruments upon which to evaluate these associated parameters are only beginning to be developed, and this is where research should currently be directed.

Even if specifying uniform definitional criteria for DLD studies were not premature, I would object to this practice for a second more essential reason: the very real possibility that DLD may not, in fact, be a distinct, qualitatively discrete disorder but may rather be on a continuum merging with other forms of developmental disorders. While I can appreciate the methodological benefits deriving from a uniform, restrictive definition of DLD, this approach may not address the real world. I believe we may also gain significant insights into the nature and causes of DLD by adopting a broader perspective to the population of children so identified. If subtle physiological bases ultimately are identified for DLD children, it would appear to me that more exaggerated forms of these disorders may be instructive in identifying the nature and causal basis for DLD. For example, recently as a part of the National Institute of Neurological and Communicative Disorders and Stroke program project on classification of DLD in which Dr. Rapin and I are investigators, we had the opportunity to study several nonverbal children for whom only very limited aspects of cognitive abilities are within normal limits. Therefore, if a rigid IQ criteria were established, these children would have been excluded. Yet through this study, we have identified one nonverbal 5-year old with bilateral cerebellar atrophy and a 4-year old with a partial deletion of the 18th chromosome. Both cases suggest potentially useful avenues for subsequent investigation of the bases of DLD in less severely involved children.

Further, children with additional developmental disorders can serve as a testing group for theoretical issues in language development and disorders. Study of language among mentally retarded populations, for example, has begun to inform us about cognitive prerequisites necessary for language, and study of severely motorically-limited children provides information relative to the importance of sensorimotor exploration as a requisite to cognitive and linguistic development. Finally, a fundamental reason for adopting a broader criterial definition for DLD is that the incidence, severity, and persistence of language disorders among children in virtually any population of more broadly defined developmental disorders is more pronounced than in a narrowly defined group (Paul, Cohen, and Caparulo, 1983; Allen and Rapin, 1980; Griffiths, 1969). Thus, the educational and societal demands of the multiply handicapped children with DLD are great and therefore should deserve significant investigative attention. In summary of this point: while I believe each investigator should provide detailed specification of subject selection criteria and should be prepared to share subject-by-subject raw data with other investigators in the field, a priori mandated specification of inclusionary and exclusionary criteria is at best premature and may in fact be counterproductive to the study of the nature and causes of DLD. The second major point I want to make concerns the need to seriously embrace the recognition of the existence of differences among DLD children and the need for sustained study of subtypes of DLD. In my mind, possibly the most serious obstacle to productive research in the area of DLD has been the practice of considering all DLD children, whatever the inclusionary criteria, to be a homogeneous group. As Dr. Rapin has already commented upon subtypes, here I only outline areas in which I suggest that DLD subtype research proceed.

- Although there have been a handful of studies attempting to objectively identify subtypes of DLD, I know of no studies that have provided any repeated or cross-validation of the subtypes once identified.
- As both Drs. Tallal and Rapin have pointed out, very little attention has been given to subtype stability over time, although it should be noted that in contrast to Tallal's findings, at least two studies have demonstrated persistence of DLD subtypes through development (Wolpaw, Nation, and Aram, 1976, Bishop and Edmundson, 1987).
- Once repeatable and potentially stable subtypes are identified, attempts to identify explanatory causal factors may then be more productive.
- If subtypes are in fact real, then the development, implementation, and assessment of intervention programs must differentially relate to the subtype addressed.

The third major direction in which I feel research in DLD should proceed is in investigation of the biological and causal bases of DLD. Dr. Tallal has outlined several levels of needed diagnosis and investigation in DLD. The level that I feel is in greatest need, in which we have next to no information, is understanding the biological basis of DLD. With few exceptions, of which Tallal's recent program project promises to make an important contribution, investigators have made few attempts to address brain structures through various imaging procedures, or brain function through—for example—electrophysiological measures.

At the level of identifying the causal factors for DLD, Tallal has summarized well the very limited knowledge available. Here I want only to underscore the importance of pursuing studies addressing the genetic, metabolic, hormonal, and neurological basis of DLD. To date, data in this area are very scant, and our understanding is as yet very rudimentary.

The final point I wish to make is the overriding importance of longitudinal investigation in this area of study. Much of the knowledge that needs to be gained can be addressed only through a long-term perspective. Among the important questions that can be answered only from longitudinal studies are those related to the developmental course of language and associated characteristics (for example: Schery, 1985; Stark, Bernstein, Condino, Bender, Tallal, and Catts, 1984) and to the long-term prognosis for DLD in terms of language, learning, and social and emotional development. While I would agree that large, multicenter, multidisciplinary program projects have their place in the study of DLD, equally important are long-term (and by this I mean 10 to 15 year) funding commitments to individual investigators, which will permit sustaining the prospective studies that are required to systematically address questions fundamental to the development, education, and eventual functioning in society of a very significant number of our country's children.

REFERENCES

Allen, D. A., Rapin, I. (1980). Language disorders in preschool children: Predictors of outcome: a preliminary report. *Brain and Language,* 2:73-80.

Aram, D. M., Nation, J. E. (1975). Patterns of language behavior in children with developmental language disorders. *Journal of Speech and Hearing Research,* 18:229-241.

Aram, D. M., Ekelman, B. L., Nation, J. E. (1984). Preschoolers with language disorders: 10 years later. *Journal of Speech and Hearing Research,* 27:232-244.

Bishop, D. V. M., Edmundson, A. (1987). Language-impaired 4-year olds: Distinguish transient from persistent impairment. *Journal of Speech and Hearing Disorders,* 52:156-173.

Garvey, M., Gordon, N. (1973). A follow-up study of children with disorders of speech development. *British Journal of Disorders of Communication,* 8:17-28.

Griffiths, C. P. S. (1969). A follow-up study of children with disorders of speech. *British Journal of Disorders of Communication,* 4:46-56.

Hall, K. H., and Tomblin, J. B. (1978). A follow-up study of children with articulation and language disorders. *Journal of Speech and Hearing Disorders,* 43:227-241.

Paul, R., Cohen, D. J., and Caparulo, B. K. (1983). A longitudinal study of patients with severe developmental disorders of language learning. *Journal of the American Academy of Child Psychiatry,* 22:525-534.

Schery, T. K. (1985). Correlates of language development in language disordered children. *Journal of Speech and Hearing Disorders,* 50:73-83.

Stark, R. E., Bernstein, L. E., Condino, R., Bender, M., Tallal, P., Catts, H. (1984). Four year follow-up study of language-impaired children. *Annals of Dyslexia,* 34:49-68.

Wolpaw, T., Nation, J. E., and Aram, D. M. (1976). Developmental language disorders: A follow-up study. *Illinois Speech and Hearing Journal,* 12:14-18.

PART IV: SOCIAL SKILLS DEFICITS

SOCIAL SKILLS AND LEARNING DISABILITIES: CURRENT ISSUES AND RECOMMENDATIONS FOR FUTURE RESEARCH

J. Stephen Hazel

and

Jean Bragg Schumaker

INTRODUCTION

Over the last decade, increasing attention has been devoted to the topic of social skills in such areas as self-help, business, industry, education, and the professions. This focus on social skills has not escaped the learning disabilities field. Previously, the way we interact with others was widely regarded as a matter of "personality," a concept related to a person's fixed character. More recently, society has accepted the notion that the way we interact with others is based on skills we have learned. Some people learn such skills quickly and easily, with seemingly little attention devoted to the learning process; others do not learn them or learn only a few of them. Those in the latter group are often considered by society to have "social problems."

Social problems of this type have been noted in learning disabled youths (Mercer, 1983) in addition to their problems in the academic realm (Kirk and Chalfant, 1984; Warner, Schumaker, Alley, and Deshler, 1980). Initially, LD youths' social problems were reported only in anecdotal accounts; recent research, however, has documented the range and severity of these types of problems.

The purpose of this paper is twofold. First, specific issues in the fields of social ability and learning disabilities, which provide a foundation for the remainder of the paper, are addressed. Second, seven areas of research related to social skills of the learning disabled population are discussed.

Each discussion is followed by suggestions for further work in the area.

OVERVIEW OF ISSUES

WHAT IS SOCIAL COMPETENCE?

A major issue for individuals interested in pursuing social skills research is that, until recently, the definitions of social skills and social competence have not been clearly specified. As Hops stated in 1983, "Our inability to agree on a precise definition of social competence in children ... has been a major impediment in our attempts to identify and treat socially problematic children." (p. 4). Fortunately, since Hops' statement, a number of authors have addressed this problem, and although there has not been sufficient time for some of their contributions to be critiqued, there seems to be increasing agreement on this important issue. Generally, social skills have been defined as cognitive functions and discrete behaviors that are performed in interacting with others (Schumaker and Hazel, 1984a) and as "the specific behaviors that an individual exhibits to perform competently on a [social] task" (Gresham, 1986, pp. 145-146). More specifically, Michelson, Sugai, Wood, and Kazdin (1983) presented an operational definition of social skills that includes the following seven components:

- Social skills are primarily acquired through learning (e.g., observation, modeling, rehearsal, and feedback).
- Social skills comprise specific and discrete verbal and nonverbal behaviors.
- Social skills entail both effective and appropriate initiations and responses.
- Social skills maximize social reinforcement (e.g., positive responses from one's social environment).
- Social skills are interactive by nature and entail both effective and appropriate responsiveness (e.g., reciprocity and timing of specific behaviors).
- Social skill performance is influenced by the characteristics of the environment (i.e., situational specificity). That is, such factors as age, sex, and status of the recipient affect one's performance.
- Deficits and excesses in social performance can be specified and targeted for intervention. (p. 3)

Thus, social skills are widely seen as discrete behaviors that are learned and performed in interactive situations. Such behaviors can include verbal responses (e.g., making a statement), overt nonverbal responses (e.g., head nods, eye contact), and covert nonverbal responses (e.g., discriminating one social cue from another) (Schumaker and Hazel, 1984a).

Social competence, the other variable to be considered in this context, is a more "value laden" construct. According to Gresham (1986), social competence is "an evaluative term based on judgments (given certain criteria) that a person has performed a [social] task adequately" (p. 146). It is closely related to the concept of social validity (Wolf, 1978), which is society's judgment that something is acceptable or "well done." A socially competent person is thus one who can perform social skills in a socially acceptable manner. Hazel, Sherman, Schumaker, and Sheldon (1985) specified that in order for a person to be considered socially competent, the person must:

- Discriminate situations in which social behavior is appropriate;
- Choose appropriate skills to be used in a given situation;
- Perform these skills fluently in appropriate combinations according to current social mores;
- Accurately perceive the other person's verbal and nonverbal cues; and
- Flexibly adjust to those cues. (pp. 228-230)

In summary, a *social skill* has been defined as a discrete learned response, whereas *social competence* is viewed as the socially acceptable performance of a smoothly flowing sequence of a variety of those responses. The following discussion is based on these definitions.

WHY IS SOCIAL COMPETENCE IMPORTANT?

The ability to interact appropriately in social situations is critical for successful adjustment in life. Research has shown that individuals who are not socially competent are at a greater risk for future problems. Van Hasselt, Hersen, Whitehill, and Bellack (1979) cited research that shows a relationship between inadequate social ability and poor long-term adjustment, including juvenile delinquency (Roff, Sells, and Golden, 1972), dropping out of school (Ullmann, 1957), "bad conduct" discharges from the military (Roff, 1961), and mental health problems in adulthood (Cowen, Pederson, Babigian, Izzo, and Trost, 1973). These long-term adjustment problems may be the result of the inability of socially incompetent individuals to form positive relationships with peers and authority figures.

In addition to causing such long-term problems, poor performance of social skills may also impede a youth's academic progress. For example, if a youth is unable to follow directions (a social skill), the youth may do poorly on academic tasks that require this skill. When Salend and Salend (1986) surveyed regular and special education teachers regarding the social skill competencies required for successful adjustment to the mainstream setting, regular educators identified 30 different social competencies and special educators identified 36 competencies as important. Example competencies include following directions, not speaking when others are talking, and communicating needs. Without such skills, a youth was considered to be at a major disadvantage in school situations. Social competence may thus form the foundation for success in both the academic and the social realms.

WHAT CAUSES SOCIAL INCOMPETENCE?

Gresham (1986) proposed that four kinds of social deficits result from four different causes. *Skill deficits* occur when an individual does not possess needed social skills in his or her repertoire. A youth who does not know how (has not learned the skill components) to greet people, for example, demonstrates a skill deficit. In contrast, a *social performance deficit* occurs when an individual has the given skills in his or her repertoire but does not have sufficient motivation or opportunity to use them. A *self-control skill deficit* occurs when an individual has not learned how to perform a social skill because of competing emotional responses. Some children, for example, may not ever learn how to interact with their peers because social anxiety prevents them from interacting at all. Finally, a *self-control performance deficit* defines situations in which an individual has learned the requisite skills but is prevented from performing them because of competing emotional responses or problems related to antecedent or consequent control. For example, a youth may have mastered the skills involved in accepting criticism, but when faced with an irate person delivering abusive criticism, the youth may become too emotionally upset to perform the skills. Another hypothesis has been recently proposed for the origin of poor social performance. Its proponents (e.g., Feingold, 1976, Schauss, 1984) suggest that poor social performance (the emission of inappropriate social behaviors) is related to certain physiological factors such as environmental sensitivities and chemical imbalances.

The disparity surrounding the causes of poor social skill performance complicates any solution to social incompetence problems. We cannot simply take an individual who appears to be socially unacceptable and instruct the person in a series of social behaviors. Such a course of treatment might be inappropriate if the person has a chemical imbalance, a food sensitivity, a social performance deficit, or a self-control performance deficit. The complexity of the problem is increased even further when one considers the possibility that a person might exhibit one kind of deficit with regard to some social skills and another kind of deficit relative to other social skills.

Do Learning Disabled Individuals Have Social Problems?

Recent research supports the notion that LD youths and young adults demonstrate social adjustment problems. Several reviews of the literature on LD children's social skills (e.g., Bryan and Bryan, 1981; Schumaker and Hazel, 1984a) have shown that, compared to their nonhandicapped peers, LD children are less well liked and more likely to be rejected by others (e.g., Bruininks, 1978a and 1978b; T. Bryan, 1974, 1976; Garrett and Crump, 1980; Gresham and Reschly, 1986; MacMillan and Morrison, 1980; Morrison, 1981; Morrison, Forness, and MacMillan, 1983; Perlmutter, Crocker, Cordray, and Garstecki, 1983; Scranton and Ryckman, 1979; Siperstein, Bopp, and Bak, 1978). In addition to concurring with this notion, Bruck (1986), in her review of the literature on LD youths' social and emotional adjustment, concluded that LD youths tend to exhibit increased levels of anxiety, withdrawal, depression, and low self-esteem compared to their nonhandicapped peers (Cullinan, Epstein, and Lloyd, 1981; Kasen, 1972; Rosenthal, 1973).

In a series of studies (Epstein, Bursuck, and Cullinan, 1985; Epstein, Cullinan, and Rosemier, 1983; and Epstein, Cullinan, and Lloyd, 1986), Epstein and his colleagues have documented the behavior patterns that characterize LD youths. The investigators concluded that although age and sex differences do occur, LD youths generally exhibit behavior problems.

In addition to the findings of researchers and scholars, people close to LD youths also recognize their problems in the social realm. In a survey of parents regarding their children's social abilities, McConaughy and Ritter (1986) found that parents of LD boys rated their children as poorer performers in the social arena than parents of nonhandicapped children. Parents rated their LD boys as having more behavior problems than typical for boys of that age. According to McConaughy and Ritter, the frequency of reported behavior problems among the LD boys in their sample fell within the range of behavior problems for children referred to child guidance clinics.

With regard to extracurricular participation, Deshler and Schumaker (1983) reported that LD adolescents are the lowest frequency participators among groups of low-frequency participators in school activities. Such social problems for LD individuals appear to continue into adulthood. White, Schumaker, Warner, Alley, and Deshler (1980) found that LD young adults participate significantly less in social and fraternal activities than their nonhandicapped peers. White et al. also noted that LD young adults were more likely to be underemployed and less satisfied with their employment than their peers.

Although these studies do not directly address the relationship between social performance and long-term adjustment, they do point to potential long-term social adjustment problems for LD individuals. Research has substantiated the contention that LD youths do have problems in the social realm.

Because social skills are important for life adjustment and because some LD individuals exhibit adjustment problems, it is important to determine whether LD youths exhibit social skill deficits in areas required for social adjustment. Numerous studies have compared LD and non-LD individuals' performance of certain social skills. In an extensive review of the findings of these studies, Schumaker and Hazel (1984a) concluded that, on the average, LD individuals exhibit deficits in social skill areas related to social competence as it has been defined in the literature. With regard to the more cognitive social skills, LD individuals have been found to choose socially unacceptable behaviors to use in social situations (e.g., J. Bryan, Sonnefeld, and Greenberg, 1981; T. Bryan, Werner, and Pearl, 1982; Pearl, Donahue, and Bryan, 1981), to be less able than peers to solve social problems and predict the consequences for their social behavior (e.g., Bruno, 1981; Schumaker, Hazel, Sherman, and Sheldon, 1982), to misinterpret social cues (e.g., Axelrod, 1982; Bachara, 1976; Bruno, 1981; T. Bryan, 1977; Gerber and Zinkgraf, 1982; Pearl and Cosden, 1982; Wiig and Harris, 1974), to fail to adjust to the characteristics of their listeners (e.g., T. Bryan and Pflaum, 1978; Donahue, 1984), and to fail to take into account the thoughts and feelings of another person (e.g., Bruck and Hebert, 1982; Dickstein and Warren, 1980; Horowitz, 1981; Wong and Wong, 1980). With regard to overt social behaviors, LD individuals have been found to perform certain nonverbal behaviors (e.g., J. Bryan and Sherman, 1980; J. Bryan, Sherman, and Fisher, 1980; Raskind, Drew, and Regan, 1983) and certain verbal behaviors (e.g., Banikowski, 1981; T. Bryan, Donahue, Pearl, and Sturm, 1981; T. Bryan and Pflaum, 1978; Donahue and T. Bryan, 1983; Donahue, Pearl, and T. Bryan, 1980; Noel, 1980; Smiley and T. Bryan, 1983a, 1983b) at significantly lower levels than their nonhandicapped peers. Their performance of certain complex sequences of social skills (e.g., persuasion, negotiation, resisting peer pressure, explaining a problem, giving and accepting criticism) is also significantly poorer than that of normally achieving peers (e.g., T. Bryan et al., 1981; Donahue, 1981; Mathews, Whang, and Fawcett, 1982; Schumaker et al., 1982) and sometimes similar to the performance of the same skills by juvenile delinquents (Schumaker et al., 1982). Finally, LD youths emit certain inappropriate social behaviors (e.g., negative comments, competitive statements) at higher levels than their peers (e.g., T. Bryan, Wheeler, Felcan, and Henek, 1976; Smiley and T. Bryan, 1983a, 1983b).

Although the methodologies of the studies cited here often do not allow one to determine how individuals within the LD population perform, how subgroups within the population perform, how LD youths might perform in natural versus contrived situations, and how poorer performance of certain skills relates to peer acceptance and overall social adjustment, results overwhelmingly lead to the conclusion that members of the learning disabled population demonstrate social deficits. Moreover, these deficits occur in both home and school settings and are perceived by LD children's teachers and parents as well as by their peers (Gresham and Reschly, 1986).

DO ALL LEARNING DISABLED INDIVIDUALS DEMONSTRATE INADEQUATE SOCIAL SKILL PERFORMANCE?

Although LD youths as a group have been found to exhibit social skill deficits, it remains unclear whether these deficits are common to all LD youths or if they are exhibited by only a certain percentage of the youths in this population. Some data on this issue have been presented by Schumaker et al. (1982), who assessed the social skill performance of LD adolescents and normally achieving adolescents with regard to eight different social skills. These authors found that, although youths in an LD group performed significantly fewer components of the majority of social skills assessed compared to their non-LD peers, the LD youths exhibited more variability in their performances. Some LD youths (26 percent of the sample) performed the social skills well compared to their nonhandicapped peers, and others performed poorly. Other researchers (Perlmutter, Crocker, Cordray, and Garstecki, 1983; Prillaman, 1981) have found that some LD youths are as well liked as their nonhandicapped peers. Thus, social skill deficits do not appear to be characteristic of all LD youths; rather, they appear to be problematic for a major subset.

ARE SPECIFIC CHARACTERISTICS ASSOCIATED WITH LEARNING DISABLED YOUTHS WHO HAVE SOCIAL SKILL DEFICITS?

If not all LD youths exhibit social skill deficits, certain characteristics may be found among those who do exhibit the deficits. Bruck (1986) identified four possible factors. One may be the pattern of cognitive functioning. LD youths with certain types of cognitive processing deficits may have more social skill problems than youths demonstrating other types of processing difficulties. A related factor may be the severity of the learning disability. Youths with more severe learning disabilities may have more social skill deficits. Sex of the youth may be another factor, with some evidence suggesting that female LD children are more likely to suffer social adjustment problems than males (Bruck, 1985). A final factor may be hyperactivity. LD children who are hyperactive may suffer more in the social arena than LD children who are not hyperactive. Bruck emphasized that while none of these factors alone accounts for social or emotional problems, in combination they may provide clues about which children are at risk.

Reviewing the characteristics of children who perform poorly in social situations, Michelson et al. (1983) cited research showing that students with appropriate social skills exhibit higher academic achievement scores. In addition, these authors listed locus of control, hopelessness, and irrationality as variables that may be related to poor social performance.

Although it may hold some credence, the notion that LD children who are most likely to exhibit social deficits share certain characteristics is not supported by empirical research. Even if such research were available, the utility of its results would be questionable since a majority of the LD population seems to exhibit social skill deficits of some kind (Schumaker et al., 1982) and since specific deficits must be assessed before social skills programming for a particular individual can be provided.

ARE SOCIAL SKILL DEFICITS PRIMARY OR SECONDARY PROBLEMS FOR LEARNING DISABLED YOUTHS?

Even if not all LD youths exhibit social skill deficits, the source of the deficits in those who experience problems remains to be determined. Two different hypotheses have been proposed. According to proponents of the first, social skill problems result from the same processes that are responsible for the academic problems of LD youths. That is, social skill deficits are seen as primary for LD youths. According to proponents of the second, social skill deficits result from LD youths' academic problems. That is, their academic problems cause LD students to become rejected or isolated from others, which prevents their social skills from developing in the same way as those of other children. After discussing these two hypotheses, Bruck (1986) concluded that either hypothesis by itself is unlikely to be correct; rather, both sources are probably responsible for the observed deficits. The author goes on to state that although there is no conclusive support for either hypothesis, data indicate that social skill deficits are not primary symptoms. Data show that social problems are not a distinguishing characteristic for all members of the LD population.

Although of some importance, the question of whether social skill deficits are primary or secondary to the condition of learning disabilities does not help identify LD youths with social skill deficits or remediate their problems. Efforts should be directed to issues that relate to more practical concerns.

WHAT MAJOR SOCIAL SKILLS ISSUES NEED TO BE ADDRESSED?

A number of issues are central to an understanding of the relationship between learning disabilities and social skill performance.

ASSESSMENT

Social skills assessment is critical to the whole process of social skill remediation. Youths who exhibit social skill deficits must be identified, the reason for the deficits must be determined, the specific social skills that should be learned must be pinpointed, and progress in a prescribed remedial program must be traced. An ideal social skills assessment tool for learning disabled youths would address all these areas and demonstrate the following characteristics: (a) it would be based on LD individuals' empirically validated social skill deficits; (b) it would be psychometrically acceptable (reliable, socially valid, sensitive to change, nonreactive); (c) it would be practical to use in school settings; (d) it would span the age ranges from preschool through secondary school; and (e) it would allow assessment of all skills required for social competence (overt verbal and nonverbal behaviors as well as cognitive skills).

To date, such an assessment tool has not been developed. In fact, no single available assessment tool appears to approach the above requirements (Arkowitz, 1981; Gresham, 1981). Several social skills assessment devices have been designed for use with youths in the general population, and some have been employed in research studies with LD youths; to date, however, no device has been specifically designed for use with the learning disabled. Many articles and chapters have been written to review available assessment devices (Arkowitz, 1981; Gresham and Elliott, 1984; Hops, 1981; Hops, Finch, and McConnell, 1985; Michelson, Foster, and Ritchey, 1981; Schumaker and Hazel, 1984a; Sprafkin, 1980). The following discussion focuses on the major kinds of assessment tools currently being used to measure social skill performance, including their advantages and disadvantages with respect to the ideal requirements specified above, and offers some recommendations for future research.

SOCIAL SKILL ASSESSMENT DEVICES

SOCIOMETRIC DEVICES

Sociometric devices have been designed to identify students who are the most and least liked within their classes. These instruments take primarily three forms. Students (a) nominate a fixed number of peers in the class whom they like the best and the least (the peer nomination method), (b) choose one peer out of each of a series of pictured pairs of peers as the preferred peer (the paired-comparison method), or (c) rate every peer in the class using Likert-type scales on some dimension of likability (the rating scale method). Sociometric devices of these types have been employed in a number of research studies to investigate the social acceptability of LD children (e.g., Bruininks,

1978a, 1978b; T. Bryan, 1974, 1976; T. Bryan and J. Bryan, 1978; Garrett and Crump, 1980; Prillaman, 1981; Scranton and Ryckman, 1979; Siperstein, Bopp, and Bak, 1978), but to date, they have not been used to identify particular LD candidates for social skill training programs or to evaluate treatment program outcomes.

Sociometric devices appear to be the most socially valid instruments for measuring social competence (Asher, Oden, and Gottman, 1976; Gottman, 1977; Gresham, 1983). In addition, they are easy and quick to administer, they have good predictive validity for school-age children (Cowen et al., 1973; Roff et al., 1972; Ullman, 1957), and they have been proven to be sensitive to changes in young children's behavior, to have concurrent validity with behavioral measures, and to have acceptable test-retest reliability (Gresham, 1981). Unfortunately, sociometric devices tend to be reactive (Gresham, 1981), and they provide no diagnostic information on why the social problems exist or which social skills should be trained. Further, such rating scales may be expensive to use with young children when pictures are required, they are insensitive to change in children above the ages of 9-10 years (Oden and Asher, 1977), and the results may vary according to the class population (Perlmutter et al., 1983). In addition, some people oppose the use of sociometric devices because of their potential for "teaching" peer rejection (Asher and Hymel, 1981). For these reasons, these devices are best limited to young populations, general screening for children at risk, and heterogeneous mainstream classes.

TEACHER RANKING SYSTEMS

Teachers use ranking systems to rank all the students in their classes according to the frequency of the social interactions in which the students engage. Such ranking systems are quick and easy to use, require only written instructions to administer (Hops et al., 1985), are stable across a one-month period, are accurate for identifying the lowest rate interactors, and are significantly correlated with other measures of interaction rates (Greenwood, Walker, Todd, and Hops, 1979). Like sociometric devices, however, they must be used with students in heterogeneous mainstream classes. In addition, they do not allow for specifying the reasons for noted skill deficits or for identifying particular skill deficits. Ranking systems have been used only with young children, and norms are not available for determining which children should receive consideration for treatment.

BEHAVIORAL RATING SCALES

Behavioral rating scales, inventories, and checklists have been designed for parents, teachers, peers, or target children themselves to report how well a target child fits a given description or emits a particular social behavior. Scales of this kind have been used in a small number of research studies to compare LD children's social skills to those of other children (e.g., Gresham and Reschly, 1986) and to identify skills to be trained (e.g., Hazel, Smalter, and Schumaker, 1983). Like most of the assessment methods reviewed above, this procedure is quick and easy, and allows measuring a person's impact on a variety of significant people in the person's life, who interact with the person in a variety of settings (school, home, community).

On some scales, teacher ratings have been found to be related to social interaction rates (Greenwood et al., 1976), to statistically discriminate children referred for social problems from nonreferred children, to be stable over time (Walker, 1983), and to be reliable and sensitive to treatment effects (Michelson et al., 1981). Most rating scales result in summary scores and/or classification of a child within a certain category; however, individual items on some scales can be used to target specific skills deficits.

Nevertheless, since most scales are devised to be global indicators of performance, they cannot be used to determine an individual's responses to certain sets of varying circumstances without becoming impractically long. Besides, they do not identify why a skill deficit is present. In addition, parent ratings seem to correlate less accurately than teacher ratings with actual social behavior (Cartledge and Wilburn, 1986), and some authors have cautioned against the use of self-report ratings because of their limitations in terms of reliability and validity (e.g., Gresham and Elliott, 1984; Michelson et al., 1981). Clearly, self-report scales or inventories that require reading and writing skills have limited utility for younger as well as some older learning disabled students.

INTERVIEWS

Another form of assessment, interviews, have been utilized with parents, teachers, and target children themselves to identify social deficits. Such interviews with parents and teachers can be helpful in targeting specific skill deficits. With the youths themselves, they can circumvent the reading and writing problems LD children may experience with paper-and-pencil instruments. In addition, they allow a child to report historical events and private thoughts and feelings, while allowing the interviewer an opportunity to observe certain basic social skills first hand. Interviews can be a convenient and easy method of gathering information.

In spite of the numerous advantages, several drawbacks must be mentioned. First, conducting interviews requires training (Cartledge and Milburn, 1986). Second, the predictive and experimental validity of interviews has yet to be determined (Hops et al., 1985). Third, LD children may have difficulty understanding interview questions and expressing their thoughts and feelings in words (Cartledge and Milburn, 1986). Thus, interviews may not be appropriate for some LD children.

Another type of assessment device, observation codes, has been employed, usually in conjunction with time-sampling methods, to record social behavior as it naturally occurs. In the LD field, observation codes have been used in conjunction with contrived situations, where youths were asked to complete an interactive task, for comparing LD and non-LD youths' performance of social skills during completion of the task (e.g., Banikowski, 1981; J. Bryan, Sherman, and Fisher, 1980). In the social skills field, observation codes have generally been used to confirm a child's need for treatment and to evaluate treatment outcomes. Usually, these codes center on a small number of observable behaviors, are very reliable as long as observers have been adequately trained (Harris and Lahey, 1978; Hartmann, 1977), can be sensitive to behavior changes (Gresham and Nagle, 1980; Strain, 1977), can be used repeatedly and often, and accurately measure how an individual behaves. Some simple measures, such as the overall rate of social interaction, have been found to relate significantly to occurrence rates of a variety of social skills, and some normative standards are available for some of these simple measures (Greenwood et al., 1976, 1979; Hops, Walker, and Greenwood, 1979). In addition, observation codes can be used to measure sequences of behaviors and the responses of others to the targeted person's behaviors (e.g., Dodge, Schlundt, Schocken, and Delugach, 1983; Tremblay, Strain, Hendrickson, and Shores, 1981).

The major disadvantage of observation codes is that they are costly and time-consuming (LeGreca and Stark, 1986). Observers must be present in the targeted student's environment for long periods of time (more than two hours according to Asher and Hymel, 1981) to obtain accurate behavior samples, and even then, many critical interactions may occur outside the observer's earshot. Some behaviors are so infrequent that waiting for them to occur is impractical. In addition, training is usually necessary for observers to become reliable users of the codes, and it is unlikely that a teacher would be able to teach children and at the same time use an observation code because of the intensity of concentration required for both tasks. Since most observation codes focus only on the frequency of occurrence of a few behaviors or categories of behaviors (for instance, positive interactions), they usually do not allow users to assess the quality of an individual's response within interactions or the kind of deficit that might be present (skill vs. performance) or to target specific component behaviors for treatment. That is, even though a child may be found to have a low rate of peer interaction, it is unclear what social skill strengths and weaknesses are present when the child does interact and whether the low interaction rate represents a skill deficit or a performance deficit. Additionally, observation codes that focus on rate of response may not be as useful for evaluating treatment outcomes as devices that focus on quality of the response because increasing the rate of a behavior may not make a person more socially competent (LaGreca and Stark, 1986).

OBSERVATION CHECKLISTS

Observation checklists have been used to record an individual's behaviors within a given interaction. Different checklists have been developed for different types of interactions (for instance, accepting criticism, resisting peer pressure, job interview), and specific verbal and nonverbal behaviors are specified for each interaction. The observer simply watches the interaction and records the occurrence of the component behaviors and, in some cases, the gross quality of the performance of those behaviors, using a simple 3-point rating scale. Observation checklists have been used to measure the overt social behaviors of LD youths in conjunction with role-playing situations (Hazel, Schumaker, Sherman, and Sheldon, 1982; Mathews, Whang, and Fawcett, 1982), contrived situations within the natural milieu (Schumaker and Ellis, 1982), and naturally occurring situations (Whang et al., 1982). They have also been used in an interview situation where LD youths were asked to "think aloud" about how they would solve a social problem (Hazel et al., 1982).

The advantages of observation checklists are that they are quick and easy to use, require little training to use, and take less than thirty seconds to complete. They can be reliably used after users have had some training. In addition, they are sensitive to changes in behavior (Hazel et al., 1982); measures derived from them have been shown to significantly correlate (r = .75) with social validity measures (Serna, Schumaker, Hazel, and Sheldon, 1985); they can be used to record sequences and timing of behavior as well as the occurrence of behavior; they can be used to pinpoint specific behaviors for treatment; they can be used repeatedly; and they can be easily used by teachers as well as by observers in a classroom or other settings. Additionally, observation checklists can be used to measure responses to varying sets of circumstances (for instance, criticism delivered by a calm person versus that delivered by an angry or belligerent person). If a behavior is present when it is measured in a role-play situation and absent in a contrived or naturally occurring situation in the natural milieu, use of observation checklists can help distinguish a performance deficit from a skill deficit. Similarly, when behavior is measured via a checklist in a series of situations, it is possible to determine how well an individual discriminates cues and chooses appropriate behaviors. Varying the responses of the other person systematically makes it possible to determine how well the target person perceives and adjusts to feedback.

In spite of their significant advantages, observation checklists suffer from certain drawbacks. First, there is usually no way to record behaviors that are not listed on the checklist. Second, a standardized set of situations to be used at varying ages has not been developed, nor are norms available for determining who needs training. Third, most observation checklists do not provide a means for recording the specific quality of a given response or for recording such socially valid factors as latency of response and speech disfluencies (Spence, 1981). Finally, since it has been noted that measures derived from checklists for behavior observed in role-playing situations do not necessarily correlate with the same measures collected for behavior observed in the natural environment (Schumaker and Ellis, 1982), care should be taken to use these instruments in the natural environment.

SUMMARY

A number of assessment devices have been developed for measuring social skills performance. Some of them have been used with LD youths; however, no instrument has been designed specifically for measuring LD individuals' social skills, nor does any one instrument meet all the requirements for an ideal assessment device. As a result, some authors (e.g., Brockman, 1985; Hops et al., 1985; Schumaker and Hazel, 1984a) have recommended using a combination of devices to adequately cover all the required functions. A global screening device, for example, might be used to identify youths at risk; another might be used for pinpointing skill deficits and measuring treatment progress. Unfortunately, no two currently available devices in combination meet all the requirements, nor are they readily available to school personnel.

RESEARCH RECOMMENDATIONS

- Research needs to be conducted to determine whether the social skill deficits of socially incompetent LD individuals differ from those of non-LD individuals also considered to be socially incompetent. Once this has been established, a decision can be made with regard to whether social skills assessment devices should be specifically developed for LD individuals. This research should employ socially validated samples of socially incompetent LD and non-LD individuals and should focus on the components of social interactions, the quality of social interactions, and the frequency of social responses. Such research should also attempt to identify the roots of the social deficits: that is, whether they are skill deficits or performance deficits and whether social performance is impaired by emotional responses.
- An assessment device or a package of assessment devices that meets the requirements specified above is needed. A primary consideration should be the usability of the device(s) for teachers, since most treatment of LD individuals takes place

in schools. In addition, such device(s) should not require resources (for instance, hiring observers) not normally present in schools. In short, what is needed is a commercially available assessment package that teachers can use, after reading a set of written instructions, to screen and diagnose social skill deficits, plan instruction, and measure progress for students of all ages. Alternatively, two assessment packages may be developed: one for elementary, the other for secondary school students. Regardless of their format, the assessment devices must be normed, and socially validated cutoff points should be available as indicators of needed training. The instrument(s) must also allow teachers to pinpoint specific social skills deficits for each youth so that the small amounts of instructional time available within most special education programs can be used efficiently. The social skills to be assessed should be skills that can be empirically and socially validated.

SKILL SELECTION

Development of useful assessment devices to identify LD individuals' social skill deficits depends partly on the availability of sound strategies for selecting skills to be assessed and trained. That is, assessment devices are needed to identify the presence or absence of specific behaviors or skills in a youth's behavioral repertoire. Hence, in order to be useful for measuring social competence, these devices must include the specific skills or behaviors that are critical determinants of social competence. Appropriate skill selection is not only necessary for developing valid assessment devices; it is also central to successful social skill training. The skills selected must be valued by LD youths and contribute to their success in social situations. Otherwise, the youths will be unlikely to use them.

In spite of the importance of skill selection, appropriate procedures in this area have yet to be identified. The discussion below reviews the procedures that have been used to select skills and provides suggestions for future research.

METHODS USED TO SELECT SKILLS FOR TRAINING

A variety of approaches have been used to identify appropriate social skills for training programs. Most common among them has been reliance on the intuition or clinical judgment of the trainer or program developer. The advantage of this approach is that ongoing observation and interaction with youths make a trainer aware of the types of problems and social skill deficits that commonly occur. The knowledge and experience gained from such contacts and interactions with youths can be invaluable in identifying potentially important skills.

Unfortunately, several disadvantages are associated with this approach. First, while the trainer may view the skills selected for training as important, they may not be perceived as important by the trainee. Adults, for example, often believe that positive social comments are important for young children; young children, however, may respond more favorably to quite different forms of social responses.

Hazel, Sherman, Schumaker, and Sheldon (1985) noted another reason why intuition may lead to poor skill selection. According to these authors, program developers may focus more on reactive or obligatory skills than on self-initiatory skills. *Reactive skills* are defined as skills demanded by a social situation. An example of a reactive skill is the skill of answering questions. If a youth fails to answer a question during a conversation, the absence of a response would be obvious to the other person in the interaction and would probably be identified as a social skill deficit. In contrast, *self-initiatory* or *optional* skills are not so clearly demanded in social situations. For example, the skill of giving constructive criticism, while potentially important to youths for maintaining friendship, might not be chosen as important by a trainer because nonperformance of the skill is not noticed. Thus, while focusing on obvious skills, developers of programs may miss skills that are equally important because of the nature of the skills themselves.

Another problem associated with selecting skills based on intuition is that it is impossible to determine whether the skills selected are indeed important until after the youths are trained to perform and use them in real-life situations (Hazel et al., 1985). In addition, success at outcome validates only that the skills taught were helpful and does not identify other skills that may need to be taught or that might be helpful to a youth.

Given the problems associated with skill selection based upon the intuitive approach, other methods are needed to determine what social skills should be taught to LD youths. An alternative to selecting skills through intuition relies on social validity. *Social validity* refers to the degree to which program participants and significant "others" in their lives agree that the goals, procedures, and effects of a program are important and acceptable (Wolf, 1978). By interviewing potential trainees, their parents, teachers, and other significant persons in the youths' lives about skills they consider to be important, a trainer can apply the concept of social validity, broaden the judgment pool upon which skill selection is based, and ultimately ensure that the skills selected for training are viewed as important by all concerned. This approach has been used, for example, by Hazel, Schumaker, Sherman, and Sheldon-Wildgen (1981b), who first asked probation officers to identify problem areas for youths and then asked parents and youths to rate the importance of the social skills related to those areas and being considered for inclusion in a social skills training program. All eight skills being considered were rated as "important" or "very important" and were included in the program (Hazel et al., 1981b).

This approach does have disadvantages. First, pooled knowledge may turn out to be pooled ignorance. That is, increasing the number of people surveyed does not guarantee that better or more appropriate skills will be selected. Although the trainer, the parents, and the trainee agree on the importance of the skill, their judgments concerning the helpfulness of a given skill in increasing social acceptance by society in general may be incorrect.

Second, it is often difficult to accurately pinpoint skills that should be taught. For example, when asked to identify problem areas, a parent might say that her child has "trouble getting along with others." The lack of specificity in this statement means that many important judgments must still be left to the discretion of the program developer.

A third approach to selecting skills for training has involved reviewing the relevant research literature to determine what skill deficits or problem areas have been identified for the target population. La Greca and Mesibov (1979), for example, studied the literature on social skill training for children and identified nine social skill areas that might be important for LD children, including smiling and laughing, greeting, joining peer activities, extending invitations, conversation skills, sharing and cooperating, verbal affection and complimenting, play skills, and physical appearance and grooming. The authors developed a training program for LD children based on these skills.

Similarly, as a result of their review of the social skill research on LD youths, Schumaker and Hazel (1984a) found three cognitive skills— choosing socially acceptable behaviors, discriminating social cues, and role-taking skills—that were common deficits among the LD population. Deficits in a number of overt behaviors were also noted, including both nonverbal skills (e.g., smiling while talking, hand illustrations while talking, forward body lean) and verbal skills (e.g., asking questions, making requests, and communicating fully) that were common problems. In addition, the authors found that many LD youths were unable to make successful positive statements and self-disclosing statements, and were lacking in the skills needed in conflict situations (persuasion, negotiation, resisting peer pressure, and explaining a problem). Finally, the review showed that LD youths tended to emit more negative comments and competitive statements than their nonhandicapped peers. A social skills program has been developed for teaching some of the skills identified by this review (Schumaker, Hazel, and Pederson, in press).

The benefit of basing the content of a social skills program on reviews of the research literature is that training decisions are backed by empirical data. Such an approach increases the likelihood of focusing on important skills. At present, however, only a few empirical studies have identified social skill deficits that are directly related to social acceptance problems for LD youths of different ages and across different situations. Although a number of studies have pinpointed skill deficits, they have not often established how these deficits relate to social acceptance.

A final approach to selection of skills for training involves observing youths during social interactions in a variety of social situations with a variety of individuals. This type of observation could help identify social problems that are common for LD individuals at different ages. Observation reduces the influence of trainer judgment because emphasis is placed on the actual rather than perceived social problems of LD youths. To date, this approach has not been used by developers of social skill programs for LD youths.

A problem inherent in the observation approach relates to our inability to observe ongoing social interactions without disrupting or altering those interactions. Thus, many peer interactions will change in the presence of an observer. A further difficulty is the infrequency of some social interactions. Youths who have social problems interact infrequently with others, and opportunities for certain types of interactions (e.g., teasing, initiating an activity) and use of certain skills might occur only once or twice a day. Thus, observation would have to extend over lengthy periods of time to allow sufficient opportunities for the behaviors to occur.

Another problem related to observation of social interactions concerns the units of behavior to be observed. As mentioned earlier, without an agreed-upon definition of social skills, it is not clear what level of analysis a trainer should apply when observing social skills. Should the number of eye blinks be recorded, or should observation focus on larger conversational units that occur during an interaction? In a similar fashion, how should social responses selected for observation be grouped? Without a taxonomy of social skills, the categorization of social responses depends on an individual clinician's judgment.

Lack of commonality of social skill deficits presents another problem. It has not been established that all LD youths have social deficits or that they all encounter problems in the same types of social situations. Observation of a limited sample might provide information that is useful only with respect to teaching social skills to that pool, and may not be generalizable outside the pool.

A final difficulty associated with observation is that while this approach may identify problem areas, it may not identify solutions. This difficulty may be partly overcome by observing socially competent youths in similar situations and by identifying the types of social skills these youths employ in these situations.

SUMMARY

Four methods or combinations of methods have been identified as appropriate for selecting skills for social skills training. Each method has strengths but also suffers from potential problems and limitations.

Consequently, research is needed to help program developers and trainers identify the most appropriate social skills to be included in social skill training programs for LD individuals.

RESEARCH RECOMMENDATIONS

- Research is needed to identify common social demands and problematic situations for LD youths. Such problematic situations could be identified by observing LD youths' interactions. Because of the changing nature of social problems at different ages and because of the different types of social problems that occur across situations, observations must occur across all age ranges and in a variety of situations. The information gathered in this manner would help identify the types of social demands and problem situations that commonly confront LD youths at different ages and across situations. Next, suggestions for potentially appropriate social skills for coping with these situations could be elicited from LD youths, non-LD youths, and significant "others" in their lives. These responses could be rated and judged for adequacy, and those deemed appropriate could subsequently be included in training programs. Following training, assessment should focus on the effects of training.
- Observational research also needs to focus on youths who are judged to be socially competent by their peers and teachers. Studies of this type should span the age range from young children to young adults in a variety of interactions with peers and with individuals who are younger or older than the target group. An attempt should be made to identify and name the skills these individuals use in various social situations, especially the situations that have been identified as problematic for LD youths through naturalistic observation methods (see La Greca and Stark, 1986, for a review of these methods). This information will tell us what skills socially successful youths use and, therefore, what skills should be taught to socially incompetent LD youths.
- Research should include the use of social validity measures as they relate to the selection of skills. The types of instruments and questions that are most helpful in identifying whether the correct skills were taught need to be determined. In addition, the best methods for obtaining judgments of social validity need to be identified. (See Gresham [1983, 1986] for reviews and proposals for research in this area.)
- Research should focus on identifying a taxonomy of social skills. That is, social skills should be organized according to scope and sequence and be related to different age groups. Research is needed to determine what type of organization is most functional for social skills.

This research should advance our understanding of how increases in a youth's ability to perform specific social skills are related to the youth's social acceptance. Are a wide variety of skills required, is there a core group of critical skills, or do youths simply need a certain number of skills regardless of specific type before being deemed socially acceptable? Answers to these questions would come from research on a functional organization of social skills and eventually would lead to the development of effective social skills training programs.

SKILL DESIGN

Once certain global skills have been identified as needed by LD youths who exhibit social skills deficits, it becomes critical to identify the components of those skills and the qualitative aspects that lead to the most positive responses from other persons. For example, after determining that positive initiations with peers are highly related to social acceptance by peers, the components of a successful initiation must be identified. Such components might include eye contact, a smile, a pleasant tone and volume of voice, a greeting, and a question or statement about an ongoing activity. Components must be organized into a sequence in which some of them occur once, while others appear throughout the interaction. In addition, the type and duration of, for example, eye contact, the timing and latency of responses, the way in which a greeting is phrased, the content of a question or statement, and the number and types of words used in verbal responses may be critical for social acceptance. In other words, a child who states, "I like this game!" might be better accepted into an ongoing activity than one who states, "This game is dumb." To further complicate the matter, acceptability of the performance of certain skill components may vary for different aged children of different sexes and in different situations.

Unfortunately, a standard method of determining the components of a social skill, the sequence in which the components should be performed, and the qualitative aspects of the components have not been specified. The discussion below reviews the methods that have been used, along with their advantages and disadvantages, and recommends future research directions.

DESIGN METHODS

For the most part, developers of social skills programs have relied on their own intuition and their professional and clinical experience in designing social skills. Although often sound and based on years of observing children's interactions, such judgments can be problematic and inaccurate. First, they often reflect an adult's point of view. Although this approach may be acceptable for judging what a child should do when interacting with an adult, it may not be appropriate for designing a skill to be used between two children. For example, in designing a skill for a child to use when someone pokes fun at or makes a pun of the child's name, an adult might design a skill that involves telling the offending person to stop making fun of the name. What may make the child more socially acceptable by peers and result in less fun being poked at the name might be a skill sequence in which the child laughs about the pun and counters with a pun about the other child's name. Second, an individual's judgment or that of a small group of people may not often reflect what is generally accepted by society at large. People's opinions of what should be said and done in certain situations vary. Third, what may be acceptable behavior for one segment of society may not be accepted in others. Certain expectations vary by cultures and often by sex. Thus, other methods must be utilized to design the qualitative components of social skills.

A method used outside the LD field involves having the youths in the target populations design the skills themselves. Minkin, Minkin, Goldstein, Taylor, Braukmann, Kirigin, and Wolf (1981) asked predelinquent girls to discuss behaviors that would improve their delivery of criticism to peers. The girls then learned the skill components they had designed, and the skill components were validated by judges who rated the girls' performances before and after training.

Hazel, Schumaker, Sherman, and Sheldon-Wildgen (1981b) used a variation of this method to design eight skills for a social skills program for adolescents. These authors designed the skills after surveying probation officers. Youths on probation were subsequently asked to critique the skill components, and the skill components were modified accordingly. Later, knowledgeable individuals in the social skills field reviewed the components, and adult judges rated the youths' before- and after-training performances to validate the appropriateness of the skills.

This method of skill design has the advantage of incorporating input from youths themselves. To be successful, however, it requires that the youths' discussions be structured properly and that participating youths have ideas and be able to express them in a group meeting. For these reasons, this approach is not appropriate for very young children or other individuals who have difficulty expressing themselves verbally in groups. In some cases, individual interviews may be a fitting alternative. Finally, it is questionable whether youths with skill deficits should design skills and whether adults should validate skills to be used between child peers. Perhaps age-relevant youths who have been selected as well liked by their peers are the most appropriate candidates for designing and validating such skills.

A further variation of this approach has involved relevant "others." Hiemberg, Cunningham, Stanley, and Blankenberg (1982), for example, asked employers to identify a series of preferred responses from employees or from job applicants. The suggested skill components were later validated by having employers rate actual performances during job interviews. This method seems to have a high degree of face validity. That is, for skills designed to be used by a youth with an adult or an authority figure, members of the senior population appear to be the most appropriate for designing the skills. Teachers, principals, parents, and employers should therefore be involved in designing skills to be used in interactions with adults. In addition, age-appropriate youths should always be consulted regarding the design of a skill because what adults prefer may be objectionable to youths. On the basis of the present authors' experience, training a youth to use a social skill is fruitless if the youth refuses to use it.

Another method of designing social skills involves direct observation of situations in which the skills are to be used, and subsequently correlating observed skill components with the reaction of peers to the individual emitting them. Dodge et al. (1983), for example, observed six responses that children used when trying to join ongoing peer activities. Through sequential analyses, the authors noted that certain entry behaviors were more likely to receive a positive response than others and that a three-step sequence involving (a) waiting and hovering, (b) imitating the group's activity, and (c) making a statement about the ongoing activity was a particularly successful strategy.

This method of designing skills has merit because it is based on what children actually do and on data concerning tactics that are actually successful. Nevertheless, some cautions are in order. First, the method requires direct access to youths' social behavior, which may be difficult to arrange, especially when older youths are the targets. Second, the method may be appropriate for simple skills but unwieldy for skills involving as many as 16 components (Hazel, Schumaker, Sherman, and Sheldon-Wildgen, 1981a). Third, the method relies on the developer's judgment in choosing the skill components to be observed. Hence, important skill components may be inadvertently ignored. Fourth, to be adequately productive, the method should be used at two different levels; that is, once successful skill components have been identified, the method should be used to identify the qualitative aspects associated with those components—for instance, to determine the optimal kind of statement a child can use when the child "makes a statement about the ongoing activity."

Finally, a method of skill design currently being tested by the present authors involves having large numbers of individuals role play what they would do in certain situations. Subjects' performances are recorded (on audiotape or videotape) and divided into parts related to certain skill components. All the responses related to a given component are then reviewed together and rated by another group of individuals, who categorize them as optimal, acceptable, or unacceptable responses. Responses rated as optimal are then analyzed to determine their common qualities. Eventually, these common qualities are built into the new social skill.

This method yields excellent information about how to design skills, but it is extremely time-consuming and needs to be refined. Nevertheless, if used with age-relevant and sex-relevant populations of youths who are well liked, the method holds promise for the design of appropriate social skills for training.

SUMMARY

A number of methods have been utilized to design social skills to be taught to children who demonstrate skill deficits. Some developers have directly involved youths and relevant "others" in the design process; other developers have relied on observation of skill usage and the results of such usage; still others have categorized responses (optimal, acceptable, and unacceptable) as the basis for further determination of common qualities of optimal skills. Most of these methods focus on the identification of skill components; only one is aimed at the identification of the qualitative aspects related to those components. All methods reviewed here have involved some sort of social validation of the skill components and/or qualitative aspects. In the design process, it is critical that age-relevant and sex-relevant youths be involved since evidence suggests that the acceptability of social performance varies according to a trainee's sex and age (LeGreca and Stark, 1986). Since structured methods of skill design have been applied to only a few skills and since the qualitative aspects of children's social skill performances are still relatively unknown, further work in this area is warranted.

RESEARCH RECOMMENDATIONS

- Research is needed to develop and apply standardized methods to the design of components of a wide variety of social skills needed by socially incompetent LD individuals at various age levels. In addition, methods for designing the sequence of the skill components should also be developed and designed. To validate skill components as acceptable and appropriate, the input of age-appropriate youths appears to be paramount.
- Additional research is needed to develop and apply standardized methods to specifying the qualitative aspects of each component of a skill. That is, such factors as response duration, latency, timing, content, and format should be considered.
- Research should address the development of means through which social skill components and their qualitative aspects can be socially validated by age-relevant populations.

COGNITIVE AND DECISION-MAKING SKILLS

The study of LD youths' social skill performance and deficits has raised the question of what role cognitive factors play in facilitating or inhibiting acquisition and performance of social responses. The cognitive factors that have been considered include thinking and reasoning processes and extend to perceptions and beliefs about events in the world.

Cognitive factors can affect a youth's social ability or performance in at least three different ways. First, cognitive deficits, which include deficiencies in cognitive processing, may influence the ability to learn a social skill. That is, some youths may have difficulty processing certain types of information, including the information necessary for appropriate social skill performance. Second, even if a youth has learned how to perform a specific social skill, certain cognitive skills may be required to successfully perform that skill in real-life situations. For example, without the cognitive skills necessary to discriminate what skill to use in a given situation, a youth may not be able to perform adequately in that situation, even though the youth was able to perform it correctly when cued to do so. Third, cognitions may play a role in regulating emotional responses, such as anxiety, in social situations. Such emotional responses can hinder acquisition and performance of social skills.

Each of these possibilities is discussed below in conjunction with relevant research. Possible directions for future research are also proposed.

COGNITIVE INFLUENCE ON SKILL ACQUISITION

Gresham (1986) proposed that some youths may perform poorly in social situations because they have failed to acquire the required social skill—they demonstrate a *skill deficit*. To date, most social skill training approaches focus on remediating skill deficits. If a social skill problem results from a skill deficit, the reason why some youths fail to learn the skill must be pursued. Is the failure to learn social skills caused by poor cognitive processing abilities? For LD youths, is the failure to acquire social skills based on the same cognitive deficits as those which account for their failure to master academic skills?

In a review of the relevant literature, Bruck (1986) concluded that available evidence does not indicate conclusively whether social problems result from the processes that lead to academic failure for LD youths or whether social deficits are the secondary result of academic failure. She stated that "...there are no definitive data to support either of the two extreme hypotheses.... Rather, it is likely that the two forces (internal psychological factors and external social factors) interact to result in social emotional problems; or, for some children, adjustment problems reflect psychological deficits, for others, problems reflect negative external conditions" (p. 365).

COGNITIVE INFLUENCES ON SKILL PERFORMANCE

Cognitions may also influence social performance because use of certain cognitive skills is necessary to perform a social skill appropriately. That is, to perform in a social situation, a youth must utilize cognitive skills and strategies to direct the overt performance of verbal and non-verbal skills. A way to conceptualize the role of cognitions in such situations is to think of a social performance as a discrete sequence of events. At the first point of the sequence is a perception of relevant social cues. If a youth is lacking in these perceptual skills, poor social performance will result. Poor perception of cues has been a noted characteristic of the learning disabled (Johnson and Myklebust, 1967) to the extent that some authors have argued that social perception deficits account for LD youths' poor social performance (Perlmutter, 1986). Nevertheless, Maheady and Sainato (1986), in a review of the literature on LD students' social perception, concluded that, because of ambiguous results and methodological problems, the evidence does not support the teaching of social-perception skills to LD youths. Given this uncertainty, further research is needed.

Cognitive skills also may be important at later points of the sequence of a social performance. After a youth perceives the cues that indicate a social situation, the youth must discriminate what skill is most appropriate in the given situation with that particular person. Choosing the correct skill requires cognitive discrimination. For example, if a youth has incorrectly discriminated that the correct skill response is to give criticism in a situation that calls for negotiation, the youth would not perform well in that social interaction and would probably not be positively reinforced for the performance.

After identifying the correct skill, the youth must decide which of several skill variations to use. That is, even though the youth may correctly discriminate what skill to use, the youth must use problem-solving skills to select the appropriate skill variation to suit the other person's age, relationship to the youth, and other factors. Problem-solving is difficult for many LD youths (see Stone and Michals, 1986, for a review of the problem-solving literature on LD children). Thus, for some LD youths, failure to make good decisions may hinder their social performance. The best way to teach these skills to LD youths has not yet been determined. Hazel, Schumaker, Sherman, and Sheldon (1982), for example, attempted to teach a problem-solving skill to LD youths, with only limited success.

After a youth decides which variation of a skill to use, the youth must initiate the skill performance. To do so, the youth must be motivated. Cognitive strategies may be a way to increase the necessary motivation. For example, the youth might say: "I know I can do it if I try." In a review of the relevant literature, Pearl (1985) concluded that cognitive methods offer promise for increasing motivation.

If a youth is motivated to perform a task, the youth must perform it while using the required cognitive skills. For example, the youth must be responsive to feedback from the other person during the social interaction and must be able to adapt his or her social skill performance to the other person's responses. The youth must decide when to stop making requests, when to accept negative feedback, and when to end a conversation. These kinds of adaptations require cognitive decision-making and problem-solving skills.

A youth must also be aware of and act in accordance with the social rules dictated by a given situation. Social rules often are those unwritten rules we follow when engaging in social interactions. A common social rule in Western society, for example, is to maintain a certain minimum distance in talking to another person. If a youth does not know this rule or does not follow it in a social interaction, the youth will be perceived as performing poorly. To learn and use these social rules properly during a social interaction requires cognitive skills.

After completing a social interaction, a youth must be able to give himself or herself accurate feedback on the performance. Through self-evaluation and feedback, the youth can improve his or her social performance. In addition, the youth must provide himself or herself with reinforcement for the performance. Such reinforcement may range from merely saying to oneself, "I did a good job," to buying oneself a soft drink or allowing oneself to call a friend. These types of self- evaluation and self-reinforcement require cognitive skills.

In summary, a variety of cognitive skills are critical for successful social skill performance. However, important questions remain regarding what types of cognitive skills are necessary for correct social performance and how to develop programs to teach these skills to LD youths who lack them.

COGNITIVE INFLUENCES ON EMOTIONAL RESPONSES

The ability to learn or use a social skill may be influenced by a youth's emotional response to a given situation. Strong emotional reactions may interfere with acquisition or performance of a skill. An emotion often identified as problematic in this regard is anxiety (Gresham, 1985); another is anger. If youths are taught how to control their emotions, they may be better able to learn new social skills and perform them successfully.

Cognitive skills may be important in influencing the strength of emotional responses to a situation. Ellis (1962), for example, argued that an individual's thoughts and beliefs about a situation largely influence that person's emotional response in the situation. Thus, strategies have been developed to teach children specific types of cognitive skills in an attempt to mediate and influence emotional responses (Kendall and Braswell, 1985). Although the research on the role of these cognitive variables as mediators of emotional responses during social interactions remains less than clear (see Stefanek and Eisler, 1983, for a review), they are potentially important.

Cartledge and Milburn (1986) identified five types of cognitive training for modifying emotions that may affect social performance. *Social perception training,* which involves learning to perceive one's own and others' feelings, is one type. Without the ability to correctly interpret and label feelings, a person encounters many problems in social interactions. A second type of training focuses on learning *problem-solving strategies.* Such skills may be important not only in helping a youth to decide what skills to use in different social situations, they also might help the youth to limit the intensity of emotional responses by following a specified problem-solving approach. In a third type, *self-instructional training,* youths are taught to make appropriate self-statements designed to modify emotional responses (Meichenbaum, 1977). Through this training, youths learn to make self-statements, such as "I can handle it" or "It's no big deal," to help them reduce the intensity of their emotional reactions. *Cognitive restructuring,* a fourth type, focuses on teaching new beliefs. While being similar to self-instructional training, this type places more emphasis on evaluation of the underlying beliefs such as "life must be fair" that contribute to emotional problems. A fifth approach, proposed by Cartledge and Milburn (1986), includes training in *self-monitoring, self-evaluation,* and *self-reinforcement procedures* that may enable youths to improve and maintain social behavior even in the presence of intefering emotions.

The above approaches appear valuable for helping youths overcome the adverse effects of emotional responses in social situations. At this time, the majority of research in this area has been conducted with children labeled "hyperactive" or "impulsive" (see Kendall and Braswell, 1985, for a review). Consequently, more research is needed that directly addresses the effects of these approaches on LD youths.

RESEARCH RECOMMENDATIONS

- Research is needed to determine how cognitive events are related to social performance. That is, how do social perception, discrimination, decision-making, problem-solving, and social awareness relate to competent social performance? How does LD youths' social performance suffer as a result of a lack of these cognitive skills?
- Research is needed to identify the exact nature of the cognitive skills that are related to social performance. Are some skills more important than others? Do some cognitive skills present

more common problems for LD youths? Research is also needed to evaluate the relative contribution of each of these cognitive skills and strategies to social skill performance.

- Research is needed to determine how these cognitive skills should be taught to best enhance social skill ability. What strategies are most effective for teaching the use of these cognitive skills? Are the instructional approaches that are useful for teaching social skills also effective for teaching cognitive skills?
- Research is needed to establish the effects of various cognitive strategies on emotional responsiveness. How do these approaches affect emotional responses and hence the acquisition of social skills? Which of these approaches is most helpful for LD youths in the acquisition and performance of social skills?
- Research is needed that assesses the effect of cognitive strategies on emotional responses as they occur in real-life situations. Emotions most often occur in the context of actual skill use. Research needs to be conducted in settings in which the emotions occur and can be studied directly.

INSTRUCTIONAL PROCEDURES

In addition to specifying the social skills needed by some LD youths, procedures for increasing the successful use of them in social situations must also be identified. A variety of intervention procedures have been developed. The choice of intervention depends on the source of the target social skill problem.

As discussed previously, Gresham (1986) proposed two sources of poor performance in social situations. The first relates to the initial learning of a social skill. If a youth has not learned the requisite skill steps, the youth cannot perform the skill. The second is the presence of competing stimuli that inhibit social skill acquisition or performance. Competing stimuli include such emotional states as feeling anxious or upset. These two causes of poor performance function independently. Consequently, although a youth may have learned to perform certain skills, inhibiting emotional reactions may hinder successful demonstrations of them in an actual social situation. Either source, alone or in combination, can lead to poor social performance.

In Gresham's scheme, social deficits fall into four categories: skill deficits, performance deficits, self-control skill deficits, and self-control performance deficits. (See above—What Causes Social Incompetence?—for further discussion of these categories). The deficit category, in turn, determines the types of remedial interventions that are needed for a given youth. If, for example, a youth demonstrates a skill deficit, intervention should focus on teaching new skills. In contrast, a performance deficit would dictate a program designed to control competing stimuli.

The following discussion focuses on various intervention approaches, with emphasis on those factors that may cause social performance problems among LD youths and on curriculum development for intervention efforts for this population. It concludes with proposed research areas.

INTERVENTION APPROACHES

In a review of the literature, Schumaker and Hazel (1984b) divided current social skill improvement approaches into three categories: (a) instructional procedures designed to teach new skills to youths who have skill deficits or self-control skill deficits; (b) approaches that focus on manipulating antecedent or consequent events to remediate social performance deficits; and (c) self-control procedures designed to increase a youth's control over his or her own social behavior and eliminate inappropriate behaviors. Since all of these approaches deal with social performance, the categories tend to overlap.

Most social skill remediation programs for LD youths are founded on the assumption that the youths do not possess certain social skills in their behavioral repertoires. Thus, most reported training attempts have focused on the instructional, or skill-acquisition, approach. Though not often noted by its developers, this approach may also be appropriate for youths with self-control skill deficits because it usually involves instruction in a nonthreatening environment.

Twentyman and Zimering (1979) categorized the training procedures commonly used in the skill acquisition approach as follows: (a) coaching, (b) modeling, (c) discussion or modeling of projected consequences, (d) cognitive modification, (e) rehearsal, (f) feedback and reinforcement, and (g) homework. *Coaching* includes a verbal description of relevant skills and how to perform them, whereas in *modeling,* a trainer shows how to perform a given skill by "acting it out." *Discussion or modeling of projected consequences* covers the outcomes of skill usage. This should enhance a person's motivation to practice and eventually use a given skill. *Cognitive modification,* in turn, focuses on changing cognitive self-statements as a means of enhancing motivation and of decreasing interfering emotions. *Rehearsal* typically involves practice of a skill in simulated situations, while *feedback and reinforcement* serve to reinforce appropriate performance and to correct errors that occur during training. *Homework* refers to out-of-class assignments to use a skill in an effort to facilitate generalization.

In different forms and combinations, these procedures have been employed in several training programs for LD youths (e.g., Cooke and Apollini, 1976; Donahue and Bryan, 1983; Gorney-Krupshaw, Atwater, Powell, and Morris, 1981; Oden and Asher, 1977; and Whang, Mathews, and Fawcell, 1981). (See Schumaker and Hazel, 1984b, for a review of these studies.) For the most part, these training programs have been effective; they have changed the youths' social behavior within the training setting.

Hazel, Schumaker, Sherman, and Sheldon (1982), for example, used six of the seven procedures specified by Twentyman and Zimering (1979) in a group social skill training program for LD youths. The instructional sequence for each skill began with an explanation of the skill (coaching) intended to orient the learners to the skill by defining terms and introducing the general characteristics of situations in which the skill could be used. The second step involved a discussion of rationales for using the skill (discussion of projected consequences), whereas step three consisted of an overview of the types of situations in which the skill could be used (coaching). This step was followed by a discussion of the verbal and nonverbal components involved in the skill (coaching). At this point, the youths received a list of the steps necessary to perform the skill. During the fifth stage, the teacher simulated a performance of the skill while interacting with one of the youths (modeling). The sixth instructional step consisted of a rapid-fire verbal rehearsal of skill steps until each youth met a mastery criterion of 100 percent correct performance in verbally listing the steps. Behavioral rehearsal was combined with feedback during the seventh step. Here, each youth was required to perform the skill in a role-play situation. After each performance, both the teacher and other youths provided positive and corrective feedback. Youths continued to practice performing the skill until each youth could perform it without making mistakes. The eighth step, planned practice outside the training setting (homework), was designed to enhance generalization of the skill to the home setting.

The results of this study showed that the LD subjects made substantial gains in their performance of six social skills in novel role-play tests following training. In addition, the youths' posttraining performances of most of the skills were comparable to those of nonhandicapped youths in the same situations (Schumaker et al., 1982).

Another application of some of the instructional procedures discussed by Twentyman and Zimering (1979) was provided by LaGreca and Mesibov (1981), who taught 12- to 16-year-old LD boys social skills (initiating interactions and conversation skills), using modeling, coaching, and behavioral rehearsal. The trainers began by modeling the target skill and then discussed how and when the youths could use the skill. The students next practiced the skill in simulated role-playing situations, which were videotaped for later review. Feedback was given as the videotapes were replayed. Practice and feedback alternated until the youths demonstrated mastery of the skill. The final training step involved practicing the skill in real-life settings outside of the training setting (homework). Again, results showed substantial increases in the LD youths' performance of the target skill in role-playing situations. Further, their performances after the training more closely resembled the performances of non-LD youths than before the training. Other social validity data indicated that the boys reported a higher frequency of interactions after training than before, and adult judges rated the boys' posttraining performances higher than pretraining performances.

To summarize, studies show that LD youths can learn to perform social skills in simulated situations at levels similar to those of their nonhandicapped peers when procedures like coaching, modeling, rehearsal, and feedback are used. The specific contribution of each of these procedures to the overall results and the configuration of the most effective "package" of procedures remain unclear.

The second kind of approach to intervention has focused on the manipulation of antecedents and consequences of behavior. When this approach is utilized, it is assumed that the youths possess the relevant skills in their behavior repertoires but fail to perform them because of lack of motivation or opportunity or because of competing emotional responses; that is, they demonstrate performance deficits. Environmental factors are manipulated to increase the likelihood of the performance of some skills or to decrease the likelihood of the emission of other less appropriate behaviors.

Strain and his colleagues (Strain, 1977; Strain, Shores, and Timm, 1977) used this approach with behaviorally handicapped preschool children. They instructed peers to initiate social interactions with the target youths by asking them to engage in activities. As a result of this environmental change, the target children emitted more positive social behaviors and initiated more interactions than during baseline.

In a different kind of environmental manipulation, Bryan, Cosden, and Pearl (1982) used cooperative goal structures to improve social behavior. Paired LD and non-LD students received incentives for their combined academic performance. As a result, social behaviors like listening, working together, and questioning increased. Martino and Johnson (1979) found similar increases in friendly interactions during free-play periods when they gave cooperative swimming assignments to paired LD and non-LD children during swimming lessons than when they gave individual assignments.

Other researchers have studied the application of systematic consequences based on youths' social behavior. Most often, a token system in which students can earn or lose tokens on the basis of their social performances has been used in these efforts. A token system implemented by Broden, Hall, Dunlap, and Clark (1970) in which appropriate classroom behavior was rewarded led to a related decrease in disruptive behaviors. Iwata and Bailey (1974) showed similar decreases in rule violations in the classroom, using both reward and cost token procedures with elementary special education students. In a more complex application, Schumaker, Hovell, and Sherman (1977) used a home-based token system. Increases in junior-high school students' appropriate social behavior in both special education and mainstream classes were noted when consequences at home were dependent on social behavior at school.

Thus, antecedents and consequences can be effectively manipulated to increase the rates of social skill performance among youths who already have the skills in their behavioral repertoires but who do not routinely perform them. To date, these procedures have been used with simple one-step social behaviors, such as raising one's hand before speaking in class or initiating an interaction. It remains unclear, however, whether they can be used effectively to promote the use of more complex social behaviors which have been identified as deficits for learning disabled children, and whether they promote long-term changes in the performance of social behavior.

A third approach to improving social skill performance has focused on reducing the rates of inappropriate social behaviors. That is, if a youth exhibits a high rate of inappropriate social behaviors, the youth may not be able to perform appropriate social behaviors, especially if the inappropriate behaviors are incompatible with appropriate ones. Specific research in this area has focused on teaching youths to self-record targeted behavior (e.g., Broden, Hall, and Mitts, 1971) and to self-evaluate their behavior (e.g., Kaufman and O'Leary, 1972). Training procedures have proved effective for reducing the rates of such behaviors as disruptiveness, out-of-seat behaviors, and talking-out behaviors; however, studies using these procedures have not been conducted with empirically validated behavioral excesses exhibited by LD youths. Thus, Schumaker and Hazel (1984a) concluded that although evidence exists that LD youths can learn to use self-control procedures to increase academic behaviors, more research is needed to study the effectiveness of this approach with social behaviors in this population.

SOCIAL SKILLS CURRICULA

A variety of curricula have been developed to address the need for effective training programs for social skill deficient youths. One such program for adolescents is the *ASSET Program* by Hazel, Schumaker, Sherman, and Sheldon-Wildgen (1981a), which consists of a leader's guide, program materials, and modeling videotapes for teaching eight social skills. Example skills include giving and receiving criticism, negotiating, and resisting peer pressure. *Getting Along With Others* by Jackson, Jackson, and Monroe (1983) targets elementary-school-aged students and focuses on 17 social skills such as introducing oneself, following directions, sharing, and compromising. *Skillstreaming the Adolescent* by Goldstein, Sprafkin, Gershaw, and Klein (1980) and *Skillstreaming the Elementary School Child* by McGinnis and Goldstein (1984) are books outlining instructional procedures for teaching 50 and 60 social skills, respectively. Example skills for adolescents include joining in, expressing one's feelings, asking permission, and responding to persuasion. Example skills in *Skillstreaming the Elementary School Child* include listening, apologizing, staying out of fights, and accepting "no."

These curricula generally utilize some combination of the instructional procedures described by Twentyman and Zimering (1979). Although not specifically developed for LD youths, evidence suggests that these curricula may be effective with this population. Hazel, Schumaker, Sherman, and Sheldon (1982), for example, found increases in LD students' social skill performances as a result of using an early version of the *ASSET Program*.

The Walker Social Skills Curriculum: The Accepts Program (Walker, McConnell, Holmes, Todis, Walker, and Golden, 1983) was specifically developed for handicapped children. The Walker program targets 28 social skills in five areas, including classroom skills, basic interaction skills, getting along skills, making friends skills, and coping skills.

Schumaker, Pederson, Hazel, and Meyen (1983) described three recently developed curricula for handicapped students, the *Marathon Program* (Abt Associates), the *Social Solutions Curriculum* (Weisgerber, Appleby, and Fong-Sue, 1984), and *Social Skills for Daily Living* (Schumaker, Hazel, and Pederson, in press), developed by the University of Kansas Institute for Research in Learning Disabilities. A major focus of these curricula is the use of a variety of instructional formats to stimulate acquisition and use of target skills. *Social Skills for Daily Living*, for example, utilizes workbooks, comic books, peer practice, and game simulations to teach social skills. Such use of novel instructional approaches is an important step toward meeting the need for innovative approaches to social skills instruction to ensure that youths' interest is maintained throughout the instructional process.

Additionally, since most social skills instruction is conducted with groups of students in educational settings, training procedures must be geared specifically for the classroom environment. Teachers need packages of materials that are easy to use in conjunction with other instructional methods and activities.

Developers of new social skill curriculum activities or materials are encouraged to consider the questions posed by Schumaker et al. (1983): (a) Does the curriculum promote social competence? (b) Does the curriculum accommodate the learning characteristics of the mildly handicapped? (c) Does the curriculum target the social skill deficits of the mildly handicapped population? (d) Does the curriculum provide training with regard to situations as well as skills? (e) Does the curriculum incorporate instructional methodologies found to be effective with the mildly handicapped? By addressing these considerations during the development of curriculum materials, it is more likely that useful and effective materials will be produced.

- Research is needed to establish the causes of poor social skills performances in LD children and adolescents. Are their deficits the result of poor learning, poor motivation, competing emotions, or combinations of these factors? If LD youths' social problems stem from multiple causes, research is needed to identify the frequency with which various causes lead to social problems and whether the use of particular skills is related to particular causes. Such research would help guide the development of effective intervention programs for LD youths by matching instruction to the targeted problems.
- Research is needed to develop programs for LD youths with self-control performance deficits and self-control skill deficits. If a significant number of LD youths do not perform well in social situations because of competing emotional responses, research is needed to validate remediation programs for youths with these kinds of problems.
- Research is needed that focuses on the development of novel instructional approaches for social skills training. Although it is relatively clear which instructional principles should be incorporated into an effective social skills training sequence, research is needed to identify practical but novel ways to integrate and use these principles in instructional settings, such as the classroom. The use of computer simulations may be promising in this regard. For example, the learner's interest may be maintained by presenting social situations in a computer game format. Other variations include games, stories, miniplays, peer tutoring, and family intervention programs. To ensure that newly developed procedures effectively teach targeted skills, motivational activities and procedures may need to be combined with other procedures. For example, computer simulations might be paired with peer practice of social skills to ensure increases in actual skill performance.
- Research is needed to design approaches to social skills instruction in the regular education classroom. In many cases, social skills instruction for LD youths is conducted in the special education classroom where LD students are isolated from regular education students. By including all students in social skills instruction, many additional benefits may accrue for LD students. For example, more opportunities would be available for LD students to practice the skills with peers with whom they interact inside and outside classes. Further, research is needed on strategies for effectively integrating social skills training within regular education classes, especially for elementary-school-aged students.

- Research is needed for the development of teacher training models that facilitate implementation of social skills training programs, with an emphasis on the rationale, content, and instructional approaches to social skill remediation. Such research should focus on both preservice and inservice models.

GENERALIZATION

Appropriate and long-term usage of social skills across a variety of settings, people, and situations should be the goal of any social skills training program for LD students. In the final analysis, social skills usage must be under the control of naturally occurring contingencies within social interactions versus contingencies external to such interactions (Hake and Olvera, 1978; Stokes and Baer, 1977). Furthermore, generalized social skills usage must lead to the social acceptance of an LD individual who prior to training was rejected, neglected, or otherwise labeled as socially incompetent. In the following discussion, studies of generalization of social skills are reviewed, including methods for promoting generalization and measures to assess generalization. Recommendations for future research are also proposed.

METHODS USED TO PROMOTE GENERALIZATION

Several researchers who have studied LD youths' generalized use of social skills after social skills instruction have reported problems in achieving the desired results. Gorney-Krupsaw et al. (1981), for example, taught LD adolescents to use social skills appropriate for the regular classroom environment. When measuring the youths' generalized use of the skills in naturally occurring situations in that environment, the authors found that the youths used either a small percentage of a skill's components or applied entire skills infrequently. In a similar study, Whang, Mathews, and Fawcett (1981) measured LD adolescents' generalized use of newly mastered social skills in naturally occurring situations in employment settings. Participating youths were found not to use the skills at levels comparable to those achieved in training although they showed some improvement over baseline levels. In a later study, Schumaker and Ellis (1982) programmed opportunities for LD adolescents' skill usage within a resource room environment and measured their generalized use of mastered skills in response to those opportunities. Finding improved usage of some skills and no improvement in others for each adolescent, the authors concluded that although LD adolescents meet mastery performance criteria in skill training sessions (that is, a skill deficit no longer exists), they do not necessarily generalize their use of social skills outside the training environment. Specific training on how to generalize newly learned skills therefore appears warranted for LD individuals receiving social skills training.

Even though a number of authors (e.g., Cartledge and Milburn, 1986; Rose and Gottlieb, 1981; Scott, Himadi, and Keane, 1983; Stokes and Baer, 1977; Stokes and Osnes, 1986) have suggested ways of promoting generalized use of social skills, only a few methods have been tried with LD youths, and results have been inconsistent. In the three studies cited above (Gorney-Krupsaw et al., 1981; Schumaker and Ellis, 1982; Whang, Mathews, and Fawcett, 1981), the authors applied principles such as teaching relevant behaviors, explaining when and where to use the behaviors, pointing out how the behaviors are related to natural contingencies, using multiple stimulus and response exemplars, and telling the youths to generalize. Nevertheless, these within-acquisition generalization methods were not sufficient to ensure generalization.

In another study in which within-acquisition generalization methods were used with elementary-school-aged LD children, Berler, Gross, and Drabman (1982) used multiple exemplars, stimuli common to both the training environment and the natural environment, and rehearsal of five skills (eye contact, responding to criticism, initiations, complimenting, and requesting new behavior) in situations spontaneously created by the children as generalization training methods during acquisition of the skills. Although the children's use of the skills generalized to untrained role-play situations, measurement of their verbalization rates in play situations and popularity as measured by sociometric devices showed no improvements related to the training. Because these authors used only a general measure (verbalization rates) without measuring the five target behaviors in the generalization setting, they may have missed actual improvements in those behaviors. Nevertheless, the results of the study by Berler et al. do show that LD children's mastery of a number of finite social skills does not necessarily translate into improved peer acceptance.

Schumaker, Hazel, Pederson, and Nolan (in prep.) used all the generalization methods employed in the studies described above combined with the practice of skills in noncued situations within the naturally occurring milieu of a resource room to promote generalized use of newly mastered skills by LD adolescents. As each opportunity was presented, the student was observed to determine whether the appropriate skill components were used. In addition, immediate feedback was provided regarding strengths and weaknesses in the students' performances. Following this generalization training, the LD adolescents began to use the skills in other noncued situations throughout the school with individuals who were not related to the training program.

Such results indicate that training methods that extend into the natural environment can successfully promote LD individuals' generalized use of social skills. To date, however, no evidence shows that social skills training impacts the social acceptance of LD individuals who were previously labeled socially incompetent, and no research has been conducted to determine whether LD individuals' use of newly acquired social skills maintains over time.

GENERALIZATION MEASURES

A reason for the dearth of research on generalization is simply that few studies have investigated social skills training of LD individuals. Further, among available studies, several have not gathered data on generalization. Several generalization measures have been suggested in the literature (e.g., Hazel et al., 1985; Scott et al., 1983). More of these should be applied in social skill training studies with LD youths. In the studies reviewed above, novel role-playing situations were used to assess participating youths' initial mastery of the targeted skills. This kind of generalization within the training setting, however, did not ensure generalization outside the training setting. Another generalization measure involved direct observation of skills as they were performed in naturally occurring and in contrived situations in the school environment. Although both methods have a certain amount of face validity, the use of contrived situations with confederates presenting situations or opportunities for skill usage seems to be the most practical way of measuring generalization within school settings. Both types of measures allow social skill trainers to get an accurate picture of how youths behave when they have not been cued to use a particular skill.

Another method used in the LD field to assess generalization of social skills consists of measuring related factors such as verbalization rates or sociometric status. Other related measures such as disciplinary problems in school, juvenile court recidivism, ratings by parents, teachers, job interviewers, and by the youths themselves have been used outside the LD field (see Hazel et al., 1985, for a review) with mixed results. Additional work is needed to determine whether social skill training programs are having a substantial impact on the lives of LD youths.

SUMMARY

To date, only a small number of studies have been conducted in the LD field with regard to generalization. Based on only a few ways of producing and measuring these effects in LD youths, studies indicate that LD youths can generalize their use of skills across people and time; however, unless generalization training is conducted outside the training setting, such effects tend to be inconsistent.

RESEARCH RECOMMENDATIONS

- Research needs to be conducted to experimentally validate the most effective methods of promoting LD students' generalized use of social skills outside the training settings at various ages. Effective combinations of generalization methods used during actual training sessions and after mastery of the skills in both training and nontraining settings need to be explored. Training methods must be practical and easy to use by teachers who serve LD individuals, so that treatment can be delivered without additional resources.

- Researchers need to develop and test ways of measuring generalization of social skills across settings, situations, people, and time. Again, such measurement systems must be simple and practical for both teachers and parents to apply, so that feedback on the generalization process can be easily obtained by the person delivering the training.
- Research needs to address how much social skills training LD youths need at various ages to impact their social acceptance by peers and others in their school and community environments. The goal of generalization training should not be simply to ensure that a youth uses social skills in a generative way. The ultimate goal is to ensure the social acceptance of the youth. Thus, it is critical to determine what kinds of interventions are needed to make this kind of impact. Training studies, therefore, should involve reliable measurement of such factors as number of friends, number of social activities, and satisfaction with social life. Since these types of measures have not been previously employed, creative methods of gathering such data are needed.

THE RELATIONSHIP BETWEEN PHYSIOLOGICAL FACTORS AND SOCIAL BEHAVIOR

Several authors have recently noted the relationship between social behavior and physiological factors. Consequently, more and more research is being devoted to the possible impact of food and other environmental sensitivities and chemical imbalances on social behavior and learning. Researchers are asking whether certain types of social behavior can be influenced by the introduction or elimination of a particular food, food additive, environmental agent (e.g., dust, pollen, lead), or nutrient (e.g., vitamins, minerals). The underlying notion here is that a youth whose body is intolerant of a particular type of environmental substance or food or who demonstrates a chemical imbalance or deficiency will feel bad physically (e.g., have a headache, stomachache, rashes, urinary disorder, or muscle and joint disorders) or psychologically (e.g., will feel weepy, depressed, angry, excessively tense, and fatigued for no apparent reason) (Alder, 1978; Schauss, 1984). As a result of these states, the youth may withdraw socially, be hyperactive, become aggressive or destructive, be noncompliant, have tantrums, be unable to sustain play activities, and display a host of other inappropriate social behaviors—most of which interfere with appropriate social interactions—even if the youth has previously learned appropriate social skills. Conceivably, if continuous, such states may interfere with a child's learning of new social behaviors. As the child becomes more isolated from peers because of inappropriate social behavior, fewer opportunities for learning through imitation and through practice of new social behaviors will occur.

This discussion is a review of the research that has been conducted to date on the relationship between social behavior and physiological factors, including interventions. Since very little research in this area has specifically focused on learning disabled children, studies in related fields are incorporated. The discussion concludes with recommendations for future research.

THE RELATIONSHIP BETWEEN SENSITIVITIES TO ENVIRONMENTAL SUBSTANCES AND SOCIAL BEHAVIOR

The possible relationship between sensitivities to environmental substances and behavior was initially brought to national attention by the late Benjamin F. Feingold, M.D. (1966, 1976, and 1981; Feingold, Suzer, and Fallman, 1968). On the basis of his clinical experience with over 1,200 cases, he claimed that children's hyperactivity and other manifested social and learning problems were related to sensitivities to certain substances in their diets. Specifically, Feingold focused his attention on the relationship between salicylates, artificial flavorings, and artificial colorings in foods and children's behavior. He designed a salicylate- and additive-free diet (known as the K-P [Kaiser Permanente] diet) to be used with hyperactive and learning disabled children, which he claimed produced dramatic improvement in the behavior of a large proportion of these children.

Following this widely publicized claim, a number of researchers investigated the relationship that he so strongly espoused. Connors, Goyette, Southwick, Lees, and Andrulonis (1976) were among the first to do a double-blind experiment with hyperkinetic children. Although they found some improvement in teachers' ratings of the children's behavior when the children were given the controlled diet in an experimentally controlled manner, they reported no change in the parents' ratings. Since they found a significant order effect and only a few children actually showed improvement, the authors advised caution with regard to the interpretation of their results. This report, which was also widely publicized, convinced the public and many physicians that Feingold's claims were disproved. This work by Conners et al. has recently been criticized for a variety of methodological flaws: inappropriate outcome measures, inadequate dosages of food dyes, the type of placebo used, the type of blood test used to determine allergies, the observation period after dosage delivery, and presenter bias (Rippere, 1983; Schauss, 1984). Such criticism is largely unknown to the public at large.

Although a number of additional studies have focused on the effects of Feingold's K-P diet, very few meet even minimal standards of adequate research methodology (Wender, 1986). Of those that do, only one conducted by Swanson and Kinsbourne (1980) has shown adverse reactions in children to food dyes. After Swanson and Kinsbourne determined that the appropriate dosages of food dyes to be administered should be three to six times as strong as those used by Connors et al. (1976) to more closely approximate the dietary intake of those substances, they used these larger dosages in a double-blind experiment with hyperkinetic children. The authors found adverse reactions in more than one-half the children on a laboratory learning task. Nevertheless, this study has also been criticized for a number of flaws (Mattes, 1983).

Since the research in this area has been so flawed, it is impossible to draw firm conclusions from it. Some authors (for instance, Wender, 1986) have even suggested that further research on the K-P diet may be inappropriate since the diet itself is flawed in terms of screening out all salicylates. Another possible problem that may doom further research in the area is the possibility that a certain category of foods might not cause behavior problems in *all* hyperactive children. That is, a variety of different substances might cause these problems in individuals. Indeed, even combinations of particular substances may cause these problems.

A few investigators have studied this possibility by challenging hyperactive children with a variety of foods and other environmental substances. O'Shea and Porter (1981), for example, challenged hyperkinetic children with intradermal and sublingual doses of a variety of foods (e.g., milk, corn, eggs, food dyes) and inhalants (dust, mold, and tree pollen) in a double-blind experiment. They found that a majority of the children exhibited behavioral changes related to such substances as food dyes (80 percent of the children) and milk (73 percent) and that smaller proportions of the group had adverse reactions to such foods as peanuts (47 percent), corn (40 percent), and chocolate (33 percent). Such data indicate that individual children's problems may be related to an individual pattern of sensitivities.

This hypothesis has been pursued by a group of researchers at London's Institute of Child Health and Hospital for Sick Children. Using a carefully controlled research protocol, including a double-blind design, Egger, Carter, Wilson, Turner, and Soothill (1983) found a relationship between migraine, other physical symptoms (joint pain, abdominal pain), and behavioral and learning problems and ingestion of particular foods. They reported that most of the children had adverse reactions to several different foods. Using a similar research protocol, Egger, Carter, Graham, Gumley, and Soothill (1985) found a relationship between certain foods and hyperactive children's behavior. Although many of the children reacted to food dyes and preservatives, none of them were sensitive to these substances alone.

Even though the research design of both of the Egger et al. studies has been described as being "too good to be true" (Podell, 1985, p. 120), the studies do provide impetus for additional work to determine the relationship of individual patterns of sensitivities to social behavior in children.

THE RELATIONSHIP BETWEEN CHEMICAL IMBALANCES AND SOCIAL BEHAVIOR

A few authors have studied the relationship of a variety of chemical excesses and deficiencies and children's socially related behavior. Iron deficiency, for example, has been found to be related to inattentiveness to environmental cues, poor problem-solving (Pollitt, Viteri, Saco-Pollitt, and Liebel, 1982), and conduct problems (Webb and Oski, 1974) in children. Additionally, when Pihl and Parkes (1977) compared the chemical content of learning disabled and normal children's hair, they found significant differences between the two groups in a number of elements. Among them, the levels of lead and cadmium were the best discriminators between the two groups, with the LD children exhibiting elevated levels of both. Since elevated lead levels have been associated with hyperactivity (Silbergeld and Goldberg, 1974), this finding is significant. Pihl and Parks also found that the LD children had significantly lower levels of cobalt than their normal peers. Low cobalt levels have been shown to be related to high levels of violent behavior in adults (Pihl, 1982; Schauss, 1984). Since LD children have not been shown to emit more aggressive behavior than their peers, this relationship is perplexing.

TREATMENT

The treatment for a particular food sensitivity or chemical imbalance usually involves either supplying the deficit substance or eliminating a suspect substance from the environment or diet. Although this approach sounds simple enough, such an intervention is often very complicated. Current methods of testing individuals for food sensitivities are crude and sometimes unreliable (Schauss, 1984). This limitation makes it difficult to determine whether a child has an adverse reaction to a particular substance and what that reaction is. Likewise, since there is a paucity of research on the effects of chemical imbalances on the behavior of LD children and since some authors suspect that the ratios of particular elements may be as important as their individual levels (Schauss, 1984), it remains unclear what deficiencies and excesses to examine in these children's body chemistries.

The treatment for children with learning problems/hyperactivity has often been based on a "spray and pray" approach. That is, the same elimination diet or the same orthomolecular treatment program has been recommended for the population as a whole. Since the research results described above have shown that children react differently to different foods and other ingestible and environmental substances and that their deficiencies differ, it appears that treatments should be designed according to individual children's needs. Although some case studies have been reported (Baker, 1985; Menzies, 1984), few experimentally sound intervention studies that might be acceptable to the medical community have been conducted in which treatments are based on individual needs. The diets that have been designed for some studies (Egger et al., 1983, 1985) have been very rigorous and specifically designed for experimental purposes; consequently, such diets would not be appropriate for widely used treatments. As a result, research must focus on methods of identifying food sensitivities and chemical imbalances that relate to social behavior in a particular LD youth as well as on practical and acceptable interventions that lead to improved social behavior in such LD individuals.

RESEARCH RECOMMENDATIONS

- Research is needed that replicates and further extends the work conducted to date on sensitivities to foods and food additives. Experimental methodologies should be improved as part of such extensions. For example, observable, reliable, and valid measures of a variety of social behaviors, especially those related to the condition of learning disabilities, need to be utilized. In addition, different experimental designs must be tried. Given the individual nature of the problem, studies employing groups of children who receive the same experimental challenge may not be appropriate (Alder, 1978). Care should be taken to ensure that, when used, placebos are indeed inert for individual subjects. In addition, sufficient time should be allowed while behavior changes are assessed since reactions can take place several hours after a substance has been ingested. Additionally, since reaction time may be related to variables such as age and since reaction severity may be related to such variables as level of vitamin C in the body, these variables must be considered in the study design. Interdisciplinary teams of medical and behavioral researchers working together are recommended to ensure acceptance of the research findings by both behavioral scientists and medical scientists.
- Research is needed that further explores the role of chemical imbalances in learning disabled children and the effects of such imbalances on their social behavior. Once imbalances are identified, methodologies such as reversal designs should be employed, using double-blind procedures with individual

children to explore the effects of the intervention. Again, interdisciplinary approaches representing collaboration between medical and behavioral researchers are needed.

- Research is needed to distinguish the differences and similarities between the sensitivities and chemical imbalances of learning disabled and other problem children. That is, do LD children constitute a subset of a population of children who exhibit these sensitivities and imbalances, or are they different from the larger population of children with sensitivities and imbalances? If so, such differences need to be to be explored to determine their effects on the children's social behavior.

- Practical and efficient methods of identifying sensitivities and chemical imbalances need to be designed so that, if the positive results reviewed here are supported, children's individual needs can be identified and treated at an early age to prevent social problems.

- Practical treatment methods need to be designed, experimentally validated, and specified in a form that is easily understood. Since parents will naturally be in charge of a child's daily treatment regimen, methods of educating parents about sensitivities and chemical imbalances and of maintaining children's treatment regimens must be developed.

- Ways of combining treatment regimens for sensitivities and chemical imbalances with social skill training programs need to be explored for those children and adolescents who continue to exhibit social skill deficits after their behavioral excesses have been eliminated through controlled diets. For example, older children who have been isolated from peers due to their inappropriate social behaviors cannot be expected to blend in with their peers immediately after those inappropriate behaviors disappear, especially if they have not learned developmentally appropriate social skills. Thus, treatment programs for these children might need to include skill training in addition to controlled diets, vitamins, and other environmental controls.

SUMMARY

The ability to perform well in social situations is a critical prerequisite for successful functioning in life. Many LD youths exhibit poor social ability in a variety of situations. However, the exact nature of these social problems, their cause, the type of remediation needed, and the role of various cognitive and emotive factors remain undetermined.

Seven issues are identified as critical to advancing our understanding of social competence and LD youths. These issues are the following:

- *Assessment instruments need to be developed and validated.* Given the multiple causes of poor social performance, the heterogeneity of the

LD population with regard to social skill performance, and the lack of an agreed-upon definition of social skills and social competence, new assessment procedures need to be developed. These procedures need to be based on LD individuals' social deficits, be psychometrically sound, be practical for school settings, and assess a wide range of skills.

- *Skill selection procedures need to be improved.* The selection of skills for training has often been based on trainer judgment rather than empirical data. Four methods of skill selection (judgment, social validity, review of relevant research, and observation) were described. Further work is needed to clarify which method or methods are most appropriate for selecting skills.

- *Skill design and qualitative aspects of skills need study.* Following the selection of skills for training, their component steps must be identified. That is, in a given situation, the components which dictate what a youth should say and do should be specified. Research is needed to validate the most effective strategies for determining these component steps.

- *Research on decision-making and cognitive skills is needed.* Cognitive skills is a somewhat neglected area in social skills training. Cognitive skills often are critical in determining what skill will be used, when it will be used, where it will be used, and how successfully it will be used. Thus, research is needed to determine the relationship between cognitive skills and social performance and the best methods for training these cognitive skills.

- *Novel instructional procedures need to be developed.* The basic strategies for social skills instruction have been developed; however, social skills curricula need to be developed that incorporate these procedures and keep the learners motivated and interested in the training. Research should focus on developing effective interventions for LD youths.

- *Procedures to enhance generalization need to be developed.* A central problem in social skills training is promoting use of the newly learned skills to the natural environment. Although procedures have been developed in this area, much work is still needed to develop additional procedures and to ensure that these procedures are incorporated into social skill training programs.

- *The relationship between physiological factors and social behavior needs further study.* The role of physiological factors in social behavior is unclear. Research efforts are needed to identify the possible effects of such variables as vitamin deficiencies, chemical imbalances, and environmental sensitivities on social performance.

The major research efforts in the field of learning disabilities have focused on the academic problems and deficits of LD youths. More recently, behavioral and social problems as well as academic problems have been noted. As this review has shown, social problems are a reality for a significant number of LD youths. Thus, research is needed to delineate the causes and cures of these problems.

BIBLIOGRAPHY

Adler, S., (1978). Behavior management: A nutritional approach to the behaviorally disordered and learning disabled child. *Journal of Learning Disabilities,* 11:49-56.

Arkowitz, H. (1981). Assessment of social skills. In Hersen, M., Bellack, A. S. (Eds.), *Behavioral assessment* (pp. 296-327). New York: Pergamon Press.

Asher, S., Oden, S., Gottman, J. (1976). Children's friendships in school settings. In Katz, L. (Ed.), *Current topics in early childhood education:* Vol. 1. Hillsdale, NJ: Lawrence Erlbaum Associates, Inc.

Asher, S., Hymel, S. (1981). Children's social competence in peer relations: Sociometric and behavioral assessment. In Wine, J. D., Syme, M. D. (Eds.), *Social competence* (pp. 125-157). New York: Guilford Press.

Axelrod, L. (1982). Social perception in learning disabled adolescents. *Journal of Learning Disabilities,* 15:610-613.

Baker, S. M. (1985). A biochemical approach to the problem of dyslexia. *Journal of Learning Disabilities,* 18(10):581-584.

Bachara, G. (1976). Empathy in learning disabled children. *Perceptual and Motor Skills,* 43:541-542.

Banikowski, A. K. (1981). *The verbal cognitive-socialization and strategies used by learning disabled and non-learning disabled junior high school adolescents in a peer-to-peer interaction activity.* Unpublished doctoral dissertation. Lawrence: University of Kansas.

Berler, E. S., Gross, A. M., Drabman, R. S. (1982). Social skills training with children: Proceed with caution. *Journal of Applied Behavior Analysis,* 15(1):41-53.

Brockman, M. P. (1985). Best practices in assessment of social skills and peer interaction. In Thomas, A., Grimes, J. (Eds.), *Best practices in school psychology.* Kent, OH: NASP.

Broden, M., Hall, R. V., Dunlap, A., Clark, R. (1970). Effects of teacher attention and a token reinforcement system in a junior high school special class. *Exceptional Children,* 36:341-349.

Broden, M., Hall, R. V., Mitts, B. (1971). The effect of self-recording on the classroom behavior of two eighth-grade students. Journal of Applied Behavior Analysis, 4:191-199.

Bruck, M. (1985). The adult functioning of children with specific learning disabilities. In Sigel, I. (Ed.), *Advances in applied developmental psychology:* Vol. 1 (pp. 91-129). Norwood, NJ: Ablex.

Bruck, M. (1986). Social & emotional adjustments of learning disabled children: A review of the issues. In Ceci, S. (Ed.), *Handbook of cognitive, social neuropsychological aspects of learning disabilities:* Vol. 1 (pp. 361-380). Hillsdale, NJ: Lawrence Erlbaum Assoc.

Bruck, M., Hebert, M. (1982). Correlates of learning disabled students' peer-interaction patterns. *Learning Disabilities Quarterly,* 5:353-362.

Bruininks, V. L. (1978a). Actual and perceived peer status of learning disabled students in mainstream programs. *Journal of Special Education,* 12: 51-58.

Bruininks, V. L. (1978b). Peer status and personality characteristics of learning disabled students. *Journal of Learning Disabilities,* 11:484-489.

Bruno, R. M. (1981). Interpretation of pictorially presented social situations by learning disabled and normal children. *Journal of Learning Disabilities,* 14:350-352.

Bryan, J. H., Sherman, R. (1980). Immediate impressions of nonverbal ingratiation attempts by learning disabled boys. *Learning Disability Quarterly,* 3:19-28.

Bryan, J. H., Sherman, R., Fisher, A. (1980). Learning disabled boys' nonverbal behaviors within a dyadic interview. *Learning Disability Quarterly,* 3(1):65-72.

Bryan, T. H. (1974). Peer popularity of learning disabled children. *Journal of Learning Disabilities,* 7:621-625.

Bryan, T. H. (1976). Peer popularity of learning disabled children: A replication. *Journal of Learning Disabilities*, 9:307-311.

Bryan, T. H. (1977). Learning disabled children's comprehension of nonverbal communication. *Journal of Learning Disabilities*, 10:501-506.

Bryan, T. H., Bryan, J. H. (1978). Social interactions of learning disabled children. Learning Disability Quarterly, 1(1):33-38.

Bryan, T. H., Bryan, J. H. (1981). Some personal and social experiences of learning disabled children. In Keogh, B. (Ed.), *Advances in special education:* Vol. 3 (pp. 147-186). Greenwich, CT: JAI Press, Inc.

Bryan, T. H., Cosden, J., Pearl, R. (1982). The effects of cooperative models on LD and NLD students. *Learning Disability Quarterly*, 5:415-421.

Bryan, T. H., Donahue, M., Pearl, R., Sturm, C. (1981). Learning disabled children's conversational skills—the T.V. talk show. *Learning Disability Quarterly*, 4:250-259.

Bryan, T. H., Pflaum, S. (1978). Social interactions of learning disabled children: A linguistic, social, and cognitive analysis. *Learning Disability Quarterly*, 1(3):70-79.

Bryan, T. H., Sonnefeld, L. J., Greenberg, F. Z. (1981). Children's and parents' views of ingratiation tactics. *Learning Disability Quarterly*, 4:170-179.

Bryan, T. H., Werner, M., Pearl, R. (1982). Learning disabled students' conformity responses to prosocial and antisocial situations. *Learning Disability Quarterly*, 5:344-352.

Bryan, T. H., Wheeler, R., Felcan, J., Henck, T. (1976). "Come on Dummy": An observational study of children's communications. *Journal of Learning Disabilities*, 9:661-669.

Cartledge, G., Milburn, J. F. (1986). *Teaching social skills to children.* New York: Pergamon Press.

Combs, M. L., Slaby, D. A. (1977). Social skills training with children. In Lahey, B. B., Kazdin, A. E. (Eds.), *Advances in clinical child psychology:* Vol. 1. New York: Plenum Press.

Conners, C. K., Goyette, C. H., Southwick, D. A., Lees, J. M., Andrulines, P. A. (1976). Food additives and hyperkinesis: A controlled double-blind experiment. *Pediatrics*, 58(2):154-166.

Cooke, T. P., Apolloni, L. (1976). Developing positive social emotional behaviors: A study of training and generalization effects. *Journal of Applied Behavior Analysis*, 9:65-78.

Cowen, E. L., Pederson, A., Babigian, H., Izzo, I. D., Trost, M. A. (1973). Long-term follow-up of early detected vulnerable children. *Journal of Consulting and Clinical Psychology*, 41:438-446.

Cullinan, D., Epstein, M., Lloyd (1981). School behavior problems of learning disabled and normal girls and boys. *Learning Disability Quarterly*, 4:163-169.

Deshler, D. D., Schumaker, J. B. (1983). *A life-planning intervention for facilitating the transition of learning disabled adolescents to post-school situations* (Grant No. G00739421-83). U.S. Office of Education.

Dickstein, E. B., Warren, D. R. (1980). Role-taking deficits in learning disabled children. *Journal of Learning Disabilities*, 13:378-382.

Dodge, K. A., Schlundt, D. C., Schocken, I., Delugach, J. D. (1983). Social competence and children's sociometric status: The role of peer group entry strategies. *Merrill-Palmer Quarterly*, 29:309-336.

Donahue, M. I. (1981). Requesting strategies of learning disabled children. *Applied Psycholinguistics*, 2:213-234.

Donahue, M. (1984). Learning disabled children's conversational competence: An attempt to activate the inactive listener. *Applied Psycholinguistics*, 5:21-35.

Donahue, M., Bryan, T. (1983). Conversational skills and modeling in learning disabled boys. *Applied Psycholinguistics*, 4:251-278.

Donahue, M., Pearl, R., Bryan, T. (1980). Learning disabled children's conversational competence: Responses to inadequate messages. *Applied Psycholinguistics*, 1:387-403.

Egger, J., Carter, C. M., Graham, P. J., Gumley, D., Soothill, J. F. (1985). Controlled trial of oligoantigenic treatment in the hyperkinetic syndrome. *Lancet*, 1:540-545.

Egger, J., Carter, C. M., Wilson, J., Turner, M. W., Soothhill, J. F. (1983). Is migraine food allergy? A double-blind controlled trial of oligoantegenic diet treatment. *Lancet*, 2:865-869.

Ellis, A. (1962). *Reason and emotion in psychotherapy.* New York: Lyle Stuart Press.

Epstein, M. H., Bursuck, W., Cullinan, D. (1985). Patterns of behavior problems among the learning disabled: In boys aged 12-18, girls aged 8-11, and girls aged 12-18. *Learning Disability Quarterly,* 8(2):123-131.

Epstein, M. H., Cullinan, D., Lloyd, J. W. (1986). Behavior-problem patterns among the learning disabled: III—replication across age and sex. *Learning Disability Quarterly,* 9:43-54.

Epstein, M. H., Cullinan, D., Rosemier, R. (1983). Patterns of behavior problems among the learning disabled: Boys aged 6-11. *Learning Disability Quarterly,* 6:305-312.

Feingold, B. F. (1968). Recognition of food additives as a cause of symptoms of allergy. *Annals of Allergy,* 26:309.

Feingold, B. F. (1976). *Why your child is hyperactive.* New York: Random House.

Feingold, B. F. (1981). Dietary management of behavior and learning disabilities. In Miller, S. A. (Ed.), *Nutrition and behavior* (ppf. 37). Philadelphia: Franklin Institute Press.

Feingold, B. F., Singer, M. T., Freeman, E. H. (1966). Variables in allergic disease: A critical appraisal of methodology. *Journal of Allergy,* 38:143.

Garrett, M. K., Crump, W. D. (1980). Peer acceptance, teacher preferences, and self-appraisal of social status among learning disabled students. *Learning Disability Quarterly,* 3(3):42-48.

Gerber, P. J., Zinkgraf, S. A. (1982). A comparative study of social-perceptual ability in learning disabled and non-handicapped students. *Learning Disability Quarterly,* 5:374-378.

Goldstein, A. P., Sprafkin, R. P., Gershaw, N. J., Klein, P. (1980). *Skill streaming the adolescent: A structured learning approach to teaching prosocial skills.* Champaign, IL: Research Press Co.

Gorney-Krupsaw, B., Atwater, J., Powell, L., Morris, E. K. (1981). *Improving social interactions between learning disabled adolescents and teachers: A child effects approach* (Research Report No. 45). Lawrence: University of Kansas Institute for Research in Learning Disabilities.

Gottman, J. (1977). Toward a definition of social isolation in children. *Child Development,* 48:513-517.

Greenwood, C. R., Walker, H. M., Todd, N. H., Hops, H.(1976). *Preschool teachers' assessments of social interaction: Predictive success and normative data* (Report No. 26). Eugene, OR: University of Oregon, Center at Oregon for Research in the Behavioral Education of the Handicapped.

Greenwood, C. R., Walker, H. M., Todd, N. M., Hops, H. (1979). Selecting a low-cost effective screening device for the assessment of preschool social withdrawal. *Journal of Applied Behavior Analysis,* 12:639-652.

Gresham, F. M. (1981). Social skills training with handicapped children: A review. *Review of Education Research,* 51:139-176.

Gresham, F. M. (1983). Multitrait-multimethod approach to multifactored assessment: Theoretical rationale and practical applications. *School Psychology Review,* 12:26-34.

Gresham, F. M. (1983). Social validity in the assessment of children's social skills: Establishing standards for social competency. *Journal of Psychoeducational Assessment,* 1:297-307.

Gresham, F. M. (1986). Conceptual issues in the assessment of social competence in children. In Strain, P., Guralnick, M., Walker, H. (Eds.), *Children's social behavior: Development, assessment, and modification* (pp. 143-186). New York: Academic Press.

Gresham, F. M., Elliott, S. N. (1984). Assessment and classification of children's social skills: A review of methods and issues. *School Psychology Review,* 13(3):292-301.

Gresham, F. M., Nagle, R. J. (1980). Social skills training with children: Responsiveness to modeling and coaching as a function of peer orientation. *Journal of Consulting and Clinical Psychology,* 48:718-729.

Gresham, F. M., Reschly, D. J. (1986). Social skill deficits and low peer acceptance of mainstreamed learning disabled children. *Learning Disability Quarterly,* 9:23-32.

Hake, D. F., Olvera, D. (1978). Cooperation, competition, and related social phenomena. In Catania, A., Brigham, T. (Eds.), *Handbook of applied behavior analysis: Social and instructional processes* (pp. 208-245). NY: Irvington.

Harris, F. C., Lahey, B. B. (1978). A method for combining occurrence and nonoccurrence interobserver agreement scores. *Journal of Applied Behavior Analysis*, 11:523-527.

Hartmann, D. P. (1977). Considerations in the choice of interobserver reliability estimates. *Journal of Applied Behavior Analysis*, 1:103-116.

Hazel, J. S., Schumaker, J. B., Sherman, J. A., Sheldon, J. (1982). Application of a group training program in social skills and problem-solving skills to learning disabled and non-learning disabled youth. *Learning Disability Quarterly*, 5:398-408.

Hazel, J. S., Schumaker, J. B., Sherman, J. A., Sheldon-Wildgen, J. (1981a). *ASSET: A social skills program for adolescents*. Champaign, IL: Research Press.

Hazel, J. S., Schumaker, J. B., Sherman, J. A., Sheldon-Wildgen, J. (1981a). The development and evaluation of a group skills training program for court-adjudicated youths. In Upper, D., Ross, S. (Eds.), *Behavioral group therapy, 1981: An annual review* (pp. 113-152). Champaign, IL: Research Press.

Hazel, J. S., Sherman, J. A., Schumaker, J. B., Sheldon, J. (1985). Group social skills training with adolescents: A critical review. In Upper, D., Ross, S. (Eds.), *Handbook of behavioral group therapy* (pp. 203-246). New York: Plenum Press.

Hazel, J. S., Smalter, M. C., Schumaker, J. B. (1983, October). *A Learner-managed social skills curriculum for mildly handicapped adolescents and young adults*. Presentation at the International Conference on Learning Disabilities, San Francisco.

Hiemberg, R. G., Cunningham, J., Stanley, J., Blankenberg, R. (1982). Preparing unemployed youth for job interviews: A controlled evaluation of social skills training. *Behavior Modification*, 6:299-322.

Hops, H. (1981). Behavioral assessment of exceptional children's development. *Exceptional Education Quarterly*, 4:31-43.

Hops, H. (1983). Children's social competence and skill: Current research practices and future directions. *Behavior Therapy*, 14:3-18.

Hops, H, Finch, M., McConnell, S. (1985). Social skill deficits. In Bornstein, P. H., Kazdin, A. E. (Eds.), *Handbook of clinical behavior therapy with children* (pp. 543-598). Homewood, IL: The Dorsey Press.

Hops, H., Walker, H. M., Greenwood, C. R. (1979). PEERS: A program for remediating social withdrawal in school. Behavior systems for developmentally disabled. In Hamerlynck, L. A. (Ed.), *School and family environments*. New York: Brunner/Mazel.

Horowitz, F. C. (1981). Popularity, decentering ability, and role-taking skills in learning disabled and normal children. *Learning Disability Quarterly*, 4:23-30.

Iwata, B. A., Bailey, J. S. (1974). Reward versus cost token systems: An analysis of the effects on students and teachers. *Journal of Applied Behavior Analysis*, 7(4):567-576.

Jackson, N. F., Jackson, D. A., Monroe, C. (1983). *Getting along with others*. Champaign, IL: Research Press.

Johnson, D. J., Myklebust, H. (1967). *Learning disabilities: Educational principles & practices*. New York: Grune & Stratton.

Kasen, E. (1972). *The syndrome of specific dyslexia*. Baltimore: University Park Press.

Kaufman, K. F., O'Leary, K. D. (1972). Reward, cost, and self-evaluation procedures for disruptive adolescents in a psychiatric hospital school. *Journal of Applied Behavior Analysis*, 5:293-309.

Kendall, P. C., Braswell, L. (1985). *Cognitive behavioral therapy for impulsive children*. New York: The Guilford Press.

Kirk, S. A., Chalfant, J. C. (1984). *Academic and developmental learning disabilities*. Denver, CO: Love Publishing.

LaGreca, A. M. (1981). Social behavior and social perception in learning- disabled children: A review with implications for social skills training. *Journal of Pediatric Psychology*, 6(4):395-416.

LaGreca, A. M., Mesibov, G. B. (1979). *Social skills intervention with learning disabled children.* Paper presented at the Annual Meeting of the Midwestern Psychological Association, Chicago.

LaGreca, A. M., Mesibov, G. B. (1981). Facilitating interpersonal functioning with peers in learning-disabled children. *Journal of Learning Disabilities,* 14(4):197-199.

LaGreca, A. M., Stark, P. (1986). Naturalistic observations of children's social behavior. In Strain, P., Guralnick, M., Walker, H. (Eds.), *Children's social behavior: Development, assessment and modification* (pp. 181-213). New York: Academic Press.

MacMillan, D. L., Morrison, G. M. (1980). Correlates of social status among mildly handicapped learners in self-contained special classes. *Journal of Educational Psychology,* 72:437-444.

Maheady, L., Sainato, D. M. (1986). Learning disabled students' perceptions of social events. In Ceci, S. (Ed.), *Handbook of cognitive, social & neuropsychological aspects of learning disabilities:* Vol. 1 (pp. 381-402). New Jersey: Lawrence Erlbaum Assoc.

Martino, L., Johnson, D. W. (1979). Cooperative and individualistic experiences among disabled and normal children. *The Journal of Social Psychology,* 107:177-183.

Mathews, R., Whang, P., Fawcett, S. (1982). Behavioral assessment of occupational skills of learning disabled adolescents. *Journal of Learning Disabilities,* 15:38-41.

Mattes, J. A. (1983). The Feingold diet: A current reappraisal. *Journal of Learning Disabilities,* 16(6):319-323.

McConaughy, S. H., Ritter, D. R. (1986). Social competence and behavioral problems of learning disabled boys aged 6-11. *Journal of Learning Disabilities,* 19(1):39-45.

McFall, R. M. (1982). A review and reformulation of the concept of social skills. *Behavioral Assessment,* 4:1-33.

McGinnis, E., Goldstein, (1984). *Skill streaming the elementary school child: A guide for teaching prosocial skills.* Champaign, IL: Research Press Co.

Meichenbaum, D. (1977). *Cognitive behavior modification: An integrative approach.* New York: Plenum Press.

Menzies, I. C. (1984). Disturbed children: The role of food and chemical sensitivities. *Nutrition and Health,* 3(1-2):39-54.

Mercer, D. C. (1983). *Students with learning disabilities* (2nd ed). Columbus, OH: Charles E. Merrill.

Michelson, L., Foster, S., Ritchey, W. (1981). Behavioral assessment of children's social skills. In Lahey, B. B., Kazdin, A. E. (Eds.), *Advances in clinical child psychology:* Vol. 3. New York: Plenum Press.

Michelson, L., Sugai, D. P., Wood, R. P., Kazdin, A. E. (1983). *Social skill assessment and training with children.* New York: Plenum Press.

Minkin, N., Minkin, B. L., Goldstein, R. S., Taylor, M. W., Braukmann, C. J., Kirigin KA, Wolf, M. M. (1981). Analysis, validation, and training of peer-criticism skills with delinquent girls. In Upper, D. and Ross, S. (Eds.), *Behavior group therapy. An annual review* (pp. 153-166). Champaign, IL: Research Press.

Morrison, G. M. (1981). Sociometric measurement: Methodological considerations of its use with mildly learning handicapped and nonhandicapped children. *Journal of Educational Psychology,* 73:193-201.

Morrison, G. M., Forness, S. R., MacMillan, D. L. (1983). Influences on the sociometric ratings of mildly handicapped children: A path analysis. *Journal of Educational Psychology,* 75:63-74.

Noel, M. M. (1980). Referential communication abilities of learning disabled children. *Learning Disability Quarterly,* 3:70-75.

Oden, S., Asher, S. R. (1977). Coaching children in social skills for friendship making. *Child Development,* 48:495-506.

O'Shea, J. A., Porter, S. F. (1981). Double-blind study of children with hyperkinetic syndrome treated with multi-allergen extract sublingually. *Journal of Learning Disabilities,* 14(4):189-191, 237.

Pearl, R. (1985). Cognitive behavioral interventions for increasing motivation. *Journal of Abnormal Child Psychology,* 13(3):443-453.

Pearl, R., Bryan, T., Donahue, M. (1983). Social behaviors of learning disabled children: A review. *Topics in Learning & Learning Disabilities*, 2:1-14.

Pearl, R., Cosden, M. (1982). Sizing up a situation: LD children's understanding of social interactions. *Learning Disability Quarterly*, 5:371-373.

Pearl, R., Donahue, M., Bryan, T. (1981). Learning disabled and normal children's responses to non-explicit requests for clarification. *Perceptual and Motor Skills*, 53:919-925.

Perlmutter, B. F. (1986). Personality variables & peer relations of children & adolescents with learning disabilities. In Ceci, S. (Ed.), *Handbook of cognitive, social and neuropsychological aspects of learning disabilities:* Vol. 1 (pp. 339-360). New Jersey: Lawrence Erlbaum Assoc.

Perlmutter, B. F., Crocker, J., Cordray, D., Garstecki, D. (1983). Sociometric status and related personality characteristics of mainstreamed learning disabled adolescents. *Learning Disability Quarterly*, 6:20-30.

Pihl, R. O. (1982). Hair element levels of violent criminals. *Canadian Journal of Psychiatry*, 27(6):533-534.

Pihl, R. O., Parkes, M. (1977). Hair element content in learning disabled children. *Science*, 198:204-206.

Podell, R. N. (1985). Food, mind, and mood: Hyperactivity revisited. *Postgraduate Medicine*, 78(2):119-125.

Pollitt, E., Viteri, F., Saco-Pollitt, C., Leibel, R. L. (1982). Behavioral effects of iron deficiency anemia in children. In Pollitt, E., Leibel, R. L. (Eds.), *Iron deficiency, brain biochemistry, and behavior* (pp. 195-204). New York: Raven Press.

Prillaman, D. (1981). Acceptance of learning disabled students in the mainstream environment: A failure to replicate. *Journal of Learning Disabilities*, 14:344-346.

Prinz, R. J., Roberts, W. A., Hantman, E. (1980). Dietary correlates of hyperactive behavior in children. *Journal of Consulting and Clinical Psychology*, 48(6):760-769.

Raskind, M. H., Drew, D. E., Regan, J. O. (1983). Nonverbal communication signals in behavior-disordered and non-disordered LD boys and NLD boys. *Learning Disability Quarterly*, 6:12-19.

Rippere, V. (1983). Food additives and hyperactive children: A critique of Conners. *British Journal of Clinical Psychology*, 22:19-32.

Roff, M. (1981). Childhood social interactions and young adult bad conduct. *Journal of Abnormal and Social Psychology*, 63:333-337.

Roff, M., Sells, S. B., Golden, M. M. (1972). *Social adjustment and personality development in children.* Minneapolis: University of Minnesota Press.

Rose, T. L., Gottlieb, J. (1981). Transfer of training: An overlooked component of mainstreaming programs. *Exceptional Children*, 48:175-177.

Rosenthal, J. (1973). Self-esteem in dyslexic children. *Academic Therapy*, 9:27-39.

Salend, S. J., Salend, S. M. (1986). Competencies for mainstreaming secondary level learning disabled students. *Journal of Learning Disabilities*, 19(2):91-94.

Schauss, A. G. (1984). Nutrition and behavior: Complex interdisciplinary research. *Nutrition and Health*, 3(1-2):9-37.

Schumaker, J. B., Ellis, E. (1982). Social skills training of LD adolescents: A generalization study. *Learning Disability Quarterly*, 5:409-414.

Schumaker, J. B., Hazel, J. S. (1984a). Social skills assessment and training for the learning disabled: Who's on first and what's on second? Part I. *Journal of Learning Disabilities*, 17(7):422-431.

Schumaker, J. B., Hazel, J. S. (1984b). Social skills assessment and training for the learning disabled: Who's on first and what's on second? Part II. *Journal of Learning Disabilities*, 17(8):492-99.

Schumaker, J. B., Hazel, J. S. (1984c). *The development of a model program to facilitate the transition of mildly handicapped adolescents from secondary to post-secondary education* (Grant No. G00739421-83). Washington, D.C.: U.S. Office of Education.

Schumaker, J. B., Hazel, J. S., Pederson, C. S. (in press). *Social skills for daily living.* Circle Pines, Minnesota: American Guidance Service.

Schumaker, J. B., Hazel, J. S., Pederson, C. S., Nolan, S. (in prep.). *Evaluation of a method for promoting generalization of newly learned social skills* (Research Report). Lawrence: The University of Kansas Institute for Research in Learning Disabilities.

Schumaker, J. B., Hazel, J. S., Sherman, J. A., Sheldon, J. (1982). Social skill performances of learning disabled, non-learning disabled, and delinquent adolescents. *Learning Disability Quarterly,* 5:409-414.

Schumaker, J., Hovell, M., Sherman, J. (1977). An analysis of daily report cards and parent managed privileges in the improvement of adolescents' classroom performance. *Journal of Applied Behavior Analysis,* 10:449-464.

Schumaker, J. B., Pederson, C. S., Hazel, J. S., Meyen, E. L. (1983). Social skills curricula for mildly handicapped adolescents: A review. *Focus on Exceptional Children,* 16(4):1-16.

Scranton, T., Ryckman, D. (1979). Sociometric status of learning disabled children in an integrative program. *Journal of Learning Disabilities,* 12:402-407.

Scott, R. R., Himadi, W., Keane, T. M. (1983). A review of generalization in social skills training: Suggestions for future research. *Progress in Behavior Modification,* 15:113-172.

Serna, L., Schumaker, J. B., Hazel, J. S., Sheldon, J. (1985). Teaching reciprocal social skills to parents and their delinquent adolescents. *Journal of Clinical Child Psychology,* 15:64-77.

Silbergeld, E. K., & Goldberg, A. M. (1974). Lead-induced behavioral dysfunction: An animal model of hyperactivity. *Experimental Neurology,* 42:146-157.

Siperstein, G. N., Bopp, M. J., Bak, J. J. (1978). Social status of learning disabled children. *Journal of Learning Disabilities,* 11:98-102.

Smiley, A., Bryan, T. (1983a). *Learning disabled boys' problem solving and social interactions during raft building.* Chicago: Chicago Institute for the Study of Learning Disabilities.

Smiley, A., Bryan, T. (1983b). *Learning disabled junior high boys' motor performance and trust during obstacle course activities.* Unpublished manuscript. University of Illinois at Chicago.

Spence, S. H. (1981). Validation of social skills of adolescent males in an interview conversation with a previously unknown adult. *Journal of Applied Behavior Analysis,* 14(2):159-168.

Sprafkin, R. P. (1980). The assessment of social skills: An overview. *School Psychology Review,* 9(1):14-20.

Stefanek, M. E., Eisler, R. M. (1983). The current status of cognitive variables in assertiveness training. In Hersen, M., Eisler, R., Miller, P. (Eds.), *Progress in behavior modification:* Vol. 15 (pp. 277-319). New York: Academic Press.

Stokes, T. F., Baer, D. M. (1977). An implicit technology of generalization. *Journal of Applied Behavior Analysis,* 10:349-367.

Stokes, T. F., Osnes, P. G. (1986). Programming the generalization of children's social behavior. In Strain, P., Guralnick, M., Walker, H. (Eds.), *Children's social behavior: Development, assessment, and modification* (pp. 407-443). New York: Academic Press, Inc.

Stone, A., Michals, D. (1986). Problem solving skills in LD children. In Ceci, S. (Ed.), *Handbook of cognitive, social & neuropsychological aspects of learning disabilities:* Vol. 1 (pp. 291-315). Hillsdale, NJ: Lawrence Erlbaum Assoc.

Strain, P. S. (1977). An experimental analysis of peer social initiations on the behavior of withdrawn preschool children: Some training and generalization effects. *Journal of Abnormal Child Psychology,* 5:445-455.

Strain, P. S., Shores, R. E., Timm, M. A. (1977). Effects of peer social initiations on the behavior of withdrawn preschool children. *Journal of Applied Behavior Analysis,* 10:289-298.

Swanson, J. M., Kinsbourne, M. (1980). Food dyes impair performance of hyperactive children on laboratory learning test. *Science,* 207:1485-1486.

Tremblay, A., Strain, P. S., Hendrickson, J. M., Shores, R. E. (1981). Social interactions of normal preschool children. *Behavior Modification,* 5:237-253.

Twentyman, C. T., Zimering, R. T. (1979). Behavior training of social skills: A critical review. *Progress in Behavior Modification,* 7:319-400.

Ullman, C. A., (1957). Teachers, peers, and tests as predictors of adjustment. *Journal of Educational Psychology,* 48:257-267.

Van Hasselt, V. B., Hersen, M., Whitehill, M. B., Bellack, A. S. (1979). Social skills assessment and training for children: An evaluative review. *Behavior Research & Therapy,* 17:413-437.

Vetter, A. A. (1983). *A comparison of the characteristics of learning disabled and non-learning disabled young adults.* Unpublished doctoral dissertation, University of Kansas, Lawrence.

Walker, H. M. (1983). *Walker problem behavior identification checklist: Test and manual* (2nd Ed.). Los Angeles: Western Psychological Services.

Walker, H. M., McConnell, S., Holmes, D., Todis, B., Walker, J., Golden, N. (1983). *The Walker social skills curriculum: The Accepts Program.* Austin, Texas: Pro-Ed.

Warner, M. M., Schumaker, J. B., Alley, G. R., Deshler, D. D. (1980). Learning disabled adolescents in the public schools: Are they different from other low achievers? *Exceptional Education Quarterly,* 1(2):27-36.

Webb, T. E., Oski, F. A. (1974). Behavioral status of young adolescents with iron deficiency anemia. *Journal of Special Education,* 8(2):153-156.

Wender, E. H. (1986). The food additive-free diet in the treatment of behavior disorders: A review. *Development and Behavioral Pediatrics,* 7(1):35-42.

Weisgerber, R., Appleby, J., Fong-Sue, S. (1984). *Social solutions curriculum.* Developed at American Institute for Research, Palo Alto, CA. Burlingame, CA: Professional Associated Resources.

Whang, P. L., Mathews, R. M., Fawcett, S. B. (1981). Teaching job-related social skills to learning disabled adolescents. *Analysis and Intervention in Developmental Disabilities,* 4:29-38.

White, W. J., Schumaker, J. B., Warner, M. M., Alley, G. R., Deshler, D. D. (1980). *The current status of young adults identified as learning disabled during their school career* (Research Report No. 21). Lawrence, KS: The University of Kansas Institute for Research in Learning Disabilities.

Wiig, E. H., Harris, S. P. (1974). Perception and interpretation of nonverbally expressed emotions by adolescents with learning disabilities. *Perceptual Motor Skills,* 38:239-245.

Wolf, M. M. (1978). Social validity: The case for subjective measurement or how applied behavior analysis is finding its heart. *Journal of Applied Behavior Analysis,* 11:203-214.

Wong, B. Y. L., Wong, R. (1980). Role-taking skills in normal achieving and learning disabled children. *Learning Disability Quarterly,* 3(2):11-18.

DISCUSSION

Tanis Bryan

Professors Hazel and Schumaker have presented a comprehensive analysis of the current state of knowledge in social skills assessment and intervention. They outline a research agenda the results of which should contribute to our ability to meet the needs of youngsters who experience problems in the social domain. A number of issues germane to the social problems of the learning disabled, however, are worthy of more intensive attention. These issues relate to (1) the rationale for providing special education services to learning disabled children for their social problems, (2) policy issues related to the assessment and intervention of social problems, (3) the relationship between social problems, theories about etiology, and the definition of learning disabilities, and (4) suggestions for alternative directions for social skills training.

RATIONALE FOR SOCIAL SKILLS INTERVENTIONS

Deficits in social skills have traditionally been treated as marginal in the field of learning disabilities. This marginal status is demonstrated by: (1) the absence of any reference to social problems in various definitions, with the recent exception of the definition developed by the Association for Children and Adults with Learning Disabilities, (2) the absence of diagnostic tests and procedures to assess social skills and status in school-based assessments, (3) the absence of either short- or long-term social skills goals in individual education plans, and (4) the absence of special training to prepare learning disability specialists to assess or intervene in the social domain.

Meanwhile, the results of research, accumulated during the past fifteen years, have consistently found learning disabled children to differ from achieving children, in ways that favor the achievers, on a variety of social status and social skills measures. Twelve of fifteen studies, for example, found the learning disabled less popular or more rejected by their classmates. The same ratio of studies found the learning disabled less skilled in communicative competence than achieving classmates. In every area of social skills that has been studied, the learning disabled consistently perform more poorly than their nondisabled peers. Of course, there are learning disabled children who do not experience social problems, and of course, there are nondisabled children who do. Nonetheless, the data are consistent that social problems are a significant factor in learning disabilities. Significant numbers of learning disabled children experience some kind of problem, the problems persist even when the child makes academic progress, and the existence of such problems has implications for both short- and long-term academic achievement and personal adjustment.

The question has been raised as to whether social problems are the result of academic failure or are part of the learning disability. Given the diversity and complexity of social problems, it seems reasonable to assume that social problems could result from frustrations and stresses experienced as a result of learning failures, and/or be part of the learning disability. In the former case, the experience of frustration may lead the child to adopt maladaptive notions about the causes of his or her successes and failures. These beliefs mediate the child's willingness to engage and persist in cognitively challenging tasks, and are very resistant to change. In the latter case, social problems resemble learning problems; that is, a child may have difficulty reading people, as the child has difficulty reading text. Underlying both causes are maladaptive or inadequate notions about the self and others.

Another important question is whether social skills training will reduce the time available for academic intervention. For elementary and secondary school children, one of the most important consequences of schooling is success in mastering the basic skills. Since the learning disabled take longer and need more trials for academic mastery, time is a very precious commodity. Hence practitioners' concern that social skills training will reduce the amount of time available for academic learning is legitimate. If practitioners believe that they must choose between academic instruction and social training, it is likely they will feel committed to allocating time to academic instruction.

It is terribly important that teachers and others concerned with the learning disabled realize that social interactions and academic instruction are intertwined; they are not separate events. The classroom is a complex social organization. Teaching and learning are social interaction events as well as cognitive events. Consider, for example, teacher questioning—a high-frequency behavior. When a teacher asks a question, the phrasing of the question, the choice of a student to answer, the length of time given the student to respond, the teacher's feedback, and the next question all communicate a teacher's evaluation of a student's cognitive capacity and worth. Children as young as first grade—high and low achievers—consensually interpret teachers' judgments (Weinstein, Marshall, Brattesoni, and Middlestadt, 1982). Furthermore, since learning disabled children spend most of their time in regular classrooms, they tend to view achieving classmates as their primary reference group (Harter, 1985) and compare their performance unfavorably to nondisabled peers. Learning disabled children do not live in an experiential vacuum.

A large body of data show that academic achievement, children's ideas about their own capabilities, and peer status are interrelated (Entwisle, Alexander, Cadigan, and Pallas, 1986). Low expectations and low peer status lead to a low utilization of academic capabilities. Children's attributions can both hinder the acquisition of knowledge as well as reduce the automatization of information processing (Kolligian and Sternberg, 1986). Learning disabled children's self-concepts, attributions, and peer status mediate their responsiveness to our attempts to educate them. The choice we make is not between social versus academic interventions. Our choice is whether we will use the extant data base in social research to facilitate academic and social development, or forge in blindly, ignoring the critical role of social factors in children's cognitive development, and never understanding why some children are hard to reach and hard to teach.

It is important that we not limit our concerns to the long-term implications of social problems for continuing education, job selection and status, and mental health, as if these were not sufficient causes for concern. It is that social factors are central to the daily activities of the classroom and home, and children's social skillfulness and adaptiveness play a significant role in their academic progress.

For theoretical and policy reasons, it is especially important to understand how the schooling process influences children's acquisition of academic skills, their self-expectations, and peer status. It is time for us to take into account the interactive nature of teaching and learning. While theoretical models of handicap traditionally focus on the characteristics of the child, we know that the child's attitudes, behaviors, and learning are the result, in part, of the child's interaction with significant "others" in the environment. To understand the nature and impact of a handicap, we must attend to the interrelationship of child, school, and family contexts. The educational decisions we make must be better informed by research that examines the nature of these complex social interactions.

POLICY ISSUES

While the rationale for addressing learning disabled youngsters' social problems is based on a solid body of research data, there are complex policy issues involved in the provision of social skills services. These issues are not just matters of science, but matters of values and resources. Since the field of learning disabilities always has been criticized for definitional problems and since schools are currently being barraged with criticism for presumably overidentifying children as learning disabled (see Pugach and Sapon-Shevin, 1986; Shepard, 1986), it is important that the educational community debate these issues. Given the abundance of data, one issue is whether the definition of learning disabilities should include references to problems in the social domain. If social problems were included in the definition, school districts would be mandated to provide social skills interventions. However, this would create the possibility that any child who is unpopular could be defined as learning disabled—an outcome that would be highly undesirable.

A second issue to consider is whether teachers' referrals and diagnosticians' evaluations are unwittingly influenced by social factors. James Bryan's research (Bryan and Sherman, 1982) on immediate impressions of the learning disabled suggests that the identification of children as learning disabled may well be influenced by factors that we are not overtly conscious of. If this is the case, the reasons we have difficulty differentiating between the learning disabled and their low achieving classmates may rest in the social domain. We need to better understand the impact of social factors in the diagnostic process.

Third, if it is accepted that learning disabled children who experience social problems should be provided with interventions, there is the question of who shall be responsible for doing what type of assessment and intervention, and at what cost. As it is, the cost of assessment, even when limited to the academic domain, is extraordinary (Shepard, 1986), and the prospect of increasing such costs may well meet legitimate resistance.

Fourth, we need to know if children with other handicaps experience similar problems in the social domain. To what extent, and in what way, are social problems generic to handicapping conditions? While children with different handicaps may experience different social problems, it seems very likely that problems would be found. Cross-categorical research that compares the social status and social problems of children with different handicaps would greatly enhance our knowledge of handicaps and of the needs of children with varying degrees and types of handicaps. Given the debate on categorical versus noncategorical programs—a debate that reflects different viewpoints as to whether handicap categories are mutually exclusive, such research would have significant implications for the classification of children, certification, and funding.

While Hazel and Schumaker deal with research issues in their paper, we must at some point address these policy issues, issues that reflect our values, goals, and resources, and drive public policy decisions.

THEORIES ABOUT THE DEFINITION AND ETIOLOGY OF LEARNING DISABILITIES AND SOCIAL PROBLEMS

Hypotheses about the causes of learning disabilities have been dominated by four models. One is the medical disease model, which contends that learning problems are the result of damage, dysfunction, or slow maturation of the brain. While unable to specify the exact location or nature of the dysfunction, various definitions include qualifiers that learning disability is an "intrinsic deficit" and not caused by external factors such as poor teaching (Kolligian and Sternberg, 1986). The second is a behavioristic model, which eschews theorizing and focuses on diagnosing the specific nature of the learning problem. The third model is a motivational/attributional model, in which the learning problem is hypothesized to result from a lack of motivation or from maladaptive notions as to the causes of academic successes and failures. The fourth is an information processing model, which focuses on such processes as attention, perception, metacognition, and language. The conceptual model that has dominated research in learning disabilities is the information processing model, and it is this model that has generated the most substantial research base in its support.

The definition of learning disabilities used in P.L. 91-230 in 1969 and again in P.L. 94-192 in 1975 states that learning disabilities is "a disorder in one or more of the basic psychological processes involved in understanding or using spoken or written language. These may be manifested in disorders of listening, thinking, talking, reading, writing, spelling or arithmetic" (P.L. 91-230, 1969). Research in learning disabilities has found that various components of information processing—in particular, attention, metacognition, and language—differentiate learning disabled from achieving children (Brown and Compioni, 1986; Hallahan and Reeve, 1980; Wong and Jones, 1982; Vellutino, Bentley, and Scanlon, 1983). While the research on social problems has not been cast in the information processing mode, listening, thinking, and talking are obviously involved in social interactions.

In theorizing about the causes of social problems, Hazel and Schumaker present four different causes: (1) lack of social skills in repertoire (the behavioristic model), (2) insufficient motivation or opportunity to use skills in repertoire (the motivational model), (3) failure to execute appropriate behavior because of competing emotional responses (the motivational model), and (4) physiological causes such as environmental sensitivities and chemical imbalances (the medical disease model). None of these proposed sources of social deficits reflect the information processing model.

While the definition of learning disabilities has suffered a great deal of criticism, it should be noted that contemporary research in the social sciences is heavily dominated by information processing theories and research. For instance, contemporary research on teaching has shifted dramatically from the perspective that teaching is a sequence of behaviors to teaching as a decision making and information processing process (Carter and Koehler, 1986). The folks who created the learning disabilities definition may well have been decades ahead of their time, and may be vindicated and venerated when we figure out how to operationalize the definition into dynamic means of information processing assessment and intervention.

In light of the definition and the results of research on information processing, it would seem appropriate to study social problems in learning disabilities from an information processing perspective. In the social domain, information processing refers to the way people handle stimuli from the environment, organize data, sense problems, and generate concepts. Though it is possible, and clearly popular, to talk about children's behavior, it is obvious that what children do is directed in no small measure by what they think. Children's behavior reflects their knowledge of the situation, their judgment as to what is appropriate, expected, and rewarded, their relationships with other significant actors in the situation, their expectation of likely outcomes, and their evaluation of the importance of various outcomes for themselves. Learning disabled children may well have deficits in behavioral repertoires, but there is no Black Hole in social behavior. Any attempts at social skills training will be mediated through the minds and motives of children, and training attempts that treat social behaviors like a Black Hole are doomed to very limited success. Because children's thought processes are the precursors of their behaviors, research and training efforts must take into account learning disabled children's information processing and decision making in social situations.

An information processing model has several advantages. First, it would allow us to relate learning disabled children's social problems to the definition. If social problems are viewed as part of the handicap, we can more easily justify directing resources into assessment and intervention. Second, it is theoretically important to understand the linkages, if any, between problems in academic and social domains. If research in academic and social development were to share a common theoretical framework, we might enhance our understanding of both. Third, there is considerable evidence that individuals' appropriate deployment of behavior is a function of their knowledge about the situations in which the strategies are to be used (Chi, Feltovich, and Glaser, 1981). Central to progress in understanding learning disabled children's social problems is analyses of their comprehension and evaluation of situations. This suggests that interventions based on teaching specific social behaviors will not be likely to lead to their appropriate use unless the learning disabled have full knowledge about the situations in which they are appropriate. And it also suggests why it is so difficult to show generalization of learning. Acquiring a repertoire of behaviors outside the social context in which they are to be used and/or in the absence of learning the principles governing the situations in which they are to be used, is not likely to be effective. An information processing paradigm should free us from trying to assess and teach—and children from having to learn—the myriad of social skills that are involved in a behavioristic model. In sum, an information processing paradigm would enhance our knowledge of learning disabilities and would provide, at least for some children, a more economic and more heuristic route to social skill assessment and intervention.

Hazel and Schumaker include physiological factors such as environmental sensitivities and chemical imbalance among the possible causes of social skills deficits. This is refreshing, insofar as the field of learning disabilities by and large has avoided consideration of physiology in learning disabilities for the past two decades. As a field, we have been pragmatic and have adopted a behavioristic model for guiding the assessment and training of academic problems. What is interesting is that several decades ago Samuel Orton hypothesized that dyslexics might experience emotional problems as a result of changes in brain processes. According to Geschwind (1982), Orton stated: "it should not be assumed that emotional disturbance is necessarily the result of the impact of the disorder on the child, but that it can be the direct result of changes in the brain" (p. 18). We do not know whether Orton's use of the term emotional disturbance is synonymous with what we are calling social skills deficits. But Orton should be given credit for recognizing that dyslexics were experiencing emotional problems and that these problems could result from the experience of frustration or from brain changes. While progress has been made in identifying the brain regions involved in emotion (Geschwind, 1982), it is still hypothetical as to whether the social skills deficits of the learning disabled are related to brain processes.

At this time, we can only speculate as to the causes of learning disabled students' social problems, but research that helps us to discover the causes and the dynamics of the problem makes it more likely that we will be able to develop effective measures and interventions.

OBSERVATIONS ON SOCIAL SKILLS TRAINING

Hazel, Schumaker, Sherman, and Sheldon (1982) divide social skill improvement approaches into three categories: (1) instructional procedures to teach new skills, (2) manipulation of antecedent or consequent events, and (3) self-control procedures. While each method holds promise for various social skills deficits, there are problems that should be considered when contemplating social skills training. First, as noted above, interventions have been developed from a behavioristic framework and they emphasize learning the sequences of behavior appropriate for various situations. The magnitude of accounting for appropriate behavioral sequences for different ages, sexes, races, socioeconomic status, and situations seems quite an overwhelming task. Further, to the extent that social skills problems reflect information processing deficits, behaviorally oriented interventions may be ineffectual.

Second, the interventions do not take into account situational variables. For instance, recent research shows that peer status is related to characteristics of the peer group: aggressive children are more popular in aggressive groups than they are in nonaggressive groups whereas nonaggressive children are more popular in nonaggressive groups than in aggressive groups (Wright, Giammarino, and Parad, 1986). A mismatch between characteristics of the group and of a child can play a significant role in eliciting peer rejection. As currently conceptualized, assessment procedures do not take into account the match of child and group characteristics. There may be nothing inherently wrong with the child's social skills, yet the child may experience social difficulties as a function of bad luck, of being in the wrong group at the wrong time. Furthermore, if the problem is related to a mismatch and if the intervention plan fails to take the mismatch into account, how can the intervention make a difference? If the intervention teaches behaviors that are not endorsed by the child's peer group, the social problems could get worse. Finally, children often adopt social strategies that fit their capabilities and social status, such as playing a passive, dependent, cooperative role among peers. One form of therapy might be programming the child with a similar peer group.

Third, interventions are adult-centered, not child-centered. It is adults and not children who select which social skills shall be learned, when the skills have been adequately demonstrated, and the criteria for program termination. While we are knowledgeable about important generic social skills that influence success in classrooms and the work place, and to a lesser extent peer friendships, the bases for children's social attraction—or our ability to control this attraction—remain problematic. Behaviors admired by "significant" peers (those peers the child is trying to befriend) may not be behaviors known or acceptable to adults. Indeed, they may not even be social!

Hazel and Schumaker call for novel instructional procedures for social skills interventions. We need novel approaches that are child-centered, that facilitate children's learning from children, and that take into account what is significant and salient to children. Since children are the most cost-effective therapists, interventions that utilize their knowledge and skills seem most likely to yield positive effects. In addition, as stressed many times by James Bryan, interventions need not focus on the learning disabled child. Interventions could be directed toward nonhandicapped children: To train compassion, sympathy, tolerance, and acceptance of individual differences and the human condition may well serve the public good in more significant ways.

Referred to in the Hazel and Schumaker paper is a study showing the positive impact of cooperative goal structures on learning disabled children's social behaviors (Bryan, Cosden, and Pearl, 1982). In fact, a large body of data shows that cooperative goal structures are very effective in increasing children's regard for themselves, their peers, and their teachers. In cooperative goal structures, classrooms are organized so that children are encouraged to cooperate with one another, and rewards are based on group, not individual, products. In comparison to reward structures based on individual goals or competitive goals, cooperative goal structures promote positive social interactions and relationships. This is very cost-effective, it does not take time away from academics, it increases the amount of time teachers have to provide individual instruction, it facilitates children's social development, it does not require singling the learning disabled child out for special treatment, and it intertwines the academic and social domains. As an intervention, cooperative goal structures should be viewed as quite promising. While there will still be children who need individualized social skills training, the use of cooperative goal structures will make it feasible for us to afford training for those in greatest need.

In sum, in spite of a relatively brief history of research, a body of information is now available that testifies to the likelihood that learning disabled children might be experiencing difficulties in their social lives. It is important that research consider how these social problems relate to information processing deficits, the definition and etiology of learning disabilities, the referral and diagnosis of learning disabilities, and the similarities and differences between social problems of children with varying degrees and types of handicap. It is critical that practitioners understand the interrelatedness of social and academic learning. Low self-concept and low peer status are intertwined with low achievement. It is further critical that practitioners understand that interventions in the social domain can be programmed within the context of everyday academic instruction. Cooperative goal structures is but one example of how this might be accomplished. While there are learning disabled youngsters who need individualized training in social skills, research is needed to establish what behaviors should be addressed and what outcomes should be strived for. Finally, the many policy issues that are generated by learning disabled children's social problems call for objective debate.

SUGGESTED RESEARCH DIRECTIONS

Research needs in the area of social factors and learning disabilities are outlined as follows:

- Basic research on the nature and dynamics of social problems, research that is based on an information processing paradigm.
- Research that is cross-categorical and compares the social status and social skills of learning and language disabled children, children with other types of handicaps, and underachieving children.
- Research that is comprehensive in scope, that examines the multiple components that make up social effectiveness, such as the relationship of syntactic deficits to communicative competence.
- Research that is interactive in nature, that includes assessment of child, teacher, and parents in creating, maintaining, exacerbating, or ameliorating social problems.
- Research that examines the role of social factors in the processes of assessment and intervention.
- Research that links social factors to research in other areas of importance, such as psychobiology and neurology.

REFERENCES

Brown, A. L., Campione, J. C. (1986). Psychological theory and the study of learning disabilities. *American Psychologist*, 41:1059-1068.
Bryan, J. H., Sherman, R. (1980). Audiences' immediate impressions of nonverbal ingratiation attempts by boys labeled learning disabled. *Learning Disability Quarterly*, 3:19-28.

Bryan, T., Cosden, M., Pearl, R. (1982). The effects of cooperative goal structures and cooperative models on LD and NLD students. *Learning Disability Quarterly,* 5:415-421.

Carter, K., Koehler, V. R. (1987). The process and content of initial year of teaching programs. In Griffin, G. A. and Millies, S. (Eds.), *The first years of teaching* (pp. 91-104). Chicago, IL: University of Illinois at Chicago-Illinois State Board of Education.

Chi, M. T. H., Feltovich, P., Glazer, R. (1981). Categorization and representation of physics problems by experts and novices. *Cognitive Science,* 5:121-152.

Entwisle, D. R., Alexander, K. L., Cadigan, D., Pallas A (1986). The schooling process: Two samples a decade apart. *American Educational Research Journal,* 23:587-613.

Geschwind, N. (1982). Why Orton was right. *Annals of Dyslexia,* 32:13-30.

Hallahan, D. P., Reeve, R.E. (1980). Selective attention and distractability. In Keogh, B. K. (Ed.), *Advances in special education:* Vol. 1. Greenwich, Conn.: JAI Press.

Harter, S. (1985). Processes underlying the construction, maintenance, and enhancement of the self-concept in children. In Suls, J., Greenwald, A. (Eds.), *Psychological perspectives on the self:* Vol. 3. Hillsdale, NJ: Erlbaum.

Hazel, J. S., Schumaker, J. B., Sherman, J. A., Sheldon, J. (1982). Application of a group training program in social skills and problem solving skills to learning disabled and non-learning disabled youth. *Learning Disability Quarterly,* 5:398-408.

Kolligian, J., Sternberg, R. J. (1986). Intelligence, information processing, and specific learning disabilities: A triarchic synthesis. *Journal of Learning Disabilities,* 20:8-17.

Pugach, M., Sapon-Shevin, M. (1986). New agendas for Special Education policy: What the National Reports haven't said. *Exceptional Children,* 53:295-299.

Shepard, L. A. (1986). The new push for excellence: Widening the schism between regular and special education. *Exceptional Children,* 53:327-329.

Vellutino, F. R., Bentley, W. L., Scanlon, D. M. (1983). Interhemispheric learning and speed of hemispheric transmission in dyslexic and normal readers: A replication of previous results and additional findings. *Applied Psycholinguistics,* 4:209-228.

Weinstein, R. S., Marshall, H. H., Brattesani, K. A., Middlestadt, S. E. (1982). Student perceptions of differential teacher treatment in open and traditional classrooms. *Journal of Educational Psychology,* 74:678-692.

Wong, B. Y. L., Jones, W. (1982). Increasing metacomprehension in learning disabled and normally achieving students through self-questioning training. *Learning Disability Quarterly,* 5:228-240.

Wright, J. C., Giammarino, M., Parad, H. W. (1986). Social status in small groups: Individual-group similarity and the social "misfit." *Journal of Personal and Social Psychology,* 50:523-536.

DISCUSSION

Frank M. Gresham

The paper by Hazel and Schumaker represents an important development in the field of learning disabilities for several reasons. First, the topic of social skills deficits as a major research area and concern for LD youths would not have been considered as one of the five major topics in a national conference of this type five years ago. Second, it has been only within the past five years that researchers have begun to develop an adequate knowledge base for understanding the social skills and peer acceptance difficulties of LD youths. It is important to note that 75 percent of all published articles in the area of social skills have appeared within the past five years (Gresham, 1987). Third, more recent research has begun to relate LD youths' social skills deficits to the more traditionally studied deficits of this population, such as specific academic deficiencies, attention deficit disorders, and physiological factors (Bursuck and Asher, 1986; Coie and Krehbiel, 1984; Reschly, Gresham, and Graham-Clay, 1984; Prinz, Roberts, and Hantman, 1980). Finally, acknowledgment of the importance of social behavior should provide increased interest in and support for research designed to more clearly understand and remediate the social skills and peer acceptance difficulties of LD youths and how these social deficits relate to specific academic deficits.

The following two sections of this critique address key issues in the areas of definition/conceptualization and etiological aspects of social skills deficits. These sections are followed by a critique of three of the most important issues described by Hazel and Schumaker: (a) assessment of social skills, (b) skill selection for social skills training, and (c) instructional procedures. These three issues were chosen for this in-depth critique because they are central to the future development and understanding of the relation between learning disabilities and social competence.

DEFINITIONAL ISSUES

Hazel and Schumaker aptly point out the difficulties in defining social skills and utilize a social validity definition that defines social skills as:

> those behaviors which, within given situations, predict important social outcomes for children and youth....Important social outcomes may include: (a) peer acceptance, (b) significant others' judgments of social skill (e.g., teachers, parents, etc.), (c) academic achievement, (d) self esteem, and (e) other social behaviors known to consistently correlate with a-d above. (Gresham, 1983, 1986, 1987).

The chief advantage of this definition is that it enables one to specify the behaviors that occur in specific situations and to relate such situational behaviors to socially valued or important outcomes.

It is critical that future research delineates the specific social behaviors and situations in which LD youths are most deficient and relates these deficiencies to socially important criteria. An emphasis should also be placed upon developmental differences in the LD population in social skill deficiencies because socially important criteria shift dramatically from the elementary school years through adolescence to adulthood.

An important conceptual development in the area of social skills is the recognition of the relation between adaptive behavior and social skills. Gresham and Reschly (1987) indicate that the construct of adaptive behavior deals with behaviors under the rubric of independent functioning and personal self-sufficiency (for instance: personal responsibility, social responsibility, economic-vocational activity, and functional academic skills). In contrast, social skills include behaviors of a more interpersonal nature such as social initiation, cooperation, assertion, peer reinforcement, and social self-efficacy. It is important to remember that adaptive behavior and social skills are related constructs, given recent research showing at least moderate relations between these two constructs (see Gresham and Elliott, in press). In addition, both adaptive behavior and social skills are related to academic achievement in school-age children and youths (Reschly et al., 1984). The complex interrelations between adaptive behavior, social skills, and academic achievement suggest a common core for academic and social deficits in LD youths. Unfortunately, we remain ignorant of the specific nature of this core and how it relates to the difficulties that LD youths encounter.

ETIOLOGICAL FACTORS

Hazel and Schumaker make a cogent point that the determination of whether social skills deficits are primary or secondary to the condition of LD is irrelevant to the identification and remediation of social skills difficulties of the LD population. Moreover, there is substantial evidence to support the fact that a significant minority of LD youths are as socially skilled and as well accepted by peers as the non-LD population. Estimates of this percentage are in the range of 2 percent to 17 percent (Gresham and Reschly, 1986). As Bruck (1986) and others have noted, there is little evidence to support the notion that social skills deficits are causative factors in LD, but rather they may be more appropriately viewed as effects of academic difficulties, frustration, and motivational deficits that result from difficulties encountered in the mastery of specific academic skills in the ecology of school settings.

Major Issues to be Addressed in Learning Disabilities and Social Skills

Hazel and Schumaker accurately state that a single ideal social skill assessment tool is not available. My position is that a single assessment tool should never be used to identify social skills deficits in this or any other population. Using a single assessment tool would be necessarily restrictive in scope and would not yield the requisite information to target specific social skills deficits or to evaluate the effects of social skills training. Campbell and Fiske's (1959) notion of convergent and discriminant validation provides a useful heuristic for guiding social skills assessment. In short, social skills should be multiply operationalized, using a variety of assessment procedures including: (a) teacher and parent ratings, (b) direct observations of social behavior in naturalistic environments, (c) self-reports, (d) interviews with significant "others," (e) self-monitoring, (f) behavioral role-play measures, and (g) sociometric assessment. Using Campbell and Fiske's (1959) definition, validity is represented by the relative agreement between different methods of measuring social skills.

Social skills assessment procedures can be classified according to the purpose of assessment: (a) identification/classification or (b) intervention/therapy (Gresham, 1986). The basis for an assessment procedure falling into one of these two categories is the degree to which the assessment procedure allows for a functional analysis of behavior (that is, the specification of the antecedent, sequential, and consequent conditions surrounding a social behavior). Assessment procedures such as direct observations, behavioral interviews, and self-monitoring allow for such a functional analysis and, as such, are classified as intervention/therapy assessment techniques. Procedures such as ratings by significant "others," self-reports, and role-plays do not allow for a functional analysis and are classified as identification/classification assessment techniques. Obviously, both types of assessment procedures are needed in the assessment of social skills.

Hazel and Schumaker's paper omits a very important development in the area of sociometric assessment, namely the work on sociometric classification by Coie, Dodge, and Coppoletti (1982). Coie et al. developed a classification system that identifies five sociometric status groups: (a) popular, (b) neglected, (c) rejected, (d) controversial, and (e) average. These groups are defined on the basis of liked most (LM) and liked least (LL) scores, which are used to define a child's social preference and social impact within groups. This system of assessment provides for a more detailed view of a child's social status in the peer group. Moreover, each sociometric group has known behavioral correlates that differentiate them. Rejected children, for example, display high rates of aggressive behavior, disruptive behavior, and acting-out behavior, and low rates of cooperative behavior, peer reinforcement, and helping others. In contrast, controversial children display a curious mixture of inappropriate behaviors and socially skilled behaviors.

Future research into the distributions of sociometric classifications and behavioral correlates would greatly benefit the field of LD. We need to know, for example, what percent of LD youths are rejected, neglected, controversial, average, and even popular in the peer group. We also need to know how, if at all, behavioral correlates of these classifications differ from those of non-LD youths.

Hazel and Schumaker indicate that research needs to focus on developing an assessment device or package of assessment devices which is: (a) based upon empirically validated social skills deficits of LD individuals, (b) psychometrically acceptable in terms of reliability and validity, (c) practical to use in school settings, (d) spans the age range from preschool through secondary school, and (e) allows for assessment of all skills required for social competence. Hazel and Schumaker suggest that this assessment device be commercially available and that it be developed for use by a teacher, by reading a set of written instructions to screen and diagnose social skills deficits, plan instruction, and measure progress for any age student.

Gresham and Elliott (in press) have developed a commercially available (via American Guidance Service) assessment package consisting of teacher, parent, and self-report rating scales known as the *Social Skills Rating Scales* (SSRS). These scales are designed for children and youths from preschool through 12th grade (ages 3-18) and were developed on the basis of empirical relations between specific social behaviors and socially important outcomes. The SSRS is standardized on a nationally representative sample stratified according to age, gender, race, geographic region, socioeconomic status, type of education (resource room, and self-contained classroom), and child status (nonhandicapped, learning disabled, mentally retarded, and seriously emotionally disturbed). The SSRS appears to meet most, if not all, of Hazel and Schumaker's five criteria for an assessment package.

SKILL SELECTION

An important aspect of social skills remediation programs is the precise selection of social skills to be taught. Hazel and Schumaker indicate that the most appropriate procedures for selecting social skills have yet to be identified. They state that most social skills training programs rely upon intuition rather than empirical data to select social skills for training. This approach, of course, does not guarantee that the most appropriate or most important social skills will be selected. Hughes (1986) reviewed 32 social skills training investigations published between 1980 and 1984 and found that 56.5 percent (18 studies) used nonempirical methods to select social skills for training and 62.5 percent (20 studies) did not attempt to verify that subjects were in fact deficient on the targeted social skills to be trained.

Gresham and Elliott (in press) have incorporated a means of selecting social skills to be trained by having teachers and parents rate the importance of each social skill on a three-point scale: (a) *Critical* for Classroom Success or for Development, (b) *Important* for Classroom Success or Development, and (c) *Unimportant* for Classroom Success or Development. This approach yields a frequency $\underline{x}$ importance matrix in which all skills receiving a 0 frequency rating and a 2 importance rating are identified as potential target social skills to be trained. Thus, the scale will identify all behaviors that never or infrequently occur but are considered critical by teachers and parents. This approach responds to the need that the social skills selected for training are those that are considered critical by significant "others" and that show empirical relations to socially important outcomes.

INSTRUCTIONAL PROCEDURES

Social skills training (SST) may be conceptualized as a four-step process: (a) promoting skill acquisition, (b) enhancing skill performance, (c) removing interfering behaviors, and (d) facilitating generalization. These steps are related to the type of social skill deficiency (that is, skill versus performance deficit), the presence or absence of interfering behaviors, and the functional control of social behaviors in specific situations.

Modeling and coaching represent the major ways in which social skill acquisition is facilitated. These procedures are typically used to remediate social skill deficits that refer to a child's not having the social skill in the repertoire or the child's not knowing a particular step in the performance of a behavioral sequence.

A number of procedures are designed to enhance the behavioral performance of social skills already in a child's repertoire. These procedures are not appropriate for remediation of performance deficits that refer to the number of times a behavior is exhibited (that is, the behavior is not performed at an acceptable level). A variety of antecedent and consequent events reviewed by Hazel and Schumaker have been used successfully to enhance behavioral performance of social skills.

The third step or phase in SST is one that is often overlooked in discussions of teaching positive social behaviors. It is often assumed that a child has no interfering behaviors that prevent or block the acquisition or performance of socially skilled behaviors. This is highly unlikely for many LD children, and one must apply contingencies for the interfering behaviors as well as teach and/or reinforce appropriate social behaviors. Interfering behaviors and socially skilled behaviors are perhaps best conceptualized using the notion of *concurrent schedules of reinforcement*. Concurrent schedules describe a situation in which two or more behaviors are reinforced according to two or more schedules of reinforcement at the same time. If interfering behaviors are on a relatively "thicker" schedule of reinforcement than socially skilled behaviors, the interfering behaviors will be performed more frequently than the socially skilled behaviors. They "block" the acquisition or performance of socially skilled behaviors. When interfering behaviors block or prevent the acquisition or performance of socially skilled behaviors, the difficulties are referred to as a self-control skill deficit and a self-control skill performance deficit, respectively.

The final stage in SST is generalization. Generalization refers to the occurrence of relevant behaviors under different, nontraining conditions (across settings, subjects, people, behaviors, and times) and without the scheduling of conditions, as in training. As Hazel and Schumaker emphasize, a much needed area of research is one which develops a technology that adequately generalizes (transfers) socially skilled behaviors trained in one situation and setting to other situations and settings. Stokes and Osnes (1986) have outlined three classes of procedures to enhance the generalization of social skills: (a) take advantage of natural communities of reinforcement, (b) train diversely, and (c) incorporate functional mediators. Future research must investigate which of these classes of procedures produces the greatest degree of generalization of LD children and youths.

SUMMARY

Hazel and Schumaker have done the field of LD a great service by comprehensively reviewing the important area of social skills for LD youths. Their review should assist public policy makers, organizations, parents, and educators in targeting specific research areas and in demanding better services for LD youths' social development. Unfortunately, the field of LD has overemphasized cognitive and academic deficits at the expense of social deficits, and there have been less research monies and support for researchers interested in the social skill and peer acceptance deficits of this population. Hopefully, the Hazel and Schumaker paper will serve as a catalyst for promoting more intensive investigations into the causes and effects of social skill deficiencies in LD children and youths.

REFERENCES

Bruck, M. (1986). Social and emotional adjustments of learning disabled children: A review of the issues. In Ceci, S. (Ed.), *Handbook of cognitive, social, and neuropsychological aspects of learning disabilities:* Vol. 1 (pp. 351-380).

Bursuck, W., Asher, S. (1986). The relationship between social competence and achievement in elementary school children. *Journal of Clinical Psychology,* 15:41-49.

Campbell, D., Fiske, D. (1959). Convergent and discriminant validation by the multitrait-multimethod matrix. *Psychological Bulletin,* 56:81-105.

Coie, J., Dodge, K., Coppoletti, H. (1982). Dimensions and types of social status: A cross-age perspective. *Developmental Psychology,* 18:557-570.

Coie, J., Krehbiel, G. (1984). Effects of academic tutoring on the social status of low-achieving, socially-rejected children. *Child Development,* 55:1465-1478.

Gresham, F. M. (1983). Social validity in the assessment of children's social skills: Establishing standards for social competency. *Journal of Psychoeducational Assessment,* 1:297-307.

Gresham, F. M. (1986). The assessment of social behavior/competence in children. In Strain, P., Guralnick, M., Walker, H. (Eds.), *Children's social behavior: Development, assessment, and modification* (pp. 143-179). New York: Academic Press.

Gresham, F. M. (1987). Social competence and motivational characteristics of learning disabled students. In Wong, M., Walberg, H., Reynolds, M. (Eds.), *The handbook of special education: Research and practice.* Oxford, England: Pergamon Press.

Gresham, F. M., Elliott, S. N. (in press). The relationship between adaptive behavior and social skills. *Journal of Special Education.*

Gresham, F. M., Elliott, S. N. (in press). *Social skills rating scales: Teacher, parent, and self-report versions for children and adolescents.* Circle Pines, MN: American Guidance Service.

Gresham, F. M., Reschly, D. J. (1986). Social skill deficits and low peer acceptance of mainstreamed learning disabled children. *Learning Disability Quarterly,* 9:23-32.

Gresham, F. M., Reschly, D. J. (1987). Social skills and peer acceptance in the mildly handicapped. In Kratochwill, T. (Ed.), *Advances in school psychology:* Vol. 5. Hillsdale, NJ: Lawrence Erlbaum.

Hughes, J. (1986). Methods of skill selection in social skills training: A review. *Professional School Psychology,* 1:235-248.

Prinz, R., Roberts, W., Hantman, E. (1980). Dietary correlates of hyperactive behavior in children. *Journal of Consulting and Clinical Psychology,* 48:760-769.

Reschly, D., Gresham, F., Graham-Clay, S. (1984). *Multifactored nonbiased assessment: Convergent and discriminant validity of social and cognitive measures with black and white regular and special education students.* Washington, D.C.: United States Department of Education, Grant No. G008110156, Assistance Catalog No. CFDA: 84-023E.

Stokes, T., Osnes, P. (1986). Programming the generalization of children's social behavior. In Strain, P., Guralnick, M., Walker, H. (Eds.), *Children's social behavior: Development, assessment, and modification* (pp. 407-443). New York: Academic Press.

DISCUSSION

Hill M. Walker

I would like to compliment Drs. Hazel and Schumacher on a most scholarly analysis of the empirical knowledge base regarding social skills and learning disabilities. Their review clearly establishes that learning disabled students are (1) often seriously deficient in critically important social process skills, (2) experience problems and conflicts in their peer relations as well as in their relationships with adults in school settings, and (3) suffer higher than average levels of peer rejection and school failure. These authors identify and describe seven important issues that need to be addressed in the social skills domain and offer valuable research suggestions for each. Their recommendations should prove useful in guiding the future efforts of scholars, researchers, policymakers, and ultimately practitioners.

I wish to cover three topics. They are (1) to discuss some conceptual and procedural issues as well as programmatic approaches to social competence that are not addressed by the authors, (2) to address several issues where I disagree with the authors' position or where I think elaboration is required, and (3) to present recommendations regarding the future direction of research and program development efforts for mildly handicapped students in the social competence domain.

These issues are less specific to LD students per se and focus more on the broad range of handicapped students in school and post-school settings, and include the mentally retarded, the learning disabled, and the behavior disordered populations. As a result of the research efforts of the past decade and, as Frank Gresham noted in his remarks, especially of the last five years, we know a great deal about the social competence of both the handicapped and the nonhandicapped student populations. Much of this knowledge, in my view, is directly applicable to the learning disabled population in school.

CONCEPTUAL AND PROCEDURAL ISSUES

I think there are some historical developments and trends that help explain the current strong interest in social behavior within school, employment, and community living settings. These include (1) the types of social behavior adjustment required of children when they enter school settings, (2) the long-term development implications of social competence problems experienced early in the school process, (3) the effect of major transitions on social behavioral adjustment, such as mainstreaming and moving from school to work and independent living, (4) the need to acknowledge that the perception of students' social competence by peers, teachers, and parents depends as much on a child's motor and language skills as it does on specific social skills levels, and (5) the need to acknowledge the limited efficacy of social skills intervention procedures and training efforts to date in producing durable, reliable changes in the social competence status of mildly handicapped children.

Interest in social skills training dates from the early 1930's. It received a gigantic boost with the invention of the sociometric test by Mareno and colleagues in the 1930's. The work of behavioral psychotherapists such as Salter, Wolpe, and Lazarus was quite instrumental in demonstrating that specific social skills could actually be taught and mastered effectively. A very powerful factor was the broad-based deinstitutionalization of adults that escalated in earnest, starting about 1967.

Followup studies of deinstitutionalized adults indicated that the best predictor of their posthospitalization adjustment status was not their psychiatric diagnosis, their behavioral characteristics while hospitalized, or the types of treatments to which they were exposed. The best single predictor of posthospitalization adjustment was the residents' level of social competence prior to entering the hospital. This finding has had quite an impact in demonstrating the importance of social skills training.

Finally, and most influential, I think, the major transitions that handicapped students and adults have been exposed to over the past 20 years in mainstreaming into less restrictive settings and moving from school to work have dramatically illustrated the social competence deficits and social skills problems of this population.

There are two types of social behavioral adjustment required of children in school. Upon entering school, they are required to adjust to instructional settings that are controlled by teachers and to free play settings that are controlled by peers. There is overlap among these adjustments, but they both make unique contributions to the socialization process.

The competencies that are required for these two types of adjustments differ markedly. To make it in an instructional setting and to receive teacher approval, a child needs to display behavioral compliance, to follow classroom rules, to make the needs of assistance known in an appropriate manner, and to produce work of acceptable quality that meets teacher standards, given the teacher's appraisal of the student's level of ability.

Handicapped children fail this important test of adjustment by the thousands. There is broad agreement among teachers regarding these behavioral demands. As a rule, in less restrictive settings, teachers' demands are not adjusted downward to accommodate handicapped children's lower competence levels in relation to them.

In contrast, peer-related social competencies that are important in effecting a good peer-related adjustment include being honest with others, offering assistance to peers, giving approval, taking turns, initiating and responding to social exchanges, playing games and pursuing activities at recess skillfully, and waiting for a natural break to join peer activities.

If a student is competent in one type of adjustment, it does not necessarily follow that the student is also competent in the other. In our social skills training efforts, we need to clearly separate out those two types of adjustments and ensure that target students are competent in both.

The long-term developmental implications of social competence problems experienced early in the schooling process are devastating to the handicapped and have been recounted in the literature by many scholars. They include low self-esteem, low achievement, school dropout, adoption of a delinquent lifestyle, bad conduct discharges from military services, and extensive mental health problems experienced in adulthood.

The effect of major transitions such as mainstreaming and moving from school to work and independent living has been dramatic in illustrating the social competence problems of the broad range of handicapped students. The students fall through the cracks. They can't meet minimum behavioral requirements, and they often go into a period of shock in attempting to make those adjustments, which incapacitates them even further.

In terms of the general evaluation of children's social competence, their motor skills and language-communication skills are of critical importance and account for as much influence as social skills—or more influence—in the judgments of parents, teachers, and peers about social competence. This is especially true at the preschool level. So, when we are diagnosing social skills deficits, it is important to look beyond social skills and also examine related pre-skills.

In terms of the effectiveness of social skills training intervention procedures, I think that the interventions that have been reported in the literature to date are extremely weak. Social skills interventions give children a vocabulary for describing their own social behavior and that of others more precisely. It teaches them to recognize social cues, but there have been precious few demonstrations that systematic social skills training leads to demonstrations of those skills in natural settings, which in turn leads to perceived changes in the child's social competence.

AREAS OF DIFFERENCE

In terms of differences with the authors of the review paper, there are three areas. One, they are somewhat critical of the use of behavioral observation procedures because of their obtrusiveness and reactivity. I think their view is valid, especially at adolescent levels. But the great bulk of what we know about correlates of social competence are derived from systematic behavioral observation procedures and teacher ratings recorded in natural settings. So, I think it is important to note that observational methodology has been critically important and will continue to be so in the development of social skills knowledge. But I fully acknowledge that the use of sociometric procedures and direct observations with adolescents is extremely problematic.

Second, the unwillingness of teachers in less restrictive settings to teach social skills is a serious problem. We have had enormous difficulties in cracking the academic curriculum in regular schools and getting teachers to see, especially in mainstream settings, that the teaching of social skills is a legitimate and very important activity.

The third issue concerns service delivery. Teachers, I think, will effectively teach social skills that facilitate adjustment to instructional settings; somebody else, however, is going to have to teach social skills that facilitate peer adjustments—school psychologists, counselors, and other professionals working in schools.

RECOMMENDATIONS

I quickly mention some general recommendations relating to social skills. First, I think we need to adopt a social-ecological approach to social skills assessment and training efforts. We also need to adopt a direct instructional approach for the cognitive teaching of key social skills. It is one of the most effective instructional methodologies ever developed, and it currently has only very limited use in social skills curricula.

We also need to provide opportunities in natural settings for the display, rehearsal, monitoring, and reinforcement of cognitively mastered social skills. The generalization problems associated with social skills training efforts are extensive. For our efforts to succeed, we need to solve this problem.

Computer-assisted video capabilities have enormous potential in social skills training. With this technology, we can create social situations, dramatize them, have children respond and make choices, show them the consequences of a choice, and then recycle them through the process.

We need to adopt a competency-correlates approach in empirically identifying critical social skills where we sample a range of forms and a range of effects associated with them. Because of the powerful role that developmental factors play in the acquisition of social competence, I would recommend that in the future, the literature on social skills be broken out in terms of preschool, elementary school, middle school, and high school because the issues are so different across these domains.

We need longitudinal studies, of course, to see how social competence levels change over time and across settings. Also, as Frank Gresham has done, we need to assess social validation preferences of teachers and students across adjustment domains in designing curricula and conducting social skills training.

In some of our work in this area, we have found that teachers and adolescent students agree very strongly about the behavioral requirements of classroom settings. However, the correlations between teacher and peer ratings regarding what's important in peer relationships are only in the neighborhood of 0.2 to 0.3. The correlations between teachers and adolescents' ratings about what is important in self-related adjustment domains, such as being organized, coping with depression, being responsible for your behavior, and so on, are zero.

PART V: HYPERACTIVITY/ ATTENTION DEFICITS

ATTENTION DEFICIT DISORDER: CURRENT PERSPECTIVES

Sally E. Shaywitz

and

Bennett A. Shaywitz

INTRODUCTION

While what we today term attention deficit disorder (ADD) has captured the imagination of investigators and clinicians alike for almost 50 years, an explosion in the number of investigations examining every conceivable facet of ADD has occurred over the past decade. Our primary goal in this report is to provide investigators and interested clinicians with a critical review of selected issues in this rapidly proliferating scientific literature so that they are able to formulate their own sense of what the disorder is about and of how best to approach specific research questions dealing with ADD. It is not our purpose to review every possible issue but rather to be comprehensive, and in some cases, almost compulsively complete in our review of those particular questions that we believe are central to the understanding of any and every aspect of ADD.

In one respect, this review is quite traditional: we begin with an historical perspective, define the disorder, and review the diagnostic assessment and clinical characteristics. We then discuss epidemiology,

ACKNOWLEDGMENTS: We are grateful to our colleagues who so generously provided us with their preprints: Russell Barkley, Ph.D., Jan Loney, Ph.D., William Pelham, Ph.D., and Alan Zametkin, M.D.

Investigations described in this report were supported in part by grants from the National Institute of Neurological and Communicative Disorders and Stroke, United States Office of Education, and National Institute of Child Health and Human Development, Connecticut State Department of Education, and National Institute of Mental Health.

etiology, management, and prognosis. However, while we believe this traditional format will provide a sense of comfort and security for the reader, we have emphasized particular components of this schema in a way that we believe best captures those controversies that form the core of current thinking and research strategies. In particular, we have focused a great deal of attention on issues of definition and syndrome validation, concepts that permeate every aspect of research related to ADD. Theoretical underpinnings of syndrome classification and validation are discussed, and the factors responsible for diagnostic disagreement are examined. We then review those principal, but not necessarily valid, assumptions upon which much of the ADD literature is based, and gently caution against the tendency for both clinicians and investigators to accept such assumptions uncritically, as they do all too often. We emphasize how subjective determinations that can critically affect the outcome of the classification enterprise are made at every step of the research process, such as selection of different criteria for sample identification, use of different scales to measure specific constructs, and use of different sources or different environments. Each may profoundly influence the results of investigations, and often produce conflicting and inconsistent results.

We also respond to those investigators who have questioned the validity of ADD. In particular, we indicate that the belief that syndrome validity requires postdictive validity—that is, a single or common etiology—is at variance with many well-established medical syndromes. Thus, as noted by Weiss, hypertension is certainly well recognized as a syndrome, yet many different etiologies are recognized. Similarly, hydrocephalus may be caused by a wide variety of factors, yet hydrocephalus has been recognized as a definite syndrome for the last 60 to 70 years. Definitional issues include a discussion of current DSM III criteria, and we review recent approaches to their empiric validation, including a diagnostic model for ADD.

Recognizing the needs of investigators for more homogeneous subgroups in ADD, we introduce the concept of uncomplicated ADD and ADD complicated by other conditions. We propose employing the term ADD to represent those children who satisfy diagnostic criteria for ADD but who do not have any other complicating feature such as conduct disorder, affective disorder, or mental retardation. For those children with ADD who have, in addition, one or more of the associated conditions just noted, we propose the term ADD-plus (ADD-P). In this way, the diagnosis would not be too restrictive and yet would allow for the more precise delineation of homogeneous subgroups critical for research purposes. We conclude this detailed definition section with a discussion of ADD with hyperactivity compared to ADD without hyperactivity, the relationship between ADD and learning disabilities (LD), and the problems involved in distinguishing ADD and conduct disorders (CD).

Assessment measures are then discussed, with a particular emphasis on those measures designed to measure ADD constructs. Our intent is to provide clinicians and investigators with the necessary background regarding the strengths and limitations of those measures so that they can knowledgeably select and utilize specific diagnostic instruments. Rating scales provide the focus for this discussion, since they have traditionally been the principal measures used in the evaluation of ADD, and we review specific rating scales including newer rating scales as well as those under development. Other measures (structured interviews, observational methods, direct measures of activity level, specific tests of attention) and their relationship to rating scales are examined as well. Our emphasis, in addition to critically reviewing the particular diagnostic instruments, is to provide the reader with a sense of the relationships between the various measures, or, as is often the case, the relatively poor correlations between measures purporting to examine the same construct. In response to some recommendations that older measures (particularly the Conners scales) be abandoned, we indicate that the acceptance of so radical an approach would tend to cut the results of present investigations off from an entire body of literature. We recommend that despite their shortcomings, it is critical to continue to employ some of these older measures in addition to newer, more methodologically sound instruments. If the present generation of investigators arbitrarily decides to ignore these methods, the relationship between current investigations and previous studies may be difficult, if not impossible, to determine.

Definitional issues pervade every other aspect of our notions of ADD, a fact immediately evident when we begin to review epidemiology, etiology, management, and prognosis. Thus, when we consider the prevalence of ADD, it is obvious that the criteria used to define ADD, assessment measures employed, and decisions regarding cutoff scores will all affect the prevalence rate. Similarly, we indicate how investigations of etiology also depend upon the definition of ADD, and that the conclusions about relationships with pre- and perinatal events or psychosocial factors will be influenced considerably by the definition of ADD employed in that particular study. Similar considerations apply to discussions of treatment and prognosis.

Although we have focused a great deal of attention on definitional issues, this has not been to the exclusion of other traditional (and even some not so traditional) domains. For example, our discussion of treatment examines nonpharmacologic approaches and a wide variety of pharmacologic therapies, and we conclude with a review of nontraditional, controversial, idiosyncratic approaches to therapy. Rather than just considering the latter as ineffective but harmless techniques, we emphasize the possibility of significant adverse effects, both immediate and long-term. In keeping with a traditional format for presentation and before addressing issues of definition and syndrome validation, we begin our review with an historical perspective, tracing the development of the concept of ADD from Still's notions of a defect in moral control, through Strauss' belief in brain damage, to Clements and Peters' appellation of minimal brain dysfunction, and follow this evolution through the DSM III.

HISTORICAL PERSPECTIVE

OVERVIEW

Although the entity we today term ADD has evolved in a fairly circuitous pattern, behavioral manifestations have always been considered to represent the core symptoms of the syndrome. Identification of the entity can be traced to the late nineteenth century with the first descriptions of behavioral disorders occurring as sequelae of an insult to the brain. When such symptoms as inattention, hyperactivity, and poor impulse control followed a head injury or a central nervous system infection, the etiology seemed obvious, and thus it is not surprising that both medical and lay opinion alike would refer to such sequelae as *brain damage*. With time, the behavioral manifestations that were considered to be specifically the result of brain damage came to be observed in children who had no history of such an insult. In order to account for this result within the popular theory of that era, the damage to the central nervous system was considered so minimal that its only manifestations were the behavioral syndrome, hence the notion of *minimal brain damage*. By the early 1960's the behavioral syndrome associated with brain damage (or minimal brain damage) and the frequently associated occurrence of learning disability were arbitrarily linked together under the rubric of *minimal brain dysfuction* (MBD), an entity that emerged within the psychiatric literature but was rapidly adopted by other disciplines. The effort to clarify MBD necessitated the disentangling of the behavioral syndrome from those cognitive aspects best considered within the domain of learning disability. Early approaches focused on the hyperactivity component of the syndrome, and the literature of the 1960's and 1970's refers to such children as exhibiting the *hyperactive child syndrome*. Our current terminology, attention deficit disorder, emphasizes the primacy of attentional dysfunction as the principal behavioral manifestation of the syndrome. In the following paragraphs, we detail the evolution of this concept.

CONCEPT OF BRAIN DAMAGE

By the beginning of this century, descriptions of the difficulties experienced by children—difficulties which are similar to what we know today as attention deficit disorder with hyperactivity (ADDH)—began to appear in the medical literature. In a remarkably prescient report, Still (1902) described children with what he termed "morbid defects in moral control."

While Still's descriptions are remarkable for their similarity to current diagnostic criteria (see below), his notions of etiology remained poorly defined. However, in that same era, other physicians were linking the description of similar behaviors to traumatic brain injury (Meyer, 1904; Goldstein, 1936), to the sequelae of von Economo's encephalitis (Hohman, 1922), or to a variety of other childhood central nervous system infections (Bender, 1942).

Perhaps the most influential and enduring support for the notion of a specific behavioral syndrome in children arising from brain damage was that provided by the work of Strauss and his associates, who in a series of reports in the 1930's and 1940's formulated the conceptual entity of the "brain-injured [damaged] child." (Werner and Strauss, 1941; Strauss and Lehtinen, 1947).

Surveying a population of mentally defective, institutionalized children and using the history or neurologic examination as support for a diagnosis of brain damage, Strauss classified children into two groups: an exogenous group in whom the neurologic examination or history was thought to provide evidence for cerebral insult, and an endogenous group for whom such information was lacking. Despite much overlap in the cognitive and emotional styles of the groups, there appeared to be an excess of hyperactive, distractable, impulsive, emotionally labile, and perseverative behaviors in the group termed exogenous or brain damaged. These vaguely defined behavioral traits based upon nonvalidated indicators of brain injury were now, in and of themselves, to be considered as indicators of brain injury or damage. Thus, according to Strauss (Strauss and Lehtinen, 1947), "all brain lesions, wherever localized, are followed by a similar kind of disordered behavior."

His theories captured the attention of many physicians and educators, and his influence persisted into the 1960's. Often forgetting or unaware of the tenuous foundation that served as the rationale for diagnosing brain damage, investigators embraced the concept of the brain-damaged child both as a research tool and a diagnostic category.

CONCEPT OF BRAIN DYSFUNCTION

By the 1950's, the behavioral consequences of learning disorders had come to dominate the educational literature of that era. At the same time, the pediatric and psychiatric medical literature was preoccupied with the behavioral disturbances seen in what today we recognize as ADD. Embedded within and often the major undercurrent of publications in that era was the decades-old struggle between those who emphasized biological causes and somatic treatments of behavioral disorders (the classic Krapelanian view adopted by most neurologists) and the belief that an understanding of the mechanisms of intrapsychic conflict could best explain the origins of behavioral disorders as well as provide the most effective means of therapy (the view promulgated by Freud and his followers and shared by the overwhelming majority of psychiatrists; see Valenstein, 1986). This conflict was now joined in a pediatric arena. On one side were arrayed an educational and pediatric community that was influenced to a considerable degree by a powerful psychiatric establishment, which emphasized the psychodynamic interpretations of behaviors almost to the exclusion of other factors. The contrasting perspective was embodied by those who believed in a primarily "neurologic" explanation of behavior, a view embraced by neurologists, child neurologists, and some psychiatrists and psychologists.

Given the predisposition of the majority of psychiatrists of that era to interpret all behaviors within a psychodynamic framework, totally ignoring or minimizing the influence of biological factors, it was not unexpected that reaction to this exclusively psychodynamic view would develop. What was surprising was not only that this reaction developed in the pediatric and educational literature but also that the psychiatric community itself provided the most impetus for change, a change toward a more neurologically based explanation for behavioral disorders. Thus the entity, hyperkinetic behavior disorder, was promulgated in the pediatric literature by Maurice Laufer (a child psychiatrist) and Eric Denhoff (a behavioral pediatrician) (Laufer and Denhoff, 1957).

Laufer and Denhoff argued that underlying the hyperkinetic syndrome was "injury to or dysfunction of the diencephalon." This concept presaged that of minimal brain dysfunction by noting that many of the same factors that produce the hyperkinetic syndrome, if not limited specifically to the diencephalon, could also go on to involve other anatomic areas and produce cerebral palsy, mental retardation, blindness, or deafness. With this belief in brain injury as the etiology of the syndrome came a clinical approach that focused on elucidating the nature of the injury; thus the authors suggested questioning the parents for such indications of cerebral insult as "high forceps delivery or severe pertussis in infancy."

Even more influential, however, were Clements and Peters (1962), who elaborated the notion of *minimal brain dysfunctions*. Their seminal paper, appearing in the *Archives of General Psychiatry* in 1962, introduced the notion of the special neurologic examination or examination for soft signs as indicators of organic brain damage. While not negating the psychodynamic interpretation, the authors urged a more balanced view that would recognize the multifactorial origin of these behavioral and learning problems. Building on the work of Strauss and of Kennard (1960) who "accepted the 'equivocal' Babinski and other signs as having the value of true neurological manifestations," Clements and Peters introduced the belief that the demonstration of abnormalities on neurologic examination, however minor, was an important indicator of the syndrome. In their view, minimal brain dysfunctions could be inferred from the presence of a cluster of symptoms, including specific learning deficits, hyperkinesis, impulsivity, and short attention span, and confirmed by findings on examination of "equivocal" neurological signs and borderline abnormal or abnormal EEG.

The term minimal brain dysfunctions was appealing to many workers in the field, often for quite different reasons. To Clements and Peters, it was an approach that would allow psychiatrists and psychologists to detect organicity or brain damage of a subtle nature. Thus, their formulation of minimal brain dysfunctions was a response to the tendency to overlook possible organic or neurologic causes of behavioral syndromes. From a somewhat different perspective, the notion of minimal brain dysfunctions appeared attractive to many investigators and clinicians who were becoming increasingly uncomfortable with the assumption that structural brain damage could be inferred on the basis of behavioral symtomatology alone. Thus, by 1962, both the Oxford International Study Group on Child Neurology (Bax and MacKeith, 1963) as well as an NIH Task Force (headed by Clements and Peters) had recommended that the term "minimal brain damage" be discarded and replaced by "minimal brain dysfunction (MBD)."

At the time, the notion of MBD was viewed as a real advance in incorporating the diverse manifestations thought to reflect the syndrome while not emphasizing a particular interpretation of the nature of the brain insult. However, this loose conglomeration of behavioral and learning symptomatology created confusion as well. Almost immediately, there developed a schism in the way the medical and the educational communities viewed the disorder. The medical literature accepted the term minimal brain dysfunction and incorporated the entity into a medical model. In contrast, the educational literature focused more on the findings of a learning difficulty and preferred to describe affected children as having a specific learning disability.

This concatenation of behavioral symptomatology with supposed indicators of brain injury beginning with Strauss' notion of brain damage and evolving to minimal brain damage and then to minimal brain dysfunction has generated a great deal of confusion and controversy. These successive rubrics became laden with multiple meanings, sometimes referring to the behavioral syndrome described by Strauss, and, in other instances, held to be indicative of certain cognitive traits, motor atypicalities, or a combination of behavioral, cognitive, and motor disturbances. As we discuss later, the relationship of specific behavioral or learning difficulties to subtle neurologic findings and, in turn, the relationship of these findings to brain dysfunction continue to be controversial. Curiously, the search for "soft" neurological signs has proven more attractive for psychiatrists than for neurologists or behavioral pediatricians, with many more papers on the subject appearing in the psychiatric than in the pediatric or neurologic literature.

The frequent appellations of "organicity" employed by many present-day psychologists and psychiatrists can be traced to this notion, which certainly had the salutary effects of focusing attention on suspected biological etiologies of a behavioral syndrome and allowing biological psychiatrists influence within their discipline.

CURRENT CONCEPTS

With time, it became increasingly apparent that the concept of MBD was seriously flawed and, in an operational sense, unworkable. Thus, the amalgamation of both the learning disability and the behavioral disorder within the diagnosis of MBD served only to compound the already existing confusion. Perhaps an even more serious criticism of the notion of MBD was the absence of any rigorous diagnostic criteria for MBD itself. In no small measure, this deficiency was a reflection of the lack of progress in the classification (or nosology) of behavioral disorders in general. Strategies for the elaboration of scientifically valid classification schemas would begin to emerge only in the 1970's, as exemplified by the work of Feighner and his colleagues (1972) on diagnostic criteria for affective disorder and schizophrenia. Such studies mandated specific inclusion and exclusion criteria that could be operationalized within the framework of both research studies and clinical practice. Their approach spread rapidly within the psychiatric community and resulted in the elaboration of research diagnostic criteria (RDC), presented rather superficially in an early Diagnostic and Statistical Manual of the American Psychiatric Association (DSM II) and elaborated in more detail in DSM III. Current approaches employing such methodology are described below.

DEFINITION AND SYNDROME VALIDATION

BACKGROUND

How is attention deficit disorder recognized? Even more importantly, is ADD a real entity? Such questions, which relate to definition and syndrome validation, have long troubled investigators and must be addressed before any other issue in research on ADD. This problem was recognized by Ross and Pelham (1981), who noted: "Most of the major questions regarding etiology, nature, treatment, and prognosis of childhood psychological disorders remain unanswered. Foremost among these are difficulties in classifying childhood disorders." This was echoed by Achenbach and Edelbrock (1984), who in their review chose to "focus on certain general problems that hinder our understanding of specific disorders." The chief problem—Ross and Pelham's "foremost difficulty"—is classifying childhood disorders.

The evolution of our notions of classification in childhood neurobehavioral disorders has been well described by Quay (1979). He notes (after Lorr, 1961) that two competing points of view are recognized: (a) the class model, where disorders are viewed as present or absent and disorders are mutually exclusive—a view held by many British investigators, and (b) the quantitative model, where disorders are viewed as a group of symptoms forming a domain and the number of symptoms present provides a measure of intensity. Quay indicates that the rationale for any classification system lies in its ability to permit useful assumptions to be made based on the child's membership in that category (or domain).

Cantwell (1980) agrees with Rutter (1977) that there is no right or natural way to classify neurobehavioral disorders of childhood. Given this inability to discover any natural system, the investigator must by necessity impose his own schema. Fortunately, thoughtful investigators have begun to address these issues seriously. Awareness not only of the existence of systematic approaches to the classsification process but also of the rationale for their development will provide a context to consider the definition and validity of ADD. Thus, Blashfield and Draguns (1976) have provided a general outline and rationale for classification of neurobehavioral disorders. They emphasize the purposes of a classification system: (a) provide communication between workers; (b) retrieve information; (c) generate scientific concepts. They first introduce the notion of a taxonomy, the theoretical structure of the classification. Classification represents the process of forming groups from a large set of entities (in this case, children with neurobehavioral disorders). The classification system represents the product of the classification process, a defined set of entities. The classification system is composed of entities being classified (patients), categories or domains (e.g., ADD, schizophrenia, affective disorder, normal), and a hierarchical set of categories. This approach incorporates intensional definitions—the symptoms the patient must have to be included in the category. Identification is the term used to represent assigning the entities to a category (or domain) and is equivalent to diagnosis. Four criteria are proposed as critical to any classification process: reliability, coverage, descriptive validity, and predictive validity. Each of these components is described below.

(a) Reliability refers to both the variability of the classification system from user to user as well as the variability of those characteristics used to assign a diagnosis. The major source of variance is disagreement among diagnosticians. Factors that contribute to this inter-diagnostician variation in agreement include:

1. Specificity of intensional definition. This is what Spitzer and Williams (1980) refer to as criterion variance, and represents the source of two-thirds of diagnostic disagreement (Ward et al., 1962). This represents the different criteria that clinicians use to make a diagnosis. For example, some clinicians might

diagnose ADD on the presence of attentional difficulties, impulsivity, and conduct disorder (CD). Other clinicians, given this same constellation of symptoms might diagnose both ADD and CD, while still others might diagnose only CD and ignore ADD.

2. Training of diagnosticians. Spitzer and Williams (1980) refer to this as observer and interpretation variance. Thus, different clinicians, even though they obtain the same information and make the same observations, differ in what they remember and how they interpret what they see and hear.
3. Amount of information or information variance. Here, differing clinicians obtain different types of information.
4. Intradiagnostician consistency. Reliability can be measured quantitatively using Cohen's Kappa, which corrects the percentage of agreement between observers for the base rates of the categories considered.

(b) Coverage designates the applicability of the classification schema for the domain of patients considered.

(c) Descriptive validity refers to the degree of homogeneity of the category of behaviors, symptoms, personality characteristics, and social history comprising all the other information used in arriving at a diagnosis. According to Blashfield and Draguns (1976), there are two major problems that need to be addressed when considering descriptive validity. The first is recognizing the limitations of defining the characteristics that are to be considered. Thus, the possible domains are (1) only those characteristics employed in what we have termed the intensional definition, and (2) all possible characteristics. The second major difficulty involves defining what is meant by the term homogeneity and deciding upon a statistical measure of the concept. Blasfield and Draguns suggested Wilk's Lambda, though other measures are applicable as well.

(d) Predictive validity. More will be said of this shortly. Here, such a measure as response to therapy is considered as a characteristic to validate the diagnosis. In a sense, this measure parallels that of construct validity, except that the construct involves homogeneity of a therapeutic response measured over time rather than a measure determined at the same time as diagnosis.

More recently, investigators have elaborated upon the schema outlined by Blashfield and Draguns to provide not only a more detailed theoretical strategy but also one that can be operationalized within current research paradigms. Thus, Skinner (1981) and Fletcher (1985) have both detailed integrated classification methodologies applicable to neurobehavioral disorders in children. In Skinner's three-stage classification paradigm, classification proceeds from theory formulation, to internal validation, and finally, to external validation. By theory formulation, Skinner means the precise definition of typal constructs, the specification of the purpose of the classification (etiological *vs.*

descriptive), and the formulation of the hypothesized linkages between types. In this component, the investigator needs to decide on the content domain of the classification schema—that is, the variables to be employed in the classification. Measures such as behavioral observations obtained via rating scales and results of psychometric testing are the kinds of variables that have been employed in research on ADD and related disorders. Other possibilities include natural history of the disorder or response to treatment. Theory formulation is also useful in hypothesizing a relationship between the groups postulated and particular external variables. For example, the direction of group differences on such variables as outcome, cognitive skills, or other variables not used to develop the typology would provide external validation of the classification. Theory formulation must proceed within the context of hypothesis-driven research. The only appropriate hypothesis is the null hypothesis—no groups exist.

The systematic approach to validation such as that described above provides a context both to evaluate and to plan for future studies of the validity of ADD. It is critically important for investigators and clinicians alike to be aware that validation of an entity such as ADD can be considered from such a rational and orderly perspective. Of particular interest is an influential report by Cantwell (1983) in which he reviews the steps in the process of validating any neurobehavioral syndrome, but with particular emphasis on ADD. As will be evident, this process described for ADD is consistent with the overall approaches just described.

As detailed by Cantwell (1983), the first step is the establishment of face validity—that is, a consensus among a group of experts regarding what the essential clinical features of a particular syndrome are. The second step, descriptive validity, describes the extent to which the essential clinical features are unique to the disorder, as opposed to their occurrence in other conditions or in normals. Predictive validity, the next step in the process, represents the extent to which knowledge that an individual has a particular disorder is useful in predicting some aspect about the future, such as the natural history, complications, or response to therapeutic interventions. Construct validity refers to the extent that evidence supporting a particular theory explains the etiology or pathophysiology; that is, it helps us to understand family-genetic, social-environmental, or biological factors. At the outset, it should be recognized that these are all relatively recent formulations and that to date, there have not been any investigations of ADD that conform to each of these steps in the validation process. However, awareness of these validation strategies provides a background within which to consider the work to date relevant to the validation of ADD.

ISSUES IN SYNDROME VALIDATION

At this juncture, it is appropriate to consider the process of syndrome validation in a more molecular fashion, particularly as it applies to ADD. The methodology of syndrome identification is inextricably joined with the tools used in the process of syndrome validation. In a sense, criticism of the validity of ADD as a syndrome has tended to overlook both the methods and the measures used in arriving at a diagnosis of ADD. It should be noted that there is a validation procedure not only for the classification of a disorder itself but also for the measures used in the classification process—in this instance, primarily behavior rating scales. Such measures must be reliable and valid. As we describe below, this unfortunately has not been the case in a large proportion of studies examining ADD, and as a result, the interpretation of some of these findings is questionable. Interpretation of these studies has often proceeded as if the written word was inviolate, when in reality, the admonition given to Alice in *Through the Looking Glass* that things are not always what they seem would have been more appropriate. Both instruments and the actual studies themselves have been accepted without the healthy skepticism that should accompany scientific inquiry.

INSTRUMENT DEVELOPMENT

Just as there is a process for syndrome validation, there are also procedures for instrument development. These generally involve first specifying the purpose of the instrument and then through both a critical review of the literature and the expert opinion of a group of judges, a set of items is selected as the original item pool. Through empiric methods such as factor analysis, the list of items is refined and ordered into scales representing particular factors or constructs. These factors are then labeled or named, and a series of investigations are undertaken to determine if these factors or scales are reliable—that is, if the items are related to other items on the scale (internal consistency) and if the findings can be replicated over time and across examiners. If a scale is not reliable, it cannot be valid. Validity is a critical factor because it is a measure of whether the instrument, as comprised of a group of scales, actually does what it purports to do. There are, as indicated above, several different kinds of validity, and validity is an ongoing process.

In evaluating the validity of a syndrome, the nature of the instruments used and the criteria against which it is measured can greatly affect the results of the outcome. In a sense, this can lead to circular reasoning; if an inadequately developed instrument or an inappropriate criterion is used as a measure, the results of the investigation will be uninterpretable. Unreliable or invalid instruments define groups that have these same shortcomings or fail to identify groups that may represent the true construct. It is important to note that for the most part, there has been no classification study that has proceeded anteroprospectively, with specific tools or instruments designed and developed to assess ADD and with populations in whom ADD was diagnosed by DSM III standards.

It is often not appreciated that at every step in the process of instrument development a judgment must be made; the results of these series of decisions can drastically affect the resulting instrument. Thus, the initial items selected for the item pool, the exact procedures used in factor analysis, and criteria for item retention and interpretation of retained factors, including especially the subsequently attached names or labels, are each subject to the investigator's judgment and particular perspective and/or biases, and hence, are not invariable. Not only will variability, if not lack of validity, be introduced as a result of judgments made by the investigator, but also the procedures themselves may be influenced by particular features of the study design. For example, the sample characteristics and nature of the informant (parent or teacher), and whether one or two sources are used to complete the ratings, may influence the number and nature of factors that emerge from a factor analysis (Loney, 1986).

With this brief description of the sensitivity of scale construction to multiple influences as a background, let us consider how awareness of these and other factors may affect the interpretation of syndrome validity as it applies to ADD. The question is not so much: Does there exist a group of children who have difficulties with concentration, impulsivity, and excess activity? But rather: Can this group of children be reliably and meaningfully differentiated from children who have other symptoms that make up what is termed the external dimension of behavioral disorders? Does ADD as defined by DSM III represent a valid classification category? Since there has not been a single classification study designed to conform to the procedures enumerated earlier, attempts to determine syndrome validity have, by necessity, been retrospective and utilized instruments or findings that have often antedated current DSM III concepts of ADD. Therefore, the relationship of the conclusions reached to the validity of ADD as a diagnostic entity is unclear. Loney and her collaborators have made significant contributions to the clarification of this issue, and we refer the reader to Loney's chapters (1983; 1986 in press) for detailed discussions of these issues.

NOT NECESSARILY VALID ASSUMPTIONS

In this section, we review some of the assumptions that have been made in discussions of the validity of ADD and how, in some instances, conclusions reached may have reflected erroneous assumptions.

(1) Samples diagnosed "according to DSM III criteria" represent relatively homogeneous groups that are comparable from study to study. While DSM III provides the category of ADD and the dimensions or symptoms that must be present for diagnosis, operational criteria that would permit the reliable determination of the presence

of each of the symptoms comprising the constructs of inattention, impulsivity, and hyperactivity are not provided for in DSM III. This means that each clinician or investigator makes his own interpretation of how to operationalize DSM III criteria. Approaches have varied from those based on an informal history or chart review, to use of specific scales on already existing instruments that preceded the current terminology, to use of scales consisting of a series of items reflecting those in DSM III. Even in the last example, uncertainty and variability exist: Are the items scored dichotomously or on a Likert-like scale; and if so, does the scale have demonstrated reliability? (We discuss the issue of validity of DSM III criteria below.)

(2) Scales labeled as hyperactivity or inattention accurately reflect those constructs as enumerated in DSM III. The most widely used instruments in studies of ADD are the series of parent/teacher rating scales developed by Conners. (The specific details of this and other instruments used in ADD research are discussed below in "Assessment Measures.") These instruments were developed primarily for use in drug studies, and most importantly, at a time when the externalizing disorders were conceptualized in a more global sense. Concern was centered on the hyperkinetic syndrome; and symptoms of aggressive, hyperactive, and inattentive behaviors were all represented on, for example, the 10-item short form, sometimes termed the Hyperkinesis Index (Goyette et al., 1978). Furthermore, original item pools were not constructed to lead to a diagnosis of ADD, and often the items that were correlated on a factor analysis had only some loose resemblance to current notions of the label that was attached to that particular scale. For example, many studies have used the hyperactivity factor or the inattention-passive factor of the 38-item Conners Teacher Rating Scale (Goyette et al., 1978), assuming that the items on these factors paralleled those indicated in DSM III. This hyperactivity factor, in addition to items corresponding to DSM III symptoms, also contains the following items: "disturbs other children"; "excitable, impulsive"; "makes inappropriate noises when he shouldn't"; "demands must be met immediately"; and "excessive demands for teacher's attention." These items are not entirely congruent with the construct of hyperactivity as it appears in DSM III. The inattention-passive factor contains items such as: "appears to be easily led by other children," "appears to lack leadership," "childish and immature," and "easily frustrated in efforts." These items clearly do not reflect the DSM III construct. Thus, samples identified on the basis of these Conners scales would not really be consistent with DSM III criteria and would represent groups heterogeneous for attentional, activity, and aggressive features. It is critical that investigators not rely on scale labels, but that they look at the actual item content before assuming that a scale has even face validity.

In the remaining examples, we focus on the symptoms of hyperactivity and aggressivity as representing the disorders of ADD and conduct disorder, respectively. Although the concern is the distinctiveness of the ADD syndrome in relation to conduct disorder, much of the relevant research has been conducted by Loney and her associates, who employed hyperactivity and aggression factors to represent ADD and conduct disorder syndromes. Therefore, in the ensuing paragraphs, syndrome validation refers to validation of hyperactivity rather than of ADD.

(3) If a syndrome is valid, a distinct single factor will emerge from factor analysis to represent that construct. However, as Loney (1986) indicates, there are a variety of methodological influences—influences separate from the syndrome validity issue—that can affect the number and the kind of factors that emerge. Failure of a distinct factor to emerge may reflect variations due to situational or source variance. Thus, hyperactive children will behave differently in one type of a setting than in another, and scores on the various items comprising a factor will reflect this. Furthermore, if the information is collected from a single source, the intercorrelations are more likely to be high and, in turn, to suggest a single factor. In addition, Langhorne et al. (1976) have shown that symptoms tend to group together by source rather than by construct. This is a reflection of hyperactive children's tending to behave differently in home and school settings.

(4) The interpretation of correlations between two dimensions is clearcut; that is, the dimensions are correlated or they are not. In reality, the dimensions of interest are not perfectly correlated, nor are they entirely uncorrelated; rather they are partially correlated—necessitating a judgment decision to be made as to what constitutes a relationship and what constitutes a nonrelationship. Loney (1986, in press) notes that source can also influence the strength of correlations between different measures; for example, teacher ratings tend to be much more highly correlated than parent measures. Sample differences, too, can influence intercorrelations between measures. Thus, some studies have found correlations between direct observation measures and hyperactivity factor ratings (Milich, Loney, and Landau, 1982), while others (Plomin and Foch, 1981; Barkley and Ullman, 1975) have not demonstrated such a relationship. These apparent discrepant findings may reflect sample differences since the Milich study sample was selected on the basis of a relatively pure hyperactivity factor, while the other studies relied on rather vague criteria denoting boys referred for evaluation of hyperactivity (Plomin and Foch, 1981) or boys said to be hyperactive by their pediatrician. The heterogeneous nature of the latter samples may have precluded significant relationships from emerging between the so-called hyperactivity factor and the observation.

Loney cautions that limitations of the instruments used not be confused with limitations of the disorder: "To what extent does the association between hyperactivity and aggression lie in our minds, in our measures and methods, and in the actual behavior of children?" (Loney, 1986, in press). The answer to this provocative question is not yet known, but at least we should be humble and aware enough to appreciate that there is a question.

(5) The children comprising the clinic samples as they appear in the literature are representative of children with the disorder and particularly of children referred for professional consultation. The transformation of the hyperkinetic disorder to an attention deficit disorder may have had farther reaching implications for the character of the current disorder than is generally appreciated. The hyperkinetic disorder as it was defined in DSM II referred mainly to a behavioral disorder in which a short attention span was not the major focus. Such children whose externalizing behaviors were not tolerated or tolerable were generally referred to psychiatrists. Many of the children referred to psychiatrists today for evaluation of possible ADD have many of these same symptoms, but by definition, they will have to manifest an attentional deficit, whether or not there is accompanying hyperactivity. However, those children now referred for assessment because of poor school work or learning difficulties rather than primarily for behavioral problems may not be triaged to psychiatrists but instead referred to other professionals such as pediatricians and child neurologists. While these professionals have had long-standing interests in hyperkinetic children, the perspective most represented in the literature on hyperkinesis has been that of the psychiatrist, the professional most likely to be referred to for children with serious externalizing disorders.

The pre-DSM III literature, therefore, may reflect children whose characteristics do not necessarily reflect the characteristics of the children currently diagnosed as ADD. However, it is also important to be aware that the children currently written about and described in the literature may not represent either all children with ADD or all children referred for consultation. Even today, the literature primarily reflects children referred to mental health clinics for assessment, who may have very serious and complex behavioral disturbances of which hyperactivity is only one component. Rather than represent children with ADD or all children referred to clinics with ADD, those evaluated in mental health settings may reflect the "tip of the iceberg" and not the entire spectrum of ADD. Therefore, the findings of the association of hyperactivity with aggressive behavior may only represent a small, severely involved subset of children with ADD. Thus, in large measure, the children with ADD reported in the literature comprise a group diagnosed and treated primarily by psychiatrists, and cannot be assumed to represent the entire universe of children with ADD.

That selective referral patterns may result in a biased sample evaluated in mental health settings is illustrated by comparing symptom presentations in clinic (mental health) and school-based samples. Loney and Milich (1982) have reported that between 63 percent and 71 percent of the children in a clinic sample displayed both aggressive and hyperactive symptoms, contrasted with 18 percent in a classroom control sample for whom teachers completed the same instrument. Further support for the selectivity of referral rates to mental health clinics favoring the most severely involved children is provided by epidemiological studies (McGee, Williams, and Silva, 1984) in which three groups of children were identified by parent and teacher ratings: hyperactive only, aggressive only, and hyperactive-aggressive. Severity of the disorder followed a progression of no problem, hyperactivity, aggression, and in the most severe cases, hyperactivity and aggression. Referral rates paralleled severity, so that for the most severely impaired boys (the mixed hyperactive-aggressive group), the referral rate was six times that for the other two groups. Moreover, the boys with both hyperactivity and aggression demonstrated more associated problems, including poorer cognitive skills. Thus, there is now very good empiric evidence to indicate that the children who are referred to mental health clinics represent the extreme of the continuum of children with ADD and as such are not representative of all children with ADD. The clear implication is that these children should not be regarded as prototypal ADD children and that generalizations made from studies of these complex, severely involved patients may not be appropriate. The range of children with ADD may best be appreciated by consideration not only of children with hyperactivity and, at times, aggression who are referred for behavioral reasons to psychiatrists but also of children with primary attentional deficits and associated learning problems who may be seen by child neurologists or pediatricians. What is needed is a multidisciplinary study including these disciplines with the addition of psychology, which may bridge both psychiatry and neurology in terms of the kinds of children referred. Such a study performed on a representative sample would provide a panoramic view of the entire range of severity and symptoms encompassed by the diagnosis of ADD.

(6) Children with ADD will be hyperactive in all situations; that is, they will demonstrate "pervasive" hyperactivity or else they should not be eligible for a diagnosis of ADD. Following the same line of reasoning just enumerated, children with pervasive hyperactivity are likely to represent those who have a more severe form of the disorder and who may not be representative of the population of children with ADD. Schachar and associates (1981) have shown that pervasively hyperactive boys are more likely to demonstrate cognitive impairment, general behavioral disturbance, and poorer prognosis than are situationally hyperactive boys. This is another indication that they represent a more severe and perhaps more globally impaired group. It may be that rather than situationally hyperactive children not warranting the diagnosis of ADD, pervasively hyperactive children represent a contaminated group that has a variety of problems in addition to their ADD. More likely, the pervasively active group represents an extreme that should be balanced with less severely affected, perhaps ADDnoH children in studies examining the characteristics of ADD children. Samples biased in the direction of these multiply involved children may provide a very misleading portrait of the ADD child. Only an epidemiological study can provide information as to how representative the pervasively and situationally hyperactive children are of all ADD children.

The view that posits variability in behavior of hyperactive children gains further support from studies examining the social behavior of these children (Barkley, 1985). Although hyperactive children tend to exhibit problematic behavior more often than nonhyperactives, this behavior varies greatly from situation to situation, and even within situations. Thus, situations in which more controlled or restrained behavior is required will enhance the emergence of symptoms of hyperactivity. In contrast, hyperactive and nonhyperactive controls may not be distinguishable in periods of free play during recess periods. Barkley (1985) summarizes these findings: "This is contrary to a belief implicit in clinical lore that hyperactive children misbehave everywhere, for if they do not they may not be hyperactive at all. Our research suggests that situational variation is a rather common finding with hyperactive children and should not, by itself, rule out the diagnosis in these children" (p. 40).

(7) More homogeneous study groups of ADD children may be identified by raising the cutoff scores to select smaller groups of children or by requiring evidence from multiple sources before diagnosing ADD. This premise has both theoretic and practical shortcomings. Since there is evidence that the emergence of ADD is influenced by interactions between the child's biologic substrate and his environment, children who have the highest levels of hyperactivity may also be those who have the least goodness of fit with their environment. Either their genetic loading for hyperactivity is great, their ability to modify their behavior is impaired because of associated deficits, or their environment is not salutary. In many cases, several or all of the above are true. The result is that children who represent the most extreme scores of hyperactivity or who meet multiple criteria for hyperactivity may also be the ones who are not only more hyperactive but are also more globally impaired, including more severe overall psychopathology as well (Loney, 1986 in press).

IMPLICATIONS

Research itself is a living, constantly changing, interactional process in which tensions between apparently contradictory phenomenon are constantly being resolved or intensified, reshaping our notions of reality as it applies both to normal and to abnormal states. Out of this process evolves an ever-expanding network of relationships that, when validated, become part of the accepted "heritage" of specific disorders. Once these relationships are accepted into the heritage or literature belonging to a disorder, they are rarely questioned again, and are used as a basis to test new hypotheses and to explore new relationships. However, as our concepts of particular disorders evolve, previously held assumptions may no longer be valid, but nevertheless they may persist. The danger is that if outmoded notions or measures based on them continue to be actively used in the testing of new concepts, the concepts rather than the measures may be discarded as not valid.

In the preceding paragraphs we have reviewed some of the assumptions upon which much of the ADD literature is both based and critiqued. The continued use of scales developed to reflect more global behavioral disturbances, but labeled with the same terminology as current quite specific behavioral constructs, is a flagrant example of such a methodological lag. Perhaps of more concern is the tendency for both clinicians and investigators to accept uncritically the kinds of assumptions we have detailed. It must be recognized that subjective determinations that can critically affect the outcome of the enterprise are made at every step of the research process, including definition and identification of study samples and selection of measures. Each of these components of the research process has many variations—variations that are not necessarily interchangeable—so that selection of different criteria for sample identification, different scales to measure specific constructs, and different sources or different environments from which to obtain the data may each profoundly influence the results of the investigation.

As a result of the acceptance of faulty assumptions surrounding sample selection, measures, and methods used in ADD studies, such studies have produced often conflicting and inconsistent results. The results of these studies have then been used as arguments against the validity of the ADD syndrome. Syndrome validation as it has been addressed in the ADD literature relates to the distinctiveness of the hyperactivity factor and the demonstration of construct, descriptive, and predictive validity, each of which is dependent on selection of appropriate samples, measures, and methods. Below, we discuss specific issues raised concerning the validity of ADD and indicate how, in some cases, faulty assumptions were responsible for findings interpreted as contrary to the notion of ADD as a valid syndrome.

OTHER POINTS OF VIEW

The great majority of investigators in the field now accept the validity of the concept of ADD. However, other points of view should be recognized. Below, we present points of view contrary to those accepting the validity of ADD as a syndrome. (The preceding discussion should provide a context within which to consider these arguments.) In addition, we present specific responses of other senior investigators, some of which may complement or reinforce the previous discussion.

Shaffer and Greenhill (1979) and Shaffer (1980), adopting Kraepelinian criteria, question the value of the concept of ADD. They argue that the disorder lacks indication of validity—specifically, postdictive validity (no common etiology), concurrent validity (the term tells little about the child's current state and does not allow differentiation from children with other disorders or normals), and predictive validity (outcomes differ widely).

Postdictive validity has also been addressed by Rapoport and Ferguson (1981), who comment that hyperactivity appears to represent a final common pathway of a variety of antecedents. In a retrospective analysis of over 200 primary school boys identified by parent and teacher questionnaires, Sandberg et al. (1980) examined the influence of biological and psychosocial parameters on hyperactivity and CD. Although both were associated with maternal mental distress, the two disorders could not be distinguished on etiological grounds. In the Dunedin multidisciplinary developmental study (McGee et al., 1984), biological etiologies did not separate HA, HA-aggression, and pure aggression in boys; psychosocial factors, however, were helpful, with aggressive boys exhibiting more parental separation and represented by more solo parents.

The belief that syndrome validity requires postdictive validity (that is, a single or common etiology) is at variance with many well established medical syndromes. As Weiss (1985) notes, such classical syndromes as hypertension do not have postdictive validity, but rather seem to result from a variety of interacting antecedent variables or etiologies. Certainly, in pediatrics and neurology, hydrocephalus is a relatively specific syndromic entity, yet it may result from a great variety of neuropathological processes.

Weiss also addresses Shaffer's concerns regarding concurrent validity, and suggests that it is possible to predict a child's clinical state by symptoms other than those that constitute the diagnosis. Thus, if a child is diagnosed as HA, the child is more likely to exhibit concommitant cognitive deficits with lower IQ, reading retardation, neurodevelopmental signs, and symptoms that endure. Regarding predictive validity, Weiss is more impressed by the similarity of results from widely different kinds of studies than in what she views as minor discrepancies in outcome. Thus, as detailed later (see "Prognosis"), most investigators agree on fundamental outcome issues, suggesting that there exists a relatively high degree of predictive validity for ADD.

Perhaps the most influential criticism of the validity of ADD was that detailed by Rutter (1982). We summarize his concerns and the evidence refuting each below.

(1) Parents, teachers, and clinicians lack agreement as to who is hyperactive. Weiss (1985) notes that this low level of agreement among teachers, parents, and clinicians as to which child is HA could have two possible explanations: (a) the observers have poor interobserver reliability; (b) the symptoms of HA may be situational.

Parenthetically, this issue of pervasive compared to situational HA has continued to plague investigators since 1968 when Werry (1968) defined HA as a problem in all social situations, both at school and at home. He suggested that if HA were present in only one situation, then it was most likely to be reactive to that situation and less likely to be true HA. Interestingly, if only pervasively HA children are studied, then better correlations are found between parent and teacher observations. It is also evident that ratings of children by physicians in the office setting may be quite different from those observed in school or at home. In the office setting, the child is usually alone with either the physician or a physician and a nurse in contrast to a classroom setting of perhaps 30 children and a single adult.

In addition, inherent in physician observations are some very obvious discipline-specific biases, both referral and diagnostic in nature. It is possible, for example, that the psychiatrist is more likely to diagnose a conduct disorder along with HA than is the pediatrician or child neurologist. Indeed, it might be argued (see above) that one of the hallmarks of the disorder is its variability, particularly in different situations. That a child might sit calmly in a quiet setting with one other person and yet fidget and squirm in a loud and noisy environment does not argue against, but rather may be suggestive that there is a disorder present. Such a variability in expression has been noted for other neurobehavioral disorders as well—for example, Tourette's disorder (Cohen et al., 1984).

(2) Different prevalence rates (1 per 1,000 on Isle of Wight compared to 5 percent to 6 percent in North America) suggest differing concepts of the diagnosis rather than a true difference in prevalence. Weiss believes that this discrepancy is more apparent than real and could be explained by the British practice of excluding hyperactive-aggressive (HA-Agg) children from HA diagnosis and including this group (HA-Agg) within the CD group. Furthermore, Weiss believes that Rutter may have confused prevalence rates for situational HA with those for pervasively HA children. Thus, Lambert et al. (1978) noted that 1.2 percent of 5,000 children living in the East Bay area of San Francisco were diagnosed HA by parents, teachers, and physicians. This prevalence rate for pervasive HA is quite similar to the 2 percent prevalence rate observed by Schachar et al. (1981) in the followup study on the Isle of Wight. Thus, when the issue of pervasive compared to situational HA is addressed, the prevalence figures for HA are remarkably consistent between Great Britain and the United States.

(3) Different measures of hyperactivity correlate poorly (Stevens et al., 1978; Sandberg et al., 1978). Thus, there is poor agreement between measurements of HA as determined by mechanical devices (actometer, watch, ballistographic cushion, photoelectric systems) and observational methods in naturalistic settings and questionnaires. Weiss comments that mechanical devices measure the quantity of activity while parent and teacher responses on questionnaires or rating scales seem to measure the quality of activity or a different kind of activity from that determined by mechanical devices. The latter (questionnaires) appear to measure a nontask oriented type of activity rather than a more focused activity determined by mechanical devices. Since the qualities of the two types of measures are so different, it is not surprising that

they are not congruent. (See "Assessment Measures" for additional discussion.)

(4) Factor analytic studies have frequently failed to obtain an overall factor for hyperactivity from different measures of hyperactivity. However, more recent studies, particularly those employing a large cohort, have identified a hyperactivity factor. Schachar et al. (1981) reported three items on Rutter's parent and teacher scales that appeared to represent HA. Furthermore, Achenbach and Edelbrock (1983) include a narrow band HA scale in the Child Behavior Checklist; Milich et al. (1982) note a factor of HA derived from symptom ratings recorded from chart reviews; and Shaywitz et al. (1986a) have reported HA as a clearly defined factor derived from parent ratings of the Yale Children's Inventory (YCI). Trites et al. (1982) factor analyzed the Conners teacher scale obtained on an epidemiological sample of 9,583 elementary school children. Not only did HA emerge as a distinct primary factor, but HA rather than CD accounted for the greatest proportion of variance, supporting the belief that HA was the most important single factor in this sample. Again, the items included, the samples studied, and sources used can significantly influence and account for inconsistencies among studies.

(5) Application of different scales (Conners, Rutter) result in selection of different children as hyperactive. This is not a surprising finding to anyone who has worked seriously at scale development in children with neurobehavioral disorders, and it simply reflects the different emphasis of the particular diagnostic instruments. More will be said of this below, but it must be recognized that scales are composed of questions, and if questions differ from instrument to instrument, it is not surprising that the composition of the scales, too, will differ. A major difficulty in interpreting the results of factor analytic studies and subsequent children identified by different scales is, as indicated earlier, the great variability between scales. For example, in the Trites study, the HA factor contained three items—"inattentive," "short attention span," and "day dreams"—that in other analyses have been seminal to the definition of an attention factor. Another example of scale-to- scale noncomparability is provided by the factor placement of a single commonly used item. The multiple versions of the Conners Teacher Rating Scales contain an item variously represented as "overly sensitive" (Conners, 1969), "overly sensitive to criticism" (Goyette, Conners, and Ulrich, 1978), and "sensitive" (Werry, Sprague, and Cohen, 1975; Trites et al., 1982). In the four factor solutions emerging from these different studies, this item appears on four differently labeled factors: an "anxiety" factor, a "conduct disorder" factor, an "unsociability" factor, and an "emotionality" factor respectively. It is therefore not surprising that this confounding obscures the relationships of the individual scales and the uniqueness/synonymity of the behavioral dimensions represented by them—particularly attention and hyperactivity, and hyperactivity and conduct disorder. The controversies described above may, in part, reflect

methodological flaws that result in equivalently labeled but not equivalently composed scales. Thus, while the number and heterogeneity of problematic behaviors to be classified have convinced researchers of the value of factor analysis as a technique to reduce and consolidate data dimensions, with the exception of statistical technique, studies have often shared little in common (very different item pools, rating sources, and subject samples).

(6) Hyperactivity and conduct disorder overlap, both in factors on rating scales and by clinician's judgment. While this is certainly true, it does not seem that the co-occurrence of HA and CD can be used to negate the validity of the concept of HA. While some investigators have suggested that HA and CD are not separable (Lahey et al., 1980; Quay, 1979), most investigators find an overlap of HA with CD in 30 percent to 65 percent of cases (Pelham and Murphy, 1986; Loney, 1986, in press), with the remainder of children exhibiting symptoms of either HA or CD (Loney and Milich, 1982; Stewart et al., 1981). Thus, Loney and the Iowa group in a series of investigations (Loney, Langhorne, and Paternite, 1978; Langhorne and Loney, 1979; Milich, Loney, and Landau, 1982; Loney and Milich, 1982) have convincingly demonstrated that when items are chosen for scales of hyperactivity and aggression to ensure both convergent and divergent validity, two distinct constructs will emerge. It may be that, in addition to children with relatively pure hyperactivity and conduct disorders, there exists a third subgroup of children with mixed symptomatology. This finding does not negate the validity of either hyperactivity or of conduct disorder as distinct entities.

Most recently, Trites and LaPrade (1983) present evidence for the existence of three such subgroups of children: hyperactive, conduct disordered, and hyperactive-conduct disordered. They argue that the delineation of a group of children with a mixture of both hyperactivity and conduct disorder does not preclude the existence of more distinct or pure forms of each of these disorders. These issues are reviewed in more detail by Pelham and Murphy (1986) and by Loney (1986, in press).

CURRENT TERMINOLOGY AND CRITERIA

The publication of DSM III represented a significant advance in efforts to establish the validity of diagnoses of HA, or more accurately, what DSM III referred to as ADD. Cantwell (1983) notes that the term ADD was developed because most investigators believed that an attentional rather than an activity problem (though the latter clearly was often prominent) was the cardinal symptom of the disorder. The entity was accordingly identified as attention deficit disorder with hyperactivity, ADDH. Furthermore, some children exhibit attentional deficits and impulsivity but no hyperactivity (attention deficit disorder without hyperactivity, ADDnoH), and older individuals often continue to exhibit inattention and impulsivity but no hyperactivity (ADDRT, attention deficit disorder residual type). Thus DSM III criteria for ADD recognize these three types, each with an attentional deficit at its core:

ADDnoH: inattention, impulsivity
ADDH: inattention, impulsivity, hyperactivity
ADDRT: inattention, impulsivity persists, hyperactivity does not.

In the DSM III paradigm for ADD, not only are the constructs necessary for diagnosis provided, but also the symptoms characterizing each of the constructs are detailed, although they are not operationalized. According to DSM III, the criteria for ADDH are:

Inattention (at least three of the following):

1. often fails to finish things he or she starts
2. often doesn't seem to listen
3. easily distracted
4. has difficulty concentrating on schoolwork or other tasks requiring sustained attention
5. has difficulty sticking to a play activity

Impulsivity (at least three of the following):

1. often acts before thinking
2. shifts excessively from one activity to another
3. has difficulty organizing work (this not being due to cognitive impairment)
4. needs a lot of supervision
5. frequently calls out in class
6. has difficulty awaiting turn in games or group situations

Hyperactivity (at least two of the following):

1. runs about or climbs on things excessively
2. has difficulty sitting still or fidgets excessively
3. has difficulty staying seated
4. moves about excessively during sleep
5. is always "on the go" or acts as if "driven by a motor"

DSM III criteria for ADD, by emphasizing the attentional component rather than focusing on the hyperactivity, represent a significant departure from previous approaches to children with difficulties in attention regulation and activity modulation. The emphasis on the attentional deficit as the core feature reflects an accumulating body of work (Douglas, 1972; Dykman, Ackerman, Clements, and Peters, 1971; Whalen and Henker, 1976) that led Douglas and Peters (1979) and Cantwell (1983) to suggest that the attentional deficit, rather than the problem in activity modulation, was of primary importance.

The development of DSM III criteria for disorders of attention regulation and activity modulation has influenced subsequent research in a number of significant ways. Clearly, it has influenced our conception of the disorder. In a sense, the label and accompanying criteria attached to any particular disorder represent a "self-fulfilling prophecy"; since children subsequently diagnosed as ADD will be identified on the basis of these criteria, they will (or should) all tend to exhibit the symptoms outlined in DSM III. It must be remembered that DSM III criteria did not arise out of an empiric base but rather represented a consensus of experienced investigators, a consensus for which validation must still be demonstrated.

The significant departure of DSM III criteria from the previously viewed hyperkinetic syndrome also has implications for the interpretation of the body of literature relating to this entity. DSM III is a relative newcomer, and current research efforts attempt, in one manner or another, to incorporate these criteria into subject selection. However, the large body of research that occurred prior to the publication of DSM III (1980) did not require the demonstration of inattention; only indications of hyperactivity were generally required for subject selection. Therefore, although studies before and after DSM III publication tend to be viewed as a continuum and the discontinuity between diagnostic criteria often blurred in the literature, significant methodological differences characterize many of these studies. Hyperactivity and attention deficit disorder tend to be used interchangeably although there are few studies to indicate that ADD or even ADDH by DSM III criteria and hyperactivity from previous formulations identify the same populations. A further confounding element has been the tendency for both clinicians and investigators to utilize the Conners instruments to identify subjects with ADD, although the items on the Conners do not parallel those detailed in DSM III.

Therefore, when interpreting studies conducted prior to the publication of DSM III criteria, it is difficult to know if the findings can be generalizable to children with ADD by current DSM III standards. The confusion is extended to post-DSM III studies as well, by the tendency of some investigators to describe their populations as conforming to DSM III criteria (see "Basic Assumptions" below) but then to select according to the presence of hyperactivity, ignoring the inattention (or impulsivity) criteria, or to utilize scales with seemingly correct labels but whose content does not conform to DSM III criteria.

EMPIRIC VALIDATION OF DSM III CRITERIA FOR ADD

Critical to the clinical evaluation of patients or to the assessment of subjects in investigations is a basic understanding of the strategy employed in the selection of a classification scheme. The following discussion is designed to provide the concerned professional with a perspective, an overview of the validation process as it applies to the development of a reliable and valid nosology for ADD.

Child rating instruments (see "Assessment Measures") have emerged as the technique of choice in efforts to develop an empirically based taxonomy for the classification of neurobehavioral disorders of childhood. Such instruments address the need for a methodology to systematize the intake of a vast array of behavioral information and organize it in a fashion relevant and pertinent to the diagnostic process. A number of child behavior rating instruments are now available to assess the broad range of deviant behavior in childhood (Revised Behavior Problem Checklist, Quay, 1983; Quay and Peterson, 1983; Child Behavior Checklist, Achenbach, 1978; Achenbach and Edelbrock, 1979; Conners Parent and Teacher Rating Scales, Conners, 1969, 1970, 1973; Goyette et al., 1978). Although the Conners instruments have been, perhaps, the most widely utilized in studies of hyperactive children, they do not provide three distinct scales paralleling DSM III constructs for ADD. Two newer instruments, the ACTeRS (Ullmann et al., 1984a) and the Yale Childrens Inventory (YCI) (Shaywitz et al., in press) have been developed to be responsive to DSM-III terminology and criteria. Our experience with the YCI is described below.

The YCI was developed in an effort to improve the ability of clinicians and researchers to characterize children presenting to child neurologists, pediatricians, and psychologists for the evaluation of school-related problems with particular emphasis on attentional deficits. Instrument development for the YCI has proceeded in an orderly fashion, examining both internal and external validity, so that scales reflecting specific constructs were both reliable and meaningful. Following initial studies establishing its reliability (Shaywitz et al., 1986a), the YCI was utilized to explore the validity of DSM III criteria for ADD. Thus, although DSM III provides a provisional guide to classification and diagnosis, there have been no studies examining the psychometric properties of DSM III criteria for ADD. Furthermore, while there appears to be tentative agreement as to the choice of these constructs now incorporated into ADD (Cantwell, 1975a; Routh, 1980), the operationalization of these constructs as sets of selected items has not been subject to empiric investigation.

Initial development of the YCI resulted in the emergence of eleven scales. Preliminary investigation, including second order factor analysis, identified two broad-band scale groupings of these eleven narrow-band YCI scales: a "behavioral" grouping containing the scales of Impulsivity, Activity, Tractability, Conduct Disorder-Socialized, Conduct Disorder-Aggressive, and Negative Affect, and a "cognitive" grouping containing the scales of Academics, Language, and Fine Motor. An important finding was that while each of nine scales could be uniquely represented on either the behavioral or the cognitive scale, the Attention scale and along with it, the Habituation scale (representing a component of attention) straddled both domains—that is, loaded equally well on both the behavioral and the cognitive broad-band scales. The finding that the attention scales overlap both broad-band domains indicates the importance and the intrinsic relationship of attention to both behavioral and cognitive function and strongly supports the DSM III nosology for ADD. These data clearly demonstrate the centrality of attention, and with it, the labeling of the disorder attention deficit disorder rather than hyperactivity. This finding parallels the observations of Quay (1983), who noted the association of the factor labeled attention problem-passivity with both the bands labeled internalizing and externalizing.

The 17 items comprising DSM III criteria for ADD were included in the YCI, and it was possible to attempt to empirically validate the diagnostic categories for ADD. However, when these items were subjected to factor analysis, only two factors, attention/impulsivity and activity, emerged. It was not possible to distinguish attention and impulsivity statistically. In contrast, a factor analysis of the items from the three corresponding YCI scales produced three clearly delineated factors, with the appropriate items loading highly onto each. A comparison of YCI to DSM III items for inattention, impulsivity, and hyperactivity is listed in Table 1.

Table 1

Structure Comparison of Attention, Impulsivity, and Hyperactivity
Constructs Between Yale Children's Inventory (YCI) Scales and
DSM III Structure

Scale/Category	YCI Factor	DSM III Criteria
Inattention:	1. Often fails to finish what s/he starts.	1. Often fails to finish what s/he starts.
	2. Hears but doesn't seem to listen.	2. Hears but doesn't seem to listen.
	3. Difficulty concentrating or paying attention unless 1:1.	3. Difficulty concentrating or paying attention unless 1:1.
	4. Asks to have things repeated.	
	5. Is easily distracted.	5. Is easily distracted.
	6. Confuses the details.	
	7. Needs a calm, quiet atmosphere in order to work.	
		A. Difficulty sticking to a play activity.
Impulsivity:	8. Frequently calls out in class.	8. Frequently calls out in class.
	9. Difficulty waiting turn in games or groups.	9. Difficulty waiting turn in games or groups.
	10. Disrupts other children.	
	11. Talks excessively.	
	12. Is extremely excitable.	
		A. Often acts before thinking.
		B. Shifts excessively from one activity to another.
		C. Needs a lot of supervision.
		D. Difficulty organizing work.
Hyperactivity:	13. Runs about and climbs on things.	13. Runs about and climbs on things.
	14. Always on the go, driven by a motor.	14. Always on the go; driven by a motor.
	15. Fidgets and squirms.	15. Fidgets and squirms.
	16. Difficulty sitting still.	16. Difficulty sitting still.
	17. Acts in a loud and noisy manner.	
	18. Must always be doing something or fidgets.	
		A. Has difficulty staying seated.
		B. Moves excessively during sleep.

The YCI scales of inattention and hyperactivity include four of five items on the corresponding DSM III scales plus three and two additional items respectively. The YCI scale of impulsivity, however, contains only two of the six DSM III impulsivity criteria plus three additional items. Impulsivity has been difficult to characterize. As indicated above, in the attempted replication of DSM III criteria, the Attention and Impulsivity scales were not distinguishable. In Loney's new scales (DACI-APD; Loney, 1986, in press), impulsivity is part of a hyperactive impulse disorder single scale, and in a recent study by Lahey et al. (1984) examining differences between ADDH and ADDnoH groups, only the ADDH group and not the ADDnoH goup differed from normals on ratings of impulsivity. ADDH children were also more impulsive than ADDnoH children, a finding at variance with DSM III criteria for the two subtypes. In a second order factor analysis of the YCI scales, impulsivity corresponded most to the "behavioral" grouping, and it may be that impulsivity is more a correlate of hyperactivity than of inattention. If this were to be confirmed in future studies, criteria for ADDnoH could reasonably be limited to the finding of inattention, with ADDH diagnosed if there were the additional findings of impulsivity and hyperactivity. These findings suggest that if ADDnoH children are chosen on the basis of impulsivity as well as inattention, they may, in fact, be hyperactive as well.

Thus, the findings of this attempt to empirically validate DSM III criteria for ADD suggest a more cautious approach in accepting these criteria. The YCI scales represent a modification of DSM III criteria; they correspond to the DSM III constructs conceptually and have many overlapping items. They represent a step forward in that they have emerged from empiric studies and have proven psychometric properties. Further studies on other populations are necessary to explore the empiric clustering of items representing the three diagnostic features of ADD (Shaywitz et al.,1986a). In the interim, we suggest utilization of instruments with established structure, such as the YCI scales, as provisional research and diagnostic tools.

DIAGNOSTIC MODEL FOR ADD

The YCI scales provide an opportunity to investigate dimensions contributing to the diagnosis of ADD and to empirically derive a definition of the disorder. Thus, three of the scales closely parallel DSM III criteria for ADD while the remaining eight correspond to features often associated with the disorder—for example, fine motor and academic difficulties, manageability problems, conduct problems, and negative affect. Using these modified DSM III scales with the addition of the other possibly contributing constructs, we wanted to determine which combination of these eleven scales best discriminated ADD from normal children.

In a series of investigations (Shaywitz et al., 1986b), the eleven YCI scales were compared among samples of ADDH, ADDnoH, and normal children in order to explore the possibility of developing a diagnostic rule for ADD. The sample consisted of 184 children (58 ADDH, 26 ADDnoH, 100 normal) ages 8-14, with no significant differences in the distribution of the sexes among the three groups. The diagnosis of ADD had been made independently by a multidisciplinary team utilizing the Best Estimate Diagnosis (Leckman et al.,1982). The scales are scored from 1 to 4, with the highest score representing the rating of most impairment. It was found that it was extremely rare for an ADD child to score < 2 on the Attention scale (2/81) and equally unusual for a normal child to score > 3 (4/100) on this scale. With this critical finding as a basis and utilizing logistic regression models, a multistage hierarchical procedure was developed.

In this model, initial risk status for ADD (high, medium, or low) is defined on the basis of scores on the core symptom, inattention. Medium-risk children are sorted into ADD-nonADD categories based on the logistic regression equation including the Fine Motor, Academics, Tractability, and Activity scales. These findings are consistent with a recent epidemiological study in which McGee et al. (1985) found that indices of academic and fine motor function were among the best predictors of inattention. In the third and final stage of this hierarchical procedure, children classified as ADD are further subdivided into ADDH and ADDnoH groups based on a second logistic equation. Interestingly, in addition to Activity, Tractability, and Habituation, higher scores on the Impulsivity scale contribute to distinguishing ADDH from ADDnoH children. This may be interpreted as another indication that impulsivity, as defined on behavior rating scales, is more a correlate of hyperactivity than it is of inattention.

Based on this procedure, the YCI scales were able to correctly classify ADD and normal children with a high degree of sensitivity (87.5 percent cases correctly classified) and specificity (94 percent normals correctly classified). Application of the model on a replication sample of entirely different children again correctly classified the children with a high degree of sensitivity (94 percent) and a good degree of specificity (76.9 percent). (The logistic regression equations are available from the authors as part of a computer program.)

In this population of children referred to pediatric neurology and learning disorders units, scales reflecting conduct problems were not selected for inclusion in the diagnostic model. It is possible that in a sample representing children referred to mental health centers, these scales and not the Fine Motor and Academic scales would have demonstrated the best discrimination between ADD and normal controls. Such results clearly require replication in future studies and on other types of samples.

The good discriminant validity shown by the YCI scales together with their sound psychometric properties represent the initial steps in the validation process for ADD. External validation studies are now in progress and may help clarify issues relating to etiology, natural history, response to treatment, and outcome. In the future, large-scale, multi-disciplinary studies employing homogeneous subgroups representing not only ADD but also conduct disorder and learning disabilities will be necessary to establish a reliable and valid nosology for ADD.

OTHER DIAGNOSTIC FEATURES

DSM III indicates that for a diagnosis of ADD to be made, age of onset is prior to 7 years with a duration of symptoms of at least 6 months. Since the diagnosis is typically made between ages 8 and 10, the onset of symptoms by age 7 appears to be reasonable. There are, however, some investigators who argue for a lower age of onset. Barkley (1981) uses findings of Sandberg et al. (1980) that hyperactive children differed from children with other psychiatric disorders in having more neurodevelopmental abnormalities, more variability in tests of impulse control, and onset of hypractivity before 5 years to suggest that children with valid diagnoses of hyperactivity are those who present with early symptoms. Employing Douglas and Peters' (1979) argument that learning disabled children develop secondary behavior problems after experiencing school failure, Barkley believes that insistence on the onset of symptoms earlier than 7 years will prevent labeling children with these reactive behavioral problems as hyperactive. A contrary view posits that these children who have the most pervasive symptoms and present earliest represent an extreme group that may not be representative of ADD children in general. While it is known that many of the children presenting to mental health centers provide a retrospective history of early-onset hyperactivity, it is unclear if this finding applies to other groups of ADD children as well—for example, children presenting to pediatricians and child neurologists. Another concern with lowering the age of onset is that children with ADDnoH might then be excluded since many do not exhibit symptoms until they have been in school for several years. In addition (as discussed in "Clinical Characteristics"), it is difficult to differentiate children with "difficult" temperaments from children who may have attentional deficits in the preschool period. Therefore, insistence on an early onset might exclude a significant number of children from the diagnosis and bias the diagnosis toward children with more extreme forms of the disorder.

The establishment of exclusionary criteria is complex. This reflects the sometimes different needs of research and clinical practice. Thus, the sole exclusionary criterion in DSM III-R is pervasive developmental disorder, a reasonable recommendation for clinical practice. However, the needs of the investigator demand more homogeneous subgroups than this would permit. A reasonable suggestion, then, is for research diagnostic criteria to incorporate the concept of uncomplicated ADD and ADD complicated by other conditions. We propose the term ADD be used to represent those children who satisfy diagnostic criteria for

ADD but who do not have any other complicating feature such as conduct disorder, affective disorder, oppositional disorder, or mental retardation. For those children with ADD who have, in addition, one or more of the associated conditions noted above, we propose the term ADD-plus (ADD-P). In this way, the diagnosis would not be too restrictive and yet would allow for the more precise delineation of homogeneous groups of ADD children.

Subtypes: ADDH/ADDnoH

The nosology provided for in DSM III marked a departure from DSM II and other previous conceptualizations of disorders of activity and attention regulation by emphasizing the attentional rather than the activity component. However, DSM III went a step further by differentiating two subtypes of the disorder based on the presence or absence of symptoms of hyperactivity: ADDH and ADDnoH respectively. In the DSM III diagnostic paradigm, children with ADDnoH meet diagnostic criteria for inattention and impulsivity while children with ADDH have the additional feature of hyperactivity. While DSM III indicates that there are two subtypes of the disorder, it is unclear whether "they are two forms of a single disorder or represent two distinct disorders" (APA, 1980; p. 41).

Since the publication of DSM III in 1980, a number of investigations have examined the distinctiveness of the two subtypes of the disorder. Consistent with other studies in this area, a number of different instruments have been used and different approaches taken. It is important to recall that a variety of methodological factors including original item pool, subjects selected, procedure, and source of ratings will influence the factors and their content that emerge from factor analytic studies. If items reflecting inattention are not included, the emergence of an inattention factor is precluded; the presence of other items will determine what the exact makeup of such a factor will be. Thus, although a number of inattention factors have emerged on different instruments, they each differ in their content and do not necessarily conform to the DSM III construct of inattention. (See also "Rating Scales.")

Overall, despite the differences in measures employed, the results of these studies are fairly consistent in demonstrating that ADD children differ from control or comparison groups, and ADDH and ADDnoH demonstrate significantly different behavioral, academic, and social patterns. The results have indicated that the inattention-passive factor accounts for a measure of independent variance in multiple regression analyses (Lahey, Green, and Forehand, 1980). Samples selected as ADDH and ADDnoH do not differ on independent measures of inattention (King and Young, 1982; Edelbrock et al., 1984). These two groups, however, present different patterns on other measures, the precise pattern being a reflection of the measures in the particular study. Edelbrock et al. (1984), using the Teacher Report Form of the Child Behavior Checklist (Achenbach, 1978; Achenbach and Edelbrock, 1979), describe ADDH boys as more impaired on the Nervous-Overactive, Unpopular, Self-Destructive, and Aggressive scales. In contrast, ADDnoH boys score higher on the Social Withdrawal scales. These boys (ADDnoH) are rated by their teachers as manifesting a poorer school performance. This finding is supported by the high rate of retention (71.5 percent), which is high even in relation to ADDH boys (16.7 percent). Teachers also rated ADDnoH boys as less happy than their ADDH counterparts. Thus, although ADDnoH children may be less visible, they appear to be at high risk for academic and social problems. Similar findings characterized ADDH-ADDnoH group differences in a study by King and Young (1982). Teacher judgments on the Conners Teacher Rating Scale (Conners, 1969) indicated that ADDH boys were significantly more impaired on the Hyperactivity and Conduct Problem scales. There were no significant differences between the groups in measures of peer perception; they were both rejected by their peers. Academic function was not assessed in this study. Most recently, Lahey et al. (1984) compared ADDH and ADDnoH children using a battery of teacher ratings (Revised Behavior Problem Checklist: Quay, 1983; Quay and Peterson, 1983) and peer ratings and self-report measures (Piers-Harris Self Concept Scale: Piers and Harris, 1964). Once again, reflecting the measures used, ADDH and ADDnoH children displayed markedly different patterns. ADDH children were rated as more deviant on the Aggression, Conduct Disorder, and Psychotic Behavior scales, while ADDnoH children were more impaired on the Anxiety-Withdrawal scale. Consistent with the Edelbrock et al. (1984) study, these ADDnoH children were rated as less proficient in both academic and sports performance. Peer perceptions of the ADDH children were also negative, and these children received more "least liked" nominations than did their ADDnoH classmates. The children's perceptions of themselves also tended to differ, with ADDH children exhibiting low self-esteem in the areas of behavior and popularity, while the ADDnoH group indicated more concerns with physical appearance, anxiety, and general happiness. Teacher nominations viewed the ADDH children as more guiltless and the ADDnoH group as more socially withdrawn and shy. A retrospective study (Maurer and Stewart, 1980) consisting of chart reviews found that 31 of 52 children rated as ADDnoH were also conduct disordered. They argue that since both ADDH and ADDnoH overlap with conduct problems, they should not be considered as separate disorders. Since this finding of conduct problems in such a high proportion of ADDnoH children is at variance with subsequent concurrent studies examining these two groups, it is difficult to interpret the results of the former and place them in the context provided by the other investigations.

In summary, despite the variability in measures and populations used, the results of these investigations appear to support DSM III nosology for two distinct subtypes of ADD. Of particular concern and importance is the nature and range of deficits reported in ADDnoH children. While they do not manifest the intrusive, externalizing behaviors of the ADDH group, they appear to be performing poorly in school and to be at serious risk for long-term academic and social problems. This is a group that has not been well studied and may present a low visibility but high-risk profile for both school and social failure. It is unclear what the relationship of ADDH is to conduct disorder. Clearly, this is the group that has been the focus of studies in the past that produced questions of whether the conduct disordered and hyperactive groups represented distinct entities. (This issue is more fully discussed in "Defintion and Syndrome Validation," "Rating Scales," and "ADD and Conduct Disorder.")

ASSOCIATED CONDITIONS

ADD AND LEARNING DISABILITIES

Historically, learning disability and hyperactivity share common roots; they were both considered manifestations of minimal brain dysfunction and later of the hyperkinetic syndrome. (See "Historical Perspective" for a complete discussion.) Therefore, it is not surprising that the prevailing assumption as reflected in the literature and in clinical lore is that there is a substantial overlap between hyperactivity and learning disabilities. (See "Epidemiology" for full details.) Reflecting the use of vague and inconsistent criteria for both learning disability and ADD, or more accurately, hyperactivity, estimates of the co-occurrence of the two disorders have varied considerably. The prevalence of learning disability in hyperactive children has ranged from highs of 80 percent to 92 percent (Silver, 1981) to more recent estimates of 9 percent to 10 percent in hyperactive boys (Halperin et al., 1984) and 11 percent in an epidemiologic sample of 8-year-old Connecticut school children (Shaywitz, 1986a). Conversely, the prevalence of hyperactivity in learning disabled populations has varied from 41 percent (Holborow and Berry, 1986) to 80 percent (Safer and Allen, 1976), with a prevalence of 33 percent reported in the epidemiological sample (Shaywitz, 1986a).

The increased association of the two disorders had led to speculation about the nature of the relationship. For example, are they both subtypes of the same disorder, does one predispose to the other, or do they share a common etiology that produces two distinct syndromes? Factor analytic studies, if they have included appropriate items, have identified separate learning disability and hyperactivity factors (Lahey et al., 1978). Studies comparing hyperactive and mixed hyperactive-reading disabled groups have found very few measures on which the two groups differed. These results are contrary to the notion that the two are discrete subgroups of ADDH (Halperin et al., 1984). Studies examining the academic achievement of hyperactive compared to control children indicate that significantly more ADDH children experience academic achievement problems. They are more likely to perform below expectations in reading and arithmetic and to be behind in their academic subjects and to be behind in more subjects than control children (Cantwell, 1978). In a more recent study examining 1,593 primary grade school children in Australia in which teachers completed the Conners Abbreviated Symptom Questionnaire (Goyette et al., 1978) and also indicated ratings of level of academic difficulty, seven times as many children rated as hyperactive were described as experiencing "very much" difficulty in all academic areas compared to their nonhyperactive classmates (Holborow and Berry, 1986).

An important recent study investigated the pupil characteristics associated with receiving special services in school (Sandoval and Lambert, 1984-5). This study demonstrated the strong correlation between externalizing behaviors and referral for special education. Thus, while lower reading achievement scores were associated with provision of services, higher levels of hyperactivity, and in hyperactive children, higher levels of aggression were correlates of receiving educational assistance. Interestingly, 33.3 percent of hyperactives compared to 17.9 percent of controls received services even when they were not learning disabled. The implications of these findings for research are significant; studies basing their subject selection for learning disabled children on system-identification will have a selection bias resulting in many children with behavioral and not necessarily learning disabilities. Data emerging from these studies will then report that hyperactivity and aggression are found in "learning disabled" children. Another caveat in making assumptions about the relationship of hyperactivity and learning is the recently reported association between extreme degrees of giftedness and increased activity (Shaywitz et al., 1986c). Comparable findings are suggested by Trites (1979), who reported that 15.6 percent of boys rated as above average in learning capacity are also hyperactive.

The implications of these findings are that hyperactivity or ADD and learning disabilities are two separate disorders and that one does not necessarily predict the other. A suggestion has been made that children with learning disability be screened out of samples of hyperactive children in order not to contaminate the homogeneity of the sample. Douglas (1983) argues that to remove all learning disabled children from hyperactivity samples would result in unrepresentative samples of hyperactive children. DSM III lists academic difficulties as an impairment associated with ADD and school failure as a complication. Axis II on DSM III provides for diagnoses of developmental reading, or arithmetic or language disorders. The importance of the overlap in the occurrence of the two disorders is that the presence of either should be a signal to consider the other and provide appropriate diagnostic testing. Even if the two are not present together initially, there is a belief that unaddressed learning problems will lead to secondary attentional and activity problems (Douglas and Peters, 1979). Others (Ross, 1976; Pelham and Ross, 1977) have suggested that poor readers have deficits in selective attention. Recent evidence (Ford, Pelham, and Ross, 1984) does not support such an assumption.

In summary, although results of many investigations indicate that there is a relationship between learning disabilities and ADD, the nature of this relationship has not been well defined. There has been a paucity of research studies utilizing well defined, nonsystem-identified learning disabled children where the diagnosis both of learning disability and of ADD was made on the basis of rigorous criteria. Such studies are necessary to provide a clearer understanding of: (a) the prevalence of the co-occurrence of ADD and LD; (b) their mechanisms of interaction, including the expression and course of one on the other; (c) most importantly, approaches to intervention in children with both disorders.

ADD AND CONDUCT DISORDER

The nature of the relationship between ADDH and conduct disorder is the subject of much controversy, and indeed, the claim that the two disorders cannot be disentangled has been the basis of claims that ADDH or hyperactivity is not a valid syndrome. This subject has been discussed extensively in other parts of this review. To summarize briefly, an inability to discern a separate hyperactivity factor, to describe differential correlations, or to separate children diagnosed as conduct disordered from children diagnosed as hyperactive on a series of external variables was considered to rule against the independence of hyperactivity from conduct disorder. A distinct hyperactivity factor has now emerged in a number of studies supporting the distinctiveness of hyperactivity as separate from conduct disorder.

Many of the difficulties in syndrome validation have been the result of nonsubstantive, primarily methodological flaws. One has been the tendency of British investigators to identify as ADDH-only cases in which there is severe and pervasive hyperactivity. Studies (Sandberg et al., 1978; Schachar et al., 1978) of these rare children indicate that they often show signs of neurologic dysfunction and decreased cognitive function. British investigators use these findings to support their contention that it is only this extreme group of hyperactive children who warrant a distinct diagnosis of hyperactivity. A contrary position (as discussed in "Definition and Syndrome Validation") argues that these children by being so extreme are not representative of hyperactive children or ADDH children, but rather represent a multiply disturbed and disabled population that is contaminated by a variety of confounding influences.

Perhaps the major obstacle to separating conduct disordered from hyperactive groups has been methodological: the absence of an instrument that represented relatively pure factors for each of these dimensions. Loney and her colleagues have succeeded in developing, through employment of convergent and divergent validation strategies, the IOWA Conners (Loney and Milich, 1982) and distinct hyperactivity and aggression factors based on chart ratings (Loney, Langhorne, and Paternite, 1978; Milich, Loney, and Landau, 1982). Following the identification of distinct hyperactivity and aggression factors, Loney et al. (1978) posited that there were three clinical groups: purely hyperactive, purely aggressive, and a mixed hyperactive-aggressive group. Loney (1986) describes approximately 45 percent mixed, 29 percent to 36 percent aggressive, and 18 percent to 36 percent hyperactive in outpatient clinic populations identified by either the IOWA or chart ratings. The selection bias in referrals to clinics was demonstrated when the IOWA was used to assign boys with externalizing behavior patterns from a normal classroom to these subgroups; the pure hyperactive group and pure aggressive group each had 45 percent of the boys, while only 10 percent of these boys from a nonclinic population fulfilled criteria for the more severe mixed group. Thus, in the nonreferred sample, the proportion of hyperactive boys who were also aggressive was only 18 percent, a decline from 71 percent in the clinic group. This suggests that the proportion of mixed hyperactive-aggressive boys found in clinic samples is an overrepresentation of the prevalence of the disorder in nonreferred samples and further suggests caution in assuming that such clinic groups are representative of all hyperactive children. This view that there are both distinct groups of hyperactive and aggressive children and also a mixed group is supported by the results of Trites' large-scale study as well (Trites and LaPrade, 1983). These investigators were also able to identify subgroups of pure hyperactivity, pure conduct problem and a mixed hyperactivity-conduct problem group. Thus, it seems most reasonable to postulate that both aggression and hyperactivity can occur independently, but that they can also occur together in rarer instances. Availability of distinct measures of each of these constructs will facilitate studies of etiology, natural history, and response to interventions. Loney et al. (1981) have demonstrated that the presence of aggression early on in hyperactive children can be associated with a poorer outcome in adolescence.

Evidence for two subtypes of hyperactivity (with conduct problems and without conduct problems) is further supported by family studies. Boys with conduct disorder but not with hyperactivity have parents who are more likely to have personality disorders and alcoholism (Stewart, DeBlois, and Cummings, 1980). Hyperactive boys who had a positive family history for antisocial disorders were more likely to be deviant on measures of conduct disorder and to have siblings who also had a high prevalence of conduct disorder (August and Stewart, 1983). In contrast, hyperactive boys with a negative family history for antisocial disturbances did not manifest conduct disturbance, nor did their siblings. These boys and their siblings did have a high prevalence of learning problems.

In summary, indications point to two distinct groups of children: one with hyperactivity, the other with symptoms of aggression. Infrequently, the two can co-occur in the same child. Further studies are needed to replicate these findings. In the interim, since aggressivity affects the prognosis in hyperactive children, it would seem reasonable to assess children for ADD by using more recently developed instruments that provide separate measures of activity and of aggression or conduct problem. This will be more relevant to children presenting to mental health clinics than to those generally seen by pediatricians and child neurologists. Exploring the family history for antisocial problems can also help suggest whether hyperactive children are also at risk for conduct problems.

ASSESSMENT MEASURES

ADD CONSTRUCTS

OVERVIEW

A child with ADD may present with pervasive difficulties that permeate every aspect of existence: his home life, his school functioning, and his relations with peers in the classroom and in the community. As pervasive and oftimes disabling as his symptoms are, they are also often elusive and are difficult to capture in an objective, reliable manner. DSM III and recent modifications (elaborated in "Definition and Syndrome Validation" above) were a major step forward in providing for the establishment of both categories and rules for identification. This discussion focuses on the development of measures that would allow for the operationalization of these constructs elaborated in DSM III: attention, activity, and impulsivity. DSM III represented a major change in our conceptualization of the disorder, emphasizing the attentional deficit and not the hyperactivity. In this discussion, we present an overview of instruments developed prior to DSM III because many of them are still in current use and continue to be the basis of the bulk of the reports in the literature. Since DSM III represented a different emphasis and presented a new set of diagnostic criteria, newer measures have been developed and introduced more recently to reflect these changes. Because of their recency, many of these instruments are still in the process of being validated and modified.

Reflecting the intrusion of ADD symptoms into both home and school life, measures have been developed to assess the ADD child's behavior in each of these environments. Sources of information include parents, teachers, and the children themselves. Methods include utilization of rating scales or questionnaires for parents and teachers, direct measurement of the construct itself through mechanical or testing procedures of the child, and direct observation methods in which the child is observed in the classroom or in the laboratory. Each of these methods offers its own unique perspective of the construct being measured, and each has its own set of drawbacks. Whalen (as quoted in Ross and Ross, 1982) captures the nuances associated with each of these varied approaches: "Rating scales are global measures that are easily influenced by the cognitive and motivational characteristics of the respondent as by the behaviors of the child." Subjectivity and bias are less likely to plague direct behavioral observations, but frequency counts of target behaviors may be too specific, time-limited, or reactive to provide a representative picture of the child's problematic patterns. Laboratory measures tend to be more objective than ratings, more sensitive than behavior observations, and perhaps the most comparable from study to study. However, they are often obtained under novel, artificial, and even anxiety-inducing conditions rather than in the child's natural environments. Thus, their ecological validity—their relevance to everyday functioning—must be documented.

RATING SCALES

ADVANTAGES AND DISADVANTAGES

Perhaps the most popular method of assessing children's behavior is through the use of behavior rating scales. Conners and Barkley (1985) have recently enumerated the advantages of these measures including: (1) the ratings will reflect the rater's in-depth knowledge of the child, having seen him over time and in a variety of situations; (2) they will reflect rare and unusual occurrences that might be missed during the limited time-frame of an observational assessment; (3) they can be collected efficiently and economically; (4) normative data are often available for comparison purposes; (5) many have accumulated information on their reliability and validity; (6) the ratings may reflect the opinion of the variety of people who are of ecological importance to the child; (7) ratings are means of quantifying behaviors of interest.

Rating scales have also met with criticism, which has been summarized by Ross and Ross (1982). They note the variable correlation between rating scales and observational methods (see "Definition and Syndrome Validation" for fuller discussion), poor interrater reliability, and the subjective nature of the judgments being made. Whalen and Henker (1976) suggest that differences between ratings appropriately reflect situational and temporal factors. Both Barkley (1986, in press) and Ross and Ross (1982) have emphasized the problems arising out of differences in the perceptions of the rater and the investigator of the base rates of the behavior being assessed. In a recent epidemiological study of kindergarteners in the State of Connecticut (Shaywitz, 1986a), the parents of 76 percent of the children rated their child as being more active than the average for the child's age.

Another issue of importance with all measures of behavior but particularly with more inferential measures that behavior ratings represent is the question of what is actually being assessed. Thus, for example, while some investigators have found increased movement in hyperactive children (Porrino et al., 1983), this finding has not been consistent across studies (Barkley and Ullmann, 1975). In addition, the correlation between behavioral ratings and direct observational measures of activity level has been variable (Sandberg et al., 1978; Whalen et al., 1978; Whalen et al., 1979). Thus, there appears to be a discrepancy between the "perception" of hyperactivity as measured by global rating scales and the direct "observation" of activity by more objective measures. Some investigators have suggested that certain behaviors of the child, behaviors that are rare but salient, significantly influence the teacher's perception of the child's hyperactivity independent of the child's actual level of movement (Collins, 1981; Collins, Whalen, and Henker, 1980). Behaviors influencing teacher's perceptions have been summarized by these authors as having four characteristics in common: they are inappropriate, salient, intrusive, and conspicuous. In an interesting experiment (Mintz and Collins, 1985), actors and actresses appearing in videotaped vignettes were rated for hyperactivity by undergraduate volunteers utilizing the Conners Abbreviated Symptom Questionnaire. They were able to influence the rater's perception of degree of movement by manipulating the context (degree of inappropriateness) or sound level. In this way, for the same vignette, if the raters were led to believe that the activity was inappropriate or if the volume of sound was turned up, the corresponding ratings indicated a higher activity level and a more negative evaluation. Mintz and Collins refer to this as an illusion of movement and a negative halo effect respectively. The authors do not suggest that all behavior ratings of movement are illusionary, but rather that the perception of movement can be influenced by these factors.

As a corollary, recent investigations (Henker et al., 1979; Henker et al., 1986) suggest that the aspect of movement that is being rated may be more related to the intensity than the amount or frequency of movement. In a study comparing these two aspects of motoric behavior (motoric style or intensity, and gross motor locomotion in medicated and nonmedicated children) measures of intensity differentiated the groups who did not differ in either off-task behavior or gross motor activity. Thus, although numerous studies indicate "improvement" in children on medication, it remains unclear just what characteristic(s) has changed or improved. As studies of behavior become more analytic in nature, the relative contributions of increased social compliance, diminished intensity, or decreased gross motor locomotion should become more evident (Henker et al., 1986). These more analytic studies of behavior will also contribute to our understanding of inconsistent findings between observed direct measures of activity and activity as defined by rating scales. These studies, reporting environmental modulators of perception of activity and child-based qualities of movement that influence the rater's perception of activity, suggest caution in interpreting both future and past studies of activity utilizing either direct observation or behavior rating scales. This is a reminder that "things are not always what they seem."

BASIC ASSUMPTIONS

A final and perhaps basic consideration that relates to all measures is that they must be reliable and valid. Reliability ensures that the results are reproducible, and validity indicates that the instrument measures what it purports to measure. Without these qualities, no matter how sound the theoretical basis or impressive the description of the results, the scales have little or no value in providing meaningful, interpretable information about the child. Further details of the standards that rating scales should meet if they are to be useful to investigators or clinicians are provided by Barkley (1981).

SPECIFIC RATING SCALES

Those measures that have been utilized most extensively or that have been developed to be consistent with DSM III criteria are briefly reviewed below. Further details of specific child behavior rating scales have been provided by Ross and Ross (1982) and more recently by Conners and Barkley (1985) and by Barkley (1986).

Child rating scales incorporate both parent and teacher measures, and each has its own set of advantages and disadvantages (Shaywitz et al., in press). Thus, parent instruments are completed by respondents who are highly motivated and informed and who have witnessed their child's behavior in a variety of situations. However, parent-based scales are also vulnerable to threats of validity due to possible parental biases arising from social desirability, subjective judgments of one's own child relative to other children, individual response tendencies, and retrospective distortions. In contrast, responses from the classroom teacher are less prone to some of these sources of potential error. The teacher has broader exposure to diverse children from which to generate an internal anchor, maintains a single response tendency across ratings, and has less personal investment in any particular child and, therefore, may be more objective. Nonetheless, the classroom teacher observes the child's behavior in a narrower context and lacks the more intimate knowledge and perspective of the parents.

PARENT RATING SCALES

The Conners series of parent rating scales have undoubtedly been the most widely used of all the parent measures. There are three forms in use, including the original 93-item version (Conners, 1970), the revised 48-item version (Goyette, Conners, and Ulrich, 1978), and the 10-item Abbreviated Symptom Questionnaire (ASQ), also referred to as the Hyperkinesis Index (Conners, 1972). The 93-item version demonstrates test-retest reliability, but factor scores decrease from the first to the second rating (Werry and Sprague, 1974), which may confound its utilization in pharmacological studies unless two baseline ratings are obtained. Scales include: Aggressive-Conduct Disorder, Anxious-Inhibited, Anxious-Immature, Antisocial-Reaction, Enuresis-Encopresis, and Psychosomatic Problems (Conners, 1970). Thus, although some of the symptoms are related to the entity of ADD, it would be difficult to make a diagnosis of ADD based on DSM III criteria using this instrument. One of the difficulties present in interpreting data based on the Conners scales is that there are many different versions bearing the same title but with slightly different wordings or factors represented. This is further discussed under the teacher ratings.

The original Conners scales were shortened to 48 items, with some additional rewording of items (Goyette, Conners, and Ulrich, 1978). Scales emerging from this instrument relevant to the diagnosis of ADD include the Impulsive-Hyperactive scale, while Conduct Problem and Learning Problem scales address associated characteristics found in ADD children. Characteristic of the semantic and labeling difficulties surrounding rating scales, this version includes a factor labeled learning problems that includes two items related to inattention: ("fails to finish things," "distractability") and two others that are only tangentially related to inattention ("difficulties in learning," "easily frustrated"). Psychometric properties including measures of both reliability and validity have not been as well described as for the longer version. Conners and Barkley (1985) caution that the Conners, as all other parent rating forms, are less sensitive to drug effects than are teacher ratings, which reflect the time of availability of the drug (while the child is in school) and the differences between the structured task situations characterizing school and the free play environment generally found at home.

The Child Behavior Checklist (CBCL) (Achenbach and Edelbrock, 1983) represents a comprehensive, well-documented parent checklist containing empirically derived factors. While there is a hyperactivity factor represented, there is no factor related to inattention—again hampering its usage in the diagnosis of ADD based on current DSM III criteria. Thus, while significantly abnormal scores were obtained on the Hyperactivity scale by hyperactive boys (Barkley, 1981), elevated scores were also found on a series of other scales including Aggression, Delinquency, and Obsessive-Compulsive, which brings into question the specificity of the parent CBCL in the diagnosis of ADD. A teacher version is also available and is discussed below.

The Revised Behavior Problem Checklist (RBPC) (Quay and Peterson, 1983) represents an expansion of the original BPC, which has resulted in increased comprehensiveness of the instrument. Good reliability and validity data support the measure. Empirically derived scales include Conduct Disorder, Socialized Aggression, Attention Problems-Immaturity, Anxiety-Withdrawal, Psychotic Behavior, and Motor Tension-Excess. Comparisons of groups of ADDH and ADDnoH children indicate strikingly different patterns on the RBPC, differences which have been invoked as evidence that these are two dissimilar disorders rather than subtypes of the same disorder (Lahey et al., 1984). While some items on the Attention Problems-Immaturity scale do correspond to the DSM III construct, other items (for example, "irresponsible, undependable," "passive, suggestible, easily led by others," "acts like he or she were much younger, immature," "childish"), while accurately reflecting the scale's title, do not conform to the intent of the inattention construct. Whether children diagnosed in this manner meet DSM III criteria for ADD awaits futher investigation. The scales can be completed by parents and teachers. A number of other parent rating scales have been developed to assess behavioral patterns in children and have recently been discussed by Barkley (1986).

TEACHER RATING SCALES

The Conners Teachers Rating Scales represent the most widely used teacher rating measures. As was described for the parent forms, several versions of the teacher rating scale exist: a 39-item and a revised 28-item version (Conners, 1969; Goyette et al., 1978, respectively), the abbreviated 10-item scale, the Abbreviated Symptom Questionnaire (ASQ) or Hyperkinesis Index (Goyette et al., 1978), and the Iowa Conners Teacher Rating Scale developed by Loney and Milich (1982). The original Conners scales have been used extensively in research on child behavior disorders, having been developed originally for use in drug studies with hyperactive children. Psychometric properties including reliability, and measures of validity are well documented. A source of confusion has been the multiple versions with different factor structures, all usually referred to by the same terminology in the literature. Studies have identified anywhere from five to eight factors, each emphasizing a different dimension. Thus, in early analyses (Werry et al., 1975; Conners, 1969), conduct problem emerged as the primary factor, while in the largest and most recent sample (Trites et al., 1982), hyperactivity accounted for the greatest proportion (36 percent) of the total variance. Conners (quoted in Barkley, 1986) suggests that the norms and factors emerging from the Trites large epidemiological survey be employed. This form assesses six factors: hyperactivity, conduct problems, emotionally over-indulgent, anxious-passive, asocial, and daydreams-attendance.

The six items comprising the original 1969 hyperactivity factor are widely used to identify hyperactive children for research studies, with a score of 1.5 designated as the cutoff to differentiate hyperactive from nonhyperactive children. The difficulty is that items on this scale reflect not only hyperactivity but impulsivity and aggressiveness as well; the result is a more global measure of misbehavior rather than a precise definition of hyperactivity. Clearly, children identified by this scale will exhibit a mixture of symptoms and not constitute a homogeneous group. The scales are drug-sensitive and have been shown to discriminate between hyperactive and normal children in numerous studies (Barkley, 1986).

A revised, shorter 28-item version is also available (Goyette et al., 1978). Interestingly, agreement between the parent and teacher versions has only been moderate, which emphasizes the effects that different environments or situations will have on the hyperactive child (Goyette et al., 1978). Scales that have emerged from these versions again emphasize the inconsistences found between the label attached to a scale and its actual item content. Thus, the inattentive-passive factor contains only three out of eight items that are consistent with current notions of inattention (Sprague et al., 1981), which makes this scale inconsistent with the operationalization of inattention as described in DSM III.

The 10-item scale, the ASQ, is brief and easy to use and thus has been quite popular with clinicians as well as investigators. This scale for use by parents and teachers was developed from the original 39-item Conners Teacher Rating Scale by the selection of the ten items that were most frequently selected by teachers when rating hyperactive children. These ten items are also referred to as the Hyperkinesis Index. The final version, the so-called IOWA (Inattention/Overactivity With Aggression) Conners' Teachers Rating Scale (Loney and Milich, 1982) consists of ten items chosen to be highly divergent on the hyperactivity and on the conduct problem factors so that children could be selected who were either purely aggressive or purely hyperactive. Although this is one of the rare measures developed to select relatively homogeneous hyperactive and aggressive groups, there have been few reports to document its psychometric properties. The construct of inattention is not reflected on the IOWA scale.

Recently, both the form and the content of the Conners instruments have been examined more critically (Ullmann et al., 1985). One concern focuses on the multiple versions of the instrument that have been used and discussed in the literature as if they were interchangeable. For example, four different versions of the ASQ are available, and this has generated considerable confusion. Ullmann and her colleagues (1985) point out that while there are multiple versions of this shortened version, the commonly utilized criterion of a score of 1.5 as a cutoff for identification of hyperactive children is empirically based on only one of the versions. However, investigators continue to use this cutoff on all versions of the instrument as if it were sacrosanct. They also indicate that procedures used to determine the cutoff score may have eliminated problematic children from the control sample so that normative values were lower than they would have been in an unbiased sample. This investigative group, composed of individuals involved in the initial normative studies of the ASQ, performed a new study to clarify some of these issues. They selected hyperactive subjects based on the 1.5 cutoff score on the ASQ and then compared this cohort with a normal sample on the Hyperactivity and Inattentive-Passive scales of the longer 39-item teacher rating scale. The two groups were found to differ markedly on the Hyperactivity scale but not on the Inattention-Passivity scale, which suggested to the investigators that the abbreviated scale is satisfactory for selecting hyperactive subjects but not for identifying children whose primary problem is inattentiveness. Thus, this instrument may be useful for recognizing children with antisocial and hyperactive features but may miss well-behaved children who do not pay attention (ADDnoH). A confounding alternative explanation is that the Inattentive-Passive scale does not accurately reflect the construct of inattention (see above).

Whichever explanation is more appealing, the issue clearly is that the labeling of the scales relevant to the items actually on the scales and the choice of items comprising the ASQ generate a great deal of confusion and make findings based on these instruments difficult to interpret. Citing the long list of difficulties enumerated above, Ullmann and associates (1985) take the radical position of suggesting abandonment of all the Conners scales. They state that this is the only way to guarantee consistency in subject selection and accurate characterization of subjects identified for research studies. The difficulty in following this advice is that the Conners series of instruments have been used in the overwhelming majority of studies that now form the literature for hyperactivity/ADD. We recommend a more moderate position; that is, in future studies a Conners instrument be utilized along with perhaps a newer instrument more consistent with current terminology and definitions of ADD. In this way, the Conners could serve as a transition instrument to increase the interpretability of newer studies in comparison to studies performed earlier using the Conners. Without such an approach, an entire body of research might be cut off from relevance to current work.

NEWER INSTRUMENTS

There currently exist two newer rating instruments developed to reflect DSM III criteria for ADD. These are the ADD-H Comprehensive Teacher Rating Scale (ACTeRS) (Ullmann, Sleator, and Sprague, 1984) and the Yale Children's Inventory (YCI) (Shaywitz et al., 1986a; Shaywitz et al., 1986b, in press). The ACTeRS has data on reliability and construct as well as discriminant validity. No information is yet available on concurrent or predictive validity. Four empirically derived scales, Oppositional Behavior, Attention, Hyperactivity, and Social Problems, were developed to be useful in the assessment of children with ADDH.

Barkley (1986) reports that the oppositional factor shares similarities with both the conduct problems factor of the Conners and the aggression factor on the CBCL. Barkley is uncertain what advantages the ACTeRS has over the much more developed Conners.

The YCI, a parent-based rating scale, was developed to help identify and measure multiple dimensions relevant to ADD and related disorders. Eleven scales, Attention, Impulsivity, Activity, Tractability, Habituation, Conduct Disorder-Socialized, Conduct Disorder-Aggressive, Negative Affect, Language, Fine Motor, Academics, were empirically derived, and demonstrate both test-retest and internal consistency (Shaywitz et al., 1986). Measures of validity, including concurrent and predictive, have also been reported, and age-graded norms are available (Shaywitz et al., in press; Shaywitz, 1986b). As described above in "Definition and Syndrome Validation," development of these scales included items represented in the DSM III criteria for attention, activity, and impulsivity and as such represent the first empiric studies of the psychometric properties of DSM III criteria. While these constructs were selected by a consensus of senior investigators, the operationalization of these constructs as selected sets of items had not been subjected to empiric investigation. Results of our investigations suggest a modification of DSM III criteria for ADD (see "Definition and Syndrome Validation"). As indicated earlier, a second order factor analysis indicated two broad bands, a behavioral band and a cognitive band, with the attentional scales overlapping both. This finding supports the relationship of attention to both behavioral and cognitive function and supports the DSM III nosology labeling the disorder ADD rather than hyperactivity. In a validation study (Shaywitz et al., 1986b), it was demonstrated that in every instance where there existed a relationship between the Activity scale and a criterion variable, there also existed a relationship between that variable and the Attention scale. This suggests that, in the population studied, where there is an activity problem, there is a high likelihood of an associated attentional problem, although it may be less visibly or outwardly disruptive. However, the converse—that is, a strong relationship between the Attention scale and a criterion—did not necessarily herald a similar correspondence between the Activity scale and that variable. These differential correlations further support the emphasis on the attentional deficit in the current nosology.

The divergence of the YCI and other report inventories such as the CBCL and RBPC reflect, for the most part, the different populations that were utilized in initial scale development. The CBCL and similar instruments were developed from items differentiating and relevant to children attending mental health centers, while the YCI is based on items differentiating children referred to pediatric neurology and learning disorders clinics that are administratively part of a pediatrics department. The inclusion in the scales of items relating to language, fine motor, and academic function reflect the types of problems prominent in these children. In the development of a diagnostic rule for ADD, these scales rather than the scales related to conduct disorder were helpful in discriminating ADD from normal children (Shaywitz et al., 1986b).

This brings up the larger issue of differences in populations given the same diagnostic label but diagnosed by different disciplines. Most of the reports in the literature on ADD and especially hyperactivity originate from specialists (psychiatrists and psychologists) associated with mental health facilities. Not surprisingly, reports emanating from these sources stress the behavioral and often the conduct problems of children referred and subsequently diagnosed as ADD. Children referred to child neurologists or behavioral pediatricians will more often have attentional difficulties and associated learning problems as their primary symptom.

At this time, it is not clear whether the designation of the disorder as ADD and the emphasis on attentional difficulties has led to the identification and referral of a previously unrecognized or perhaps undiagnosed group of children. What the relationship of the primarily behaviorally disordered children referred to mental health facilities and given a diagnosis of ADD is to those groups of children presenting with primary attentional and learning problems is as yet unclear. Do they have the same disorder and represent opposite ends of a continuum, or are they representative of two categorically different entities? Studies are currently underway, utilizing the Conners scales, the CBCL, and the YCI, to compare the characteristics of children identified as ADD on each of the measures. Also ongoing is an investigation of children diagnosed ADD by different disciplines and in different settings including an in-patient child psychiatry unit, a hospital-based learning disorders unit, and out-patient private pediatric and child psychologist practices. Since the literature regards all patients diagnosed as ADD as representing a unitary entity, it will be of great importance to clarify whether these different groups of children diagnosed as ADD share common characteristics. It is only in this way that findings relevant to etiology or outcome will have relevance to all groups of children diagnosed as ADD.

INSTRUMENTS UNDER DEVELOPMENT

The development or further refinement of behavioral measures that would provide reliable and valid assessment of constructs relevant to current notions of ADD is a subject of active investigation. Under the aegis of the American Psychological Association, three senior and highly experienced investigators are in the process of developing a factorially-derived classification system for a range of neurobehavioral disorders affecting children (Achenbach et al., 1985).

Another group under the direction of Loney (1986) has begun work on the development of three scales to identify children with attention problem disorder, hyperactive impulse disorder, and aggressive behavior disorder. The scales, the Divergent and Convergent Interview for Attention Problem Disorder (DACI-APD), based on a structured interview, the DICA-P (The Diagnostic Interview for Children and Adolescents: Parent Version, 1981), were formed with a particular emphasis on achieving both convergent and divergent validity for the Attention Problem and Aggressive Behavior scales. However, the Hyperactive Impulse Disorder scale meets criteria for convergent but not for divergent validity. As the author indicates, the instrument is in a preliminary developmental stage, and by nature, many of the decisions affecting scale composition have had to be somewhat arbitrary in nature. In its current format, the questions are presented to mothers in a structured interview format. Much of the data driving the development were obtained retrospectively, and the investigators recognize that measures of both concurrent and predictive validity and cross-validation studies will be important in establishing the validity of this diagnostic approach.

An important and troubling issue concerns the current approaches to revision of DSM III criteria. The Work Group to revise DSM III (chaired by Robert L. Spitzer) was appointed by the American Psychiatric Association (with representation from the Child Neurology Society and the Neurology Section of the American Academy of Pediatrics) and is completing its recommendation for revision of DSM III criteria for attention deficit disorder (DSM-III-R, American Psychiatric Association, in press). As indicated in other sections of this report, a serious limitation of current DSM III criteria was that the criteria did not emerge from large-scale empiric investigations but rather represented a preliminary step in syndrome validation in providing both categories and rules for identification based on predominantly consensual agreement. The rationale for emphasizing attentional deficits as the core feature was provided by a growing body of work indicating that attentional rather than motoric problems were of most diagnostic relevance and that a focus on hyperactivity served to obscure the often prevalent and disabling attentional deficits.

The new formulation, now termed "attention deficit-hyperactivity disorder" (ADHD), is placed within "disruptive behavior disorders," which includes ADHD, oppositional-defiant disorder, and conduct disorder, the latter itself subdivided into "solitary aggressive, group and undifferentiated types." The new terminology does away with what DSM III termed ADDnoH, though it recognizes that many of the children so classified would now be included within ADHD. Rather than three separate qualities (inattention, impulsivity, and hyperactivity), a diagnosis of ADHD is made on the presence of any 8 of 15 symptoms, representing inattention, impulsivity, and hyperactivity. Severity is graded as mild, moderate, or severe, according to how many symptoms are present (though the number is not specified).

Despite the obvious care which the Work Group has taken to hear the views of many of the principal investigators in the field, the new terminology was arrived at principally by consensus, and there is no empiric evidence to suggest that the proposed diagnostic criteria are superior to DSM III. Furthermore, the elimination of ADDnoH and the elevation of hyperactivity back into a prominant position in the terminology represent what many believe to be a regressive step, one which is likely to lead to still more confusion. Though the criteria are said to have emerged after field trials, they can be considered only as very preliminary.

It is particularly unfortunate that the terminology of DSM III was changed because the validation process was essentially at the stage of what Skinner (1981) and Fletcher (1985) call the theory formulation component of a classification process. In essence, the Work Group and its various advisory committees have performed this first step; it is what Loney (1986) notes as the first stage in any validation strategy, "the accumulation of a pool of potential items or questions....with both face and consensual validity,...items which appear to a group of experts to describe the dimension or disorder in question." What is now necessary is to progress to the internal and external validation phases of the classification process.

In no small measure, the impetus to rename ADD as ADHD reflects the continuing controversy over the relative importance of inattention and hyperactivity in contributing to the clinical picture. Another problem has been the difficulty in validating each of the three constructs proposed in DSM III, a necessary preliminary step in the validation process of the syndrome itself. It is reasonable to believe that it has been the insensitivity of the instruments to identify and differentiate these constructs that has led to this frustration. Clearly, the acceptance of ADD as a valid entity mandates the development and availability of instruments capable of measuring the behavioral characteristics comprising the syndrome.

As detailed previously, the concept of ADD evolved from that of hyperactivity. Despite the change in terminology promulgated by DSM III, the instruments used to diagnose ADD were the same ones used to define hyperactivity; there was a lag in the development of measures to reflect the newer constructs. Now that the syndrome was conceptualized as comprised of three distinct dimensions or symptoms, instruments that were available that had been useful in studying what initially appear to be the same constructs proved to be otherwise. For example, as our notions of behavioral disorders have evolved, there has been a refinement in just what is meant by such behaviors as hyperactivity. Appreciation of the classification process has underscored the necessity of identifying homogeneous subgroups for biologic and other studies of etiology, response to treatment, and outcome, each of which is predicated upon availability of relatively pure and uncontaminated study groups.

As we have noted above, many of the instruments used do not have scales that conform to constructs found in DSM III. Thus, many of the available scales developed prior to DSM III appear to measure much more global qualities of externalizing behaviors—for example, a mixture of hyperactivity, aggressivity, and inattention. In addition, though individual scales may be labeled as if they were synonymous with DSM III symptoms, examination of their item content indicates otherwise. Finally, instruments are becoming available (YCI, DACI-APD, ACTeRS) that provide relatively distinct measures of inattention, hyperactivity, and impulsivity as described in DSM III. Availability of such measures should now permit internal and external validation studies of the syndrome.

Studies of the DSM III constructs are only now beginning to emerge. It is hoped that this new change in terminology will not create still more confusion and that the advances made by DSM III will not be abandoned prematurely.

STRUCTURED INTERVIEWS

Structured interviews have been developed in recent years to provide diagnoses according to DSM III. Many are still in the process of revision and modification and have not been a constant feature of the clinical or research settings evaluating children with ADD. The Diagnostic Interview Schedule for Children (DISC) reflects modifications by Costello et al. (1984). It is not designed for general clinical usage but rather for large-scale screening of populations for a variety of mental health problems. There are both parent and child editions. The interview is lengthy, and interviewers should be trained for reliability. Reliability measures are moderately high, but the major concern rests with the divergence of clinicians' judgments and diagnoses based on the interview. Active investigations are currently underway, and it may be that this issue will be resolved in the near future. The Kiddie SADS-E (K-SADS-E), a semistructured interview, also provides for a diagnostic category for ADD. It, too, is lengthy and tiresome for some children. These and other structured interviews are discussed in detail by Orvaschel et al. (1980).

DIRECT OBSERVATION METHODS

The most direct approach to measuring the core features of ADD is provided by observations of the child's behavior in a naturalistic environment—that is, in the child's home or classroom, or in a laboratory setting. As with other measures, a critical question is what is being assessed and what the relationship is to other methods of assessment. Considerable controversy surrounds the issue of direct observations in both clinical and research contexts. Some investigators (Vincent et al., 1981) suggest that the observational approach may be the most appropriate method for research, rather than for clinical purposes. Thus, while some observational methods may not be appropriate because they are expensive and complicated, and have the potential to be intrusive and affect the behavior being measured, some observational approaches (Abikoff, Gittelman-Klein, and Klein, 1977; Whalen et al., 1978) may be more practical for classroom observation purposes (Ross and Ross, 1982).

Although the home is theoretically the most "naturalistic" of all environments, few studies have reported home observations, and fewer have compared these with clinical assessments of the same child. In one such study, Rapoport and Beboit (1975) observed 20 hyperactive children in their home environment and correlated these observations with parent and teacher ratings as well as with ratings made by a psychiatrist and a psychologist. Mothers also maintained 4-day diaries. The home observations measured both relatively noninferential actions (activity shifts) and more inferential occurrences (negative interactions) as well as global impressions. The global observations demonstrated the strongest correlations, but the other measures were also correlated with ratings by the psychologist, psychiatrist, and teacher, and with mothers' diaries.

Advantages of classroom observational methods include their objectivity, simplicity, reliability, and relative lack of bias, while disadvantages include the high demands made on the observer, necessity for continual vigilance, and high cost (Ross and Ross, 1982). Behaviors of low frequency but high saliency (Whalen et al., 1979; also see "Clinical Characteristics"), which may influence, for example, teacher and peer perceptions, might also be missed during the limited observation period. Observation systems vary in their inclusion of categories and types of behavior to be measured, scoring criteria, and reliability. Two of the systems most frequently referred to in the literature are the Classroom Observation System (Whalen et al., 1978) and the Revised Stony Brook Observation Code (Abikoff, et al., 1977). An outstanding feature of the former is its incorporation of both stylistic as well as quantitative activity measures in keeping with the notion that it may be the qualitiative aspect of the interaction that influences perceptions of the hyperactive child.

Attempts to relate classroom observations to teacher ratings have shown mixed results, some reporting at least moderate correlations (Jacob et al., 1978; Whalen et al., 1979), while others (Abikoff et al., 1977) report poor correlations between individual items observed and the hyperactivity factor score on the Conners. However, in this latter study, global observational scores differentiated affected from control children, although there was a high rate of false negatives (42 percent). In a more recent study focusing on children identified by operationalization of DSM III criteria (Atkins et al., 1985), objective classroom measures discriminated between teacher-identified ADD and non-ADD children. False negatives, although less than in previous investigations, were again problematic, occurring in 24 percent of the cases. In this study, the only two behavioral observations differentiating the ADD and control children were behaviors coded as verbal intrusion or attending, which the investigators interpret as paralleling DSM III symptoms of impulsivity and inattention and as supporting DSM III nosology for ADD. Measures from several classroom sources including direct behavioral observation, academic work, and organization of belongings entered into the final discriminant function identifying ADD children. The investigators suggest that such "multimethod" approaches may improve classification rates for ADD.

DIRECT MEASURES OF ACTIVITY LEVEL

Intuitively, measurement of activity by mechanical means should offer the most direct and unbiased assessment of movement. Porrino et al. (1983), reviewing laboratory measurements of hyperactive behaviors, conclude that there are a number of factors that can influence these measurements. They include the type of activity being measured, the method used, the length of time of the observation period, and the nature of the setting itself. A variety of instruments and devices have been used: actometers, stabilometric cushions, and pedometers. Consistent with direct observation methods, hyperactive children demonstrate increased movement in structured situations, but not during free play (Schulman and Clarinda, 1964; Schulman and Reisman, 1969; Barkley and Ullmann, 1975, Routh and Schroeder, 1976). Other techniques such as ultrasound or photoelectric cells are complicated, expensive, and not necessarily reliable. One of the problems with such apparently simple and direct techniques is that these measures often do not correlate well with each other, or the correlations are quite inconsistent (Shaffer et al., 1974; Barkley and Ullmann, 1975; Ullmann et al., 1978). Both Porrino et al. (1983) and Ross and Ross (1982) emphasize that techniques to measure activity fail to provide information on the qualitative aspects of the activity. These features may be more critical in characterizing the ADD child than the more quantitative measure of activity.

Recently, the development of an actometer that measures truncal activity over a prolonged period of time has provided investigators with an opportunity to clarify the nature of activity patterns in hyperactive children compared to control children (Porrino et al., 1983). This naturalistic assessment demonstrated that, overall, hyperactive boys move more than their controls. This is an important finding, complementing other studies using observation systems that indicate that the activity of hyperactive children is also qualitatively different from that of nonhyperactives. Porrino et al. also address the question of the situational nature of hyperactivity by demonstrating that, across a variety of situations, hyperactives move more than control children. Hyperactive children differ most from their nonhyperactive peers during times when they are in structured classroom situations, particularly during academic subject times. During relatively unstructured activities (for example, lunch or recess), both hyperactive and normal children increase their activity level and do not differ from one another in this aspect. This finding is consistent with that of other investigators (Zentall, 1975; Schleifer, Weiss, and Cohen, 1975), who found that raters were able to differentiate hyperactives from controls only in structured situations. It is suggested that it may be only in structured settings that the behavior of hyperactives is qualitatively different from and more disturbing than that of normals. Therefore, this is the setting in which the more inferential rating scales are likely to identify these children as hyperactive. Porrino et al. (1983) review previous findings of a lack of correlation between parent (home) and teacher (school) ratings (Goyette, Conners, and Ulrick, 1978; Sandberg, Rutter, and Taylor, 1978) and suggest that utilization of multiple measures rather than only parent and teacher ratings contributed to the findings of increased activity across situations. The Porrino et al. (1983) findings are influential in furthering our understanding of the nature of the activity in children labeled as hyperactive and the relationship between direct measures and more inferential techniques. These findings need to be replicated. A difficulty in using actometers has been the problems in standardization and in their frequent breakdown. Hopefully, these difficulties can be resolved and replication studies carried out and completed.

MEASURES OF ATTENTION

THEORETICAL ISSUES

Although DSM III emphasizes the primacy of the attentional deficit in ADD, attention is a complex construct both to measure and to comprehend. As Douglas (1983) has summarized, the change in diagnostic terminology from hyperkinesis to attention deficit disorder has reflected research findings that hyperactivity is accompanied by more subtle, but at times more disabling, deficits in attention. Attention is a broad construct encompassing many components, with difficulties in any or all resulting in effects on the "children's behavior, academic achievement and cognitive functioning" (Douglas, 1983; p. 280). Obstacles to our better comprehension of the nature of the attentional deficit in ADD children include: (a) significant differences among investigators in the definition and measurement of these components; (b) the nature of the relationships among the different components of attention; and (c) the relationship between a component of attention as it is measured in the laboratory and as it is perceived and labeled by parents or teachers rating a particular child. Douglas and Peters (1979) have described four components of the attentional process that may be affected in ADD: (1) how the child invests in and maintains attention, (2) the inhibition of impulsive response tendencies, (3) the modulation of arousal, and (4) sensitivity to reinforcement. Other difficulties reflect heterogeneous samples utilized in studies;

indeed, in an earlier study documenting differences in sustained attention, subject selection was based on narrative descriptions rather than on quantitative measures of hyperactivity (Sykes et al., 1973). Perhaps the strength of such studies was that, even in the face of such heterogeneous populations, the finding of inattention was so strong that it emerged anyway. Douglas (1983) believes that the primary and secondary effects of the attentional deficit are often confused. As secondary deficits she includes: impaired development of higher order strategies and concepts; impaired metacognition; and as a response to frustration and continued failure, diminished motivation for mastery (Douglas, 1980a; Douglas and Peters, 1979; Tant and Douglas, 1982). These effects on the children's cognitive and coping styles may increase differences between hyperactive and control children over time if interventions are not undertaken. Awareness of both the primary and the secondary effects of the attentional deficit can be useful in understanding (and hopefully ameliorating) the ADD child's poor performance on a task. While in some instances, true inability is the responsible cause, more often it may be that the ADD child is failing to make use of the abilities that the child does possess. It has been demonstrated that certain modifications to the testing procedure will improve performance—for example, the presence of an adult or an authority figure during testing, performing individually rather than as part of a group situation, increasing the saliency of the task, and the use of rewards.

As suggested earlier, one of the prime difficulties in attempts to understand the mechanisms of inattention has been the confusion surrounding terminology. The complexity of the situation is illustrated by confusion over the term "sustained attention." Douglas considers sustained attention to involve the ability of the individual to maintain attention over time. Others have considered aspects of intensity and organization of attentional processes as part of sustained attention. Similarly, the terms "selective attention" and "distractibility" have generated some confusion. While ADD children are often identified because they are rated as "distractable" by observers, attempts to demonstrate this finding in the laboratory have not been universally successful (Douglas and Peters, 1979). These authors feel that even in those instances in which ADD children perform more poorly in the presence of a distractor, the poor performance can be ascribed to mechanisms other than distractibility, such as impaired concentration, inhibition, arousal, or reinforcement. Another component of attention, inhibition control, is associated with an impulsive response style in ADD children. This can manifest itself in a response style in which children answer before they completely hear or understand a problem and/or have given themselves enough time to reflect on the correct response. The difficulties that this can present in a classroom situation are evident. The fourth component of attention that may be affected in ADD children involves the ability to modulate their own arousal state to be compatible with the demands of a particular task or situation.

Douglas (1983) emphasizes the methodological difficulties in attempting to ascribe a particular result to a deficit in a specific component of attention. She points out that there is a long list of experimental variables that may influence the child's performance on a specific task. These include the influence of order effects in "distraction" studies so that ADD children perform more poorly on the second administration of a task, regardless of the presence or absence of a distractor. In other settings, investigators have demonstrated the importance of duration of the task (Hiscock et al., 1979) and of how demanding the task is on performance (Loiselle et al., 1980). Douglas (1983) argues, therefore, that the interpretation of, for example, distractability on a particular task may be more reflective of task characteristics than of the presence of a distractor. Douglas (1983, p. 297) believes that the behaviors exhibited by ADD children, both in the laboratory and in the community, can best be summarized by a formulation which emphasizes "a child's inclination to seek salience, novelty, and immediate reinforcement."

The understanding of the factors influencing the emergence of the child's attentional deficit on a task has clinical and investigational implications. Douglas (1983) advocates cognitive training as the ideal method to provide the child with the strategies and problem-solving techniques not spontaneously acquired because of a primary attentional deficit. In addition, attentional studies have clarified what factors influence the child's often variable performance. Factors associated with improved performance include: tasks that are more salient or challenging and less boring; provision of consistent feedback; and child-paced rather than investigator-paced tasks. Furthermore, research has demonstrated that ADD children may require more time to habituate; therefore, their performance will frequently improve after a "shaky" start. This information is important to both the child and teacher in approaching classroom activities, particularly tests.

Review of the research findings clearly indicates that hyperactive children have problems paying attention. What is less clear, and what the preceding review illustrates, is that the terminology for and mechanisms underlying particular aspects of the construct of attention are far from being completely understood or agreed upon. Nevertheless, a number of "tests of attention" have indicated differences between hyperactive and control populations and are useful measures in investigations of ADD. These difficulties in part reflect the complicated nature of the deficit in ADD, but also reflect discipline-related issues in cognitive psychology. Active work is now underway in attempts to develop better and theoretically more meaningful tests of attention for use with ADD populations. However, there is a core of tasks that have been used and continue to be used, particularly in pharmocological studies, which we now briefly review.

Continuous performance tests, originally developed by Rosvold et al. (1956) to study schizophrenia, have been used extensively to study hyperactive children. In these tasks, the child is asked to sustain attention, over a set period of time, to a series of auditory or visual stimuli and then indicate when a preassigned, infrequent stimulus appears and refrain from signaling when the stimulus is not present. In the limited age range of 3-7 years, children make fewer errors as they get older. In a large number of investigations, hyperactive children have been found to make more errors than controls. The continuous performance test is a sensitive discriminator between hyperactive and nonhyperactive children (Whalen and Henker, 1976; Rosenthal and Allen, 1978). Hyperactives make more errors of commission in some instances (Hoy et al., 1978), while in other cases, reports indicate an increased frequency of both errors of omission and of commission (Loiselle et al., 1980). Although these measures have formed a cornerstone of the laboratory evaluation of inattention in children, Taylor (1986) questions what the clinical implications are of performance on this kind of task. He doubts the relevancy of such tasks for either classroom or social learning.

The Matching Familiar Figures Test (MFFT) is another measure that has been consistently helpful in differentiating hyperactive from nonhyperactive children. This matching-to-sample test requires the child to match a standard figure to one of a series of highly similar figures, each of which, except one, differs from the standard in very minor ways. The child's response is scored for accuracy and latency of response time. An interaction of the errors and response latency is used to characterize the child as reflective (response time longer, fewer errors) or impulsive (shorter response time, more errors). Reliability measures have been inconsistent (Egeland and Weinberg, 1976; Berry and Cook, 1980), and there has been controversy over just what processes the MFFT measures (Douglas, 1983). However, there is a consensus (Messer, 1976) that there is a relationship between performance on the MFFT and hyperactivity. Differences between hyperactives and controls appear to be present from preschool through high school age (Aman, 1978; Douglas and Peters, 1979; Messer, 1976; Sandoval, 1977), as reported by Douglas (1983). Followup studies (Hopkins et al., 1979) indicate that these differences persist. A newer version of the MFFT (Cairns and Cammock, 1978) appears to be more reliable and a better predictor of academic function.

The paired-associate learning (PAL) test has also been frequently used in psychopharmacological studies. In this task, stimulus-response pairs of common items are presented to the child, and the child is asked to learn the assigned response to each item. Trials are repeated until a criterion is reached and errors are scored for each trial. The PAL differentiates control from hyperactive children (Conners, 1973; Douglas et al., 1986) and has been useful in pharmocological studies (Swanson and Kinsbourne, 1976; Swanson et al., 1978). There has been an inconsistent relationship between response to medication as assessed by behavioral measures and as measured by responses on the PAL (Gittelman-Klein, 1975; Swanson et al., 1983). A variety of other tasks have been utilized in studying ADD children. Some of these are discussed by Douglas and Peters (1979), Taylor (1986), Douglas (1983), and particularly the tasks useful in psychopharmacological studies, by Swanson (1985).

In summary, while the precise mechanisms of the attentional deficits await further investigation, it has been clearly demonstrated that hyperactive children are inattentive and that there exist measures of the components of attention that differentiate hyperactive from control children. A word of caution is urged in attempting to prematurely utilize the results of group differences on specific measures as an indication that these measures are valid diagnostic instruments for ADD. As has been indicated previously (Sebrechts et al., 1986), the construct of attention is represented by many different components, and no single measure of attention provides a complete assessment of attentional deficits. Thus, some children with ADD will perform adequately on one specific measure and perform poorly on another; therefore, a child's performance on any one measure should not, in and of itself, be used to diagnose ADD. This caveat takes on a particular cogency now that commercially marketed "diagnostic" tests of some of the aspects of attention have become available. Milich and colleagues (1986, in press) discuss some of these concerns in a recent paper.

OTHER MEASURES

PHYSICAL EXAMINATION

It would be remiss not to discuss the routine physical examination. As one might expect, this is usually normal, but the possibility of symptomatology resembling ADD but secondary to impairment of hearing or vision should be considered in the evaluation of children for attentional problems. Thus, if a child has difficulty hearing his teacher or is unable to see the blackboard from the back of the room, he may appear inattentive and restless. Examination for the features of sex-linked genetic disorders such as Klinefelter's and Turner's syndromes that are associated with ADD or learning problems may be productive as well. Thus, assessment of physical growth characteristics as well as sexual maturation should be incorporated into the general examination. The most recent study of the physical development of hyperactive boys (McGee et al., 1985) indicates no difference in stature, weight, or skeletal maturity assessed by bone age in hyperactive boys at age 7 years compared to controls. However, hyperactives had significantly smaller triceps skin fold measures, suggesting a leaner body mass.

There has been some suggestion that the examination for minor congenital anomalies may be useful. Minor congenital anomalies are physical characteristics (for example, small palpebral fissures, malformed ear lobes, clinodactyly) that are of no medical or cosmetic consequence to the patient and are often overlooked on routine general physical examination.

A number of investigators have used the presence of a high number of minor congenital anomalies to distinguish various groups of normal and disabled children as well as to suggest a prenatal origin to the difficulties experienced by the high-anomaly group. Of particular interest has been the recurring association of high anomaly scores with difficulties of modulation of activity, impulsivity, and aggression. Waldrop et al. (1978) have found minor anatomic defects observed during the newborn period to predict difficulties with attention, aggression, and impulsivity at 3 years of age. Significant relationships have also been reported between preschool anomaly scores and hyperactivity at both 2.5 (Waldrop et al., 1978) and 7.5 years of age (Waldrop and Halverson, 1971), negative peer judgments (Halverson and Victor, 1976), early onset of hyperkinesis (Quinn and Rapoport, 1974), and increased dopamine-b-hydroxylase (DBH) activity in plasma (Quinn and Rapoport, 1974). Others (Mattes et al., 1980) have not been able to confirm the latter finding.

Firestone et al. (1978) noted that hyperactive and retarded children exhibit an increased number of minor physical anomalies compared to controls. A later study (Firestone and Prabhu, 1983) compared hyperactive (defined as a score of 15 on Conners teacher questionnaire), psychoneurotic, and control boys, their siblings, and parents. They found an increased number of minor physical anomalies in hyperactive children compared to normal controls, with the psychoneurotic children falling between the hyperactives and controls but not different from either. Despite these results, the authors conclude with the admonition that "the present study does not support the conclusion that MPA [minor physical anomalies] alone are sufficiently accurate to be used as 'markers' for children at risk for hyperactivity."

In a more recent study, Fogel et al. (1985) rated activity levels and minor physical anomalies in 10-13 year olds. Their results suggested a significant relationship between activity levels in normal boys and minor physical anomalies. Unfortunately, the same pediatric neurologist both assessed the children for anomalies and rated their activity after examination, presenting a potentially serious bias. The authors recommend against the use of minor physical anomalies in clinical screening or diagnosis.

It must be emphasized that the decision as to what constitutes an anomaly remains very arbitrary, and while it is possible to elaborate criteria during investigations (Shaywitz, 1982) and develop the necessary reliability needed for such a determination, this is extremely difficult to effect during a routine clinical examination. Thus, while the findings of minor congenital anomalies are interesting from an investigational perspective, most investigators (Firestone and Prabhu, 1983; Fogel et al., 1985; Shaywitz, 1982) have concluded that such an examination is not helpful clinically, and may, in fact, be counterproductive.

NEUROLOGIC EXAMINATION

Results of the routine neurological examination are usually normal in children with ADD. There is, however, a long history of attempts to document subtle neurologic abnormalities in disorders of cognition and behavior, reflecting the notion that the examination for minor neurologic abnormalities offers a window on central nervous system (CNS) functioning. Thus, over the last 50 years, a seemingly unending series of attempts have been made to delineate minor abnormalities of the neurological examination in children. Such findings, termed neuromaturational signs, are considered to be minor, often occur in normal young children, and need not be related to any structural lesion in the brain. These generally include such diverse indices of CNS function as laterality, choreiform movements, mirror or overflow phenomena, diadochokinesis, and performance on a variety of fine and gross motor tasks.

It was originally hoped that these abnormalities might have heuristic value in furthering the understanding of behavior and learning difficulties, although just what these findings of irregularities on neuromaturational examination indicate has often been unclear. For the most part, investigations have been flawed by poor methodology, including a lack of uniformity in describing abnormalities or determining their presence or absence, inadequate control groups, and failure to consider the effects of intelligence, social class, and other environmental factors. More importantly, there has existed a vagueness in interpreting the significance of the findings reported. Thus, from time to time, the findings of minor neurologic abnormalities have been used to indicate pathogenesis, with some clinicians equating these findings with the diagnosis of brain damage or organicity, and others interpreting these signs as merely suggesting brain dysfunction (see "Historical Perspective"). However, both the theoretical and the practical limitations of such an approach are well recognized.

The choreiform syndrome, which emerged in the 1960's, embodies the controversy surrounding the significance of minor neurologic abnormalities. First noted as muscle artifact on the EEG of hyperactive children referred for poor school performance, these irregular, arrhythmic muscle jerks of short duration were termed choreiform movements and related to reading problems and histories of prenatal or perinatal complications (Prechtl and Dijkstra, 1960; Prechtl and Stemmer, 1962). However, Rutter, Graham, and Birch (1966) were not able to replicate these findings. The relationship between neuromaturational signs and ADD continues to remain controversial. Some investigators (Hart et al., 1974; Lucas et al., 1965; McMahon and Greenberg, 1977; Mikkelsen et al., 1982; Peters et al., 1975) report an increased frequency of soft signs in children with ADD, while others (Camp et al., 1978; Werry and Aman, 1976; Wikler et al., 1970) fail to note any difference. Waber and Mann (1985) report an association between motor overflow and task-related performance in normal third and fifth grade children. Thus, children with high overflow scores exhbited difficulty in focusing attention, distractibility, and impulsivity.

Most recently, Shaffer et al. (1985) examined adolescents who were indexed at age 7 as exhibiting minor neurological abnormalities as part of the Collaborative Perinatal Project. While they reported a significant relationship between later affective or anxiety disorder and soft signs at age 7, such a relationship did not emerge for ADD. Adolescents with soft signs were more likely to have a lower IQ (performance affected most), a phenomenon noted by others as well (Rutter et al., 1966; Shaywitz et al., 1984).

In practical terms, many investigators and clinicians believe that the significance of a neuromaturational examination (NME) relates to its ability to differentiate groups rather than individual children as either ADD or normal. At the present time, it is reasonable to suggest inclusion of such aspects of the neuromaturational examination as finger agnosia, laterality, and fine motor function, including rapid sequential finger tapping, synkinesis, and figure drawing (Shaywitz et al., 1984). However, examination of such gross motor function as balance during passive stance, heel or toe walking, or any of the gross motor items on the Lincoln-Oseretsky test (Stott, 1966) does not appear to be useful in the diagnosis of ADD (Colligan, 1981) .

The NME may be a helpful adjunct in the examination of the school age child, particularly if a systematic, consistent format with a well delineated scoring protocol is utilized. The clinician can then develop his own internal anchor as to what responses are appropriate at different ages. Primarily, the NME is useful to the clinician as a vehicle to observe the child in a structured format over a period of time. As instructive, or more instructive than any of the particular responses to a specific task, is the manner in which the child conducts himself, his behavioral style. How does he respond to directions? Is he impulsive? Does he give up early? Since the physician is being called upon to evaluate problems that occur in a school setting, the NME gives the clinician an opportunity to get as close as possible to the issues modulating a child's school function—his ability to follow instruction, his response to failure, his persistence. It is these responses that may be helpful in a formulation. Under no circumstances should the presence or a lack of presence of any of the so-called soft signs be invoked, in and of themselves, as reason for designating a child as having ADD.

In addition to the history, physical examination, and neurologic examination, psychometric testing is critical in the evaluation of the child suspected of having ADD. This component of the examination assesses ability, achievement, and information processing characteristics. Psychologic assessment of ability and achievement indicates whether a learning problem is secondary to a learning disability in which there is a discrepancy between ability and achievement, or if the academic performance problems reflect a more general retardation of cognitive ability in which achievement is low but not disproportionate to ability. In instances of a suspected attentional disorder, psychometric testing is helpful in gaining an understanding of the full range of attentional deficits and their influence on cognitive ability and academic achievement.

Diagnostic or therapeutic decisions for children with possible ADD should never rest on group ability or achievement tests alone. The inappropriateness of a group test to assay ability in children who function less than optimally in group situations, who may have basic difficulties in understanding and following directions, who are inattentive, distractable, disorganized, and fail to persist in a task, is self-evident. Thus, discrepancies between group and individualized tests favoring the latter may be helpful in documenting an attention deficit disorder. Similarly, it is important to obtain an assessment of academic achievement using an individually administered test battery. It is not uncommon to find inattentive children who are unable to score well on achievement tests administered to an entire class and yet who demonstrate significant progress when tested individually. The same case should be made for assessing a child's performance using untimed measures. Since slowness in performance may be the hallmark of the attentionally disabled child, the child should always be permitted an opportunity to demonstrate what he knows in an untimed format as well. The contrast between the child's performance in the timed and untimed settings may have implications for both diagnosis and intervention.

SPECIFIC MEASURES

Although traditionally, intelligence has been assessed by both the Stanford Binet and the Wechsler Intelligence Scales for Children—Revised (WISC-R) test batteries, most clinicians and investigators usually find the WISC-R to be more instructive, because in contrast to the primarily verbal emphasis of the Stanford Binet, the ten subtests of the WISC-R provide a broad survey of both verbal and performance skills. Many children with ADD exhibit a characteristic profile recognizable by relatively poor scores on the subtests of arithmetic, coding, information, and digit span, collectively referred to as the ACID profile, or, excluding the information subscale, referred to as the freedom from distractability factor (Kaufman, 1975). These subtests are considered to be especially sensitive to deficits in attention, concentration, and alertness to the environment, the latter reflected particularly by low scores on the information subtest. Much has been written about particular profiles diagnostic of children with learning disabilities. Perhaps the most frequently cited characteristic is that of a significant discrepancy between the Verbal and Performance scales. However, despite the possible clinical and theoretical meaningfulness of differential strengths and weaknesses exhibited by learning disabled children on WISC-R subscales, neither the interpretation of regrouped composite WISC-R subscale scores (Henry and Wittman, 1981) nor the presence of inter- or intra-scale scatter (Kaufman et al., 1981) has been shown to be particularly useful in the differential diagnosis of learning or attentional difficulties. More recently, investigators have employed the Kaufman ABC battery designed to provide a culture-free measure of intelligence. This battery has been criticized because of its omission of a verbal component, since it is generally this component that provides the most robust measure of predictive validity to later academic performance (Sternberg, 1984).

While a number of academic achievement tests are available, the Woodcock-Johnson Psychoeducational Battery is particularly useful since its achievement scores can be converted to standard scores with a mean of 100 and a standard deviation of 15, allowing for comparability of academic achievement relative to intellectual ability as measured by the Wechsler scales. The Peabody Individual Achievement Test (PIAT) and the revised Wide Range Achievement Test (WRAT) are also widely used for measuring academic achievement.

A variety of other measures are available and may be useful, particularly those pertaining to language such as the Peabody Picture Vocabulary Test (PPVT-R), a well-standardized measure of receptive language; the Boston Naming Test, a confrontation naming task sensitive to dysnomic problems; and the Token Test, which provides an index of the child's comprehension of directions, particularly prepositions. Although most current conceptualizations of reading disability posit a linguistic basis, it is nevertheless instructive to obtain a measure of visual perceptual function. The most commonly utilized test for this is the Beery Developmental Test of Visual-Motor Integration (VMI), which provides age-equivalency scores from ages 3-15 years. Specific, more analytic measures of reading, arithmetic, and writing skills are frequently helpful in pinpointing the precise area of difficulty and developing an educational instructional plan. The problem is that many of these instruments have been poorly standardized. More complete discussion of these tests is provided by Berk (1984) and Sparrow et al. (1986).

ELECTROENCEPHALOGRAPHIC STUDIES

In his comprehensive review of EEG abnormalities in dyslexia and related disorders, Hughes (1978) cites two investigations suggesting that 90 percent of hyperkinetic children exhibit abnormal EEGs. Review of these (Anderson, 1963) indicates that almost one-half the children described had clinical seizures, one-half had evidence of perinatal asphyxia, and one-half had slow motor and speech development. Some had only borderline normal intelligence. Thus, it is clear that these clinical findings would have excluded the children from ADD as we define it today. Later studies, involving more appropriately defined hyperactive children, indicated no EEG differences between hyperactives and controls, either by the frequency of abnormalities or the type of abnormality (Satterfield et al., 1972; Werry et al., 1972).

Not surprisingly, more recent investigations have employed more sophisticated electroencephalographic testing paradigms. Thus, Halliday et al. (1983; 1984) utilized visual evoked repsonses to examine methylphenidate effects in hyperactive children. These event related potentials (ERP) were influenced more by age than by drug dose, but the response to medication could be predicted by the ERP. The importance of maturational effects on electrophysiological responses was noted as well by Satterfield et al. (1984).

In a recent series of experiments, Klorman and his associates (Klorman et al., in press; Peloquin and Klorman, 1986) examined the effects of methylphenidate on a variety of electrophysiological measures in normal children, children with ADD, and normal young adults. Methylphenidate administration prior to the subject's performing on a continuous performance test resulted in an increase in amplitude but no change in latency of the P3b component of the evoked response.

OTHER LABORATORY STUDIES

With the advent of computed tomography (CT), there was expectation that this technique might prove clinically useful in demonstrating anatomical evidence of brain dysfunction in ADD children. To date, however, CT studies have been normal (Shaywitz et al., 1983). The addition of other investigative measures (hematologic indices, endocrine studies, lead levels, chromosomes) is primarily dependent on the individual patient's manifestations and the need to consider other causes of attentional difficulties.

CLINICAL CHARACTERISTICS

DSM III View

As defined by DSM III criteria, the essential clinical features of ADD are "signs of developmentally inappropriate inattention and impulsivity" (DSM III, APA, 1980). This diagnostic paradigm delineates three subtypes of the disorder: ADD with hyperactivity (ADDH), ADD without hyperactivity (ADDnoH), and ADD residual type (ADDR) for individuals who once met criteria for ADDH, who are no longer hyperactive, but who still demonstrate other characteristics of the disorder. The DSM III provides an overview of the characteristics of children with ADD as they present in both home and school settings. At home, ADDH children demonstrate attentional problems, problems expressed by their failure to follow through on parental requests and/or instructions and by their inability to stay with most activities, including play, for time periods appropriate to their developmental stage. In school, the difficulties maintaining attention are reflected by the child's lack of persistence in completing his work, his tendency to be off task, and his poor organization. Such children often appear not to be listening or not to have heard a direction or instruction. As a reflection of their impulsivity, work is sloppy. Problems of this nature are evident on, as described by DSM III, individually administered tests, but perhaps, more so, on group tests. A range of errors may be present as indicators of the impulsivity characterizing such children. Generally falling under the rubric of "carelessness," these errors include omissions, insertions, poor performance on easy items with better performance on sometimes more difficult tasks, and misplacement and/or misinterpretation of arithmetic signs. It is further emphasized that these difficulties are not secondary to motivational factors and that they may be accentuated in group situations and when sustained attention is required. Unfortunately for affected children, both of these stressors are present in the usual classroom situation. In young, hyperactive children, gross motor activity such as running and climbing is increased. Descriptive terms such as "always on the go" or "running like a motor" are frequently applied to such affected children. Characteristically, this overactivity is not focused and is described as haphazard and frenetic. In contrast to the ontogeny of the attentional deficit that persists, the large muscle activity diminishes with maturation so that by preadolescence, running and climbing may have been replaced by a quality of restlessness and fidgetiness. DSM III indicates that in unstructured situations in which a high level of activity is to be expected, such as on the playground, ADDH children may not be discernable from children without the disorder. The variability of the symptoms is also emphasized so that in any one child the symptomatic expression of the disorder may vary with the situation or the time. Indeed, this great variability is the rule rather than the exception: "It is the rare child who displays signs of the disorder in all settings or even in the same setting at all times" (DSM III, APA 1980, p. 42). Associated features corresponding to poor compliance (obstinacy, negativism, stubborness, bossiness, and lack of response to discipline), mood lability (low frustration tolerance, temper outbursts), and low self-esteem are also described as part of the clinical syndrome. Age of onset is young (typically by age 3), and the course may be complicated by impairments in school and social functioning. Specific inclusion criteria for ADD reflect this clinical picture by providing for symptoms of inattention and impulsivity, and in the case of ADDH, symptoms of hyperactivity.

While DSM III was a major step forward in the development of a nosology for disorders of attention regulation and activity modulation, this diagnostic formulation did not emerge from empiric studies but rather reflected a consensus among experienced investigators. Therefore, it is important to review the components of the clinical picture as portrayed by the DSM III formulation and consider the empiric basis for each of these assumptions. According to DSM III, the cardinal features of ADD are signs and symptoms of developmentally inappropriate inattention, impulsivity, and in the subtype ADDH, hyperactivity. The disorder is envisioned as occurring in very young children, frequently by the age of 3 and always by the age of 7 according to inclusion criteria. DSM III stresses the great variability in presentation of symptoms, indicating that the precise clinical picture presented by any one child will reflect a number of factors, including the developmental level of the child, the environmental context, and the specific demands being made on the child's capacities. Thus, the symptoms may vary within a child from day to day and from situation to situation. The cardinal symptoms of the disorder are often accompanied by features indicating poor compliance, emotional lability, and diminished self-esteem, and may further be associated with both academic and social impairments.

EMPIRIC BASIS FOR DSM III FORMULATION OF ADD

Research that would permit the finer delineation of the basic clinical components of the disorder has been beset by a number of difficulties, not the least of which are the only recent provision of guidelines for inclusion and exclusion criteria for diagnosis and the shift of the conceptualization of the disorder from one focused primarily on hyperactivity to one centering on inattention as the core characteristic. Thus, investigators have employed a variety of criteria to identify target children, sometimes focusing on the hyperactivity and at other times on global behavioral problems including conduct disorder and less often on inattention. Not only has there been inconsistency affecting which constructs to consider in defining a sample; the inconsistency has extended to include operationalization of symptoms within each of the constructs as well. Yet, what has emerged from all of this seeming confusion is some order in the form of agreement from several lines of investigation on a number of features of the disorder.

Review of the literature suggests that perhaps the most impressive characteristic of the clinical features of ADD is the great variability in expression. Clinical presentation will vary both as a function of time or developmental stage and of place or particular environmental situation. This finding is certainly not surprising in a disorder characterizing an organism, the child, whose fundamental nature is to change, and is consistent with research into other developmental disorders. The clinical picture presenting at any one time will reflect the dynamic interaction between the innate characteristics of the child and the attributes of his environment. This theoretical model, termed interactional by Thomas and Chess (1977) and transactional by Sameroff and Chandler (1975), has achieved a consensus among investigators following the repeated demonstration that other simpler, static models are inadequate to "conceptualize sequences of human development and the transformation of psychological attributes over time" (Chess and Thomas, 1984, p. 20). This theoretic framework has been perhaps best articulated by Schneirla (1957, p. 79), as quoted in Chess and Thomas: "For an adequate perspective in the methodology of research and theory, we cannot accept a priori definition of behavioral development either as an unfolding of the innate, with gains through learning presumably superimposed in superior phyla, or as a continuum expanding mainly through the pressure of environmental forces, with the genes merely contributing an initial push to the process. Rather, a defensible generalization is that a species' genetic constitution contributes in some manner to the development of all behavior in all organisms, as does milieu, developmental context or environment." With this transactional model as a framework, we can proceed to consider first the developmental ontogeny of the symptoms of ADD.

INFANCY

There are two issues of concern regarding infants: one is whether events occurring prior to or at the time of birth can be used to predict which infants will have difficulties, often equated with "hyperactivity in infancy"; the second, a corollary, is whether specific behaviors in infancy are predictive of hyperactivty or ADD as the child matures. The first issue has been reviewed by Rapoport et al. (1979). In their view, research (Werner et al., 1971; Graham et al., 1957, 1962) has shown that pre- or perinatal factors alone have a weak but significant relationship to some developmental, emotional, or neurological indices in the first three years of life. However, more importantly, these relationships tend to disappear by school age. Therefore, their significance as predictors of long-term behavioral difficulty in general and of hyperactivity or attentional deficits in particular is questionable. Rapoport and her colleagues also emphasize the complex nature of the relationships between early events and later outcome. As discussed below in "Etiology," data from at least two important longitudinal studies, the Kauai Study (Werner et al., 1971) and the Collaborative Project of the National Institute of Neurological and Communicative Disorders and Stroke (NINCDS) (Nichols and Chen, 1981), indicate that the home environmental factors must be considered along with the effect of pre- and perinatal events.

Again, it should be understood that these studies focused on broad descriptors of outcome, and it remains difficult to evaluate how the findings apply more specifically to ADD or hyperactivity. For example, in the Kauai study, hyperkinetic symptoms were identified through behavior checklists "filled out by parents and teachers and confirmed by personality tests administered by clinical psychologists" (Werner et al., 1971, p. 22). These criteria were adequate for the time but clearly lacked in the demonstration of reliability or validity, which are prerequisites of current measures. Similarly, in the NINCDS study, the measures relating to ADD or hyperactivity included one termed minimal brain dysfunction and another termed hyperactivity (Nichols and Chen, 1981). Minimal brain dysfunction was identified by a constellation of features: hyperactivity, learning difficulties, and poor coordination and gait difficulties that emerged from a factor analysis of 26 signs and symptoms thought to be associated with the disorder. The authors point out that the association among these three factors was weak and the resultant group defined by these criteria quite heterogenous. A diagnosis of hyperactivity was determined by behavior ratings completed by the clinical psychologist following the 7-year psychological examination. Nichols and Chen (1981) themselves point out that a number of investigators (Wender, 1973; Kenny et al., 1971; Klein and Gittelman-Klein, 1975) have emphasized that hyperactivity may be absent in a 1:1 situation and that this symptom is frequently overlooked by clinicians who base their diagnosis solely on behavior in the clinician's office rather than on a consideration of the reports of parents and teachers (Sleator and Ullmann, 1981). In addition, the cutoff scores were entirely arbitrary and not based on any empiric findings. Therefore, the relationship of the disorders described by Nichols and Chen to either ADD or hyperactivity as generally referred to in the literature remains unclear.

As reviewed by Ross and Ross (1982), a number of studies have indicated that certain patterns of physical attributes and/or behavior evident in infancy may be predictive of later hyperactivity (Rapoport et al., 1979; Routh, 1978). Rapoport and associates review their findings on the possible association of minor congenital anomalies discerned in infancy and later hyperactivity. They indicate that behavioral measures in infancy are more apt to describe a globally "difficult" child than to clearly differentiate a "distractable" infant from an infant whose behavior was "intense negative," and that their comparisons between high and low anomaly infants on behavioral measures, while statistically significant, were also "numerically small" (Rapoport and Ferguson, 1981, p. 113). Thus, they conclude that a measure of minor congenital anomalies will not be clinically useful in identifying infants at risk for later hyperactivity. The investigators also emphasize that since the rate of false positives (infants with high anomaly scores who do not develop behavioral difficulties) is fairly high, identification of vulnerable children by this method alone might have the danger of providing a "self-fulfilling prophecy." Ross and Ross (1982) caution against applying a diagnostic label in infancy; they note that most, if not all, infants exhibit these "difficult" behaviors at some time and to some degree. Thus, these behaviors may be transient, with some increasing with time while others diminish as the child matures. The nature of the reports associating early behavioral difficulties to later hyperactivity are mainly of a retrospective nature based on reports by parents (Stewart et al., 1966) and clinicians (Weiss and Hechtman, 1979) about the behavior as infants of children later diagnosed as hyperactive. The retrospective nature of the majority of reports detailing the infant behavior of later diagnosed hyperactive children makes the information difficult to interpret and to generalize to all children with either ADD or hyperactivity. Having had a child identified as hyperactive or who currently displays behaviors consistent with hyperactivity can certainly selectively color a parent's recollections of that child's behavior as an infant. Even if these remembrances were generally accurate, what is lacking is a controlled longitudinal study in which both the predictive and the outcome behaviors were documented in an anterospective manner. While children later identified as having behavioral problems may have exhibited certain symptoms in infancy, what is unclear is what proportion of a normal population free of the outcome behavioral manifestations may also have exhibited the same "difficult" infant symptoms earlier on. What is also unclear is whether the presence of symptoms as early as infancy is confined to a small subgroup of hyperactive or attentionally disordered children or is representative of the general group of children who receive diagnoses of ADDH.

The symptoms described in infancy range across the entire "response repertoire" (Ross and Ross, 1982) and include activity modulation, sleep, feeding, and emotional responsivity. Movements are described as jerky or jittery, cries as shrill or piercing, sleep patterns as irregular, meals as interminable and difficult, and smiling as infrequent. Clinical experience and reports in the literature point to the unmistakable reality of children who were hyperactive while still in utero, who were squirmers from birth, who rocked incessantly in their cribs so that the crib would jolt across the room, who bit their mothers' breasts rather than suckled, who ran as soon as they could walk, whose piercing cries brought the neighbors running, and whose meals were a veritable battle, leaving the parent exhausted and the kitchen with smeared and flung foods resembling the remains of a combat scene. While these descriptions of the infancy of hyperactive children are clinically appealing and intuitively satisfying, empiric data that would indicate that such behaviors are an invariable component of the natural history of either ADD or hyperactivity are, for the most part, lacking. What remains to be determined is what the natural history of these disorders is. The historical component in infancy is particularly difficult because the diagnosis is generally not made until years later.

At this point, while there are some data suggesting that a "difficult" infancy may characterize the early development of some children who are later diagnosed as hyperactive, the data may also characterize the infancy of children who grow up free of such symptomatology. Furthermore, children later diagnosed as hyperactive may not have exhibited any indications of a "difficult" infancy. Until prospective epidemiologic studies with well defined diagnostic criteria are conducted, such questions will remain a matter of conjecture. Thus, while Ross and Ross (1982) are convincing in their delineation of the social toll extracted by the effects of the behavior of the "difficult" child on the interaction of the mother-child dyad, the generalizability of this effect to the early experience of all children later diagnosed as ADD or hyperactive is debatable.

The findings of the New York Longitudinal Study, too, provide a cautionary note in a somewhat different sense of attempts to predict later behavior from characteristics noted in infancy. Thus, Thomas and Chess (1977) indicate that children with particular constellations of tempermental attributes were at a higher risk for behavioral disturbances. They then go on to state, however, that "any temperamental trait or pattern in any individual child could significantly enter into the development of a behavior disorder if the environmental demands and expectations were sufficiently dissonant with the child's behavioral style.... In no case did a given pattern of temperament, as such, result in behavioral disturbance. Deviant behavior was always the result of the interaction between a child's individual makeup and significant features of the environment" (pp. 37-38). They proceed to provide a number of examples, based on their findings from the New York Longitudinal Study, to support this statement. Overall, they indicate that temperament is not necessarily a consistent attribute over the course of development and that children who are characterized as exhibiting a particular temperament do not "universally," but rather "predominantly," display this behavioral pattern. These investigators also emphasize the interactional nature of the effects of temperament and environment on symptom formation. Inclusion in the sample of two different sociocultural groups—a middle-class and a Puerto Rican working-class—helped to define the significant role of environmental influences. For example, at the age of 9 years, 31 percent of the middle-class sample in contrast to 10 percent of the Puerto Rican sample had been diagnosed as having a behavioral difficulty. Thomas and Chess ascribe these differences to a combination of factors: less preoccupation with theories of child development and pathology, and less stress on or pressure for task performance in the working-class group. In contrast, almost three times the number of working-class as did middle-class children presented with symptoms of hyperactivity. In this instance, the investigators ascribe the environmental living conditions as the stress leading to the development of the symptom. They reason that in the cases of children with similar temperaments, those living in crowded, small apartments would be penalized for the temperament and appear "hyperactive" while those middle-class children living in more spacious suburban homes would be able to run about and not appear to be problematic. While the development of particular symptoms is dependent on interactions between the child and his environment, the behavioral manifestation of a particular symptom will reflect the child's intrinsic temperament. The difficulties with predicting from early to later childhood were also evident in the great variability of outcomes for children diagnosed as having behavior problems in the childhood period. Of 42 such cases followed into adolescence, 19 recovered, 5 improved, 3 were unchanged, 8 worsened somewhat, and 7 became significantly worse. These empiric results emphasize the difference between correlational data, which suggest that two factors may be related, and also the reality of being able to predict the outcome in any one particular individual based on early behavioral functioning. Finally, Thomas and Chess (1977) review methodological problems (as noted by Rutter, 1970) in attempting to predict later behavior from data in infancy. Methodological factors include: (1) at the time of infancy, much psychological development has yet to occur and may be influenced by later experiences; (2) effects of pre- and perinatal adversity may still be present in infancy but wash out over time; (3) children develop at different rates, resulting in great variations in the correlation of specific variables in infancy and later childhood; and (4) the difficulties of measuring the same attribute at different developmental stages when they may take on widely differing expressions, and the difficulties of interpreting the same behavioral patterns at different developmental levels when they may represent a response to different stresses or influences. The dilemma of predicting from early on to later development is summarized by Thomas and Chess (1977): "The problem, therefore, is one of determining when dissimilar behavior over time reflects the same characteristic—whether it be temperament, motivation, cognition, values and standards, or psychopathology—and when the same behavior reflects different characteristics at different age periods" (p. 159).

In summary, review of data, both those that focus on developmental issues in general and those concerned more with hyperactivity, strongly suggests that while infants may be born with a particular vulnerability, it is premature to assume either that hyperactivity can or should be diagnosed in infancy or that certain behavioral patterns demonstrated in infancy form the earliest manifestations of the unfolding of a natural history of attention deficit disorder, or more precisely, of hyperactivity, since almost all relevant studies have focused on this symptom. Studies reviewed have indicated that while there is a relationship between behavioral patterns in infancy and later behavioral outcome, the precise nature of this relationship and its generalizability remain a matter for future investigations. The most important finding regarding the predictability of later behavior from patterns manifest in infancy is that of the mutual influences or interactional nature of the environment and specific attributes of the child on each other. Thus, any attempts to interpret the behavior of infants as prescient of later behavioral functioning must be made in the context of such an interactional model. By the same token, adherence to an interactional model would strongly favor therapeutic interventions to attempt to improve the goodness of fit between a mother and her infant. Such a view acknowledges the detrimental effects of the interactive process between a "difficult" infant and a mother expressing negative affect and recognizes the importance of instituting measures to either prevent or interrupt such a negative cycle.

PRESCHOOL AGE

As in the studies of infancy, many of the investigations of preschoolers have centered on the "difficult" child, representing a clustering of behaviors: irregular rhythms, poor adaptability, withdrawal rather than approach, high intensity, and negative mood (Thomas et al., 1968). Taylor (1986) points out that while this constellation of behaviors may be the most appropriate for describing preschoolers referred by their parents for professional help, "difficulty" represents "a considerably wider idea than inattentiveness and restlessness" (p. 149) and may not be as specific as hyperactivity. Interpretation of many of the studies of this developmental period must be made with this cautionary note in mind. Another difficulty is that relatively few studies, particularly of a prospective nature, have been conducted on the early clinical characteristics, environmental correlates, or ontogeny of hyperactivity in preschool children (Campbell et al., 1986; Taylor, 1986). Campbell has reviewed in detail (Campbell et al., 1982) the difficulties in attempting to identify hyperactivity in children before they enter school. School is for many hyperactive and inattentive children the stressor that brings their difficulties to the fore, and for young preschool children, these symptoms may not yet be evident or present for long enough to indicate that they represent a pattern of chronicity. At this stage, there is no clear distinction between what represents normal toddler or "terrible 2's" behavior and what is aberrant; and furthermore, there exists a paucity of objective behavioral measures that would function to reliably differentiate problematic from normal behavior. Parental concerns of disobedience, increased activity, and temper tantrums characterize this developmental period, and it has not yet been demonstrated how to differentiate those children for whom these behaviors represent a normal transient developmental phase and those for whom these behaviors are indicative of a more long-lasting pathology.

Developmental studies support the appropriateness of the interactional model for understanding the contributing factors to the evolution of later behavioral patterns. Campbell and associates (1986) have reviewed the evidence indicating the importance of family factors in the evolution of deviant behavioral patterns and the consistency of their own findings with such a perspective. A number of lines of investigation have converged to emphasize the importance of family characteristics; these include evidence that negative family interactions are associated with the identification of a particular child's behavior as deviant and with initial referral for evaluation (Hartsough and Lambert, 1982) and evidence that there is more negative interaction among family members in the homes of hyperactive preschoolers than in the family environments of nonhyperactives (Cohen and Minde, 1983; Schleifer et al., 1975). Richman and associates (Richman et al., 1982) have demonstrated that hyperactive, acting-out behaviors identified as early as the preschool age persist and that both the nature of the child's initial symptoms and the family interactional factors influence outcome by the time the child is of school age. The most recent report by Campbell et al. (1986) confirms and extends these previous findings. In this study, multiple indicators of family disruption and maternal stress were associated with higher ratings of hyperactivity and aggression. Campbell and colleagues suggest that the stress experienced by the mother secondary to family factors reduces her tolerance and ability to cope with hyperactive and impulsive behaviors, which in turn is reflected in her disciplinary practices and interactions with her child. Such mothers will tend to be more directive with their children, rate them higher on measures of hyperactivity and aggression, and react more negatively to them. The longitudinal course of the Campbell group's studies support the persistent nature of these effects, at least through age 6. Not only do these relationships persist, but the pattern of relationships are also fairly consistent through this age period and suggest that children who first exhibit "externalizing" behaviors at this time will demonstrate a constellation of problems including inattention, impulsivity, disobedience, and aggression through the preschool years (Campbell et al., 1986). The authors also indicate that not only may family stress influence maternal attitudes toward children's behavior but also that family discord as well as family disciplinary practices may contribute to children's symptom development and persistence (Richman et al., 1982). The persistent nature of the difficulties experienced, at least in this cohort of children and in groups as well (Halverson and Waldrop, 1976; Kohn, 1977), suggest that these problematic "externalizing" behaviors are not necessarily outgrown.

A complicating factor at this as at other developmental periods is the relationship between hyperactivity and aggressive behavior. The question is whether hyperactivity and aggression are two entirely separate disorders or represent different aspects of the same disorder, the conduct disorder (Sandberg et al., 1978). Loney and Milich (1982) suggest that aggressive behavior may occur as a secondary phenomenon in hyperactive children and may significantly influence the course and outcome of the disorder in affected children. In the agglomeration of problem behaviors that causes parents of preschoolers to seek professional help, hyperactivity and aggression appear to be strongly intertwined, and Campbell et al. (1982) suggest that "distinctions among them (symptoms of conduct disorder, attention deficit and hyperactivity) are difficult, if not impossible, to make."

Studies of preschool children have also shed light on the ontogenic pattern of hyperactivity itself. While activity level appears to increase from infancy through age 3, from this point onwards the level of activity (in an experimental playroom with mother present) declines (Routh, 1980). A number of studies have now indicated that in free play situations, there are no discernable differences observed between children identified as hyperactive and controls (Shleifer et al., 1975; Routh and Shroeder, 1976). In a structured activity, children who had been reported to be hyperactive by their parents and also by teachers and psychiatrists were found to be more aggressive and more off task and away from their tables than controls. This finding is supported by Campbell et al. (1982), who noted that hyperactive children did not exhibit an increased amount of gross motor activity in a free play situation, but demonstrated a higher actometer score in a laboratory setting.

During this developmental stage, children become socialized and begin to interact with their peers outside the family setting. A striking finding of preschool hyperactive children has been their unpopularity (Rubin and Clark, 1983; Campbell and Paulauskas, 1979; Battle and Lacey, 1972). The emanative effects of the child's failure to adjust to group settings and his exclusion by his peer group may lead to the development of secondary symptoms of lack of self-esteem (Cantwell, 1979).

In summary, studies of the preschool period strongly support the influence of environmental factors on the expression and persistence of hyperactivity and associated behaviors. In particular, stressful home environments appear to be associated with a diminished maternal tolerance for these behaviors, leading to more negative mother-child interactions and more controlling behavior on the part of the mother. Hyperactive behavior was almost inseparable from aggressive and defiant behavior, and as such, it is difficult to determine what role each of these behaviors plays in the genesis of secondary symptoms of peer rejection and low self-esteem, which become evident at this stage. What is clearer is the association that aggressive behaviors have with a poorer long-term outcome. The persistence of these symptoms and the associated secondary symptoms argue for intervention during this period. The data suggest that both parent and child require active assistance in improving the "goodness of fit."

SCHOOL AGE

This is the time for the full-blown expression of an attention deficit disorder. This low visibility but pervasive disorder affects virtually every niche of the child's existence including home, school, and peer group. It is at this time that the child is most frequently brought for professional consultation. Referral may be made by the child's parents, school personnel, or the child's primary physician. The intrusiveness of the child's problematic behaviors into every aspect of his life is evidenced by the broad range of disciplines that are called upon to assess his performance, including pediatricians, psychologists, child neurologists, and child psychiatrists. Generally, the component of the core features of the syndrome that is most disruptive to the child and his family will preselect the specialist who is called upon for consultation. Thus, if an attentional deficit is most disabling and school function is impaired, a child neurologist or pediatrician will be consulted; if the child's hyperactivity and impulsivity are presenting management problems, the assistance of a child psychiatrist or psychologist will be sought. If the child's problems are persistent and interfere with his functioning in both behavioral and academic spheres, it is not unusual for the family to visit a range of specialists seeking "The Answer." The intrusion of his symptomatology into every sphere of his existence, his failure to get on with parents and siblings, and his failures at school and with peers are a source of mounting frustration and disappointment to the child and his parents. Several factors coalesce to make this a particularly frustrating and puzzling disorder for parents and children to understand. Attention deficit disorder is characterized as a so-called low visibility disorder—that is, the child appears "normal" in outward appearances, he may be quite bright intellectually and therefore should "know better," and his symptoms are unpredictable, often varying from minute to minute and from place to place. Thus, from all outward appearances, from all the ways we generally judge a person's "wellness," the ADD child appears to be just like any of his well-functioning peers, and the expectation is for him to perform appropriately.

This is the developmental period that has been most intensively studied and best characterized for ADD. This state of knowledge reflects the better differentiation of ADD symptomatology at this time, in contrast to the more global behavior patterns evident early on; the presence of school as a catalyst or perhaps more of a stressor to bring about the emergence of ADD symptomatology; and the availability of measures with which to assess each of the components of the disorder. It is primarily at this age that studies focused specifically on ADD rather than on hyperactivity or "difficult" children have been conducted.

While DSM III inclusion criteria for ADD represented a significant step in providing criteria for identification of affected children, more recent empiric studies suggest a modification of these criteria (Shaywitz et al.,1986a; Shaywitz et al , 1986b). Results of these investigations support the centrality of an attentional deficit as the core clinical feature of ADD. Children with such deficits may be characterized as being easily distractable, failing to finish what they start (be it a book or a puzzle), requiring a calm atmosphere in order to concentrate, and frequently having to have things repeated. Another aspect of the attentional deficit will be manifest as a difficulty in habituating or adjusting to a new situation or change in routine. Mood flunctuations and a seeming slowness to repond are observed as well. Particularly disruptive are the child's impulsive behaviors expressed as disruptions of other children's activities, difficulties waiting his turn, calling out or making noises in class, and talking excessively. While DSM III describes a single construct of hyperactivity, results of empiric studies (Shaywitz et al., 1986a) indicate that it may be more helpful to consider two dimensions of hyperactivity: one that is descriptive of the activity itself, and the other that describes the social consequences of the increased activity. We refer to the descriptive component as Activity and to the second component as Tractability. Manifestations of Activity include fidgeting or squirming, climbing on cabinets and furniture, running rather than walking, and doing things in a loud or noisy way. In contrast, the Tractability dimension encompasses difficulties taking the child for a visit to friends or shopping, or leaving him with a babysitter, and indications that the child requires constant supervision or is destructive. Consideration of the social consequences of hyperactive behavior is supported by the findings of Routh and Shroeder (1976) that behavioral rating scales used for hyperactive children correlated with measures of "noncompliance" rather than with measures of activity level. Barkley (1985) in reviewing these findings suggests that it is this social noncompliance that is so distressing to parents and teachers and that it is this aspect of the child's behavior that leads to eventual referral.

At home, depending on the focus of his symptomatology, he will present all degrees of management difficulties. If he is primarily inattentive but not necessarily hyperactive, he will leave behind him a trail of unfinished business: toothpaste uncovered, toys and clothes wherever he last used or dropped them, games begun and unfinished, and clothes mismatched with shoelaces untied. If hyperactivity or impulsivity is present, the house will often be in a general state of disarray, toys scattered or broken, walls marked, and family activities constantly ending prematurely in anger and frustration. Meals will be disrupted by the child's inability to sit still, or there will be fights at the table through an entire meal; and car rides will be disastrous. In contrast, the same child may be able to sit through Saturday morning cartoons or to fish for surprisingly long periods of time. Finding an appropriate extracurricular activity becomes a mission: the child is not interested, is impatient, or disrupts the game. Nothing is more discouraging to the parent of an ADD child than to see him up at bat, hit the ball, and then proceed to race around the bases, passing, and seemingly oblivious of his teammates still on the bases. In contrast to baseball, the constant movement associated with soccer seems to be more accommodating of the ADD child's need to run.

The DSM III lists "moves about excessively during sleep" as one of the criteria for hyperactivity, which reflects clinical lore suggesting that children with ADDH have a range of sleep difficulties including problems falling or staying asleep, and restless or interrupted sleep (Barkley, 1981; Salzarulo and Chevalier, 1983). In our analytic studies of the factor structure of DSM III criteria for ADD, we found that the item related to sleep did not load with the other hyperactivity items and removed it from the modified criteria currently utilized in our studies. Although some studies indicate that sleep patterns of ADDH children may be different from those of nonhyperactive children (Luisada, 1969), an extensive review of the literature by Greenhill et al. (1983) indicates that the results were not entirely clear. Thus, while there is some suggestion that hyperactive children experience a restless sleep (Porrino et al., 1983), Greenhill's own investigations (1983) failed to document any difference in the sleep architecture pattern between groups of ADDH and control children. Another associated finding reflects the child's impulsivity. This impulsivity and seeming failure to appreciate danger result in accidents and mishaps both in and out of the home (Stewart et al., 1970).

HOME

Clearly the presence of such a child in the home will be a source of concern, anxiety, and often anger experienced by the parents. A number of studies have examined the parent-child and, most commonly, the maternal-child relationship in ADD. In view of the interactional model, the nature of this relationship takes on particular importance in influencing the course of the disorder in affected children. As detailed above in "Preschool Age," a number of studies have indicated that mothers of hyperactive children are distant, critical, and disapproving (Barkley, 1985; Ross and Ross, 1982). Conjecture as to the relationship of this maternal behavior to the child's symptomatology has ranged from ascribing the child's hyperactivity to his mother's behavior (Bettelheim, 1973) to suggestions that the mother's behavior was a response to the child's hyperactive behavior (Bell and Harper, 1977). Campbell (1975) observed the mother-child interaction in a laboratory setting during structured task situations. In contrast to mothers of nonhyperactive children, mothers of study children were more likely, particularly on difficult tasks, to provide directions, supervision, and structure. Similarly, distinct from their nonhyperactive controls, hyperactive children were more noncompliant and more needing of assistance or direction. To better comprehend the sequential order of the antecedent-reaction interaction, Cunningham and Barkley (1979) introduced a medication and a placebo condition. Under these experimental conditions, it was clearly demonstrated that the maternal controlling behaviors were the reaction to the antecedent noncompliant behavior of the child. On medication, the child was more compliant and less dependent. As a consequence, mothers reacted with more positive and less directive behavior. Mash and Johnston (1981), cited in Ross and Ross (1982), included siblings in their laboratory observations of hyperactive boys and their mothers. Not surprisingly, the interactions between the hyperactive boys and their brothers demonstrated higher rates of negative interactions and conflict than did the nonhyperactive-sibling pairs. Of particular interest was the interaction of the mothers of the hyperactive boys with their nonhyperactive sons; these mothers were also more negative and more distant with their nonhyperactive children compared to mothers of control children. Ross and Ross (1982) relate this to the spread of "negative affect phenomenon in the hyperactive child's social environment" (p. 41), confirming what others had previously described (Barkley, 1978; Cantwell, 1979, Whalen et al., 1981).

The difficulties in both parent-child and sibling-child relationships appear to diminish as the ADDH child matures (Mash and Johnston, 1982, 1983). Barkley, in a series of studies, has also examined the developmental aspects of parent-child interactions (Barkley et al., 1984, 1985a,b; Barkley, Karlsson, and Pollard, 1985a,b). He observed that hyperactive children become more compliant and independent as they mature (ages 4 or 5 through 9 years); in turn, their mothers become less directive, respond less negatively, and spend more time simply observing rather than correcting them. Consistent with the results of the drug studies (see above), developmental investigations demonstrate that the controlling and negative behavior characterizing mothers of hyperactive children diminishes when the child is able to exert his own self-control. This exquisite responsivity between the child's behavior and controlling forces in his environment once again attest to the appropriateness of the interactional model.

PEERS

Indications from a variety of sources suggest that the ability of the hyperactive child to form and maintain friendships is impaired. This information reflects parent reports (Battle and Lacey, 1972; Conners, 1970; Schleifer et al., 1975) and self-report (Campbell, Endma, and Bernfeld, 1977), child interview (Campbell and Paulaukas, 1979, Hoy, Weiss, Minde, and Cohen, 1978), and sociometric data (Mainville and Friedman, 1976, Klein and Young 1979, Pelham and Milich, 1980). Direct observational measures have also confirmed that hyperactive children display less socially appropriate behavior and more negative behavior than do controls (Hinshaw et al., in press) and that these behaviors are associated with negative peer ratings (Pelham et al., 1984). Peer difficulties include peer rejection or dislike and low peer acceptance and unpopularity. Pelham and Milich (1984) interpret this as reflecting both increased externalizing behaviors that lead to rejection and diminished social skills that in turn lead to low acceptance. These findings are of particular concern since peer relationships are considered to be an important index of later adjustment (Cowen et al., 1973) and peer rejection a predictor of later psychopathology (Milich and Landau, 1982).

Pelham and Bender (1982) provide some useful insights into the genesis of peer difficulties experienced by hyperactive children. Comparisons of peer judgments between groups of hyperactive and nonhyperactive boys revealed that the items that best discriminated between the groups were those related to peer interactions rather than to teacher-pupil interactions. Thus, hyperactive boys are judged by their peers to "try to get other people into trouble," "bother other people who are trying to work," and "start a fight over nothing." Pelham and Bender (1982) comment that this provides, in a sense, concurrent validation of the same types of immature, aggressive, and impulsive behaviors that teachers and parents report for hyperactive children. Observational studies by the same investigators demonstrated that in a play situation, hyperactive children engage in high rates of aggressive and annoying behaviors directed toward their peers, behaviors associated with extreme ratings of dislike and rejection by these peers. Results to date have failed to clarify the relative role of the aggressive and of the bothersome behaviors in the genesis of the negative peer ratings. Attempts to clarify the developmental aspects of peer relationships in hyperactive children suggest that the presence of an aggressive component may influence how the child is viewed as he matures. Thus while an initial cross-sectional study of hyperactive children did not demonstrate that peer relations changed as a function of age (Johnston et al., 1985), a followup study of a subsample of these children found that certain children were rated less negatively (Johnston and Pelham, 1986). Children rated to be relatively more aggressive by their teachers initially continued to receive negative peer nominations; however, those children judged to be less aggressive at referral demonstrated significant improvements on their peer ratings later on. Pelham and Milich (1984) interpret this finding as consistent with data indicating that there is an age-related improvement in the core symptoms of ADDH, while aggressiveness tends to be stable with time (Olweus, 1979). Thus, they argue that children who are primarily hyperactive and rejected by their peers because of their hyperactivity will meet lower rates of peer rejection as they mature and their hyperactivity diminishes. However, those hyperactive children who are also highly aggressive will be rejected on the basis of both their hyperactivity and their aggressiveness. Since the aggressive characteristic does not diminish with time, they will continue to be rejected by their peers.

Several recent studies have also examined the peer relationships of ADDH and ADDnoH children. ADDH children are clearly more aggressive and intrusive compared to ADDnoH children, as perceived both by their teachers (Edelbrock et al., 1984) and by their peers (Pelham and Milick, 1984). While both ADDH and ADDnoH children differ from their peers on popularity ratings, ADDH children received the lowest peer popularity rating (Lahey et al., 1984). Ratings of impulsivity appear to be highly correlated with problems in peer relationships, and in fact, impulsivity may be more closely related to these problems than is hyperactivity (Pelham and Bender, 1982).

In addition to the possible role of aggressive behavior in the genesis and persistence of negative peer perceptions, Ross and Ross (1982) review other hypotheses that have been suggested. Thus, Patterson et al. (1965) have speculated that high activity levels preclude the development of necessary social skills, and Whalen et al. (1979) have enumerated the types of difficulties experienced by hyperactive children that impair their ability to participate successfully with their peers in group activities. Whatever the etiology of their peer difficulties, a significicant possible consequence is the development of secondary symptoms of poor self-esteem, depression, and antisocial behaviors. Cantwell (1979) has suggested that these secondary symptoms may be more refractory to treatment than the initial symptoms and that the child may develop an avoidance response to social situations that too may be difficult to treat.

SCHOOL

The difficulties experienced by the ADD child in school, both in the classroom and on the playground, are responsible in large measure for the high number of referrals in this period. Each of the core components of the disorder interfere with his ability to successfully adjust to the demands of the school environment. A large number of studies have confirmed that the hyperactive child is a disruptive influence in the classroom (Campbell et al., 1977; Cohen et al., 1981; Klein and Young, 1979; Whalen et al., 1979; Whalen et al., 1981). Direct observation in the classroom has also indicated differences in attentiveness, verbal intrusion, and accuracy of academic work between teacher-identified hyperactive children and their classmates (Atkins et al., 1985). Specific classroom behaviors described have included: increased movement, calling out and making noises, increased contacts with classmates, and frequent fidgeting (Whalen et al., 1979).

Attentional difficulties including problems sustaining attention, distractability, and deficits in selective attention all interfere with his ability to successfully master his academic tasks. Work remains incomplete after an initial effort, and any slight noise or movement is enough to attract his attention away from his assigned work. Impulsivity leads to academic errors as well as social disruptions. The lack of reflectivity is evidenced by the frequent erasures and errors, even on easy items. Calling out, making noises, and raising his hand even when he does not know the answer are a source of ongoing friction between student and teacher. Frequently he does perform up to ability and falls behind peers of similar ability (Cantwell and Satterfield, 1978; Minde et al., 1971).

446

As detailed later (see "Prognosis"), the initial sanguine assumptions (Laufer and Denhoff, 1957) that symptoms would be outgrown in adolescence are no longer tenable. Thus, evidence from a number of investigative groups now supports the belief that as adolescents, a significant number of children with ADD continue to exhibit behavioral, academic, and language difficulties, though hyperactivity usually decreases (Hechtman et al., 1976; Hechtman et al., 1980; Hoy et al., 1978; Weiss et al., 1975; Weiss et al., 1971; Weiss, et al, 1978; Weiss et al., 1979; Kramer and Loney, 1978; Langhorne and Loney, 1979; Loney et al., 1978; Loney et al., 1981; Paternite et al., 1976; Paternite and Loney, 1980). Secondary problems relating to aggression, poor self-concept, poor peer relationships, and poor school functioning may now become prominent components of the clinical picture. Hyperactive adolescents may be frequently sad and depressed (Cantwell, 1979; Sassone et al., 1981), though the co-occurrence of depression and ADD in younger children is quite low (Anderson et al., 1987).

Ross and Ross (1982) review the methodological difficulties inherent in studying antisocial problems in hyperactive adolescents. These include the similarity between hyperactivity and conduct disorder in younger children that might lead to mistaken diagnoses of hyperactivity rather than conduct disorder. These children would then erroneously be considered as hyperactives at followup, and any antisocial behaviors would be considered as consequences of the hyperactivity. Confounding effects of demographic variables such as socioeconomic status and family status have also often failed to be considered.

Data emerging from studies with well-thought-out methodologies are somewhat contradictory. Some indicate an increase in antisocial behaviors and trouble with the police (Milich and Loney, 1979; Weiss et al., 1971; Ackerman et al., 1977), while others conclude that hyperactive adolescents do not have an increased likelihood of becoming delinquent (Loney et al., 1981).

ADULTS

Discussion of the clinical characteristics and natural history of ADD does not end with adolescence. Indeed, DSM III incorporates a category for residual type hyperactivity, termed ADDRT. In recent years, much interest has centered on this group, so much so that in 1979, a major conference was held on what was then termed minimal brain dysfunction in adults (Bellak, 1979). Overall, studies indicate that maturation to adulthood carries with it many of the same symptoms (inattention, restlessness, fidgetiness, impulsivity, poor self-esteem, and difficulties with social interactions) characterizing older children with ADD. The detailed studies of Weiss et al. (1985) are reviewed below ("Prognosis"). We summarize them here by indicating that, in general, previously hyperactive young adults fare better as adults than they did as children. The workplace where they can choose the situation is far more accommodating than the classroom, where the goodness of fit is generally poor. Morrison (1979) in a retrospective study of psychiatric patients with and without a previous history of hyperactivity reports an association between childhood hyperactivity and later sociopathy, hysteria, and personality disorders. Cantwell (1978a) has reviewed the data on childhood hyperactivity and the later development of antisocial disorders and concludes that there is a relationship between the two occurrences.

SUMMARY

ADD is a low visibility but high prevalence disorder that can permeate every dimension of a child's life. In a sense, the term low visibility is a misnomer; it refers to the "normal" appearance of ADD children, not to the impact that the disorder may have on the child, his family, his class, and his community. The basic features of the disorder—inattention, impulsivity, and at times, hyperactivity—may interfere with the child's adjustment in every phase of his existence, both through time and across situations and experiences. First as an infant, the ADDH child may present as a "difficult" baby who does not sleep or eat well, whose rhythms are irregular, and who is a source of continued frustration to his parents, especially his mother, who does not understand where she has gone wrong. The so-called "difficult" child continues as a toddler and preschooler to manifest high intensity, poor adaptability, and negative moods in association with increased activity and perhaps poor compliance to demands, first of his parents and then of his teachers. Studies performed at this developmental stage already indicate the mutual influences or interactional nature of the environment and specific attributes of the child on one another. Thus, in families of hyperactive children, there are more negative interactions between the child and his mother, and more family disruptions and maternal stress. A picture emerges of a self-perpetuating cycle in which an already overburdened mother with diminished tolerance must cope with a hyperactive and impulsive child to whom she responds with controlling and negative behaviors of her own, which further perpetuate the child's difficulties. Developmental studies and intervention strategies have both indicated that when the child's behavior improves, whether as a reflection of maturation or of medication, maternal behavior toward the child becomes less controlling, less negative, and less distant. As the child leaves the circle of his family and enters the community of peers, his difficulties now have a larger arena or sphere in which to manifest themselves. Thus, as early as the preschool period, hyperactive children manifest difficulties adjusting to group settings and begin to experience peer rejection.

The developmental demands on the school-age child both academically and socially produce the full-blown expression of an attention deficit disorder. Each one of the prime symptoms, inattention, impulsivity, and hyperactivity, interferes with the child's ability to be a "good citizen" of his class, to attend to his studies, and to initate and develop friendships and win acceptance by his group of peers. This is the time when most ADD children are brought to professional attention, and depending on whether the academic or behavioral problems are more salient, a range of "specialists" will be consulted. The intrusion of the child's symptomatology into every sphere of his existence, his failure to get on with family members, and his failures at school and with peers are a source of mounting frustration and disappointment to the child and his parents. A confounding feature is that to all outward appearances the child "looks normal," his intelligence is good, and at times he performs commendably. There is a discrepancy between the child's outward appearance, which suggests that all is well, and the tremendous turmoil and disruption surrounding the child, beginning with his own sense of himself and proceeding to envelop his interactions with his family, his teacher, and his peer group. The lack of obvious external indicators of a problem, the subtle and yet pervasive nature of the child's symptoms, and the variability of his symptoms lead to the questioning of whether there really is a problem, and at times, to the suggestion that it may all be motivational. Thus, while the parent of a preschooler may be told that the child will outgrow his symptoms, the difficulties of the school-age child may be ascribed to poor motivation in lieu of a referral for evaluation that might lead to a diagnosis of ADD. Although the disorder may change in its manifestations as the child matures, it does not go away. Peer relationships are characterized by both low acceptance and rejection. These findings are of particular concern since peer relationships are considered to be an important index of later adjustment. Thus, studies of adolescents indicate that while certain symptoms may diminish, primarily the hyperactivity, academic and learning difficulties, behavioral problems, poor peer acceptance, low self-esteem, and at times, depression may persist. Indeed, secondary problems relating to aggression, poor self-concept, impaired peer relationships, and poor school functioning now may become prominent components of the clinical picture. Long-term studies indicate that, although many of the symptoms persist, previously hyperactive young adults fare better in the workplace than they did in the classroom.

In addition to specific symptoms of the disorder, certain overall trends or characterisitcs are also evident. The symptoms diagnostic of ADDH manifest a developmental trend; that is, up until age 3, activity levels increase but then continue a downward trend so that by adolesence, gross motor hyperactivity is no longer present. However, attentional deficits persist. Awareness of this developmental pattern is particularly important because it is at times mistakenly assumed that since the child is no longer hyperactive, he is free of problems and no longer needy of, for example, special education services. It is critically important that parents and professionals, particularly educators, appreciate the differential ontogeny of the activity and attentional components of the syndrome.

Along with the variability in symptoms over time is the situational variability of the features of the disorder. Both the environmental context and the task demands placed on the child will influence his symptomatic expression at any particular time. Thus, ADD children may not be differentiated from controls in a playground but will be significantly more active and off task in a structured academic situation. The variability not only extends to different settings and situations but also refers to the frequent lack of predictability of the child's behavior from minute to minute or day to day, even in similar situations.

While the thrust of recent investigations point to an inherent vulnerability, indications are that the expression of this vulnerability will very much be dependent on the so-called "goodness of fit" between the child and his environment. An interactional model in which both the child and his environment are constantly influencing one another and modulating the behavior of the other appears most appropriate for understanding symptom emergence in ADD and as such has significant implications for intervention.

A number of research issues are yet to be resolved, and not surprisingly, they relate to definition and diagnosis. An especially problematic area is that of the diagnosis of ADD in younger children and in turn the prognostic significance of specific behaviors found in so-called "difficult" young children. Since there is more natural variability in symptoms and wider latitude in what is considered developmentally appropriate in young children, it has been very difficult to determine which symptoms may be transient and which may presage more enduring problems. In addition, the more global patterns of symptomatology make it difficult to determine if these symptoms reflect a final common pathway for a myriad of influences (that is, a rather nonspecific response of the young organism to a range of stressors), and conversely if such patterns represent the earliest symptoms of ADD or other more severe emotional disorders, or in some cases, if they are a transient phenomenon. There is a great need for a better understanding of these early manifestations including their natural course, correlates, and implications. Measures are necessary to be able to better tease apart these global presentations so that, for example, hyperactivity and aggressive components can be clarified and monitored over time. It is equally important to expand our investigations to include a more representative range of young ADD children rather than the often most severely impaired who present to mental health clinics for early assessment.

Review of the clinical characteristics of the ADD child indicate that ADD is a very serious disorder. ADD may affect children from their earliest infancy, through toddlerhood and school to adulthood. The intrusion of symptoms into every aspect of a child's life and their interference initially with his relationships with his parents and siblings and later with his teachers and peers produces a world of unhappiness, frustration, and failure. Both the depth and the breadth of the ADD child's difficulties mandate a clearer understanding of the evolution of the disorder and the influences on the expression of symptoms. This is predicated on improved ability to define the symptoms of the disorder and study their natural course over time and under different conditions. It is only in this way that better and more appropriate strategies will be developed for intervention.

EPIDEMIOLOGY

METHODOLOGICAL ISSUES

Although it is obvious to all investigators that many of the issues listed here are essential in evaluating the prevalence of ADD, such critical factors are often ignored when epidemiological data (for example, prevalence, sex ratios, association with other disorders such as learning disability and conduct disorder) are discussed. These issues include:

(1) Which criteria were used to define ADD (or, since many studies were performed prior to DSM III formulation, hyperactivity or MBD)? These issues are discussed in detail above and are not repeated here.

(2) What cutoffs were employed? It is obvious that if a cutoff of 1.5 standard deviations above the mean is selected, this selection will dictate a prevalence rate of 9 percent, assuming a normal distribution; and if a cutoff of 1.0 standard deviations is employed, the corresponding rate will be 16 percent. Though obvious, this simple fact is often forgotten when prevalence rates are discussed.

(3) Who provided the information for the diagnosis (parent, teacher, physician, independent observer)? Clearly, the source of the information has been demonstrated as having significant influence on diagnosis (Langhorne et al., 1976).

(4) What age subjects were studied? This relates to diagnostic criteria, since some of the cardinal features of ADD, most notably hyperactivity, abate as the child matures.

(5) What are the selection biases of the population being studied? (Clinic [child guidance, learning disorders, etc.] populations, broad population, participation rate.) These factors are among those that have been shown to be particularly significant (Firestone et al., 1986; Pelham and Murphy, in press).

Such problems make it extremely difficult to present any simple compilation of prevalence rates for ADD. In the remainder of this discussion, we consider prevalence rates in North America (arbitrarily divided in chronological fashion by the appearance of DSM III), prevalence rates in other countries, explanations for sex differences, a description of ADD in girls, and the commonality of learning disability and ADD.

PREVALENCE OF ADD

PRE-DSM-III ERA

In one of the first studies of the epidemiology of hyperactivity, Lapouse and Monk (1958) questioned the mothers of 6- to 12-year-olds, and 57 percent of boys and 42 percent of girls were considered "overactive." The criteria for classification, however, were not described. A frequently quoted figure for the prevalence of ADD is 20 percent, based upon the studies of Huessy (1967). He studied 500 Vermont second graders by asking the teachers to rate the children on a 21-item five-point scale. Those children with a total score above the 80th percentile were considered hyperkinetic, and thus it is obvious that 20 percent of their population was thus arbitrarily defined as hyperkinetic! Thus, not only was the prevalence of hyperactivity predetermined, but also its criteria were never validated. By age 10 years, parents and teachers rated 6 percent of the children in the Kauai study (9 percent of boys and 3 percent of girls—Werner et al., 1968) as exhibiting the hyperkinetic syndrome. Precise definition was not specified, but hyperactivity, distractibility, and irritability formed the core of the diagnosis.

In his influential book published in 1971, Wender noted a prevalence rate for problems of restlessness (15 percent) and attention span (22 percent) reported by teachers of first through sixth grade children. No criteria were specified for either characteristic, and no rating scale was identified. Utilizing the Quay-Petersen checklist, Werry and Quay (1971) asked teachers to rate all children in grades K through 2 in the Urbana, Illinois, school system. Symptoms of short attention span, inability to sit still, and distractibility were reported in approximately 50 percent of boys and 30 percent of girls. When more stringent diagnostic criteria for hyperactivity were applied by Miller et al. (1973), 9 percent of boys and 1.5 percent of girls in grades 3 through 6 in suburban St. Louis were diagnosed by their teachers as hyperactive.

Lambert et al. (1978) examined a population of K through grade 5 children in the East Bay area of San Francisco. Parents were asked "if their child was considered to be hyperactive," school personnel (teachers, psychologists, principals, nurses, special educators) were asked separately to identify "children known to be considered hyperactive in their school district," and physicians were asked to "refer to us any children they identified as hyperactive." The maximum prevalence rate was betweem 12 and 13 percent, with boys identified from 6 to 8 times more frequently than girls. School-identified hyperactivity was most common, and no difference was noted for socioeconomic status or for grade level. Bosco and Robin (1980) asked parents and teachers of one-half the elementary, middle, and junior high school students in Grand Rapids, Michigan, to participate in a three-step process designed to determine the prevalence of hyperkinesis and therapy in a school population. In the first step of the process, parents were questioned about the presence or absence of a medical diagnosis of a learning or behavior problem. In the second stage, parents were asked to check any of the eleven diagnostic terms most frequently used for hyperkinetic children. The final step in the process asked about medications used. Not surprisingly, such stringent criteria resulted in the identification of only 3 percent as hyperkinetic. Boys outnumbered girls by 4 to 1. Socioeconomic status was reassuringly not a factor in medication use.

In a massive study of over 14,000 Canadian children from pre-K through grade 6, Trites (1979) asked teachers to complete the 39-item Conners rating scale. In the version used by Trites, the hyperactivity factor was composed of 6 items, of which only 2 could be considered as reflecting purely activity. Hyperactivity was diagnosed using a criterion of > 15. Prevalence ranged between 1 and 16 percent, depending on school district, with 21 percent of boys and 7.5 percent of girls satisfying diagnostic criteria. As in previous studies, no differences were noted across grade levels. Nichols and Chen (1981) reported that symptoms of hyperactivity and short attention were reported by the examining psychologist in 9.3 percent and 12.5 percent, respectively, of the National Collaborative Perinatal Project (NCPP) population at age 7 years. A diagnosis of hyperactivity-impulsivity (HI) was made in 6 percent of children, but this is not terribly surprising since, as we describe later, a cutoff of the upper 8 percent of those scoring highest on the HI factor score was established as the basis for diagnosis.

DSM-III ERA

Shekim et al. (1985) administered structured interviews to randomly selected 9-year-olds (Diagnostic Interview Schedule for Children [DISC], Costello et al., 1984) and their parents (DISC-P, Costello et al., 1984) in two rural midwestern counties. A diagnosis of ADDH was made in 16 children, nearly always by parent interview, with twice as many boys diagnosed as girls. Shapiro and Garfinkel (1986) studied all children in grades 2 through 6 in a rural Minnesota school. Teachers completed the 39-item Conners TRS, and the ADD portion of the DICA structured interview was given to the children (Herjanic and Campbell, 1977). In addition, all children performed a continuous performance test, a computerized progressive maze, and a sequential organization test. Apparently a criterion score of 1.5 standard deviations above the mean on the CTRS was employed, resulting in approximately 3 percent of children satisfying criteria for either hyperactivity or aggression, or for both.

Most recently, we have determined the prevalence of ADD in an epidemiologic, longitudinal sample of 445 children followed from K through grade 3 (Shaywitz, 1986b, Connecticut Longitudinal Study of Learning Disability). Applying a diagnostic rule for ADD developed on a validated population of well-diagnosed ADD children (Shaywitz et al., 1986b), we found an overall prevalence rate of 23 percent in the epidemiologic sample.

CROSS-CULTURAL STUDIES

Prechtl and Stemmer (1962), utilizing choreiform movements on examination and "behavioral problems" as criteria, found 20 percent of boys and 10 percent of girls to exhibit difficulties. Holborow et al. (1984) compared teacher ratings on three different rating scales (Conners 10-item ATQ, Queensland adaptation of Davids, 1971 scale, and the Pittsburg Adjustment Scale [Miller et al., 1973]) in Australian children in grades 1 through 7. Using a 1.5 cutoff on the Conners, 12 percent of the entire population satisfied criteria for hyperactivity (18 percent of boys and 5 percent of girls). In general, a comparison of items on each scale indicated a general agreement. Thus, "restless and overactive" was noted 18 percent on Conners and 24 percent on Queensland. Short attention was seen 17 percent on Conners, 26 percent on Queensland, and 23 percent on Pittsburg. Using Rutter's teachers and parent scales, McGee et al. (1984) found 20 percent of 7-year-olds (25 percent boys, 15 percent girls) in Dunedin, New Zealand, to be aggressive and/or hyperactive. This finding is difficult to interpret since factor scores and criteria are not as well studied in this instrument as in others.

A number of investigators have defined hyperactivity on the basis of cutoff scores on the Conners Abbreviated Teacher Rating Scale (ATRS). Ullmann et al. (1985) have criticized this instrument primarily for (1) too low a cutoff score (1.5 in most studies), (2) its inability to assess inattention, and (3) the inconsistency among its versions. Despite such problems, studies employing the ATRS provide important data regarding the prevalence of hyperactivity across populations around the world. Utilizing teacher ratings on the Conners ATRS with a cutoff of above 1.5, prevalence rates for hyperactivity have been reported as 17 percent in the United States (Ullmann, 1983, quoted in O'Leary et al., 1985), 8 percent in West Germany (Sprague et al., 1977), 13 percent in New Zealand (Werry and Hawthorne, 1976), 12 percent in Italy (O'Leary et al., 1985), 16 percent in Spain (Arias and O'Leary, 1983, quoted in O'Leary et al., 1985), and 10 percent in Great Britain (extrapolated from rates of 14.6 percent in boys and 5.7 percent in girls, cited in Holborow and Berry, 1986).

Yu-Cun et al. (1985) utilized a modification of a Conners scale and a Rutter scale modified for use in the Chinese culture. Apparently it contained only four items (poor concentration, short attention span, hyperactivity or very restless, impulsive emotion), scored from 0-4 on severity. Employing a cutoff of 2 standard deviations above the mean, they not surprisingly obtained a prevalence rate consonant with that cutoff, with a boy-girl ratio of 7:1. Socioeconomic status did influence prevalence rate, with rates of 6 percent in children of scientific and technical professionals but 16 percent in children of peasants. Since a standard Conners ATQ was not used (allowing a cutoff of 1.5 as in the studies described above), it is difficult to compare the prevalence in China with that described in other countries. Probably the most appropriate comparisons here are with the Lambert et al. (1978) and Bosco and Robin (1980) studies in this country. The similarity in prevalence rates between those and Yu-Cun's suggest that Ross and Ross's notion of culturally based ADD (see "Etiology") needs to be reevaluated.

The extremely low prevalence of hyperactivity noted in British studies stands in stark contrast to the general agreement in prevalence from other parts of the world. Thus, Rutter et al. (1970) reported hyperactivity to occur in less than 1 per 1,000 children in his population survey on the Isle of Wight. Barkley (1981, p. 9) and Taylor (1986) cite as the most reasonable explanation for this phenomenon the difference in diagnostic practice between the United Kingdom and the United States. Thus, children likely to be diagnosed as having ADD in the United States are diagnosed as conduct disordered in the United Kingdom.

SEX DIFFERENCES

As noted above, the prevalence rates for hyperactivity range between 12 percent and 24 percent for boys and 3 percent and 13 percent for girls (Arias and O'Leary, 1983, quoted in O'Leary et al., 1985; Holborow and Berry, 1986; Langsdorf et al., 1979; Sprague et al., 1977; Ullmann et al., 1985; Werry and Hawthorne, 1976), with boys outnumbering girls in every study and with sex ratios ranging between 2:1 and 8:1. Reasons for this gender discrepancy remain enigmatic, though suggestions include greater vulnerability of the male CNS to developmental failures (Stewart, 1970), biologically determined sex differences in response to intrauterine insults (Halverson and Victor, 1976), and polygenetic inheritance, with girls having a higher threshold for phenotypic expression of disorder (Omenn, 1973). It is also possible that selective referral of boys may represent an important factor in determining sex ratio, with boys referred because they exhibit more disruptive behaviors that are troublesome to adults than girls do. Boys may be under greater pressure to succeed at school (Hoffman, 1977), and this might make them more vulnerable to the effects of stress (Taylor, 1986, p. 139).

In addition to the difference in prevalence rates between boys and girls, good evidence suggests that the clinical presentation of ADD is different for boys and girls. Thus, Berry et al. (1985) compared characteristics of ADD boys and girls. While in most respects the clinical profiles were similar, ADD girls exhibited greater cognitive and language deficits and greater social liability. Boys with ADD exhibited more physical aggression and loss of control, while inappropriate and anti-social behavior was observed in both sexes. Such findings suggest that girls with ADD represent an underidentified and as a consequence, underserved group of children who are at significant risk for long-term academic, social, and emotional difficulties. Similar findings have also been noted in a recent study by deHaas (1986), who reports that girls with ADD exhibit more conduct problems than normal girls.

PREVALENCE OF SUBTYPES

As noted previously, within the current DSM III classification scheme, three major subtypes of ADD are recognized: ADDH, ADDnoH, and ADD residual type. Considerable controversy still exists over the validity and stability of these subtypes. Using DSM III criteria, both King and Young (1982) and we (Shaywitz, 1986b) report that ADDnoH occurs approximately one-fourth as frequently as ADDH, and Maurer and Stewart (1980) noted ADDnoH in 17 percent of child psychiatry outpatients, occurring one-fifth the frequency of ADDH.

CO-OCCURRENCE OF LD AND ADD

It is generally assumed (Wender, 1973; Keogh, 1971) that the prevalence of learning disabilities in the ADD population is substantial. Lambert and Sandoval (1980), examining the hyperactive population described earlier (Lambert et al., 1978), noted that 43 percent of hyperactive children were achieving below grade level and 53 percent were underperforming. Silver (1981) evaluated the relationship between learning disabilities, hyperactivity, distractibility, and behavioral problems in populations of children selected as either LD or hyperactive. Of school-system-identified LD, 26 percent were hyperactive, 41 percent distractible, and 24 percent both hyperactive and distractible. In contrast, 92 percent of hyperactive children had learning disabilities as defined by what current standards would consider fairly vague criteria (1975 Federal guidelines). Halperin et al. (1984) examined the relationship between reading disability and hyperactivity in a group of 8.5-year-olds who scored 1.8 on the Conners TRS. Reading disability, defined as reading (on the Wide Range Achievement Test) more than 1 standard deviation below the FSIQ (WISC-R), was found in 9 percent of the hyperactive children. A striking finding was the relationships between age and reading disability in the hyperactive children. The hyperactive reading disabled group tended to increase in frequency with age, with approximately 10 percent of hyperactive children found to be reading disabled between 7.5 and 9.5 years. Others have estimated hyperactivity in an LD population to range from 41 percent (Holborow and Berry, 1986) to 80 percent (Safer and Allen, 1976).

In our epidemiologic sample of 445 children followed from K through grade 3 (Shaywitz, 1986), 11 percent of ADD children were classified as LD in either reading or arithmetic. LD was diagnosed utilizing a regression method for a discrepancy of >1.5 standard deviations between IQ measured by WISC-R and achievement measured by Woodcock-Johnson. Conversely, 33 percent of LD children satisfied criteria for ADD. Such findings suggest a considerable overlap between attention disorders and LD.

SUMMARY

Despite the significant problems in definition discussed above, there now appears to be general agreement on a number of epidemiologic issues. When similar rating scales are employed and teachers are used as raters, the prevalence of ADD in school-age populations appears to range between 10 percent and 20 percent. If parents are the source of information, prevalence rates appear to be higher, perhaps as high as 30 percent. The low rates found in some studies (3 to 5 percent) seem to be too stringent and represent a very skewed portion of the ADD population—that is, diagnosed as hyperactive by a professional. While a prevalence rate of 20 percent might seem to be identifying a very large segment of the school-age population, it should be noted that recent epidemiologic surveys of affective disorder (depression) in adult populations using structured clinical interviews have found similarly high prevalence rates (Weissman and Myers, 1978).

It is also evident that ADD is more common in boys, with boy-girl ratios of from 2:1 to 4:1 as reasonable. While there are a number of possible explanations for this phenomenon, it is evident from recent investigations that the underidentification of ADD in girls may be a major concern. The clinical characteristics of girls with ADD indicate that, despite attentional problems similar to those of boys with ADD, the characteristics are less intrusive, exhibit fewer aggressive symptoms, and thus, are less likely to come to the attention of their teachers or other professionals who are likely to diagnose their condition. Clearly, the identification of girls with ADD remains one of the more pressing problems in the field.

The overlap between LD and ADD is real, though recent studies suggest that it is not reasonable to believe that all, or even a majority of ADD children have LD. Recent evidence suggests that perhaps 10 percent of ADD children satisfy criteria for LD, while, conversely, one-third of LD children also exhibit symptoms of ADD. Thus in many cases, parents, school personnel, and professionals who must deal with the child must appreciate the complexity of his condition and the multidisciplinary nature of any management regimen.

ETIOLOGY

At the outset, it must be recognized that the studies described below for etiology suffer from the same major weakness of those described under prevalence: a lack of diagnostic rigor in the formulation of ADD. Many of them were begun prior to the formulation of diagnostic criteria for ADD and were initiated to examine hyperactivity or even MBD; and as indicated above, such terms represent more heterogeneous groups of behavioral disorders in children than does ADD. As discussed previously, a critical need exists to more precisely define ADD if we are to obtain any meaningful information about such issues as prevalence, etiology, pathogenesis, management, and prognosis. With this caveat, the causes of ADD are most reasonably considered within the context of primarily biologically mediated disturbances or primarily psychosocial factors.

BIOLOGIC (CONSTITUTIONAL) FACTORS

GENETIC INFLUENCES

KNOWN GENETIC DISORDERS

Studies of patients with known genetic abnormalities provide good evidence for genetic influences in ADD. Boys with an extra Y chromosome (XYY) show depression of both verbal and performance abilities and an increased incidence of hyperactivity (Hier, 1980). In contrast, girls with 45,XO do not manifest verbal deficits but rather depressed performance IQ scores. They tend to have problems with handwriting and copying tasks (Pennington and Smith, 1983) and manifest attentional deficits. Boys with a fragile X chromosome exhibit abnormal speech and language development not explained solely by their mental retardation (McLaughlin and Kriegsman, 1980; Wagerman et al., 1985). Hyperactivity and attention disorders have been described as well (Kerbeshian et al., 1984). Children with neurofibromatosis are reported to have a high incidence of learning and attentional problems including visual-perceptual and language impairments (Eliason, 1986).

FAMILY, TWIN, AND FOSTER REARING STUDIES

Evidence from a number of diverse but complimentary research strategems involving family studies, twin studies, and adoptee-foster rearing strategies have all converged to suggest an important genetic contribution to ADD. Family studies (Morrison and Stewart, 1971; Cantwell, 1972) noted an increased risk of ADD in parents and second degree relatives of children diagnosed as ADD and in the siblings of ADD boys (Welner et al., 1977). Twin studies represent still another research strategy to examine the role of genetic influences in ADD. The rationale for these studies presumes that the difference in concordance rate for monozygotic (MZ) compared to dizygotic (DZ) twins represents the effects of genetic over environmental factors. While several twin studies have noted a higher concordance rate for activity levels in MZ compared to DZ twins (Buss and Plomin, 1975; Rutter et al., 1963; Torgersen and Kringlen, 1978; Scarr, 1966; Vandenberg, 1962; Willerman, 1973), such studies reflect activity levels in normal rather than hyperactive children. Serious methodological problems make the only twin study involving hyperactive children difficult to interpret (Lopez, 1965).

Adoptee and foster rearing studies represent what some observers (DeFries and Plomin, 1978) believe to be the most influential evidence bearing on the genetic influences in ADD. Such studies are designed to elucidate the respective roles of environmental and genetic characteristics by comparing the prevalence of ADD in the biologic relatives compared to the nonbiologic relatives of probands with ADD. Both Morrison and Stewart (1971) and Cantwell (1975b) noted an increased rate of ADD in the biologic parents of ADD probands compared to that found either in the parents of normals or in the adoptive (non-biological) parents of ADD children adopted at an early age. Safer (1973) compared ADD in full siblings (same father) and one-half siblings of children with ADD who had been placed in a foster home at an early age. More than one-half the full siblings exhibited symptoms of ADD, compared to less than 10 percent of one-half siblings, adding further support for a genetic component in ADD.

Results from the National Collaborative Perinatal Project also suggest an inherited component in the group considered hyperactive-impulsive (HI). Thus, the risk to siblings of probands classified as severe HI was over two times the expected risk, and "lend[s] some support to a polygenic basis" (Nichols and Chen, 1981). Attentional and impulsivity characteristics of the biological and adoptive parents of hyperactive and normal children were examined by Alberts-Corush et al. (1986). Biological parents of ADD children exhibited more attentional difficulties but no differences in impulsivity from other parents.

In a family history study of a large cohort of children with ADD, we (Pauls et al., 1983) found an increased incidence of ADD in siblings of girls with ADD. Furthermore, we noted an increased risk of ADD in siblings if either the mother or both parents had ADD. Such findings not only support the hypothesis that there is a strong familial clustering for ADD, but the patterns also suggest that vertical transmission occurs and that the sex differences observed for the disorder might be explained by a threshold effect, with girls requiring a more pronounced genetic loading before the disorder is expressed. Thus, although girls are affected much less frequently, when they are affected, their genetic loading is high, as indicated by the more frequent occurrence of ADD in their families and, perhaps, by what is only a clinical impression of an increased severity of ADD in girls.

Most recently, Pauls and Leckman (1986) have noted a distinctly different inheritance pattern for ADD with Tourette's syndrome compared to Tourette's syndrome alone, which suggests distinct patterns of heritability for ADD and Tourette's syndrome.

NEUROCHEMICAL STUDIES

Utilizing the rationale that was quite productive in elucidating biochemical abnormalities in disorders with presumed genetic components such as phenylketonuria (PKU), it is not unreasonable to believe that the presumed genetic etiology in many cases of ADD suggests a relationship to biochemical abnormalities. For this reason, we have chosen to discuss the body of studies relating to neurochemical measures in children with ADD within the domain of genetic influences.

MONOAMINES: BASIC NEUROPHARMACOLOGY

It is beyond the scope of this review to examine the neurochemistry and neuropharmacology of the catecholamines, and the interested reader is referred to Cooper, Bloom, and Roth's text (1986) for details. The compounds that have received most attention are the monoamines, comprising the catecholamines (dopamine and norepinephrine) and the indoleamine, serotonin. Catecholamines in the brain originate from the precursor amino acid 1-tyrosine, which is transported to the brain via blood and concentrated within neurons. Dopamine (DA) formation proceeds via the enzyme tyrosine hydroxylase acting on tyrosine and resulting in the formation of 1-dihydroxyphenylacetic acid (1-DOPA), which is then decarboxylated to DA. Norepinephrine (NE) formation proceeds from DA via dopamine-b-hydroxylase (DBH). Nerve stimulation or stimulation by drugs results in release of the neurotransmitter into the synaptic cleft with subsequent inactivation by reuptake mechanisms and metabolism. The catecholamines are metabolized by two enzymes, monoamine oxidase (MAO) and catechol-o-methyltransferase (COMT). In the brain, the principal metabolite of DA is homovanillic acid (HVA) and for NE is 3-methoxy-4-hydroxy-phenylglycol (MHPG). The indoleamine, serotonin, originates from the amino acid 1-tryptophan, which in a series of metabolic steps analagous to those for the catecholamines forms serotonin (5HT). This is metabolized by monoamine oxidase to 5-hydroxyindoleacetic acid (5-HIAA). Advances in neuropsychopharmacology have allowed the determination of many of these compounds in children's urine, blood, or cerebrospinal fluid.

Evidence from several lines of investigation suggests that brain monoaminergic systems play a central role in the pathogenesis of ADD. The earliest evidence suggesting a role for brain monoamines (primarily catecholamines) derived from the observation that stimulants produce

460

an often remarkable ameliorative effect on the symptoms of ADD (reviewed in detail in "Treatment"). Considerable evidence supports the belief that stimulant agents affect central catecholaminergic mechanisms. Investigations in animals (Kuczenski, 1983) demonstrate that stimulants act via central monoaminergic systems to: (1) inhibit reuptake, (2) increase release of amine, and (3) to some extent inhibit monoamine oxidase (MAO) activity. All are actions that serve to increase the concentration of catecholamine (both dopamine and norepinephrine) at the synaptic cleft. Thus, alterations in plasma and urinary concentrations of either catecholamines, their metabolites, or compounds believed mediated by catecholamines may provide an index of the function of that particular catecholamine system. This commonality between the effects of stimulants on the symptoms of ADD and their known mechanism of action suggested that brain catecholaminergic mechanisms could be influential in the genesis of ADD (Wender, 1971).

Animal models, too, provide evidence for a relationship between brain catecholamines and ADD. Thus, utilizing the neurotoxin 6-hydroxydopamine, it is possible to produce a selective depletion of brain dopamine in the neonatal rat (Shaywitz et al., 1976a). The behavior of these animals is remarkably similar to behavior observed in children with ADD, including hyperactivity that abates with maturity and learning deficits that persist. Administration of amphetamine (Shaywitz et al., 1976b) or methylphenidate (Shaywitz et al., 1978) reverses the hyperactivity. Selective depletion of brain norepinephrine results in performance deficits but normal activity (Shaywitz et al., 1984).

More direct evidence is provided by examination of monoamines, their metabolites, and related enzymes in blood, urine, and cerebrospinal fluid of children with ADD. Further evidence is provided by pharmacological studies termed pharmacological probe studies. These are discussed below.

DOPAMINERGIC MECHANISMS

Abnormalities in central dopaminergic systems have been suggested by reports of reduced concentrations of homovanillic acid, the principal metabolite of dopamine in cerebrospinal fluid of children with ADD (Shaywitz et al., 1977). This suggests an abnormality in DA turnover. Pharmacological studies using a dopamine agonist (DOPA) indicate a weak effect (Langer et al., 1982). More recent studies have employed methylphenidate as a pharmacological probe and the hormone prolactin as an index of central dopaminergic activity. Prolactin increases activity of tuberoinfundibular DA neurons. These neurons, in turn, release DA, which inhibits prolactin. Methylphenidate acts to release DA and NE. DA inhibits prolactin, resulting in reduction in prolactin levels. Results of this study suggest significant relationships between the symptoms of ADD and alterations in prolactin concentration (Shaywitz et al., 1982).

Considerable evidence supports the belief that central noradrenergic mechanisms play a role in the genesis of ADD. Good evidence indicates that 60 percent of urinary MHPG is derived from the brain (Maas and Leckman, 1983), and thus it is reasonable to believe that determination of urinary MHPG in children will provide an index of brain NE. In fact, urinary MHPG is reduced in children with ADD compared to controls (Shekim et al., 1977; 1979; Yu-Cun and Yu-Feng, 1984). The pressor response to standing is greater in ADD children, suggesting to Mikkelson et al. (1981) increased alpha 2 receptor sensitivity. Pharmacological studies, too, suggest a role for noradrenergic mechanisms. Thus amphetamine reduces urinary MHPG in ADD children (Brown et al., 1981; Shekim et al., 1977, 1979; Zametkin et al., 1985b), a reduction observed primarily in those who responded positively to the agent (Shekim et al., 1983). Administration of the tricyclic antidepressant agent desmethylimipramine results in decreases in both plasma and urinary MHPG, which correlated with behavioral improvement (Donnelly et al., 1986). Support, too, derives from examination of the behavioral effects of different monoamine oxidase inhibitors. Two types of MAO are now recognized, differentiated on the basis of their substrate specificity. MAO A acts on NE and 5HT while MAO B acts on DA (as well as phenylethylamine). Clorgyline (primarily an MAO A inhibitor) and tranylcypromine (an inhibitor of both MAO A and MAO B) are both effective in ADD (Zametkin et al., 1985). However, deprenyl (an MAO B) inhibitor is not effective in ADD (Donnelly, personal communication, cited by Zametkin and Rapoport, in press).

SEROTONERGIC MECHANISMS

To date, there is little evidence to suggest a role for serotonin in ADD. No changes have been noted in 5-HIAA concentrations in cerebrospinal fluid (Shaywitz et al., 1977; Shetty and Chase, 1976) or platelets (Irwin et al., 1981; Rapoport et al., 1974). Fenfluramine, an agent that reduces brain serotonin, has no effect on behavior, though chemical measures of serotonin were reduced (Zametkin and Rapoport, in press).

QUESTIONS REMAINING

The reader should recognize that despite the relatively strong evidence suggesting a role for central catecholaminergic mechanisms in ADD, questions still remain. Some studies have not found decreases in urinary MHPG in ADD (Rapoport et al., 1978), while others report decreased 5HT in blood (Coleman, 1971). Furthermore, tricyclics are more specific for NE, yet they are not as effective as the stimulants in the treatment of ADD. Finally, there is often a dissociation between the biochemical and the behavioral effects. For example, cessation of stimulants (or an MAO inhibitor) results in an abrupt worsening in behavior, yet urinary MHPG continues reduced (Zametkin et al., 1985). In addition to its effects on serotonin noted above, fenfluramine results in reduction in MHPG, but with no concommitant behavioral effects. Newer methodologies, described below, may circumvent some of these problems.

As noted above, a number of investigators have employed stimulants such as amphetamine and methylphenidate as well as other drugs with well-characterized mechanisms of action as pharmacological probes to examine the role of brain catecholamines in children with ADD. This strategy, termed the pharmacological probe method, is predicated on the belief that administration of the pharmacologic probe will result in alterations in the particular neurotransmitter systems affected by the agent. In previous studies, investigators have measured concentrations of neuroendocrine-related compounds, for example, growth hormone and prolactin, which appear to be mediated by central catecholaminergic systems. However, while prolactin is a relatively specific measure of DA effect, its decrease after methylphenidate or amphetamine is limited by a "floor effect." Growth hormone response is less specific, since growth hormone is mediated by DA, NE, and 5HT. Thus, it is necessary to develop a strategy that will permit not only the more precise delineation of the specific CA system involved, but one which will permit examination of brain (central) rather than peripheral catecholaminergic (CA) systems.

A NEW STRATEGY: PHARMACOLOGIC PROBE COUPLED WITH DEBRISOQUIN

Recent advances offer for the first time the possibility of stimulating specific central (brain) catecholaminergic systems in children, measuring the effects of this stimulation on compounds present in plasma and urine, and differentiating the effects in brain from those occurring in the peripheral nervous system. The first is technological: it is now possible, utilizing a combination of gas chromatography coupled with mass fragmentography, to measure catecholamines and their metabolites in blood at concentrations as low as 10-50 fematomoles (10-15M)! Furthermore, high performance liquid chromatographic techniques coupled with electrochemical detection provide a relatively inexpensive assay of monoamines and their metabolites in the low picogram range.

The second major advance is the development of strategies to differentiate peripheral from central catecholaminergic systems, a problem considerably more troublesome in the DA than in NE systems. Thus, brain NE is metabolized preferentially to MHPG, while NE in the peripheral nervous system is metabolized to vanillylmandelic acid (VMA). Furthermore, urinary NE is derived almost exclusively from peripheral NE, since NE under normal circumstances does not cross the blood-brain barrier. Thus, plasma and urinary MHPG is a useful marker of brain NE while urinary VMA and NE reflect peripheral NE metabolism. In the DA system, we are not so fortunate. Here, both brain DA and DA originating in the peripheral nervous system are metabolized to HVA, which appears in blood and urine. The discovery of a compound that blocks the peripheral nervous system contribution to plasma and urinary HVA provides a unique opportunity to examine brain DA systems in man. The agent, debrisoquin, is a weak MAO inhibitor that does not cross the blood-brain barrier and, thus, acts only on peripheral CA systems. Evidence suggests that at predebrisoquin, 33 percent of plasma HVA is derived from the brain, but at postdebrisoquin, this rises to 75 percent (Swann et al., 1980). Thus, the measurement of HVA in blood and urine predebrisoquin will yield measures reflecting both central + peripheral DA systems. The elimination of HVA from the peripheral nervous system by the administration of debrisoquin means that urinary and plasma HVA concentrations postdebrisoquin reflect primarily brain DA activity.

Though such studies are just in their infancy, it has already been documented (Riddle et al., 1986; Shaywitz et al., 1986) that, as predicted, administration of debrisoquin results in significantly reduced concentrations of HVA and MHPG in plasma. Together with the pharmacologic probe strategy described previously, the debrisoquin strategy provides the investigator with a "window" on brain CA systems, for the first time offering a unique opportunity to examine the relationships between particular behaviors in ADD and brain DA and NE functioning.

EARLY INSULTS

For many years, the view that there was a "continuum of reproductive casualty" (Lilienfeld and Pasamanick, 1955), in which more severe perinatal insults led to profoundly poor outcomes and less serious injury to more minimal sequalae, was invoked as explanation for such frequent but low-morbidity disorders as ADD. However, the findings of the Kauai study suggested that unfavorable environment even more than perinatal stress may be more influential on later learning and attentional problems (Werner et al., 1968). Based in part upon their review of such studies, Sameroff and Chandler (1975) proposed the notion of a continuum of caretaking casualty, suggesting that environmental and social factors are important predictors of the neurological outcome of low birth weight infants and that perinatal events have less influence. As we discuss in more detail below, a more reasonable model posits an interaction between the early insult and environmental factors. Thus, in some cases the early insult will be the more influential factor in predicting later outcome, while in others, environmental influences are predominant; but in all cases, both the biological and the environmental factors must be considered.

Werry (1968) reported that 34 percent of children diagnosed as MBD had a history of some abnormal perinatal event, and more recent studies of low birth weight babies again suggest a relationship between perinatal factors and ADD. Thus, Neligan et al. (1976) have noted that low birth weight or prematurity is associated with hyperactivity, distractibility, and aggressive behavior at age 7 years (Neligan et al., 1976). Dunn et al. (1986), reporting on the results of the Vancouver study, noted that BD was the most common neurological sequelae for low birth weight children, with the prevalence of MBD 18 percent in low birth weight children compared to a rate of 6.5 percent in full birth weight children. Dunn diagnosed MBD if 2 to 4 of the following four findings were present: abnormal neurological signs; abnormal behaviors typical of "organic brain syndrome" (inattention, hyperactivity, distractibility, low frustration tolerance); psychological findings similar to those seen in organic encephalopathies (verbal-performance discrepancies on WISC-R greater than 20 points, draw-a-person test significantly lower than WISC-R); and abnormal EEG. Dunn et al. (1986) believe that "there might very well be a relationship between adverse perinatal factors and subsequent mild dysfunction."

By far the largest prospective study to examine the relationship between early events and later outcome is the National Collaborative Perinatal Project (NCPP) (Broman et al., 1985; Nichols and Chen, 1981; Rubin and Balow, 1977). Although current diagnostic criteria were not available during the study, Nichols and Chen were able to approximate many of the symptoms using data available at the 7-year-old evaluation. Thus, behavioral measures (hyperactivity, hypoactivity, impulsivity, short attention span, emotional lability, withdrawal, socioemotional immaturity) were assessed from the psychologist's observations after psychometric testing (itself providing measures used to determine learning disability). Neurologic examination provided an additional index. Factor analysis of these items yielded four factors, three of which were used in analysis. For the most part, the factors represented the particular domains examined: behavioral (hyperactivity, impulsivity, inattention, emotional lability), psychometric testing (reading, spelling, and arithmetic scales of the wide-range achievement test), and neurologic examination. Based upon arbitrarily defined cutoffs of the top 8 percent (or 3 percent for severe), these three factors were then employed to define three groups of children termed hyperactive-impulsive (HI), learning disability, and neurologic signs (NS). The HI group represents those children most closely related to what we today recognize as ADD. Analysis indicated that a number of prenatal factors were represented in the HI group more frequently than in non-HI children. These included more maternal cigarette smoking, convulsions during pregnancy, low fetal heart rate during the second stage of labor, lower placental weight, more breech presentations, and more chorionitis. Toxemia was marginally related. These findings provide important evidence supporting a role for prenatal influences in the emergence of ADD.

It is reasonable to believe that the effects of early insults to the nervous system could be demonstrated by neuroanatomical methods in individuals with a history of ADD. While convincing reports of anatomic disturbances have been noted for dyslexia (Galaburda et al., 1985; Galaburda and Kemper, 1979), to date, no pathological reports have appeared for children with ADD. Studies of CT scans in such children, however, have been performed. Although an initial study suggested abnormalities in as many as 30 percent of cases, more recent studies employing double-blind evaluations and control groups have indicated that CT scans do not distinguish between ADD and non-ADD children (Shaywitz et al., 1983; Harcherak et al., 1985).

Positron emission tomography (PET) provides a unique opportunity to examine metabolic factors in vivo in a variety of disorders. Such a procedure involves adminstration of radioactive products, and its use in the United States is not permitted in well children. Results are available from such studies performed in Sweden by Lou et al. (1984) on 13 children with learning and attention problems. The clinical profiles are not detailed, but measures of regional cerebral blood flow (rCBF) by PET scanning indicate regions of hypoperfusion in the periventricular white matter and in watershed areas between major cerebral vessels. Methylphenidate increased perfusion in mesencephalon and basal ganglia while decreasing perfusion in cortical areas. The authors suggest that their findings represent sequelae of hypoxic-ischemic encephalopathy. Most recently, Zametkin et al. (1986) examined glucose utilization by PET in 9 parents of children with ADD. The parents, who themselves satisfied Wender Utah critieria for ADD residual type, were compared to 27 age-matched controls. Whole brain glucose utilization was reduced significantly in the ADD group, etiology decreased in right frontal areas but increased in posterior medial orbital areas. Together, with the epidemiological studies discussed above, these PET studies add support for the belief that perinatal factors may play a role in the genesis of ADD.

INFECTIOUS AND METABOLIC DISORDERS

A wide variety of etiologies have been linked to the emergence of the symptoms of ADD. While the concept of "brain damage" as the principal etiology of ADD is no longer tenable (see "Historical Perspective"), it is clear that, in some cases, damage to the central nervous system may be followed temporally by the emergence of behaviors whose symptoms satisfy diagnostic criteria for ADD. In such cases, the relationship between the insult to the nervous system and the subsequent development of ADD is irrefutable. Thus, as noted previously, symptoms similar to those now described for ADD were noted as the sequelae of von Economo's encephalitis (Hohman, 1922) and following CNS complications of nearly all of the common viral diseases of childhood (Bender, 1942) as well as Sydenham's chorea (Aron et al., 1965). Although earlier studies suggested that children who suffered from *Haemophilus influenzae meningitis* exhibited a higher percentage of behavioral disturbances (including ADD) and school problems than controls (Sproles et al., 1969), the results of a more recent study suggest a more complicated scenario. Thus, Taylor and associates (1984), in a study employing siblings as controls, found that although full-scale and performance IQ scores were reduced in children following *H. influenzae meningitis,* their behavior and academic achievement was indistinguishable from their sibling controls.

Chronic otitis media with effusion has been implicated as a cause of delayed development in speech, language, and cognition, though these effects appear related to socioeconomic status (SES) (surprisingly those in the highest SES groups appeared to be more at risk—Teele et al., 1984). Most recently, Paradise and Rogers (1986) suggest that serious methodologic concerns make conclusions of Teele et al. (1984) difficult to accept, and at the present time the issue remains unresolved.

Learning and attentional problems may occur following metabolic encephalopathies, such as Reye syndrome, though in this case the symptoms are usually transient (Shaywitz et al, 1982). There is also a suggestion that such children may have had learning and attention disorders preceding their Reye syndrome (Quart et al., 1985). ADD has also been associated with rare metabolic encephalopathies such as hyperammonemias, though in such cases associated neurologic problems occur as well (Batshaw et al., 1980; Bernar et al., 1986). Most recently Realmuto et al. (1986) have described ADD in 9 of 13 children treated since early life for phenylketonuria. Such a finding suggests that children with PKU may be at risk for ADD and other childhood psychiatric diseases even when treatment begins early and is maintained.

EXOGENOUS TOXINS, DEFICIENCY STATES, AND DIET

Exogenous toxins represent another potential etiology for dyslexia and ADD. Exposure may occur in utero, for example, from maternal ingestion of ethyl alcohol, an entity described as the expanded fetal alcohol syndrome (EFAS) (Shaywitz et al., 1980; Streissguth et al., 1978). The amount of alcohol that must be consumed by the mother and the time during gestation when alcohol is believed to exert its damaging effects, however, remain unclear. Furthermore, some investigations fail to find such an association. Thus, Hesselbrock et al. (1985) have reported that while ADD occurring before age 12 years may predict the onset of alcoholism, there was no difference in the rate of ADD between the offspring of alcoholics compared to the offspring of nonalcoholics. At the present time, prudence dictates following the most recent recommendations by the National Institute of Alcohol and Alcohol Abuse, which suggest that pregnant women refrain from any alcoholic consumption.

Lead poisoning represents a more controversial etiology for attentional difficulties. It has long been recognized that children who survive the effects of acute lead intoxication are frequently left with significant neurological handicaps and intellectual sequelae. Less well appreciated are the studies that indicate that persistently elevated lead levels without clinical evidence of encephalopathy may also be associated with cognitive and behavioral difficulties (Needleman et al., 1981; Bellinger and Needleman, 1983). Considerable controversy exists over whether the small decrements in performance IQ demonstrated by Needleman's studies are clinically significant, and, in fact, whether factors related to lead are responsible for the changes (Ernhart et al., 1981). The most recent studies suggest that low lead levels are associated with ADD but that this association is quite weak (Gittelman and Eskenazi, 1983). A major limitation in the interpretation of such studies has been the confounding effects of body lead burden with other dependent variables, such as social class. Thus, at the present time, it is reasonable to suggest that while low lead levels may affect behavior and cognition, it is factors common to both lead and behavior problems, such as social adversity, that better explain these findings (Taylor, 1986).

Though not a common etiology in this country, the role of malnutrition in the genesis of learning and behavior problems has been examined by many investigators, most recently by Galler and her associates (1984). Their results suggest a relationship between early severe protein calorie malnutrition and later ADD and learning problems. Anecdotal reports have also linked ADD to transient folic acid deficiency (Shapira et al., 1983).

Although the role of diet in the genesis of ADD continues to receive attention, at the present time, there appears to be no significant relationship between ingestion of such products as food colorings (Kavale and Forness, 1983) or sucrose (Barling and Bullen, 1985) and the emergence of ADD. This subject continues to remain a popular one, however, and reports of apparent links between food allergy and behavioral disturbances continue to appear (Egger et al., 1985). While it is possible that rare instances occur where there may be a relationship between ingestion of food products and the immediate emergence of ADD, such occurrences are inadequately documented or are described in an anecodotal manner that provides little empiric validity to the claims made. More will be said of this below (see "Treatment").

The belief that unshielded fluorescent lighting might provoke hyperactivity in children (what Ross and Ross, 1982, refer to as "radiation stress") was first proposed by Ott (1968, 1976). Despite initial suggestions of such an effect (Mayron et al., 1974), a subsequent study by O'Leary et al. (1978) provided solid evidence to refute this claim. To date, Ott's suggestion has received no further support, and has, for all intents and purposes, been laid to rest.

NEUROLOGICAL PROBLEMS ASSOCIATED WITH ADD

HEAD TRAUMA

Head trauma represents still another insult often implicated in the genesis of attentional difficulties. Not only is there little relationship between the anatomic site of head injury and later cognitive and attentional deficits (Chadwick et al., 1981; Shaffer et al., 1975), but as was the case for lead intoxication, controversy exists over the causal relationship between head trauma and the development of disorders of attention, activity, and cognition. Furthermore, although clinical lore suggests behaviors similar to those described as sequelae of Reye syndrome, such a notion has been difficult to document (Rutter et al., 1983). Furthermore, for minimal degrees of head trauma, it is difficult to decide whether the behavioral and cognitive deficits observed are the consequences of the injury or simply represent the fact that children with attentional difficulties and hyperactivity are more likely to behave in a manner that may lead to accidents.

SEIZURE DISORDERS

While a number of studies have documented an increased incidence of learning and behavior disorders in children with epilepsy (Rutter et al., 1970), it is not at all clear whether any specific behavioral disorder occurs more frequently than another, and if a particular learning or behavioral disorder is associated with a particular type of epilepsy (Stores and Hart, 1976; Corbett and Trimble, 1983). It should be noted that controversy surrounding the kinds of behavior and learning problems exhibited by individuals with epilepsy is certainly not restricted to the pediatric literature (Dodrill and Batzel, 1986; Lesser et al., 1986).

Most recently, Kinney et al. (1985) indicate that the degree of inattention, hyperactivity, and impulsivity is similar in children with seizures and ADD compared to those with ADD without seizures. However, those children with both ADD and seizures exhibited a significantly lower IQ as measured by WISC-R than those with ADD alone.

Confounding the issue of the relationship between ADD and seizures is the question of the role of anticonvulsant medications in the genesis of both disorders. Few studies are available in children, and, as noted by Reynolds (1983), those in adults have been confounded by factors such as the severity of the seizure disorder as well as the simultaneous use of several anticonvulsant agents. Thompson et al. (1981) and Thompson and Trimble (1981; 1982) noted deficits in memory and processing speed after therapeutic doses of phenytoin, sodium valproate, carbamazepine, and clobazam in normal adults. Thus, since nearly all children with seizure disorders are receiving anticonvulsant medications, any behaviors attributed to the seizure disorder could as easily be attributed to medication effects. The anticonvulsant medications themselves may influence the emergence of learning and attention problems. Such questions are difficult to resolve. Prospective studies addressing, for example, the issue of phenobarbital and behavior in children with febrile seizures are currently in progress (Farwell, personal communication). Most recently, O'Dougherty et al. (personal communication) have demonstrated deficits in memory scanning and learning new information in children with newly diagnosed complex partial epilepsy receiving therapeutic doses of the anticonvulsant agent carbamazepine. This effect appeared to be dose related, and suggests that anticonvulsant agents need to be employed at the lowest effective therapeutic dose in order to minimize any potential cognitive and behavioral side effects.

ENVIRONMENTAL AND CULTURAL FACTORS

While it is reasonable to suppose that environmental and cultural factors play an important role in the genesis of ADD, such a relationship has not always been easy to document. Campbell and Redfering (1979) were unable to relate hyperactivity (assessed by the teacher) to such variables as birth order, number of siblings, times moved, family income, mother's age, mother's educational level, or the father's educational level. Similar findings have been reported as well by Goyette et al. (1978). Campbell and Redfering did, however, suggest a possible relationship between hyperactivity and marital status, though in a more recent investigation (Prinz et al., 1983), marital discord failed to explain the aggressive behavior of hyperactive boys.

Findings from the longitudinal National Collaborative Perinatal Project (see "Early Insults" above) provide evidence for environmental influences in the emergence of ADD (Broman et al., 1985; Nichols and Chen, 1981). Thus, the HI group was more likely to come from homes where the father was absent, a finding noted as well in the Kauai study (Werner and Smith, 1977). Such data provide support for the belief that the behavioral manifestations of ADD are linked to adverse social conditions, primarily disruptive family relationships. Further support is provided by Deutsch et al. (1982), who noted the prevalence rate of ADD in nonrelative adoptees at 13 percent and 21 percent in two separate populations, compared to a rate of 2.3 percent in controls. They suggest that factors such as stress placed on adoptive families (Mech, 1973) or a result of separation anxiety (Yarrow, 1964; 1965) or substance abuse by the biological mother could play a role in this observation. However, it is possible that genetic influences could explain such findings as well. Horn et al. (1975) note that 88 percent of the biological mothers of nonrelative adoptees are unwed mothers and that the unwed mother is characterized by a substantial elevation in psychopathology, as measured by the Minnesota Multiphasic Personality Inventory.

Other studies, too, suggest a relationship between low socio-economic status and the behaviors characteristic of ADD (Schachar et al., 1981) or poor performance on a continuous performance test (Levy, 1980) in children with ADD.

It is also reasonable to believe that what Ross and Ross (1982) term "cultural" factors and Mintz and Collins (1985) refer to as a "social psychological hypothesis" may significantly influence the perception of ADD. Ross and Ross suggest that hyperactivity is less likely to occur in those cultures characterized by a consistency of the basic tenets of the society across institutions within that culture—that is, a consistency within the home, school, church, mass media, and other major organizational structures of society. In their view, those cultures characterized by high consistency tend to be high on group cohesiveness and seem to offer acceptance to individuals because of their membership in the cultural group rather than on the basis of individual performance. By minimizing the difference between children with ADD and their normal peers, such cultures provide what Whalen et al. (1979) describe as a rarefaction ecology and Chess (1979) terms a goodness of fit situation. The converse—inconsistency in the ecosystem—results in a provocation ecology (Whalen et al., 1979) or poorness of fit (Chess, 1979) for the child with ADD. Citing hyperactivity to be "virtually non-existent" in China, urban Japan, and Salt Lake City, and among Mexican groups in the Southwest, Ross and Ross believe they exemplify cultures representing a consistent, rarefaction, goodness of fit ecology in contrast to the inconsistency of contemporary American and Western European society. However, references to the "virtually nonexistent" hyperactivity in these "consistent" cultures represent personal communications or reports at meetings, which to date have not yet been published in peer reviewed journals. Furthermore, a recent study from China indicates a prevalence rate of ADD similar to that in this country and Europe (see "Epidemiology").

While the data clearly do not support the notion of cultural consistency as a primary cause of ADD, good evidence supports the belief that cultural influences do, indeed, play a role. Thus, Mintz and Collins (1985) demonstrated that loudness and contextual inappropriateness led to the perception of hyperactivity and a more negative evaluation of behaviors. Furthermore, recent studies by Whalen and Henker and their associates (reviewed by Whalen and Henker, 1984) support the belief that cultural factors play an important role in the way children with ADD are perceived by their parents, teachers, peers, and themselves.

A particularly intriguing theory posits that hyperactivity may represent a learned response to an emotionally depriving environment that then becomes generalized to the classroom or other group situations (Taylor, 1986). Support for this theory comes from Tizard and associates (Tizard and Hughes, 1978; Tizard and Rees, 1974) in studies of hyperactivity in institutions. However, documentation of hyperactivity in school as a result of institutionalization has not been published, though Taylor cites a presentation by Roy (1983).

Summary

It is clear that ADD results from a wide variety of influences. Although for ease of presentation, these are considered as either biologic or psychosocial factors, current evidence indicates that an interactional model, one considering both domains, is the most reasonable approach. Among the biologic factors, genetic influences are extremely important. From a clinical perspective, they often permit the clinician to make a reasonable statement to parents about the suspected cause of the child's problems: "Your child was born that way. You seem to have had similar problems too." Recognition of the importance of genetic factors is important from the perspective of learning more about the mechanisms responsible for ADD. Thus, the strong evidence suggesting genetic influences is consonant with the neurochemical studies supporting a role for brain catecholaminergic mechanisms in the genesis of the disorder. The development of newer strategies, particularly pharmacological probes coupled with the use of debrisoquin, offers a unique opportunity to better elucidate these mechanisms.

Results of recent longitudinal studies of low birth weight babies as well as the results of the National Collaborative Perinatal Project indicate that insults to the brain occurring in the perinatal period may play a role in some cases. Rarely, infections, metabolic disorders, exogenous toxins, or deficiency states may also be implicated. While the relationship between maternal alcoholism and ADD seems established, the relationship between chronic low lead levels and ADD remains controversial, though, if there are effects, they are minimal. Such etiologies seem to be the ones most approachable by preventive measures, but the number of cases of ADD that each etiology is responsible for is so small that no appreciable effects on the number of children with ADD would be discerned. The occurrence of ADD in children with seizures is well established, though it is often not clear if the anticonvulsant medications used for treatment of the seizures may not play an important role. Recent evidence suggests that even at therapeutic blood levels of relatively "safe" anticonvulsants, decrements in cognitive function are apparent. This suggests caution in prescribing anticonvulsants, but if unavoidable, using them at the lowest possible effective dose.

Environmental and cultural factors clearly play a role in the genesis of ADD. Thus, the same longitudinal studies that demonstrated the importance of perinatal insults also demonstrated the link between ADD and adverse social conditions. The goodness of fit between the child

472

and his society clearly plays an important role in the genesis of ADD. In contrast, the notion that ADD is not found in certain "consistent" cultures does not appear to be tenable, since the prevalence data indicate a consistent rate across cultures. Certainly cultural factors play a critical role in the way the children with ADD are perceived by their parents, teachers, peers, and themselves.

Current research supports an interactional, transactional model for the genesis of ADD, incorporating both biological as well as psychosocial factors. In this context, for example, a child's genetic endowment provides the biologic basis for particular behaviors. However, the clinical expression of these behaviors is influenced considerably by the child's environment. Thus, given a heavy loading of biologically determined behaviors for ADD, we might expect to see ADD expressed under most environmental conditions. Conversely, given a moderate loading for biologically determined behaviors consistent with ADD, we might expect to see the symptoms only in stressful environments. Finally, a particularly damaging environment may provoke symptoms even in children with very little biologically determined loading.

TREATMENT

Management of ADD represents a complex and intricate balance of a variety of treatment strategies encompassing educational, cognitive-behavioral, and pharmacological interventions. Establishing the diagnosis comprises the initial focus of management, and once this has been accomplished, the diagnosis and its implications must then be interpreted to the child, his parents and critical school personnel. For purposes of this paper, generally accepted management of ADD encompasses two general domains: (a) nonpharmacologic (educational and cognitive-behavioral and other psychological and psychiatric approaches); (b) pharmacologic therapies. Our review of management would not be complete without a discussion of still a third general class of therapies, what we have termed (c) nontraditional, controversial, idiosyncratic approaches.

NONPHARMACOLOGIC THERAPIES

EDUCATIONAL MANAGEMENT

We begin with the recognition that, from an educational perspective, ADD is a serious disorder that will not resolve spontaneously. However, given this consideration, what is not at all clear is precisely what approach would provide the most effective specific educational strategy in any particular child. In fact, the number of possible special education programs is almost overwhelming. As Deshler et al. (1983) suggest, the sheer number of programs may reflect the demands of P.L. 94-142, which mandated programming not only in an extremely short time but also in a very visible public climate. This resulted, unfortunately, in the development of a great number of programs, each based on extremely limited research. The programs range from broad-based systems to very specific remediation of reading, writing, and arithmetic. The interested reader is referred to Myers and Hammill (1982) for a critical review of instructional strategies. All successful approaches must recognize and deal effectively with not only academic issues but also social and behavioral problems as well.

Current educational practices have most recently been reviewed by Smith (1986), who organizes the issues within three general domains. The first, referred to as "orientations to improving basic school performance," includes (1) underlying process and behavioral orientations, (2) interactional approaches, (3) assessment for instruction, (4) learning strategies approach, (5) developing talents and special expertise, and (6) enhancing motivation. A second major domain includes environmental, medical, and neuropsychological interventions. Adolescent and adult interventions are considered separately. As a minimum, it is critical that those professionals undertaking the care of the child with ADD be aware of such general educational approaches as (a) the role of self-contained classrooms for children with ADD as opposed to mainstreaming in a regular classroom, (b) strategies for providing structured classroom environment, (c) techniques for removing the child from distracting stimuli, and (d) optimal timing and specific recommendations for making curriculum modifications.

COGNITIVE-BEHAVIORAL THERAPIES

Cognitive-behavioral therapy (CBT), a term representing a host of cognitive components and behavioral strategies including operant techniques (positive and negative reinforcement) and parent counseling, has come to represent the most widely employed alternative to pharmacotherapy. Cognitive strategies encourage the active participation of the child in the learning and monitoring process. Training addresses such issues as problem definition, problem approach, focusing of attention, choosing an answer, and self-enforcement and coping (Kendall and Braswell, 1985). As noted by Whalen et al. (1985), this enthusiasm for CBT comes both from the recognition that while stimulant medications are often effective, their actions are often circumscribed, and both physiological and psychologic toxicity may occur. Thus, in addition to side effects observed with medications (discussed below in "Pharmacotherapy"), medications may alter the way the child with ADD views himself and the way that parents perceive their child, effects that Whalen and Henker (1984) refer to as emanative effects of pharmacotherapy of ADD. Furthermore, medications are effective in at most 70 percent of children, and many others may either refuse medication or discontinue it shortly after initiation (Firestone, 1982). With its focus on self-guidance and problem solving, CBT offers an attractive long-term coping strategy for the child with ADD that is both durable and generalizable. Intuitively, one would expect synergy between both types of therapies; unfortunately, both short- and long-term gains with CBT have been quite limited, and a number of investigators have questioned whether CBT combined with pharmacotherapy offers any advantages to pharmacotherapy alone (Abikoff and Gittelman, 1985; Brown et al., 1985). However, formidable methodologic difficulties plague such studies (Pelham and Murphy, in press) and may obscure the effects of combined CBT and pharmacotherapy. Firestone et al. (1986) noted the importance of considering all subjects, including those who drop out of a study. Thus, in their investigation comparing stimulant medications and parent training in ADD, medications were superior, but when the data were reanalyzed taking into consideration those who dropped out of the study, no differences were noted between the two treatment regimens. Furthermore, recent studies suggest that CBT may, in fact, be a useful adjunct to pharmacotherapy (Hinshaw et al., 1984; Schell et al., 1986). In addition, CBT may be helpful when children are tapered off medication (Rosen et al., in press).

PSYCHOTHERAPY

Individual psychotherapy may be a helpful component of therapy in some children who have serious psychiatric problems or are unable to cope with their disability. While the exclusive use of psychotherapy is rarely employed in ADD, what Satterfield et al. (1980; 1982) term "multimodality" therapy has been demonstrated to be quite effective indeed. As employed by his group, multimodality therapy includes: (a) individual and group psychotherapy for the child, (b) individual education therapy for the child, (c) individual and group psychotherapy for the parents, (d) family psychotherapy, and (e) medication. Satterfield et al. (1981) compared outcome after three years in children receiving multimodality therapy for 34 months with those receiving similar therapy for only 9 months. Those receiving less therapy were more anti-social and more inattentive than the group receiving longer duration therapy, which suggests a benefit from treatment. These issues are discussed in more detail and by Cohen and his associates (Hunt and Cohen, 1984; Hansen and Cohen, 1984).

PHARMACOTHERAPY

SCOPE AND PREVALENCE OF USE

Medication, used either alone or in combination with CBT or psychiatric or psychologic therapy, is the most widely utilized modality employed in the managment of ADD. Estimates suggest that drug treatment prevalence rates range from 0.75 percent to 2.6 percent, depending upon the location and age-group surveyed (Gadow and Kalachnik, 1981). While some have observed an increase in drug use for the treatment of ADD in children between 1971 and 1977, such estimates are difficult to substantiate. In preparing this paper, we assessed drug use in several ways. One estimate was obtained from the U.S. Drug Enforcement Agency (DEA), which is responsible for tracking the prescriptions for all controlled drugs, including the stimulants amphetamine and methylphenidate. Data are available since 1980 on both the amount of methylphenidate ordered by pharmacists (termed ARCOS) and the kilograms of methylphenidate requested by pharmaceutical companies (quota data). In general, these data indicate a relatively constant amount of methylphenidate available for this 6-year period.

The most detailed estimate of drug use in hyperactivity was obtained from a survey of physicians in office-based practice performed by IMS America, Ltd. These data, generously provided by Stephan Chappell, Senior Vice President, provide information on individual drug use by category of primary childhood behavioral disorders. Thus, drug use in the combination of hyperactive childhood behavior (HCB) and minimal brain dysfunction (MBD) represents one of these categories. Information from 1970 to 1985 was requested. We calculated the percent drug use (for Ritalin, methylphenidate, or Ritalin-SR) as a percent of total patient visits. In 1970, for example, 413,000 visits were recorded for HCB/MBD. In that same year, 171,000 uses of Ritalin were reported. Ritalin, therefore, was used in 41 percent of HCB/MBD visits.

Although there was some fluctuation from year to year, calculations using a goodness-of-fit analysis indicate no significant change in methylphenidate use between 1970 and 1985, which is consonant with that provided by the DEA.

We begin our discussion with a review of the effects of stimulants (amphetamine, methylphenidate, pemoline) generally regarded as the most effective and, not surprisingly, the most widely utilized agents in the management of ADD. We review their mechanism of action, clinical effects, and pharmacokinetics, and indicate a reasonable and practical clinical approach to their use. Potential toxicity and side effects are discussed as well. We then turn our attention to tricyclic agents, which are assuming increasing importance in the therapeutic armamentarium, and finally discuss a variety of miscellaneous pharmacologic agents.

STIMULANTS

EFFECTS ON ACTIVITY AND ATTENTION

As noted earlier ("Etiology"), evidence from several lines of investigation have converged to suggest a role for central monoaminergic mechanisms in the genesis of ADD. In no small measure, much of this

476

evidence relates to the commonality of the mechanism of action of the stimulants and their therapeutic effects in children with ADD. Thus, investigations in animals (Kuczenski, 1983) demonstrate that amphetamine and methylphenidate act via central monoaminergic systems to (1) increase release of amine, (2) inhibit reuptake, and (3) to some extent, inhibit monoamine oxidase activity, all actions that serve to increase the concentration of catecholamine (both dopamine and norepinephrine) at the synaptic cleft. The actions of pemoline are not nearly as well studied, though it is now clear that the early suggestion that pemoline preferentially stimulates dopamine synthesis is not supported by more recent studies. These indicate that pemoline reduces catecholamine turnover and may inhibit catecholamine uptake (Fuller et al., 1978; Molina and Orsingher, 1981). Historically, a stimulant, d-amphetamine, was the first agent found to be effective in the treatment of hyperactivity (Bradley, 1937), and since that initial report, abundant evidence from many investigative groups supports the belief that stimulants (amphetamine, methylphenidate, pemoline) are effective in reducing activity levels and improving attention in 60 percent to 70 percent of children with ADD (Barkley, 1977; Conners and Werry, 1979; Gadow, 1983; Rosenthal and Allen, 1978; Weiss et al., 1979; Whalen and Henker, 1976; Kavale, 1982; Ottenbacher and Cooper, 1983).

Investigations employing continuous monitoring of truncal activity recorded automatically for 24 hours per day for 7 days (Porrino et al., 1983) indicate that this reduction in activity levels occurs during academic studies in structured on-task activities and that activity during physical education is actually increased. Furthermore, the reduction in activity appears to be related to a reduction in perceived intensity of activity (Henker et al., 1986; Whalen et al., 1979; Whalen et al., 1981). This finding is consonant with the observations of Barkley et al. (1985) that stimulants enhance appropriate or rule-governed behavior—that is, result in a general increase in improving compliance of ADD children to their mothers' commands or in the duration of this compliance.

EFFECTS ON CONGNITION

In contrast to the plethora of studies documenting the salutary effects of stimulants on attention and activity in children with ADD, their effects on cognitive function remain controversial. In assessing such effects, one reasonable strategy compares the effects of the stimulant in children with ADD compared to children referred primarily for learning disability. Some investigators have failed to note any positive effects of stimulants in primarily learning disabled children (Huddleston et al., 1961; Gittelman-Klein and Klein, 1976; Gittelman, 1980). However, others (Ackerman et al., 1982) have found that while hyperactive subjects demonstrated a more marked clinical response to the stimulant methylphenidate than a group of primarily learning disabled children without hyperactivity, all subject groups exhibited "substantial improvement" on the tests of attentiveness. Such findings suggest not only that attentional problems are a significant component in the children selected primarily for reading disability but also that stimulants may be effective in those children with reading difficulty regardless of the presence of hyperactivity. Such findings are generally consonant with those of Gittelman et al. (1983) and suggest that methylphenidate may provide some benefit in the treatment of reading disabled children, though such results still remain somewhat tenuous.

Clearly the examination of drug effects on academic achievement in children with ADD provides an even more direct strategy to examine the effects of stimulants on cognitive processes. Despite some early studies suggesting a positive effect of stimulants on learning or academic achievement (Conners, 1972; Weiss et al., 1971), other investigations reported no significant drug effects on academic achievement (reviewed by Barkley, 1981; Rie et al., 1976a,b). Employing what has been termed meta-analysis of 61 studies of the effects of drugs on hyperactivity, Ottenbacher and Cooper (1983) indicate that those measures classified as tapping "IQ achievement" were improved by stimulants, although to a considerably lesser degree than were such qualities as "behavioral social," "perceptual motor," and "impulse attention." In contrast, Kavale (1982), employing similar meta-analytic techniques, suggests that "cognitive outcomes" are affected almost as much by stimulants as are behavioral outcomes.

As noted by Pelham (1983) and Douglas et al. (1986), explanations for these apparent discrepancies may be found in such methodological issues as (a) insufficient items on an achievement test to detect short term changes, (b) failure to control for order effects, and (c) testing performed in a relatively artificial laboratory setting. Utilizing an experimental design that minimized such problems, Douglas et al. (1986) noted methylphenidate-induced improvement on mathematical computations and word discovery. In classroom tasks, children on methylphenidate attempted and completed more work, indicating a more efficient performance. Other investigators, too, have now provided evidence suggesting that stimulant administration to children with ADD results in improvement in academic performance in reading, arithmetic, and spelling (Ballinger et al., 1984; Pelham, 1986; Rapport et al., 1986; Sebrechts et al., 1986; Stephens et al., 1984).

EFFECTS ON CONDUCT AND SOCIAL BEHAVIOR

Despite the half-century of experience with stimulants in children, their effects on aggressive kinds of behaviors are still not clear. Aggressive behavior, as determined by 5-minute observations during relatively short-term amphetamine administration is, indeed, reduced (Amery et al., 1984). As reviewed by Pelham and Murphy (1986), it is likely that combined pharmaco- and behavioral therapy is more effective than either alone in children with both CD and ADD. To date, however, our inability to define CD more precisely (to say nothing of the difficulties in defining ADD) makes it impossible to determine with certainty those target populations employed in such investigations and the degree to which CD and ADD are confounded.

Social interactions are significantly affected by stimulants. Thus, methylphenidate is effective in improving the compliance of ADD children to their mothers' commands (Barkley et al., 1985), though sociability may be decreased (Barkley and Cunningham, 1979). Peer relationships may be affected as well, though it may be difficult to discern if the measures and the setting are not well suited for such observations. Thus, a number of investigators (Cunningham et al., 1985; Pelham and Bender, 1982; Riddle and Rapoport, 1976) have not been able to document that stimulant medications affect peer interactions. Such studies, however, employed either relatively insensitive observational methods or simulated classroom settings. Utilizing a naturalistic setting and more sensitive observational methods, Whalen and her associates (1979, 1981) noted that methylphenidate reduced both the intensity and positive affect of boys with ADD. Taken together with what Whalen and Henker (1984) have termed "emanative effects," such studies support the belief that stimulants exert significant influences on a variety of social interactions.

ONTOGENY OF STIMULANT EFFECTS

While the effects of stimulants in ADD have been described, for the most part, in school-age children, an emerging literature has begun to document the effects of stimulants in both younger (preschool) and older (adolescent) children as well as in adults. Clinical lore suggests that stimulants are not effective in the preschool child, and this notion is supported by studies such as that of Schliefer et al. (1975), which failed to document improvement in nursery school behavior after methylphenidate. Clearly, more studies are needed at this age, but until diagnostic criteria for ADD in the preschool child are formulated, such studies will be difficult indeed. Those issues relating to diagnosis are discussed above and reviewed by Campbell et al. (1986).

In contrast, studies of stimulant effects in adolescents suggest that these pharmacological agents are as effective here as in the school-age child (Garfinkel et al., 1986; Varley and Trupin 1983). This is not surprising, given the now well-established phenomenological information core that documents a reduction of activity with maturation but a persistence of inattention and impulsivity.

Despite the initial optimism that ADD in adults might respond to stimulants, this result has not been realized. In a recent study, Mattes et al. (1984) examined the effects of stimulant therapy in adult psychiatric patients with and without a childhood history of ADD. Methylphenidate appeared to benefit 25 percent of the subjects, regardless of their history of childhood ADD. However, even in those who responded, the effects were not as pronounced as those observed in childhood ADD. Again, as in the preschool ADD, diagnostic criteria for adult ADD have not been well established and it is not at all clear whether the term when applied to adults is describing a particular syndrome or is confounded by the large number of character disorders identified in adult psychiatric practice.

PRACTICAL CONSIDERATIONS

To a great extent, the decision to initiate pharmacotherpy is based upon a number of diverse and difficult-to-define general factors such as the physician's clinical judgment, his understanding of the child, the family, and the school environment, and his knowledge of educational practices within his community. However, two very specific considerations are:

(1) Proper class placement. This represents, perhaps the most critical factor in the success of pharmacotherapy since stimulant therapy will almost certainly be ineffective unless the child's educational placement is satisfactory. Thus, it is vital for the physician to do everything to ensure that the school system has properly evaluated the child and that the most appropriate school placement has been effected.

(2) Focus on target symptoms. Before beginning medication, the physician must determine which particular symptoms are the targets of the treatment and decide at which times these symptoms are most troublesome. Contrary to popular notions, hyperactivity alone is seldom a sufficient reason for initiation of pharmacotherapy. In fact, hyperactivity tends to abate with increasing age, no matter what treatment is employed.

In general, stimulants are more effective in the amelioration of attentional difficulties in school than in improving the child's behavior or performance at home. In part, this dichotomy between satisfactory improvement at school with relatively less improvement at home correlates with the biological availability of the stimulant. It also reflects the fact that those characteristics of attentional deficit that are most amenable to the effects of stimulants—for example, being able to follow a complicated set of directions amid the distractions caused by 25 other children—are put to the test in school. It is rare for the child to be placed in a similar stressful situation at home.

Not surprisingly, prediction of clinical response to stimulants does not appear to depend on either an abnormal neurological examination or abnormal electroencephalogram. Some investigators have suggested that such prediction can be reliably determined using double-blind, placebo-controlled methodology to assess the child's performance on specific tests conducted in a laboratory setting (Swanson et al., 1978). While such procedures may be advantageous in particular situations, they are generally too complex, and a large majority of experienced clinicians would consider the administration of medication in the child's real life setting as the only valid therapeutic trial. Parenthetically, it should be noted that a positive response to stimulants may be observed in nonhyperactive children (Rapoport et al., 1978; Werry, 1982), and thus improvement in symptoms with therapy should not be construed as implying that the diagnosis of ADD was, indeed, correct.

Children with ADD characteristically are extremely sensitive to alterations in their environment and need more time to adjust to new situations. Thus, we recommend initiation of pharmacotherapy only if the child has had an opportunity to adjust to any environmental alteration. This means that, in most cases, medication should not be initiated simultaneously with the child's beginning a new school year or with his entrance into a classroom setting that has just been changed. Such a practice not only allows the physician to determine the child's baseline functioning without medication, but more importantly, it also gives the child an opportunity to adjust to his new environment prior to beginning stimulant therapy. However, if past experience suggests that pharmacotherapy has made such a difference in the child's behavior that entry into a new class without medication would probably result in the child's being viewed by his new teachers in a negative fashion, it would seem most reasonable to consider beginning medication prior to entry into the new environment. In practice, such a situation is most likely to arise when the child enters, for example, a middle or a junior high school setting and must contend with the additional stresses of a new setting, departmentalized programs, and older peers.

Since the details of peak concentrations and elimination half-lives at any given dosage are just beginning to emerge (see below) and blood levels of methylphenidate (MPH) are not yet generally available, the physician must decide upon dosage empirically and modify the initial dosage depending upon the clinical situation. This is further compli-cated because an optimum dosage for one target symptom may not be optimum for a different symptom. Thus, Sprague and Sleator (1977) have suggested that while high doses of MPH (1.0 mg/kg) may produce improvement in global measures of activity, scores on memory tasks and performance on attentional tests may be poorer at a high dose com-pared to a low dose (0.3 mg/kg). However, other investigators have found that within a range of 0.3-0.8 mg/kg, performance on both behavioral and cognitive tasks improves in a dose-related fashion (Charles et al., 1981; Cunningham et al., 1985; Rapport et al., 1985; Sebrechts et al., 1986; Shaywitz et al., 1982).

PHARMACOKINETICS

The recent development of a gas chromatographic assay for MPH (Hungand et al., 1978; Shaywitz et al., 1982) has facilitated the deter-mination of blood levels and permitted the initiation of studies de-signed to explore a number of clinically relevant issues, including the pharmacokinetics of MPH and the relationship between MPH concentrations and behavioral response.

Several investigative groups have examined the pharmacokinetics of oral MPH (Shaywitz et al., 1982; Sebrechts et al., 1986; Gualtieri et al., 1984; Winsberg et al., 1982). After a lag phase of about 0.5-1.0 hour, MPH reaches a peak plasma concentration 2.5 hours after administration. Two- and three-hour concentrations are on the average within 80 percent and 90 percent of the observed peak, with maximal concentrations averaging 11.2 ng/ml at a dose of 0.34 mg/kg and 20.2 ng/ml at a dose of 0.65 mg/kg. Single point specimens obtained 2 hours after administration in children chronically taking medication approximate those found at the same time period after a single acute dose (Shaywitz et al., 1982). Elimination half-life averages 2.5 hours (Shaywitz et al., 1982). Swanson et al. (1978) have reported a "behavioral half-life- between 2 and 4 hours which is quite consistent with the biological half-life observed for MPH. This effect constrasts with that observed after d-amphetamine, which demonstrates a much higher peak concentration (65.9 ng/ml after 0.45 mg/kg dose) and a longer half-life (about 7 hours). In contrast to MPH, the behavioral effects observed after d-amphetamine were reported not to correlate with peak drug levels (Brown et al., 1979).

More recently, several investigative groups have examined the pharmacokinetics of pemoline. A wide individual variation was observed, with maximum plasma concentrations occurring approximately 3 hours after administration and peak concentrations averaging 4.3 mg/L. In contrast to previously reported studies in adults where elimination half-life averaged 11-13 hours, pemoline half-life in children averaged 7.0-8.5 hours (Sallee et al., 1985; Collier et al., 1985).

ADMINISTRATION AND DOSAGE

In contrast to previous recommendations that MPH must only be given 30 minutes before breakfast when the stomach is empty to ensure absorption, recent studies (Swanson et al., 1983; Chan et al., 1983) have demonstrated that both the pharmacokinetics and the behavioral effects of the drug are indistinguishable whether it is given with breakfast or 30 minutes before breakfast. A reasonable approach is to begin with an initial dosage of 0.3 mg/kg given in the morning immediately before the child leaves for school. Thus, by the time the child reaches school, MPH should be absorbed and peak levels attained within 2-3 hours. The school should be encouraged to place the child in academic subjects during these morning hours so that the effects of the drug on attentional processes will be maximal when the child needs the most help. Thus, by lunchtime, and in afternoon classes (ideally, nonacademic subjects), the medication effect will be waning, but the need for the drug is not as great. Clinical response is monitored by obtaining weekly feedback from the parents and, most importantly, from the school. This may be accomplished most efficiently via weekly rating scales (for example, Conners, 1972; or Yale MIT, Shaywitz, 1986) filled out by the child's primary academic teacher(s). If the child is not responding satisfactorily after 2 weeks of treatment, MPH dosage should be increased to 0.6-0.8 mg/kg. If there is no response after 2 weeks at this dose, the physician should consider switching to another medication and possibly reassessing the patient.

At least one study documents what many clinicians know only too well: poor compliance in taking stimulant medications may be a significant problem in children with ADD. Kaufman et al. (1981) studied medication compliance over an 18 week period in 12 school-age boys with ADD assigned to methylphenidate, amphetamine, or placebo. The percent of children compliant for a given week ranged between 25 percent and 83 percent. Furthermore, they found 5 of 12 children taking methylphenidate when they were supposed to be taking placebo. Poor compliance in taking medications may explain some of the variability and conflicting results of various studies of the effects of stimulants.

On many occasions the child will do well in the morning at the 0.3 mg/kg dose, but the effects appear to wear off by early afternoon. In this situation, it is reasonable to add another 0.3 mg/kg dose in the morning (for a total morning dose of 0.6 mg/kg). If afternoon function is still problematic, a second 0.3 mg/kg dose may be given 3 hours later. Experience has shown that "piggy-backing" a second dose in this manner before the initial dose has worn off eliminates the problems seen with decreasing availability of the medication. Another option would be to employ a stimulant with a longer duration of action, such as amphetamine or pemoline. Although d-amphetamine has an apparent biological half-life of 6.6 hours for tablets and 8.4 hours for sustained release, the behavioral effects last no longer than 4 hours with either preparation (Brown et al., 1979).

Still another possibility is to consider the use of what is advertised as the "sustained-release" preparation of MPH, SR-20. An early study claiming that SR-20 was equivalent to regular MPH failed to incorporate such standard methodology as placebo controls, diagnostic criteria of the cohort, and equivalent mg/kg dosages (Whitehouse et al., 1980). Most recently Pelham et al. (in press) compared the behavioral effects of SR-20 to 10 mg MPH administered at breakfast and 4 hours later. The standard preparation was found to be more effective than SR-20 in 7 of 10 children who responded to MPH. Such findings suggest that at the present time, standard MPH is the preparation of choice, and we would not recommend the use of the SR-20 form of MPH in the treatment of ADD.

Pemoline will also provide a longer duration of action. Though not as widely used as methylphenidate and amphetamine, the improvement rate in ADD following pemoline is similar to that observed with the other stimulants. Furthermore, its action may be continued even after treatment is stopped (Conners and Taylor, 1980). It is supplied in capsules of 18.75, 37.5, and 75 mg. Dosage varies between 0.5-3.0 mg/kg (Zametkin et al., 1986), with a starting dose of 18.75 mg/day and a dosage range between 37.5 and 112.5 mg/day.

Another important issue that must be considered is whether medication should be administered daily or just on school days, with drug holidays when the child is away from school. Administration solely during school offers the advantage of limiting potential toxicity while maximizing the effect of MPH when it is most needed, which is during the school day. Our routine is to prescribe MPH each school day but omit the drug on weekends, school holidays, during the summer, and for the first 4 to 6 weeks of the new school year. Discontinuing MPH at the end of one school year enables us to evaluate how the child will do off medications and offers a regular opportunity to discontinue medications permanently. Thus, if it appears that he is doing well without medication during the initial portion of the new school year, we do not resume pharmacotherapy. However, careful followup is critical since as the school year continues and academic pressures increase, initial sanguine assumptions about the lack of a need for medication may prove to be overly optimistic.

Clearly, such a procedure may need to be modified in particular situations. On occasions, when a particular child's impulsivity and activity are preventing optimum peer and family interaction, we have continued MPH on weekends. Furthermore, if the physician believes that the child's response to medication has been so dramatic and that starting a new school year without medication would be detrimental to the best interests of the child, he may decide that medication should be initiated as soon as school begins.

Physicians have come to rely on blood levels of a number of pharmacological agents (e.g., anticonvulsants), and the development of an assay for MPH suggested initially that blood levels of MPH might be helpful in the management of ADD. Although we (Sebrechts et al., 1986) and others (Winsberg et al., 1982) have found a significant positive correlation between blood levels and response on tests of attention, blood levels are so well correlated with oral dosage that there does not appear to be any real advantage of plasma levels over simply adjusting dose. Thus, except in unusual circumstances, we do not find MPH blood levels of practical utility in the pharmacotherapy of ADD.

SIDE EFFECTS

Insomnia or sleep disturbances and decreased appetite represent the most frequently observed side effects of stimulants, with weight loss, irritability, and abdominal pains almost as common. These and a host of other less frequent side effects (such as headaches, nausea, dizziness, dry mouth, and constipation) usually disappear as the child becomes tolerant to the medication, or they resolve if the dosage is reduced (Golinko, 1984). Although significant cardiac arrhythmias have been reported in young adults following intravenous methylphenidate (Lucas et al., 1986), cardiovascular function in ADD children receiving oral stimulants is reassuringly normal (Brown et al., 1984). Whether stimulants affect growth remains an important question. Mattes and Gittelman (1983) noted a signficant decrease in height percentile after 2, 3, and 4 years of MPH therapy. Furthermore, they emphasized that the reduction in height was related to the total yearly dose of MPH. This latter study supports conclusions reached by a Food and Drug Administration subcommittee, and suggests that the effects of MPH appear to be dose-related, with higher doses administered for prolonged duration producing the greatest decrement in height. This problem may be minimized if the drug is discontinued for a time to allow catchup growth to occur. In practice, this suggests that if the medication could be omitted for long periods (e.g., summer vacations, holidays, weekends), the total yearly dose would be reduced, and presumably the detrimental effects on stature lessened. Similar effects on growth have been reported with pemoline as well (Friedmann et al., 1981).

In contrast to these effects, which are either transient or are reversed by a reduction in drug dosage, the emergence of Gilles de la Tourette's syndrome (TS) is of more concern, and instances of TS appearing in association with the administration of MPH have been reported (Lowe et al., 1982). Since MPH acts via central catecholaminergic mechanisms and TS may result from stimulation of supersensitive dopaminergic or noradrenergic neurons, it is reasonable to believe that the onset of the tics after MPH was more than simply coincidental. Good evidence suggests that TS occurs more frequently in the offspring of parents with TS and in the siblings of affected individuals. Thus, in those children with ADD whose parents or siblings have a history of tics, caution must be used in the administration of stimulants (Cohen et al., 1984). Tics have also been reported as a consequence of combinations of stimulants plus other neuroleptics (amphetamine + haloperidol; methylphenidate, imipramine, thioridazine) in two children with ADD (Gualtieri and Patterson, 1986). In light of the well-established relationship between TS and obsessive-compulsive disorders, a recent report (Koizumi, 1985) of the emergence of obsessive-compulsive symptoms in three children—two following d-amphetamine and one following methylphenidate—adds further support for a possible relationship between ADD and TS.

TRICYCLIC ANTIDEPRESSANTS

Tricyclic antidepressants act to inhibit reuptake of catecholamines, primarily norepinephrine, thus increasing concentration of transmitters at the synaptic cleft. These actions are similar to those described for the stimulants. Although an earlier report had suggested that such agents might be useful in ADD (Rapoport et al., 1974), more recent investigations now provide good support for such a notion. Thus, in an open trial of desimpramine, a good response in both behavioral and attentional components was observed by the fourth week of therapy (Gastfriend et al., 1984). Further support for tricyclics in ADD is provided by a double-blind comparison of methylphenidate with two tricyclics, clomipramine and desipramine (Garfinkel et al., 1983). While methylphenidate was superior to both tricyclics in improving teacher ratings of ADD children, MPH was not as effective as the other agents in relieving depression and helping self-esteem. Most recently, Donnelly et al. (in press), utilizing a non-crossover, double-blind procedure, noted a marked improvement in classroom behavior and hyperactivity to desipramine, evident as early as day 3 and sustained for the full 2 weeks of the trial. Plasma concentrations of desmethylimipramine did not correlate either with clinical changes or with the reduction in urinary MHPG reported. Imipramine has been reported helpful in patients with both ADD and Tourette's syndrome, with 50mg/day resulting in improvement in the symptoms of ADD without any negative effect on Tourette's syndrome (Dillon et al., 1985).

The effective dose of desipramine in these studies ranged between 0.5-3.0 mg/kg with a maximum dose of 5 mg/kg. It is given in an initial dose of 25 mg with weekly increments to a total dose of 25 mg four times a day. Side effects include elevations in pulse and diastolic blood pressure (Donnelly et al., in press). Others have noted that although intraventricular conduction defects of the right bundle branch type are common (24 percent), no clinically significant cardiovascular effects are observed with desipramine. However, clinically significant cardiovascular effects are generally not found (Biederman et al., 1985).

OTHER MEDICATIONS

Clonidine, an agent that acts as both an alpha adrenergic agonist at low concentrations and antagonist at higher concentrations, appears to ameliorate some of the symptoms of ADD (Hunt et al., 1985). It has been employed primarily in children with both ADD and Tourette's syndrome because of the concern (see above) that stimulants and tricyclics may increase the risk of exacerbating the Tourette's symptoms. The drug is begun at a dose of 0.05 mg/day and increased every other day until a dose of 4 to 5 mg/kg/day (0.05 mg four times a day) is achieved. Full improvement may take as long as 8 weeks.

Monoamine oxidase inhibitors act to inhibit the class of enzymes termed monoamine oxidases, which are important in the degradation of serotonin, dopamine, and norepinephrine. Clinical effects of these agents appear related to MAO inhibition rather than to the chronic changes in receptor function known to occur with long-term administration. Thus, like the stimulants, the clinical effects of these agents appear related to their effects on central monoaminergic systems.

At least two types of MAO are known: MAO A, acting primarily on serotonin and norepinephrine, and MAO B, acting primarily on phenylethylamine and dopamine. Present evidence suggests that clorgyline (a selective inhibitor of MAO A) and tranylcypromine (an inhibitor of both MAO A and MAO B) result in pronounced effects on sustained attention as measured in the laboratory and by classroom behavior. The effects are comparable to those observed with amphetamine (Zametkin et al., 1985). However, early reports indicate that deprenyl, a selective inhibitor of MAO B, does not appear to ameliorate the symptoms of ADD. Both medications were given at a dosage of 5 mg twice a day.

Piracetam, an agent chemically related to the neurotransmitter gamma-amino butyric acid (GABA), represents the only agent other than the stimulants that have been studied in dyslexia. Although initial reports were optimistic (Dimond and Brouwers, 1976; Wilsher and Milewski, 1983; Rudel and Helfgott; 1984), more recent studies (Chase et al., 1984; Wilsher et al., 1985) suggest that, at best, piracetam improves certain components of the reading process only marginally, and for the most part, has no consistent effect. Thus, at the present time, piracetam does not appear to be indicated in the overall management of dyslexia, and there seems to be no evidence to support its use in ADD.

As noted earlier (see "Etiology"), considerable evidence suggests a role for brain monoamines in the genesis of ADD. It is reasonable to suggest that administration of precursors of these compounds may have some effect in children with ADD. Nemzer et al. (1986) compared adminstration of tyrosine (the precursor of catecholamines) and of tryptophan (the precursor of indoleamines) with placebo and amphetamine in children with ADD. Teacher ratings on the Conners teacher rating scale markedly improved after amphetamine, but no differences were evident between placebo and either of the precursor amino acids. Parent ratings indicated that both tryptophan and amphetamine improved scores on the hyperkinetic factor of the Conners short-form parent questionnaire. The precursor aminoacid levodopa, administered as Sinemet, may also improve behavior in children with ADD (Langer et al., 1982).

Other medications tried in ADD include bupropion and alprazolam (Ferguson and Simeon, 1984), ACTH 4-9 (Butter et al., 1984), and vasopressin (Eisenberg et al., 1984). In general, their actions have been at best only weakly effective.

Whether the methylxanthine caffeine should be considered as an effective stimulant in ADD remains controversial. Initial studies (Schnackenberg, 1973; Reichard and Elder, 1977) suggested that caffeine is effective, but later studies (Arnold et al., 1978; Conners, 1979; Firestone et al., 1978; Gross, 1975) found no significant effect of caffeine over placebo. Most recently, Schechter and Timmons (1985) noted that high doses (600 mg/day) of caffeine were as effective as d-amphetamine in improving performance on a continuous performance test and parent ratings on the Conners APQ. This finding is somewhat at variance with that of Garfinkel et al. (1981), indicating that low doses of caffeine were as effective as methylphenidate.

NONTRADITIONAL, CONTROVERSIAL, AND IDIOSYNCRATIC THERAPIES

DEFINITION

This category encompasses a wide range of therapies, which Golden (1984) defined operationally as sharing the following characteristics:

- Their theoretical justification is not consistent with modern scientific knowledge.
- The effectiveness of therapy is claimed for a broad range of problems that are usually not rigorously defined.
- The possibility of adverse effects are minimized since the treatment usually relies on the use of "natural" substances (vitamins, special diets), exercises, or simple manipulations of the body.
- Their initial presentation is often in media other than in peer-reviewed scientific journals.
- Controlled studies that do not support the therapy are discounted as being improperly performed or biased because of the unwillingness of the medical and scientific establishment to accept "novel" ideas.
- Support for the therapy is provided by the emergence of lay organizations that proselytize new members and attempt to develop special-interest legislation and regulations.

Golden notes that investigations suggest that the orientation of groups advocating such therapies may reflect as much a social movement as a medically oriented one (Vissing and Petersen, 1981). Characteristics include testimonials, antiprofessionalism, and an often expressed view that there is a conspiracy between the government and the medical establishment to withhold the therapy.

We have chosen to categorize such therapies as (a) dietary and (b) what Silver (1986) terms neurophysiologic retraining.

DIETARY TREATMENTS

FOOD-ADDITIVE-FREE DIET (FEINGOLD DIET)

The belief that food colorings and other food additives influence the behavior of children with ADD had its origins more than a decade ago with the anecdotal reports by Feingold in his book entitled *Why Your Child Is Hyperactive* (Feingold, 1975). In her recent review of the

13 studies to date addressing the Feingold diet, Wender (1986) concludes that there is "little, if any, effect of food colorings and other additives on the behavior of hyperactive children." She recognizes, however, that belief in the "efficacy of dietary treatment is widespread and firmly held," in part because of the power of food as a conditioned stimulus (Zametkin et al., 1985). Others have come to similar conclusions (Kavale and Forness, 1983; Mattes, 1983).

SUGAR AND ADD

Many clinicians and investigators believe that sugar has replaced food additives as the major dietary concern of both parents and teachers of children with ADD. An editorial in the influential *American Psychologist* refers to sugar as "the most ubiquitous toxin" (Buchanan, 1984), and a recent survey indicates that 45 percent of practicing pediatricians and family practioners periodically recommend low-sugar diets when treating children with ADD (Bennett and Sherman, 1983). In general, the scientific approach to the evaluation of such claims incorporates double-blind, placebo-controlled "challenge" studies involving administration of the substance in question, in this case sucrose. In a study of 21 boys (both normal and behaviorally disordered) who had an alleged history of adverse response to sugar, Behar et al. (1984) noted a slight but significant decrease in motor activity. Similarly, Wolraich et al. (1985) found only 1 of 37 dependent variables affected by the sugar challenge, and on this, the children performed better on the sugar day.

Two studies have noted significant negative effects of sugar. Conners et al. (1984) found a significant increase in total motor activity after a challenge with either sucrose or fructose in 12 children who were inpatients on a children's psychiatric ward, but in a larger replication, he noted that sucrose reduced fine motor activity and that fructose reduced gross motor activity. Goldman et al. (1984), examining normal preschool children, found that sugar challenge resulted in more errors on a continuous performance test.

Most recently, Milich and Pelham (1986) investigated the effects of sugar challenge on 16 boys with ADD. No significant effects were observed on measures of classroom behavior, academic productivity and accuracy, noncompliance with adult requests, and peer interactions. Thus, at the present time, we would agree with Milich et al. (1986) that "the empirical evidence to date has not established any consistent adverse behavioral effects of sugar."

OTHER DIETARY TREATMENTS

Both Golden (1984) and Silver (1986) review the use of massive doses of vitamins to treat behavioral disorders, a therapy termed megavitamin therapy. Suggestions by Cott (1971, 1985) that megavitamin therapy is helpful in learning disabled children have never been confirmed. In fact, a recent double-blind, placebo-controlled study by Haslem et al. (1984) convincingly demonstrated that megavitamins were ineffective in the management of ADD. Furthermore, their findings of elevations in serum transaminase in 42 percent of subjects receiving megavitamins suggested that such treatment may result in potential hepatotoxicity.

What Egger et al. (1985) term "oligoantigenic treatment" was reported to normalize behavior in 21 of 76 hyperactive children. Diagnosis was made by the first author based on his clinical observations and a score of   14 on the Conners scale, though it is not specified who scored this instrument (parent?, teacher?, physician?). Some 48 different foods were implicated, and clearly, "counselling and advice concerning management of the child's behavior" (Egger et al., 1985, p. 545) were part of the management plan. Thus, it is reasonable to suggest that factors other than dietary modifications were responsible for the improvements noted by Egger et al.

NEUROPHYSIOLOGIC RETRAINING

Patterning, a regimen proposed by Doman and Delacato (1968), is critically reviewed by Silver (1986). Controlled studies by Sparrow and Zigler (1978) provide ample evidence for the conclusion of the American Academy of Pediatrics (1982) "that the patterning treatment offers no special merit, that the claims of its advocates are unproven, and that the demands on families are so great that in some cases there may be harm in its use."

Though aimed primarily at learning disability, the vestibular dysfunction hypothesis popularized by Levinson (1980; 1984) advocates antimotion sickness medication for the treatment of dyslexia. Most recently, Polatajko (1985) compared vestibular function in learning disabled and normal children. His findings demonstrate no significant differences either in the intensity of vestibular responsivity or the incidence of vestibular dysfunction between groups. Thus, we would agree with Silver's summary (1986) that "at this time there is no evidence supportive of the vestibular theories nor of the proposed treatment approaches."

ADVERSE EFFECTS

Such therapies are clearly quite appealing, not only to parents but to professionals as well, and although not helpful, at least they are seemingly innocuous. Even brief reflection, however, provides good evidence of real harm from such approaches. Perhaps the greatest harm results from the parents' investing inordinate energy in nonproductive treatments, leaving little time and energy for well-documented effective management methods. Thus, the parent whose energies are bound up in an idiosyncratic management regimen may not have the energy to ensure that the child's classroom is optimal and that the teacher is providing the most effective school environment. It may be that parents omit pharmacotherapies that have proven effective, even, as noted by Golden (1984), to the point of omitting anticonvulsants in a child who has a seizure disorder.

Given the poor self-image characterizing many children with ADD, and recognizing that food is a very important component of the child's interaction with society, there is a real danger that some of the dietary therapies may serve to further isolate the child from his peers and others in his environment.

The effects of dietary therapy are obvious, not only on the child who is the particular target of the therapy but also on other children and adults in the family constellation. The preparation and implementation of a special diet for one child in the family often means that the other children not only must eat the same meals but also that they are denied the time and attention necessary for their well-being. Thus, the time and energy necessary for the preparation of special diets might be more productively spent on other family activities. Still another negative effect is the expense involved in many of these unproven treatment modalities. Special diets are indeed expensive, and they may create an additional reason for the parents and siblings to be angry at the child with ADD.

Evaluation of the safety of such idiosyncratic therapies must also take into consideration the possibility that, though seemingly innocuous now, they may be shown later to have significant and permanent side effects. As noted by Golden (1984), the use of oxygen to treat respiratory problems in premature infants was initially believed to be not only effective but also to have no side effects. We all know now that oxygen therapy may result in retrolental fibroplasia and blindness, but who would have predicted that the use of such a "natural" substance could produce such severe side effects? One has only to reflect on the history of such treatments as lobotomy or the use of diethylstilbestrol (DES) (see Valenstein, 1986) to recognize how difficult it is to accurately predict the long-term safety of any therapy.

SUMMARY

We have reviewed above two major classes of therapies employed in ADD. Educational management represents an important priority and often forms the cornerstone of all other therapies, nonpharmacologic or pharmacologic. Cognitive-behavioral therapies represent the most widely employed alternative to pharmacotherapy. Although the effects of CBT alone are disappointing, recent studies suggest that such therapies may provide a useful adjunct to pharmacotherapy and may be helpful when children are tapered off medication. Psychotherapy or a combination of psychotherapy and medication (termed multimodality therapy) may also be useful.

Pharmacotherapy for ADD originated 50 years ago, and at this time, the ameliorative effects of medications in ADD are well established. Despite concerns in the early 1970's that medication, primarily stimulants, were being prescribed too frequently, recent data and the experience of most clinicians indicate that this is not the case. The general scepticism of experienced clinicians, coupled with a climate where parents are reluctant to medicate children, serves to limit their use except where indicated. While the effects of stimulants on attention and activity seem well established, effects on cognition, conduct, and social behavior are more controversial. Within recent years, a great deal has been learned about the pharmacokinetics of stimulants in children with ADD, providing a rational basis for administration. It is also clear that side effects are minimal, the most serious being the possibility of the emergence of tics. While stimulants are clearly the most effective agents, tricyclic antidepressants and monoamine oxidase inhibitors may also be effective.

Nontraditional, controversial, and idiosyncratic therapies continue to be used in ADD, both by professionals and laymen alike. To date, there is no indication that such approaches as a food-additive-free diet, elimination of sugar, megavitamin therapy, patterning, or treatment of alleged vestibular dysfunction have any benefit above their placebo effects. Though appealing for their simplicity, their adverse effects are not often recognized. Thus, they may divert parents' energies from more effective management strategies, are often expensive, and may have long-term side effects not apparent now.

PROGNOSIS

From both a theoretical and practical perspective, investigations of the outcome of ADD are critical in our understanding of the entity. Thus, as noted earlier, predictive measures represent important components in the validation of ADD (predictive validity). Furthermore, an appreciation of its natural history is obviously a necessary prerequisite in the evaluation of the long-term effects (both benefits and possible side effects) of any treatment modalities. Throughout the 1960's and early part of the 1970's, clinical lore, influenced considerably by Laufer and Denhoff's (1957) belief that the symptoms of hyperactivity "wane spontaneously and disappear," considered ADD to be limited to childhood. Within the last decade, a number of investigations, employing both retrospective and prospective methodologies, have begun to provide a better picture of the natural history and long-term response to therapy in adolescents and young adults diagnosed as ADD at school age. Others who have reviewed this subject (Weiss, 1985; Weiss et al., 1985) have recognized that it is most easily discussed in relation to adolescent and adult outcome, with retrospective studies noted first, then the methodologically more sophisticated prospective investigations. We follow this practice as well.

OUTCOME IN ADOLESCENTS

In one of the first studies of outcome, Mendelson et al. (1971) retrospectively evaluated teenagers (mean age 13 years) diagnosed as hyperactive 2 to 5 years earlier. Although hyperactivity tended to abate, the majority still exhibited symptoms of distractibility and restlessness, along with school learning difficulties, low self-esteem, and problems with peer relations. Antisocial characteristics were seen in from 25 percent to 50 percent as well. Such characteristics were noted as well by Blouin et al. (1978) in another retrospective study. These investigators also reported an increase in alcohol use by adolescents diagnosed as ADD in childhood. This problem is discussed in more detail below. Feldman et al. (1979), reporting on a followup of Denhoff's patients, noted a high incidence of learning difficulties but considerably less antisocial problems than reported in the studies just discussed.

Prospective investigations are clearly superior in design to the vagaries of retrospective studies, and to date, several investigative groups have examined the long-term outcome of children diagnosed as ADD in childhood. The longest and certainly the most detailed studies are those of Gabrielle Weiss and her associates at the Montreal Children's Hospital (summarized in the introduction and discussion in Weiss et al., 1985). In a series of investigations, they report on the followup of a cohort of children diagnosed between 1962 and 1965 as hyperactive. This HA group, primarily representing a relatively untreated cohort, was then compared with a control group of age- and sex-matched controls recruited slightly later (1968), and in other studies with a group of children with hyperactivity recruited 5 years later and treated for at least 3 years with methylphenidate. The 5-year followup of this group, placing the cohort in their early teens (14 years), indicated that these children continued to exhibit impulsivity, distractibility, poor school performance, poor self-esteem, and antisocial behaviors (Cohen et al., 1972; Hoy et al., 1978; Minde et al., 1971, 1972; Weiss et al., 1971). Reporting on a group of teenagers of a similar age (14 years old), Dykman and Ackerman (1980) also noted a high percentage with antisocial problems in the group originally seen at school age with both learning disabilities and ADD.

Such findings are also observed in followup studies performed in the later teenage years. In the 10-year followup of the Montreal cohort (mean age 19 years), it was found that although hyperactives had completed less education, those who were working were judged by their employers to be no different from controls. While one-half were judged to be functioning well, a minority exhibited significant symptoms of antisocial personality disorder (Hechtman et al., 1980, 1984a,b; Weiss et al., 1978; 1979). Satterfield et al. (1982), reporting on followup of hyperactivity in a cohort from Los Angeles evaluated in the later teenage years (mean 17 years), noted a much higher percentage of antisocial activities compared to the Montreal studies. Weiss (1985) suggests that this difference might reflect the lesser liklihood of Montreal teenagers to carry handguns. It is likely that other influences also play a role, since even in a primarily rural U.S. population, a high prevalence of antisocial problems has been noted (Howell et al., 1985). As noted by Loney et al. (1981) and discussed by her more recently (Loney, 1986), much of this confusion in the prevalence of antisocial problems may reflect the initial agglomeration of ADD with conduct disorders. This issue was previously discussed (see "Definition and Syndrome Validation").

OUTCOME IN ADULTS

In general, both retrospective and prospective studies of hyperactives followed into adult life indicate a continuation of the pattern described in studies in adolescents. Thus, in a retrospective study comparing hyperactive men with their brothers (mean age 30 years), Borland and Heckman (1976) noted many of the probands exhibited symptoms of nervousness and restlessness, and although they were all steadily employed and self-supporting, they had entered the work force at a lower level, and their socioeconomic status was significantly less than that of their brothers. In an early retrospective study of young adults (mean age 24 years) considered hyperactive as children, Menkes et al. (1967) noted significant sequelae including major psychoses and mental retardation. This report has been criticized, however, for its lack of a control group, and its inclusion of retarded and prepsychotic children and chaotic families (Weiss et al., 1985). Reporting a prospective study of 101 boys with hyperactivity, Gittelman et al. (1985) noted that symptoms of ADD with hyperactivity were still present in one-third of the probands, compared to only 3 percent of normal controls. Furthermore, the boys with ADD also exhibited conduct disorders and substance abuse disorders, though the substance abuse seemed to follow the conduct disorder. Substance abuse was not observed in the Montreal population (Hechtman et al., 1984). Most recently Weiss et al. (1985) have reported their 15-year followup (mean age 25 years). As young adults, HA's continue to exhibit educational and work difficulities (though their employers rate them no different from controls) and evidence of impulsive lifestyles (increased moves, more job changes, more debt). While they clearly do not exhibit severe psychiatric disturbances, a significant percentage (23 percent) have evidence of antisocial personality.

EFFECTS OF THERAPY

To date, only the Montreal group has evaluated the long-term outcome after therapy. Hechtman et al. (1984) compared outcome in young adults (mean age 22 years) derived from three groups of children: (a) hyperactives who received stimulants for at least 3 years;

(b) hyperactives who had not received any sustained stimulant therapy; (c) controls matched to the long-term treated hyperactives. A confounding problem was that the stimulant-treated hyperactives and their controls were recruited 5 years after the untreated hyperactives entered the study. Major differences were observed between hyperactives (both groups) and controls (discussed in previous section). Treated hyperactives compared to untreated hyperactives had fewer car accidents, viewed their childhood more positively, in elementary school had less stealing, exhibited better social skills, better self-esteem, fewer problems with aggression, and less need for psychiatric treatment as adults. Hechtman et al. summarize their results: "Stimulant treatment in childhood seems to have no significant negative effects but may in fact result in less social ostracism with subsequent better feelings toward themselves and others."

SUMMARY

In general, these studies indicate what Weiss et al. (1985) refer to as "a fairly good" outcome. Thus, despite school difficulties evident in their early teenage years, by the time they are adults, most subjects with ADD were not only working and self-supporting, but their employers did not differentiate them from the non-ADD population. Drug abuse and alcoholism did not appear to be a problem, nor did serious psychiatric disturbance.

Mild to severe residual problems associated with ADD were present in the remaining one-half of subjects. These ranged from poor self-esteem, impulsive behavior, and lower socioeconomic status, to antisocial problems that may be severe. The frequency of antisocial difficulties may relate to the inclusion of large numbers of aggressive, conduct disordered children in the original cohorts. Clearly, better discrimination of ADD from CD is needed if we are to better prognosticate the degree of antisocial difficulties associated with ADD. Long-term (3 years or longer) treatment with stimulants may improve self-esteem and prevent early social ostracism.

Perhaps the most important facet of these outcome studies is their general agreement, which, as much as anything else, provides strong evidence of the validity of ADD as a syndrome. Thus, it is clear that at an early age (6-12), a group of children can be identified who when followed for up to 15 years can be shown to evidence a particular constellation of behaviors. Furthermore, therapy focused on specific symptoms believed to represent core characteristics of the syndrome can influence the outcome.

SUMMARY AND IMPLICATIONS

We introduced this review by indicating that our primary goal was to provide a critical examination of selected issues in the rapidly proliferating scientific literature on ADD. We believe that enough information is now available to generate a consensus about the most critical issues in the field, and to offer suggestions on how best to approach them. Considered as critical issues and needs in ADD, they are most reasonably classified as follows.

- Definition and syndrome validation. Definition occupies the central place in any formulation of ADD, and indeed, influences and pervades every other aspect of our notions of the disorder. This fact is immediately evident from the preceding review of epidemiology, etiology, management, and prognosis. We have focused a great deal of attention on issues best considered as involving classification, including definition and syndrome validation. Such issues form the core of current thinking and represent concepts that affect every facet of research related to ADD. We emphasized how subjective determinations made at every step of the research process often produce conflicting and inconsistent results, which may profoundly influence the results of the classification enterprise. Until a generally accepted, valid, and reliable classification for ADD is in place, such conflicts and inconsistencies are inevitable.

We believe that such evidence mandates that investigations of the classification and definition of ADD are among the most critical needs, if not a prerequisite for any other studies of children with ADD. Both the theoretical approaches to classification and the more operational concerns (assessment measures) for their implementation are currently available. As we have noted, subject selection and the need to be inclusive rather than exclusive in the classification enterprise require that such a study be multidisciplinary, incorporating the views and expertise of a number of professionals including educators, behavioral pediatricians, psychologists, child psychiatrists, and child neurologists.

- Homogeneous subgroups. The need for the delineation of homogeneous subgroups is critical, too, in the research process. In a sense, this can also be considered as an issue in definition. Recognizing the needs of the clinician for a diagnosis that would not be too restrictive and the needs of the investigator for more homogeneous subgroups in ADD, we proposed the term ADD-plus (ADD-P) for those children with ADD who have, in addition, one or more of the associated conditions (conduct disorder, affective disorder, or mental retardation) while we reserve the term ADD for those children who satisfy diagnostic criteria for ADD but who do not have any other complicating feature.
- Reliable and valid assessment measures. This requirement is the operationalization of the definitional issue, and was discussed in detail within that context. While it is clear that newer measures will be needed and are, in fact, being employed, older measures should not be abandoned. The acceptance of so

radical an approach would tend to cut the results of present investigations off from an entire body of literature, studies that have proven valuable in our better comprehension of ADD. We recommend that despite their shortcomings, it is critical to continue to employ some of these older measures in addition to newer, more methodologically sound instruments. If the present generation of investigators arbitrarily decides to ignore these older methods, the relationship between current investigations and previous studies may be difficult, if not impossible, to determine.

- External validation, including other biologic approaches must be incorporated into any classification paradigm. Advances in technology have provided noninvasive techniques that permit examination of neuroanatomical, neurochemical, and neurophysiological measures. Such techniques as magnetic resonance imaging and positron emission tomography offer the possibility not only of imaging the brain in better detail than ever before but also of providing information about regional brain metabolism and blood flow. Furthermore, neurochemical measures, particularly those involving brain catecholaminergic mechanisms, offer for the first time an opportunity to examine central catecholaminergic systems in children with ADD. Clearly, the success of such a strategy depends on the better delineation of clinically homogeneous subgroups as described above.

- Learning disabilities and ADD not only represent the two most common and serious disorders of childhood; they also often occur in the same child. Previous studies examining the relationship of LD and ADD were seriously limited by the inadequacy of the definition and assessment measures employed. Methods are now available to more precisely and operationally define each. What is critically needed is a broad-based investigation, utilizing operational criteria that will permit a more precise delineation of each of these groups. This is a prerequisite for understanding the influence and interaction of one on the other. Such studies may lead to a better appreciation of the mechanisms of each of these disorders, which, in turn, may lead to the development of more rational approaches to intervention.

- Reputable professionals must begin to recognize the adverse effects of nontraditional, controversial, idiosyncratic approaches to therapy. Rather than just considering these as ineffective but harmless techniques, professionals should appreciate their potential for significant adverse effects, both immediate and long-term.

In summary, what is needed are large scale studies of representative samples of both normal and clinic populations in which the clinic populations reflect the full range of severity and associated features characteristic of ADD. By necessity, such studies require a multi-disciplinary approach, involving the full range of disciplines that are called upon to evaluate and manage the child with ADD. Assessment measures are now available to select homogeneous subgroups of children according to operational definitions of ADDH and ADDnoH children, with and without complicating features of, for example, conduct disorder and learning disabilities. Identification of relatively homogeneous subgroups of children selected in this manner would represent a first step in a classification process for ADD. The validity of such a nosology could then be further examined through internal and external validity studies. An important component of such studies would be a longitudinal strategy in which the sample, the symptomatology, and the outcome measures are clearly defined from the onset. Incorporation of these methodologies would, we believe, represent the most efficient and productive approach to the elucidation of the mechanisms and to the optimal management of ADD.

BIBLIOGRAPHY

Abikoff, H., Gittelman, R. (1985). Hyperactive children treated with stimulants. Is cognitive training a useful adjunct? *Archives of General Psychiatry,* 42:953-961.

Abikoff, H., Gittelman-Klein, R., Klein, D. F. (1977). Validation of a classroom observation code for hyperactive children. *Journal of Consulting and Clinical Psychology,* 45:772-783.

Achenbach, T., Edelbrock, C. (1979). The child behavior profile: II. Boys aged 12-16 and girls aged 6-11 and 12-16. *Journal of Consulting and Clinical Psychology,* 47:223-233.

Achenbach, T. A., Conners, C. K., Quay, H. (1985). The ACQ Behavior Rating Scale. University of Vermont.

Achenbach, T. M. (1978). The child behavior profile: I. Boys aged 6-11. *Journal of Consulting and Clinical Psychology,* 46:478-488,

Achenbach, T. M., Edelbrock, C. S. (1983). *Manual for the child behavior checklist and revised child behavior profile.* Burlington, VT; T. M. Achenbach.

Achenbach, T. M., Edelbrock, C. S. (1984). Psychopathology of childhood. *Annual Review of Psychology,* 35:227-256.

Ackerman, P. T., Dykman, R. A., Holcomb, P. J., McCray, D. S. (1982). Methylphenidate effects on cognitive style and reaction time in four groups of children. *Psychology Research,* 7:199-213.

Ackerman, P. T., Dykman, R. A., Peters, J. E. (1977). Teenage status of hyperactive and nonhyperactive learning disabled boys. *American Journal of Orthopsychiatry,* 45:577-596.

Alberts-Corush, J., Firestone, P., Goodman, P. T. (1986). Attention and impulsivity characteristics of the biological and adoptive parents of hyperactive and normal control children. *American Journal of Orthopsychiatry,* 56:413-423.

Aman, M. G. (1978). Drugs, learning and the psychotherapies. In Werry, J. S. (Ed.), *Pediatric psychopharmacology: The use of behavior-modifying drugs in children* (pp. 79-108). New York: Brunner/Mazel.

American Psychiatric Association (1968). *Diagnostic and statistical manual of mental disorders* (Second edition) (DSM II). Washington, DC: APA.

American Psychiatric Association (1980). *Diagnostic and statistical manual of mental disorders* (Third edition) (DSM III). Washington, DC: APA.

Amery, B., Minichello, M. D., Brown, G. L. (1984). Aggression in hyperactive boys: Response to d-amphetamine. *Journal of the American Academy of Child Psychiatry,* 23:291-294.

Anderson, J. C., Williams, S., McGee, R., Silva, P. A.(1987). DSM-III disorders in pre-adolescent children. *Archives of General Psychiatry*, 44:69-76.

Anderson, W. W. (1963). The hyperkinetic child: A neurological appraisal. *Neurology*, 13:968-973.

Arnold, L. E., Christopher, J., Huestis, R., Smeltzer, D. (1978). Methylphenidate versus dextroamphetamine versus caffeine in minimal brain dysfunction. *Archives of General Psychiatry*, 35:463-475.

Aron, A. M., Freeman, J. M., Carter, S. (1965). The natural history of Sydenham's chorea. *American Journal of Medicine*, 38:83-95.

Asbury, A. (1981). Diagnostic considerations in Guillain-Barre syndrome. *Annals of Neurology*, 9 (supp):1-5.

Atkins, M. S., Pelham, W. E., Licht, M. H. (1985). A comparison of objective classroom measures and teacher ratings of attention deficit disorder. *Journal of Abnormal Child Psychology*, 13 (1):155-167.

August, G. J., Stewart, M. A. (1983). Familial subtypes of childhood hyperactivity. *Journal of Nervous and Mental Disease*, 171:362-368.

Ballinger, C. T., Varley, C. K., Nolen, P. A. (1984). Effects of methylphenidate on reading in children with attention deficit disorder. *American Journal of Psychiatry*, 141:1590-1593.

Barkley, R. A. (1977a). The effects of methylphenidate on various types of activity level and attention in hyperkinetic children. *Journal of Abnormal Child Psychology*, 5:350-369.

*Barkley, R. A. (1977b). A review of stimulant drug research with hyperactive children. *Journal of Child Psychology and Psychiatry*, 18:137-165.

Barkley, R. A. (1978). Recent developments in research on hyperactive children. *Journal of Pediatric Psychology*, 3:158-163.

Barkley, R. A. (1981). A specific guideline for defining hyperactivity in children. In Lahey, B., Kazdin, A. (Eds.), *Advances in child clinical psychology*. New York: Plenum.

Barkley, R. A. (1985). The social behavior of hyperactive children: Developmental changes, drug effects, and situational variation. In McMahon, R., Peters, R. (Eds.), *Childhood disorders* (pp. 218-243). New York: Brunner/Mazel.

Barkley, R. A. (1986). A review of child behavior rating scales and checklists for research in child psychopathology. In Rutter, M., Tuma, M., Lann, I. (Eds.), *Assessment and diagnosis in child and adolescent psychology*. New York: Guilford Press.

Barkley, R. A., Cunningham, C. E. (1979). The effects of methylphenidate on the mother-child interactions of hyperactive children. *Archives of General Psychiatry*, 36:201-208.

Barkley, R. A., Karlsson, J., Pollard, S. (1985). Effects of age on the mother-child interactions of ADD-H and normal boys. *Journal of Abnormal Child Psychology*, 13:631-637.

Barkley, R. A., Karlsson, J., Pollard, S., Murphy, J. V. (1985). Developmental changes in the mother-child interactions of hyperactive boys: Effects of two dose levels of Ritalin. *Journal of Child Psychology and Psychiatry*, 26:705-715.

Barkley, R. A., Karlsson, J., Strzelecki, E., Murphy, J. V. (1984). Effects of age and Ritalin dosage on the mother-child interactions of hyperactive children. *Journal of Consulting and Clinical Psychology*, 52:750-758.

Barkley, R. A., Ullman, D. G. (1975). A comparison of objective measures of activity and distractibility in hyperactive and nonhyperactive children. *Journal of Abnormal Child Psychology*, 3 (3):231-244.

Barling, J., Bullen, G. (1985). Dietary factors and hyperactivity: A failure to replicate. *Journal of Genetic Psychology*, 146:117-123.

Batshaw, M. L., Roan, Y., Jung, A. L., Rosenberg, L. A., Brusilow, S. W. (1980). Cerebral dysfunction in asymptomatic carriers of ornithine transcarbamylase. *New England Journal of Medicine*, 302:482-485.

Battle, E. S., Lacey, B. A. (1972). A context for hyperactivity in children over time. *Child Development*, 17:757-773.

Bax, U., MacKeith, R. C. (1963). "Minimal Brain Damage"—A concept dysfunction. In MacKeith, R. C., Bax, M. (Eds.), *Minimal cerebral dysfunction*. London: SIMP with Wm Heinemann.

Behar, D., Rapoport, J., Adams, A., Berg, C., Cornblath, M. (1984). Sugar challenge testing with children considered behaviorally "sugar reactive." *Journal of Nutrition and Behavior,* 1:277-288.

Bell, R. Q., Harper, L. V. (1977). *Child effects on adults.* Hillsdale, NJ; Erlbaum.

Bellak, L. (1979). *Psychiatric aspects of minimal brain dysfuntion in adults.* New York: Grune and Stratton.

Bellinger, D. C., Needleman, H. L. (1983). Lead and the relationship between maternal and child intelligence. *Journal of Pediatrics,* 102:523-527.

Bender, L. (1942). Post encephalitic behavior disorders in childhood. In Bender, L. (Ed.), *Encephalitis: A clinical study* (pp. 361-384). New York: Grune and Stratton.

Bennett, F. C., Sherman, R. (1983). Management of childhood "hyperactivity" by primary care physician. *Journal of Developmental and Behavioral Pediatrics,* 4:88-93.

Berk, R. A. (1984). *Screening and diagnosis of children with learning disabilities.* Springfield: Charles C. Thomas.

Bernar, J., Hanson, R. A., Kern, R., Phoenix, B., Shaw, K. N. F., Cederbaum, S. D. (1986). Arginase deficiency in a 12 year old boy with mild impairment of intellectual function. *Journal of Pediatrics,* 108:432-435.

Berry, C. A., Shaywitz, S. E., Shaywitz, B. A. (1985). Girls with attention deficit disorder: A silent minority? A report on behavioral and cognitive characteristics. *Pediatrics,* 76:801-809.

Berry, K., Cook, V. J. (1980). Personality and behavior. In Rie, H. E., Rie, E. D. (Eds.), *Handbook of minimal brain dysfunctions.* New York: Wiley.

Bettelheim, B. (1973). Bringing up children. *Ladies Home Journal,* 90:28.

Biederman, J., Gastfriend, D., Jellinek, M. S., Goldblatt, A. (1985). Clinical and laboratory observations: Cardiovascular effects of desipramine in children and adolescents with attention deficit disorder. *Journal of Pediatrics,* 106:1017-1020.

Blashfield, R. K., Draguns, J. G. (1976). Evaluative criteria for psychiatric classification. *Journal of Abnormal Psychology,* 85:140-150.

Blouin, A., Bornstein, R., Trites, R. (1978). Teenage alcohol use among hyperactive children: A 5 year follow-up study. *Journal of Pediatric Psychology,* 3:188-194.

Borland, B. L., Heckman, H. K. (1976). Hyperactive boys and their brothers: A 25-year follow-up study. *Archives of General Psychiatry,* 33:669-675.

Bosco, J. J., Robin, S. S. (1980). Hyperkinesis: Prevalence and treatment. In Whalen, C. K., Henker, B. (Eds.), *Hyperactive children: The social ecology of identification and treatment* (pp. 173-187). New York: Academic Press.

Bradley, C. (1937). The behavior of children receiving benzedrine. *American Journal of Psychiatry,* 94:577-585.

Broman, S., Brien, E., Shaughnessy, P. (1985). *Low achieving children: The first seven years.* Hillsdale, NJ: Lawrence Erlbaum Associates, Inc.

Brown, G. L., Ebert, M. H., Hunt, R. D., Rapoport, J. L. (1981). Urinary 3-methoxy-4-hydroxyphenylglycol and homovanillic acid response to d-amphetamine in hyperactive children. *Biological Psychiatry,* 16:779-787.

Brown, G. L., Hunt, R. D., Ebert, M. H., Bunney, W. E., Kopin, I. J. (1979). Plasma levels of d-amphetamine in hyperactive children. *Psychopharmacology,* 62:133-140.

Brown, G. L., Murphy, D. L., Langer, D. H., Ebert, M. H., Post, R. M., Bunney, W. E. Jr. (1984). Monoamine enzymes in hyperactivity: Response to d-amphetamine. Presented at American Academy of Child Psychiatry, Annual Meeting, Toronto, Canada.

Brown, R. T., Wynne, M. E., Medenis, R. (1985). Methylphenidate and cognitive therapy: A comparison of treatment approaches with hyperactive boys. *Journal of Abnormal Child Psychology,* 13:69-87.

Buchanan, S. (1984). The most ubiquitous toxin. *American Psychologist,* 39:1327-1328.

Buss, A. H., Plomin, R. A. (1975). *A temperament theory of personality development.* New York: Wiley.

Butter, H. J., Lapierre, Y., Firestone, P., Blank, A. (1984). Efficacy of ACTH 4-9 analog, methylphenidate and placebo an attention deficit disorder with hyperkinesis. *Progress in Neuropsychopharmacology and Biological Psychiatry,* 8:661-664.

Cairns, E., Cammock, T. (1978). Development of a more reliable version of the Matching Familiar Figures Test. *Developmental Psychology,* 14:555-560.

Camp, J. A., Bialer, I., Sverd, J., Winsberg, B. G. (1978). Clinical usefulness of the NIMH physical and neurological examination for soft signs. *American Journal of Psychiatry,* 135:362-364.

Campbell, E. S., Redfering, D. L. (1979). Relationship among environmental and demographic variables and teacher-rated hyperactivity. *Journal of Abnormal Child Psychology,* 7:77-81.

Campbell, S. B. (1975). Mother-child interaction: A comparison of hyperactive, learning disabled, and normal boys. *American Journal of Orthopsychiatry,* 45:51-57.

Campbell, S. B. (1979). Mother-infant interaction as a function of maternal ratings of temperament. *Child Psychiatry and Human Development,* 10:67-76.

Campbell, S. B., Breauz, A. M., Ewing, L. J., Szumowski, E. K. (1986). Correlates and predictors of hyperactivity and aggression: A longitudinal study of parent-referred problem preschoolers. *Journal of Abnormal Child Psychology,* 14:217-234.

Campbell, S. B., Endman, M. W., Bernfeld, G. (1977). A three-year follow-up of hyperactive preschooler into elementary school. *Journal of Child Psychology and Psychiatry,* 18:239-249.

Campbell, S. B., Paulauskas, S. (1979). Peer relations in hyperactive children. *Journal of Child Psychology and Psychiatry,* 20:233-246.

Campbell, S. B., Szumowski, E. K., Ewing, L. J., Gluck, D. S., Breaux, A. M. (1982). A multidimensional assessment of parent-identified behavior problem toddlers. *Journal of Abnormal Child Psychology,* 10(4):569-592.

Cantwell, D. P. (1975). Genetic studies of hyperactive children. In Fieve, R. R., Rosenthal, D., Brill, H. (Eds.), *Genetic research in psychiatry.* Baltimore: Johns Hopkins University Press.

Cantwell, D. P. (1972). Psychiatric illness in the families of hyperactive children. *Archives of General Psychiatry,* 27:414-417.

Cantwell, D. P. (1975a). The hyperactive child syndrome: Clinical aspects. In Cantwell, D. P. (Ed.), *The hyperactive child:* Part 1 (pp. 3-64). New York: Spectrum.

Cantwell, D. P. (1975b). Genetics of hyperactivity. *Journal of Child Psychology,* 16:261-264.

Cantwell, D. P. (1978a). Hyperactivity and antisocial behavior. *Journal of the American Academy of Child Psychiatry,* 17:252-262.

Cantwell, D. P. (1978b). CNS activating drugs in the treatment of the hyperactive child. In Bradu, J. P., Brodie, H. K. (Eds.), *Controversy in psychiatry.* Philadelphia: Saunders.

Cantwell, D. P. (1979). Use of stimulant medication with psychiatrically disordered adolescents. In Feinstein, S. C., Giovacchini, P. L. (Eds.), *Adolescent psychiatry: developmental and clinical studies:* Vol. 7 (pp. 375-388). New York: Basic Books.

Cantwell, D. P. (1980). The diagnostic process and diagnostic classification in child psychiatry—DSM-III. *Journal of the American Academy of Child Psychiatry,* 19:345-355.

Cantwell, D. P. (1983). Diagnostic validity of the hyperactive child (attention deficit disorder with hyperactivity) syndrome. *Psychiatric Developments,* 3:277-300.

Cantwell, D. P., Satterfield, J. H. (1978). The prevalence of academic underachievement in hyperactive children. *Journal of Pediatric Psychology,* 3:168-171.

Chadwick, O., Rutter, M., Brown, G., Shaffer, D., Traub, M. (1981). A prospective study of children with head injuries: II. Cognitive sequalae. *Psychological Medicine,* 11:49-61.

Chan, Y. M., Swanson, J. M., Soldin, S. S., Thiessen, J. J., MacLeod, S. M., Logan, W. (1983). Methylphenidate hydrochloride given with or before breakfast: II. Effects on plasma concentration of methylphenidate and ritalinic acid. *Pediatrics,* 72:56-59.

Charles, L., Schain, R. J., Zelniker, T. (1981). Optimal dosages of methylphenidate for improving the learning and behavior of hyperactive children. *Behavioral Pediatrics,* 2:78-81.

Chase, C. H., Schmitt, R. L., Russell, G., Tallal, P. (1984). A new chemotherapeutic investigation: Piracetam effects on dyslexia. *Annals of Dyslexia,* 34:29-48.

Chess, S. (1979). Development theory revisited: Findings of a longitudinal study. *Canadian Journal of Psychiatry,* 24:101-112.

Chess, S., Thomas, A. (1984). *Origins and evolution of behavior disorders.* New York: Brunner/Mazel.

Clements, S. D., Peters, J. E. (1962). Minimal brain dysfunctions in the school-aged child. *Archives of General Psychiatry,* 6:185-187.

Cohen, D. J., Riddle, M. A., Leckman, J., Ort, S., Shaywitz, B. A. (1984). Tourette's syndrome. In Jeste, D. V., Wyatt, R. J. (Eds.), *Neuropsychiatric movement disorders* (pp. 19-52). Washington, DC: American Psychiatric Press.

Cohen, N. J., Minde, K. (1983). The "hyperactive syndrome" in kindergarten children: Comparison of children with pervasive and situational symptoms. *Journal of Child Psychology and Psychiatry,* 24:443-456.

Cohen, N. J., Sullivan, S., Minde, K. K., Novak, C., Helwig, C. (1981). Evaluation of the relative effectiveness of methylphenidate and cognitive behavior modification in the treatment of kindergarten-aged hyperactive children. *Journal of Abnormal Child Psychology,* 9:43-54.

Cohen, N. J., Weiss, G., Minde, K. (1972). Cognitive styles in adolescents previously diagnosed as hyperactive. *Journal of Child Psychology and Psychiatry,* 13:203-209.

Coleman, M. (1971). Serotonin concentrations in whole blood of hyperactive children. *Journal of Pediatrics,* 78:985-990.

Collier, C. P., Soldin, S. J., Swanson, J. M., MacLeod, S. M., Weinberg, F., Rochefort, J. G. (1985). Pemoline pharmacokinetics and long term therapy in children with attention deficit disorder and hyperactivity. *Clinical Pharmacokinetics,* 10:269-278.

Colligan, R. C. (1981). Prediction of reading difficulty from parental preschool report: A 3-year follow-up. *Learning Disability Quarterly,* 4:31-37.

Collins, B. E. (1981). Hyperactivity: Myth and entity. In Brewer, M. B., Collins, B. E. (Eds.), *Scientific inquiry in the social sciences: A volume in honor of Donald T. Campbell* (pp. 385-412). San Francisco: Jossey-Bass.

Collins, B. E., Whalen, C. K., Henker, B. (1980). Ecological and pharmacological influences on behaviors in the classroom: The hyperkinetic behavioral syndrome. In Salzinger, S., Antrobus, J., Glick, J. (Eds.), *The Ecosystem of the "sick" child* (pp. 103-113). New York: Academic Press.

Conners, C. K. (1969). A teacher rating scale for use in drug studies with children. *American Journal of Psychiatry,* 126: 152-156.

Conners, C. K. (1970). Symptom patterns in hyperkinetic, neurotic and normal children. *Child Development,* 41:667-682.

Conners, C. K. (1972). Symposium: Behavior modification by drugs. II. Psychological effects of stimulant drugs in children with minimal brain dysfunction. *Pediatrics,* 49:702-708.

Conners, C. K. (1973). Rating scales for use in drug studies with children. *Psychopharmacology Bulletin* (Special Issue):24-29.

Conners, C. K. (1979). The acute effects of caffeine on evoked response, vigilance, and activity level in hyperkinetic children. *Journal of Abnormal Child Psychology,* 7:145-151.

Conners, C. K., Barkley, R. A. (1985). Rating scales and checklists for child psychopharmacology. *Psychopharmacology Bulletin,* 21:809-812.

Conners, C. K., Taylor, E. (1980). Pemoline, methylphenidate, and placebo in children with minimal brain dysfunction. *Archives of General Psychiatry,* 37:922-930.

Conners, C. K., Werry, J. S. (1979). *Pharmacotherapy.* In Quay, H. C., Werry, J. S. (Eds.), *Psychopathological disorders of childhood.* New York: John Wiley and Sons.

Conners, C. K., Wingler, M., Schwab, E., Leong, N., Blouin, A. (1984). Some effects of sugar and nutrition on behavior of ADD/H children. Paper presented at the meeting of the American Psychological Association, Toronto.

Cooper, J. R., Bloom, F. E., Roth, R. H. (1986). *The biochemical basis of neuropharmacology.* New York: Oxford University Press.

Corbett, J. A., Trimble, M. R. (1983). Epilepsy and anticonvulsant medication. In Rutter, M. (Ed.), *Developmental neuropsychiatry* (pp. 112-129). New York: Guilford Press.

Costello, A., Edelbrock, C., Dulcan, M., Kalas, R. (1984). Testing of the NIMH Diagnostic Interview Schedule for Children (DISC) in a clinical population: Final report. National Institute of Mental Health, Bethesda, MD.

Cott, A. (1971). Orthomolecular approach to the treatment of learning disabilities. *Schizophrenia,* 3:95-107.

Cott, A. (1985). *Help for your learning disabled child: The orthomolecular treatment*. New York: Huxley Institute.

Cowen, E. L., Pederson, A., Babijian, J., Izzo, L., Trost, M. A. (1973). Long-term follow-up of early detected vulnerable children. *Journal of Consulting and Clinical Psychology*, 41:438-444.

Crain, S., Shankweiler, D. (in press). Syntactic complexity and reading acquisition. In Davison, A., Green, G., Herman, G. (Eds.), *Critical approaches to readability: Theoretical bases of linguistic complexity*. Hillsdale, NJ: Erlbaum.

Cunningham, C. E., Barkley, R. A. (1979). The interactions of normal and hyperactive children with their mothers in free play and structured tasks. *Child Development*, 50:217-224.

Cunningham, C. E., Siegel, L. S., Offord, D. R. (1985). A developmental dose-response analysis of the effects of methylphenidate on the peer interactions of attention deficit disordered boys. *Journal of Child Psychology and Psychiatry*, 26:955-971.

Davids, A. (1971). An objective instrument for assessing hyperkinesis in children. *Journal of Learning Disabilities*, 4:499-501.

Davie, R., Butler, N., Goldstein, H. (1972). *From birth to seven: A report of the national child development study*. London: Longman.

DeFries, J. C., Plomin, R. (1978). Behavioral genetics. *Annual Review of Psychology*, 29:473-515.

deHaas, P. (1986). Attention styles and peer relationships of hyperactive and normal boys and girls. *Journal of Abnormal Child Psychology*, 14:457-467.

Denckla, M. B., LeMay, M., Chapman, C. A. (1985). Few CT scan abnormalities found even in neurologically impaired learning disabled children. *Journal of Learning Disabilities*, 18:132-135.

Denckla, M. B., Rudel, R. G. (1976). Rapid "automatized" naming (RAN): Dyslexia differentiated from other learning disabilities. *Neuropsychologia*, 14:471-479.

Deshler, D. D., Warner, M. M., Schumaker, J. B., Alley, G. R. (1983). Learning strategies intervention model: Key components and current status. In McKinney, J. D., Feagans, L. (Eds.), *Current topics in learning disabilities* (pp. 245-283). Norwood, NJ: Ablex Publishing Corporation.

Deutsch, C. K., Swanson, J. M., Bruell, J. H., Cantwell, D. P., Weinberg, F., Baren, M. (1982). Overrepresentation of adoptees in children with the attention deficit disorder. *Behavioral Genetics*, 12:231-238.

Dillon, D. C., Salzman, I. J., Schulsinger, D. A. (1985). The use of imipramine in Tourette's syndrome and attention deficit disorder: Case report. *Journal Clinical Psychiatry*, 46:348-349.

Dimond, S., Brouwers, E. (1976). Increase in the power of human memory in normal man through the use of drugs. *Psychopharmacology*, 49:307-309.

Dodrill, C. B., Batzel, L. W. (1986). Interictal behavioral features of patients with epilepsy. *Epilepsia*, 27(S2):64-76.

Doman, G., Delacato, C. (1968). Doman-Delacato philosophy. *Human Potential*, 1:113-116.

Donnelly, M., Zametkin, A. J., Rapoport, J. L., Ismond, D. R., Weingartner, H., Lane, E., Oliver, J., Linnoila, M., Potter, W. Z. (1986). Treatment of childhood hyperactivity with desipramine: Plasma drug concentrations, cardiovascular effects, plasma and urinary catecholamines and clinical response. *Journal of Pharmacology and Experimental Therapeutics*, 39:72-81.

Douglas, V. (1972). Stop, look, and listen: The problem of sustained attention and impulse control in hyperactive and normal children. *Canadian Journal of Behavioral Science*, 4:259-282.

Douglas, V. I. (1975). Are drugs enough? To treat or train the hyperactive child. *International Journal of Mental Health*, 4 (1-2):199-212.

Douglas, V. I. (1980). Treatment and training approaches to hyperactivity: Establishing internal or external control. In Whalen, C. K., Henker, B. (Eds.), *Hyperactive children: The social ecology of identification and treatment* (pp. 283-317). New York: Academic Press.

Douglas, V. I. (1980). Higher mental processes in hyperactive children: Implications for training. In Knights, R. M., Bakker, D. J. (Eds.), *Rehabilitation, treatment and management of learning disorders*. Baltimore: University Park Press.

Douglas, V. I. (1983). Attention and cognitive problems. In Rutter, M. (Ed.), *Developmental neuropsychiatry* (pp. 280-329). London: The Guilford Press.

Douglas, V. I., Barr, R. G., O'Neill, M. E., Britton, B. G. (1986). Short term effects of methylphenidate on the cognitive, learning and academic performance of children with attention deficit disorder in the laboratory and the classroom. *Journal of Child Psychiatry and Psychology,* 27:191-211.

Douglas, V. I., Peters, K. G. (1979). Toward a clearer definition of the attentional deficit of hyperactive children. In Hale, G., Lewis, M. (Eds.), *Attention and the development of cognitive style* (pp. 173-247). New York: Plenum Press.

Drake, W. E. Jr. (1968). Clinical and pathological findings in a child with a developmental learning disability. *Journal of Learning Disabilities,* 1:9-25.

Drillen, C. M. (1961). The incidence of mental and physical handicaps in school-age children of very low birth weight. *Pediatrics,* 27:452-464.

Dunn, H. (1986). *Sequelae of low birthweight: The Vancouver Study.* Philadelphia: JB Lippincott Co.

Dunn, H. G., Crichton, J. U., Robertson, A. M., Traynor, M. E., Tredger, E. (1971). Late prognosis in children of low birthweight. *Proceedings of the XIIIth International Congress of Pediatrics, Vienna* (pp. 33-38). Vienna: Vienna Academy of Medicine.

Dunn, H. G., Ho, H. H., Schuzer, M. (1986). Minimal brain dysfunction. In Dunn, H. G. (Ed.), *Sequelae of low birthweight: The Vancouver Study.* Oxford: Blackwell.

Dykman, R., Ackerman, P. (1980). Long-term followup studies of hyperactive children: A 5-year followup study. In Camp, B. W. (Ed.), *Advances in behavioral pediatrics.* Greenwich, CT: JAI Press.

Dykman, R. A., Ackerman, P. T., Clements, S. D., Peters, J. E. (1971). Specific learning disabilities: An attentional deficit syndrome. In Myklebust, H. R. (Ed.), *Progress in learning disabilities* (pp. 56-93). New York: Grune and Stratton.

Edelbrock, C., Costello, A. J., Kessler, M. D. (1984). Empirical corroboration of attention deficit disorder. *Journal of the American Academy of Child Psychiatry,* 23:285-290.

Egeland, B., Weinberg, R. A. (1976). The Matching Familiar Figures Test: A look at its psychometric credibility. *Child Development,* 47:483-491.

Egger, J., Graham, P. J., Carter, C. M., Gumley, D. , Soothill, J. F. (1985). Controlled trial of oligoantigenic treatment in the hyperkinetic syndrome. *Lancet,* 2:540-545.

Eisenberg, J., Chazan-Gologorsky, S., Hattab, J., Belmaker, R. H. (1984). A controlled trial of vasopressin treatment of childhood learning disorder. *Biology-Psychiatry,* 19:1137-1141.

Eliason, M. J. (1986). Neurofibromatosis: Implications for learning and behavior. *Developmental and Behavioral Pediatrics,* 7:175-179.

Ernhart, C., Landa, B., Schell, N., Norman, B. (1981). Subclinical levels of lead and developmental deficit—A multivariate follow-up reassessment. *Pediatrics,* 67:911-919.

Feighner, J. P., Robins, E., Guze, S. B. (1972). Diagnostic criteria for use in psychiatric research. *Archives of General Psychiatry,* 18:746-756.

Feingold, B. F. (1975). *Why your child is hyperactive.* New York: Random House.

Feldman, S., Denhoff, E., Denhoff, J. (1979). The attention disorders and related syndromes: Outcome in adolescence and young adult life. In Denhoff, E., Stern, L. (Eds.), *Minimal brain dysfunction: A developmental approach* (pp. 133-148). New York: Masson.

Ferguson, H. B., Simeon, J. G. (1984). Evaluating drug effects on children's cognitive functioning. *Progress in Neuropsychopharmocology and Biological Psychiatry,* 8:683-686.

Firestone, P., Crowe, D., Goodman, J. T., McGrath, P. (1986). Vicissitudes of follow-up studies: Differential effects of parent training and stimulant medication with hyperactives. *American Journal of Orthopsychiatry,* 56:184-194.

Firestone, P., Peters, S., Rivier, M., Knights, R. M. (1978). Minor physical anomalies in hyperactive, retarded and normal children and their families. *Journal of Child Psychology,* 19:155-160.

Firestone, P., Prabhu, A. N. (1983). Minor physical anomalies and obstetrical complications: Their relationship to hyperactive, psychoneurotic and normal children and their families. *Journal of Abnormal Child Psychology,* 11:207-216.

Fletcher, J. (1985). External validation of learning disability typologies. In Rourke, B. P. (Ed.), *Learning disabilities: Advances in subtypal analysis*. New York: Guilford Press.

Fodor, J. A. (1983). *The modularity of mind*. Cambridge, MA; MIT Press.

Fogel, C. A., Mednick, S. A., Michelsen, N. (1985). Hyperactive behavior and minor physical anomalies. *Acta Psychiatrica Scandanavica*, 72:551-556.

Ford, C. E., Pelham, W. E., Ross, A. O. (1984). Selective attention and rehearsal in the auditory short-term memory task performance of poor and normal readers. *Journal of Abnormal Child Psychology*, 12:127-142.

Friedmann, N., Thomas, J., Carr, R., Elders, J., Ingdahl, I., Roche, A. (1981). Effect on growth in pemoline-treated children with attention deficit disorder. *American Journal of Disturbed Children*, 135:329-332.

Frith, U .(1981). Experimental approaches to developmental dyslexia. *Psychological Research*, 43:97-109.

Fuller, R. W., Perry, K. W., Bymaster, F. P., Wong, D. T. (1978). Comparative effects of pemoline, amfonelic acid, and amphetamine on dopamine uptake and release in vitro on brain 3, 4-dihydroxy-phenylacetic acid concentration on spiperone-treated rats. *Journal of Pharmacy and Pharmacology*, 30:197-198.

Gadow, K. D. (1983). Effects of stimulant drugs on academic performance in hyperactive and learning disabled children. *Journal of Learning Disabilities*, 16:290-299.

Gadow, K. D., Kalachnik, J. (1981). Prevalence and pattern of drug treatment for behavior and seizure disorders of TMR students. *American Journal of Mental Deficiency*, 85:588-595.

Galaburda, A. M., Kemper, T. L. (1979). Cytoarchitechtonic abnormalities in developmental dyslexia: A case study. *Annals of Neurology*, 6:94-100.

Galaburda, A. M., Sherman, G. F., Rosen, G. D., Aboitiz, F., Geschwind, N. (1985). Developmental dyslexia: Four consecutive patients with cortical anomalies. *Annals of Neurology*, 18:222-233.

Galler, J. R., Ramsey, F. , Solimano, G. (1984). The influence of early malnutrition on subsequent behavioral development. III. Learning disabilities as a sequel to malnutrition. *Pediatric Research*, 18:309-313.

Garfinkel, B. D., Brown, W., Klee, S. H., Braden, W., Beauchesne, H., Shapiro, S. K. (1986). Neuroendocrine and cognitive responses to amphetamine in adolescents with a history of attention deficit disorder. *Journal of the American Academy of Child Psychiatry*, 25:503-508.

Garfinkel, B. D., Webster, C. D., Sloman, L. (1981). Responses to methylphenidate and varied doses of caffeine in children with attention deficit disorder. *Canadian Journal of Psychiatry*, 26:395-401.

Garfinkel, B. D., Wender, P. H., Sloman, L., O'Neill, I. (1983). Tricyclic antidepressant and methylphenidate treatment of attention deficit disorder in children. *Journal of the American Academy of Child Psychiatry*, 22:343-348.

Gastfriend, D. R., Biederman, J., Jellinek, M. A. (1984). Desipramine in the treatment of adolescents with attention deficit disorder. *American Journal of Psychiatry*, 141:906-908.

Gittelman, R. (1980). Indications for the use of stimulant treatment in learning disorders. *Journal of the American Academy of Child Psychiatry*, 19:623-636.

Gittelman, R., Eskenazi, B. (1983). Lead and hyperactivity revised. An investigation of disadvantaged children. *Archives of General Psychiatry*, 40:827-833.

Gittelman, R., Klein, D. F., Feingold, I. (1983). Children with reading disorders. II. Effects of methylphenidate in combination with reading remediation. *Journal of Child Psychology and Psychiatry*, 24:193-212.

Gittelman, R., Mannuzza, S., Shenker, S., Bonagura, N. (1985). Hyperactive boys almost grown up. I. Psychiatric status. *Archives of General Psychiatry*, 42:937-947.

Gittelman-Klein, R., Abikoff, H., Pollack, E., Klein, D. F., Katz, S., Mattes, J. (1980). A controlled trial of behavior modification and methylphenidate in hyperactive children. In Whalen, C. K., Henker, B. (Eds.), *Hyperactive children: The social ecology of identification and treatment* (pp. 221-243). New York: Academic Press.

Gittelman-Klein, R., Klein, D. F. (1976). Methylphenidate effects in learning disabilities. *Archives of General Psychiatry*, 33: 654-655.

Gittelman-Klein, R., Klein, D. G. (1985). Are behavioral and psychometric changes related in methylphenidate-treated, hyperactive children? *International Journal of Mental Health,* 4:182-198.

Golden, G. S. (1974). Gilles de la Tourette's syndrome following methylphenidate administration. *Developmental Medicine and Child Neurology,* 16:76-78.

Golden, G. S. (1984). Controversial therapies. *Pediatric Clinics of North America,* 31:459-469.

Goldman, J. A., Lerman, R. H., Contois, H. J., Udall, J. N. (1984). The behavior of preschool children following ingestion of sucrose. Paper presented at the Annual Meeting of the American Psychological Association, Toronto.

Goldman-Rakic, P. S., Rakic, P. (1984). Experimentally modified convolutional patterns in nonhuman primates: Possible relevance of connections to cerebral dominance in humans. In Geschwind, N., Galaburda, A. M. (Eds.), *Biological foundations of cerebral dominance* (pp. 179-192). Cambridge, MA: Harvard University Press.

Goldstein, K. (1936). Modification of behavior consequent to cerebral lesion. *Psychiatric Quarterly,* 10:539-610.

Golinko, B. E. (1984). Side effects of dextroamphetamine and methylphenidate in hyperactive children—a brief review. *Neuropsychopharmacology Biology and Psychiatry,* 8:1-8.

Goyette, C. H., Conners, C. K., Ulrich, R. F. (1978). Normative data on revised Conners Parent and Teacher Rating Scales. *Journal of Abnormal Child Psychology,* 6:221-236.

Graham, F., Ernhart, C., Thurston, D., Carft, M. (1962). Development three years after perinatal anoxia and other potentially damaging newborn experiences. *Psychological Monographs* (Serial 522), 76:3-10.

Graham, F. K., Caldwell, B. M., Ernhart, C. B., Pennoyer, M. M., Hartman, A. F. Sr. (1957). Anoxia as a significant perinatal experience: A critique. *Journal of Pediatrics,* 50:556-569.

Greenhill, L., Puig-Antich, J., Goetz, R., Hanlon, C., Davies, M. (1983). Sleep architecture and REM sleep measures in prepubertal children with attention deficit disorder with hyperactivity. *Sleep,* 6:91-101.

Gross, M. (1975). Caffeine in the treatment of children with minimal brain dysfunction or hyperkinetic syndrome. *Psychosomatics,* 16:26-27.

Gualtieri, C. T., Hicks, R. E., Mayo, J. P., Schroeder, S. R. (1984). The persistence of stimulant effects in chronically treated children: Further evidence of an inverse relationship between drug effects and placebo levels of response. *Psychopharmacology,* 83:44-47.

Gualtieri, C. T., Patterson, D. R. (1986). Neuroleptic-induced tics in two hyperactive children. *American Journal of Psychiatry,* 143:1176-1177.

Hagerman, R., Kemper, M., Hudson, M. (1985). Learning disabilities and attentional problems in boys with the fragile X syndrome. *American Journal of Diseases of Children,* 139:674-678.

Halliday, R., Callaway, E., Naylor, H. (1983). Visual evoked potential changes induced by methylphenidate in hyperactive children: Dose/response effects. *Electroencephalography and Clinical Neurophysiology,* 55:258-267.

Halliday, R., Callaway, E., Rosenthal, J. H. (1984). The visual ERP predicts clinical response to methylphenidate in hyperactive children. *Psychophysiology,* 21:114-121.

Halperin, J. M., Gittelman, R., Klein, D. F., Rudel, R. G. (1984). Reading disabled hyperactive children: A distinct subgroup of attention deficit disorder with hyperactivity? *Journal of Abnormal Child Psychology,* 12:1-14.

Halverson, C. F., Waldrop, M. (1976). Relations between preschool activity and aspects of intellectual and social behavior at age 7 1/2. *Developmental Psychology,* 12:107-112.

Halverson, C. F. Jr., Victor, J. B. (1976). Minor physical anomalies and problem behavior in elementary school children. *Child Development,* 47:281-285.

Hansen, C. R., Cohen, D. J. (1984). Multimodality approaches in the treatment of attention deficit disorders. *Pediatric Clinics of North America,* 31:499-513.

Harcherik, D. F., Cohen, D. J., Ort, S., Paul, R., Shaywitz, B. A., Volkmar, F. R., Rothman, S. L. G., Leckman, J. F. (1985). Computed tomographic brain scanning in four neuropsychiatric disorders of childhood. *American Journal of Psychiatry,* 142:731-737.

Hart, A., Rennick, P. M., Klinge, V., Schwartz, M. (1974). A pediatric neurologist's contribution to evaluations of school under-achievers. *American Journal of Diseases of Children*, 128:319-323.

Hartsough, C. S., Lambert, N. M. (1982). Some environmental and familial correlates and antecedents hyperactivity. *American Journal of Orthopsychiatry*, 52(2):272-287.

Haslem, R. M., Dalby, J. T., Rademaker, A. W. (1984). Effects of megavitamin therapy on children with attention deficit disorders. *Pediatrics*, 74:103-111.

Hechtman, L., Weiss, G., Finklestein, J., Wener, A., Benn, R. (1976). Hyperactives as young adults: Preliminary report. *Canadian Medical Association Journal*, 115:625-630.

Hechtman, L., Weiss, G., Perlman, T. (1980). Hyperactives as young adults: Self-esteem and social skills. *Canadian Journal of Psychiatry*, 25:478-483.

Hechtman, L., Weiss, G., Perlman, T. (1984a). Young adult outcome of hyperkinetic children who received long-term stimulant treatment. *Journal of the American Academy of Child Psychiatry*, 23:261-269.

Hechtman, L., Weiss, G., Perlman, T. (1984b). Hyperactives as young adults: Past and current substance abuse and antisocial behavior. *American Journal of Orthopsychiatry*, 54:415-425.

Henker, B., Astor-Dubin, L., Varni, J. W. (1986). Psychostimulant medication and perceived intensity in hyperactive children. *Journal of Abnormal Child Psychology*, 14:105-114.

Henker, B., Whalen, C., Collins, B. (1979). Double-blind and triple-blind assessments of medication and placebo response in hyperactive children. *Journal of Abnormal Child Psychology*, 7:1-13.

Henry, S. A., Wittman, R. D. (1981). Diagnostic implications of Bannatyne's recategorized WISC-R scores for identifying learning disabled children. *Journal of Learning Disabilities*, 14:517-520.

Herjanic, B. (1981). *The diagnostic interview for children and adolescents: Parent version (DICA-P)*. St Louis: Washington University.

Herjanic, B., Campbell, J. (1977). Differentiating psychiatrically disturbed children on the basis of a structured interview. *Journal of Abnormal Child Psychology*, 5:127-135.

Hesselbrock, V. M., Stabenau, J. R., Hesselbrock, M. N. (1985). Minimal brain dysfunction and neuropsychologic test performance in offspring of alcoholics. *Recent Developments in Alcoholism*, 3:65-82.

Hier, D., LeMay, M., Rosenberger, P., Perlo, V. (1979). Developmental dyslexia: Evidence for a subgroup with reversal of cerebral asymmetry. *Archives of Neurology*, 35:90-92.

Hier, D. B. (1980). Learning disorders and sex chromosome aberrations. *Journal of Mental Deficiency Research*, 24:17-26.

Hinshaw, S. P. (1986). On the distinction between attentional deficits/hyperactivity and conduct problems/aggression in child psychopathology. (Submitted.)

Hinshaw, S. P., Henker, B., Whalen, C. K. (1984). Cognitive-behavioral and pharmacologic interventions in hyperactive boys: Comparative and combined effects. *Journal of Consulting and Clinical Psychology*, 52:739-749.

Hiscock, M., Kinsbourne, M., Caplan, B., Swanson, J. M. (1979). Auditory attention in hyperactive children: Effects of stimulant medication on dichotic listening performance. *Journal of Abnormal Psychology*, 88:27-32.

Hoffman, L. W. (1977). Changes in family roles, socialization and sex differences. *American Psychologist*, 32:644-657.

Hohman, L. B. (1922). Post encephalitic behavior disorders in children. *Johns Hopkins Hospital Bulletin*, 380:372-375.

Holborow, P., Berry, P. (1986). A multinational, cross-cultural perspective on hyperactivity. *American Journal of Orthopsychiatry*, 56:320-322.

Holborow, P. L., Berry, P., Elkins, J. (1984). Prevalence of hyperkinesis: A comparison of three rating scales. *Journal of Learning Disabilities*, 17:411-417.

Holborow, P. L., Berry, P. S. (1986). Hyperactivity and learning difficulties. *Journal of Learning Disabilities*, 19:426-431.

Hopkins, J., Perlman, T., Hechtman, L., Weiss, G. (1979). Cognitive style in adults originally diagnosed as hyperactives. *Journal of Child Psychology and Psychiatry*, 20:209-216.

Horn, J. M., Green, M., Carney, R., Erickson, M. T. (1975). Bias against genetic hypotheses in adoption studies. *Archives of General Psychiatry,* 32:1365-1367.

Howell, D. C., Hussy, J. R., Hassuk, B. (1985). Fifteen-year followup of a behavioral history of attention deficit disorder. *Pediatrics, 76:185-190.*

Hoy, E., Weiss, G., Minde, K., Cohen, N. (1978). The hyperactive child at adolescence: Emotional social, and cognitive functioning. *Journal of Abnormal Child Psychology,* 6:311-324.

Huddleston, W., Staiger, R. C., Frye, R., Musgrove, R. S., Stritch, T. (1961). Deanol as aid in overcoming reading retardation. *Clinical Medicine,* 8:1340-1342.

Huessy, H. R. (1967). Study of the prevalence and therapy of the choreiform syndrome of hyperkinesis in rural Vermont. *Acta Paedopsychiatrica,* 34:130-135.

Hughes, J. R. (1978). Electroencepalographic and neurophysiological studies in dyslexia. In Benton, A. L., Pearl, D. (Eds.), *Dyslexia: An appraisal of current knowledge* (pp. 205-240). New York: Oxford University Press.

Hungund, B. L., Henna, M., Winsberg, B. G. (1978). A sensitive gas chromatographic method for the determination of methylphenidate (Ritalin) and its major metabolite a-phenyl-2-piperidine acetic acid (ritalinic acid) in plasma using a nitrogen-phosphorous detector. *Psychopharmacological Communications,* 2:203.

Hunt, R. D., Cohen, D. J. (1984). Psychiatric aspects of learning difficulties. *Pediatric Clinics of North America,* 31:471-497.

Hunt, R. D., Minderaa, R. B., Cohen, D. J. (1985). Clonidine benefits children with attention deficit disorder and hyperactivity: Report of a double-blind placebo-crossover therapeutic trial. *Journal of the American Academy of Child Psychiatry,* 24:617-629.

Irwin, M., Belendink, K., McCloskay, K., Freedman, D. X. (1981). Tryptophan metabolism in children with attention deficit disorder. *American Journal of Psychiatry,* 138:1082-1085.

Jacob, R. G., O'Leary, K. D., Rosenblad, C. (1978). Formal and informal classroom settings: Effects on hyperactivity. *Journal of Abnormal Child Psychology,* 6:47-59.

Johnston, C., Pelham, W. E. (1986). Teacher ratings predict peer ratings and aggression at 3 year follow-up in boys with attention deficit disorder with hyperactivity. *Journal of Consulting and Clinical Psychology,* 54:571-572.

Johnston, C., Pelham, W. E., Murphy, H. A. (1972). Peer relationships in ADDH and normal children: A developmental analysis of peer and teacher ratings. *Journal of Abnormal Child Psychology,* 13:89-100.

Katz, R. B. (1982). Phonological deficiencies in children with reading disability: Evidence from an object-naming task. Unpublished doctoral dissertation, University of Connecticut, Storrs, Connecticut.

Kaufman, A. (1981). The WISC-R and learning disabilities assessment: State of the art. *Journal of Learning Disabilities,* 14:520-526.

Kaufman, A. S. (1975). Factor analysis of the WISC-R at 11 age levels between 1/2 and 16-1/2 years. *Journal of Consulting and Clinical Psychology,* 43:135-147.

Kaufman, R. E., Smith-Wright, D., Reese, C. A., Simpson, R., Jones, F. (1981). Medication compliance in hyperactive children. *Pediatric Pharmacology,* 1:231-237.

Kavale, K. (1982). The efficiency of stimulant drug treatment for hyperactivity: A meta-analysis. *Journal of Learning Disabilities,* 15:280-289.

Kavale, K. A., Forness, S. R. (1983). Hyperactivity and diet treatment: A meta-analysis of the Feingold hypothesis. *Journal of Learning Disabilities,* 16(6):324-330.

Kendall, P. C., Braswell, L. (1985). *Cognitive-behavior therapy for impulsive children.* New York: Guilford Press.

Kennard, M. A. (1960). Value of equivocal signs in neurologic diagnosis. *Neurology,* 10:753-764.

Kenny, T. J., Clemmens, R. L., Hudson, B., Lentz, G. A. Jr., Cicci, R., Nair, P. (1971). Characteristics of children referred because of hyperactivity. *Journal of Pediatrics,* 79:618-622.

Keogh, B. K. (1971). Hyperactivity and learning disorders: Review and speculation. *Exceptional Children,* 38:101-109.

Kerbeshian, J., Burd, L., Martsolf, J. (1984). A family with fragile X syndrome. *Journal of Nervous and Mental Disease,* 172:549-551.

Khan, Q. U., DeKirmenjian, H. (1981). Urinary excretion of catecholamine metabolites in hyperkinetic child syndrome. *American Journal Psychiatry*, 138:108-112.

King, C., Young, R. D. (1982). Peer interaction in a communication task and peer popularity: A comparison of hyperactive and active boys. Unpublished manuscript, Indiana University.

Kinney, R. O., Shaywitz, B. A., Shaywitz, S. E. (1985). Cognitive deficits independent of behavioral difficulties in children with epilepsy and attention deficit disorder. *Pediatric Research*, 19:391a.

Klein, A. R., Young, R. D. (1979). Hyperactive boys in their classroom Assessment of teacher and peer perceptions. *Journal of Abnormal Child Psychology*, 7:425-442.

Klein, D. F., Gittelman-Klein, R. (1975). Problems in the diagnosis of minimal brain dysfunction and the hyperkinetic syndrome. *International Journal of Mental Health*, 4:45-60.

Klinkerfuss, G. M., Lang, P. H., Weinberg, W. A., O'Leary, J. L. (1965). EEG abnormalities of children with hyperkinetic behavior. *Neurology*, 15:883-896.

Klorman, R., Brumaghim, J. T., Coons, H. W., Peloquin, L. J., Strauss, J., Lewine, J. D., Borgstedt, A. D., Goldstein, M. G. (In press). The contributions of event related potentials to understanding effects of stimulants on information processing in attention deficit disorder. In Sergent, J., Bloomingdale, R. L. (Eds.), *Attention deficit disorder*. New York: Spectrum.

Kohn, M. (1977). *Social competence, symptoms and underachievement in childhood: A longitudinal perspective*. Washington, DC; VH Winston.

Koizumi, H. M. (1985). Obsessive-compulsive symptoms following stimulants. *Biological Psychiatry*, 20:1332-1333.

Kramer, J., Loney, J. (1982). Childhood hyperactivity and substance abuse: A review of the literature. In Gadow, K., Bialer, I. (Eds.), *Advances in learning and behavioral disabilities*. Greenwich, CT: JAI Press.

Kuczenski, R. (1983). Biochemical actions of amphetamines and other stimulants. In Crease, I. (Ed.), *Stimulants: neurochemical, behavior and clinical* (pp. 31-63). New York: Raven Press.

Lahey, B. B., Green, K. D., Forehand, R. (1980). On the independence of ratings of hyperactivity, conduct problems, and attention deficits in children: A multiple regression analysis. *Journal of Consulting and Clinical Psychology*, 48:566-574.

Lahey, B. B., Schaughency, E. A., Strauss, C. C., Frame, C. L. (1984). Are attention deficit disorders with and without hyperactivity similar or dissimilar disorders? *Journal of the American Academy of Child Psychiatry*, 23:302-309.

Lahey, B. B., Stempniak, M., Robinson, E. J., Tyroler, M. J. (1978). Hyperactivity and learning disabilities as independent dimensions of child behavior problems. *Journal of Abnormal Psychology*, 87:333-340.

Lambert, N. M., Sandoval, J. (1980). The prevalence of learning disabilities in a sample of children considered hyperactive. *Journal of Abnormal Child Psychology*, 8:33-50.

Lambert, N. M., Sandoval, J., Sassone, D. (1978). Prevalence of hyperactivity in elementary school children as a function of social system definers. *American Journal of Orthopsychiatry*, 48:446-463.

Langer, D. H., Rapoport, J. L., Brown, G. L., Ebert, M. H., Bunney, W. E. Jr. (1982). Behavioral effects of carbidopa/levodopa in hyperactive boys. *Journal of the American Academy of Child Psychiatry*, 1:8-10.

Langhorne, J. E. Jr., Loney, J. (1979). A four-fold model for subgrouping the hyperkinetic/MBD syndrome. *Child Psychiatry and Human Development*, 9:153-159.

Langhorne, J. E. Jr., Loney, J., Paternite, C. E., Bechtoldt, H. P. (1976). Childhood hyperkinesis: A return to the source. *Journal of Abnormal Psychology*, 85:201-209.

Langsdorf, R., Anderson, R. F., Walchter, D., Madrigal, J. F., Javrez, L. J. (1979). Ethnicity, social class and perception of hyperactivity. *Psychology in the Schools*, 16:293-298.

Lapouse, R., Monk, M. (1958). An epidemiological study of behavior characteristics in children. *American Journal of Public Health*, 48:1134-1144.

Laufer, M., Denhoff, E. (1957). Hyperkinetic behavior syndrome in children. *Journal of Pediatrics*, 50:463-474.

Leckman, J. F., Sholmskar, D., Thompson, D., Belanger, A., Weissman, M. M. (1982). Best estimate of lifetime psychiatric diagnosis. *Archives of General Psychiatry,* 39:879-883.

LeMay, M., Kido, D. (1978). Asymmetries of the cerebral hemispheres on computed tomograms. *Journal of Computer Assisted Tomography,* 2:471-476.

Lesser, R. P., Luders, H., Wylic, E., Dinner, D. S., Morris, H. H. III (1986). Mental Deterioration in epilepsy. *Epilepsia,* 27 (s2):105-123.

Levinson, H. N. (1980). *A solution to the riddle of dyslexia.* New York:Springer, Verlag Inc.

Levinson, H. N. (1984). *Smart but feeling dumb.* New York: Warner Books.

Levy, F. (1980). The development of sustained attention (vigilance). *Journal of Child Psychology and Psychiatry,* 21:77-84.

Liberman, I. Y. (1982). A language oriented view of reading and its disabilities. In Myklebust, H. (Ed.), *Progress in learning disabilities.* New York: Grune and Statton.

Liberman, I. Y., Mattingly, I. G. (in press). The motor theory of speech perception revised. *Cognition.*

Liberman, I. Y., Shankweiler, D., Fischer, F. W., Carter, B. (1974). Explicit syllable and phoneme segmentation in the young child. *Experimental Child Psychology,* 18:201-212.

Lilienfeld, A. M., Pasamanick, B., Rogers, M. (1955). Relationship between pregnancy experience and the development of certain neuropsychiatric disorders in childhood. American Journal of Public Health, 45:637-643.

Loiselle, D. L., Stamm, J.S., Maitinsky, S. (1980). Evoked potention and behavioral signs of attentive dysfunctions in hyperactive boys. *Psychophysiology,* 17:193-201.

Loney, J. (1983). Research diagnostic criteria for childhood hyperactivity. In Guze, S. B., Earls, F. E., Barrett, J. E. (Eds.), *Childhood psychopathology and development* (pp. 109-115). New York: Raven Press.

Loney, J. (1986). Hyperactivity and aggression in the diagnosis of attention deficit disorder. In Lahey, B. B., Kazdin, A. E. (Eds.), *Advances in Clinical Child Psychology.* New York: SUNY at Stony Brook (in press).

Loney, J., Kramer, J., Milich, R. (1981). The hyperkinetic child grows up: Predictors of symptoms, delinquency, and achievement at follow-up. In Gadow, K. D., Loney, J. (Eds.), *Psychosocial aspects of drug treatment for hyperactivity.* Boulder, CO: Westview Press.

Loney, J., Langhorne, J. E., Paternite, C. E. (1978). An empirical basis for subgrouping the hyperkinetic/MBD syndrome. *Journal of Abnormal Psychology,* 87:431-441.

Loney, J., Milich, (1982). Hyperactivity, inattention, and aggression in clinical practice. *Advances in Development and Behavioral Pediatrics,* 3:113-147.

Loney, J., Prinz, R. J., Mishalow, J., Joad, J. (1978). Hyperkinetic/aggressive boys in treatment: Predictors of clinical response to methylphenidate. *American Journal of Psychiatry,* 135:1487-1491.

Lopez, R. E. (1965). Hyperactivity in twins. *Canadian Psychiatric Association Journal,* 10:421-426.

Lorr, M. (1961). Classification of the behavior disorders. In Farnsworth, P. R., McNemar, O., McNemar, Q. (Eds.), *Annual Review of Psychology.* Palo Alto, CA: Annual Reviews, Inc.

Lou, H. C., Henriksen, L., Bruhn, P. (1984). Focal cerebral hypoperfusion in children with dysphasia and/or attention deficit disorder. *Archives of Neurology,* 42:825-829.

Lowe, T. L., Cohen, D. J., Detlor, J., Kremenitzer, M. W., Shaywitz, B. A. (1982). Stimulant medications precipitate Tourette's syndrome. *Journal of the American Medical Association,* 247:1729-1731.

Lucas, A. R., Rodin, E. A., Simson, C. B. (1965). Neurological assessment of children with early school problems. *Developmental Medicine and Child Neurology,* 7:145-156.

Lucas, P. B., Gardner, D. L., Wolkowitz, O. M., Tucker, E. E., Cowdry, R. W. (1986). Methylphenidate-induced cardiac arrhythmias. *New England Journal of Medicine,* 315:1485.

Luisada, P. V. (1969). REM deprivation and hyperactivity in children. *Chicago Medical School Quarterly,* 28:97-108.

Maas, J. W., Leckman, J. F. (1983). Relationships between central nervous system noradrenergic function and plasma and urinary MHPG and other norepinephrine metabolite. In Mass, J. (Ed.), *MHPG: Basic mechanisms and psychopathology* (pp. 33-43). New York: Academic Press.

Mainville, F., Friedman, R. J. (1976). Peer relations of hyperactive children. *Ontario Psychologist*, 8:17-20.

Mann, V. A., Liberman, I. Y., Shankweiler, D. (1980). Children's memory for sentences and word strings in relation to reading ability. *Memory and Cognition*, 8:329-335.

Mash, E. J., Johnston, C. (1982). A comparison of the mother-child interactions of younger and older hyperactive and normal children. *Child Development*, 53:1371-1381.

Mash, E. J., Johnston, C. (1983). Parental perceptions of child behavior problems, parenting self-esteem, and mothers' reported stress in younger and older hyperactive and normal children. *Journal of Consulting Clinical Psychology*, 51:68-99.

Mattes, J. A. (1983). The Feingold diet: A current reappraisal. *Journal of Learning Disabilities*, 16:319-323.

Mattes, J. A., Boswell, L., Oliver, H. (1984). Methylphenidate effects on symptoms of attention deficit disorder in adults. *Archives of General Psychiatry*, 41:1059-1063.

Mattes, J. A., Gittelman, R. (1983). Growth of hyperactive children on maintenance regimen of methylphenidate. *Archives of General Psychiatry*, 40:317-321.

Mattes, J. A., Gittelman, R., Levitt, M. (1980). The interrelationship of physical anomalies, DBH and genetic factors in childhood hyperkenesis: An attempt at replication. In Shopsin, B., Greehil, L. (Eds.), *The psychobiology of childhood: A profile of current issues.* New York: Spectrum Publications.

Maurer, R. G., Stewart, M. A. (1980). Attention deficit without hyperactivity in a child psychiatry clinic. *Journal of Clinical Psychiatry*, 41:232-233.

Mayron, L., Ott, J. N., Nations, R., Mayron, E. L. (1974). Light, radiation and academic behavior. *Academic Therapy*, 10:33-47.

McGee, R., Birbeck, J., Silva, P. A. (1985). Physical development of hyperactive boys. *Developmental Medicine and Child Neurology*, 27: 364-368.

McGee, R., Williams, S., Silva, P. A. (1984). Background characteristics of aggressive, hyperactive, and aggressive-hyperactive boys. *Journal of the American Academy of Child Psychiatry*, 23:280-284.

McLaughlin, J. F., Kriegsmann, E. (1980). Developmental dyspraxia in a family with X-linked mental retardation (Renpenning syndrome). *Developmental Medicine and Child Neurology*, 22:84-92.

McMahon, S. A., Greenberg, L. M. (1977). Serial neurological examination of hyperactive children. *Pediatrics*, 59:584-587.

Mech, E. V. (1973). Adoption: A policy perspective, In Caldwell, B. M., Ricciuti, H. N. (Eds.), *Review of child development research*. Chicago: University of Chicago Press.

Mendelson, W., Johnson, M., Stewart, M. (1971). Hyperactive children as teenagers: A followup study. *Journal of Nervous and Mental Diseases*, 153:272-279.

Menkes, M., Rowe, J., Menkes, J. (1967). A 25-year followup study on the hyperkinetic child with MBD. *Pediatrics*, 38:393-399.

Messer, S. B. (1976). Reflection-impulsivity: A review. *Psychological Bulletin*, 83:1026-1052.

Meyer, A. (1904). The anatomical facts and clinical varieties of traumatic insanity. *American Journal of Insanity*, 60:373-441.

Mikkelsen, E. J., Brown, G. L., Minichiello, M. D., Millican, F. K., Rapoport, J. L. (1982). Neurologic status in hyperactive, enuretic, encopretic and normal boys. *Journal of the American Academy of Child Psychiatry*, 21:75-81.

Mikkelson, E., Lake, C. T., Brown, G. L., Ziegler, M. G., Ebert, M. H. (1981). The hyperactive child syndrome: Peripheral sympathetic nervous system function and the effect of d-amphetamine. *Psychiatry Research*, 4:157-169.

Milich, R., Landau, S. (1982). Socialization and peer relations in the hyperactive child. In Gadow, K., Bialer, I. (Eds.), *Advances in learning and behavioral disabilities*. Greenwich, CT: JAI Press.

Milich, R., Lindgren, S., Wolraich, M. (1986). The behavioral effects of sugar: A comment on Buchanan. *American Psychologist*, 41 (2):218-220.

Milich, R., Loney, J., Landau, S. (1982). Independent dimensions of hyperactivity and aggression: A validation with playroom observation data. *Journal of Abnormal Psychology,* 91:183-198.

Milich, R., Pelham, W. E. (1986). Effects of sugar ingestion on the classroom and playgroup behavior of attention deficit disordered boys. *Journal of Consulting and Clinical Psychology,* 54:714-718.

Milich, R., Pelham, W. E., Hinshaw, S. P. (in press). Issues in the diagnosis of attention deficit disorder: A cautionary note on the Gordon Diagnostic System. *Psychopharmacology Bulletin.*

Milich, R. S., Loney, J. (1979). The role of hyperactive and aggressive symptomatology in predicting adolescent outcome among hyperactive children. *Journal of Pediatric Psychology,* 4:93-112.

Miller, R. G., Palkes, H. S., Stewart, M. A. (1973). Hyperactive children in suburban elementary schools. *Child Psychiatry and Human Development,* 4:121-127.

Minde, K. K., Lewin, D., Weiss, G., Lavigueur, J., Sykes, E. (1971). The hyperactive child in elementary school: A 5-year controlled followup. *Exceptional Children,* 38:215-221.

Minde, K. K., Weiss, G., Mendelson, N. A. (1972). A 5-year followup study of 91 hyperkinetic school children. *Journal of the American Academy of Child Psychology,* 11:595-610.

Mintz, L, I., Collins, B. E. (1985). Qualitative influences on the perception of movement: An experimental study. *Journal of Abnormal Child Psychology,* 13:143-153.

Molina, V. A., Orsingher, O. A. (1981). Effects of Mg-Pemoline on the central catecholaminergic system. *Archives Internationales de Pharmacodynamie,* 251:66-79.

Morrison, J. R. (1979). Diagnosis of adult psychiatric patients with childhood hyperactivity. *American Journal of Psychiatry,* 136:955-958.

Morrison, J. R., Stewart, M. A. (1971). A family study of the hyperactive child syndrome. *Biological Psychiatry,* 3:189-195.

Myers, P. I., Hammill, D. D. (1982). *Learning disabilities: Basic concepts, assignment practices and instructional strategies.* Austin, TX: Pro-Ed.

Needleman, H. L., Bellinger, D., Leviton, A. (1981). Does lead at low dose affect intelligence in children? *Pediatrics,* 68:894-896.

Neligan, G. A., Kolvin, I., Scott, D., Garsida, R. F. (1976). Born too soon or born too small. In Heinemann, W. (Ed.), *Clinics in developmental medicine.* Philadelphia: JB Lippincott.

Nemzer, E. D., Arnold, L. E., Votolato, N. A., McConnell, H. (1986). Amino acid supplementation as therapy for attention deficit. *Journal of the American Academy of Child Psychiatry,* 25(4):509-513.

Nichols, P. L., Chen, T. C. (1981). *Minimal brain dysfunction: A prospective study.* Hillsdale, NJ; Lawrence Erlbaum Associates Inc.

O'Leary, K. D., Rosenbaum, A., Hughes, P. C. (1978). Flourescent lighting: A purported source of hyperactive behavior. Journal of Abnormal Child Psychology, 6:285-289.

O'Leary, K. D., Vivian, D., Nisi, C. (1985). Hyperactivity in Italy. *Journal of Abnormal Child Psychology,* 13:485-500.

Olweus, D. (1979). Stability and aggressive reaction patterns in males: A review. *Psychological Bulletin,* 86:852-875.

Omenn, G. S. (1973). Genetic issues in the syndrome of minimal brain dysfunction. *Seminars in Psychiatry,* 5:5-17.

Ott, J. N. (1968). Responses of psychological and physiological functions to environmental radiation stress: Part II. *Journal of Learning Disabilities,* 1:348-354.

Ott, J. N. (1976). Influence of flourescent lights on hyperactivity and learning disabilities. *Journal of Learning Disabilities,* 9:417-422.

Ottenbacher, K. J., Cooper, M. M. (1983). Drug treatment of hyperactivity in children. *Developmental Medicine and Child Neurology,* 25:358-366.

Orvaschel, H., Sholomskas, D., Weissman, M. M. (1980). The assessment of psychopathology and behavioral problems in children: A review of scales suitable for epidemiological and clinical research (1967-1979). Rockville, MD: National Institute of Mental Health.

Paradise, J. L., Rogers, K. D. (1986). On otitis media, child development and tympanostomy tubes: New answers or old questions? *Pediatrics*, 77:88-92.

Paternite, C. E., Loney, J. (1980). Childhood hyperkinesis: Relationships between symptomatology and home environment. In Whalen, C. K., Henker, B. (Eds.), *Hyperactive children: The social ecology of identification and treatment* (pp. 105-141). New York: Academic Press.

Paternite, C. E., Loney, J., Langhorne, J. E. (1976). Relationships between symptomatology and SES-related factors in hyperkinetic/MBD boys. *American Journal of Orthopsychiatry*, 46:291-301.

Patterson, G. R., Jones, R., Whittier, J., Wright, M. A. (1965). A behavior modification technique for the hyperactive child. *Behavior Research and Therapy*, 2:217-226.

Pauls, D. L., Leckman, J. F. (1986). The interaction of Gilles de la Tourette syndrome and associated behaviors: Evidence for autosomal dominant transmission. *New England Journal of Medicine*, 315:993-997.

Pauls, D. L., Shaywitz, S. E., Kramer, P. L., Shaywitz, B. A., Cohen, D. J. (1983). Demonstration of vertical transmission of attention deficit disorder. *Annals of Neurology*, 14:363.

Pelham, W. E. (1983). The effects of psychostimulants on academic achievement in hyperactive and learning-disabled children. *Thalamus: (International Academy for Research in Learning Disabilities Journal)*, 3:1-47.

Pelham, W. E., Bender, M. E. (1982). Peer relationships in hyperactive children: Description and treatment. In Gadow, K., Biale, E. (Eds.), *Advances in Learning and Behavioral Disabilities* (pp. 365-436). New York: JAI Press.

Pelham, W. E., Milich, R. (1984). Peer relations in children with hyperactivity/attention deficit disorder. *Journal of Learning Disabilities*, 17:560-567.

Pelham, W. E., Ross, A. O. (1977). Selective attention in children with reading problems: A developmental study of incidental learning. *Journal of Abnormal Child Psychology*, 5:1-8.

Pelham, W. E., Schnedler, R. W., Bologna, N. C., Contreras, A. (1980). Behavioral and stimulant treatment of hyperactive children: A therapy study with methylphenidate probes in a within-subject design. *Journal of Applied Behavior Analysis*, 13:221-236.

Pelham, W. E. Jr., Murphy, H. A. (1986). Attention deficit and conduct disorders. In Hersen, M. (Ed.), *Pharmacological and behavioral treatment: An integrative approach* (pp. 108-148). New York: Wiley.

Peloquin, L. J., Klorman, R. (1986). Effects of methylphenidate on normal children's mood, event-related potentials, and performance in memory scanning and vigilance. *Journal of Abnormal Psychology*, 95:88-98.

Pennington, B. F., Smith, S. D. (1983). Genetic influences on learning disabilities and speech and language disorders. *Child Development*, 54:369-387.

Peters, J. E., Romine, J. S., Dykman, R. A. (1975). A special neurological examination of children with learning disabilities. *Developmental Medicine and Child Neurology*, 175:63-78.

Piers, E. V., Harris, D. B. (1964). Age and other correlates of self-concept in children. *Journal of Educational Psychology*, 55:91-95.

Plomin, R., Foch, T. T. (1981). Hyperactivity and pediatrician diagnoses, parental ratings, specific cognitive abilities, and laboratory measures. *Journal of Abnormal Child Psychology*, 9:55-64.

Polatajko, H. J. (1985). A critical look at vestibular dysfunction in learning-disabled children. *Developmental Medicine and Child Neurology*, 27:283-292.

Porrino, L. J., Rapoport, J. L., Behar, D., Sceery, W., Ismond, D. R., Bunney, W. E. Jr. (1983). A naturalistic assessment of the motor activity of hyperactive boys: I. Comparison with normal controls. *Archives of General Psychiatry*, 40:681-693.

Prechtl, H., Dijkstra, J. (1960). Neurological diagnoses of cerebral injury in the newborn. In tenBerge, B. (Ed.), *Prenatal care*. Groningen, Netherland: Noordhoff.

Prechtl, H. F. R., Stemmer, C. J. (1962). The choreiform syndrome. *Developmental Medicine and Child Neurology*, 4:119-127.

Prinz, R. J., Myers, D. R., Holden, E. W., Tarnowski, J. J., Roberts, W. A. (1983). Mental disturbance and child problems: A cautionary note regarding hyperactive children. *Journal of Abnormal Child Psychology*, 11:393-399.

Public Law 94-142. Education for All Handicapped Children Act, S.6, 94th Congress [Sec 613 (a) (4)], 1st Session, June, 1975, Report No. 94-168.

Quart, E. J., Cruickshank, W. M., Sarnaik, A. (1985). Prior history of learning disabilities in Reye's syndrome survivors. *Journal of Learning Disabilities*, 18:345-349.

Quay, H. C. (1979). Classification. In Quay, H. C., Werry, J. S. (Eds.), *Psychopathological disorders of childhood* (pp. 1-42). New York: Wiley.

Quay, H. C. (1983). A dimensional approach to behavior disorder: The revised behavior problem checklist. *School Psychology Review*, 12:244-249.

Quay, H. C., Peterson, D. R. (1983). *Interim manual for the revised behavior problem checklist*. Coral Gables; University of Miami.

Quay, H. C., Peterson, D. R. (1983). Appendix I to the *Interim manual for the revised behavior problem checklist*. University of Miami. Unpublished manuscript.

Quinn, P., Rapoport, J. (1974). Minor physical anomalies and neurologic status in hyperactive boys. *Pediatrics*, 53:742-747.

Rapoport, J. L., Benoit, M. (1975). The relation of direct home observations to the clinic evaluation of hyperactive school age boys. *Journal of Child Psychology and Psychiatry*, 16:141-147.

Rapoport, J. L., Buchsbaum, M. S., Zohn, T. P., Weingartner, H., Ludlow, C., Mikkelson, E. J. (1978). Dextroamphetamine: Cognitive and behavioral effects in normal prepubertal boys. *Science*, 199:560-563.

Rapoport, J. L., Ferguson, H. B. (1981). Biological validation of the hyperkinetic syndrome. *Developmental Medicine and Child Neurology*, 23:667-682.

Rapoport, J. L., Mikkelsen, E. J., Ebert, M. H., Brown, G. L., Weise, V. L., Kopin, I. J. (1978). Urinary catecholamine and amphetamine excretion in hyperactive and normal boys. *Journal of Neurology and Mental Disease*, 166:731-737.

Rapoport, J. L., Quinn, P. O., Bradbard, G., Riddle, D., Brooks, E. (1974). Imipramine and methylphenidate treatments of hyperactive boys. *Archives of General Psychiatry*, 30:789-793.

Rapoport, J. L., Quinn, P. O., Burg, C., Bartley, L. (1979). Can hyperactives be identified in infancy? In Trites, R. L. (Ed.), *Hyperactivity in children: Etiology, measurement, and treatment implications* (pp. 103-116). Baltimore: University Park Press.

Rapoport, J. L., Quinn, P. O., Scribanic, N., Murphy, D. L. (1974). Platelet serotonin in hyperactive school age boys. *British Journal of Psychiatry*, 125:138-140.

Rapoport, J. L., Zametkin, A. (1980). Attention deficit disorder. *Psychiatric Clinics of North America*, 3:425-441.

Rapport, M. D., Stoner, G., DuPaul, G. J., Birmingham, B. K., Tucker, S. (1985). Methylphenidate in hyperactive children: Differential effects of dose on academic, learning and social behavior. *Journal of Abnormal Child Psychology*, 13:227-244.

Rapport, M. D., Tucker, S. B., DuPaul, G. J., Merlo, M., Stoner, G. (1986). Hyperactivity and frustration: The influence of control over and size of rewards in delaying gratification. *Journal of Abnormal Child Psychology*, 14:191-204.

Raskin, L. A., Shaywitz, S. E., Shaywitz, B. A., Anderson, G. M., Cohen, D. J. (1984). Neurochemical correlates of attention deficit disorder. *Pediatric Clinics of North America*, 31:387-396.

Realmuto, G. M., Garfinkel, B. D., Tuchman, M., Tsai, M. Y., Chang, P. N., Fisch, R. O., Shapiro, S. (1986). Psychiatric diagnosis and behavioral characteristics of phenylketonuric children. *Journal of Nervous and Mental Disease*, 174:536-540.

Reichard, C. C., Elder, S. T. (1977). The effects of caffeine on reaction time in hyperkinetic and normal children. *American Journal of Psychiatry*, 134:144-148.

Reynolds, E. M. (1983). Mental effects of antiepileptic medication: A review. *Epilepsia*, 24 (Suppl 2):S85-S95.

Richman, N., Stevenson, J. S., Graham, P. J. (1982). *Preschool to school: A behavioral study*. London: Academic Press.

Riddle, K. D., Rapoport, J. L. (1976). A 2 year followup of 72 hyperactive boys. *Journal of Nervous and Mental Disease*, 162: 126-134.

Riddle, M. A., Leckman, J. F., Cohen, D. J., Anderson, M., Ort, S. I., Caruso, K. A., Shaywitz, B. A. (1986). Assessment of central dopaminergic function using plasma-free homovanillic acid after debrisoquin administration. *Journal of Neural Transmission*, 67:31-43.

Rie, H., Rie, E., Stewart, S., Ambuel, J. (1976). Effects of ritalin on underachieving children: A replication. *American Journal of Orthopsychiatry*, 46:311-313.

Rie, H., Rie, E., Stewart, S., Ambuel, J. (1976). Effects of methylphenidate on underachieving children. *Journal of Consulting and Clinical Psychology*, 44:250-260.

Robinson, N. M., Robinson, H. B. (1965). A follow-up study of children of low birthweight and control children at school age. *Pediatrics*, 35:425-433.

Rosen, L. A., O'Leary, S. G., Conway, G. (In press). The withdrawal of stimulant medication for hyperactivity: Overcoming detrimental attributions. *Behavior Therapy*.

Rosenberger, P., Hier, D. (1980). Cerebral asymmetry and verbal intellectual deficits. *Annals of Neurology*, 8:300-304.

Rosenthal, R. H., Allen, T. W. (1978). An examination of attention, arousal, and learning dysfunctions of hyperkinetic children. *Psychological Bulletin*, 85:689-715.

Ross, A. L. (1976). *Psychological aspects of learning disabilities and reading disorders*. New York: McGraw-Hill.

Ross, A. O., Pelham, W. E. (1981). Child psychopathology. *Annual Review of Psychology*, 32:243-78.

Ross, D. M., Ross, S. A. (1982). *Hyperactivity: Research, theory and action*. Wiley: New York.

Rosvold, H. E., Mirsky, A. F., Saranson, I., Bransome, E. D., Beck, L. H. (1956). A continuous performance test of brain damage. *Journal of Consulting Psychology*, 20:343-350.

Routh, D. K. (1978). Hyperactivity. In Magrab, P. R. (Ed.), *Psychological management of pediatric problems*. Baltimore: University Park Press.

Routh, D. K. (1980). Developmental and social aspects of hyperactivity. In Whalen, C. K., Henker, B. (Eds.), *Hyperactive children: The social ecology of identification and treatment* (pp. 55-73). New York: Academic Press.

Routh, D. K., Schroeder, C. S. (1976). Standardized playroom measures as indices of hyperactivity. *Journal of Abnormal Child Psychology*, 4(2):199-207.

Roy, P. (1983). Is continuity enough? Substitute care and socialization. Paper presented at the Spring Scientific Meeting, Child Adolescent Specialist Section, Royal College of Psychiatrists, London.

Rubin, K. H., Clark, M. L. (1983). Preschool teachers' ratings of behavioral problems: Observational, sociometric, and social-cognitive correlates. *Journal of Abnormal Child Psychology*, 11:273-286.

Rubin, R. A., Balow, B. (1977). Perinatal influences on the behavior and learning problems in children. In Lahey, B., Kazdin, A. E. (Eds.), *Advances in child clinical psychology*. New York: Plenum.

Rubin, R, A., Rosenblatt, C., Balow, B. (1973). Psychological and educational sequelae of prematurity. *Pediatrics*, 52:352-363.

Rudel, R. G., Helfgott, E. (1984). Effect of piracetam on verbal memory of dyslexic boys. *Journal of the American Academy of Child Psychiatry*, 23:695-699.

Rutter, M. (1970). Psychological development: Predictions from infancy. *Journal of Child Psychology and Psychiatry*, 11:49-62.

Rutter, M. (1977). Classification. In Rutter, M., Hersov, L. (Eds.), *Child psychiatry: Modern approaches* (pp. 359-384). London: Blackwell Scientific Publications.

Rutter, M. (1982). Temperament: concepts, issues, and problems. *In Symposium 89, Ciba Foundation: Temperamental differences in infants and young children* (pp. 1-16). London: Pitman Books.

Rutter, M., Chadwick, O., Shaffer, D. (1983). Head injury. In Rutter, M. (Ed.), *Developmental neuropsychiatry* (pp. 83-111). New York: Guilford Press.

Rutter, M., Graham, P., Birch, H. (1966). Interrelations between the choreiform syndrome, reading disability and psychiatric disorder in children of 8-11 years. *Developmental Medicine and Child Neurology*, 8:149-159.

Rutter, M., Graham, P., Yule, W. (1970). *A neuropsychiatric study in childhood: Clinics in developmental medicine*. London: SIMP with Wm Heinemann.

Rutter, M., Korn, S., Birch, M. G. (1963). Genetic and environmental factors in the development of "primary reaction patterns." *British Journal of Social and Clinical Psychology*, 2:161-173.

Safer, D. J. (1973). A familial factor in minimal brain dysfunction. *Behavior Genetics*, 3:175-186.

Safer, D. J., Allen, R. D. (1976). *Hyperactive children: Diagnosis and management*. Baltimore: University Park Press.

Sallee, F., Stiller, R., Perel, J., Bates, T. (1985). Oral pemoline kinetics in hyperactive children. *Clinical Pharmacology Therapy*, 37:606-609.

Salzarulo, P., Chevalier, A. (1983). Sleep problems in children and their relationship with early disturbances of the waking-sleeping rhythms. *Sleep*, 6:47-51.

Sameroff, A. J., Chandler, M. J. (1975). Reproductive risk and the continuum of caretaking casualty. In Horowitz, F. D., Heterington, M., Scarr-Salapatek, S., Siegel, G. (Eds.), *Review of child development research* (pp. 187-244). Chicago: University of Chicago Press.

Sandberg, S. T., Rutter, M., Taylor, E. (1978). Hyperkinetic disorder in psychiatric clinic attenders. *Developmental Medicine and Child Neurology*, 20:279-299.

Sandberg, S. T., Wieselberg, M., Shaffer, D. (1980). Hyperkinetic and conduct problem children in a primary school population: Some epidemiological considerations. *Journal of Child Psychology and Psychiatry*, 21:293-311.

Sandoval, J. (1977). The measurement of hyperactive syndrome in children. *Review of Educational Research*, 47:293-318.

Sandoval, J., Lambert, N. M. (1984-85). Hyperactive and learning disabled children: Who gets help? *Journal of Special Education*, 18:495-503.

Satterfield, J., Hoppe, C., Schell, A. (1982). A prospective study of delinquency in 110 adolescent boys with attention deficit disorder and 88 normal adolescent boys. *American Journal of Psychiatry*, 139:795-798.

Satterfield, J. H., Satterfield, B. T., Cantwell, D. P. (1980). Multimodality treatment: A two-year evaluation of 61 hyperactive boys. *Archives of General Psychiatry*, 37:915-918.

Satterfield, J. H., Satterfield, B. T., Cantwell, D. P. (1981). Three year multimodality treatment study of 100 hyperactive boys. *Journal of Pediatrics*, 98:650-655.

Satterfield, J. M., Cantwell, D. P., Lesser, L. I. (1972). Physiological studies of the hyperkinetic child. *American Journal of Psychiatry*, 128:1418-1424.

Satterfield, J. M., Schell, A. M., Backs, R. W., Hidaka, K. C. (1984). A cross-section and longitudinal study of age effect of electrophysiological measures in hyperactive and normal children. *Biological Psychology*, 19:973-990.

Scarr, S. (1966). Genetic factors in activity motivation. *Child Development*, 37:663-673.

Schachar, R., Rutter, M., Smith, A. (1981). The characteristics of situationally and pervasively hyperactive children: Implications for syndrome definition. *Journal of Child Psychology and Psychiatry*, 22:375-392.

Schechter, M. D., Timmons, G. D. (1985). Objectively measured hyperactivity: II. Caffeine and amphetamine effects. *Journal of Clinical Pharmacology*, 25:276-280.

Schell, R. M., Pelham, W. E., Bender, M. E., Andree, J. A., Law, T., Robbins, F. R. (1986). The concurrent assessment of behavioral and psychostimulant interventions: A controlled case study. *Behavioral Assessment*, 8:373-384.

Schleifer, M., Weiss, G., Cohen, N. J., Elman, M., Cvejic, H., Kruger, E. (1975). Hyperactivity in preschoolers and the effect of methylphenidate. *American Journal of Orthopsychiatry*, 45:38-50.

Schnackenberg, R. (1973). Caffeine as a substitute for schedule II stimulants in hyperactive children. *American Journal of Psychiatry*, 130:796-798.

Schneirla, T. C. (1957). The concept of development in comparative psychology. In Harris, D. B. (Ed.), *The concept of development*. Minneapolis: University of Minnesota Press.

Schulman, J. L., Clarinda, S. M. (1964). The effect of promazine on the activity level of retarded children. *Pediatrics*, 33:271-285.

Schulman, J. L., Reisman, J. M. (1969). An objective measure of hyperactivity. *American Journal of Mental Deficiency*, 64: 455-456.

Sebrechts, M. M., Shaywitz, S. E., Shaywitz, B. A., Jatlow, P., Anderson, G. M., Cohen, D. J. (1986). Components of attention, methylphenidate dosage, and blood levels in children with attention deficit disorder. *Pediatrics*, 77:222-228.

Shaffer, D. (1980). An approach to the validation of clinical syndromes in childhood. In Salzinger, S., Antrobus, J., Glick, J. (Eds.), *The ecosystem of the "sick" child* (pp. 31-45). London: Academic Press.

Shaffer, D., Chadwick, O., Rutter, M. (1975). Psychiatric outcome of localized head injury in children. In Porter, R., FitzSimmons, D. W. (Eds.), *Outcome of severe damage to the central nervous system*. Amsterdam, Holland: Elsevier/Exceptional Medicine.

Shaffer, D., Greenhill, L. (1979). A critical note on the predictive validity of "the hyperkinetic syndrome." *Journal of Child Psychology and Psychiatry and Allied Disciplines*, 20:61-72.

Shaffer, D., McNamara, N., Pincis, H. H. (1974). Controlled observations on patterns of activity, attention and impulsivity in brain-damaged and psychiatrically disturbed boys. *Psychological Medicine*, 4:4-18.

Shaffer, D., Schonfeld, I., O'Connor, P. A., Stokman, C., Trautman, P., Shafer, S., Ng, S. (1985). Neurological soft signs: Their relationship to psychiatric disorder and intelligence in childhood and adolescence. *Archives of General Psychiatry*, 42:342-351.

Shankweiler, D., Liberman, I. Y., Mann, S. L., Fowler, L. A., Fisher, F. W. (1979). The speech code and learning to read: Human learning and memory. *Journal of Experimental Psychology*, 5:531-545.

Shapira, Y., Meagan, C., Statter, M., Ben-Zvi, A. (1983). Minimal brain dysfunction: A possible late sequelae of infantile transient folic acid deficiency. *Journal of Pediatrics*, 103:671-672.

Shapiro, S. K., Garfinkel, B. D. (1986). The occurrence of behavior disorders in children: The interdependence of attention deficit disorder and conduct disorder. *Journal of the American Academy of Child Psychiatry*, 25:809-819.

Shaywitz, B. A., Cohen, D. J., Bowers, M. B. (1977). CSF monoamine metabolites in children with minimal brain dysfunction: Evidence for alteration of brain dopamine. *Journal of Pediatrics*, 90:67-71.

Shaywitz, B. A., Klopper, J. H., Yager, R. D., Gordon, J. W. (1976). Paradoxical response to amphetamine in developing rats treated with 6-hydroxydopamine. *Nature*, 261:153-55.

Shaywitz, B. A., Shaywitz, S. E., Byrne, T., Cohen, D. J., Rothman, S. (1983). Attention deficit disorder: Quantitative analysis of CT. *Neurology*, 33:1500-1503.

Shaywitz, B. A., Shaywitz, S. E., Gillespie, S. M., Anderson, G. M., Riddle, M. A., Leckman, J. F., Cohen, D. J., Jatlow, P. (1986). Effects of methylphenidate during debrisoquin loading on plasma and urinary concentrations of monoamines and their metabolites in children with attention deficit disorder. *Annals of Neurology*, 20:416.

Shaywitz, B. A., Yager, R. D., Klopper, J. H. (1976). Selective brain dopamine depletion in developing rats. An experimental model of minimal brain dysfunction. *Science*, 191:305-308.

Shaywitz, S. (1982). Assessment of brain function in clinical pediatric research: Behavioral and biological strategies. *Schizophrenia Bulletin*, 8:205-235.

Shaywitz, S. E. (1986). Prevalence of Attentional Deficits in an Epidemiologic Sample of School Children (unpublished raw data).

Shaywitz, S. E. (1986). Early recognition of vulnerability-EREV. Technical report to the Connecticut State Department of Education.

Shaywitz, S. E., Cohen, D. J., Shaywitz, B. A. (1980). Behavior and learning difficulties in children of normal intelligence born to alcoholic mothers. *Journal of Pediatrics*, 96:978-982.

Shaywitz, S. E., Hunt, R. D., Jatlow, P., Cohen, D. J., Young, J. G., Pierce, R. N., Anderson, G. M., Shaywitz, B. A. (1982). Psychopharmacology of attention deficit disorder: Pharmacokinetic, neuroendocrine, and behavioral measures following acute and chronic treatment with methylphenidate. *Pediatrics*, 669:688-694.

Shaywitz, S. E., Schnell, C., Shaywitz, B. A., Towle, V. R. (1986). Yale Children's Inventory (YCI): An instrument to assess children with attentional deficits and learning disabilities I. Scale development and psychometric properties. *Journal of Abnormal Child Psychology,* 14:347-364.

Shaywitz, S. E., Sebrechts, M. H., Jatlow, P., Anderson, G. M., Young, J. G., Cohen, D. J., Shaywitz, B. A. (1982). Clinical response to methylphenidate (MPH) is related to plasma prolactin and growth hormone levels: Support for catecholaminergic influences in attention deficit disorder (ADD). *Annals of Neurology,* 12:196.

Shaywitz, S. E., Shaywitz, B. A., Jamner, A. H., Gillespie, S. M. (1986). Diagnosis of attention deficit disorder: Development and validation of a diagnostic rule utilizing the Yale Children's Inventory. *Annals of Neurology,* 20:415.

Shaywitz, S. E., Shaywitz, B. A., Jamner, A. H., Towle, V. R., Barnes, M. A. (1986c). Heterogeneity within the gifted: Boys with higher IQ exhibit increased activity, impulsivity, and parenting problems. *Annals of Neurology,* 20:415.

Shaywitz, S. E., Shaywitz, B. A., McGraw, K., Groll, S. (1984). Current status of the neuromaturational examination as an index of learning disability. *Journal of Pediatrics,* 104:819-825.

Shaywitz, S. E., Shaywitz, B. A., Schnell, C., Towle, V. R. (in press). Yale Children's Inventory (YCI): An instrument to assess children with attentional deficits and learning disabilities. II. Concurrent and predictive validity. *Pediatrics,*

Shekim, W. O., DeKirmenjian, H., Chapel, J. L. (1977). Urinary catecholamine metabolites in hyperkinetic boys treated with d-amphetamine. *American Journal of Psychiatry,* 134:1276-1279.

Shekim, W. O., DeKirmenjian, H., Chapel, J. L. (1979). Urinary MHPG excretion in minimal brain dysfunction and its modification of d-amphetamine. *American Journal of Psychiatry,* 136:667-671.

Shekim, W. O., Javaid, J., Dans, J. M., Bylund, D. B. (1983). Urinary MHPG and HVA excretion in boys with attention deficit disorder and hyperactivity treated with d-amphetamine. *Biological Psychiatry,* 18:707-714.

Shekim, W. O., Kashani, J., Beck, N., Cantwell, D. P., Martin, J., Rosenberg, J., Costello, A. (1985). The prevalence of attention deficit disorders in a rural midwestern community sample of nine-year-old children. *Journal of the American Academy of Child Psychiatry,* 24:765-770.

Shetty, T., Chase, T. N. (1976). Central monoamines and hyperactivity of childhood. *Neurology,* 26:1000-1002.

Shleifer, M., Weiss, G., Cohen, W., Elmen, M., Cvejic, H., Kruger, E. (1975). Hyperactivity in preschoolers and the effect of methylphenidate. *American Journal of Orthopsychiatry,* 45:38-50.

Silver, L. B. (1981). The relationship between learning disabilities, hyperactivity, distractibility and behavioral problems. A clinical analysis. *Journal of the American Academy of Child Psychiatry,* 20:385-397.

Silver, L. B. (1986). Controversial approaches to treating learning disabilities and attention deficit disorder. *Learning Disabilities,* 140:1045-1052.

Skinner, H. A. (1981). Toward the integration of classification theory and methods. *Journal of Abnormal Psychology,* 90:68-87.

Sleator, E. K., Ullmann, R. K. (1981). Can the physician diagnose hyperactivity in the office? *Pediatrics,* 67:13-17.

Smith, C. R. (1986). The future of the LD field: Intervention approaches. *Journal of Learning Disabilities,* 19:461-472.

Sparrow, S. S., Fletcher, J. M., Cicchetti, D. V. (1986). Psychological assessment of children. In Michaels, R., Cavenar, J. D. Jr. (Eds.), *Psychiatry* (pp. 1-12). Philadelphia: J. B. Lippincott.

Sparrow, S. S., Zigler, E. (1978). An evaluation of patterning treatment for retarded children. *Pediatrics,* 62:137-150.

Spitzer, R. L., Williams, J. B. W. (1980). Classification of mental disorders and DSM-III. In Freedman, A. M., Sadock, B. J. (Eds.), *Comprehensive textbook of psychiatry.* Baltimore: Williams and Wilkins.

Sprague, R., Cohen, M., Eichlseder, W. (1977). Are there hyperactive children in Europe and the South Pacific? Paper presented to the American Psychological Association, San Francisco.

Sprague, R. L., Sleator, (1977). Methylphenidate in hyperkinetic children: Differences in dose effects on learning and social behavior. *Science*, 198:1274-1276.

Sprague, R. L., Ullman, R. K., Sleator, E. K. (1981). Characteristics of subjects selected by using a cut-off point on the Conners Teacher Rating Scale. Unpublished manuscript. University of Illinois.

Sproles, E. T. III, Azerrad, J., Williamson, C., Merrill, R. E. (1969). Meningitis due to hemophilus influenzae: Long-term sequalae. *Journal of Pediatrics*, 75:782-788.

Stephens, R. S., Pelham, W. E., Skinner, R. (1984). State-dependent and main effects of methylphenidate and pemoline on paired-associate learning and spelling in hyperactive children. *Journal of Consulting and Clinical Psychology*, 52:104-113.

Sternberg, R. J. (1984). The Kaufman Assessment Battery for Children: An information processing analysis and critique. *Journal of Special Education*, 18:269-279.

Stevens, T. M., Kupst, M. J., Suran, B. G., Schulman, J. L. (1978). Activity level: A comparison between actometer scores and observer ratings. *Journal of Abnormal Child Psychology*, 6:163-173.

Stewart, M. A. (1970). Hyperactive children. *Scientific American*, 222:94-99.

Stewart, M. A., Cummings, C., Singer, S., deBlois, C. S. (1981). The overlap between hyperactive and unsocialized aggressive children. *Journal of Child Psychology and Psychiatry*, 22:35-45.

Stewart, M. A., deBlois, C. S., Cummings, C. (1980). Psychiatric disorder in the parents of hyperactive boys and those with conduct disorder. *Journal of Child Psychology and Psychiatry*, 21:283-292.

Stewart, M. A., Pitts, F. N. Jr., Craig, A. G., Dieruf, W. (1966). The hyperactive child syndrome. *American Journal of Orthopsychiatry*, 36:861-867.

Stewart, M. A., Thach, B. T., Freidin, M. R. (1970). Accidental poisoning and the hyperactive child syndrome. *Diseases of the Nervous System*, 31:403-407.

Still, G. F. (1902). The Coulstonian Lectures on some abnormal physical conditions in children. *Lancet*, 1:1008-12, 1077-82, 1163-68.

Stores, G., Hart, J. (1976). Reading skills in children with generalized or focal epilepsy. *Developmental Medicine and Child Neurology*, 18:705-716.

Stott, D. H. (1966). A general test of motor impairment for children. *Child Neurology*, 8:523-531.

Strauss, A. A., Lehtinen, L. E. (1947). *Psychopathology and education in the brain-injured child.* New York: Grune and Stratton.

Streissguth, A. P., Herman, C., Smith, D. W. (1978). Intelligence, behavior and dysmorphogenesis in the fetal alcohol syndrome: A report on 20 clinical cases. *Journal of Pediatrics*, 92:363-367.

Studdert-Kennedy, M., Shankweiler, D. (1970). Hemispheric specialization for speech perception. *Journal of the Acoustical Society of America*, 48:579-594.

Swann, A. C., Maas, J. W., Hattox, S. E., Landis, D. H. (1980). Catecholamine metabolites in human plasma as indices of brain function: Effects of debrisoquin. *Life Sciences*, 27:1857-1861.

Swanson, J., Kinsbourne, M., Roberts, W., Zucker, M. A. (1978). Time-response analysis of the effect of stimulant medication on the learning disability of children referred for hyperactivity. *Pediatrics*, 61:21-29.

Swanson, J. M. (1985). Measures of cognitive functioning appropriate for use in pediatric psychopharmacology research studies. *Psychopharmacology Bulletin*, 21:887-890.

Swanson, J. M., Kinsbourne, M. (1976). Stimulant-related state-dependent learning in hyperactive children. *Science*, 192:1354-1357.

Swanson, J. M., Sandman, C. A., Deutsch, C., Baren, M. (1983). Methylphenidate hydrochloride given with or before breakfast: I. Behavioral, cognitive, and electrophysiologic effects. *Pediatrics*, 72:49-55.

Sykes, D. H., Douglas, V. I., Morgenstern, G. (1973). Sustained attention in hyperactive children. *Journal of Child Psychology and Psychiatry*, 14:213-220.

Tant, J. L., Douglas, V. I. (1982). Problem solving in hyperactive, normal and reading disabled boys. *Journal of Abnormal Child Psychology*, 10:285-306.

Taylor, E. A. (1986). Attention deficit. In Taylor, E. A. (Ed.), *The overactive child* (pp. 73-106). Philadelphia: Lippincott JB, Co.

Taylor, H. G., Michaels, R. H., Mazur, P. M., Bauer, R. E., Liden, C. B. (1984). Intellectual, neuropsychological, and achievement outcomes in children six to eight years after recovery from haemophilis influenzae meningitis. *Pediatrics*, 74:198-205.

Teele, D. W., Klein, J. O., Rosner, B. A. (1984). Otitis media with effusion during the first three years of life and development of speech and language. *Pediatrics*, 74:282-287.

Thomas, A., Chess, S. (1977). *Temperament and development*. New York; Brunner/Mazel.

Thomas, A., Chess, S., Birch, H. G. (1968). *Temperament and behavior disorders in children*. New York: New York University Press.

Thompson, P., Huppert, F. A., Trimble, M. (1981). Phenytoin and cognitive function: Effects on normal volunteers and implications for epilepsy. *British Journal of Clinical Psychology*, 20:155-162.

Thompson, P. J., Trimble, M. R. (1981). Further studies on anticonvulsant drugs and seizures. *Acta Neurologica Scandanavica*, 89:51-58.

Thompson, P. J., Trimble, M. R. (1982). Anticonvulsant drugs and cognitive functions. *Epilepsia*, 23:531-544.

Tizard, B., Hughes, J. (1978). The effect of early institutional rearing on the development of eight-year-old children. *Journal of Child Psychology and Psychiatry*, 19:99-118.

Tizard, B., Rees, J. (1974). A comparison of the effects of adoption, restoration to the natural mother and controlled institutionalization on the cognitive development of four-year-old children. *Child Development*, 45:92-99.

Torgersen, A. M., Kringlen, E. (1978). Genetic aspects of temperamental differences in infants, a study of same-sexed twins. *Journal of the American Academy of Child Psychology*, 17:433-444.

Torgesen, J. K. (1986). Learning disabilities theory: Its current state and future prospects. *Journal of Learning Disabilities*, 19:399-407.

Trites, R. L. (1979). Prevalence of hyperactivity in Ottawa, Canada. In Trites, R. L. (Ed.), Hyperactivity in children (pp. 29-52). Baltimore: University Park Press.

Trites, R. L., Blouin, A. G. A., Laprade, K. (1982). Factor analysis of the Conners Teacher Rating Scale based on a large normative sample. *Journal of Consulting and Clinical Psychology*, 50:615-623.

Trites, R. L., LaPrade, K. (1983). Evidence for an independent syndrome of hyperactivity. *Journal of Child Psychology and Psychiatry*, 24:573-586.

Ullmann, D. G., Berkley, R. A., Brown, H. W. (1978). The behavioral symptoms of hyperkinetic children who successfully respond to stimulant drug treatment. *American Journal of Orthopsychiatry*, 48:425-437.

Ullmann, R. K., Sleator, E. K., Sprague, R. L. (1984a). A new rating scale for diagnosis and monitoring of ADD children. *Psychopharmacology Bulletin*, 20:160-164.

Ullmann, R. K., Sleator, E. K., Sprague, R. L. (1984b). ADD children: Who is referred from the schools? *Psychopharmacology Bulletin*, 20: 308-312.

Ullmann, R. K., Sleator, E. K., Sprague, R. L. (1985). A change of mind: The Conners abbreviated rating scales reconsidered. *Journal of Abnormal Child Psychology*, 13:553-565.

Valenstein, E. S. (1986). *Great and desperate cures*. New York: Basic Books.

Vandenberg, S. G. (1962). The heredity abilities study: Heredity components in a psychological test battery. *American Journal of Human Genetics*, 14:220-237.

Varley, C. K., Trupin, E. W. (1983). Double-blind assessment of stimulant medication for attention deficit disorder: A model for clinical application. *American Journal of Orthopsychiatry*, 53:542-547.

Vellutino, F. (1979). *Dyslexia: Theory and research*. Cambridge; The MIT Press.

Vincent, J. P., Williams, B. J., Harris, G. E. Jr., Duval, G. C. (1981). Classroom observations of hyperactive children: A multiple validation study. In Gadow, K. D., Loney, J. (Eds.), *Psychological aspects of drug treatment for hyperactivity*. Boulder, CO: Westview Press.

Vissing, Y. M., Petersen, J. C. (1981). Taking laetrile: Conversion to medical deviance. *CA: A Cancer Journal for Clinicians, 31*:365-369.

Waber, D. P., Mann, M. B. (1985). Motor overflow and attentional processes in normal school-age children. *Developmental Medicine and Child Neurology, 27*:491-497.

Waldrop, M. F., Bell, R. Q., McLaughlin, B., Halverson, C. F. (1978). Newborn minor physical anomalies predict short attention span, peer aggression, and impulsivity at age 3. *Science, 199*:563-565.

Waldrop, M. F., Halverson, C. F. (1971). Minor physical anomalies and hyperactive behavior in young children. In Hellmuth, J. (Ed.), *Exceptional infant* (pp. 343-389). New York: Brunner/Mazel.

Ward, C. H., Beck, A. T., Mendelson, M., Mock, J. E., Erbaugh, J. K. (1962). Reasons for diagnostic disagreement. *Archives of General Psychiatry, 7*:198-205.

Weber, D. P., Mann, M. B., Merola, J. (1875). Motor overflow and attentional processes in normal school-age children. *Developmental Medicine and Child Neurology, 27*:491-497.

Weiner, G. (1968). Scholastic achievement at age 12-13 of prematurely born infants. *Journal of Special Education, 2*:237-250.

Weiss, G. (1985). Hyperactivity. Overview and new directions. *Psychiatric Clinics of North America, 8*:737-753.

Weiss, G., Hechtman, L. (1979). The hyperactive child syndrome. *Science, 205*:1348-1354.

Weiss, G., Hechtman, L., Milroy, T., Perlman, T. (1985). Psychiatric status of hyperactives as adults: A controlled prospective 15-year followup of 63 hyperactive children. *Journal of the American Academy of Child Psychiatry, 24*:211-220.

Weiss, G., Hechtman, L., Perlman, T. (1978). Hyperactives as young adults: School, employer and self-rating scales. *American Journal of Orthopsychiatry, 48*:438-445.

Weiss, G., Hechtman, L., Perlman, T., Hopkins, J., Wener, A. (1979). Hyperactives as young adults: A controlled prospective ten-year followup of 75 children. *Archives of General Psychiatry, 36*:675-681.

Weiss, G., Kruger, E., Danielson, U., Elman, M. (1975). Effects of long-term treatment of hyperactive children with methylphenidate. *Canadian Medical Association Journal, 112*:159-165.

Weiss, G., Minde, K., Douglas, V., Nemeth, E. (1971). Studies on the hyperactive child. *Archives of General Psychiatry, 24*:409-414.

Weissman, M. M., Myers, J. K. (1978). Affective disorders in a US urban community: The use of research diagnostic criteria in an epidemiological survey. *Archives of General Psychiatry, 35*:1304-1311.

Welner, Z., Welner, A., Stewart, M. A., Palkes, H., Wish, E. (1977). A controlled study of siblings of hyperactive children. *Journal of Nervous and Mental Disease, 165*:110-117.

Wender, E. H. (1986). The food additive-free diet in the treatment of behavior disorders: A review. *Journal of Developmental and Behavioral Pediatrics, 7*:35-42.

Wender, P. H. (1971). *Minimal brain dysfunction in children*. New York: Wiley.

Wender, P. H. (1973). Minimal brain dysfunction in children: Diagnosis and management. *Pediatric Clinics of North America, 20*, 187-202.

Werner, E., Bierman, J. M., French, F., Simonian, K., Connor, A., Smith, R. S., Campbell, M. (1968). Reproductive and environmental casualties: A report on the 10 year followup of the children of the Kauai pregnancy study. *Pediatrics, 42*:112-127.

Werner, E. E., Biermann, J. M., French, F. E. (1971). *The children of Kauai: A longitudinal study from the prenatal period to age ten*. Honolulu: University of Hawaii Press.

Werner, E. E., Smith, R. S. (1977). *Kauai's children came of age*. Honolulu: University of Hawaii Press.

Werner, H., Strauss, A. A. (1941). Pathology of the figure-background relation in the child. *Journal of Abnormal and Social Psychology, 36*:236-248.

Werry, J. (1968). Studies on the hyperactive child. IV. An empirical analysis of the minimal brain dysfunction syndrome. *Archives of General Psychiatry, 19*:9-16.

Werry, J., Hawthorne, D. (1976). Conners Teacher Questionnaire: Norms and validity. *Australian and New Zealand Journal of Psychiatry, 10*:257-262.

Werry, J. S. (1982). An overview of pediatric psychopharmacology. *Journal of the American Academy of Child Psychiatry, 21*:3-9.

Werry, J. S., Aman, M. G. (1976). The reliability and diagnostic validity of the physical and neurological examination for soft signs (PANESS). *Journal of Autism and Childhood Schizophrenia*, 6:253-263.

Werry, J. S., Minde, K., Guzman, K., Weiss, G., Dogan, K., Hoy, E. (1972). Studies on the hyperactive child. VII: Neurological studies compared to normal and neurotic children. *American Journal of Orthopsychiatry*, 42:441-451.

Werry, J. S., Quay, H. C. (1971). The prevalence of behavior symptoms in younger elementary school children. *American Journal of Orthopsychiatry*, 41:136-143.

Werry, J. S., Sprague, R. L. (1974). Methylphenidate in children-effect of dosage. *Australian and New Zealand Journal of Psychiatry*, 8:18-20.

Werry, J. S., Sprague, R. L., Cohen, M. N. (1975). Conners Teacher Rating Scale for use in drug studies with children: An empirical study. *Journal of Abnormal Child Psychology*, 3:217-229.

Werry, J. S., Weiss, G., Douglas, V. (1964). Studies on the hyperactive child: Some preliminary findings. *Canadian Psychiatric Association Journal*, 9:120-129.

Whalen, C. K. (1982). Hyperactivity, learning problems, and the attention deficit disorder. In Ollendick, T. H., Hersen, M. (Eds.), *Handbook of child psychopathology*. New York: Plenum Press.

Whalen, C. K., Collins, B. E., Henker, B., Alkus, S. R., Adams, D., Stapp, S. (1978). Behavior observations of hyperactive children and methylphenidate (Ritalin) effects in systematically structured classroom environments; Now you see them, now you don't. *Journal of Pediatric Psychology*, 3:177-184.

Whalen, C. K., Henker, B. (1976). Psychostimulants and children: A review and analysis. *Psychological Bulletin*, 83:1113-1130.

Whalen, C. K., Henker, B. (1984). Hyperactivity and the attention deficit disorders: Expanding frontiers. *Pediatric Clinics of North America*, 31:397-427.

Whalen, C. K., Henker, B., Collins, B. E., Finck, D., Dotemoto, S. (1979). A social ecology of hyperactive boys: Medication effects in structured classroom environments. *Journal of Applied Behavior Analysis*, 12:65-81.

Whalen, C. K., Henker, B., Collins, B. E., McAulliffe, S., Vaux, A. (1979). Peer interaction in structured communication task: Comparisons of normal and hyperactive boys and of methylphenidate (Ritalin) and placebo effects. *Child Development*, 50:388-401.

Whalen, C. K., Henker, B., Dotemoto, S. (1981). Teacher response to the methylphenidate (Ritalin) versus placebo status of hyperactive boys in the classroom. *Child Development*, 52:1005-1014.

Whalen, C. K., Henker, B., Dotemoto, S., Vaux, A., McAuliffe, S. (1981). Hyperactivity and methylphenidate: Peer interaction styles. In Gadow, K. D., Loney, J. (Eds.), *Psychosocial aspects of drug treatment for hyperactivity* (pp. 381-415). Boulder, Colorado: Westview Press.

Whalen, C. K., Henker, B., Finck, D. (1981). Medication effects in the classroom: Three naturalistic indicators. *Journal of Abnormal Child Psychology*, 9:419-433.

Whalen, C. K., Henker, B., Hinshaw, S. P. (1985). Cognitive-behavioral therapies for hyperactive children: Premises, problems and prospects. *Journal of Abnormal Child Psychology*, 13:391-410.

Whitehouse, D., Shah, U., Palmer, F. B. (1980). Comparison of sustained-release and standard methylphenidate in the treatment of minimal brain dysfunction. *Journal of Clinical Psychiatry*, 41:282-285.

Wikler, A., Dixon, J. F., Parker, J. B. Jr. (1970). Brain function in problem children and controls: Psychometric, neurological and electroencephalographic comparisons. *American Journal of Psychiatry*, 127:94-105.

Willerman, L. (1973). Activity level and hyperactivity in twins. *Child Development*, 44:288-293.

Wilsher, C., Akins, G., Manfield, P. (1985). Effect of piracetam on dyslexic's reading ability. *Journal of Learning Disabilities*, 18:19-25.

Wilsher, C. R., Milewski, (1983). Effects of piracetam on dyslexics' verbal conceptualizing ability. *Psychopharmacology Bulletin*, 19:3-4.

Winsberg, B. G., Kupietz, S. S., Sverd, J. (1982). Methylphenidate oral dose plasma concentrations and behavioral response in children. *Psychopharmacology,* 70:329-332.

Witelson, S. F. (1985). The brain connection: The corpus callosum is larger in left-handers. *Science,* 229:665-667.

Wolf, M. (1981). The word-retrieval process and reading in children with aphasia. In Nelson, K. (Ed.), *Children's language.* New York: Gardner Press.

Wolraich, M. L., Milich, R., Stumbo, P., Schulz, F. (1985). The effects of sucrose ingestion on the behavior of hyperactive boys. *Journal of Pediatrics,* 106:675-682.

Yarrow, I. J. (1964). Separation from parents during early childhood. *Development Research, Russell Sage Foundation. (Hoffman and Hoffman)* 11:89-136.

Yarrow, I. J. (1965). Theoretical implications of adoption research. In *Adoption research.* New York: Child Welfare League.

Yu-Cun, A., Yu-Feng, W. (1984). Urinary 3-methoxy-4-hydroxyphenylglycol sulfate excretion in seventy-three school children with minimal brain dysfunction syndrome. *Biological Psychiatry,* 19:861-870.

Yu-Cun, S., Yu-Feng, W., Xiao-Ling, Y. (1985). An epidemiological investigation of minimal brain dysfunction in six elementary schools in Beijing. *Journal of Child Psychology and Psychiatry,* 26:777-787.

Zametkin, A., Nordahl, T., Gross, M., Semple, W., Rapoport, J. L., Cohen, R. (1986). Brain metabolism in hyperactive parents of hyperactive children. American Academy of Child and Adolescent Psychiatry Annual Meeting, Abstract 23.

Zametkin, A., Rapoport, J. L., Murphy, D. L., Linnoila, M., Ismond, D. (1985). Treatment of hyperactive children with monoamine oxidase inhibitors. *Archives of General Psychiatry,* 42:962-966.

Zametkin, A. J., Karoum, F., Linnoila, M., Rapoport, J. L., Brown, G. L., Chuang, L. W., Wyatt, R. J. (1985). Stimulants, urinary catecholamines and indoleamines in hyperactivity: A comparison of methylphenidate and dextroamphetamine. *Archives of General Psychiatry,* 42:251-255.

Zametkin, A. J., Linnoila, M., Karoum, F., Sallee, R. (1986). Pemoline and urinary excretion of catecholamines and indoleamines in children with attention deficit disorder. *American Journal of Psychiatry,* 143:359-362.

Zametkin, A. J., Rapoport, J. L. (1986). The pathophysiology of attention deficit disorder with hyperactivity: A review. *Advances in Clinical Child Psychology,* 9:177-216.

Zametkin, A. J., Rapoport, J. L. (In press). The neuropharmacology of attention deficit disorder with hyperactivity: A review.

Zentall, S. (1975). Optimal stimulation as a theoretical basis of hyperactivity. *American Journal of Orthopsychiatry,* 45:550-563.

DISCUSSION

Carol K. Whalen

High Risk, But Also High Potential: The Plight and the Promise With Attention Deficit Hyperactivity Disorders

First, let me offer—for all of us—our sincere appreciation to Sally and Bennett Shaywitz. They have done an admirable job of gleaning the mounds of data that are accumulating on attention deficit disorder and integrating the numerous puzzle pieces in a meaningful and highly useful fashion. What I would like to do is highlight three broad concerns, first elaborating two important points made by the Shaywitzes, and then adding a third and perhaps controversial message that deserves consideration.

The first point is that children with attention deficit hyperactivity disorder are multiproblem children who need multimodal treatments. In almost every arena of daily life, these children experience, at least some of the time, confrontation or failure (Whalen and Henker, 1984). The majority have learning difficulties, serious behavior problems, social skill deficits, and problems regulating motivation and affect. They have difficulty controlling their own actions, are socially ostracized by peers, and are frequently in trouble with parents and teachers (Whalen and Henker, 1985). As you would expect, over time such adverse experiences take their toll, seriously circumscribing the child's opportunities for building self-esteem and positive perceptions of his own competence or efficacy.

To borrow an analogy from Scarr and Weinberg (1986), a nutritional model is more appropriate here, in many ways, than the more traditional medical model. In this context, the term *nutritional* has nothing to do with the additive-free or sugar-free diets advocated by Feingold and others. The term is, instead, a metaphor for conceptualizing the problems and needs of children with ADD.

There are at least four ways in which the nutritional metaphor applies. First, any healthy diet requires a balanced blend of diverse ingredients, and hyperactivity requires multiple interventions. An intervention diet targeted exclusively on building academic skills, enhancing social competence, improving self-control, or teaching parents effective management techniques will be inadequate. Hyperactive children's problems pervade diverse domains of functioning, and each problem interferes with optimal development in other areas. The effects of remedial education will be quite limited, for example, until the child learns to read the subtle social cues that signal appropriate responses in the classroom. And neither academic nor social skills training will succeed with a child unable to inhibit his initial impulses and regulate his emotional and motoric reactivity.

Our many contacts with desperate parents underscore the fact that there are few ongoing services for hyperactive children and their families, nor is there adequate coordination among those that are available. Hyperactive children tend to fall between the safety nets that are constructed, often in isolation, by the professions that serve these youngsters—education, medicine, and psychology (Henker and Whalen, 1980). Unfortunate historical developments and "turf problems" seem to prevent optimal communication and integration across disciplinary bounds. We need to build formal structures to bridge these gaps, structures and mechanisms that will probably require radical shifts in our service delivery system. (Dr. Swanson describes an ongoing multimodal program, illustrating the promise and the possibilities.)

A second facet of the nutritional model concerns individualization. Just as dietary vulnerabilities, needs, and proclivities are emphatically individual, there is also broad heterogeneity of skills, deficits, and needs within the group of children designated hyperactive or attention deficit disordered. Nutrients required by one child may be less useful or even contraindicated with another. Some children need intensive intervention to help them regulate aggression, while others may need to learn to modulate a vigorous and irrepressible style that often disrupts or dismays other people. Some need to learn how to tackle a task, while others need help protecting their attention until the task is completed. Some need to learn to recognize their own failures, while others might need antidotes against the debilitating effects of failures.

A third aspect of the nutrition metaphor is that management is a lifelong endeavor. There is no possibility of a "quick fix," no matter how scrumptious a meal or how masterful a 6-week treatment program. We have learned that, for many individuals, attention deficit disorder is a protracted condition, with needs and approaches changing as the individual progresses from one developmental phase to the next. We need treatments that endure if we are to have outcomes that endure.

A final ingredient of this nutritional model follows from these other points: Evaluation must be multidimensional, using nontraditional as well as traditional criteria. The disappointing long-term treatment outcomes of hyperactive children have taught us that it is not enough to focus on ratings and standard test scores. We need to assess a host of other facets, including goal orientation, response to challenge, self-perceived competence, problem-solving strategies, and the abilities to nurture intimacy and sustain friendships. We need to examine not only what the child is *doing,* but also what he is *thinking* and *feeling* about what he is doing, and about what is being done to him. Because of the potent impact that children with attention deficit disorder have on others, optimal treatment evaluations will span the child's social ecology, including a focus on classroom productivity and family harmony, as well as on the well-being of classmates and teachers, siblings and parents. These domains are, of course, much more difficult to measure than the more traditional areas, but this fact does not lessen the need to do so.

Multidimensional assessments are also required for monitoring inadvertent treatment effects. When we talk about medication toxicity, for example, we must keep alert to the possibilities of much more than growth retardation, tics, or specific decrements in cognitive performance. Treatment is a salient event, and children, like people in general, have a need to explain things that happen to them. What is the message of medication? Does the child view it as analogous to wearing glasses, understanding that the pills help but will not do the reading for him? Or does he see it as confirming a deficit that he is powerless to correct through his own efforts? Should cognitive self-regulation training begin before a medication trial so that a child will have an internal attributional anchor for the changes he and others notice? This type of sequential approach to treatment might encourage him to view improvements as under his own control, due to his developing competencies, rather than as dependent on a somewhat magical or mystical chemical process. All interventions—be they educational, psychological, or medical—convey messages, and a careful consideration of such potential emanative effects when presenting a therapeutic program to a child and his family can ensure that the implicit messages facilitate, rather than impede or counteract, positive outcomes (Whalen, Henker, and Hinshaw, 1985).

The other point made by the Shaywitzes that I would like to underscore is the value of studying the interactions between the child and the environment. The goodness-of-fit construct is an apt one. Hyperactivity does not reside in the child, and it certainly does not reside in the environment. We are talking about vulnerable children who are at serious risk for problem development. But these problems are expressed in a context rather than in a vacuum. The problems become worse in some settings and are not even noticeable in others.

This means that we have more than one avenue for change. We can change the child, but we can also change the environment. Parents and siblings can and certainly do learn to adjust. Academic tasks can be presented in many different ways, tailored to harness a child's strengths or to accommodate his weaknesses. Some classroom regimens seem to provoke problematic behaviors in hyperactive children, while others seem to diminish them.

Along these lines, research is needed to increase our understanding of differences among hyperactive children who seem to "outgrow" their problems, those who continue to have mild social and occupational difficulties, and those who may even adopt criminal lifestyles. The research mandate is for systematic studies of the natural histories, the lifelong careers, of people with attention deficit hyperactivity disorders. Longitudinal research is, of course, very difficult to conduct, particularly in these days of funding cutbacks. The followup studies by Dr. Weiss and her colleagues serve as exemplary models. But there are still many unanswered questions. What are the personal, family, and environmental attributes that distinguish those with good from those with poor outcomes? Is goodness of fit one of the critical ingredients for success, and if so, how is a good person-environment match achieved? Are there some as-yet unidentified children who were born with the same vulnerabilities but happened to be placed in different environments and never developed problems? Are there other children who would develop disabilities no matter what environments they encountered? These questions comprise an important research agenda for the future.

Although the goodness-of-fit notion is certainly appealing, we must also remember that it is applicable only within a bounded range. Environments are not infinitely elastic, and even if such infinite elasticity were a possibility, it is unlikely that it would be in the best interests of the hyperactive child. Learning to modulate one's own behavior in accord with situational cues and demands is a critical component of socialization. In other words, it is important that the demise of the "blame the child" thesis not be replaced by a "blame the family or the environment" stance that has merely shifted the target of victimization.

The third and final point is that children with attention deficit hyperactivity disorders are very high-risk youngsters, but they also have high potential. They are quite different from retarded or autistic or severely disabled youth. With varying types and amounts of help, they can become fully functional and productive individuals. The hyperactive child's problems are often described in terms of noncompliance, but we also know that noncompliance can be adaptive if it is thoughtful and modulated. Even the intensity that we hear so much about in a negative context has its positive aspects. Moreover, there may be a link between hyperactivity and giftedness, as the Shaywitzes suggest, and some individuals with attention deficit hyperactivity disorders may achieve a status alongside society's most creative and innovative contributors. The long-term data have been described as discouraging, but they also tell us that many hyperactive children do indeed make it. Our mandate is to discover why and how, so that we can increase the proportion who succeed. An equally important need is to ensure that our interventions, which are often designed to enhance manageability, do not stifle unique talents and creative styles.

In closing, the comprehensive review provided by the Shaywitzes makes it clear that hyperactive children have suffered from the luck of the draw—they are burdened by far more than an average share of problems. But we could also say that these youngsters are fortunate indeed, because their enigmatic styles continue to challenge and intrigue, to pique the curiosity of so many talented scientists and child specialists, including those who are here today.

REFERENCES

Henker, B., Whalen, C. K. (1980). The changing faces of hyperactivity: Retrospect and prospect. In Whalen, C. K., Henker, B. (Eds.), *Hyperactive children. The social ecology of identification and treatment* (pp. 321-363). New York: Academic Press.

Scarr, S., Weinberg, R. A. (1986). The early childhood enterprise: Care and education of the young. *American Psychologist,* 41:1140-1146.

Whalen, C. K., Henker, B. (1984). Hyperactivity and the attention deficit disorders: Expanding frontiers. *Pediatric Clinics of North America,* 31:397-427.

Whalen, C. K., Henker, B. (1985). The social worlds of hyperactive (ADDH) children. *Clinical Psychology Review,* 5:447-478.

Whalen, C. K., Henker, B., Hinshaw, S. P. (1985). Cognitive-behavioral therapies for hyperactive children: Premises, problems, and prospects. *Journal of Abnormal Child Psychology,* 13:391-410.

DISCUSSION

Gabrielle Weiss

Dr. Bennett Shaywitz has presented a thoughtful and comprehensive review of the growing literature on this syndrome. He has appropriately drawn our attention to the difficulties of defining the syndrome and the need to have improved methods of measurements without discarding the old ones. That would result in discontinuity of previous, current, and future research findings. He has also emphasized how ADD or ADDH children referred to psychiatrists, neurologists, pediatricians, or learning clinics may differ in the differential severity of the various symptoms of the syndrome and also in the associated symptoms. Those seen in child psychiatry clinics, for example, may have more oppositional and conduct problems, and those seen in learning clinics are likely to have more specific learning disabilities such as reading and language disorders and perhaps more severe or different kinds of attentional problems. That different professionals may be somewhat blind to the total spectrum of difficulties and see only "part of the elephant" is something very real and sheds light on some of the discrepancies of different research findings, depending on the referral base.

I choose five issues in Dr. Shaywitz's presentation for discussion.

THE TIP OF THE ICEBERG

That the referred children who are diagnosed as ADD or ADDH represent only the worst of the children with this disorder may be correct. However, identifying those children who have a less severe attentional deficit disorder (including possibly more girls) presents, I think, some difficulties.

Those referred are already quite numerous and are not yet well treated. By that, I mean that they frequently do not receive the comprehensive services they require. Yet they are the children who, because of severity and disruptive behavior, have the worst prognosis. I would like to see us begin to provide better services to those referred, before enlarging the group with children identified as having milder forms of the syndrome. The exception to this might be some girls who are severely "underachieving" in school as a result of severe attentional difficulties, since some of them can be helped and are at risk by virtue of their increasing academic failure over their school years.

If all children with attentional difficulties were identified, we would probably find not a diagnostically homogeneous group but rather a heterogeneous group of children, which might include 30-50 percent of all boys. My concern would be that the use of stimulants might increase from 3 percent of all school children (current figues) to a much higher percentage. I do not think this is desirable.

Dr. Shaywitz has drawn our attention to the need for homogenous subgroups of the syndrome for the purpose of research. I most certainly agree with him. However, speaking as a clinician with 25 years of experience with these children, I would like to suggest why this has been difficult to achieve. Firstly, multiple diagnoses are very common with disturbed children, and the child with a single diagnosis may be more rare than researchers think. Secondly, children are in the process of constant development as they mature, and this development is associated with change. A child who is oppositional (even meriting this diagnosis) at age 5 years may no longer have the diagnosis or oppositional symptoms 2 years later. The groups therefore may be relatively "homogeneous" at the start of a study but no longer so a few years later. In addition, a child who may be oppositional in a situation with a given teacher at about the time his parents are having marital difficulties would present as no longer oppositional when his parents' marriage improves or he starts with a new teacher. The exception to this relative instability is when a child with ADDH is severely aggressive by age 9 years or so. It is highly likely that the aggression will continue (severe aggression is a stable dimension) and affect outcome negatively.

ATTENTION DEFICIT AS THE CORE SYMPTOM OF THE SYNDROME

I have difficulties in seeing the attentional disorder as the heart of the syndrome, based on clinical experience and our long-term followup research. I see attention deficit as one part of the syndrome but not its most enduring part. Attention is not a unitary construct. The attention deficit of ADD children is often very selective. The children have particular difficulties with paying attention in a group, have less difficulties in a one to one situation, and have problems with school work that they see as boring, difficult, or unrewarding. They can pay attention however to tasks they enjoy (TV, outings with Dad, sometimes even reading the right book). Motivation and paying attention are difficult to sort out. In our followup studies, none of the adult hyperactives spontaneously complained of difficulties in paying attention at work or for other activities, while many complained about impulsive control and restlessness. In our study, we did not measure attention in the laboratory (e.g., on a CPT) when our ADDH subjects whom we had followed for 15 years into their 20's and 30's were reevaluated. All these subjects had impaired performance on the CPT and had severe attentional problems in elementary and secondary school. Finally, I have seen learning disabled children have attentional disorders until they were placed in the appropriate learning situation for their needs, when the disorder improved markedly.

TREATMENT ISSUES

Dr. Shaywitz reviews treatment studies as thoroughly as he reviews other research on the syndrome, such as syndrome definition, prevalence, etiology, etc. Of the total length of his review, only about 15 percent or less is devoted to this crucial area. This is not a bias of the review, but reflects the reality that so little research has focused on treatment issues other than the many acute drug studies demonstrating efficacy of the stimulants. We might ask: How do we study treatment of a condition we have not succeeded in defining? I do not agree with this point of view. We know already that children referred and diagnosed as ADDH have difficulties in most of the following areas: goal-directed activity, attention to rote tasks, impulse control, social skills, compliance, and self-esteem. As a result, they make themselves rejected by siblings, parents, teachers, and peers, no matter how well meaning the home or the school. Often parents blame one another since they have found that nothing works.

· This is a syndrome that requires remedial educational, social skills training, parent groups and family counselling, and various other interventions. Only one study has addressed the efficacy of multimodality treatment, and only a handful of centers is working on nonpharmacological treatments and seeking innovative means to improve generalizability. I would like to see funding for treatment research.

PREVENTION

Since the children we followed who had ADDH are now grown up, several of them have come to us for help with their small children. The children of adults with ADDH are at risk genetically. Many of their fathers have symptoms of impulse control and restlessness, which are modeled. It may be possible to intervene with some degree of success in helping these fathers (or mothers) to recognize how to model the behaviors to their children and to improve their parenting.

I would like to thank those who invited me to be a discussant for Dr. Shaywitz' outstanding review of our current knowledge of the syndrome. It is indeed a privilege to partake in this conference.

DISCUSSION

James M. Swanson

The massive review by Shaywitz and Shaywitz provides an excellent summary of the literature on hyperactivity and attention deficit disorder, and it also suggests some fresh and interesting new perspectives for consideration. In this discussion, I address only one of the topics brought to the forefront by Shaywitz and Shaywitz. They propose that the group of ADD children seen by psychologists and psychiatrists may be different from the group of ADD children seen by pediatricians and neurologists. Due to an understandable referral bias, these cases may be more likely to represent attention deficit disorder complicated with conduct disorder (or some other psychiatric condition). They suggest that the term ADD be reserved for the uncomplicated cases of ADD and that the term ADD-plus be used for the complicated cases of ADD. They also suggest that in these ADD-plus cases, a more severe form of attentional deficits may be manifested, and that due to its severity, this attentional dysfunction may differ in important ways from the attentional dysfunction manifested in the "pure" ADD cases seen by pediatricians and neurologists.

Thus, Shaywitz and Shaywitz suggest that the "typical" children in the United States with psychiatric diagnoses of attention deficit disorder may represent only the "tip of the iceberg" of a larger clinical group of children with less complicated attentional deficits.

It should be noted that there are no controlled comparative studies of populations of ADD children from these different settings, such as referrals to psychiatrists and psychologists versus referrals to pediatricians and neurologists, to confirm the proposed difference in patterns of symptoms. However, the hypothesis is plausible and makes sense, and it deserves to be tested in a controlled study.

Two of the many recommendations made by Shaywitz and Shaywitz were directed toward remedies for the "tip of the iceberg" problem. In this discussion, we suggest that the recommendation for an ADD-plus category may be related to the need for an adequate diagnostic label for conduct disorder (CD) in young children (under the age of 12 years). The new diagnostic category (oppositional defiant disorder [ODD]) created in the recent revision of the *Diagnostic and Statistical Manual* of the American Psychiatric Association (DSM IIIR, 1987) may fill this need. If this category is used and becomes widely accepted, the mechanism may provide a way to implement the major part of the ADD-plus suggestion. Thus, it appears that the suggestion by Shaywitz and Shaywitz will achieve widespread acceptance.

The author wishes to thank Stephen Simpson, M.A., Ronald Kotkin, Ph.D., Marc Lerner, M.D., and Dennis Cantwell, M.D., who contributed to this discussion.

The recommendation by Shaywitz and Shaywitz for an exclusive focus on inattention as the defining characteristic for the label of ADD may meet with more resistance. First, the DSM III (1980) focus on inattention and impulsivity as the necessary symptoms of ADD has been changed in DSM IIIR (1987), and the DSM III label for "pure" ADD (without hyperactivity) has been dropped. This deemphasis of attentional symptoms goes counter to the suggestion by Shaywitz and Shaywitz for an exclusive emphasis on attentional symptoms, which is not likely to be accepted by the psychiatrists and psychologists who have preempted the ADD label for the mixed disorders of attention and conduct. In addition, according to the estimates given by Shaywitz and Shaywitz, the use of the "pure" ADD criteria would increase the prevalence of the disorder (so defined) from 3 percent of the elementary school-aged children up to between 20 and 30 percent of this group. Since our colleagues in the United Kingdom (see Taylor, for example, 1986, for an up-to-date review) already believe that our definition is too broad, this suggestion may meet some resistance from abroad.

THE "TIP OF THE ICEBERG"

In this paper, we discuss the type of ADD-plus children typically seen by psychologists and psychiatrists—those extreme children with concurrent aggression or conduct disorder. These ADD-plus children demand treatment in the short-term, and they are at risk for serious antisocial behavior as they grow older (Loney et al., 1978; Satterfield et al., 1981). We add to the discussion by Shaywitz and Shaywitz about the recognition and treatment of children with mixed attention and conduct disorders by providing the following: (a) a more detailed description of the IOWA Conners scale (Loney and Milich, 1982), (b) a discussion of differences between DSM III and ICD 9 in their definitions of conduct disorder as well as ADD/hyperkinetic disorder; and (c) a discussion of the new DSM IIIR criteria for disruptive behaviors of childhood.

THE IOWA CONNERS

Loney and Milich (1982) have presented data that may explain why the term ADDH has been used clinically as a label (at least in the United States) for children with conduct disorder. In a factor analysis of the Conners Teacher Rating Scale, many of the inattention/overactivity items loaded on the same factor with many of the aggression/defiance items. The list of items that overlapped in this way are shown in Table 1. These are the "typical" symptoms of ADDH that parents and teachers report, and about which the clinician inquires during the initial assessment for ADDH. These items are not exclusively associated with ADDH; they are also highly correlated with aggressive behavior in children (Loney and Milich, 1982).

Table 1

Mixed I/0 & A Items	Pure I/0 Items	Pure A Items
1. Restless or overactive	1. Fidgeting	1. Quarrelsome
2. Excitable, implusive	2. Hums and makes other odd noises	2. Acts "smart"
3. Disturbs other children	3. (Excitable, implusive)*	3. Defiant
4. Mood changes quickly	4. Inattentive, easily distracted	4. Uncooperative
5. Teases other children and interferes with their activities.	5. Fails to finish things (short attention span)	5. Temper outbursts (explosive and unpredictable behavior)

*The "Excitable, impulsive" item loaded on both factors, but it was included as an "1/0" item for practical reasons in the formulation of the IOWA Conners. (From Loney and Milich, 1982.)

Loney and Milich (1982) defined "pure" disorders of inattention/overactivity (I/O) and aggression (A) by using divergent as well as convergent criteria to select items to define these two separate dimensions of behavior. The resulting IOWA Conners questionaire is composed of 5 items for inattentive/overreactive behavior, and 5 items for aggressive behavior. These 10 items are also presented in Table 1.

As pointed out by Shaywitz and Shaywitz, in clinic samples, a majority of the cases referred to psychologists and psychiatrists may have significant symptoms of both I/O and A symptoms, but in classroom samples, subgroups of "pure" I/O cases and "pure" A cases may represent the majority of cases. The mixed I/O-A (or ADD-plus) cases represent the more extreme cases described by Shaywitz and Shaywitz—the tip of the iceberg—and are more likely to be referred for treatment than the pure cases.

DIMENSIONS OF BEHAVIOR (I/O AND A) AND CATEGORICAL DIAGNOSIS (IN DSM III AND ICD 9)

How are the A items in the IOWA Conners related to a DSM III diagnosis of conduct disorder? The A items describe disruptive behavior, but their presence may not be sufficient to warrent a diagnosis of CD in DSM III. The examples of behaviors proposed in DSM III (1980) for the CD diagnosis may be age-appropriate for adolescents but not for children under the age of 12 years.

A dramatic change in the definition of CD occurred when DSM III (1980) was formulated, from an emphasis on childhood symptoms of CD in DSM II (1968) to an emphasis on adolescence symptoms of CD in DSM III (1980). This change in emphasis for the CD definition of ADDH occurred at the same time as the dramatic change in the definition of ADDH, away from an emphasis on hyperkinesis (in DSM II) to an emphasis on attention deficit (in DSM III). The DSM III definition of CD also differs substantially from the definition of CD specified in the current International Classification of Diseases, Ninth Edition (ICD 9) (Rutter et al., 1975).

The contrast among the DSM III (1980), DSM II (1968), and the ICD 9 definitions of conduct disorder is presented in Table 2. The symptoms of conduct disorder in ICD 9, which are manifested by younger children (for example: defiance, fighting, lying, stealing) may be precursors for the symptoms of conduct disorder given in DSM III, which are those manifested by older individuals (for example: vandalism, persistent truancy, substance abuse, rape, gas station robbery). The ICD 9 and DSM II symptoms of CD, but not the DSM III symptoms of CD, although not identical, seem to be related to the dimension of aggression specified by the IOWA Conners.

Swanson and Taylor (1987) have proposed that the difference in definitions of conduct disorder between DSM III and ICD 9, perhaps even more than the difference in the definitions for ADD/hyperkinesis, has contributed to the large cross-cultural difference (United States versus United Kingdom) in diagnostic rates of ADD/hyperkinesis (Sandberg and Taylor, 1980), despite a similar prevalence of I/O and A behaviors in children in the two countries.

A collaborative study directed by Judy Rapoport from the National Institute of Mental Health and Eric Taylor from the Institute for Psychiatry in London (Prendergast et al., submitted) concluded that "British clinicians evaluating American research on ADDH should remember that many such cases would correspond to their own diagnoses of conduct disorder. American clinicians studying British writings on conduct disorder should make the corresponding translation." Thus, even if the clinical cases in the United States and the United Kingdom are similar, they may be labeled differently.

Table 2

DSM III CD Examples:	ICD 9 CD Examples:
1. Vandalism	1. Defiance
2. Rape	2. Disobedience
3. Breaking and entering	3. Quarrelsomeness
4. Fire-setting	4. Aggression
5. Mugging	5. Destructiveness
6. Assault	6. Tantrums
7. Extortion	7. Solitary stealing
8. Purse-snatching	8. Lying
9. Armed robbery	9. Bullying
10. Persistent truancy	
11. Substance abuse	DSM II CD Examples:
12. Running away from home overnight	1. Hostile disobedience
13. Persistent lying	2. Quarrelsomeness
14. Stealing without confrontation	3. Physical and verbal aggression
	4. Vengefulness
	5. Destructiveness
	6. Temper tantrums
	7. Solitary stealing
	8. Lying
	9. Hostile teasing

DSM III (REVISED)

The American Psychiatric Association's revision of DSM III (DSM IIIR, 1987) provides new definitions for "disruptive behaviors of childhood." Changes from DSM III include the following: (a) a new diagnostic label—oppositional defiant disorder (ODD)—was proposed; (b) the three classes of symptoms of ADDH in DSM III (inattention, impulsivity, and overactivity) were merged, and a single diagnosis—attention deficit/hyperactivity disorder (ADHD)—replaced the two DSM III diagnoses (ADD with H or ADD without H); and (c) the four subtypes of conduct disorder (based on the presence or absence of socialization and aggressiveness) were dropped, and a single set of symptoms for CD was established.

The DSM IIIR definitions for ADHD, ODD, and CD are presented in Tables 3, 4 and 5.

In the near future, the young (5- to 12-year old) "tip of the iceberg" cases described by Shaywitz and Shaywitz may be given the dual diagnoses of ADHD and ODD in DSM IIIR. The DSM IIIR symptoms of CD still seem to represent characteristics of disruptive children (or adolescents) who are past the age of puberty.

The new ODD diagnosis, along with a small subset of the DSM IIIR symptoms of CD (for instance: lying, stealing, and cheating), may offer an "age-appropriate" set of symptoms for conduct disorder for the 5- to 12-year old age group.

A controlled study of the outcome of the pure (ADHD and ODD) and mixed (ADHD plus ODD) subgroups of children with disruptive behaviors of childhood is clearly needed to elucidate the risk and protective factors of, as well as the different routes into, antisocial behavior in adolescence and adulthood.

TREATMENT

Evidence is accumulating that intensive treatment may be required to alter the poor prognosis of ADHD and/or ODD children (for instance, Satterfield et al., 1982). However, no adequate long-term treatment study has been conducted to prove this point. In spite of that, these children demand treatment.

Shaywitz and Shaywitz have reviewed the common treatments for these children, including educational therapy, cognitive-behavioral therapy, and psychotherapy as well as pharmacotherapy. The intensity of these therapies varies in clinical practice and in research studies, but typical treatments provided so far have been insufficient to demonstrate long-term benefits. Recently, more intensive interventions for ADHD and ODD children have been developed and are being implemented. These programs are described below.

Table 3

Diagnostic Criteria for 314.01 Attention Deficit Hyperactivity Disorder

Note: Consider a criterion met only if the behavior is considerably more frequent than that of most people of the same mental age.

A. A disturbance of at least 6 months during which at least eight of the following are present:

   (1) often fidgets with hands or feet or squirms in seat (in adolescents, may be limited to subjective feelings of restlessness)
   (2) has difficulty remaining seated when required to
   (3) is easily distracted by extraneous stimuli
   (4) has difficulty awaiting turn in games or group situations
   (5) often blurts out answers to questions before they have been completed
   (6) has difficulty following through on instructions from others (not due to oppositional behavior or failure of comprehension), e.g., fails to finish chores
   (7) has difficulty sustaining attention in tasks or play activities
   (8) often shifts from one uncompleted activity to another
   (9) has difficulty playing quietly
   (10) often talks excessively
   (11) often interrupts or intrudes on others, e.g., butts into other children's games
   (12) often does not seem to listen to what is being said to him or her
   (13) often loses things necessary for tasks or activities at school or at home (e.g., toys, pencils, books, assignments)
   (14) often engages in physically dangerous activities without considering possible consequences (not for the purpose of thrill-seeking), e.g., runs into street without looking

Note: The above items are listed in descending order of discriminating power based on data from a national field trial of the DSM-III-R criteria for disruptive behavior disorders.

B. Onset before the age of 9.

C. Does not meet the criteria for a pervasive developmental disorder.

Criteria for severity of attention deficit hyperactivity disorder:

   Mild: Few, if any, symptoms in excess of those required to make the diagnosis and only minimal or no impairment in school and social functioning.

   Moderate: Symptoms or functional impairment intermediate between "mild" and "severe."

   Severe: Many symptoms in excess of those required to make the diagnosis and significant and pervasive impairment in functioning at home and school and with peers.

STANDARD TREATMENTS

Most ADD children receive stimulant drugs, although in up to 50 percent of the cases, this treatment may not result in improved attention on cognitive tasks (Sprague and Sleator, 1977; Swanson et al., 1983). Evidence is emerging that stimulant medication may be more effective for attention/activity problems (i.e., ADHD) than for aggression and defiance (i.e., ODD) (Taylor et al., 1987).

A common clinical practice in place of medication or in combination with medication (e.g., Pelham et al., 1980) is to provide brief outpatient behavior therapy for ADD children and their families. To implement this treatment, the basic principles and techniques of behavior

Table 4

Diagnostic Criteria for 313.81 Oppositional Defiant Disorder

Note: Consider a criterion met only if the behavior is considerably more frequent than that of most people of the same mental age.

A. A disturbance of at least 6 months during which at least five of the following are present:

(1) often loses temper
(2) often argues with adults
(3) often actively defies or refuses adult requests or rules, e.g., refuses to do chores at home
(4) often deliberately does things that annoy other people, e.g., grabs other children's hats
(5) often blames others for his or her own mistakes
(6) is often touchy or easily annoyed by others
(7) is often angry and resentful
(8) is often spiteful or vindictive
(9) often swears or uses obscene language

Note: The above items are listed in descending order of discriminating power based on data from a national field trial of the DSM-III-R criteria for disruptive behavior disorders.

B. Does not meet the criteria for conduct disorder, and does not occur exclusively during the course of a psychotic disorder, dysthymia, or a major depressive, hypomanic, or manic episode.

Criteria for severity of oppositional defiant disorder:

Mild: Few, if any, symptoms in excess of those required to make the diagnosis and only minimal or no impairment in school and social functioning.

Moderate: Symptoms or functional impairment intermediate between "mild" and "severe."

Severe: Many symptoms in excess of those required to make the diagnosis and significant and pervasive impairment in functioning at home and school and with other adults and peers.

modification are taught to parents in 8 to 10 weekly group sessions, and in addition, consultation with the classroom teacher for the development and implementation of behavioral programs in the classroom may be provided (e.g., O'Leary and O'Leary, 1977; Forehand et al., 1980; Barkley, 1981). Pelham and Bender (1982) have suggested that these typical behavioral interventions are often provided in their most simplified form in order to make them practical for application in the natural environment. These concessions to practicality may preclude effectiveness. Intensive interventions in the school, however, suggest that behavior therapy may be more effective for aggressive behavior than for inattentive/overactive behavior (Abikoff et al., 1984).

Cognitive therapy has been reviewed in a special issue of the *Journal of Abnormal Child Psychology* (Harris, Wong, and Keogh, 1985). The consensus presented there is that cognitive therapy may work in

Table 5

Diagnostic Criteria for Conduct Disorder:
        312.10 group type
        312.00 solitary aggressive type
        312.90 undifferentiated type

A. A disturbance of conduct lasting at least 6 months, during which at least three of the following have been present:

(1) has stolen without confrontation of a victim on more than one occasion (including forgery)
(2) has run away from home overnight at least twice while living in parental or parental surrogate home (or once without returning)
(3) often lies (other than to avoid physical or sexual abuse)
(4) has deliberately engaged in fire-setting
(5) is often truant from school (for older person, absent from work)
(6) has broken into someone else's house, building, or car
(7) has deliberately destroyed others' property (other than by fire-setting)
(8) has been physically cruel to animals
(9) has forced someone into sexual activity with him or her
(10) has used a weapon in more than one fight
(11) often initiates physical fights
(12) has stolen with confrontation of a victim (e.g., mugging, purse-snatching, extortion, armed robbery)
(13) has been physically cruel to people

Note: The above items are listed in descending order of discriminating power based on data from a national field trial of the DSM-III-R criteria for disruptive behavior disorders.

B. If 18 or older, does not meet criteria for antisocial personality disorder.

Criteria for severity of conduct disorder:

    Mild: Few if any conduct problems in excess of those required to make the diagnosis, and conduct problems cause only minor harm to others.

    Moderate: Number of conduct problems and effect on others intermediate between "mild" and "severe."

    Severe: Many conduct problems in excess of those required to make the diagnosis, or conduct problems cause considerable harm to others, e.g., serious physical injury to victims, extensive vandalism or theft, prolonged absence from home.

---

the therapy situation but seldom generalizes to extra-therapy situations. However, several programs exist for implementing cognitive behavioral therapy with ADD children (for example: Hindshaw, Henker, and Whalen, 1984; Kendall and Braswell, 1984; Meichenbaum and Cameron, 1982.)

Recently, Satterfield et al. (1981) have suggested that multimodality therapy may be essential for successful long-term intervention. Shaywitz and Shaywitz classified "multimodality therapy" as psychotherapy, but the term suggests a broader combination of multiple interventions as well as continuation of treatment over long periods of time—for years, not weeks.

Over the past 5 years, intensive, school-based day-treatment programs have been developed and offered as summer programs for ADD at the University of California, Los Angeles, by Barbara Henker, Stephen Hindshaw, and Carol Whalen, at Florida State University and the University of Pittsburgh by William Pelham, and at the University of California, Irvine, by James Swanson, in collaboration with the other two groups. These summer programs provide intensive short-term (6 to 8 weeks) intervention for the "tip of the iceberg" type of ADHD/ODD children.

These are "multimodality" treatment programs, and include (1) intensive behavior modification, based on a structured token system in a model classroom; (2) parent training, delivered in weekly group and individual sessions with parents to teach principles and techniques of behavior modification; (3) cognitive and social skills training, delivered in daily group therapy sessions with the children; (4) generalization training, on the playground, in the classroom, and at home; (5) medication assessment, using a double-blind protocol and cognitive tests to screen for adverse effects ("cognitive toxicity").

Evaluation of the effectiveness of specific multimodality treatment programs is essential. In particular, the evaluation of effects of treatment on subgroups of "pure" and "mixed" subgroups of ADD and ADD/ODD children is needed, to determine if specific components of multimodality treatment programs are particularly effective and necessary for specific subtypes of ADD/ODD children.

DESCRIPTION OF A SPECIFIC INTENSIVE TREATMENT PROGRAM

Based on a history of four summer programs (1982 to 1985) at Irvine and modeled after the University of California, Los Angeles, and Florida State University programs described above, an extended multimodality treatment program was established at Irvine in 1985. Clinical impressions suggested that the intensive 6- to 8-week summer program interventions provided effective short-term treatment, but concern still existed about the lack of maintenance and generalization of effects after treatment ceased (Whalen, Henker, and Hindshaw, 1985). The extension of this approach at Irvine was based on a much longer intervention (the length of treatment was extended from 8 weeks to 1 year) and on the use of planned generalization training on a daily basis in the classroom and on the playground.

The program at Irvine provides a year-long intensive multimodality intervention for 40 ADHD and/or ODD children per year. The characteristics of the children and the parents who are treated in this program are summarized in Table 6.

Table 6

The Parent Training Program

A. Characteristics of parents entering program:

  (1) Higher than average risk for child abuse
  (2) High incidence of marital conflicts:
    (a) Breakdown in communication within family
    (b) High incidence of separation and divorce
  (3) One parent frequently notes having similar behavior problems as child
  (4) Limited repertoire of interventions
  (5) Lack of consistency in dealing with their child's problems
  (6) History of participation in short-term treatment programs
  (7) Parental feelings of anger, frustration, anxiety, embarrassment, inadequacy, guilt, and fear of social situations

B. Target behaviors parents frequently identify:

  (1) Noncompliance
  (2) Physical and verbal aggression
  (3) Not doing chores
  (4) Not doing homework
  (5) Stealing, lying
  (6) Not following daily routines
  (7) Not making and keeping friends

C. Six-week parent training class focusing on:

  (1) Identifying present parenting styles
  (2) Identifying successful and unsuccessful parenting styles
  (3) Developing a parenting style that parent(s) will consistently follow and expand
  (4) Targeting, prioritizing, and measuring behavior(s)
  (5) Identifying effective reinforcers
  (6) Collecting baseline data
  (7) Exploring range of interventions
  (8) Implementing and collecting data of selected intervention
  (9) Evaluating effectiveness of intervention
  (10) Generalizing interventions and strategies

D. Goals of parent training:

  (1) Provide consistent home program supported by both parents
  (2) Help parents develop ability to analyze own home program and modify as needed
  (3) Provide consistency across home, school, and social skills for generalization to new settings

The program is supported by a combination of educational and clinical funds. The Department of Pediatrics of the University of California, Irvine (UCI), provides a building of 6,500 square feet and the clinical staff. The Orange County Department of Education (OCDE) provides the educational staff. The multimodality treatment includes direct intervention with ADHD/ODD children on a daily basis in the classroom, daily social skill and cognitive training sessions in small groups, frequent interactions with parents (3 to 5 hours per week), and careful assessment of the use of medication, which results in removal of medication from many but not all of the children.

Children in the UCI-OCDE collaborative program are in the classroom, on the playground, or in group therapy from 8:30 a.m. until 3:00 p.m. An outline of the schedule followed over this period of the day is given in Table 7. A sophisticated token system is used by teachers and staff over this period of time.

A specific social skills/cognitive training program is provided in a daily group therapy session, which is coupled with an intensive generalization training program in the classroom and on the playground. An outline of this program is presented in Table 8. Once a day, for 1 hour, small groups of children (4 or 5) meet with a counselor, and specific training procedures (e.g., Oden and Asher, 1977; Pelham and Bender, 1982; Hindshaw, Whalen, and Henker, 1981 and 1984) are implemented to teach children the appropriate social and cognitive skills that they lack. However, we and others (see the special issue of the *Journal of Abnormal Child Psychology* [Harris et al., 1985]) have found that teaching children "the propositions about performance" (Tharp and Gallimore, 1985) is not sufficient to obtain generalization. So, in a limited and controlled setting of the UCI-OCDE school, intensive generalization training is provided.

Table 7

The UCI-OCDE Classroom Point System

A. Target behaviors for earning points every 30 minutes in the classroom:

  (1) Getting started (2 points)
  (2) Following directions (4 points)
  (3) Interacting with others (4 points)
  (4) Completing assignment (4 points)
  (5) Stopping, cleaning up, and transition (2 points)

B. Charting target behaviors and points:

  (1) Point checks: Every 30 minutes, students reveal the points they have assigned to themselves.
  (2) Match game: If student's evaluation matches teacher evaluation, bonus points are given.

C. Recess and lunch point system: Outside the classroom, points are earned in the following ways:

  (1) Behavior is recorded at five minute intervals
  (2) Zero points are awarded for nongoal directed behavior, aggressive behavior, noncompliant behavior
  (3) One point is awarded for isolated play (goal directed)
  (4) Two points are awarded for cooperative play
  (5) Bonus points are awarded for participation in designated group game.

D. Reinforcement: The points (tokens) are totaled for the day and traded in for the following backup reinforcers:

  (1) Daily reinforcers (computer games, time with staff, special privileges)
  (2) Weekly reinforcers (outings)
  (3) Level II reinforcers (special group recognition)
  (4) Level III reinforcers (freedom from external monitoring and special privileges)

Table 8

Social Skills and Cognitive Training

A.   Social Skills

1.   Children are taught social skills through:

(1)   Observation
(2)   Modeling
(3)   Feedback
(4)   Reinforcement

2.   In daily group therapy sessions, points (tokens) are given or taken away for the following categories of behavior:

(1)   Following rules
(2)   Participation
(3)   Good sportsmanship
(4)   Following directions
(5)   Helping
(6)   Sharing
(7)   Saying something nice to someone
(8)   Contributing to a problem solution
(9)   Raising hand/patience
(10) Ignoring
(11) Interrupting
(12) Cursing/swearing
(13) Name calling/teasing
(14) Lying
(15) Aggression
(16) Destruction of property
(17) Leaving the group without permission
(18) Not following directions

B.   Cognitive Skills

1.   Children learn self-monitoring and self-evaluation through:

(1)   Match game: Child's self-evaluation is matched with counselor's evaluation
(2)   Level system: Children, whose weekly point totals exceed 90 percent, and who demonstrate a specific level of competence at the match game, move to Level III without external monitoring.

2.   Sample topics for emotional control:

(1)   Dealing with anger
(2)   Recognizing anger in someone else
(3)   Accepting consequences for one's behavior
(4)   Dealing with tension
(5)   Avoiding a fight

Outside the group therapy setting—in the classroom and on the playground—trained staff help the ADHD/ODD children put newly acquired cognitive and social skills into practice. Every 30 minutes, for 5 days per week for a period of 1 year, the children in this program are asked to recall their recent behavior and to assign themselves points to evaluate their behavior. In this way, a systematic self-monitoring and self-evaluation program is implemented, and the intensive staff monitoring and evaluation of the original token system is shifted to the child.

We consider this frequent practice of cognitive and social skills to be "generalization training," and it is our attempt to follow the advice of Whalen, Henker, and Hindshaw (1985) to go beyond the traditional procedures that have not proved to be effective outside the therapy situation.

Psychological and educational interventions are stressed in the UCI-OCDE collaborative program. However, medical interventions, including pharmacotherapy, are provided. An outline of the medical part of the UCI-OCDE program is outlined in Table 9.

Table 9

Medical Assessment and Treatment

A. Diagnosis

    1. Structured interview by a psychiatrist, with parent and child separately, to establish DSM IIIR and ICD 9 diagnoses.

    2. Physical and neurodevelopmental assessment by a pediatrician, to establish maturation level.

    3. Psychoeducational assessment by a psychometrician and the school principal, to establish levels of ability and current achievement.

B. Selective treatment with medication:

    1. Usual (in 30% to 40% of the cases):
       (1) Stimulants (Ritalin, Cylert, Dexedrine)

    2. Unusual:
       (1) Antidepressants (Tofranil, Elavil)
       (2) Other (Clonodine, lithium)

C. Double-blind procedure for assessing effects of stimulant medication

    (1) Gather baseline data on:

       (a) Behavior at home (Parent Rating Scale)
       (b) Behavior at school (Teacher Rating Scale)
       (c) PAL, paired associate test in the laboratory

    (2) Implement 3-week double-blind assessment using capsules to disguise two different dosages of medication and placebo (1 week on each condition)

    (3) Under each condition, gather data on:

       (a) Behavior at home (5 times per week)
       (b) Behavior at school (3 times per week)
       (c) PAL, paired associate test (1 per week)

    (4) Break medication code and analyze data from each condition

    (5) Inform parents of children's behavior (from ratings) and performance (from learning tests) in each medication condition

    (6) Make recommendation on appropriateness of medication. Using this, approximately 50 percent of the children in the UCI-OCDE program manifest an adverse or non-response and are taken off medication.

Treatment programs for ADHD/ODD children are not typically provided in public schools. The UCI-OCDE collaborative program is a partial exception to this rule, since part of its funding comes from the OCDE, which is the umbrella organization for the 29 school districts of Orange County. The education funds are channeled through the Juvenile Court School program of the OCDE and are based on average daily attendance rates amounting to approximately $4,600 per year. The clinical funds are derived from fees for service, which over the first 2 years of the program amounted to approximately $100 per week.

The summer treatment programs at the University of California, Los Angeles, the University of Pittsburgh, and the University of California, Irvine, were developed prior to a controlled evaluation of their effectiveness and have been stimulated by research interests as well as a significant clinical demand for intensive treatment programs for ADHD/ODD children. As these interventions mature, they will require a long-term prospective followup of treated and untreated cases to document effectiveness.

CONCLUSION

The review by Shaywitz and Shaywitz made recommendations for more specific criteria for ADD, which if adopted would broaden the clinical population by including less severe cases and emphasizing "pure" ADD cases uncomplicated by behavioral or conduct problems. This discussion, authored by a multidisciplinary group associated with the UCI-OCDE collaborative treatment program, has focused on the "tip of the iceberg" instead of on a redefinition of the disorder. The paper has described the use of the Loney and Milich (1982) criteria and the DSM IIIR (1987) criteria to form pure and mixed subgroups of children with ADHD and/or ODD, and described treatment programs for the severe and complicated attention and behavior disorders that represent the "tip of the iceberg."

The use of the new DSM IIIR criteria, to establish groups of "pure" and "mixed" cases of ADHD and ODD, may provide a short-term solution to the nosological problems outlined by Shaywitz and Shaywitz. Long-term evaluation of treatment programs for these subgroups should provide answers in the future about the wisdom of this approach.

REFERENCES

Abikoff, H., Gittleman, R. (1984). Does behavior therapy normalize the classroom behavior of hyperactive children? *Archives of General Psychiatry,* 41:449-454.

Barkley, R. A. (1981). *Hyperactive children: A handbook for diagnosis and treatment.* New York: Guilford Press.

DSM II: *Diagnostic and Statistical Manual of Mental Disorders* (Second Edition) (1968). American Psychiatric Association: Washington, D.C.

DSM III: *Diagnostic and Statistical Manual of Mental Disorders* (Third Edition) (1980). American Psychiatric Association: Washington, D.C.

DSM IIIR: *Diagnostic and Statistical Manual of Mental Disorders* (Third Edition, Revised) (1987). American Psychiatric Association: Washington, D.C.

Forehand, R., Wells, K. C., Griest, D. L. (1980). An examination of the social validity of a parent training program. *Behavior Therapy*, 11:488-502.

Gittleman, R., Mannuzza, S., Shenker, S., Bonagure, N. (1985). Hyperactive boys almost grown up. I. Psychiatric status. *Achieves of General Psychiatry*, 42:937-947.

Harris, K. R., Wong, B. Y. L., Keogh, B. (1985). Cognitive-behavioral modification with children: A critical review of the state-of-the-art. *Journal of Abnormal Child Psychology*, 13:327-476 (Special Issue).

Hindshaw, S. P., Henker, B., Whalen, C. K. (1984). Self-control in hyperactive boys in anger-inducing situations: Effect of cognitive-behavioral training and methylphenidate. *Journal of Abnormal Child Psychology*, 12:55-77.

Kendall, P. C., Braswell, L. (1984). *Cognitive-behavioral therapy for impulsive children*. New York: Guilford Press.

Loney, J., Milich, R. (1982). Hyperactivity, inattention and aggression in clinical practice. *Advances in Developmental and Behavioral Pediatrics*, 3:113-147.

Meichenbaum, B., Cameron, R. (1982). Cognitive behavior therapy. In Wilson, F. (Ed.), *Contemporary behavior therapy*. New York. New York: JAI Press.

Oden, S., Asher, S. (1977). Coaching children in social skills for friendship making. *Child Development*, 48:495-506.

O'Leary, K. D., O'Leary, S. G. (1977). *Classroom management: The successful use of behavior modification*. New York: Pergamon Press.

Pelham, W. E., Schnedler, R., Bologna, N., Contreras, A. (1980). Behavioral and stimulant treatment of hyperactive children: A therapy study with methylphenidate probes in a within-subject design. *Journal of Applied Behavior Analysis*, 13:221-236.

Pelham, W. E., Bender, M. E. (1982). Peer relationships in hyperactive children: Description and treatment. In Gaidow, K. (Ed.), *Advances in learning and behavioral disabilities*, (pp. 365-436). New York: JAI Press.

Pelham, W. E., Murphy, H. A. (1986). Attention deficit and conduct disorders. In Hersen, M. (Ed.), *Risk in intellectual and psychosocial development*. New York: Pergamon Press.

Prendergast, M., Taylor, E., Rapoport, J., Zametkin, A., Donally, M., Aist, M. B., Bartko, J., Dunn, G., Wiessenberg, H. M. In the eye of the beholders: A U.S.-U.K. cross-national study of DSM III and ICD 9 psychiatric diagnosis of children with disruptive behavior. (Submitted.)

Satterfield, J., Hoppe, C., Schell, A. (1982). A prospective study of delinquency in 110 adolescent boys with attention deficit disorder and 88 normal adolescent boys. *American Journal of Psychiatry*, 139:795-798.

Satterfield, J., Cantwell, D. P., Satterfield, B. T. (1981). Three-year multimodality treatment study of 100 hyperactive boys. *Journal of Pediatrics*, 98:650-655.

Sprague, R. L., Sleator, E. K. (1977). Methylphenidate in hyperkinetic children: Differences in dose effects on learning and social behavior. *Science*, 198:1274-1276.

Swanson, J. M., Sandman, C. A., Deutsch, C., Baren, M. (1983). Methylphenidate hydrochloride given with or before breakfast: I. Behavioral, cognitive and electrophysiological effects. *Pediatrics*, 72:49-55.

Swanson, J. M., Taylor, E. (1987). Classification of ADD/hyperkinesis in the USA (DSM III) and UK (ICD 9). (Submitted.)

Taylor, E., Schachar, R., Thorley, G., Wieselberg, M., Everitt, B., Rutter, M. Which boys respond to stimulant medication? A controlled trial of methylphenidate in boys with disruptive behavior. (Submitted.)

Tharp, R. G., Gallimore, R. (1985). The logical status of metacognitive training. *Journal of Abnormal Child Psychology*, 13:455-466.

Whalen, C. K., Henker, B., Hinshaw, S. P. (1985). Cognitive-behavioral therapies for hyperactive children: Premises, problems and prospect. *Journal of Abnormal Child Psychology*, 13:391-410.

PART VI: SUPPLEMENTARY INFORMATION

REVISED DEFINITION OF LEARNING DISABILITIES

[Editors' Note: An overarching concern of the National Conference on Learning Disabilities and of the Interagency Committee itself was the problem of definition. Following extensive discussions, the Committee decided to recommend in its Report to Congress, submitted in August 1987, the adoption of a new definition of learning disabilities. Excerpted below is the portion of the Committee's Report discussing the problem of definition and recommending the new definition.]

A foremost consideration that has impact on all areas of the requested recommendations is the issue of definition. The concept of learning disabilities is one that has evolved over time. One of the first formal definitions was developed in 1967 by the National Advisory Committee on Handicapped Children and later incorporated into legislation in P.L. 94-142. This definition has been the standard applied in determining eligibility for services under that law. It reads as follows:

> "Specific learning disability" means a disorder in one or more of the basic psychological processes involved in understanding or in using language, spoken or written, which may manifest itself in an imperfect ability to listen, think, speak, read, write, spell, or to do mathematical calculations. The term includes such conditions as perceptual handicaps, brain injury, minimal brain dysfunction, dyslexia, and developmental aphasia. The term does not include children who have learning problems which are primarily the result of visual, hearing, or motor handicaps, of mental retardation, of emotional disturbance, or of environmental, cultural, or economic disadvantage.

As more has been learned about learning disabilities from research, and as people have attempted to apply this definition in a variety of settings, numerous shortcomings of the definition have become apparent. It wrongly implies that learning disability is a homogeneous condition rather than a heterogeneous group of disorders. The use of "children" in the definition fails to recognize that for most people a relative disability persists and affects them throughout adulthood as well. It does not indicate that, whatever the etiology of learning disabilities, the final common path is an inherently altered process of acquiring and using information, presumably based on an altered function within the central nervous system. Finally, though properly recognizing that learning disabilities do not include problems with learning as a consequence of mental retardation, sensory or motor handicap, emotional disturbance, or socioeconomic or cultural disadvantage, the definition does not clearly recognize that persons with those conditions may have learning disability in addition to, if not as a consequence of, their other handicap.

In an attempt to deal with these concerns, the National Joint Committee for Learning Disabilities in 1981 developed a revised definition. This definition has been endorsed by most professional and lay organizations in this field, and all organizations and individuals who addressed the issue of definition at the Public Hearing held [on October 15, 1986] by the Interagency Committee urged the Committee to adopt the revised definition. That definition is as follows:

> Learning disabilities is a generic term that refers to a heterogeneous group of disorders manifested by significant difficulties in the acquisition and use of listening, speaking, reading, writing, reasoning, or mathematical abilities. These disorders are intrinsic to the individual and presumed to be due to central nervous dysfunction. Even though a learning disability may occur concomitantly with other handicapping conditions (e.g., sensory impairment, mental retardation, social and emotional disturbance) or environmental influences (e.g., cultural differences, insufficient or inappropriate instruction, psychogenic factors), it is not the direct result of those conditions or influences.

The Committee believes that this new definition represents a substantial improvement and reflects the conceptual advances that have emerged from research in the past two decades. However, some problems remain. In recent years, there has developed a consensus that social skills deficit also represents a specific learning disability. The Committee has included this disability among the topics it has reviewed in this report, and believes it should be added to the definition. Second, the relationship between attention deficit disorder (with or without hyperactivity) and learning disabilities is not addressed. The Committee believes that there is evidence that attention deficit disorder may be best considered in the same category with other conditions that may either accompany learning disabilities or cause learning *problems* (but not disabilities), and thus should be added to the definition. Finally, the fact that these handicapping conditions cause learning *problems* but not what is intended by the term learning *disabilities* is not clear in the definition, and should be specified.

Therefore, the Interagency Committee proposes a modification of this revised definition of learning disabilities, and believes that it should be considered for use in epidemiologic studies of the prevalence of the condition, in diagnosis, in research, in administrative actions, and in future legislation. The modified definition is as follows (changes underlined):

> Learning disabilities is a generic term that refers to a heterogeneous group of disorders manifested by significant difficulties in the acquisition and use of listening, speaking, reading, writing, reasoning, or mathematical abilities, or of social skills. These disorders are intrinsic to the individual and presumed to be due to central nervous system dysfunction. Even though a learning disability may

occur concomitantly with other handicapping conditions (e.g., sensory impairment, mental retardation, social and emotional disturbance), with socioenvironmental influences (e.g., cultural differences, insufficient or inappropriate instruction, psychogenic factors), and especially with attention deficit disorder, all of which may cause learning problems, a learning disability is not the direct result of those conditions or influences.

CONTRIBUTORS

Duane F. Alexander is Director of the National Institute of Child Health and Human Development at the National Institutes of Health in Bethesda, Maryland. He earned the M.D. at the Johns Hopkins University School of Medicine in 1966, and he is a diplomate of the American Board of Pediatrics (1973) and a Medical Director in the U.S. Public Health Service. He is also a member of the American Academy of Pediatrics, the Society for Developmental Pediatrics, the Association for Retarded Citizens, and the American Pediatric Society. His numerous awards and honors include the Public Health Service Commendation Medal, the Public Health Service Meritorious Service Medal, and the Public Health Service Special Recognition Award. He is listed in *Who's Who in America.*

As Director of the NICHD, he oversees programs relating to the reproductive, developmental, and behavioral processes that determine the health of children, adults, families, and populations. The programs include multidisciplinary research on the development of communicative abilities, both normal and abnormal. A significant portion of this research relates to dyslexia and other learning disabilities.

Dorothy M. Aram is Associate Professor and Vice Chair for Research in the Department of Pediatrics at Case Western Reserve University School of Medicine and also holds appointments in the Department of Neurology and the Department of Communication Sciences. She received the B.S. and M.A. degrees in speech pathology from Northwestern University and completed the Ph.D. and a 2-year NIH postdoctoral fellowship in speech pathology at Case Western Reserve University. She has coauthored two books with James Nation, *Diagnosis of Speech and Language Disorders* and *Child Language Disorders,* and has published 35 research articles and chapters on topics related to developmental and acquired language disorders in children. She is a recent recipient of the Javits Neuroscience Investigator Award to support her continued work addressing linguistic sequelae of unilateral brain lesions in children. She serves as a coinvestigator on two additional NIH- supported studies: a multicenter program project grant addressing the nosology of higher cerebral function disorders in children, and a followup study at Case Western Reserve University of very low birth weight children and brain growth. Dr. Aram is an associate editor of *Brain and Language,* and she serves on the Sensory Disorders and Language Study Section of the National Institutes of Health.

Tanis Bryan is Professor of Education and Associate Dean for Research and Program Development at the University of Illinois at

Chicago. She received the Ph.D. in communication disorders from Northwestern University in 1970.

Dr. Bryan has published two textbooks with her husband James: *Understanding Learning Disabilities,* and *Exceptional Children. Understanding Learning Disabilities* is currently in its third edition and has been used at more than 100 universities.

Dr. Bryan has focused her research efforts on social factors in learning disabilities. This research has addressed learning disabled students' self concepts and attributions, social cognition, communicative competence, and social interactions. Her research has been supported by the State of Illinois through the Department of Mental Health and Developmental Disabilities, and by Federally funded grants. She was Principal Investigator and Director of the Chicago Institute for the Study of Learning Disabilities. The Chicago Institute was one of the five learning disabilities research centers funded by the Office of Special Education Programs from 1977 to 1982.

Currently, Dr. Bryan has extended her research interests to consider learning disabled and nondisabled students' vulnerability to crime victimization. A series of research studies is examining adolescents' attitudes, experiences, knowledge and strategies for coping with situations in which they might become involved in various antisocial acts.

In a different vein, Dr. Bryan is conducting classroom-based prereferral intervention research to identify the classroom (teacher and student) factors that lead teachers to refer individual children for special education evaluations. The goal of this research is to identify classroom factors that distinguish children who are referred from those who are underachieving but not referred, and to develop interventions that will better enable classroom teachers to program for heterogeneous classes of children.

Dr. Bryan has also been involved in the development of an Urban Educational Research and Development Center at the University of Illinois at Chicago. The goals of the Center are to address critical urban education problems through programs of educational research, technology transfer, and minority recruitment and retention.

Katharine G. Butler is Director of the Center for Research, School of Education, Syracuse University, and is Professor of Communication Sciences and Disorders. She received the Ph.D. in hearing and speech science from Michigan State University, and the B.A. and M.A. from Western Michigan University in communication disorders. She has served as President of the American Speech-Language-Hearing Association (ASHA); President of Division of Children with Communication Disorders (DCCD), Council of Exceptional Children; President of the National Association for Hearing and Speech Action; and President of the California Speech-Language-Hearing Association; and is currently President of the International Association of Logopedics and Phoniatrics and the New York State Speech-Language-Hearing Association. She is a Fellow of ASHA and of the International Academy for Research in Learning Disabilities, and holds the Honors of CSHA and of DCCD. She has also received Distinguished Alumni awards from both Michigan State and Western Michigan Universities. She has served as Chair of the National Joint Committee on Learning Disabilities.

Throughout her academic career, she has served in a number of clinical and administrative capacities, first as Assistant Professor of Psychology at Western Michigan University and then as Director of the Speech and Hearing Clinic at San Jose State University, Chairman of Special Education, Associate Dean for the School of Education, Associate Dean for the Graduate School, and Acting Dean, San Jose State University; Director of the Division of Special Education and Rehabilitation, and Director of the Center for Language Research at Syracuse University.

Her publications include more than 70 articles and books, the most recent being *Childhood Language Disorders* (1986), *Language Learning Disabilities in School Aged Children* (1984) edited by G. Wallach and K. Butler; and "Language Research: A Major Contribution to Special Education Theory and Practice," in *Special Education: Research and Trends* (1986), edited by R. B. Morris and B. Blatt. She serves as Editor of *Topics in Language Disorders* and as Redactor for *Folia Phoniatrica*, and is a member of several editorial boards, including *The Journal of Learning Disabilities*.

Dr. Butler has made major presentations on the topic of language learning disabilities in Tokyo, Hong Kong, Taipei, Barcelona, Edinburgh, and Dublin, and in Sweden, Switzerland/France, Italy, and Canada. She is an active member of the American Psychological Association, Orton Dyslexia Society, American Educational Research Association, Society for Research in Child Development, International Association for the Study of Child Language, International Association of Applied Linguistics, and the International Reading Association.

Carl W. Cotman is Professor of Psychobiology, Neurology, and Psychiatry and Director of the Neuroscience Association at the University of California, Irvine. His research centers on brain plasticity and recovery of cognitive function after injury. Dr. Cotman's work has illustrated that the brain is plastic throughout life and possesses regenerative capabilities that compensate for partial cell loss due to injury, disease, and aging. Recently, his studies have focused on the ability of transplanted fetal neurons and glial cells to facilitate the recovery of function in mature CNS circuits. Synaptic plasticity is probably aided by growth factors, called neurotrophic factors, which Dr. Cotman and others have shown to participate in the healing process after injury. Cotman and colleagues at Irvine have also recently demonstrated that synaptic regrowth occurs in Alzheimer's disease. Thus, in a predominantly degenerating disease, regenerative growth can occur which may help to preserve residual circuit functions.

Dr. Cotman obtained the Ph.D. from Indiana University with a major in biochemistry. He has close to 300 publications in the general area of synaptic plasticity and his most recent honors include the Allied Health Award (1987), UCI Distinguished Faculty Lectureship (1987), Wellcome Visiting Professorship (1985), the Pattison Prize in Neuroscience (1984), and the American Paralysis Association's Steven Camhi Award for Regeneration (1983). He has served as chairman of the scientific advisory committee for the American Paralysis Association, among others, and is a member of numerous professional scientific organizations. He has served as editor on six journals and reviewer on many others.

Albert M. Galaburda, who was born in Santiago, Chile, in 1948, came to the United States in 1963, at which time he finished high school and entered the combined program in liberal arts and medicine at Boston University. After graduating with the B.A.-M.D. degree with honors in 1971, Dr. Galaburda carried out clinical training in internal medicine and in neurology at the Boston City Hospital, the latter under the direction of the late Norman Geschwind, the Putnam Professor of Neurology at Harvard Medical School. Dr. Galaburda is currently Associate Professor of Neurology, Harvard Medical School. In 1977, after receiving board certification in internal medicine and in neurology, Dr. Galaburda began a research career first under the tutelage of the late German neuroanatomist Friedrich Sanides for studies in cerebral architectonics, next under Thomas Kemper for studies in neuropathology and developmental neuroanatomy, and later under Deepak Pandya for studies in cerebral connectivity. With Sanides, he published papers on the organization of the human auditory cortex and on architectonic cortical asymmetries in the human brain; with Pandya, he published on the connectional and architectonic organization of the primate auditory cortex; and with Kemper, he reported on the first detailed anatomical study of the brain in developmental dyslexia.

Over the past eight years, Dr. Galaburda has published over 90 papers and coedited four books on the subject of language and the brain, cerebral lateralization, comparative primate neuroanatomy, and developmental dyslexia. Current research is focused on disclosing developmental mechanisms for the production of brain asymmetry, anomalies in the development of brain asymmetry, anomalies in neuronal assemblies and their relationship to behavior, with special attention to developmental cognitive disturbances, and immune-brain interactions during development.

Dr. Galaburda is a member of the American Neurological Association, American Academy of Neurology, Society for Neuroscience, AAAS, American Association of Anatomists, and several other professional and research organizations. He is on the Scientific Advisory Council of the Orton Dyslexia Society and serves as liaison to the AAAS for this organization. He was the recipient of the 1983 Pattison Prize for Neuroscience and the 1987 Scientist of the Year award from the Association for Children With Learning Disabilities. Dr. Galaburda is also on the editorial board of *Neuropsychologia,* and serves as referee for several professional journals.

Frank M. Gresham is Professor of Psychology in the Department of Psychology at Louisiana State University in Baton Rouge. Dr. Gresham received the Ph.D. in psychology with a specialization in school psychology from the University of South Carolina in 1979. He is a Fellow of the American Psychological Association and a member of the National Association of School Psychologists and the American Educational Research Association. Dr. Gresham received the Lightner Witmer Award in 1982 from the American Psychological Association for outstanding scholarly research contributions by a school psychologist and received the Phi Kappa Phi award for outstanding scholarly contributions in the humanities and social sciences at Louisiana State University. He has served as a consultant to various school districts and state school psychological associations in over 30 states and Canada, presenting inservice training and workshops on social skills assessment and training, mainstreaming, and behavioral consultation. He is a licensed psychologist and a certified school psychologist.

Dr. Gresham serves on the editorial boards of seven journals, including the *Journal of School Psychology, School Psychology Review,* and *Journal of Behavioral Assessment and Psychopathology.* He serves as a frequent guest reviewer to 13 other journals including *Exceptional Children, American Journal of Mental Deficiency, Applied Research in Mental Retardation, Developmental Psychology, Child Development,* and *Review of Educational Research.*

Dr. Gresham has published 86 journal articles, books, or book chapters, primarily on the topics of social skills assessment and training, the relationship between social skills deficits of mildly handicapped children and mainstreaming outcomes, and social skills and self-efficacy of mildly handicapped children in mainstreamed and self-contained settings.

J. Stephen Hazel received the Ph.D. in psychology from the University of Illinois (1978). He was a postdoctoral fellow in the Department of Human Development and Family Life at the University of Kansas from 1978 through 1979. During that time, he began, with Jean Schumaker and other colleagues, to research the development of social skills training programs for adolescents.

He has continued research in social skills assessment and training of adolescents with disabilities and has published review and research articles in the field. In addition, he has coauthored two social skill training programs for adolescents: *ASSET: A Social Skills Program for Adolescents* and *Social Skills for Daily Living.*

Dr. Hazel is a Research Associate with the Institute for Research in Learning Disabilities and a Courtesy Assistant Professor in the Department of Human Development and Family Life at the University of Kansas. Currently, he is collaborating in the development of training programs for adolescents with disabilities, including a self-advocacy program, a transition curriculum, and a program for families with children with learning disabilities. In addition to his research interests, Dr. Hazel maintains a private practice in psychology focusing on children and adolescents.

Doris Johnson, Ph.D., is currently Professor and Program Head in Learning Disabilities at Northwestern University, Evanston, Illinois. Her professional preparation included degrees in speech/language pathology, learning disabilities, and counselor education from Augustana College in Rock Island, Illinois, and from Northwestern University. In addition, she received a certificate from the Child Care Program of the Chicago Institute for Psychoanalysis.

Dr. Johnson has spent most of her professional career at Northwestern, where she has done clinical supervision, teaching, and research. Her major research interests have been in the areas of oral language, reading, and written language. Currently, she is investigating patterns of problems among children in the early childhood years.

Dr. Johnson has numerous publications and is coauthor, with H. R. Myklebust, of *Learning Disabilities: Educational Principles and Practices*, a textbook which has been widely used in the United States and has been translated into several other languages. Most recently she coauthored, with Jane Blalock, *Adults With Learning Disabilities: Clinical Studies*. She is a member of several professional organizations and has received numerous awards. These include Outstanding Achievement awards from the National Association for Children and Adults with Learning Disabilities, the Illinois ACLD, the New Mexico ACLD, and the Augustana College Alumni Association. In addition, she was made a fellow in the American Speech-Language-Hearing Association. She has held numerous offices in professional organizations including the Professional Advisory Board of ACLD, which she now chairs, and the executive committee of the International Academy for Research in Learning Disabilities. In the past, she held various offices in the Council for Exceptional Children at the local, state, and national levels. She has been a guest lecturer in many universities and school systems in the United States and abroad, including Australia, New Zealand, Canada, Panama, South Africa, and Europe. She also has been appointed to several task forces dealing with issues in learning disabilities.

James F. Kavanagh is the Associate Director of the Center for Research for Mothers and Children of the National Institute of Child Health and Human Development, National Institutes of Health. He served as the Executive Secretary for the Interagency Committee on Learning Disabilities, which prepared *Learning Disabilities: A Report to the U.S. Congress,* as required by P.L. 99-158.

Dr. Kavanagh received the Ph.D. degree in speech and hearing from the University of Wisconsin at Madison where he also had postdoctoral research training in speech science, audiology, and psychology. He taught and directed graduate research at three universities before joining the NICHD as Health Scientist Administrator for Human Communication Research.

He has served as the Institute's Training Officer, Chief of the Growth and Development Program, and Chief of the Human Learning and Behavior Branch. He has published over 60 scientific articles and has edited or coedited twelve books including *Language by Ear and by Eye, Otitis Media and Child Development,* and *Biobehavioral Measures of Dyslexia,* which are in the series called Communicating by Language.

Dr. Kavanagh is a member of the National Advisory Board for Child Abuse and Neglect and a member of the Board and former Cochairman of the Extramural Associates Program. He is a Fellow in the American Speech-Language-Hearing Association, a member of the Editorial Board for *Topics in Language Disorders,* and a frequent reviewer for *Public Health Reports* and other professional journals.

Isabelle Y. Liberman is Professor Emeritus of Educational Psychology at the University of Connecticut and a research associate at Haskins Laboratories, New Haven, Connecticut. She earned the Ph.D. in psychology at Yale University in 1946. She is a Fellow of the American Psychological Association and also of the International Academy for Research in Learning Disabilities. In 1986, she was a Fulbright Scholar, invited to lecture at Lund, Gothenburg, and Umea Universities in Sweden, Oxford University in England, and Hebrew University in Israel. She has served on the editorial review boards of the *Reading Research Quarterly, Journal of Learning Disabilities, Annals of Dyslexia,* and *Remedial and Special Education,* and has also been consulting editor for other related journals in psychology and education. She is currently on the national board of directors of the Orton Dyslexia Society and was a member of the organizing committee of the Third World Congress of Dyslexia, which met in Crete, June 28-July 2, 1987.

Dr. Liberman's language-oriented view of reading and its disabilities has been widely influential in directing attention to the phonological aspects of literacy. She has published numerous journal articles and chapters of books on her research relating phonological awareness to reading acquisition and to the prediction, prevention, and remediation of reading problems.

Gary S. Lynch received the B.A. from the University of Delaware (1965) and the Ph.D. from Princeton University (1968), where he was Research Associate and Lecturer the following year. He then joined the faculty of the University of California, Irvine, where he is now Professor of Psychobiology. Dr. Lynch's research is focused on identifying the processes used by networks in the mammalian brain to encode memory, and he has authored or coauthored over 250 articles and chapters. He has been a Councilor of the Neuroscience Society and is on the Advisory Board of the Cognitive Neurosciences Institute. He is also an advisor to the E. I. duPont Co. and to Scientific Pharmaceutics, Inc. In 1975, he received the Outstanding Teacher Award at the University of California, Irvine.

Isabelle Rapin, who is a native of Switzerland, is currently Professor of Neurology and Pediatrics (Neurology) and Attending Neurologist and Child Neurologist at the Albert Einstein College of Medicine and its affiliated hospitals, Bronx, New York, where she has been since 1958. She graduated from medical school in Lausanne, Switzerland, and had a pediatric internship at New York University-Bellevue Medical Center and three years of neurology residency and one year of pediatric neurology fellowship at the Neurological Institute of Columbia-Presbyterian Medical Center, New York City. She founded the Child Neurology Service and Fellowship Training Program at Einstein and served as its Director from 1958-1972. Her research interests have been and are genetic disorders and disorders of higher cerebral function in children, in particular communication disorders and autism. She has worked for many years as a consultant at St. Joseph School for the Deaf in the Bronx. She is the author of the book *Children with Brain Dysfunction, Neurology, Cognition, Language, and Behavior* (Raven Press, New York, 1982) and of over 120 papers and chapters, many of them concerned with children with communication disorders. With R. B. David, M.D. (St. Mary's Hospital, Richmond, Virginia), she is coprincipal investigator for the multi-institutional multidisciplinary program project Nosology: Higher Cortical Function Disorders in Children supported by the National Institute of Neurological and Communicative Disorders and Stroke. Dr. Rapin is currently a member of the National Advisory Neurological and Communicative Disorders and Stroke Council, was Secretary-General and Vice-President of the International Child Neurology Association, First Vice-President of the American Neurological Association, President of the Tri-State Child Neurology Society, and a Board Member of the Child Neurology Society and of the International Neuropsychology Society. She has given over 200 lectures and served as visiting professor in many universities in the United States and abroad, and as a consulting editor to several professional journals. She was nominated to receive the Hower Award of the Child Neurology Society in October 1987.

Carrie Rozelle is the Founder and President of the Foundation for Children with Learning Disabilities, a national voluntary organization devoted to increasing public awareness of learning disabilities.

The FCLD provides grants to innovative programs serving children with learning disabilities and their families across the country.

The Foundation is a direct outgrowth of Mrs. Rozelle's personal experience as the mother of learning disabled sons. Mrs. Rozelle and her husband, NFL Commissioner, Pete Rozelle, live in a suburb of New York.

Mrs. Rozelle is a member of both International United Way and National United Way of America Board of Governors. She is Chair of the Volunteer Involvement Committee of United Way of America's Second Century Initiative and serves on the Long Range Planning Committee as well as the United Way Tri-State Board of Directors. Mrs. Rozelle is Chair of the Committee on Youth in Voluntarism for United Way of America. She serves on the Advisory Board of Family Service of America. Locally, Mrs. Rozelle serves on committees of Irvington House, New York (cancer research), is a member of the United Hospital of Westchester Women's Auxiliary, and a member of the National Women's Political Caucus. She serves on the Professional Advisory Board of New York Medical Center, Valhallah, New York, and the Board of Directors of Gannett Foundation in Rochester, New York.

While living in Los Angeles, she served as a member of the Assistance League, Southern California, the Blue Ribbon 400 of the Los Angeles Music Center, and was a member of the Women's Committee Hemophilia Foundation, California.

Carrie Rozelle was born in Toronto, Canada, educated in Canada and England and is a Registered Nurse, specializing in surgery.

Jean Bragg Schumaker received the Ph.D. in developmental and child psychology from the University of Kansas in 1976. Since then, her work has focused on adolescents and their problems, including juvenile delinquency, social skill deficits, and low achievement in school. She has been the Coordinator of Research at the Institute for Research in Learning Disabilities since 1978 and is a Courtesy Associate Professor in the Department of Human Development at the University of Kansas. Working with Dr. Stephen Hazel and other colleagues, Dr. Schumaker has conducted a programmatic line of research in the area of social skills for the last ten years. That research has resulted in more than fifteen articles and chapters as well as two social skills curricula for adolescents: *ASSET: A Social Skills Program for Adolescents* and *Social Skills for Daily Living*. Additionally, Dr. Schumaker, along with her colleague, Dr. Donald Deshler, has developed the Strategies Intervention Model (SIM), a program for remediating the academic deficits of learning disabled and other low-achieving adolescents. During the course of the development of this model, she has authored six books and numerous articles. She has been principal investigator on twelve grants and contracts. Her current research focuses on methods for remediating social skill deficits and academic skills deficits within mainstream classrooms, learning strategies, math strategies, transitions from secondary school to postsecondary life, self-control, and family interventions.

Bennett A. Shayitz is a graduate of Washington University (A.B. 1960, M.D. 1963). He trained first in pediatrics and then child neurology at the Albert Einstein College of Medicine and served as Lieutenant Colonel in the Air Force before joining the Yale University faculty in 1972. He has served as Chief of Pediatric Neurology since 1975 and is currently Associate Professor of Pediatrics, Neurology and Child Study Center. Dr. Shaywitz' primary and long-standing research has focused on the neurobiological influences in learning and attention disorders, and the great majority of his over 150 articles and chapters emphasize the relationships between brain neurotransmitters and disorders of learning and attention. His most recent area of investigation involves the nosology and classification of learning and attention disorders. He serves on advisory boards of the National Institute of Neurological and Communicative Disorders and Stroke and the National Academy of Sciences, the Professional Advisory Board of the Foundation for Children With Learning Disabilities and of the Reye Syndrome Foundation, and the Editorial Board of *Pediatric Neurology*. A dedicated naturalist, Dr. Shaywitz, along with his wife and three sons, has photographed wildlife throughout North America.

Sally E. Shaywitz is a graduate of the City University of New York (B.S. 1962) and the Albert Einstein College of Medicine (M.D. 1966), where she also completed her residency in pediatrics and a fellowship in neurobehavioral pediatrics. Dr. Shaywitz' interest in learning and attention disorders in children has provided the focus for both her clinical and investigational activities. She is the author of over 60 articles and chapters relating to learning and attention disorders, with a particular interest in their epidemiology. In addition, she has studied girls with attention disorder and has most recently called attention to the gifted-learning disabled child. She established the Learning Disorders Unit in the Department of Pediatrics at Yale University School of Medicine in 1976 and continues to serve as its Director as well as Associate Professor of Pediatrics, and Child Study Center. She serves on the Professional Advisory Board of the Foundation for Children with Learning Disabilities, the Editorial Board of the *Journal of Learning Disabilities*, the Yale University Resource Committee on People with Disabilities, and as a consultant to the National Institute of Neurological and Communicative Disorders and Stroke. An avid sportswoman, Dr. Shaywitz along with her husband and three sons have sailed competitively.

Margaret Jo Shepherd received the B.S. and Ed.M. in special education from the University of Illinois in 1955 and the Ed.D. in special education from Teachers College, Columbia University, in 1969. Since 1970, she has been the Director of the Learning Disabilities Program in the Department of Special Education at Teachers College. From 1977 through 1983, she was on the staff of the Institute for Research on

Learning Disabilities at Teachers College, which was one of five Federally funded institutes for research on learning disabilities. Her research has dealt with memory strategies and memory strategy instruction. A summary of that research has recently been published in a volume entitled *Memory and Learning Disabilities: Advances in Learning and Behavioral Disabilities, Suppl. 2*, edited by H. D. Swanson and published by JAI Press. She has recently finished two summary articles, one on developmental reading disorder and the other on developmental writing disorder. Both will be published in *The Comprehensive Textbook of Psychiatry (5th Edition)*, edited by H. I. Kaplan and B. J. Sadock and published by Williams and Wilkins. She is a trustee of The Churchill School and Center, and The Gateway School, which are private schools for learning disabled children in New York City, and serves on the Professional Advisory Board for the Foundation for Children With Learning Disabilities and the Association for Children and Adults With Learning Disabilities. She is also a Fellow of the International Academy for Research on Learning Disabilities and worked on the revision of the section on specific developmental disorders for the DSM-III-R.

James M. Swanson received the Ph.D. from Ohio State University in 1970. He was on the faculty of the University of Texas at Austin from 1970 to 1974. From 1975 to 1980, he was a Research Scientist in the Research Institute of the Hospital for Sick Children in Toronto, Canada. In 1980, he joined the faculty of the University of California, Irvine (where he is a Professor of Pediatrics, Psychiatry, and Social Science) and the State Developmental Research Institute (where he is a Research Scientist). At UCI, he is also Director of the Child Development Center, and at SDRI he is the Director of the Computer and Learning Laboratories.

Since 1975, Dr. Swanson has focused on the study of attention deficit disorder/hyperactivity in children. His early work at the Hospital for Sick Children was in collaboration with Dr. Marcel Kinsbourne, a pediatric neurologist. Together, they developed methods for the double-blind assessment of the effects of stimulant medication on ADD/hyperactive children. Their methods relied on the use of laboratory learning tests to document the cognitive effects of stimulant medication, and in a series of publications pointed out that a significant minority of ADD/H children manifested an adverse or nonresponse when objective, double-blind procedures were used to supplement the subjective reports of parents and teachers. These procedures are now in regular clinical use at the Hospital of Sick Children and at the University of California, Irvine.

Since 1980, Dr. Swanson has concentrated his efforts on developing clinical procedures for intensive intervention with ADD/H children and their families. At the UCI Child Development Center, in collaboration with the public school system of Orange County, he and Steve Simpson have established a school-based day-treatment program for

45 ADD/H children with serious attention and behavior problems. The goal of this combined clinical and educational program is to prevent these at-risk children from developing more serious antisocial behavior as the they mature.

Dr. Swanson is the Editor of a new monograph series published by the *Journal of Child Psychology and Psychiatry,* entitled *Developmental Psychopathology: Attention and Conduct Problems in Children,* which evolved out of the annual Bloomingdale meetings on ADD/H.

Paula Tallal received the B.A. from New York University, where she majored in art history, minored in psychology, and completed the requirements for premedical studies. While an undergraduate, she gained laboratory research experience in physiological psychology, working at the Rockefeller University. After completing the B.A., she became a Research Associate in the Department of Anatomy at Cambridge University, England. Dr. Tallal was accepted as a graduate student in the Department of Experimental Psychology at Cambridge University, where she received the Ph.D. in 1974.

After completing the Ph.D., she was granted an NIH postdoctoral fellowship at the Kennedy Institute at Johns Hopkins School of Medicine and was later awarded a major NIH research grant to continue and expand her studies on the neurological basis of language development and disorders. In 1977, Dr. Tallal was selected as the Distinguished Young Scientist of the Year by the Maryland Academy of Sciences. She also received a Mayor's Citation for her research in Baltimore, was awarded the President's Medal for Creativity from Notre Dame College, and was selected to participate on the National Panel of Outstanding Women in Science. In 1978, Dr. Tallal joined the faculty of the University of California, San Diego, where she is presently Professor of Psychiatry and is Director of the Language Research Center at San Diego's Children's Hospital.

Dr. Tallal has published over 75 papers on the neurological basis of language. She presently is the principal investigator of two major NINCDS-funded programs. The first is a longitudinal study evaluating the outcomes of preschool impairments in language. In this study, over 200 children with normal or impaired language development are being followed longitudinally from ages 2.5 to 9 years to determine the effect of language disorders on subsequent linguistic, neuropsychological, intellectual, academic achievement, and social and emotional development. The second is a Research Center for Neurodevelopmental Studies. The first of its type in the United States, this Center was developed specifically to facilitate collaborations between scientists across many different disciplines to focus on the biological basis of neurodevelopmental disabilities. Neuroanatomical, neurochemical, neurological, neurophysiological, neuropsychological, and neurolinguistic studies of a variety of children with neurodevelopmental disorders form the basis of this research.

Dr. Tallal has recently been appointed Codirector of Rutgers University's new Center for Molecular and Behavioral Neurosciences.

Richard F. Thompson is Keck Professor of Psychology and Biological Sciences at the University of Southern California. Prior to this, he was Bing Professor of Human Biology and Professor of Psychology at Stanford University, where he served as Chair of the Human Biology Program from 1980-1985. Previous positions include Professor of Psychobiology in the School of Biological Sciences at the University of California, Irvine, Professor of Psychology (Karl Lashley's chair) at Harvard University, and Professor of Medical Psychology and Psychiatry at the University of Oregon Medical School. He received the B.A. degree at Reed College, the Ph.D. in psychobiology at the University of Wisconsin, and did postdoctoral research in the laboratory of neurophysiology at the University of Wisconsin and in the laboratory of neurophysiology at the University of Goteborg in Sweden.

His area of research and scholarly interest is the broad field of psychobiology, with a focus on the neurobiological substrates of learning and memory. He has written several texts, edited several books and published over 200 research papers. Honors and societies include the National Academy of Sciences, the Distinguished Scientific Contribution Award of the American Psychological Association, Councilor of the Society for Neuroscience, member of the Society of Experimental Psychologists, Chair of the Psychonomic Society, President of Division 6 of the American Psychological Association, and a Research Scientist Career Award from the National Institute of Mental Health.

He has been involved in a wide range of scientific-administrative activities at the national level, including the Assembly of Behavioral and Social Sciences of the National Research Council, a Presidential Task Panel on Research in Mental Health, Chair of the Board of Scientific Affairs of the American Psychological Association, Chair of the Committee on Animal Research and Experimentation of the American Psychological Association, Chair of the Psychology Section of the AAAS, Chair of the Psychology Section of the National Academy of Sciences, previously Chief Editor of *Physiological Psychology* and *The Journal of Comparative and Physiological Psychology*. He is currently Chief Editor of *Behavioral Neuroscience*, Regional Editor of *Physiology and Behavior* and *Behavioral Brain Research*, and Associate Editor of the *Annual Review of Neuroscience*. He is on the editorial board of a number of other scientific journals. Dr. Thompson also has served on several research and training grant panels for the National Science Foundation and the National Institutes of Health and on committees of the National Research Council/National Academy of Sciences.

Joseph K. Torgesen received the Ph.D. in clinical and developmental psychology from the University of Michigan in 1976. At present he is Professor and Director of the School Psychology Program in the

Department of Psychology at Florida State University. Dr. Torgesen is best known for his research describing learning disabled children's difficulties in using efficient cognitive strategies on intellectual tasks. He is also well known for his conceptualization of learning disabled children as "inactive" or "maladaptive" learners. His recent research focuses on the phonological processing disabilities of children with severe reading difficulties. In addition to an extensive series of empirical studies on this topic, he has published a recent review of the area (with Richard Wagner) in the *Psychological Bulletin*, entitled "The nature of phonological processing and its causal role in the acquisition of reading skills." Dr. Torgesen is also studying methods to remediate reading disabilities through the use of computer assisted instruction. With Bernice Wong, Dr. Torgesen is the editor of a book recently published by Academic Press entitled *Psychological and Educational Perspectives on Learning Disabilities*, and he has published over 50 chapters and journal articles in the field. For the past several years, Dr. Torgesen has edited a series of review papers for the *Journal of Learning Disabilities*, and he is currently serving as an Associate Field Editor for that journal.

Tom J. Truss, Jr., received the B.A. *magna cum laude* (1948) and the M.A. (1950) from Vanderbilt University and the Ph.D. (1957) from the University of Wisconsin. His teaching career began in 1952 as Instructor in English at the University of South Dakota, and in 1957 he joined the faculty of the University of Mississippi, where he served in numerous capacities, including Director of Freshman English. After advancing to Professor of English, he joined the Washington Office staff of the American Association of University Professors (AAUP) in 1966, where he was Associate Editor of the *AAUP Bulletin*. He was also conference coordinator for the AAUP, looked after its Reference and Information Office, and served as staff liaison for several Association committees. In 1980, he accepted an appointment at the National Institutes of Health. Since then, he has edited over fifteen NIH publications, including the Ninth and Tenth Reports of the Director, National Heart, Lung, and Blood Institute (NHLBI), which received awards from the D.C. Chapter of the Society for Technical Communications. In 1987, he was cited by the National Heart, Lung, and Blood Institute for his contribution to the quality of NHLBI publications and for enhancing the Institute's standards of excellence in writing.

Dr. Truss' publications early in his career are in the area of Victorian studies. More recently, he has published musical criticism and reviews in the Washington area.

He is a member of Phi Beta Kappa and Omicron Delta Kappa.

Hill M. Walker received the Ph.D., with honors, in special education from the University of Oregon in 1967. He is currently a Professor of Special Education at the University of Oregon, where he has been a faculty member since completing his graduate training. Since 1982,

Dr. Walker has been Associate Dean for Special Education and Rehabilitation, Director of the Center on Human Development, and UAF director at the University of Oregon.

During this period, he has been either the principal investigator or coprincipal investigator on 14 Federally funded research, demonstration, and training grants. He is the author of four books, two social skills curricula, and three tests. He has published over 60 articles in refereed journals. He is the author of *The Acting Out Child, The Walker Problem Behavior Identification Checklist*, the *ACCEPTS* and *ACCESS* social skills training programs, and the *Walker-McConnell Social Skills Rating Scale for Teachers*.

He has chaired the Oregon Social Learning Center Board of Directors since 1982. He was recently elected to the governing board of the American Association of University Affiliated Programs. Since 1975, he has consulted extensively across the country on colleagues' research projects. He will be a keynote speaker at the 1988 Australian National Conference on Special Education in Sydney.

Dr. Walker's research interests include assessment and intervention in school-related behavior disorders, mainstreaming and social integration, and social skills training. His professional contributions are generally balanced across these three broad areas.

Carol K. Whalen is Professor of Social Ecology at the University of California, Irvine. She received the B.A. in psychology from Stanford University, and the M.A. and Ph.D. in clinical psychology from the University of California, Los Angeles. She serves on the National Academy of Sciences' Committee on Child Development Research and Public Policy and on the National Heart, Lung, and Blood Institute's Data and Safety Monitoring Committee for the Dietary Intervention Study in Children. She is also a Fellow of the Clinical Psychology and Health Psychology divisions of the American Psychological Association and a past member of the NIMH Treatment Development and Assessment Research Review Panel. For the past two decades, her research has focused on both childhood psychopathology and normal development, with an emphasis on social behavior and child therapies. She has special expertise in the areas of hyperactivity and attention deficit disorders. She has published numerous papers on these topics in such journals as *Science, Pediatric Clinics of North America, Journal of Consulting and Clinical Psychology, Child Development, Clinical Psychology Review*, and the *Journal of Abnormal Child Psychology*. She is also coeditor, with Professor Barbara Henker, of a volume entitled *Hyperactive Children: The Social Ecology of Identification and Treatment* (Academic Press, 1980).

Gabrielle Weiss, M.D., Professor of Psychiatry, McGill University, and Director, Department of Psychiatry, Montreal Children's Hospital, has been involved in research related to hyperactive children for 25 years. Initially in 1962, she and Dr. John S. Werry started to look at differences in the gestation and birth of hyperactives as well as possible differences in electroencephalograms. Later, they conducted controlled drug studies with Chlorpromazine, Dextromphetamine, and Methylphenidate. With Dr. Lily Hechtman, she followed both treated and untreated hyperactives for 5, 10, 15, and 20 years, assessing them at these different ages. She has published 36 articles and 10 chapters, and recently with Dr. Hechtman, she has published *Hyperactive Children Grown Up* (Guilford), which describes the sum total of their research with these children and adults.

INDEX

(Page numbers in italics indicate material in tables or in figures.)

Acetylcholine, possible role in learning disability, 48–49
Aciduria, 221
ADD. *See* Attention deficit disorder (ADD); Auditory Discrimination in Depth (ADD) program
ADHD. *See* Attention deficit/hyperactivity disorder
Alcohol, fetal effects of, 224–25
Alzheimer's disease, 39, 55
American Psychiatric Association. *See Diagnostic and Statistical Manual (DSMII); Diagnostic and Statistical Manual (DSMIII).*
Amnesia. *See also* Memory
  drug-induced, 56
  hippocampal lesions and, 5, 43
  memory-blocking drugs and, 24, 26
  memory formation and study of, 38
  rodent models of primate and human, 43–46
Aphasia
  developmental, 182
  research on, 200
Aplysia californica (sea snail), learning and memory in, 8–10
Association for Children and Adults with Learning Disabilities (ACLD), 81
Attention deficit disorder (ADD). *See also* Hyperactivity; Oppositional defiant disorder (ODD)
  associated conditions, 401–403, 403–405
  brain dysfunction and, 373–76, 466
  clinical characteristics, 430–51
  cross-cultural studies and, 454–55, 535
  current concepts of, 376
  current terminology and criteria, 391–93
  definition and syndrome validation, 376–87
  deficiency states and, 468
  diagnostic features, 396–99
  diet and, 468
  environmental and cultural factors and, 470–72
  environmental and perinatal factors in, 464–66
  epidemiology of, 451–58
  exogenous toxins and, 467–68
  genetic influences on, 458–60
  historic perspectives on, 372–73

infections and metabolic disorders in, 466–67
learning disabilities and, 456–57
neurochemical abnormalities and, 460–64
neurological problems and, 469–70
opinions on validity as a syndrome, 387–91
prevalence of, 452–54
prognosis of, 492–95
residual type hyperactive (ADDRT), 447–48
sex differences in, 455–56
as a syndrome, 387–91, 530
treatment of, 473–77, 477–80, 480–92, 526, 531, 536–45
types of, 392–99, 399–401, 456
Attention deficit disorder assessment measures, 403–406
  direct measures, 417–20
  instruments under development, 414–17
  laboratory measures, 430
  measures of attention, 420–24
  minor congenital anomalies and, 425–26
  neurological examination, 426–27
  physical examination, 424
  psychometric examination, 428
  rating scales, 406–414
  specific measures, 428–30
  structured interviews, 417
Attention deficit disorder with hyperactivity (ADDH), 372
  criteria for, 392
Attention deficit/hyperactivity disorder, 536–38, 540–45
Auditory Discrimination in Depth (ADD) program, 249
Auditory processing disorders, 231

Behavioral rating scales, 302–303
Behavioral teratogenicity, 223
Behavior problems, 278–79, 536. *See also* Attention deficit disorder (ADD); Conduct disorder; Hyperactivity; Oppositional defiant disorder (ODD)
Behavior Rating Scale (Hardin and Busch), 99
Bender Gestalt test, 98
Biochemical disorders and ADD, 460–64
Biochemical memory encoding mechanisms, 49–50
Birth complications, LD and, 92

Birth weight, LD and, 91
"Black" English, 125
Brain. *See also names of specific brain parts or regions*
  abnormal endocrine signals and development of the, 221–22
  activity-dependent developmental changes in, 32, 54
  age and effect of cortical lesions in, 231
  areas critical to memory formation, 38
  chemistry of memory in, 4
  computerized tomography of the, 116–18, 430
  developmental effects of chemicals and drugs on the, 223–25
  dyslexia and characteristics of the, 116
  early visual input and changes in, 32, 54
  electroencephalographic studies and, 117–18
  inherent capacity for repair in, 51
  lateralization and development of, 222–23
  local structural changes associated with learning, 30
  mapping of electrophysiological responses in, 16
  mathematics-learning disorders and, 133–34
  memory capacity of, 6
  memory circuits in, 5–6
  olfactory cues accessing memory-related structures of the, 44–45
  roles of cortical and subcortical regions in memory, 5, 75
  Wernicke's area development, 222
Brain cortex
  age and lesions of, 231
  calcium and plasticity of, 34
  correlates of learning in circuitries of, 35–46
  as storage site, 5
Brain damage
  ADDH and, 372–73
  developmental language disorders and, 230–35, 275
Brain electrical activity mapping (BEAM) in dyslexics and in learning disabled subjects, 118
Brain injury, 50–51, 231
Brain structures, olfactory cues accessing memory-related, 44–45
Brain wave patterns. *See* Electroencephalographic studies

Calcium
  anatomic changes in response to elevated levels of, 56
  synapses and, 25
Calpain (calcium-activated protease), 26

Cerebellum
  anatomical inputs to, 74
  association areas of cerebral cortex and, 75
  learning and, 16, 74
  mossy fiber system of, 18–19
  as site of memory trace for a conditioned reflex, 17
Cerebral cortex, cerebellum and association areas of, 75
Cerebral palsy, 275
Childhood illnesses, learning disabilities and, 95–96
Chloride deficiency, 225
Clinical syndromes, primate models of, 37–43
CMV. *See* Cytomegalovirus
Cognition
  in children with impaired verbal skills, 273–74
  language-impaired children and, 200–202
  olfaction to detect dysfunction in brain systems crucial to, 45
Cognitive factors in social skills, 316–20
Cognitive learning, vulnerability to neuropathological conditions, 55
Cognitive learning deficits, odor memories in rodents and humans, 45–46
Cognitive therapy, 538–39
Columbia University Institute, 136
Composition (written discourse), 126–28
Computer-assisted video, 365
Computerized tomography (CT) of brain, 116–17, 430
Computer simulations
  of learning in neural networks, 46–47
  research recommendations for, 58
Computers and word processors, written discourse and, 127–28
Conditioned reflex(es) (CR)
  abolition by morphine, 16
  biochemistry of, 16, 19
  GABA and, 19
  memory trace in cerebellum, 17
  model of, 16, *17*
Conditioned stimulus (CS), 15
  electromicrostimulation of mossy fiber system as, 18–19
Conditioning
  of eye blink response, 14, 15–19
  of forearm position, *14*, 19–21
  formation of new synapses with, 20
  molecular and cellular basis for, 9, 12
  red nucleus and avoidance, 20
Conduct disorder, *539*
  ADD and, 403–405
Conners Teacher Rating Scale, 533–34

Content knowledge, impact of children's, 174
CR. *See* Conditioned reflex(es) (CR)
Cross-cultural studies, 90, 118–19, 454–55
CS. *See* Conditioned stimulus (CS)
CYCLE (language test), 211
Cytomegalovirus, SES and effect of, 97

Day care centers, intervention in, 98
Decoding and word recognition research, 105–107
de Hirsch index, 98–99
Developmental age, 99
Developmental disorders, 166
Developmental dyslexia. *See also* Reading disability
    brain and, 115–18, 232–34
    cross-cultural studies of, 118–19
    neurodiagnostic procedures in study of, 115
    recent approaches and theories, and, 103–105
    research on, 200
    sex differences in, 119–20
    studies on learning strategy and, 110–11
Developmental dysphasia, 232, 273–74, 276–81, 281. *See also* Developmental language disorders; Dysphasia
Developmental language delay (DLD), 276, 281
    diagnosis of, 207–208, 208–211, 211–13, 273
    differential diagnosis of, 211–13
    discrepancies indicative of specific, 212
    emotional and behavior problems and, 278–79
    etiology of, 274–76
    nature of, 276
    patterns of language disorder in, 213
    prevalence of, 213–15
    research in, 183, 287
    subtypes of, 276–78
Developmental language disorders
    brain and, 230–35
    developmental reading disorders and, 200
    etiology of, 215–16, 216–36
    language-impaired children and phonology and, 184–86
    prognosis for, 253–54
    research in, 285
Diagnostic and Statistical Manual (DSM-II), 183
Diagnostic and Statistical Manual (DSM-III), 183, 381–82, 392–96, 430–33, 453–54, 536
DLD. *See* Developmental Language Delay (DLD)
Drug exposure, intrauterine, 224

Dynamic assessment of learning disability, 86
Dyslexia. *See* Developmental dyslexia
Dyslexics. *See* Poor readers
Dysphasia, 275–76. *See also* Developmental dysphasia

Electroencephalographic studies, 117–18, 230–31, 430
Emotional and behavior problems, 278–79. *See also* Attention deficit disorder (ADD); Conduct disorder; Hyperactivity; Oppositional defiant disorder (ODD)
Endocrines, developmental language disorders and, 221–23
Environment, arborization of cortical neurons and enriched, 54
Environmental factors
    learning disability and, 94
    ADD and early, 464–66
Epilepsy, interneurons and, 48
Ethylmalonic aciduria, 221
Eyeblink response, 15–19
Eyelid conditioning, 55
Eye movement research, 112–15

Familial patterns, learning disability and, 94. *See also* Genetic factors
Forearm position conditioning, 19–21

GABA. *See* Gamma-aminobutyric acid (GABA)
Galactosemia, 220
Gamma-aminobutyric acid (GABA), conditioned reflexes and, 19
Genetic factors
    in developmental language disorders, 216–19
    in learning disability, 94–95
Gesell School Readiness Screening Test, 99

Handwriting, 120, 121, 122
Head trauma, 96
Haemophilus influenzae meningitis, 467
Hearing impairment, 227–29
Hermissenda (sea slug), learning and memory in, 10–12
Hippocampus
    amnesia and, 5, 43
    fact memories and, 5, 7
    long-term potentiation of, 24–26
Hisky-Nebraska Test of Learning Aptitude, 212
Histidinemia, 220
Hormones. *See* Endocrines
4-hyroxybutyric aciduria, 221
Hyperactivity, 330–34, 372. *See also* Attention deficit disorder (ADD)
    criteria for, 392

Infections. *See also names of specific infections* (*e.g.*, Cytomegalovirus; Otitis media)
in ADD, 466–67
in developmental language disorders, 225–30
Inhibitory interneurons, 49
Intelligence
assessment of language and of, 211
nonverbal tests of, 212
tests of, 83–85
Intervention
cognitive, 538–39
in day care centers, 98
for dysphasics, 279
with learning disability, 135–38
for language impairment, 237–38, 237–41, 241–53
multimodal, 539
reading, 111

Jansky-de Hirsch test battery, 98–99

Knowledge, 1
children's, 174

Language
assessment of intelligence and, 211
standardized measures of, 208, 210
Language delay. *See* Developmental language delay
Language development
otitis media and, 226–30
phonological development and, 183
Language disorders, 182, 183. *See also* Developmental language disorders
nomenclature (DSM-III), 18
Language-impaired (LI) children
cognitive characteristics of, 200–202
left-hemisphere lesions and, 234
lexical acquisition and, 191
linguistic subgroups of, 194–96
morphology and word formation and, 186–87
neuropsychological (perceptual) motor characteristics, 196–99
nonverbal tests for, 211–12, 213
phonology and, 184–86
reading profiles of, 199–200
research on, 206–207
semantics and, 190–91
social-emotional characteristics of, 202–205
syntax and, 187–90
ungrammatical utterances and, 188
use of language in context and, 191–94
vocabulary acquisition and, 191
Language impairment (LI). *See also names of specific types of impairment*
diagnosis of, 207–208, 208–211, 211–13

future research and, 254–255
intervention for, 237–38, 238–41, 241–53
prognosis in, 253–54
psychogenic effects of, 235–36
SES and, 235
specific, 182
Language learning, radio and television and, 137–38
Language testing, 208–11
Laurence-Moon-Beidl syndrome, 221
LD. *See* Learning disabled (LD) children; Learning disabilities
Lead poisoning, 223–24
Learning, 2. *See also* Conditioned reflex(es) (CR); Memory; Models of Learning
associative, 10, 20
basic neurobiological mechanism of (in vertebrates), 21–23
cellular mechanisms, of, 8, 11
cerebellum and skill, 74
computer simulation of, 46–47
cortical circuitries and correlates of, 27–35
early olfactory, 28–31
essential memory trace circuit and, 17–19
invertebrate models of, 8–14
local structural changes in brain and, 30
long-term potentiation and, 26
neural model of associative, 13
neurobiological changes and early, 27–34
neurobiological descriptions to explain, 3
sprouting of new synapses as mechanism for, 23
Learning deficits, odor memories in rodents and human cognitive, 45
Learning-disabled (LD) children, 79
assessment of, 85–86
career awareness for, 143
discrepancy between ability and achievement and, 86–87
definition of, 80–82
gifted, 141
incidence and identification of, 80–82
IQ levels of, 83–84
prognosis and outcomes for, 138
program eligibility and, 82
underachievers and, 138
Learning disabilities, 164–67, 175, 549–51. *See also* Reading disability
ADD and, 401–403
from agents acting at various levels, 71
biochemical factors in, 117
birth complications and, 92–94
birth weight and, 91
childhood illnesses and, 95–96

environmental factors and, 94
etiology of, 90–98, 248–51
familial patterns and genetic factors in, 94–95
interaction of biological, social, cultural, and educational factors in, 96–98
intervention in, 51–53, 98, 135–38
maternal factors in, 92–94
medication and, 92–94
neurobiological causes of, 47–51
otitis media and, 95–96
predicting, 98–101
prospects for correction of, 51–53
research in, 87–90
tests to measure, 82–83
Learning strategies, 110–11
Learning theory, 176
Leiter International Performance Scale, 212
LI. See Language impairment
LIMAX simulation (of neural model of associative learning) program, 13
Limax (terrestial mollusc), learning and memory in, 12–13
Longitudinal studies, need for, 97
Long-term potentiation (LTP)
blocking by NMDA receptor antagonist, 25
learning and, 26, 56
major events in, 25–26
memory and, 24
synaptic facilitation and, 23

McCarthy Scales of Children's Ability, 211, 212
Magnetic resonance imaging, 118
Maternal behaviors
ADD and, 443–44
verbally unresponsive, 96
Mathematics (learning), 128–29
arithmetic, 131–32
language and, 129–30
logical reasoning and, 129
neuropsychological perspectives and, 132–34
predicting achievement in, 134
visual-spatial factors in, 130–131
Memory. See also Amnesia; Aphasia; Conditioning; Learning
in Aplysia californica, 8–10
brain structures essential for fact vs. rule, 39–40
categories and disturbances of, 2
cellular mechanisms of, 7, 11
endocrines and, 48
essential memory trace circuit and, 17–19
fact, 2, 39, 75
olfaction to detect dysfunction in brain systems crucial to, 45
olfactory cues and, 44–45
poor readers and, 170

possible origins of, 24
procedural, 2, 19
process of formation of, 24
rule, 39
short-term, 74
skill, 19, 75
of spatial location, 74
systems of, 3
tests of, 214–15
Memory-blocking drugs, 24
Memory deficits, primate vs. man, 40–43. See also Amnesia
Memory encoding systems, biochemical, 49–50
Metabolic encephalopathies, ADD and, 466, 467
Metabolic errors in developmental language disorders, 219–21
3-methylgutaconic aciduria, 221
Metropolitan Readiness Test, 98, 100
Minimal brain dysfunction (MBD), 372, 374–76
Models
animal, 55
of associative learning, 13
invertebrate, 8–14, 53
primate, 37–43
rodent, 43–46
Monoaminergic deficiency, 116
Morphine, abolition of CR by, 16
Mossy fiber system. See Cerebellum, mossy fiber system of

National Joint Committee on Learning Disabilities (NJCLD), 81
Neural experience, organization of developing visual system and, 32
Neurobiological changes following learning, 27–34
Neuromodulation, molecular events and activity-dependent, 10
Neurons. See also Synapses
arborization of cortical, 54
structural response to environment, 35
NMDA antagonist, 31
NMDA receptors, 27, 28
N-methyl-D-aspartate (NMDA), 25
Nomenclature. See Terminology and Terms
Nonverbal tests of intelligence, 211–12, 213
Norepinephrine and learning disability, 48–49

Ocular dominance, 33
ODD. See Oppositional defiant disorder (ODD)
Odors, activation of glomerular layer of olfactory bulb by, 29
Odor memories, 45–46
Olfaction to detect impaired brain systems crucial to cognition, 45

Olfactory bulb, 28, 29–30, 31
Olfactory pathways, *44*
Opioids, role in learned fear, anxiety, and aversive learning, 16, 55
Oppositional defiant disorder (ODD), 536, 537, *538. See also* Attention deficit disorder (ADD)
Otitis media (OM)
    ADD and, 467
    language development and, 226–30
    learning disabilities and, 95–96

Parents' role in language development, 235–36
Parent training program for ADHD and/or ODD children, 540–41
Peabody Picture Vocabulary Test, 211, 212
Peer acceptance and peer relations, 355, 362, 363, 366
    ADD and, 444–46
Perceptual/motor characteristics of LI children, 196–99
Phenobarbital, 225
Phenylketonuria (PKU), 220
Phonological awareness, 171
Phonological development, language development and, 183
Phonological structure, 169
Phonology, LI children and, 184–86
Pictorial Test of Intelligence, 212
Poor readers. *See also* Dyslexics; Reading disability
    memory problems of, 170
    training in comprehension skills and, 176
Positron emission tomography (PET), 466
Pragmatics, LI children and, 191–94
Prediction
    of learning disability, 98–101
    of mathematics achievement, 134
    planning research on, 100
    of reading disability, 98, 99, 100
Prenatal infections, 225–26
Primates
    brain structure and circuitries for different types of learning, *42*
    memory deficits in, 40–43
    for models of clinical syndromes, 37–43
Psychogenic factors in developmental language disorders, 235–36
Psychotropic drugs in treating reading disorders, 137

Radio, language learning and, 134–35
Ravens Colored Progressive Matrices for Children, 212
Reading, education of teachers and, 171
Reading comprehension research, 107–110

Reading disability. *See also* Dyslexia; Learning disability; Poor readers
    heredity and, 95
    neurophysiological correlates and, 112–18
    predicting, 98, 99, 100
    psychotropic drugs to treat, 137
    recent approaches and theories, 103–105
    research on, 101–118
    subtypes of, 111–12
Red nucleus (RN), 20
    new cortical synapses grown into, 23
    reactive synaptogenesis in, *22*
    synaptic rearrangements in, 23
Reflexes, 9
Reliability, 377–78
Research. *See also specific subjects being investigated*
    on biological foundation of dyslexia, 90
    control of, 285
    DLD subtype, 287
    dyslexia, 101–118
    on LD children, 87–90, 142
    on LI children, 206–207, 236–37, 254–55
    need for longitudinal, 97, 283, 288
    new fields of, 282
    on physiological factors in behavior, 334–35
    Piagetian theory and, 89
    planning (on prediction of reading ability), 100
    on reading, 87–90
    on reading disabilities, 101–118
    recommendations for learning and memory, 56–59
    on samples for review, 175
    social skills, 311–12, 315, 319, 326, 329–30, 353
    support for, 283
Rubella, 226

San Diego Longitudinal Evaluation of Outcomes of Preschool Impairments in Language, 189–90, 194, 199, 204, 210–11, 217, 224
Satz test battery, 99
School, predicting success in, 99
Semantics, LI children and, 190–91
Serotonin, possible role in learning disability, 48–49
SES. *See* Socioeconomic status
Simulations. *See* Computer simulations
Skill learning, cerebellum and, 74
Social behavior, 362
    physiological factors in, 330–35
Social competence and social skills, 247–48, 294–96, 362–64
    assessment of, 301–306, 351–60
    cognitive factors in, 316–20

instruction in use of, 320–26, 351–54

LD individuals' social skill deficits, 307–310

learning disability and, 245–47, 297, 298–300, 312–15

methods to promote generalization of, 327–30

Socioeconomic status, 96, 97, 235, 471–72

Specific developmental language disorders. *See* Developmental dyslexia; Developmental language delay; Developmental language disorder

Speech impairment. *See* Developmental dysphasia; Dysphasia

Spelling, research in, 122–25

Stanford-Binet test, 211, 212

Synapses. *See also* Neurons
calcium and, 25
conditioning and changes in, 21
conditioning and formation of new, 20, 22
environmental influence on, 35–37
growth of new (following injury), 4, 23
loss and replacement of, 36–37
LTP alterations in, 25–26
memory mechanisms in, 3, 4, 13
molecular events and heterosynaptic facilitation, *10*
rearrangement of (in red nucleus), 23

Synaptic contacts, changes in, 25–26

Synaptic facilitation, LTP as stable form of, 23

Synaptic mechanism of learning, 21–23

Synaptic plasticity, 23–27

Synaptic transmission, long-term modification of, 10

Syntax
LI children and, 187–90
written, 125–26

Teachers
of LD pupils, 142
of reading, 171

Television, influence of, 137–38

Teratogenic factors in developmental language disorders, 223–25

Terminology and terms, 164–67, 175, 183, 281, 284, 391–93, 549–51. *See also Diagnostic and Statistical Manual* (DSM-II); *Diagnostic and Statistical Manual* (DSM-III)

Tests and instruments. *See also names of specific tests*
cognitive achievement, 85
development of, 380
flaws in speech and language, 209
intelligence, 83–85
language-loaded intelligence, 211–12
for memory, 214–15
nonverbal, 211, 212, 213
of social skills, 301–306

Therapy. *See* Intervention

Tyrosinemia, oculocutaneous, 221

Unconditioned reflexes (UR), 15, 16

Underachievers, LD and, 139

Validity, 278–80

Verbal skills. *See also* Developmental dysphasia; Dysphasia
cognition in children with impaired, 273–74

Videotape libraries for teachers and parents, 143

Visual cortex, 32–33

Visual experience, early, 31–34

Vocational rehabilitation, 143

Wechsler Intelligence Scales for Children, 212

Wechsler Preschool and Primary Scale of Intelligence (WPPSI), 100

Word processors, written discourse and, 127–28, 138

Word recognition research, 105–107

Words, analysis into constituent elements, 169

Written discourse, 126–27, 127–28

Written language, research in, 120–26

Yale Children's Inventory (YCI), 394–97